My Years WITH JOHN PAUL II

Personal Notes

My Years WITH JOHN PAUL II

Personal Notes

JOAQUÍN NAVARRO-VALLS

Scepter

Published by Scepter Publishers, Inc.
info@scepterpublishers.org
www.scepterpublishers.org
800-322-8773
New York

Text and cover design by Rose Design

Library of Congress Control Number: 2023946815
ISBN: (pbk) 978-1-59417-517-6
ISBN: (ebook) 978-1-59417-518-3

Printed in the United States of America

CONTENTS

BRIEF BIOGRAPHICAL PROFILE

Physician and Journalist

JOAQUÍN NAVARRO-VALLS WAS A DOCTOR who became a journalist. He was born in Cartagena, Spain on November 16th, 1936, and he died in Rome, Italy on July 5th, 2017. As a journalist, he directed the press office of the Holy See for twenty-two years. He was spokesman for St. John Paul II (1984–2005) and Benedict XVI (2005–2006). He dedicated the last stage of his life to promoting the teaching and practice of medicine, as president of the advisory board of the Campus Bio-Medico University in Rome.

Navarro-Valls completed his primary, elementary, and high school studies at the "La Sagrada Familia" school run by the Marist Brothers and at the *Deutsche Schule* in his hometown, Cartagena. In 1961 he graduated summa cum laude in Medicine and Surgery, degrees he had studied at the universities of Granada and Barcelona. Afterwards, he began his doctoral studies in psychiatry. Although he developed some activity as an assistant professor of psychiatry, his interest in the world of communication and international politics led him to also study journalism; in 1968 he obtained his degree at the University of Navarra.

He was founder and deputy editor of the university magazine *Diagonal* (1964), later foreign correspondent of the magazine *Nuestro Tiempo* (1972) and, from 1977 to 1984, of the newspaper *ABC,* for Italy and the Eastern Mediterranean. He covered, among other events, the assassination of Egyptian President Sadat and, as special envoy, the crisis in Warsaw and the introduction of martial law in Poland in December 1981 under the threat of Russian tanks. In 1978 he wrote *Fumata bianca,* a reportage book chronicling the three popes who had succeeded each other in a few months: Paul VI, John Paul I, and John Paul II.

In 1983, his colleagues, other foreign correspondents in Rome, elected him president of the Foreign Press Association in Italy, an appointment that was repeated the following year. It was in his capacity as president of the foreign journalists that John Paul II came to know him. The Pope asked him for advice on Vatican communication and, shortly afterwards, appointed him director of the Press Office (*Sala Stampa).* Navarro-Valls accepted with only one condition: he must have direct access to the Pope.

For almost a quarter of a century, he facilitated the professional work of the four hundred journalists accredited to the Holy See, and of the thousands of others who covered the Pope's major events and trips. He was also involved in some "special missions": he participated in the first Vatican delegation to Soviet Moscow and in the Holy See's delegations to various international conferences organized by the UN; he also worked in the preparation of John Paul II's trip to Fidel Castro's Cuba.

During his years as director of the press office of the Holy See, he also participated in numerous congresses on psychiatry and communication. In addition, beginning in 1996 he was a visiting professor at the Faculty of Institutional Communication of the Pontifical University of the Holy Cross in Rome.

When Benedict XVI accepted his resignation in 2007, he returned to medicine, collaborating with the Bio-Medical Campus, a university specializing in Health Sciences. Although the university was only a few years old, it had already developed an innovative and avant-garde identity that captivated him.

He had a proven ability as a brilliant conversationalist, he had a mastery of languages, and a fondness for classical music, tennis and underwater fishing. He was passionate about theater, which he practiced during his university years especially. In his leisure reading, stories of sailors and explorers occupied a prominent place.

Joaquín Navarro-Valls was a man of deep religious convictions. His membership in Opus Dei helped him to strengthen and grow these convictions and make them more solid. In 1970 he moved to Rome, where he was able to live with St. Josemaría Escrivá and Blessed Álvaro del Portillo. He always considered himself a privileged man for having been able to deal with and know in some depth three saints: St. John Paul II, St. Josemaría and Blessed Álvaro del Portillo.

PRESENTATION

A Short History of Some Notes

"NOW THAT YOU ARE ASCENDING TO THE ALTARS, will you write your book of personal memories of a saint?" the *ABC* correspondent in Rome asked Joaquín Navarro-Valls. The beatification of John Paul II was a week away. "You touch on a subject that weighs heavily on me and that I feel as a moral imperative," the former spokesman replied. "I have some 600 pages of notes taken during those years. Much has already been written about him, but his person, his rich human profile, is still, at least in part, to be discovered."[1]

Luigi Accattoli, a veteran "Vaticanist" for *Corriere della Sera,* also knew about the existence of those notes and says they spoke about it several times: "During the last telephone interview I did with him, on the occasion of Fidel Castro's death [Nov. 25, 2016], I asked him: 'How are you doing with the memoirs?' He replied: 'They are not progressing. I have become lazy.' Maybe it was his way of indicating to me that he was not well. But he didn't say so explicitly, and until the news of his death I didn't know of his illness."[2]

That work that was "not progressing" is the book that the reader now has in his hands. It consists of quick notes, taken almost always as events unfolded, covering the twenty-three years that Navarro-Valls was the Pope's spokesman. They are written in his native language, Spanish, but peppered with numerous phrases and expressions in Italian, his adopted language. It is surprising that, in the midst of an undoubtedly intense activity, he found time to write these notes. In fact, he did not always succeed: there are many relevant dates in the pontificate of John Paul II that lack annotations. Even so, once transcribed, they would take up several hundred pages. Fortunately, the transfer from paper to digital was carried out by the author himself: not an insignificant detail, since his handwriting lived up to the stereotype of doctor's scrawl.

When he left his post at the Holy See, an American publisher insisted that he write a memoir of his years with the Pope. Navarro-Valls devoted a few days

1. Juan Vicente Boo, "Navarro-Valls: John Paul II never told me 'don't communicate this,'" *ABC,* April 24, 2011.

2. Luigi Accattoli, "From paper to digital" in Rafael Navarro-Valls (Ed.), *El Portavoz,* Ed. Rialp, Madrid, 2019.

to this task, using his notes as a basis. However, he soon gave up. He had been too optimistic in accepting the challenge. He realized that he had to dedicate many hours to this work, and what he wanted and needed at that stage of his life was a change of routine. Back to his first love, medicine. He rescinded the contract he had already signed.

He was even on the point of getting rid of those pages, but the desire to do "something useful" weighed heavily on him: he saw it as a "moral imperative," as he said in the interview mentioned at the beginning of the book. He was aware that, through his account, he could contribute to a better understanding of the human profile of John Paul II, who is the true protagonist of the book.

From the Faculty of Communication of the Pontifical University of the Holy Cross, where he had agreed years before to be a visiting professor, we offered him a hand with the notes. It was no longer a matter of constructing a memoir from the notes, but of converting that same material into something publishable. We limited ourselves to arranging those notes, cleaning up their wording, confirming the dates, introducing—if necessary—some brief explanations of the context. Since it is a book made up of unequal contributions over more than twenty years, and without having at any time an overall view, it was also necessary to cut out the inevitable repetitions.

This review was carried out without haste. A large part was carried out during Navarro-Valls' lifetime, although the pace slowed down as his illness progressed. The rest was completed some time later, following the same criteria. The distribution into fifty chapters was added, which follow a chronological order, with a title that gives a certain unity to the annotations; each one of these is presented, in turn, with a heading and the date. Some chapters have a common theme, such as those dedicated to the trip to Moscow with the delegation of the Holy See, to Mikhail Gorbachev's visit to the Vatican, to the preparation of the Pope's trip to Cuba, or to the assassination of the commander of the Swiss Guard.

Twelve chapters narrate the days of summer vacation in the mountains. The scenery changes and John Paul II sleeps under a tree, suffers for the situation in Lebanon, talks about philosophy, contemplates nature from the top of a mountain, and reveals an adventurous spirit that, for some, borders on recklessness. On one of those days the Pope's secretary surprises Navarro-Valls taking notes in a notebook and warns the others with an ironic tone: "Be careful with what you say and with the comments you make! In a few years you will see it all written down and published in a book by Dr. Navarro!"

Implicit in the whole process of revising the originals was that the book would be published—"in case anyone was interested," Navarro-Valls said—after his death, even years later. I think he wanted to avoid even the appearance of wanting to appear as *the* communicative model of the Holy See, precisely at a time when everything related to Vatican communication was being rethought and reorganized.

His point of view was well known: he considered it essential for his work to have direct access to the Pope. As Father Federico Lombardi explained years later: at that time no one in the Vatican "was aware of the close relationship that existed between government and communication: in the sense that the effectiveness of a line of government, whether in the disciplinary or organizational field, or in the pastoral field, inevitably depends on its communication [. . .]. Dr. Navarro was absolutely aware of this and that is why he insisted on establishing an intense relationship, in the first place, with the Pope. But in a complex reality like that of the Vatican, nothing is easy."[3]

In Navarro-Valls's annotations there are some references to these difficulties, which stem, above all, from the lack of sensitivity towards communicative aspects by some decision-makers within the Holy See. For many years, these questions were solved, when necessary, by going directly to the Pope. However, in the last years of his pontificate, taking into account the state of John Paul II's health, he preferred to spare him that burden.

In any case, he did not see his access to the Pope as a privilege, but as something essential to achieve and improve his harmony with the Holy Father and to better transmit his thoughts. The collaboration of John Paul II's secretary, Msgr. Stanisław Dziwisz, was decisive in achieving this, as the annotations profusely demonstrate. They made use above all of informal means, such as lunches and dinners, or the days of summer rest.

Navarro-Valls avoided the temptation to rewrite his notes with the perspective of time and reflection. What he did do, in a few cases, was to add a footnote to clarify a situation: for example, when the Pope's secretary, Stanisław Dziwisz, first asked him his opinion about an eventual resignation of John Paul II. The spokesman replied that he thought it was crazy. In the note he adds: "That's what I thought then. Naturally, almost twenty years later, history would show another very different scenario." These remarks are recorded in the book as "Author's Note," to distinguish them from the others, introduced by the editor.

In one of the first "Author's Notes," about a meeting between John Paul II and the journalist Indro Montanelli, Navarro-Valls states that he tried to

---

3. Federico Lombardi, *Papi, Vaticano, Comunicazione. Esperienze e riflessioni*, Ancora Editrice, Milano, 2021, p. 98.

"transcribe the Pope's answers as accurately as possible." It is an observation that extends to the rest of the work's dialogue and is consistent with the good work of a spokesman who, in addition, had worked for years as a reporter. This record of professional excellence is the credibility that supports the numerous phrases of John Paul II contained in this book, without pretending that each and every one of them is one-hundred percent verbatim.

One last observation about the edition: the treatments have been kept as they appear in the original. In general, the author names people by their surname, and usually avoids formulas of office or courtesy (monsignor, archbishop, cardinal, etc.) that could hinder the flow of the narrative. In the case of the Pope's secretary, he usually alternates the surname Dzwisz with the given name, Stanisław.

Human Profile

The fragmentary origin of the notes does not prevent us from perceiving some traits of John Paul II's human profile that have remained constant over the years. One of them is his sense of humor. For example, on one occasion, upon arriving at the papal apartment, Navarro-Valls records greeting the Pope and telling him: "'Every time you invite me to lunch I consider it a gift.'" The text continues: "He interrupts me, smiling: 'I have calculated the number of times I have invited you to lunch. It's a lot. It's about time for you to invite me oncexii. . . .'" (30.VI.1989).

Another characteristic is the Pope's total abandonment into the hands of God, which manifests itself not only in transcendent moments, such as illness, but also in more domestic circumstances. On one of the first occasions in which Navarro-Valls observes the Pope peacefully taking a nap during his excursions in the mountains, he notes: "I am impressed to see him sleeping in holy peace, abandoning the helm of the Church to God" (18.VII.1988).

This attitude of abandonment was accompanied at the same time by the will to do everything as well as humanly possible so that goodness, justice, and truth would prevail. One evening he notes: "I leave the Papal apartment after more than an hour of conversation on a wide variety of questions, which reveal the Pope's universal interest [. . .] He does not wait passively for favorable historical circumstances to arise: he puts the means at his disposal to direct history towards Jesus Christ" (12.III.1994).

It is not just the character of the Pope which comes out in the notes. There are many details that show Navarro-Valls' character as well, especially his admiration for the human and spiritual stature of John Paul II, whom he never heard speak ill of anyone; or who showed that he knew how to listen as if he had nothing else to do, or who trusted in the efficacy of prayer to God with the innocence of a child. . . . But these were not only details of simple admiration, but expressions of the affection of a son for his father. Like when he went around the stores in Rome looking for a good cane for the Pope, who was beginning to need it; or when he put on a clown's nose to make him laugh so he could take a photo of him without showing the stiffness that Parkinson's disease was causing in his face.

On other occasions, these proofs of affection appear unexpectedly. For example, an episode that occurred in the midst of the Lefebvre schism crisis: "I began to read to him," writes Navarro-Valls, "a dispatch from the *Reuters* agency that included some of Lefebvre's words about the Pope: a heretical Pope, who no longer had the Catholic faith, etc. I could not finish reading these things. I got a lump in my throat and tears came to my eyes. Dziwisz told me to continue. I hid the agency text in my folder and did not continue reading" (15.VI.1988). He cannot stand that the Pope should be slandered in this way and that, moreover, a bishop was responsible for it.

As in every family, the conversations with the Pope turn from the divine to the human, from jokes to illness. One day, as Navvarro-Valls leaves the dining room, he notices that the Pope is ostentatiously making noise with his shoes. It's a way of sympathetically teasing Dziwisz. "It's just that he doesn't want me to make noise when I walk . . . ," the Pope tells him laughing. The secretary explains to him that the Pope sometimes wears those shoes because they are very comfortable, but they are a size too big for him and so they make a little noise when he walks. It is Friday. Shortly after these jokes, the Pope informs Navarro-Valls that on Sunday he will be admitted to the hospital. It will be the Pope himself who will communicate it to the faithful at the Angelus of the same Sunday (10.VII.1992).

As a Father

John Paul II was much more than a boss or a superior for the Spokesman. There is no doubt that a peculiar paternal-filial relationship was established between the two, which also had affective manifestations. One that comes to mind—for those of us who lived through those moments—is the reaction of the spokesman during the last press conference that preceded the death of the Pope:

> When at 12:30 PM I have the briefing with the journalists, there is a great silence. I say that I suppose they will have many questions, but I will answer

> only a couple of them. The first question I don't remember. The second was asked by Andreas English, a German journalist: "And from a personal point of view, how do you live this moment?" It is then that the tension escapes me and my emotions get out of control. . . . [The] words come out broken and with a lump in my throat, which appears live on TV in half the world. . . . An element of truth, of true humanity, was introduced, which I had certainly not intended to deliberately communicate (1.IV.2005).

It is recognized that among the achievements of his long work as spokesperson is the overcoming of the taboo on the health of the Popes (in perfect harmony with the thinking of John Paul II). Throughout the various admissions to the Gemelli Polyclinic, and during the years of the last illness, information was abundant, despite the difficulties. It was he who told journalists—during a trip to Hungary in 1996—that the Pope was suffering from Parkinson's, information that had not been previously authorized and that, according to the chroniclers of the time, caused deep unease in the Secretariat of State. This is how he mentions this episode in his notes, in which he is perhaps too severe with himself, since that decision favored transparency, which later everyone praised:

> I ended up talking too much. [. . .] Undoubtedly, the ambiguity with which the state of the Pope's health is reported—or not reported—is a mistake on my part. I hope this will be useful and helpful in the future. And I am not referring only to "technical" aspects, but also to the search for holiness, because it is something that hurts and humiliates me" (9.IX.1996).

There is no lack in his notes of acknowledgment of his own mistakes. One such case occurred during John Paul II's trip to Guatemala, when he reported an audience with the Pope that, although planned, had not actually taken place: "Good blunder on my part! It serves as a lesson for me not to forget that, in this profession, one must never act 'by rote'" (6.II.1996).

Sometimes it is the Pope himself who corrects the spokesman. On one occasion, on the last day of one of the summer periods in the Aosta Valley, Navarro-Valls comments to the Pope that he has the impression that some of the documents published by the Vatican departments "seem to be written only to justify working." "No—says the Pope—they are documents made with great care, with time. . . ." And the spokesman concludes: "It has been a good correction to my imprudence in formulating a hasty judgment: I have never heard from your lips a critical judgment on the Curia or on the people of the Curia" (20.VII.1990).

If Stanisław Dziwisz was Navarro-Valls' usual channel of access to John Paul II, it is evident from the notes that this relationship sometimes takes on a fraternal dimension. On one occasion, the spokesman passed him a copy of an article published in an Italian newspaper—now defunct—entitled "All the Powers of Don Dziwisz." In the article, the secretary was presented as "the all-powerful man" of the Curia, as if he commanded more than the cardinals themselves. "I give it to him telling him not to worry, that it is of no importance. In the afternoon, he calls me at home: 'You know that nothing of what is stated in that article is true. But if you ever see anything in my way of acting that could give rise to it, you must tell me fraternally.'" And Navarro-Valls concludes: "It is an act of humility that impresses me" (17.VII.1992). Other annotations show the spokesman's uneasiness at the secretary's loneliness dealing with the uncertainties and sufferings surrounding the Pope's illnesses.

Joaquín Navarro-Valls' "Personal Notes" unveil situations of daily life around John Paul II, and offer an interesting glimpse into the backroom of the daily work of the Holy See. But they do not contain any glaring revelations. Therefore, I think anyone expecting a Vatican version of *The West Wing* TV series will be disappointed.[4] The Pope is not a political leader, the tools he uses are only based on persuasion (messages, appeals, letters . . . and the material means at his disposal are inversely proportional to the greatness of his mission. Moreover, for a full understanding of the figure of John Paul II, it is necessary to be open to another dimension, which also appears naturally in these pages: prayer to God, a true weapon of which he makes constant use.

The spokesman shows that his main objective was to support the Pope, even though he knew that John Paul II did not need that help, being such a powerful communicator. The conclusion of the book shows his awareness of having been privileged for many reasons—above all—"because I was able to see a holy man up close."

Diego Contreras[5]

---

4. *The West Wing* was a popular TV series (1999–2006) created by Aaron Sorkin and set in the West Wing of the White House, where the Oval Office and the offices of the main collaborators of the President of the United States are located, especially the communications and press department

5. José Miguel Cejas (†), Marc Carroggio, Jaime Cárdernas and Miguel Castellvì collaborated at different times in the editing work, which was carried out within the scope of the "Cátedra Navarro-Valls" of the Faculty of Communication of the University of the Holy Cross. Navarro-Valls gave the original annotations, with a letter, to the Chancellor of the University, who passed them on to the Faculty of Communication.

1

An Unexpected Twist

My First Lunch with John Paul II

November 18, 1984

It's raining in Rome and I have to retrieve my car (yesterday it was towed away), before the start of Giovanni Agnelli's conference[1] at the Foreign Press Association, which I have to moderate, as I am currently the president. I rescue the car and manage to arrive minutes before the start of the event.

In the middle of the conference, when I had recovered from the rush, Maria Teresa Lazzaro, the secretary of the Association, passes me a note: they had just phoned, inviting me to lunch with the Pope at half past one in the Vatican. I hide my surprise as best I can. I discreetly glance at the clock: more than an hour to go. Time passes and Agnelli continues talking. Shortly after, another furtive glance: I'm approaching the limit. Even though Agnelli is about to finish, every second feels like an eternity. As soon as he says the last word, I conclude the session, say goodbye quickly, take a cab, and arrive at the *Portone di Bronzo*, the most direct access to the Pope's Apartment, minutes before the scheduled time.

I go up to the Courtyard of San Damaso, where the main entrance to the Apostolic Palace is located. A baroque and picturesque elevator, with a bench upholstered in red satin and, naturally, with an elevator operator. I pass through the second floor, where the Secretary of State's quarters are located. On the second floor are the rooms where the Pope receives guests: the Consistory Hall, the Clementine Hall. . . .

The elevator stops at the third floor. Opposite the offices of the Secretariat of State is the Papal Apartment, the Pope's residence: an anteroom, a reception room, a large office for his private secretaries and one for himself, from whose window he prays the Angelus many Sundays of the year. Beyond are the

1. Giovanni Agnelli (1921–2003) was a well-known Italian businessman, president of the automobile company *FIAT*, founded by his grandfather, Giovanni Agnelli, in 1899.

bedroom and the private chapel. They lead us to the dining room, a sober and spacious room.

The Holy Father receives us cordially. Four of us had lunch with him: Crescenzio Sepe;[2] an Italian journalist of Polish descent, Gian Franco Svidercoschi;[3] the substitute of the Vatican Secretariat of State, Eduardo Martínez Somalo;[4] and myself.

The Pope asks me about the life and activities of the Foreign Press Association and we exchange a few words about the correspondents, including the Soviet ones. Soon he directly proposes the topic: what can be done to improve the information provided by the Holy See Press Office? At a certain point, he mentions the work of Deskur, whom he has known for many years.[5]

I tell him I have nothing prepared and will have to improvise. He doesn't seem to care. Notes are taken. Two days later, I bring a report with me, which gives a more orderly account of my ideas.

An Unexpected Call

November 30, 1984

I am working in my office in *Piazza* Navona when I receive a telephone call from the Vatican. The *Sostituto,*[6] Martínez Somalo—I am told—wants to see

---

2. Crescenzio Sepe (Italy, 1943). At that time he worked in the Secretariat of State. Years later, he was appointed Advisor to the Secretary of State, then Secretary of the Congregation for the Clergy and Prefect of the Congregation for the Evangelization of Peoples. He was Secretary General of the Committee for the Jubilee Year 2000 and Archbishop of Naples (2006–2020). He has been a cardinal since 2001.

3. Gian Franco Svidercoschi (Italy, 1936) was deputy editor of *L'Osservatore Romano* and collaborated with John Paul II on *Gift and Mystery* (1996); he is co-author of: *Stanislao Dziwisz, A Life with Karol. Conversations with Gian Franco Svidercoschi* (2007). Among his best known books is *Letter to a Hebrew Friend* (1993).

4. Eduardo Martínez Somalo (Spain, 1927–2021). He was Substitute for the Vatican Secretary of State until 1988, when he was appointed Prefect of the Congregation for Divine Worship and the Discipline of the Sacraments. In 1992, the Pope appointed him prefect of the Congregation for Institutes of Consecrated Life. In 1988 he was elevated to the cardinalate and served as Camerlengo (administrator in Sede Vacante) from 1997 to 2007.

5. Andrzej Maria Deskur (Poland, 1924–2011) was, in 1983, president emeritus of the then Pontifical Commission for Social Communications. He had a close friendship with John Paul II, whom he had known since before he was elected Pope. Precisely the day before the conclave of October 1978, Deskur suffered a stroke that left him partially paralyzed for the rest of his life. He was created a cardinal in 1985.

6. Substitute of the Secretariat of State: this name is given to the official of the Holy See who heads the first section of the Secretariat of State, the Section for General Affairs.

me as soon as possible. "It's urgent." I head for the offices of the Secretariat of State with my head in the clouds. I had never been there before. Before getting down to business, Martínez Somalo, as is his style, spends a few minutes commenting on some details of the place and then, out of the blue, he hands me a document: I see that it bears the Pope's signature in red ink, and that of Casaroli[7] and Martínez Somalo himself, in blue. I read it: John Paul II has appointed me Director of the Holy See Press Office, the *Sala Stampa*. My first reaction is one of perplexity, but the conversation continues and I begin to answer some questions about when I should take office, without realizing that I am accepting.

I am not fully aware of the responsibility I had just assumed. It dawned on me half an hour later, when I was returning home in a cab. In a shadowy space, the window glass reflects my face. The face of a man who has just turned forty-eight and now . . . my life takes another turn.

I understand that it is an opportunity to exercise my profession in direct service to the Church, but if I had been told this some time ago I would have thought it was a joke. I was born in Cartagena on November 16, 1936, in the middle of the Spanish Civil War. I studied in many different institutions: high school at the *Deutsche Schule,* medicine in Granada and Barcelona, journalism in Pamplona.

I have been a member of Opus Dei since my university years, and I had the good fortune to live in Rome with the founder, Josemaría Escrivá, and with his successor, Álvaro del Portillo.

From 1977 to 1984 I was correspondent for the Spanish newspaper *ABC* for Italy and the Eastern Mediterranean. This allowed me to get to know first-hand the political and cultural vicissitudes of Egypt, Greece, Israel, Algeria, and Turkey. In 1979 I was elected a member of the board of directors of the Foreign Press Association (*Stampa Estera*) in Italy, and in 1983 and 1984, president.

But no, this is not a joke. And I, who was thinking of returning to my specialty, psychiatry, am going to devote myself to a task that had never crossed my mind: directing the information policy on the activity of the Pope and the Holy See.

I travel to Madrid and tell the people at the newspaper that I am going to stop working for them, without being able to explain the reason, because my appointment will not be made public until December 4. In a way, I prefer it: to resign without sharing the real reason. I imagine their questions and their surprised faces. A surprise that I share with them: I still haven't quite got used to the idea.

---

7. Agostino Casaroli (Italy, 1914–1998). He was Secretary of State of the Holy See from 1979 to 1990. Known as the architect of the so-called *Ospolitik* of the Vatican towards the Communist countries of Eastern Europe. Cardinal since 1979.

Director of *Sala Stampa*

December 18, 1984

On December 6, two days after I was appointed director of the *Sala Stampa*, I attended Mass celebrated by the Pope in the chapel of his Apartment. In addition, following Vatican custom, after receiving my appointment, I requested an audience with the Holy Father. This morning, I received the answer. The Pope's secretary, Stanisław Dziwisz,[8] tells me by telephone that the Pope invites me to dine with him tonight.

During dinner—in which, in addition to Martínez Somalo, there are his two secretaries, Stanisław Dziwisz and Emery Kabongo—,[9] I tell him, in a generic way, about the possibilities I have been seeing during the last few weeks. No big issues come up, because I am still settling into my new job.

I make a concrete suggestion, which the Pope agrees with. I suggest that we encourage meetings of journalists with the cardinals who are in charge of *dicasteries*.[10] I tell the Pope that it is a matter of putting the sources of the news in functional contact with the reporters.

An Unforgettable Memory

January 2, 1985

The Pope returned yesterday from Castelgandolfo. In the afternoon, Dziwisz called me to confirm that my extended family would be able to participate today in the Mass he is celebrating in his private chapel.

There are twelve of us in total: my parents, Joaquín and Conchita, my brothers Javier and Juan Carlos, my sisters-in-law, my nephews and nieces, and

---

8. Stanisław Dziwisz (Poland, 1939) was already his personal secretary when Karol Wojtyla was auxiliary bishop of Krakow. Wojtyla himself had ordained him a priest in 1963. When he was elected Pope, John Paul II appointed him private secretary and, in 1998, prefect of the Pontifical Household. Benedict XVI appointed him archbishop of Krakow (2005–2016) and, in 2006, cardinal. He has published a book of memories of the Pontiff: *A Life with Karol* (2007).

9. Emery Kabongo Kanundowi (Republic of Congo, 1940) was second secretary to the Pope from 1982 to 1988. He was appointed bishop of Luebo in 1988. In 2003 he resigned for health reasons and returned to Rome, where he is a canon bishop of St. Peter's Basilica.

10. "Dicastery" is the generic denomination of the great organisms of the Roman Curia: the Secretariat of State, the Congregations, the Tribunals, the Pontifical Councils and the Offices. The "Roman Curia" is the group of dicasteries and agencies that assist the Pope in the exercise of his pastoral office.

me. My brother Rafael, a professor at the Faculty of Law of the Complutense University, is away on a trip.

The Pope greeted us at the end of the Mass and asked us to take a picture with him. These moments are hard to describe. All of us, especially my parents, left very excited.

A Few Sentences in Calcutta

February 1–10, 1986

From the very beginning, I have accompanied the Pope on practically all his trips.[11] He has just returned from India. I remember his visit to Calcutta, where he met Mother Teresa and comforted some dying people being cared for by the Missionaries of Charity. There, he pronounced these words that impressed me:

> The suffering body and soul cry out: "Why, why must we die?" And the answer we hear, amidst the silence of kindness and compassion, brims with honesty and faith: I cannot give you an answer. I cannot relieve all your pain. But I am sure of this: God loves you with infinite love. You are a precious gift to him. I also love you in him. For in God we are all truly brothers and sisters.

During the meeting with journalists on the return trip, Orazio Petrosillo[12] asks the Pope if it is true that his two "traveling companions" in India were Gandhi—to show that the Gospel is compatible with Hindu culture—and Mother Teresa of Calcutta—to show how the Gospel can transform India. The Pope likes that observation and tells Orazio that he has formulated it very well. At another point, he stresses that he has learned much from Gandhi throughout his life and is not ashamed to say: "Gandhi is more Christian than many Christians."

With Ostellino, director of *Corriere*

March 1986

One day in March, I don't remember the exact date, I accompanied Piero Ostellino,[13] director of *Corriere della Sera*, to dinner with the Pope. He sent a driver

---

11. I went more than a year without taking notes: I soon realized that these notes would never be a "diary." [Author's Note]

12. Orazio Petrosillo (Italy, 1947–2007) was, at that time, Vaticanist for the Roman newspaper *Il Tempo* and later for *Il Messaggero*. Author of several books on the Shroud of Turin.

13. Piero Ostellino (Italy, 1935–2018), journalist and writer, edited *Corriere della Sera* from 1984 to 1987.

to my home to take me to the Roman headquarters of the *Corriere,* where he was waiting for me: from there we went together to the Vatican.

Although Piero—who is not a Catholic—is a determined man, this afternoon he was nervous: "What should I call him?" "Should I kiss his hand?" I reassured him, telling him to do whatever he wants and sees fit.

The Pope was very friendly and affectionate with him. The conversation revolved around China and Russia, two countries where Ostellino has worked as a correspondent.

A few weeks ago, during the 27th Congress of the Soviet Communist Party, Gorbachev[14] proposed two goals for the USSR: *Perestroika* (reform) and *Glasnost* (transparency). We agree that something serious is happening in Russia. We will have to wait for these generic declarations to become concrete facts to make any greater judgement.

At the end, the Holy Father gave him a rosary for his wife and children. "They are Catholics," said Piero, visibly happy.

Indro Montanelli with the Pope

JUNE 13, 1986

The Pope has invited Indro Montanelli to dinner tonight.[15] I will accompany him. The Roman traffic is once again doing one of its worst things to me: traffic jams, traffic jams and blocked streets. I arrive at Montanelli's office—in *Piazza di Pietra,* very close to the Pantheon—at ten past seven; and dinner is at half past seven. I don't know how, but we manage to be on time.

The Pope greets Indro with great cordiality: "You see," he jokes, "when the director of the *Sala Stampa* thinks I have behaved well, he brings me a journalist for dinner." We go straight to the dining room, because he knows that Montanelli is not a believer. Out of delicacy with him, he omits his usual brief visit to the Blessed Sacrament in his private chapel.[16]

---

14. Mikhail Sergeyevich Gorbachev (Russia, 1931–2022), Russian lawyer and politician, was General Secretary of the Communist Party of the Soviet Union from 1985 to 1989, and President of the Soviet Union from 1989 to 1991.

15. Indro Montanelli (Italy, 1909–2001) was one of the great Italian journalists and writers of the 20th century. He covered the wars in Abyssinia, Spain, Finland and part of World War II. During the German occupation of Italy he was imprisoned and sentenced to death. After the war, he returned to his work at the *Corriere,* and his chronicles on the anti-communist uprising in Hungary and the Prague Spring were especially important. Years later, he left the *Corriere* and founded a newspaper, *Il Giornale.* In the last stage of his life he returned to *Corriere.*

16. It was the only time I saw him omit this visit to the chapel, which invariably preceded dinner [Author's Note].

At the beginning of the dinner—at which Dziwisz is present—Poland is discussed. Montanelli recounts his experiences of the time he lived in Warsaw in 1939. "Poles and Italians," he says at one point, "are alike. The Poles are tragic Italians, and the Italians are comic Poles." The Pope is amused by the comparison and considers it apt. Indro asks him about the private audiences with Gierek[17] and Jaruzelski.[18]

Gierek—the Pope said—told him during the conversation: "There is an east wind blowing here. You could help me by bringing wind from the west." This was, in short, the conversation between the Pope and Montanelli:[19]

—"Are you homesick for Poland?"—Montanelli asks him.

—"My nostalgia," answered the Pope, with a serious expression, "has turned into concern. When I contemplate what is happening there, I ask myself what could be done. When I receive the Polish bishops, I am surprised to see that they are not worried: they work, they live . . . and perhaps they do not realize what is happening.[20] But from here I observe the situation and I worry."

—"A possible trip to Russia?"

—"In the current circumstances it cannot be done. There is a police structure that controls everything, subjecting it to the state. In this situation I cannot go."

—"Did you have a hard time adjusting to Rome?"

---

17. Edward Gierek (Poland, 1913–2001), a prominent leader of the Polish Communist Party and of the regime's *nomenklatura*, within which he held the line of adapting Moscow's directives to Polish idiosyncrasy.

18. General Wojciech Witold Jaruzelski (Poland, 1923–2014) was prime minister (1981–85), chairman of the Council of State (1985–89) and president of Poland (1989–90)

19. In my notes, I took only the general concept of the questions asked to the Pope, while I tried to write down his answers as accurately as possible. I transcribe this interview—and the rest of those that appear in these pages—according to what I took down in my notes [Author's Note].

20. From July to September 1980, strikes had been taking place in Warsaw, Gdanks and Silesia. At last an agreement was reached between the government of the Polish People's Republic and the strike committee headed by Lech Walesa. In September Kania relieved Gierek as head of the party and in October there were registrations in the Solidarity trade union, the first independent trade union in a Soviet bloc country. In 1981 General Jaruzelski was elected prime minister. The peasants founded an agrarian solidarity. Social tensions worsened, as did the fear of Russian intervention. This led to the proclamation of martial law in December. In 1982, the government banned the *Solidarity* trade union. Martial law lasted until July 1983. Two years later, in 1985, Jaruzelski was appointed president of the Council of State (the equivalent of head of state), amid a climate of strong political tensions.

—"It was only during the summer of 1979, in Castelgandolfo, when I remembered my vacations in Poland: the mountains, the lakes, the excursions. I realized that I had lost that forever. It was hard then. But here, at the Vatican, it's not, because with this rhythm of work, in which I go from one thing to another without interruption," he says, smiling, "I have no time left for nostalgia."

—"Was there uneasiness in the conclave?"

—"Yes; especially in the first one."

—"Ah, has your name already appeared in the first one?"

—"Yes, and before. In the first conclave I was uneasy. In the second I was more serene."[21]

—"What do you think of Ali Agca?"

—"He has the feeling that he is playing his role. He is surprised that he didn't manage to kill me and he keeps thinking about it. He asked me the day we were talking, implicitly acknowledging that there was a power greater than his own that prevented him from doing so. When he tried to kill me, he did not know what the thirteenth of May meant."[22]

—"Are you all right now?"

—"Yes; I have not had any *sequelae* (after effects). After the second operation I recovered completely. Maybe in the future I will start to feel some pain, but for now I feel fine."

—"Do you always eat so little?"

—"Yes, I have very little dinner at night."

—"What time do you get up?"

—"Always before six o'clock."

The Pope asks Indro how he sees the situation of the Christian faith in Italy:

"Badly; this is a country of skeptics," says Indro.

"And that attitude, is it recent or ancient?"

---

21. Yes, and before: this is what the Pope said, without giving further explanations or historical references. I never spoke with him about this question, the scope of which I do not know [Author's Note].

22. The attack on the Pope, by the Turkish Ali Agca, took place on May 13, 1981, the same date of the first apparition of the Virgin Mary in Fatima (Portugal), May 13, 1917.

"Very ancient: since the end of the Middle Ages!" Indro says; and he makes a wide-ranging comment on the men of the Italian Renaissance and their attitude toward the faith; the Pope listens attentively.

When we finish dinner, the Pope asks us to take some pictures. We continue talking, standing by the dining room door. I tell the Pope—and Montanelli hears me—that Indro lost his mother a few years ago. She was a deeply religious woman and I am sure, I tell him, that Indro would like to pray in the chapel with the Pope for his mother's soul. The Pope looks at Montanelli and Montanelli, moved, tells him that he was about to propose it. The Pope goes to the chapel, we follow him and he begins to pray the Our Father. Indro, on his knees and with his hands on his face, responds as best he can.

On leaving the Papal Apartments he tells me, in an amused and cordial tone, that everyone thinks he is a non-believer (a *miscredente*), "when in reality I am a *Ghibelline*!"[23]

Two days later, Montanelli sent me a splendid article on that dinner and asked permission to publish it in his newspaper. I consulted with the Pontifical Apartment and the conclusion was that it was preferable to keep the meeting in a personal and private context. I communicated this to Montanelli. The article was not published.

The Nevado Volcano and Human Dignity

July 1986

We are in the middle of our trip to Colombia and Santa Lucia. Two special moments: the meeting with indigenous people in Popayán and the prayer in Chinchiná for the victims of the Nevado del Ruiz volcano.[24]

Today, July 7, we came to Castries, the capital of St. Lucia, a small volcanic island with a tropical climate, which only became independent from the United Kingdom in 1979.

During the trip from Pereira to Medellín, I prepared a short text for the press, ten lines long, and I showed it to the Pope. It is something I often do

23. In the Middle Ages the *Ghibellines,* supporters of the German emperors, fought against the *Guelphs,* who defended the popes. Montanelli's expression is best understood in the Italian cultural context: while everyone considered him an "unbeliever," an agnostic, in reality he was a supporter of the separation between Church and State, "a Ghibelline."

24. Nevado del Ruiz is an active volcano that erupted on November 13, 1985, killing some 25,000 people in what is considered the most catastrophic volcanic eruption of the 20th century.

on these occasions, to summarize the meaning of the trip. The Pope told me that I had to enrich it with new ideas. When we were a little short of landing in Medellin, I approached him again and he commented to me:

> —In the visits I make to the countries of this continent, I always speak about freedom, thinking of all Latin America. What I say can be found in the document on Christian freedom and liberation."[25]
>
> "We cannot accept any other type of liberation, because of our conception of human freedom. Therefore, my words are not a political reflection, nor sociological, nor circumstantial: they are an actualization of the content of the Christian faith."
>
> "Man is free from his constitutive act," the Holy Father continued. "God has decided to accept man's sin rather than deprive him of his freedom. And with his freedom, man can do good or evil. He can sin. And since there is nothing on this earth that can grant man this freedom, every human project must recognize this original freedom of man and direct its efforts in this direction."
>
> "That is the reason"—he concluded—"why historical materialism cannot be considered as a human project of liberation."

I was still leaning over the Pope's seat, taking notes of his words, when the plane began to land. The Pope continued speaking until Father Tucci[26] approached him to tell him that we were all ready at the Medellin airport.

I do not remember if on this occasion the Pope spoke in Italian or in Spanish. What I have recorded are not literal expressions, because what mattered to me at that time was not to record his exact words, bur rather to know his thoughts, in order to transmit them to the journalists as faithfully as possible.

JULY 10. Today we have returned to Rome and, as is his custom after every trip, the same day of our arrival (or the following day, if we return late), the Pope invites us to lunch. He wants to make a first assessment of the trip and also to know what has been published, what reactions there have been to his preaching, etc. We are Martínez Somalo, Dziwisz, Mario Agnes[27] and myself.

---

25. The second of the documents that the Holy See dedicated to liberation theology (*Libertatis conscientia,* 1986). The first—Libertatis *nuntius*—was published in 1984.

26. Roberto Tucci (Italy, 1921–2015), Jesuit priest. In 1973 he was appointed director general of Vatican Radio and from 1982 was in charge of organizing papal trips outside Italy. He was appointed cardinal by John Paul II in 2001.

27. Mario Agnes (Italy, 1931–2018), was director of *L'Osservatore Romano* from 1984 to 2007.

We tell him our impressions and points of view from each of our respective fields of work. I tell him about the difficulties encountered by journalists: the program is usually so dense and tight—some have told me—that it is impossible for them to cover all the events. The Pope comments with humility and a touch of humor: "I always say it: on these trips, the Pope works less than those who accompany him, because he leaves Rome with all the work done."

I ask him what he experienced in Armero when he saw the town buried by the avalanche of the Nevado del Ruiz volcano.

> It impressed me to contemplate that immense tomb, of twenty-five thousand people. . . . To see man crushed, martyred. But man cannot be crushed completely, because God himself has been crushed and crushed in Christ. This is difficult to understand: a whole God martyred on a cross! Not even Peter understood it.

He says these words with a singular force that comes from his soul. This profound conception of man—I think—constitutes the foundation, the basis of his spiritual hope and his human optimism.

He then tells us about the strong reactions to his latest encyclical *Dominum et vivificantem*, published a few weeks ago, in which he states that scientific materialism is linked to the sin against the spirit.[28] The Czech communists were the first to protest.

---

28. The encyclical is dated May 18, 1986 and closes the Trinitarian cycle of John Paul II's first three encyclicals: *Redemptor hominis* (March 2, 1979), dedicated to Jesus Christ, Son of God; *Dives in misericordia* (November 30, 1980), dedicated to God the Father; and *Dominum et vivificantem*, dedicated to the action of the Holy Spirit in the Church and in the world.

2

A Pope Must Make Decisions

Wilton Wynn's Questions

August 21, 1986

I accompany Wilton Wynn, an American journalist, to dinner at Castelgandolfo with the Pope.[1] Wynn has been *Time's* Roman bureau chief for years. We met on the occasion of the Pope's travels, when I was a working journalist, and we hit it off right away. He is a sincerely religious man; a Baptist Christian, married to Leila, an Arab and also a Baptist. We were together in Cairo covering the assassination of Sadat.[2]

Wilton is writing a book about the Popes he has known—-John XXIII, Paul VI, John Paul I and John Paul II.[3] Some time ago he hinted to me that it would be useful for him to be able to talk to John Paul II for documentation. I mentioned this to Dziwisz, and a few days later he informed me that the Pope would receive us today at Castelgandolfo at eight o'clock in the evening. As he usually has dinner at half past seven, I thought he would receive us later. But the fact is that we had dinner with him.

Wilton arrived exultant. Dziwisz accompanied us around the house for a few minutes and told us that the Pope is working hard during these days of August: writing, above all. "He tackles the problems of the Church," Dziwisz told us, "without being anxious. He knows how to keep them on an objective plane, preserving serenity, which is a decisive trait of his character and helps him to bear the enormous task entrusted to him. I have known him for many

1. Wilton Wynn (United States, 1920–2011). He headed the Department of Journalism at the American University in Cairo from 1945 to 1947, where he met his wife. He was correspondent of *Associated Press* in Beirut; and of *Time* in Rome (1962 to 1974). After a further stay in Cairo he returned to Rome, where he worked for *Time* until his retirement in 1991.

2. Anwar el-Sadat (Egypt, 1918–1981) was president and prime minister of Egypt from 1970 until 1981, when he was assassinated during a military parade by radical Islamists.

3. The book was published under the title *Keeper of the Keys: John XXIII, Paul VI and John Paul II: Three who changed the Church* (1988).

years and I have never seen him lose his sense of humor or become overwhelmed by events."

He leads us to a room next to the dining room. The Pope arrives a few minutes later, relaxed and smiling, as usual. He is not wearing the pectoral cross or the white skullcap, as an external manifestation—I think—that he is "on vacation." In the dining room, small and modest, he has introduced only one change: a small painting depicting the Tatra Mountains. It was given to him—I understand—by General Jaruzelski.

Wilton starts asking questions from the very first moment, with a clear desire to make the most of this time with John Paul II. We converse in English. The Pope is not fluent in English, but he makes an effort to answer him in his own language. Wilton does not take any notes: he trusts his good professional memory.

I am transcribing part of the text of that dinner, translating the Pope's words from English as literally as possible. I only include the main ideas of the questions asked by Wynn:

—"Being pope means assuming an immense responsibility."

—"It is true; but I have a conviction born of faith. When God our Lord entrusts us with a burden, he also gives us the grace to bear it. But it is not something specific to ecclesiastical responsibilities. I think, for example, of the responsibility of a husband or wife when he or she says: "I accept you as my wife or I accept you as my husband and I want to be faithful to you as long as I live." The dimension of responsibility is the same: it is a personal commitment for life. This happens in marriage, in the priesthood. . . ."

—"Now, along with the task of guarding the faith, it must face the challenge posed by new situations: the progress of science is posing very complex moral problems, especially in the field of the manipulation of human biology."

—"Yes, certain questions pose a great challenge for moral theology. The central point of our responsibility is to highlight the transcendent character of the human person, who runs the risk of being understood as a product, as a simple object. It is necessary to defend the specific features of the human person, human respect, human responsibility. This is at the heart of my teaching. But my task is not new: Pius XII and subsequent Popes had to respond in their time to the challenges posed by the development of science and technology."[4]

4. Precisely during those months the Pope was studying the document *Donum Vitae. On respect for nascent human life and the dignity of procreation*, which Joseph Ratzinger, as Prefect of the Congregation for the Doctrine of the Faith, would promulgate the following year, on February 22, 1987.

—"Theologian Curran says that, as the Church's moral teaching is not infallible, there could be evolutions and changes. . . ."[5]

—"He affirms that there has not been a solemn declaration of the ecclesiastical Magisterium on these points; only successive positions taken by the ordinary Magisterium. His argument, like that of other theologians who take this line, is that for a given doctrine to be accepted by all it must first be declared a dogma of faith. But, following this argument, by the same rule of three it could be said that the Decalogue could change in the future, because none of the Ten Commandments has been officially declared a dogma of faith."[6]

"No. We cannot change what has been the ordinary Magisterium of the Church for centuries. We cannot change the commandments of God's Law. We cannot change 'Thou shalt not kill.' This is part of the perennial Magisterium of the Church. If we were to accept only the dogmatic declarations of the Magisterium, the faith would be almost devoid of content."

—"Perhaps the Curran case has caused such intense debate in the US Church because certain Americans approach these moral questions with political guidelines?"

—"They live in a democratic system in which everything is resolved by voting, in a social environment in which the decisions of the majority must be accepted, and some try to apply this system to establish what is true or not in the area of faith. They try to substitute the 'sensus fidei' with 'consensus' on the truths of faith and moral principles.[7]

—"Some Americans complain. They say that the doctrine and teachings of his pontificate are too strict. . . ."

—"I am responsible for ensuring that these teachings are faithful to the doctrine of Christ. That is my task as Pope and that is the task of the bishops:

5. Charles E. Curran (United States, 1934), a theologian whose faculty to teach Catholic theology in Catholic schools was withdrawn in 1986 by the Congregation for the Doctrine of the Faith because of his positions on certain moral issues.

6. In reality, the dogmas of faith are very few: most of them are included in the "Creed." Over the centuries, a few others have been defined: the last was the dogma of the Assumption of the Virgin Mary, solemnly declared by Pius XII on November 1st, 1950. But the content of the Christian faith is not limited to these dogmas. John Paul II mentions the ordinary and universal magisterium: that is, when, even without a solemn act, all the bishops in union with the Pope agree that some truth must be considered definitive and binding for believers.

7. "Sense of faith." Expression that indicates the capacity of the faithful to recognize that a certain truth is part of the content of faith.

we have the responsibility to transmit those teachings as we have received them, as Christ taught them. We cannot change them, because they are not ours. We follow in the footsteps of Christ, who said: 'My teaching is not mine but His who sent me'. We teach in His name and we cannot transmit something contrary, different, to what He said."

—"On that day in 1978, when you agreed to become Pope, you took on your shoulders a weight that will be at times thankless. . . ."

—"Yes, but this is not exclusive to my pontificate. Remember what happened to Paul VI with *Humanae Vitae*, and the great response that his Encyclical Letter unleashed. How comfortable, how easy it would have been for him to write what so many wanted! But he could only write what he wrote."

—"During your pontificate there have been a series of *affairs*: Schillebeeckx, Küng, Curran, Boff. . . . Was it necessary for them to break out, after a period of certain confusion in the Church?"[8]

—"It was necessary to show the doctrine clearly. I have been a professor and I know the importance of freedom of research. But, in this case, it is not a problem of freedom of research, but of freeing the faithful from the confusion caused by hearing all kinds of personal opinions about the faith from those who should be transmitting the teachings of the Church to them."

"Public opinion accepts more easily what is easier to live with, which in many cases contradicts the traditional teaching of the Church, especially in the moral field. But the Church has the duty to teach and defend her own Magisterium, without generating confusion among the faithful. It is a doctrinal duty and a pastoral duty."

—"A Pope must make decisions . . ."

—"And sometimes, complicated decisions."

—"And what has been the most difficult decision of your pontificate so far?"

—(After a pause). "One of these questions arose in Latin America with liberation theology. A great confusion arose. For the Church it is necessary to have a liberation theology that is free from the influence of ideologies. It is a very important problem. Not so much because of the decision

8. Along with Curran, the media frequently echoed the controversies of other theologians with the Holy See, especially Edward Schillebeeckx (Belgium, 1914–2009), Hans Küng (Switzerland, 1928–2021) and Leonardo Boff (Brazil, 1938). Generally, these were problems that had arisen in the previous decade.

that had to be made, which was difficult, but because of the situation in those countries."

The dialogue has been so fluid throughout the dinner, that we have dragged on without realizing it and the Pope did not make any sign to finish. Dziwisz discreetly indicated to me that it was getting late and we had to finish. I tell the Pope that we do not want to tire him any more and shortly afterwards we say goodbye.

Wilton is very grateful to have had this opportunity to speak with the Pope in such a direct and clear way. Before we said goodbye, back in Rome, we talked about personal matters. "Wilton," I told him, "I have been praying for you for years." At that time, Wilton was considering, as was his wife, the possibility of joining the Catholic Church. He asked my advice and I suggested that he call Msgr. Rigali[9] and make an appointment with him. Wilton gave me a hug, assuring me that he would.[10]

About *Sala Stampa*

September 11, 1986

I had asked Dziwisz for the possibility of commenting to the Holy Father on some issues concerning *Sala Stampa*: positive experiences of these last two years; some problems due to lack of coordination; the extension of our interest beyond the framework of the Italian press; concrete results regarding efforts to have a greater impact on public opinion; and the possibility for *Sala Stampa to* take a step forward and comment on the activities of the Pope and the Holy See, without limiting itself to transmitting speeches and documents.

These are the themes of today's dinner at Castelgandolfo. The Pope agrees: this step forward, he says, is necessary in the present circumstances. He agrees when I explain to him that in order to take it, I need to have more information, which should come from the Secretariat of State and from the Section for

9. Justin Rigali (United States, 1935) was then president of the Pontifical Ecclesiastical Academy, the diplomatic school of the Holy See. He later became secretary of the Congregation for Bishops, and archbishop of St. Louis, Missouri and then of Philadelphia, Pennsylvania. He was appointed cardinal in 2003.

10. Several months later, he and his wife joined the Catholic Church in an intimate ceremony that took place in the chapel of the Pontifical Academy. There were four of us: he, his wife, Msgr. Rigali and myself. Weeks later, the two of them attended Mass with the Pope in his private chapel. [Author's note]

General Affairs.[11] He agrees and tells me to send him a note with the issues we have discussed.

Before I leave, Stanisław accompanies me to greet Emery Kabongo. The Pope's second secretary had a serious bicycle accident in the garden of Castelgandolfo and has not yet fully recovered.

From France: Peace Day in Assisi

October 1986

From October 4 to 7, 1986, the Pope traveled to various French cities. From Lyon he made an appeal to the world, announcing the Prayer Meeting for Peace in Assisi: together with prayer, he asked "that those who promote hostilities today be ready to take an active part in this initiative." And—on the feast day of St. Francis, Apostle of Peace—he launched an urgent appeal "to achieve, at least during October 27, the date of the meeting, a complete cease-fire in all wars."

A few days later, on October 11 and 12, an unusual meeting was held in Reykjavik between US President Ronald Reagan and Gorbachev. Coincidence?

The Longest Trip

November 18 to December 1, 1986

It has been an extremely hard trip, the longest so far, both in time and distance. We spent two nights on the plane, trying to sleep. The continuous time changes—with jumps of five, six and more hours—have been terrible.

November 19. Bangladesh. The Pope celebrated Mass in a stadium in Dhaka, where there were priestly ordinations. He had meetings with people and groups of all kinds—among them, the delegation of the Church in Burma[12]—and the next day we went to Singapore. On the 21st we were in the Fiji Islands; on the

---

11. The Secretariat of State, the first organism of the Curia—also from the historical point of view—assists the Pope in his mission and in the relationship with the rest of the dicasteries. It is presided over by the Cardinal Secretary of State, an office appointed by the Pope, which lasts for a five-year term. At that time, the Secretariat of State had two sections: the first, for general affairs, under the direction of the substitute, assisted by an advisor. The second section, for relations with states, has its own secretary, assisted by an undersecretary. In 2017, Pope Francis introduced a third section, headed by a delegate, dedicated to the diplomatic personnel of the Holy See.

12. Present-day Myanmar, which at the time was a socialist republic with limited religious freedom.

22nd we were in New Zealand. When we got there—and we had only been traveling for five days—I was physically exhausted.

And I was not the only one. Some, like the Pope's valet, Angelo Gugel,[13] became dizzy from fatigue, an inexorable law that also applied to the Holy Father.

The trip continued as planned, and after various liturgical ceremonies, meetings and receptions in Auckland, Wellington, and Christchurch, three cities located in different parts of the islands of New Zealand, we arrived at Fairbairn airport in Canberra, the capital of Australia, on November 24.

After Canberra and Brisbane, we were in Sydney, where I was able to speak with the Pope for a few minutes in the entrance courtyard of St. Mary's Presbytery. He had just driven in to have lunch with the Australian bishops, and when he saw me he came up to me, smiling: "What do journalists have to say to each other?"

—"They want to know," I told him, "if the Pope is very tired."

—"The first few days, yes," he told me, "because of the continuous change of schedule. But now less so."

NOVEMBER 29. AUSTRALIA. We left by plane from Melbourne very early in the morning. We crossed the whole of Australia from north to south and arrived in Darwin. The Pope celebrated Mass in sweltering heat. Shortly afterwards we were back on board the plane for a flight of several hours that took us to Alice Springs, in the geographical center of Australia. There we had a meeting with the aborigines, in the middle—in this case—of a big storm, with lightning and rain. This delayed our return.

We returned to the plane in the afternoon, heading for Adelaide, a city located at the southern tip of the continent. We landed very late at night, after having traveled almost eight hours, four cities, crossing Australia twice, in only twenty-four hours!

The Pope invited me to have dinner with him on the plane during the flight from Alice Springs to Adelaide. On this occasion there was only Dziwisz. He was interested when I summarized how his words had been received by the media, especially the Australian media. I told him several anecdotes and gave him an overview of those days. The media response had been very positive. Whenever any laudatory reference to him was mentioned, he deflected attention by saying "Deo gratias," and changed the subject.

---

13. Angelo Gugel (Italy, 1935) was valet (a figure, in a certain sense, equivalent to that of a butler) to John Paul I (1978), John Paul II (1978–2005), and Benedict XVI (2005–2006).

I also told him that some media had referred to the economic cost of the trip.

—"The Successor of Peter," the Pope told me, "brings the message of Redemption, and Redemption has cost an immeasurable price: all the blood of Jesus Christ."

In the climate of trust fostered by the conversation, I told him that my prayer during these trips was always the same: "Lord, I ask you whatever the Pope asks of you at this moment."

—"I thank you very much," he replied.

On the flight from Darwin to Alice Springs, after celebrating Mass, the Pope wrote the draft for the general audience next Wednesday in Rome. In the afternoon of the same day, during the flight between Alice Springs and Adelaide, he corrected the draft and left the text ready. Once again, I was in awe of his mental order and his capacity for work.

A few days later, on our way back to Rome from the Seychelles, Dziwisz told me that the Pope wanted to have dinner with a journalist. I immediately thought of Victor Simpson of the *Associated Press*, who has accompanied the Holy Father on almost every trip. He is Jewish, married to Daniela, a Catholic, and a few months ago lost his twelve-year-old daughter Natascia in a terrorist attack at Rome's Fiumicino airport.[14]

Victor readily agreed and was especially appreciative.

---

14. The terrorist attack took place on Friday, December 27, 1985, at Leonardo da Vinci airport in Fiumicino, near Rome. Victor, then forty-three years old, was on his way to New York with his family—his wife Daniela and his other son, Michael—when the terrorists fired indiscriminately. Sixteen people were killed, and numerous others wounded.

3

Stronger than Hate

Uruguay, Chile, Argentina

March 31–April 12, 1987

The press is dominated by a climate of political reductionism around the trip: the issue is how, when, and in what way the Pope will meet with Pinochet.[1] I understand that interest, but when that is the *only thing* that seems to matter about this trip, I think that the Redemption ends up being enclosed in a political scheme.

The Pope was in Uruguay, Chile, and Argentina from March 31 to April 12, the day of the second World Youth Day in Buenos Aires. So far, it has been the third longest trip. The media attention was focused on Chile.

Serious incidents in Santiago during the solemn Mass for the beatification of Sister Teresa de Jesús de los Andes. A group of some three hundred opponents of Pinochet raised banners against the regime, threw stones at journalists and set tires and stubble on fire. The police intervened with charges and tear gas. The Pope remains collected and serene. Tear gas reaches the altar and makes us all cry, including the Pope. With Buzzonetti,[2] the Pope's doctor, we thought of soaking some gauze with water to alleviate the symptoms of the gas. But it was not necessary.

At the end of the Mass, the Pope remains kneeling in front of the altar. The Chilean Cardinal Fresno approaches him and says: "Holy Father, forgive us." But the Pontiff replies: "Why? Your people have followed the ceremony, they have participated in the Holy Mass. The only thing not to do

1. Augusto Pinochet Ugarte (Chile, 1915–2006) was a military officer who came to power in Chile through a coup d'état. His dictatorship (1973–1990) ended gradually after a plebiscite in 1988.

2. Renato Buzzonetti (Italy, 1924–2017) was personal physician to John Paul II throughout his pontificate and for four years, until his retirement, to Benedict XVI. Previously, he had been second physician to Paul VI and John Paul I.

in these situations is to surrender to the agitators." Returning to the nunciature, the Pope takes the microphone of the *popemobile* and repeats three times: "Love is stronger than hatred." And then: "I congratulate you for having reacted as Christians to violence." Cardinal Fresno tells him: "Today you have wounded my heart," and the Holy Father replies: "No, it is a great victory," because "the words of my homily—on reconciliation—were a commentary on what was happening."

The day after arriving in Rome, Martínez Somalo tells me that we will have lunch with the Pope. Mario Agnes, Martínez Somalo, Dziwisz and I are there. In reference to the trip, I tell the Pope that it is difficult for journalists to confront in their comments the two goals—eschatological and historical—of the Church. The Pope took the floor and made some remarks, from which I quote a few sentences:

> The salvation of man is for *this* man who lives on *this* earth, whose life is closed by death. Eternal salvation comes through what man does on this earth. But all of this is subordinate to the beatific vision, to redemption.
>
> The moral message to man is: order your actions according to justice, and not according to one ideology or another. There is a prejudice which thinks all temporality must be entrusted to Marxism or ideologies. The Church, they say, serves for the hereafter, but not for the here. The Marxists in my country say: go to the sacristies, but do not try to fix the world. Leave that to us. It is not so, because Christ has come to save the world, and not only the separated soul.
>
> Secular thinking, secularized, does not accept that man dies. It is the difference between Christ and non-believers: Christ knows that he must die.
>
> All that pertains to the true temporal good—truth, justice, beauty—being temporal, constitutes a preparation for the future kingdom.

Commenting on some press reports about the trip to Chile and Argentina, he said: "We had to defend our Chilean and Argentine friends from [ideological] colonialism." He referred to Pinochet as "*questo piccolo dittatore*" (this little dictator), no doubt in comparison to the dictatorships of the East.

Germany: Salt of the Earth

April 30–May 4th, 1987

A few weeks later, the words of the previous entry came to mind when the Pope visited several cities in Germany, and beatified Teresa Benedicta of the Cross (Edith Stein)[3] and the Jesuit Rupert Mayer.[4]

During the homily he made an appeal to the responsibility of Germans in public life, from which I select this paragraph:

> Sanctifying life also means that we feel a common responsibility to bring the spirit of Christ into public life. No Christian should remain indifferent to events in the world. [. . .] You must be the salt of the earth and bring the light of God's truth into all areas of life. This is a service we owe to the world. You cannot live without God! [. . .] You live in one of the richest nations on earth. . . . Do not let your hearts be hardened by wealth, as you contemplate the reality of so many needy and marginalized people throughout the world.

United States: Discipline or Faith?

September 10–21, 1987

Sept. 21. It is his second trip to the United States as John Paul II and the fourth for Karol Wojtyla. It has been exhausting, as usual. Suffice it to mention the places he has been in just ten days: Miami, Columbia, New Orleans, San Antonio, Phoenix, Los Angeles, Monterrey, Carmel, San Francisco, Detroit, and Fort Simpson in Canada's Northwest Territories (with indigenous people from Canada). In San Antonio, after a very long Mass, under a blazing sun, I asked him if he was tired. "I don't know," he said laughing.

---

3. Edith Stein (Germany, 1891–1942), philosopher, Carmelite, and martyr of Hebrew origin. She was a collaborator of the philosopher Husserl. She converted to Catholicism at the age of thirty. Some time later she became a Carmelite nun in Cologne, under the name of Teresa Benedicta of the Cross. She was arrested by the Nazis in the Netherlands and imprisoned in the Auschwitz-Birkenau concentration camp, where she was murdered along with her sister Rosa in 1942. She was canonized in 1998 by John Paul II, who declared her co-patroness of Europe.

4. Rupert Mayer (Germany, 1876–1945), a Jesuit priest who was arrested three times by the Gestapo, accused of preaching against Nazism. During the last arrest, when he was already sixty-three years old, his health deteriorated so much that, in order to avoid making him a martyr, the Nazi authorities transferred him from a concentration camp to the Benedictine Abbey of Ettal, where he was released in May 1945. He died a few months later while celebrating Mass.

Some media have presented this trip to the United States and Canada in a confrontational way, placing the Pope in conflict with American Catholics on issues related to moral theology (specifically, the morality of marriage and sexuality). Many of the questions from journalists, on the outbound trip, go in this direction. "The press says it will be a difficult trip," observes one of the special envoys. "I am obedient to the press," replies the Pope with humor: "If the trip is difficult, we must pray and ask for prayers."

Although, apparently, the most burning issues of this journey concern the field of moral theology, in my opinion the deep roots of many of the questions raised are of an ecclesiological nature. The people of America need to understand what the Church is. I have the impression that there has been during the last decades a strong horizontalist reductionism, so to speak. This attitude tries to make some essential aspects of the Church merely disciplinary; and, therefore, open to historical changes (such as the ordination of women).

The sense of the ecclesiastical magisterium has been lost and many do not accept either the authority of the bishop or that of the Pope: perhaps this insistence on dialogue and on "being heard" in order to reach "a final consensus" is due, to a certain extent, to this attitude.

I have also noticed that the Americans often use socially and politically democratic approaches when speaking of the Church. I speculate that this stems from a reality of diverse character; one the one hand the notable influence of Protestant thought; and on the other hand a mistaken notion of the separation between Church and State. Many Americans, in their daily lives, make false choices between *their conscience as Christians* and *their conscience as citizens*.

To summarize, the trip was very interesting. In one of the Pope's meeting with journalists, someone told him that, in the United States, there is a community on the margins of the Church that is waiting for some words from the Pope: the homosexuals. I took note of his answer: "They are not on the margins. You know that people in difficulty are always at the center, at the heart of the Church. They are not marginalized."

When we were flying to Detroit, the Pope asked me what echoes I had heard from his Hollywood speech, given to those working in the film industry. He asked because he had received some negative comments. I told him that my impression, on the contrary, was very positive: I learned that *Le Monde* had commented on it at the editorial meeting and that *The New York Times* had published the entire speech.

Vice President Bush was waiting for him in Detroit for the farewell ceremony. He wanted to talk to him alone for a few minutes. Some have interpreted his presence as a simple *gesture* for his upcoming election campaign.[5] That may be all it is. I do not know. But it is worth remembering, on the other hand, that he is one of the few American politicians who has taken a clear pro-life position in the abortion debate.

SEPTEMBER 22, 1987. BALANCE AT CASTELGANDOLFO. The Pope invited Mario Agnes and myself to lunch at Castelgandolfo. Those of us who have accompanied him during this trip are frankly exhausted. Even the Pope looks tired, despite his enormous resilience. 'I still don't know if I'm in America or in Europe," he tells us at one point.

We talk about everything. He is interested in analyzing this trip from an outsider's point of view. I give him my opinion and the reactions I have observed in different sectors of American society: bishops, "normal Catholics," Jews, Protestants, homosexual groups.

I think that his meeting with the nuns in Los Angeles caused him pain: it had a distant atmosphere, manifested even by some details of coldness. He also suffered during his meeting with the priests in Miami. The presenter, a priest named Frank McNulty, introduced his speech with less-than-orthodox comments on the ordination of women and priestly celibacy. These were received with great applause, and the Pope, who is not as fluent in English as he would have liked, was not able to clarify things as he would have liked.

The Absence of the Czechoslovakian Bishops

OCTOBER 3, 1987

This morning I received a note explaining why the Czechoslovakian bishops will not participate in the synod on the laity.[6] The tone seems to me to be excessively *kind*.

---

5. George H. W Bush (United States, 1924–2018) was the 41st president of the United States (1989–1993), and father of President George W. Bush. At the time he was vice president with Reagan and was preparing for the 1988 presidential election.

6. This synod lasted from October 1st to October 30th, 1987. It was entitled: "Vocation and Mission of the Laity in the Church and in the World Twenty Years after Vatican II" and generated the apostolic exhortation *Christifideles laici* (December 30, 1988). An apostolic exhortation is a document of universal character, but somewhat less solemn than encyclicals. They are exhortative in nature and always bear the signature of the Pope.

The Pope spoke openly about this matter in his speech to Cardinal Tomášek,[7] who made his *ad limina* visit[8] two days ago: the Czechoslovak bishops are not coming because they are prevented by the Communist authorities, which is not clearly stated in that note.

I learn that the note comes from Cardinal Casaroli. I decide to call him to explain the reasons why I think he should not have it published: it will be misinterpreted by the press, and some may consider it as a "backward step" and a clarification of the Pope's words. He nods, but does not seem very convinced. In the end, the note is published by *L'Osservatore Romano*, but it is not distributed by *Sala Stampa*.

This episode leads me to reflect on the different visions of the problem that the Pope and Casaroli have, born of two life experiences that seek the good of the Church and the freedom of Christians by different paths. Both have their risks.

Casaroli tries not to confront the Czechoslovakian authorities, thinking, perhaps, that taking a stand in defense of one's trampled rights does not usually produce concrete results. He maintains that the best thing for the Church is to try to resolve this type of situation in the most diplomatic way possible.

The Pope, for his part, is outraged by the actions of the Communist authorities towards the Catholic hierarchy in Czechoslovakia, which he considers unjustifiable. For him, in this case, the priority is to make the truth known. This is more important to him than acting diplomatically for possible future gains.

His experience in Poland with the Communist authorities explains his way of acting. And now that, as Pope, he has a voice to defend those who have none, he is unwilling to remain silent: "Is it possible that the successor of Peter, to whom the solicitude for the Universal Church has been entrusted, should look on such a situation with indifference?" he said in his October 1st meeting with Tomášek.

The Pope's Rest

December 21, 1987

I am going to the Pope's apartment at 9:30 AM to meet with Stanisław. I am interested in updating him on some issues and projects of the office, which had been discussed in previous meetings with the Holy Father.

7. František Tomášek (Czech Republic, 1899–1992) was an archbishop and cardinal of Prague who maintained a prudent yet bold opposition to the Czechoslovak Communist regime.

8. The *visit ad limina Apostolorum* is the visit that all diocesan bishops must make to "the threshold of the gates (limina) of St. Peter and St. Paul." During this visit they report to the Pope, every five or ten years, on the state of the diocese they govern.

In the conversation, the subject of the Pope's capacity as an administrator comes up, which is something that is beginning to be commented on in the press. Laughing, he tells me that "maybe it is true that the Pope is a bad administrator? In reality, it is clear, and he sees it this way too, that the tasks of administration belong to his collaborators, above all to his most immediate ones." Before saying goodbye, he tells me that what he is concerned about is the Pope's rest. That also leaves me thoughtful.

Visit to *Stampa Estera*

January 16–18, 1988

Working dinner with the Pope in the Pontifical Apartment. Crescencio Sepe was also there. It was about preparing his visit to the Foreign Press Association, the *Stampa Estera*. He wants to know which people will attend, what questions they can ask him. I tell him that it is likely that he will be asked about his possible trip to the Soviet Union and about the Palestinian question, very present these days in the media.[9]

In the end, those will be two of the three questions he is asked. At dinner, the Pope speaks of some documents that are being prepared, such as the letter on the Christian Millennium of Russia. About a hypothetical trip of his to Russia, he says that, at the present time, the difficulties come not only from the Soviet authorities, but also from the Orthodox leaders.

The next day, I have dinner again with the Pope to talk over his visit to the *Stampa Estera* with him. The Pope comments: "Don Stanisław tells me that the climate among the journalists is very good." I agree, and I tell him about the detailed preparation for the visit and my own observations of the atmosphere afterwards.

On *Sollicitudo rei socialis*

March 10, 1988

During dinner, I ask the Pope about the "biography" of his latest encyclical, *Sollicitudo rei socialis*, published last February 19. He gives me a broad and detailed answer: he likes this kind of question.

---

9. On December 9, 1987, the first *Intifada* or rebellion of the Palestinians began. It was the so-called "war of the stones." Day after day, the news showed street battles between Palestinians and Israeli army soldiers.

"When I read *Mater et Magistra*[10] I said to myself: '*Ecco lo Spirito Santo*!" ('Here is the Holy Spirit!')." The Pope explains to me that before John XXIII, the social doctrine of the Church sought—above all—the way to resolve *the workers' question*; it considered the problem as a conflict between social classes.

"With *Mater et Magistra*," he points out, "there was a change in approach: in addition to seeking justice among the various strata of society in each country, justice had to be sought between the two *worlds* that had come into being: the developed world and the poor world. The Church's doctrine was placed in a much broader context.

With this conception—he continues—John XXIII responded to the pretension of Marxism without even naming it. Marxism tries to present itself as the solution to global injustice. *Mater et Magistra* rejects this pretension and indicates the new direction that the search for social justice should take.

Populorum Progressio[11]—he goes on to explain—was less satisfactory to him. The Communist press received it positively, because it especially emphasized the responsibility of the rich in the matter of poverty. "But, in my opinion, this perspective is incomplete. And I thought: we have to complete this world view."

He points out that new issues, such as foreign debt and liberationism, have also arisen since *Populorum Progressio*. These require a new response and they have influenced the preparation of this encyclical. He also mentions the Marxist and capitalist systems. "They are to blame for the fact that humanity is facing a threatening future. It is not only a question of war, because the poor countries of the South cannot militarily oppose the rich countries of the North, but of the slavery to which so many poor people are subjected."

And he explains that this slavery is twofold at the present time: there are many slaves of capitalism, and the confrontation between the two blocs also enslaves thousands of men. For this reason, he wished to show in the encyclical how all these factors interact with each other, going beyond a dialectical vision between social classes or between the great blocs. "Providence has acted in *its own way*. Certainly, with Gorbachev it is almost coming to a Soviet self-criticism, at least in the application of its principles." In this context he adds that he considers Marxist-rooted liberationism "an unjust answer to an unjust situation."

10. John XXIII's encyclical *Mater et Magistra* (*Mother and Teacher*) was published on May 15, 1961.

11. Paul VI's encyclical *Populorum Progressio* (The Development of Peoples), dated March 26, 1967, addresses—from a Christian perspective—cooperation among peoples and the problems of developing countries.

He also speaks about some of the people who collaborated in the encyclical, such as Calvez, Etchegaray, Mejía or Buttiglione.[12] And, last of all, the Pope points out that social justice was a topic that some episcopates, such as the Canadian one, wanted him to address.

Christianity in Russia

March 30, 1988

It is Holy Week Wednesday. Thousands of pilgrims are walking the streets of Rome. The Pope has invited me to lunch. He has arrived in the red cape he usually wears during general audiences. Mario Agnes and the two secretaries, Dziwisz and Kabongo, were there.

I wanted to discuss some issues that have been in the public eye in recent weeks: the reception of the encyclical *Sollicitudo rei socialis* and the apostolic letter *Euntes Mundum,* on the millennium of Christianity in Russia, published at the end of January.

The Pope spends a good part of the lunch talking about Christianity in Russia from the historical point of view. It is clear that this is a subject he has mastered. "The problem is the lack of knowledge that exists, even at the episcopal level. They tell me that they were not aware of all this." And he recalls that the commemoration of the millennium is an extraordinary event.

At another point in the meal, he told me that he was preparing a document on women.[13] I did not know anything about it and I find the very idea extraordinary.

I noticed some details. The forks, spoons, and knives are made of nickel silver. And the bread has been replaced by *grissini.*[14] He usually pours a little water into the glass of wine before drinking, and when he speaks, he moves the plate when he finishes before it is taken away. The wine is usually white, not branded. From the label, it is clear that it is a gift wine, handmade.

---

12. Jean-Yves Calvez (France, 1927–2010) was a Jesuit priest and expert in Marxism. Cardinal Roger Marie Etchegaray (France, 1922–2019) was, among other positions, president of the Pontifical Council "Justice and Peace" and of the Pontifical Council "Cor Unum." Cardinal Jorge María Mejía (Argentina, 1923–2014) was an expert in the social doctrine of the Church; he was later librarian of the Vatican Library and archivist of the Vatican Secret Archives. Rocco Butttiglione (Italy, 1948) in addition to being a university professor, has been an MEP and vice-president of the Italian parliament.

13. It was published on August 15, 1988, under the name *Mulieris dignitatem.*

14. This is the name given in Italy to *breadsticks,* thin and elongated in shape.

When the Pope asks questions at dinner, he raises issues in general, leaving time for his interlocutor to give his opinion. I don't know if he is more attentive to what is being said or the person who is saying it. He is very attentive to the argument and, at the same time, I get the feeling that he is trying to understand the mental structure and personality of the person he is talking to. In any case, he shows great interest in those he speaks with, and in what the other is saying.

On the USSR and the Holy See

April 14, 1988

Public opinion is frequently concerned with relations between the USSR and the Holy See. I believe the fact that John Paul II is a Slav, the presence of Gorbachev in Russia, and the Pope's repeated references to his desire to visit Catholics in the Soviet Union have all contributed to this climate.

The Roman daily *La Republica* published a news item today along the same lines: Anatoly Krasikov, vice-president of the *TASS* news agency, will be in Rome on the 20th. He will give a lecture at the *Stampa Estera* on relations between the Soviet Union and the Holy See. The journalist states that he will possibly conduct an interview with John Paul II, which will be published on the occasion of the anniversary of the Christian Millennium in Russia. The idea of the interview is nice, but—in reality—nothing has been arranged.[15]

Uruguay, Bolivia, Peru and Paraguay

May 7 to 19, 1988

May 7 to 9. Uruguay. A country with a secularist tradition and little religious practice. The Pope had already been here a year ago to commemorate the Montevideo Agreements, which in 1978 prevented the war between Chile and Argentina over the Beagle Channel dispute. On the occasion of that visit he celebrated a Mass in a central square of Montevideo, the Esplanade of the Three Crosses. The large cross that presided over the ceremony had been installed in the square. A few months ago there was a parliamentary debate to decide whether it should remain or not. Those in favor of leaving it won. On this trip, President Julio Maria Sanguinetti attended the Pope's Mass, despite declaring himself an agnostic.

15. In fact, nothing will be done [Author's Note].

At the Montevideo airport, a girl sneaks into the papal plane. She is discovered by one of our security. She just wanted to give the Pope a gift; a wind-up alarm clock with a piece of paper written on it: "Thank you, Pope, for having woken up Uruguay."

Pope ordains priests in Florida[16] and celebrates Mass at Mattos Neto Park in Salto. On the ninth he moves to Bolivia.

May 10. La Paz (Bolivia). In La Paz, he celebrated a Mass for families attended by thousands of Bolivians. He sets a high horizon for them: "Do not allow yourselves to be seduced by the easy recourse to divorce, nor reject the grace of the sacrament, opting for forms of union contrary to God's will and to the natural law, such as concubinage, where full love cannot be present."

May 11. Oruro (Bolivia). They tell me by telephone that the Minister of Foreign Affairs of Paraguay has published in the government newspaper *Patria* a letter to the Nuncio[17] to inform him, on behalf of the government, that the Pope's meeting with the so-called "builders of society" has been cancelled for reasons of public order.

That meeting was scheduled for May 17, at the National Sports Palace, on the second day of the Pope's stay in Asuncion. This decision is a sign of the existing tensions between some bishops and President Stroessner.[18]

He immediately informed Dziwisz and Martínez Somalo. On the return trip to Cochabamba, Dziwisz informed the Pope.

We are residing in a Franciscan convent. I get up to attend the Mass that Piero Marini[19] was going to celebrate in the small chapel of the convent and when I enter—it is twenty past six o'clock—I see the Pope praying on his knees on one of the kneelers. Mass is not celebrated there so as not to interrupt him. The Pope remains at the tabernacle until a quarter to eight, when breakfast is served.

---

16. Florida is a department in Uruguay, analogous to an American state.

17. Apostolic nuncios are stable representatives of the Pope in various countries. They are archbishops, have Vatican citizenship and diplomatic status as ambassadors. The diplomatic service of the Holy See is the oldest in the world.

18. Alfredo Stroessner Matiauda (Paraguay, 1912–2006) was president of the Republic of Paraguay from 1954 to 1989, when he was overthrown by a military insurrection. He died in exile in Brazil. His dictatorship lasted thirty-five years.

19. Piero Marini (Italy, 1942) was the Pope's *Cerimoniere*—the Master of Liturgical Celebrations—from 1987 to 2007.

At eleven o'clock in the morning, he celebrates Mass at the airport of Cochabamba with the attendance of thousands of people. Afterwards, he has lunch at the National Seminary. After a brief rest, he summons Casaroli and Martínez Somalo to discuss the Paraguay question. He indicated that I should be present, to advise them how to approach the matter in a way that comes off well to the press, taking into account our imminent and necessary communication with the press. The Pope encourages us to resolve the situation. If not, he says, we will have to consider suspending the trip to Paraguay.

In the afternoon, while the Pope held the scheduled meeting with priests and seminarians at the Diocesan Seminary of Cochabamba, Martínez Somalo and I went with a police car to the convent of San Francisco, where we spent the night, to make several phone calls.

Martínez Somalo speaks with Rome so that they transmit the Pope's indications to the Nuncio in Asunción. He considers that the most opportune thing to do is to send Father Tucci to Asunción so that he can personally address the problem.

May 12. Sucre and Santa Cruz (Bolivia). We continued our trip: first to Sucre, where a Mass was celebrated on the occasion of the 450th anniversary of the beginning of evangelization in Bolivia. Then, we go on to Santa Cruz, where we met with representatives of the intellectual world.

We continue with the negotiations. We have difficulties connecting with Rome because of our continuous traveling. Hours go by and no answer is received. It occurs to me to try and put pressure on the authorities.

I am making a statement to the international agencies in the hope that the Paraguayan authorities will reconsider their attitude. I write: "For now, I must express the shock provoked by an unprecedented decision regarding the Pope's pastoral activity." I think that these words—which I say to journalists, underlining especially the "for now"—leave all options open to us while still pushing to change the situation.

May 13. More Arrangements. At 7:30 AM Piero Marini is called from the Presidential Palace in Asuncion and he passes the call to me. It is Ambassador Pappalardo, Stroessner's chief of protocol, who has just read my statement to the press.

He thinks it is a "very well-considered" statement and begins to explain to me why the meeting with the "builders of society" in Asunción has been suspended. In addition to his disagreements with some members of the ecclesiastical hierarchy, he tells me that there have been numerous anomalies in the distribution of invitations: that they—those of the Colorado Party—are many more than those of the opposition and, nevertheless, the first part of the event is taken up by a group of "rabid leftists," etc.[20]

I try to make him see that there are two priorities in this matter: firstly, the good international reputation of Paraguay; and secondly, the pastoral freedom of the Pope. He speaks to me of a series of local problems and I answer him that these issues—which may be real—should be solved by bringing together the Nuncio, Georg Zur,[21] and some bishops to reach an agreement. From the conversation, I deduce that it is easier for him to talk to Zur than to the bishops, and that the bishops do not know how to fix the situation.

I insist on the need for dialogue and I ask Ambassador Pappalardo to try to reach a solution before two o'clock in the afternoon, so that I can communicate it to the Pope.

At four o'clock in the afternoon, as a result of the efforts of both sides, Ambassador Pappalardo calls me from Asunción to tell me that everything is settled. Then Zur does the same, reading me the text of the agreement over the phone. I communicate it to Casaroli and I am present when he transmits the news to the Pope, who comments with his usual good humor:—So? Will they let me go to Paraguay?

On May 17, "the builders of society" meeting took place at the Sports Palace in Asuncion. I took note of some lines from the Pope:

> To engage in this solidarity commitment means that you must stand on the side of the most needy in your country, to defend their rights and meet their just demands. Everyone is called to take his or her place in this peaceful campaign, which must be carried out by peaceful means, in order to achieve development in peace, and to safeguard nature itself and the world around us.
>
> The situations of poverty that characterize large areas of some countries, as is the case in yours, cry out to heaven, and are fertile ground for confrontation between brothers. For this reason, in addition to the call to dedicate all your forces to and to use your position of leadership in favor of the integral development of your country, for the benefit of all citizens,

20. The Colorado Party is a right wing Paraguayan party

21. Archbishop Georg Zur (Germany, 1930–2019) had been pronuncio to Malawi and Zambia, and at this time was nuncio, in addition to Paraguay, in numerous countries, such as India, Mexico, Burundi, Uganda, Russia and Austria.

> I would like to remind you of the call of your bishops to enter into constructive dialogue, capable of creating bridges of understanding based on mutual respect and freedom.

Among the journalists accompanying the Pope is Richard Denton, a British producer, and a team of professionals from the *BBC* in London who are preparing a program on the first ten years of the pontificate. I have been with them for a whole day. I also see how they weep, as they work, during the Pope's meeting with the sick in the cathedral. "Regardless of one's beliefs," the cameraman tells me in the evening, "this man is exceptional." None of them is Catholic.

In one of the Pope's many encounters with the people, a child greets the Pope and asks him: "Are you the same one who is on TV?"

On Thursday, on the return flight, the Pope addressed a few words of thanks to all of us who had accompanied him, including the four ambassadors of the countries, and especially the three present on the plane, from Bolivia, Paraguay and Peru. He recalls a saying in Polish: "A horse, when it returns home, walks faster and faster." And he jokes that this also happens to us: "It seems that this plane is like a horse trying to get home as soon as possible."

May 20. We had dinner with the Pope, Mario Agnes, Martínez Somalo and the two secretaries. Although the trip has been very hard, I find the Pope as usual: vigorous and cheerful. He has not given himself a single day of rest, also as usual. Today he had a meeting with Ratzinger, as he does every Friday. It occurs to me to think that one of the topics of the meeting may have been the outcome of the Lefebvre case, which, according to the comments I have received, is practically resolved.[22]

22. Marcel-François Marie Lefebvre (France, 1905–1991) was an archbishop known for his positions contrary to various teachings of the Second Vatican Council. During that time it was thought that Lefebvre would accept the protocol requested by the Holy See, but this was not the case. In 1970, Lefebvre created the Priestly Fraternity of St. Pius X, which had its own seminary, that of Ecône. But his harsh criticism of the Holy See and the Council led to an apostolic visitation of the seminary. Afterwards, the diocesan bishop, Msgr. Mamie, withdrew recognition of the Fraternity, stripping it of juridical support. Despite this illegal situation, Lefebvre continued to ordain deacons and priests, for which he was suspended *a divinis* on June 29, 1976. On October 11 of that year he was received by Paul VI: after that audience he said that he had reconciled with the Pope, but soon after he continued his attacks on "modernist Rome" and the council. In 1977 he published a book entitled *J'acusse le Concile.* John Paul II tried to resume dialogue with Lefebvre as soon as he was elected Pope; but following the celebration of the First Interconfessional Day in Assisi on October 27, 1986, Lefebvre's followers redoubled their criticism. On May 5th, 1988, Cardinal Ratzinger and Msgr. Lefebvre signed an agreement, but soon after Lefebvre changed his mind again.

4

A Visit to the Kremlin

In Moscow for the Millennium

June 8–13, 1988

On the millennium anniversary of Christianity's beginnings in Russia in 988, the Moscow Patriarch asked the Soviet authorities for permission to celebrate the date with special solemnity. Gorbachev, who has been in power for three years, granted permission.

The Orthodox Patriarch invited the various Christian confessions to Moscow for the celebration. They did not formally invite the Pope, but asked him to send a delegation for the event. To show the importance he gave to this anniversary, the Pope decided that the delegation of the Holy See would be headed by the Secretary of State, Agostino Casaroli, instead of Johannes Willebrands, as would be normal because of his position as president of the Pontifical Council for Christian Unity.[1]

The Pope also made another important decision. He wrote a personal letter to Gorbachev to be delivered by hand, if the occasion arose. On a personal level, I was suprised when, a few days ago, Casaroli asked me on behalf of the Pope to accompany them as part of the delegation.

In addition to Casaroli and Willebrands, the other members of the Holy See delegation are as follows: the secretary of the Council for Christian Unity, Pierre Duprey;[2] and Salvatore Escribano, a member of that Council; Roger Etchegaray, from the Pontifical Council for Justice and Peace; the vice-rector of the Pontifical Oriental Institute, John Long; Faustino Sainz, of the Council

1. Johannes Willebrands (Holland, 1909–2006) dedicated a good part of his life to ecumenical relations. He was president of the Secretariat for Christian Unity (later Pontifical Council) from 1969 to 1989. Elevated to the cardinalate in 1969, he combined his posts in Rome with that of archbishop of Utrecht during the period 1975–83.

2. Pierre Duprey (France, 1922–2007), of the Society of the Missionaries of Africa (White Fathers), was secretary of the Pontifical Council for Christian Unity (1983–1999).

for the Public Affairs of the Church;[3] the vice-secretary of that Council, Audrys Backis; and Father Szlowieniec, of the same Council.

Wednesday, June 8. I arrive at the airport. Optimistic atmosphere. We leave mid-morning for Moscow on an *Aeroflot* plane. On that flight are Casaroli, Etchegaray, Backis, Sainz, Szlowienec, and myself. The rest of the delegation is already there.

Lunkov, USSR ambassador to Italy, has come to see us off at the airport, where he speaks with Casaroli. The Cardinal told him that he is carrying a letter from the Pope to Gorbachev, and that he is open to interviews and meetings with various people. We do not know if this letter can be delivered to him, because no meeting with him is foreseen. The program only indicates, in a generic way, that there will be an "official reception in the Kremlin" on Monday the 13th.

Casaroli says, "but we do not know exactly what it will be. We assume that it will be a reception for all delegations. We will see what happens."

When we have already taken off, Alceste Santini, Vaticanist of the newspaper *L'Unità*, of the Italian Communist Party, comes to greet me. He is the *link* between Casaroli and the Soviet Embassy in the present situation, in which there is no regular channel of communication between the Holy See and the USSR government. He speaks to me because he wishes to interview the Cardinal. I make the arrangements and ask him a few questions, noting his responses. More than an interview for publication, he is interested in knowing the Cardinal's thoughts on various issues in order to discuss them with the Soviet authorities later.

When they finish talking, I provide Casaroli with some photocopies of the news that has appeared in the last few days: interviews with Gorbachev and Soviet news summaries.

We arrive in Moscow around 4:00 PM. It is hot. We are met at the airport by Josef Poustoutoff, Archimandrite of the Moscow Patriarch. He is a young and cordial man, who speaks magnificent French and is a good friend of Father Duprey and Willebrands. He will be our interpreter during these days.

We are welcomed by Karcev, Chairman of the Council for Religious Affairs (Minister of Worship, in official terminology), who greets us on behalf of the State and expresses his wish that Casaroli's stay in Moscow will serve to improve relations between the Soviet Union and the Holy See.

---

3. In 1991, the Council for the Public Affairs of the Church was renamed the Section for Relations with States (the Second Section of the Secretariat of State).

Shortly afterwards, Metropolitan Philarete of Minsk[4] arrived to give us "a fraternal embrace and welcome to Moscow, where we will celebrate together the Millennium of Christianity in Russia."

We go to the VIP lounge of the airport for a cup of tea and some sandwiches. The Austrian TV correspondent discreetly approaches me and tells me that he is in contact with some Ukrainian Catholics of the Eastern Rite, who have come to Moscow with the desire to talk to the Secretary of State. I tell him to send me a list of these people at the hotel.[5]

We leave the airport in official cars of the Patriarch—although in reality, they belong to the government—towards the *Sovietskaya Hotel,* which will be our residence during these days. The cars smell of gasoline: I don't know if it is a carburetor defect or bad quality gasoline. Heat and humidity: the usual Moscow weather in June, it seems.

We are then driven to the *Hotel Ukraine,*[6] one of "Stalin's seven skyscrapers," where we check in and pick up our credentials.

Before dinner, Casaroli decides to take a short walk, but our hosts take him by car to Red Square. I think of the Western TV stations: they would have given anything to film the Secretary of State of the Holy See walking in front of the Kremlin, symbol of Soviet power.

I take a shower and start working: I have brought a list of telephone numbers belonging to foreign correspondents in Moscow. One by one, I start contacting them. I have dinner at the *Belgrade 2 Hotel* with a group of Italian journalists: Accattoli, Melli, Mandillo, Marinaro, del Colle, among others. It is a very noisy dinner with a westernized orchestra that does not let us speak. The atmosphere becomes more and more frivolous as time goes by, with ladies going back and forth beside our table. I decide to leave before the end of the dinner.

THURSDAY, JUNE 9. Mass at St. Louis of the French, the only Catholic church in Moscow. Fifty people, mostly of Polish origin or, at least, speaking Polish. A climate of enthusiasm: it is the first time they have ever seen the Secretary of State of the Holy See. They ask him for autographs. In the building across the street, about eighty meters away, I notice a fixed TV camera, focusing on the

4. Kirill Varfolomeyevich Vakhromeev, Metropolitan Filarete (Russia, 1935) has been leader of the Belarusian Orthodox Church (1989–2013).

5. The Ukrainian Greek Catholic Church is the largest of the autonomous Eastern Catholic Churches in full communion with the Holy See. During the Soviet regime it was severely persecuted.

6. It is now called the *Radisson-Royal Hotel.*

entrance of the church. I don't know if it continues to work. Possibly, in the past, it may have relayed the images of Catholics attending Mass in this church to some obscure outbuilding in the nearby Lubyanka, the KGB building.

After breakfast at the hotel, we leave for Zagorsk monastery—of the Holy Trinity and St. Sergius—which is located about forty-five kilometers [twenty-eight miles] from Moscow. It is a sunny and pleasant morning. We headed there with all the delegations present for the events of the Millennium, forming a long caravan of black cars. We ride in Volgas and Chaikas, the cars used by the members of the government and the hierarchs of the regime. Today, the State has put them the disposal of the Orthodox Church for this event.

The monastery of Zagorsk is a marvel. We venerated the relics of St. Sergius, kissing them through a green veil.

We spent the rest of the morning, together with members of other delegations, in the monastery hall where the closing of the Extraordinary Synod is taking place. There are numerous metropolitans, archimandrites and other members of the Russian Orthodox hierarchy. On our side are Casaroli, Willebrands, Etchegaray, Duprey, O'Connor (Archbishop of New York), and Glemp (Primate of Poland), among others. Martini (Archbishop of Milan) will arrive in a few days.

Karcev, the Minister of Worship, is seated in the chair, together with the hierarchy of the Orthodox Church. During the ceremony we agreed to create the creation of a fund of one million rubles for the families of the victims of the war in Afghanistan.[7] We discussed the complex duty to educate children and also the "restoration of the Leninist principles of socialism in the face of Stalinist deformations and errors." A letter was sent to Gorbachev formally supporting this *perestroika*[8] process: "We have urged all our faithful to support this process of renewal."

At mid-morning, Archimandrite Josef Poustutof asks Casaroli and the rest of us to leave the classroom for a brief meeting with the elderly Patriarch Pimen, who resides in the adjacent building and is quite ill.[9]

7. The Afghan-Soviet war (1979–1989), which ended with Moscow's withdrawal, is considered the "Soviet Vietnam."

8. The literal meaning of perestroika is "reconstruction." The term refers to the restructuring of the Soviet political and economic system, in an attempt to end the economic stagnation of the Russian economy in the eighties.

9. Pimen I—Sergey Mikhailovich Izvekov—(Russia, 1910–1990) was the 14th Patriarch of Moscow, a position he held almost entirely under the Soviet regime.

After lunch at the monastery, we return to Moscow in the early afternoon. At the hotel I am handed the list of names I asked the Austrian TV correspondent for. I pass it to Willebrands, who compares these names with those on a small handwritten list prepared for him by Lubachivsky in Rome.[10] It is a list of the clandestine hierarchy of the Catholic Church in Ukraine. Some names match. After talking it over with others, Willebrands decides to receive several of them at the hotel: two bishops and three priests are coming.

Casaroli is only with them for a few moments. I think that the meeting has been organized in this way because Casaroli, who wishes to establish contacts with the Soviet authorities, would not like these contacts to cease because he has received people "unpleasant" for the *Nomenklatura*.

FRIDAY, JUNE 10TH. Holy Mass in the church of San Luis. There are more people. Greetings, families, and some shouts of "Long live the Pope!" I look at the TV camera that focuses on us from the building across the street and I am no longer so sure that it is an instrument of the past: has it changed its position with respect to yesterday, or is it my imagination? Breakfast with Domenico del Rio.[11]

We leave for the Bolshoi Theater. At five past ten in the morning the hall is packed. The seats in the theater are armchairs, not seats in the style of *La Scala* in Milan. At the front, above the stage, there is a Soviet emblem with two portraits of Lenin. There is also a date, which recalls the antiquity of this building: 1856.

A gong sounds, the curtain opens, and I contemplate an unusual spectacle: in the center of the long table that runs from one end of the stage to the other is Pimen, Patriarch of all the Russias. To his right, Karcev, Minister of Worship. Next to him, a senior Party official. To his left, Raisa Gorbachev, the wife of the General Secretary. Behind, in four staggered rows of seats, members of the representations of the various Christian and religious denominations: among them, Casaroli and Willebrands.

Pimen thanked the State for its collaboration in the celebration of the Millennium, echoing the words of Gorbachev. He greeted the representatives of the various churches with quotations from the Bible, and thanked the members of the diplomatic corps and the municipality for their presence.

---

10. Cardinal Myroslav Ivan Lubachivsky (Ukraine, 1918–2000) was Major Archbishop of Lviv and head of the Ukrainian Greek Catholic Church. He lived in exile in Rome until 1991. He was named cardinal in 1985.

11. Domenico del Rio (Italy, 1926–2003) was the Vaticanist of the Italian daily *La Repubblica* from 1975 to 1993.

He passed the floor to Filarete.[12] Filarete: "We are pleased with the direction being taken by those in charge of the State and we are pleased to be able to participate in this process." He shows strong support for the transformations underway, and his satisfaction with the agreement reached by Reagan and Gorbachev.

Then Metropolitan Juvenaly speaks:[13] "The relations between the State and the Church have not always been the same within the socialist State; there were certain difficulties at the beginning because we were not aware of the importance of the great Russian Revolution." He adds that among the victims there were "thousands and thousands of Party members; faithful of the Orthodox Church and members of the clergy."

He underlines that there were also internal problems, and mentions the split of the Orthodox Church. "We ask God and mankind for forgiveness, praying for the day to come soon when the separation of the Churches can be overcome. And he emphasizes in conclusion: "It was the Church that stimulated resistance in the face of foreign invaders; that contributed to the victory and that made, at the end of the war, an appeal to Christians all over the world to reach the desired harmony."

The meeting closes in the early afternoon. Pimen takes the floor again to recall that "our dear homeland is going through a period of transformation, of *perestroika,* of democratization. We appreciate the contacts we have had with the state authorities. We wish to contribute with our moral and ethical values."

Final song, standing. On the curtain, a large acronym: CCCP, next to the hammer and sickle, under a large photograph of Lenin.

We go out. It is raining. We drive back to the hotel. Light lunch. Still no news on whether or not there will be a meeting with Gorbachev.

At seven o'clock in the evening a concert is scheduled at the *Bolshoi,* on the occasion of the Millennium. I decide to catch up on my sleep. Before going to bed I wonder where all this will lead us. There is a certain union, a certain concordance and confluence of peoples and individuals in the name of God. We Westerners, I conclude, must broaden our *field of vision.* We look too much to the West (sometimes exclusively), and the way of living and reasoning here is alien to us. By visiting this part of the planet our conception is enlarged, both culturally and from the Christian and religious point of view. This is the East.

12. Metropolitan of Kiev

13. Metropolitan Juvenaly (Vladimir Kirillovich Poyarkov) (Russia, 1935) was appointed Metropolitan of Krutitsy and Kolomna in 1977.

At the same time, I perceive that in the parliaments of Pimen, Filarete and Juvenaly there is a common element: with them we are not dealing with a universal Church but with something that is, above all, national.

SATURDAY, JUNE 11TH. In the morning I am told that the concert I missed yesterday at the *Bolshoi* was spectacular. The program has undergone some changes: this very morning there will be a meeting between the delegations and President Gromyko at the Supreme Soviet.

During this meeting, Gromyko uses the term *ecumenism* and responds to written questions. He then gives the floor to those present.[14] Willebrands comments:

> —"You spoke about ecumenism. In the same vein, I must ask you about the situation of Catholics in the Soviet Union; specifically, those living in Belarus, Ukraine, and other territories. You know that for a Church to live it is necessary to have a hierarchy, seminaries, priests? Could you give me an answer on this?" (Some applause).
>
> Casaroli asks indirectly: "A new law on worship is being drafted. Is there any intention to consult religious communities on this issue?"
>
> Gromyko answers without committing himself. To the first question: "That question will have to be taken into account." To the second: "Of course, etc."

A total of twenty-five people took the floor.

At four o'clock in the afternoon, Casaroli, Backis, Sainz, and I met in a hotel room. There is still no word on Monday. It seems that there will be no official meeting in the Kremlin involving Gorbachev, after this morning's meeting with Gromyko. What to do with the Pope's letter?

We are talking about this when the telephone rings: the Ministry of Foreign Affairs announces that at twelve o'clock next Monday morning, Gorbachev will receive Cardinal Casaroli. He will be accompanied by Backis. They say—and they repeat it twice—that we must take care of the press and that the journalists we accredit must contact Mr. Vonogradov, who works at the Ministry of Foreign Affairs, by telephone. They should be at the Spaski Tower in the Kremlin by 11:20 AM.

---

14. Andrei Andreyevich Gromyko (Belarus, 1909–1989) served as Soviet Foreign Minister for more than twenty-five years, in several terms. In recent years he was chairman of the Presidium of the Supreme Soviet of the USSR (1985–88), replaced by Gorbachev himself.

The ministry calls again to confirm that we can make it. They ask if I can accompany the Cardinal in the same car. Affirmative. They will not give the news and I must not say anything to the press.

Shortly afterwards, when I am in my room, I receive a phone call from a person who does not speak any Western language. He tells me in Latin: *Ego episcopus ucranianus sum. . . .* It is Ivan Markitis, from the Zacarpaska region of Ukraine, who wants to see Casaroli. I take note of his address in Moscow and his telephone number. He explains to me, in a worried and anxious voice, that he has located me through a certain Nicolai Murator (whom I do not know).

I consult with Willebrands. In his handwritten list of members of the Ukrainian Catholic hierarchy there is no Ivan Markitis. After weighing the pros and cons, they decide not to receive him. The problem is not only that his name does not appear on the list. Above all, they do not want to give the Soviet authorities any excuse to break off the dialogue, especially when they have managed to arrange an interview with Gorbachev for Monday. This situation causes me infinite sorrow.

We dined with Juvenaly at the Novodevicy Monastery in Moscow, which has not yet been fully returned to the Orthodox Church. All the members of the Holy See delegation plus O'Connor attended. Splendid place. Juvenaly's residence is small and well appointed. He shows us the chapel: iconostasis, votive lamps, icons. Willebrands intones the Salve.

Juvenaly is a cordial man, very religious, who treats us with great confidence and spontaneity. He offers us a splendid dinner, typically Russian: caviars, vodkas—in plural—smoked fish . . .

"All this," he tells us, referring to the current relations between the Orthodox Church and the Catholic Church; and in particular, to the presence of our delegation at the celebration of the Millennium, "has been possible thanks to Pope John (he refers to John XXIII), Cardinal Bea, Cardinal Willebrands and the *ostpolitik* of Cardinal Casaroli.[15] The foundation stone of a church in Moscow, located in an area where more than one million people live, will be laid on the 13th in memory of the Millennium. It is the first church to be built in Moscow since the October Revolution."

15. The term originally refers to the policy of the Federal Republic of Germany, specifically that of the former Foreign Minister and Chancellor Willy Brandt, to normalize relations with the countries of Eastern Europe in the period 1969–1975. By extension, one speaks of "Vatican Ostpolitik" in reference to the action, directed above all by Casaroli, aimed at negotiating "possible solutions" with the governments of the Communist bloc.

Juvenaly continues speaking in a relaxed manner: "Some would like—he jokes—that church to be bigger than St. Peter's Basilica." He recalls that the second millennium of the Church is approaching and asks: Is something being prepared in Rome for this occasion? Casaroli says there is still a long way to go. . . . "No, it has not been decided for now."

"For the Russian people," Juvenaly commented, "this millennium has meant a great mobilization. Our leader has paid great attention to the problems of the Church. We have to pray for Gorbachev." About the Orthodox churches, he says that they have ceased to be museums and are being restored. Two years ago the authorities decided to restore some monasteries as well.

> Canonizations: "We have decided to continue doing them. The canonization of the imperial family has been slower, to avoid sensitivities. They died for their faith and we did not want to turn it into something political. But the time will come when we will be able to express our thoughts on their martyrdom."
>
> *Perestroika*: it gets slower as you move away from Moscow. "But there is a real renaissance going on in our country. There are no longer protests against the government, but only against things that are not working. For us here this constitutes a kind of honeymoon. Radio, TV and newspapers report every day on the Millennium celebrations, despite the negative reactions of atheists. We have decided to carry out Christian charitable works publicly, in churches and hospitals. In the legislative texts being prepared by Gorbachev there is talk of this. Many years have passed and we have no experience of these things. But Holy Russia is more alive than ever. There are ideas, initiatives, enthusiasm. And we wish to strengthen ties with the Catholic Church."
>
> Toast: "Today the Russian Church is celebrating."

We say goodbye. When we go out into the garden it is still daylight. In the car, on the way back to the hotel, we pass by the small cemetery where Khrushchev is buried. Later, we contemplate the walls of a beautiful church that is still in the hands of the State. Next to it is another smaller church: the cathedral. There we prayed and sang before an image of the Virgin.

Arriving at the hotel in the evening, Casaroli, Backis, Sainz, and I take a short walk to get some fresh air in the nearby streets. No one is there. Suddenly, there is a unanimous shout: "Goooool!" All of Moscow is watching the Soviet Union team in the European Championship on TV.

Casaroli wonders whether he should go to see Gorbachev tomorrow in a suit or dressed as a clergyman. He asks me and I do not choose one option or the other: the only thing I give him is that this photograph will appear in the press all over the world. He decides for the suit.

SUNDAY, JUNE 12. Open-air liturgical ceremony in the monastery of St. Danilov. Possibly the first open-air liturgical ceremony to be held in Moscow since 1917. The various delegations are present. Pimen joins the ceremony from the building across the street due to his health condition. It is cold and, at times, drizzling.

Casaroli leaves before the end of the ceremony because he has arranged a private meeting with Karcev, Minister of Worship. When we finish, we go to the restaurant Praga, in the Arbat district, where Pimen offers us a great reception. I get up from the table without finishing, when I am told that Casaroli has returned. After talking to him, I give a communiqué informing him of the meeting and indicating that "it has been agreed to continue the dialogue that has begun."

The *internal message* of this communiqué is clear: there is a need to establish a regular channel to discuss issues as they arise. Karcev would also like it to exist, but he does not have sufficient authority to create it.

In the evening, another dinner out of program: Metropolitan Filarete of Minsk invites us to his country house, the *dacha*. We go by car. The house, surrounded by woods, had belonged to Nicodim,[16] who died in Rome in the arms of John Paul I. We are accompanied by Kuznetsov, Karcev's collaborator, and two military men.

Filarete is an expansive and good-humored man. In the middle of dinner he makes a long toast: "Enlighten my heart, Lord, so that it will not speak nonsense. Let the heart speak." And he continues: "The invitation we sent to the Pope and his magnificent response have made this meeting possible, this historic event. Everything is the Lord's work. I send His Holiness the sympathy and recognition of our Patriarch, and I thank you for having accepted our invitation."

The dinner is long. It starts with vodka, the typical Russian drink. Every time a new dish is brought, the waiter refills the glasses. I decide to stop at the second course and tell him not to serve me any more.

16. On September 5th, 1978, the Orthodox Archbishop Nikodim of Leningrad, now St. Petersburg, died suddenly, aged 48, of a heart attack, during an audience at the Vatican, while conversing with John Paul I.

We return to the hotel in good spirits, with our minds already on tomorrow's interview. Willebrands and Duprey have been informed—with delay—of this interview: they are more concerned with relations with the Orthodox Church than with the Government. With Casaroli the opposite is true. I go to sleep, but the phone starts ringing: it is some journalists who do not know anything yet about the interview and call to explore. I tell them to go to sleep quietly.

Monday, June 13. In the morning, first thing in the morning, Mass at St. Louis des Français. I have asked a small representation of the journalists to be at eleven o'clock at the Spanski gate of the Kremlin, as agreed with the Soviet authorities. I have told the others to be at our hotel at one o'clock.

At a quarter to twelve, two black *Chaika* arrive at the hotel to take us to the Kremlin. A Spanish-speaking ambassador acts as chief of protocol. Our interpreter is Valeri M. Koulikov, from the USSR Ministry of Foreign Affairs. Casaroli, Backis, and I are in one of the cars. We enter the Kremlin and are driven to a small building where Gorbachev's private office is located.

On the second floor, Lenin's office is preserved intact, just as he left it when he died. We take the elevator upstairs and pass Anatoly Dobrynin, until recently Soviet ambassador in Washington, who has just left Gorbachev's office. It is twelve o'clock. Gorbachev and Shevardnadze, Minister of Foreign Affairs, exchange a few words with the group of journalists we have accredited.[17]

After the handshake, we sit around a small table: Gorbachev, Shevardnadze, an official who takes notes, Casaroli, Backis, the interpreter, and myself. Casaroli hands him the Pope's letter, which he reads immediately: "These are interesting ideas to which I will pay due attention" he says. He leaves for later the reading of the dossier that accompanies the letter.

He comments that both he and Shevardnadze are baptized, and that in that same room he had met Reagan a few days before. He talks about his childhood and the icon of the Virgin they had in their house. Underneath was a picture of Lenin. He explains his vision of society and human relations: these are the central ideas of *perestroika*. He speaks of the need to establish permanent contact with the Holy See to discuss various issues. He strikes me as a man who is strikingly self-confident, optimistic, and open.

---

17. Eduard Amvrosiyevich Shevardnadze (Georgia, 1928–2014) was foreign minister of the USSR from 1985 until 1991, when it was dissolved. He was president of Georgia from 1995 until November 2003.

From the window of the room, I can see a few cannons from Napoleon's Russian campaign. On all the white telephones is engraved the symbol of the hammer and sickle. There is no mention of a possible trip of the Pope to the USSR and only a few problems are mentioned in passing: the situation of the Ukrainian Catholics; the Catholics of the Latin rite; the freedom of religion and thought, etc.

When we leave the room, the interpreter comments to Casaroli: "Your Eminence, I am convinced that I have witnessed an historic event." The Cardinal looks satisfied. We return in the same car and in silence to the hotel. The room is full of journalists. They are frustrated that they did not know about the meeting earlier, but it was only possible to bring a small group to the Kremlin. Casaroli sits in the center of the table, together with Willebrands and Etchegaray, so that there is no exaggeratedly "political" perception of the trip. Thankfully, the aspect of the trip which we are particularly interested in is highlighted: the relations with the Russian Orthodox Church.

Casaroli is asked several questions. He underlines the cordial, friendly, and open tone with which both Gorbachev and Shevardnadze have received him. He describes the novelties that the Secretary General wishes to introduce in the political and social sphere, as well as his cooperation with the Church. He expresses his hope to be able to discuss the problems on both sides in the near future and notes that a channel of communication for further contacts has not yet been formalized.

"We have come on behalf of the Pope—he specifies—to join in the celebration of a religious event of the Russian Orthodox Church, to which we feel very close, both physically and spiritually."

He was asked about the Pope's letter. He explains that it was a list of the various points of mutual interest, such as the appointment of bishops. And he clarified that it was only a first contact, in which no specific point was addressed. Together with the letter, a memorandum was given to him containing various questions of interest to the Holy See. Gorbachev spoke of the principle of freedom of conscience, and gave the impression that he was very convinced. He recalled that the Secretary General had insisted, above all, on two things: firstly, the proper conception of relations between power and society (distinguishing between the *State* and the *Fatherland*); and, secondly, on the centrality of man: "It is people—he said—who build society and the State."

I have invited Anatoly A. Krasikov, Deputy Director General of the *TASS* news agency, to the press conference. He asks to speak to Casaroli for a moment. I take him to the Cardinal's room: he wants to express his fears and perplexities about the recent appointment of the Lithuanian cardinal; he says that it is better that these things be known first to avoid sensitivities.[18]

Then Antonio Natoli gives me a short interview for the first *RAI* Italian news program. We have a quick bite to eat because our plane leaves very soon. At the airport, Karcev, the Minister of Culture, is waiting for us again. There is a delay in the departure so we take advantage of it to talk with him. Filarete is there also.

> —"Have you told Gorbachev that we want to establish relations in the future," he asks Casaroli.
>
> —"Yes," answers the Cardinal.

Karcev mentions again the construction of the Orthodox church in a neighborhood of one million people in Moscow. They asked Gorbachev and within a month they received a positive answer. They thought of three different sites, and in the end they chose the best one, on a five-hectare plot. Karcev adds that atheism does not mean, *per se*, a fight against the Church; it is a conception with materialistic roots that must respect all other conceptions. "Whoever wants to demonstrate the truth, let him do so, but without fighting against believers. The dictatorship of the proletariat has not been put into practice; it has been put into practice, but in the wrong way. Stalin applied it in the wrong way. It is the same with atheism: atheism is a conception that has the same value as the others." To prove his point, he recalls that the Ministers of Worship of the friendly countries were here: Cuba, Yugoslavia, Mongolia, Poland. . . .

The plane takes off. Long flight with layover in Milan. We land in Rome in the early morning.

Some personal impressions: something is happening in Russia. Something decisive, which contrasts with the eras of Stalin, Khrushchev, and Brezhnev. On Russian TV these days, unprecedented things have been seen, such as images of the religious delegations (by the way, on the evening news, only the Muslim speaker was shown: will they have problems with the Soviet Muslims?) On Saturday, at 12:30 PM, the TV showed the film "Xrahm" ("*The Temple*"), trying to explain what makes up the Christian religious experience.

Not everything is transparent: in the translations of the words of the Bolshoi, some phrases have been changed; the newspaper *Pravda*, reporting the

18. This refers to Vincentas Sladkevicius (Lithuania, 1920–2000), elevated to the rank of Cardinal on June 28, 1988. He was archbishop of Kaunas (1989–1996). He suffered persecution during communism and was under house arrest from 1963 to 1982.

statements in the meeting with Gromyko, has silenced Willebrands' reference to the Catholic-inhabited regions, such as Belarus or Ukraine.

But facts indicate a certain liberalization, together with the recognition of realities outside the Party, which are part of Soviet society. The Orthodox Church wants to take advantage of the occasion to make itself visible in hospitals, schools, and social welfare. They asked the Catholic Church for advice and experience on how to make known their work in these fields.

5

Witness of a Schism

A Hectic Afternoon

June 15, 1988

Dinner with the Pope. I arrive a few minutes early and I am greeted by Msgr. Thu.[1] The Pope is in the Clementine Hall with a group of Poles. I have had a hectic afternoon. I have been waiting a long time in the *Sala Stampa* for Marcel Lefebvre to announce, at the press conference he has called in Ecône, his decision to ordain four bishops against the will of the Pope.

Shortly afterwards, while he was in front of the cameras doing an interview with me on the Lefebvre case, Dante Alimenti, the Vatican reporter for *RAI*, felt unwell, fainted, and fell to the ground. I interpreted the situation as serious and arranged for him to be taken, unconscious, in a cab to the nearby *Santo Spirito* Hospital.[2]

As we made our way to the dining room, I thanked the Pope for including me in the Russian delegation. During the first part of the dinner he asked me about the trip to Moscow. We had just returned in the early hours yesterday morning. I told him about Casaroli's interview in the Kremlin, which he already knew about, and about the two unscheduled dinners with Juvenaly and Filarete.

He was happy to know that we had sung the Salve in the chapel of the Juvenaly residence. I then read him a paragraph from a statement I made to *Reuters*, in which I said that all this was made possible by the Pope's personal decision to send a delegation to the Millennium, with a letter to Gorbachev. In these statements I emphasized that, thanks to the Pope's insistence, the reality of Catholics in Ukraine has ceased to be a subject for specialists and has become front-page news in many newspapers.

---

1. At that time, the Pope's second secretary became Vincent Tran Ngoc Thu (Vietnam, 1918–2002), replacing Emery Kabongo. He held that post from 1988 until his retirement in 1996.

2. In fact, Dante Alimenti died several days later, on June 27, as a result of the cerebral stroke he had suffered [Author's Note].

I mentioned to him the episode of Ivan Markitis, the bishop with whom I spoke on the phone in Latin, and he said he knew him.

After the chapter on the USSR, I describe an idea I have been working on for months: the creation of a Holy See agency tasked with informing the bishops of the whole world about the activity of the Pope and the Holy See. He is interested. Tomorrow, he tells me, he will receive Piet Derksen, who will finance the project.[3]

And so we came to today's topic. The Pope knew, prior to the Ecône press conference, that Lefebvre was going to announce his decision to ordain those four bishops. I told him that I had read his letter to the Pope, and that we would release both letters the next day, that is, the one from Lefebvre and the one the Pope wrote in response.

I began to read a dispatch from the *Reuters* Agency which included some of Lefebvre's words about the Pope: a heretical Pope, who no longer had the Catholic faith, etc. I could not finish reading these things. I got a lump in my throat and tears came to my eyes. Dziwisz told me to continue. I hid the dispatch in my folder and did not continue reading.

The Pope was serious. I don't know what he thought when he saw me sobbing. There was a strange silence. He said something, slowly, about illness (Lefebvre's). I replied that, as a doctor, I could understand illness, but that it also came to my mind that the devil could act in history through illness.

The Pope related that when Cardinal Gagnon[4] returned from his mission to Ecône as his delegate, he had commented to him: "There are two things that frighten me. One is the people with good intentions who go after Lefebvre. The other is Lefebvre's pride." And the Pope—from whom I have never heard a critical or moral judgment on a person—added that he was referring to "pride in the sense of his obstinate character, of the stubbornness with which he approaches the problem."

"It is a test," said the Pope, "one more. . . . (and he did not complete the sentence). A few days ago," he continued, "when I was with Cardinal Ratzinger, we decided to leave in Our Lady's hands the solution, whether it was better for Lefebvre to remain within the Church or to leave.

3. The agency would be the *Vatican Information Service* (VIS). Piet Derksen (Holland, 1913–1996) was a Catholic businessman, who dedicated part of the profits of his companies to sponsoring Catholic media.

4. Édouard Gagnon (Canada, 1918–2007) was a Canadian cardinal who, among other positions, presided over the Pontifical Council for the Family (1983–1990).

In other words, they did not know whether it was better to accept a merely formal reconciliation on the part of Lefebvre or not to do so. The Pope realized the risk involved in letting the Fraternity of St. Pius X remain within the Church, in an agreed juridical framework, when there had been no real change in the moral disposition of Lefebvre. Doubtless, he would have continued publicizing his misleading books, as well as his strongly critical stances towards Vatican II and the Pope.

I was impressed by the supernatural sense of the Pope and Cardinal Ratzinger, leaving this question—humanly unsolvable—in the hands of Our Lady. And he went on to say: "Our Lady wanted many things to happen during this Marian Year, like the Millennium . . . ; and among them, this."[5]

Shortly after, he reflects on the statements I have read from Lefebvre and comments: "In some of my trips I have seen banners calling me the Antichrist. No wonder. Christ himself was called Beelzebub."

Throughout this conversation the Pope has been serious, but at no time tense or uneasy. This very morning Ratzinger told me that the Pope was very serene. And so he is.

As we leave, we walk in silence. He enters the chapel and his prayer—on his knees, as always—is, on this occasion, a little longer than usual.

In Austria, Under the Shadow of Lefebvre

June 23 to 27, 1988

When I was told about the Pope's trip to Austria, I thought that it would have an impact on public opinion on three levels: the question of the Jews (with the controversy of last year, when Austrian President Kurt Waldheim went to the Vatican);[6] the question of Catholics in Eastern European countries, Austria's neighbors; and the situation of the Church in Austria.

The first one arises upon arrival, with the presence of President Waldheim at the airport. There is the natural agitation among the photographers

5. The Pope had instituted the celebration of a Marian Year for the whole Church, in preparation for the 2000th anniversary of the birth of Christ, which was celebrated from June 7, 1987 to August 15, 1988.

6. Kurt Josef Waldheim (Austria, 1918–2007), politician and diplomat, was Secretary General of the United Nations (1972–1981) and President of Austria (1986–1992). In those years, the controversy about Waldheim's past and his alleged involvement in war crimes was alive and well. An international committee cleared him of these accusations, but as a politician he was isolated on the international scene.

to see which one of them captures the best picture of Waldheim and the Pope shaking hands. After the usual speeches at the airport, in the rain, the Pope visits the cathedral, followed by a reception at the Hofburg, the presidential palace. There he meets briefly with Waldheim and some members of his family. I see his wife, a younger couple and three children. The atmosphere is cordial and familiar.

The next day, in the morning, the Pope had a meeting at the nunciature with representatives of the Jewish community in Austria. They are a bit tense because, due to a mistake in the schedule, they have been made to wait outside the door. And then, to make matters worse, they have been introduced in a room with no one to attend them. I told Casaroli, who quickly went to greet them and stayed with them until the Pope arrived. Immediately, the atmosphere changes: the contrast with the first meeting they had with the Pope is evident. "The ice has dissolved," the rabbi said later at a press conference.

The rabbi's speech remains on the level of vindication. I am told that the text has undergone at least four revisions, because at the beginning it was very harsh. The Pope responds with a speech in which he tackles head-on issues such as relations with Israel, the Palestinian right to a homeland, the rejection of the accusation that the Church is to blame for the *Shoah*.

In the afternoon, visit to the Mauthausen concentration camp. The text of the Pope's speech seems splendid to me. He does not make a historical judgment, but a moral judgment. But he does not remain anchored only in the moral judgment, but he asks himself about those facts in their current projection.

There is no denying that the representatives of the Jews here expected more: they wanted the Pope to make an act of acknowledgment of guilt on the part of the Church and a formal accusation of Austria for its historical responsibility. They ask for a *vergangen heitsbewaltigung*; a reckoning with the past. The Pope responds at a higher level: "No man can overcome his own past; only God with forgiveness."

Second issue: the Slavic peoples neighboring Austria, with numerous pilgrims, and their bishops, present in the country these days. In Transdorff there were 17,000 Austrians and 70,000 foreigners. Slovenian bishops, Croatian communities? Some Austrians do not take kindly to people from these countries moving to their own country and causing a social burden. The Pope has spoken to them of their responsibility, and he has told them that he is with these people, with these peoples.

And the third question: the Church in Austria. The Pope has endeared himself to people in Austria, because he has a virtue that some call "normality." I would say that, in reality, it is a profound humility and a great sympathy. In Salzburg, one of the cities of the Counter-Reformation, people have seen that the Pope has no "imperial" pretensions. He even reminded the bishops that they are not allowed to make aggressive criticisms. They had expected an attendance of 16,000 people at the Mass; there were 25,000.

On the 26th, in Salzburg, as we were finishing lunch, Stanisław tells me that the Pope asked him, "What does Navarro say about all this?" It's a nice way of asking me to accompany him.

The Holy Father is still having lunch with the bishops. When he leaves, I am waiting for him in the next room. I give him my view of the three dimensions the trip is taking on. He says the most important is the third, what he is saying to the Austrian Catholics. He knows perfectly well the situation of the Church here. He tells me that he had spoken with Cardinal Ratzinger recently, and they had studied the report sent by the Austrian bishops after the *ad limina* visit: "There has been some improvement. It is a slight improvement, but it is an improvement."

Kurt Krenn, auxiliary bishop of Vienna, told me during dinner at Salzburg Castle, organized by the civil authorities, that the superior of the Fraternity of St. Pius X, Schmidberger, had telephoned him from Switzerland, asking him to mediate in order to avoid the excommunication that would follow Lefebvre's ordination of bishops. Krenn discussed it with Ratzinger and called Schmidberger: the latter gave him to understand that perhaps the ordination of bishops could be delayed, but then added his well-known criticisms of the Pope and, among them, his opposition to the day of prayer in Assisi.

Krenn asks me to inform the Pope of all this, in case something can be done to prevent the schism. If anything can be done? The evidence is that both the Pope and his collaborators are doing everything they can to prevent it from happening. The curious thing is that that same night all the journalists knew about the contacts between Krenn and Schmidberger. I have not yet clarified from which of the two the indiscretion came.

A detail from the Pope: when we were flying from Rome, he commented that the funeral for Dante Alimenti, the *RAI* journalist who had died a few days earlier, was taking place at 5:00 PM. He mentioned him to all of us who accompanied him on the flight and asked us to join him in his prayer.

Lefebvre Ordains Four Bishops

June 30, 1988

A group of journalists, invited by an Italian press association, asked me about the possibility of being received by the Pope. There was no objection and I told them so, suggesting a private audience, without speeches, standing up. Today that meeting took place and the Pope presented them with a silver medal.

At the end of the day, I will have dinner with the Pope. Lefebvre ordained the four bishops this morning.[7] The schism has been consummated. The Pope is serene.

Carmen Hernandez[8] was waiting for him in a small room near the dining room. The Pope affectionately told us that she had brought him a cake, as a gesture of affection in these painful circumstances for the life of the Church. He says she also brought him two letters: "A longer one for Ratzinger and a shorter one for him." At the end of dinner, he goes to chat with her.

Perestrioka News

July 12, 1988

The Pope receives Nikolai M. Lunkov, the Soviet Ambassador, to Italy, who was with Casaroli on the 9th. The purpose of the audience is to update the Pope on the recent meeting of the Soviet Communist Party, at which Gorbachev again presented *perestroika*. The Pope tells me that Lunkov has spoken to him almost exclusively about this issue.

We have prepared and disseminated a documented list of the contacts and initiatives carried out by the Holy See in relation to the Soviet Union from 1979 to the present day.

---

7. Lefebvre ordained four bishops without pontifical mandate, contrary to canon law, despite the Pope's express entreaties and orders. In accordance with canon law, on July 2nd, 1988, John Paul II excommunicated Lefebvre and the four priests involved: Bernard Fellay, Bernard Tissier de Mallerais, Richard Williamson and Alfonso de Galarreta.

8. María del Carmen Hernández Barrera (Spain, 1930–2016) was, together with Kiko Argüello, the founder of the Neocatechumenal Way.

6

ON VACATION WITH THE POPE

In the Dolomites

JULY 13–22, 1988

The Pope is taking a few days of rest—nine to be precise—in Lorenzago di Cadore, a small town in the Italian province of Belluno, surrounded by the Dolomite mountains.

We left on the 13th, at half past four, for Ciampino airport, fifteen kilometers [nine miles] from Rome. From there we flew in a DC-9 of the Italian Military to the military airport of Treviso. Then, in two helicopters of the S.A.R.,[1] we get to Lorenzago in about thirty-five minutes. We stayed at Mirabello, a house relatively close to the village, which I don't think has more than five hundred inhabitants.

Accompanying persons: Stanisław Dziwisz; Tadeusz Styczeń;[2] the Pope's valet, Angelo Gugel; the head of security, Camillo Cibin;[3] the chief police inspector of the *Ispettorato di Pubblica Sicurezza presso il Vaticano*,[4] Enrico Marinelli; the physician, Dr. Proietti; and myself.

1. S.A.R. (*Search and Rescue*) is a marine and alpine rescue service, equipped with various means, including helicopters.

2. Professor Tadeusz Styczeń (Poland, 1931–2010) was a disciple and later successor of Karol Wojtyla in the chair of ethics at the Catholic University of Lublin in Poland.

3. Camillo Cibin (Italy, 1947–2009) was the head of Vatican security when Ali Agca attempted to assassinate the Pope. While two agents were protecting the Pontiff, Cibin jumped over the wooden fences and managed to subdue Agca, helped by some assistants. After the attack, he presented his resignation to the Pope, who rejected it as a manifestation of his esteem. In 1982 he was appointed head of the Central Surveillance Office and later Inspector General, in charge of the Pope's security on all his apostolic trips abroad and on many of those within Italy. During the Pope's stay in Fatima his presence was again pivotal, when he defended the Pope against an unbalanced priest who attempted to stab the Pontiff. He retired in 2006. The funeral was held in St. Peter's Basilica, officiated by Cardinal Lajolo.

4. Inspectorate of Public Security at the Vatican, under the Italian State.

In Lorenzago, a small number of people are waiting for us, and some journalists: "Are you tired after a year of intense work? Will you walk in the mountains, like last year?"

—"My legs are not what they used to be," the Pope prudently says. However, the facts will prove otherwise in the following days.

First night in the calm of the mountains. Light dinner. Early sleep. Uncertain weather, tending to rain. No concrete plan for the next day.

THURSDAY. JULY 14. Rainy dawn. Shall we go out or stay at home? We go out. We have to walk. Cibin decides the itinerary. The doctor, a Vatican security agent, and myself drive ahead at about ten AM and head for a plateau near Mirabello. We park the car and wait. Half an hour later, the three cars arrive. The Pope gets out of the *Range Rover* with his white cassock on, which he takes off for the excursion: gray pants, gray priest's shirt with collar, brown hiking boots, white cap, white anorak.

We start walking in single file and—as will be the norm during these days—in silence. Two young policemen in civilian clothes march ahead, at some distance. Then comes the Pope, who advances with his right hand resting on a bamboo cane, and his left hand protected inside the pocket of his white anorak. A damp mist drenches everything. Occasionally, raindrops. Great peace. Arturo Mari, the photographer of *L'Osservatore Romano,* captures the scene in a magnificent photograph.

We walk along some open trails for three quarters of an hour. We meet a cow herder who greets us: I don't know if he recognized the Pope. We enter a forest of fir trees. The rain is pouring down. We pause. The Pope takes shelter under a tree and sits down next to the trunk. I took a raincoat out of my backpack and we put it between the branches over his head to protect him from the rain. We pray the Angelus and continue walking.

An hour and a half later it starts to rain heavily. We are protected by the trees. We find a log hut: a manger for the deer to eat salt. A seat is improvised for the Pope, who is sheltered from the rain. The rest of us settle in as best we can. We light a small fire to warm ourselves. We open our backpacks and have lunch in the pouring rain, which falls outside the shelter. We take, as we do every day of the excursion, a sausage or ham sandwich, a portion of local cheese, a glass of white wine and an apple. The Vatican security people carry half a bottle of whiskey. Almost all of us like it, except the Pope.

Cibin makes an *overdraft,* as they say in military jargon, to reconnoiter the terrain. We spend a long time contemplating the marvelous spectacle of the rain between the trees. The peace and well-being—physical and spiritual—of these moments is unspeakable.

When the meal is over, Gugel takes a sleeping bag out of his backpack, which he gives to the Pope. Moments later, the Pope sleeps peacefully on the ground. The rest of us follow him in a silent communication.

He wakes up forty minutes later. He is offered a cup of tea with some sugar in a plastic cup. He asks for the breviary and prays it.[5] We chat briefly in the warmth of the fire. Then we continue walking in a fine, refreshing rain along the forest path.

We begin to descend. Some slip on the twists and turns of the road. The Pope stumbles and falls sideways on some bushes. He gets up and continues walking. An hour later we arrive at a place with two streams. Cibin and one of the security guards have put up some boards to cross them. The Pope passes, determined. Arturo Mari captures the moment on camera. We continue walking to the place where the cars are waiting for us.

On the way back, we find that the road is obstructed by a crane carrying out construction work. We wait for about twenty minutes. The workers go on about their business, oblivious to who is occupying the cars. As it seems that their task is going to take a long time, we return to Lorenzago by another road, adding another thirty kilometers [nineteen miles] to our trip. Shortly after arriving, I brief the journalists on the first day of the Pope's visit.

Friday, July 15. Heavy rain. Can't go out. I go with Arturo Mari to the village, where they develop the photographs he took yesterday. There are three that could be distributed to the press. We return and I ask Dziwisz for his opinion. He says he would like to show them to the Pope first; but, as it is Friday, he is in the chapel doing the Stations of the Cross and we don't know how long he will take. Since there is no time, and the journalists are waiting, we decide to give them the photos. Great joy among the press: they are magnificent.

The weather clears up at lunchtime. The itinerary is set: we drive to the St. Anthony Pass; and from there, to the little church of St. Anne, to end up at the small alpine lake of Aiarnola. Between the outbound and return journey, we have been gone about three and a half hours.

5. Liturgical book composed of psalms, hymns, prayers and readings, arranged according to the time of day and liturgical seasons. It is also called "Liturgy of the Hours."

The sun rises. We approach the lake. The view is magnificent: mountains, forest, water. Voices and laughter of young scouts in the distance. The Pope sits down and asks for the breviary. A glass of tea, a brief chat, much contemplation. A break of forty minutes. We return making a detour to avoid meeting the people who, at the sight of the cars, intuit that the Pope is in the area.

Near the road, we come across a mushroom hunter. One of our security tries to entertain him with questions, but only manages to alert him even more, until he discovers the Pope, and greets him briefly and cordially, with great naturalness:

> —"Good morning, Papa! If you only knew the efforts of the past year to find you . . . and today, I find you all of a sudden!"

When I get home, as it has become quite late, I update the journalists by phone.

SATURDAY, JULY 16. Two days of intense pastoral activity: Adamello, diocese of Belluno, Pietralva and Stava. Four dioceses in two days. In Adamello, the Pope celebrates Mass for mountaineers and local people. Splendid scenery with snow.

Lunch at the refuge, at just over 3,000 meters. Martino, the manager, is an "old friend" of the Pope, who had been here in April 1984 with Sandro Pertini, then President of the Italian Republic. Brief rest after lunch. In the meantime, the mountaineers leave the site. We return by helicopter and land in a deserted meadow, halfway up the mountain, to walk for another thirty-five minutes.

But the area is not as deserted as we thought: soon after, four people, astonished and delighted at the same time, greet the Pope, who is in a white cassock, walking alone.

SUNDAY, JULY 17. The Pope goes to pray at the Marian Shrine of Pietralva—in Alto Adige—and in the afternoon he goes to Stava. He speaks about human sorrow, evoking the natural disaster that caused about two hundred deaths three years earlier: the walls of a waste containment dam cracked, razing a hotel and some houses to the ground. When we return, it is almost night.

MONDAY, JULY 18TH. Nice day. We leave relatively early, in the direction of Col Audoi (1,560 m), walking from home without the need to resort to cars. The Pope wears the white cassock. After a while he takes it off and continues. Some of us go ahead and prepare a seat for him with two logs, in a place where a long chain of mountains can be seen.

We met no one on the way. The Pope arrives at the Col at about half past one. We have "panini" with ham and cheese, a glass of wine, and a cup of tea, in a plastic cup. The Pope rests for a short nap in his sleeping bag. I am impressed to see him sleeping in holy peace, abandoning the helm of the Church to God. Dziwisz jokes: "You are witnesses of something historic, who has ever seen a Pope sleep like this on the middle of the mountain? I tell him that it is a gift for the Church that he can sleep like that."

We descend through a forest and meadows. The Pope stops for a moment to rest. When he sees these mountains he remembers his country: "The landscape is very similar to the Tatra Mountains, although those form a mountain range of about twenty kilometers [twelve miles], and these are much wider. But more than the rocks, I like the forests and the water." And he says: "Perhaps here nature is better preserved. He recalls his excursions with the young people, when they spent several days in the bush. On the way back, I ask him if I can take a picture of him. He gladly agrees, but when I try to focus the camera on him, he jokes by turning sideways and hiding from the lens, with his usual good humor.

TUESDAY, JULY 19. We took the longest hike so far, from Pian di Buoi to Calalzo di Cadore: six and a half to seven hours of hiking. Heat. From afar we see a group of mountaineers watching us: we've been spotted. We cross paths with a couple of people who do not recognize the Pope. Around half past one we start looking for a good place to have lunch. We find it on a small landing, almost without vegetation, at the edge of a road running up a steep slope.

Some hot pasta is prepared for the Pope. Two groups of Italian boys—three and then another three—spot us. They don't see the Pope, but they sense that he must be nearby and sit down to see what's going on. The policemen become uneasy and tell them to leave; and as they insist on staying, they end up asking them for their papers. . . . In view of the situation, Dziwisz asks me to go to them and "*faccia bella figura*," resolve this in the nicest possible way.

I approach: "you know that the Pope is here, don't you?" They confirm it to me and I ask them to let him rest, as a sign of affection for him. They answer me that they do not want to bother him; they would just like to greet him for a "little while," even if it was only for a few seconds. . . . I suggest that they offer the small sacrifice of forgoing the meeting for his intentions instead. Amused, because they no longer know what to say or how to argue, one of them comes up with an ingenious excuse, typical of Italian inventiveness: "*Ma io mi voglio confessare con Lui!* (But I want to confess to him!)."

Amazed by their quick reflexes, I play along and tell them that one of our policemen—specifically, one of the ones who has just asked them for their papers, who is now calmer—is a priest and they can go to confession with him if they wish. They laugh; I give them a rosary and they go away happy. In part, I am sorry, but these things have to be done to defend the Pope's rest.

After lunch we continue walking. There is a somewhat difficult pass that we overcome with the help of a "ferrata" fixed in the rock.[6] It is hot and we have run out of water. I suppose the Pope is thirsty, but he doesn't say so. We continue like this for several hours. We pass near the refuge. There is a small box of fruit juice left in the backpack, which the Pope drinks through a straw. He walks and drinks the juice. As the container is small, it runs out quickly. He asks if we have some tea, but we carry the thermos in another backpack. A little later we pass by a spring—the only one we have found during the day—and he gladly drinks a glass of fresh water.

As we descend, he chats with Tadeusz. He walks like a boat on the waves, bobbing. He is relaxed. Behind, Tadeusz follows him, speaking in Polish and gesticulating; the Pope asks a question from time to time, without turning to his interlocutor, and Don Tadeusz answers him, continuing with his explanation. They talk about philosophical and theological questions: on this occasion, about relativism in moral philosophy and theology. The next day, the Pope told me that he is taking advantage of his vacation to "update" himself in this field, and that Father Tadeusz is helping him.

At nine o'clock in the evening they have organized a concert in the newly restored village church in honor of the Pope. Dziwisz tells me that the Pope will not be there. I do not know the reason why. Perhaps the Pope is exhausted after these seven hours of excursion; although it is also possible that Dziwisz has convinced him not to go, with the intention that he should rest.

He asks if I can accompany him. We get dressed up and go down to the village. When we arrive, Dziwisz sees that the Bishop of Treviso has come for the occasion, which he did not expect. He starts the concert and asks the bishop's secretary to contact the house to ask the Pope if he could come down for a moment.

At the end of the concert, the Pope arrives at the church, to the great joy of the audience. The concert performers, delighted, repeat a small part of the piece. At the end, during the greetings, the Pope jokes and says that it is better

6. A ferrata, which literally means "iron way" in Italian, is an iron pin placed into rock to assist hikers and climbers. They are popular in European climbing routes.

that he has come at the end, because this way the people have been more attentive to the music.

The inspector and the doctor were having a drink in a bar in the village and, when they heard that the Pope had come down, they arrived running. . . . Here everything is improvised, informal, familiar.

Wednesday, July 20. Highlight of these days: ascent to Pieralva peak, 2,694 m. We leave by car to a nearby refuge. Halfway up the road we are stopped by some soldiers: "*Guardia forestale di Venezia*!" As soon as they notice the situation, they greet us with a smile.

The ascent begins. Around 12:00 PM we are in front of a black image of the Virgin before which we pray the Angelus. We continue climbing. Then difficulties begin: we come to a very narrow pass over the cliff. The group splits up. Doubts arise as to whether we should continue or not. The Pope continues walking.

Dziwisz asks me to tell the delayed group that, if they want, they can wait there for the Pope's return. I tell Inspector Marinelli and the doctor. They react with suprise:

—"But . . . Is the Pope going up to the top?"

—"I don't know," I tell them. "I'll let them know what happens on the walkie-talkie later."

We continue climbing. New level of difficulty. I decide to leave my backpack to keep my hands free for climbing. We come across an Austrian couple: the woman is attached to a climbing rope held by the man.

Angelo Gugel is irritated with poor Cibin for having brought the Pope this way. But the fault does not lie with Cibin, who, besides having saved the Pope's life in St. Peter's Square, is more zealous than anyone else for his safety! The Pope had decided to climb to the top a long time ago.

We see, a little further up, a very steep and snowy pass. We make a stop and have a sandwich, which the Pope appreciates. I thought that we would turn back, but the Pope resumes the march and the rest of us walk behind him, on the snow.

"It's useless to try to stop him," Dziwisz tells me. He has decided to go to the top. You try it, because he won't listen to me." I approach him, but I don't say anything at that moment. He has the soul of a mountaineer and is enjoying himself enormously, something that comforts me, after seeing him day after day carrying all the weight of the Church.

One of our company brings me my backpack and I put it back on my back. We climb up the snow clinging to a *ferrata*. The Pope stumbles. It's not a big deal but Dziwisz and I are getting more and more anxious.

We get past the steep and snowy pass and reach a small landing. We hope that here we can convince him to give up. He looks happy though. He accepts two cups of tea with sugar and contemplates the cross that crowns the summit. That cross is like a magnet for him.

Two German tourists approach us. The man—about 40 years old—recognizes the Pope, who is sitting on a rock. "*—Der Papst!!!*" They speak in German for a few minutes. The woman is excited. When they leave, the Pope looks again at the cross at the top. We make him see that there are difficult steps left.

> —"But people get there."
>
> —"Yes, Holy Father," I dare to say, "but they are usually young people, who have not been locked up in the Vatican for ten years."
>
> —"That's true, but up there is the cross and. . . . We must go up!"—he says with determination.

He adds, a few seconds later:

> —"Besides, we are all young here! Our average age is fifty-two, more or less!"

We contemplate a splendid landscape: "*Che bellezza!*" says the Pope, looking at the mountains, strongly illuminated by the sun.

In the meantime, Don Tadeusz has gone ahead of us and has reached the summit. The Pope stands up and decides to continue climbing. I leave my backpack there and accompany him.

> —"But what were you going to say to the journalists this afternoon," he says to me, laughing, as we are about to reach the summit, "when they ask you whether the Pope has reached the summit or not?"

At a quarter past three we reach the summit. The Pope prays the *Gloria* three times, then the *Regina Coeli* and three times the *Requiem*. Looking at the landscape, he says: "I had to do it . . ." And he remains silent. These are particularly joyful moments for him. He sits on a rock, covering his head with the hood of his anorak to protect himself from the sun. We stay there for about twenty minutes.

I take some pictures of it, next to the iron cross. Next to it there is a bell and an image of the Virgen de las Cumbres. We open the metal receptacle where the book of signatures is. We present it to the Pope, who writes: *Joannes Paulus II*. And the date: *20–VII–88*.

The rest of us all signed, adding, at Dziwisz's suggestion—another of his kindnesses—the name of the inspector, who stayed downstairs. Soon we began to descend. After a few stumbles and small slips, Coali and Biocca, two of our security, strong and experienced climbers, help the Pope. The descent is as difficult as the ascent. At a quarter past five we overcome the last difficult stretch and reach the grassy meadow near the refuge.

I take a deep breath and drive ahead to Lorenzago, where I am meeting the journalists. I arrive for our briefing at 5:50. The inspector calls me on the walkie-talkie to inform me that the Pope has sat down to rest near the Madonna by the shelter, after praying for a long time before that image. After the late lunch he had come to greet the family that manages the shelter.

We all returned late, happy, and tired. The fear—why not say it—is behind us. Before going to bed, I think of some words that Dziwisz said to me as we were heading towards the summit: "This is how the Pope leads the Church: slowly, without jerks, but with tenacity and his eyes fixed on the goal. He listens to everyone, asks everyone for advice, but then decides in his prayer and does not take his eyes off the goal."

Thursday, July 21st. Last day. Walk around Lorenzago. I talk with the Pope, as we walk, about the TV program that the *BBC* is preparing for the 10th anniversary of his election, and about other editorial projects.

He asks me about the latest echoes of the Lefebvre case, regarding its possible impact on the life of the Church. He says that Cardinal Lustiger's initiative in Paris—not to break ties with Lefebvre's followers—has been useful and courageous, and that we should insist on the same line.

I ask him if he has read Gorbachev's speech at the Communist Party conference. He tells me no, that it was too long and he is waiting for a summary.

We continue walking in silence. The Pope stops occasionally to contemplate the landscape. Sometimes he makes a gesture that is very much his own: he rests his chin on his hands, fixed on the handle of his cane, and remains pensive. Once I see him make the sign of the cross while he sees a small village in the distance. When he returns, he spends a long time chatting in Polish with Tadeusz and Dziwisz.

After asking Dziwisz if the Pope likes ice cream, I talk on the radio with the chief of police and we carry out the plan we had planned since yesterday: to bring some magnificent ice cream with *frutti di bosco* from a nearby town, arriving in time for dessert.

In the evening, some young people from Catholic Action in Treviso came to pray the rosary with the Pope. At the end he spoke to them about these Dolomite mountains, where "one can rest while tiring oneself out." And he adds, "This blessed fatigue of Cadore's mountain hikes! May he be able to come at least some days of the year!"

The next morning, Mass with about seventeen priests celebrating the fortieth anniversary of their ordination. In attendance are the nuns of this residence, the police officers accompanying us and a few other people. Among them is Luigia Costola, the mother of the local doctor, who has given the Pope a pair of mountain pants, a shirt and some socks. . . . (and, I must confess, he also gave me a pair of hiking pants, which I have found very useful).

After lunch, a short visit to Lorenzago to give thanks in the village church and greet the people. Helicopter to Treviso; flight to Rome-Ciampino and from there to Castelgandolfo. The next day, general audience. On Sunday, great ceremony at St. Peter's. The vacation is over for Karol Wojtyla, who has never stopped *being Pope,* as he himself acknowledged. Nor did he stop praying a lot, as all of us who have accompanied him during these days have been able to see.

7

"Do You See How the Pope Is Not So Bad?"

With the *BBC*

September 9, 1988

I spent the whole morning at Castelgandolfo, accompanying the *BBC* professionals who are making a documentary series on the Pope. We went to the Mass he concelebrated with a group of American bishops who are on an *ad limina* visit. Then Dziwisz asked me if I wanted to have breakfast with the Pope. There I saw once again the sobriety with which he lives. A cup of coffee with milk, a small portion of jam and some untoasted bread. Then a slice of mozzarella and some fruit.

I had talked to the Pope about this series and the possibility of him giving them a short interview. I read him the questions and he agreed.

I asked the *BBC* for the text of the Pope's answers, in which he pointed out a suggestive idea: experiencing a certain anxiety—he said, speaking of his election—betrays a deep sense of responsibility. He explained that he had lived his election with serenity and without anxieties; but then, for the sake of nuance, he added this idea.

He also clarified that they should not seek in the Church a homogenizing uniformity in the face of the diversity of peoples, customs and traditions of Catholics, who live scattered throughout the world, but a *pluralistic unity,* a unity in plurality. The essence of the Church, he stressed, is "communion," not uniformity.

A Landing in "Apartheid"

September 10 to 19, 1988

September 10. Rome-Zimbabwe. We left Rome at eight o'clock in the morning. We have an eight and three-quarter hour flight to cover the 6,916 km that separate us from Harare, the capital of Zimbabwe, which has a population of 1.6

million. The Pope comes down the aisle to greet the journalists accompanying him on the flight. The questions revolve around *apartheid* in South Africa, the current situation in Poland[1] and the upcoming anniversary of his pontificate (October 16 will be the tenth anniversary of his election).

In the evening, at the Dominican convent in Harare, a meeting was held with the organization that brings the bishops of the countries of Southern Africa together. The bishops have just drawn up a *communiqué* on the meeting of these days in which they announce a future document of a pastoral nature. The Pope takes up the same ideas as the bishops, but I see that he changes the order: he mentions in the first place the priority of the spiritual life in facing problems; and he cites the conclusions of the Extraordinary Synod of 1985: without personal holiness, there is no apostolic efficacy.

The trip is full of splendid details. I realize that the Pope's presence in a place makes some things happen; I am convinced that they would not happen if the Pope were not there. And this almost regardless of what the Pope says.

We see ecumenism in action. In the meetings with leaders of Christian denominations, the human climate improves, susceptibilities and suspicions fade, and there is not even the shadow of confusion in matters of doctrine.

September 13. Botswana. All kinds of people gather at the cathedral of Gaborone, capital of Botswana, to greet the Pope. In the afternoon he celebrates the Eucharist at the National Stadium.

September 14. Lesotho. We leave Gaborone for Lesotho late: the Air Zimbabwe pilot says there is a storm over Maseru (Lesotho) and we have to wait. After a long wait, the plane takes off. The bad weather conditions are confirmed by radio. We start to fly over Maseru: low clouds and very poor visibility. The ground facilities are insufficient and one of the approach radars is not working. The pilot tries to land: impossible.

We have two options: to land in Johannesburg or in Bloemfontein, closer to Maseru. The second possibility is excluded and the plane heads towards Johannesburg.

Interestingly, it was just earlier that I had handed journalists an addendum from the Pope for his speech in Maseru, in which he said that he "wished to visit South Africa in the not too distant future . . ."

1. That year, private companies and political opposition to the Communist Party had been authorized.

A few minutes later I inform everyone that, due to weather difficulties, we are going to land in Johannesburg. Naturally, there is an explosion of applause. The word South Africa has been very present throughout the trip; and now we are going to land precisely there. The surrealistic thing is that some journalists don't quite believe the bad weather and start to speculate and imagine hidden strategies.

The Pope stays serene. I had the impression, when we landed in Johannesburg, that he was feeling a little ill; perhaps he is a little dizzy from the incidents of the flight, and the twists and turns over Maseru. We land. The plane approaches the terminal. At first, no one is there. Then the airport manager arrives, who makes himself available for whatever we need.

I do not know what decision will be made in the end. Tucci and Cassidy[2] get off the plane and talk to Pik Botha, the South African Minister of Foreign Affairs, who has just arrived and is very accommodating. A solution is adopted which, despite its inconvenience, seems the safest: to organize a caravan of buses from Johannesburg to Maseru: 380 kilometers [237 miles], with an approximate duration of five and a half hours.

The Pope gets off the plane and waits at the airport terminal. I take care of the journalists, who are in an uproar. Some prefer to stay in Johannesburg and two are ill: Domenico del Rio is still dizzy and Federico Mandillo has suffered an apparent cerebral spasm with momentary loss of consciousness and partial paralysis. Seeing his condition, I decide that it is preferable for him to stay in Johannesburg; I contact the representative of his agency (*ANSA*) in South Africa and leave him in the hands of the Alitalia[3] representative, hoping for a speedy recovery.[4]

A few hours later we left for Maseru. The Pope goes in front, with Dziwisz and Cibin, in a BMW, preceded by two police cars. Behind, in the first bus, goes the entourage; and in a second bus, most of the journalists. Not all of them, because some of them are still transmitting the news from the airport and will leave a little later.

---

2. Edward Idris Cassidy (Australia, 1924–2018) had been appointed a few months earlier, on March 23, as substitute Secretary of State, a post he held until December 12, 1989, when he was appointed president of the Pontifical Council for Promoting Christian Unity. He was created a cardinal in 1991.

3. Alitalia was an Italian airline, reborn at ITA in 2021.

4. So it was. Mandillo died many years later, in 2003, of a stroke, while guiding a group of visitors on a tour of the Basilica of St. John Lateran [Author's Note].

The trip is long and monotonous. The Pope's BMW stops at a gas station to refuel. The buses don't make any stops. We arrive in Maseru at night, at about eight o'clock on September 14. What to do? It is the Pope who decides to go to Rome, a city 50 km away, to celebrate Mass. It is quite late, it is raining and cold. I am informed that in Maseru yesterday, terrorists hijacked a bus of nuns and school children who were on their way to see the Pope.

When we arrived in this African Rome, in the middle of the darkness and under the incessant rain, the small church was surrounded by several thousand people who could not believe what they were seeing: the Pope in their city! Inside the church there is room for a couple of hundred people at the most. After Mass, we return to Maseru by the same road, in total darkness.

The Kidnapping. News of the kidnapping of the bus of nuns and school children: the South African special forces opened fire and three terrorists and one of the kidnap victims were killed. After Mass the following day, the Pope goes to the hospital to visit the wounded. Some have amputated limbs and others are very seriously injured.[5]

In these circumstances so painful for everyone—for the wounded, for their families, for the pilgrims, and for the Pope—someone asks me if John Paul II does not feel responsible for this. It seems to me a cynical and inadmissible question that does not deserve an answer.

September 15. Beatification. Ceremony of beatification of Joseph Gérard (1831–1914), Oblate missionary, evangelizer of Basutoland, now called Lesotho, at the Maseru Hippodrome.

September 16, Swaziland (Esuatini). The Pope celebrates Mass at *Somhlolo Stadium* in Mbabane, which is the administrative capital of the country. He then moves to Manzini, the most populated city. During the meeting in the cathedral he praises the hospitality of the country's inhabitants towards the refugees coming from nearby countries.

September 17. Mozambique. A country divided and broken by war. The government is Marxist. We are in Nampula, a small city. A nun tells me that they needed this visit from the Pope because they were desperate and tempted to leave everything.

A priest from Maputo, the capital of Mozambique, told me: "Even if the Pope had not come, I would have been satisfied." And he explains to me what

5. Two days later another hostage died.

he means: so much has been achieved in preparation for the trip that we have seen the fruits even before the Pope arrived.

I tell him these anecdotes the day after arriving in Rome, when he invites me to have dinner with him to discuss the trip.

Shroud of Turin

October 3, 1988

Today the theme of the dinner is very clear: the Holy Shroud. The Cardinal of Turin, Anastasio Ballestrero, a Carmelite, was in Rome, bringing with him a letter from Professor Tite, of the British Museum, in which he says that the results of the *carbon-14* analysis on some samples of fabric from the *Sindone* indicate that the fabric is from the 13th century or the beginning of the 14th century. At dinner are the two secretaries, Cardinal Casaroli and the Substitute, Cassidy.

Tite is the coordinator of the analyses commissioned by Ballestrero, custodian of the Shroud, to three laboratories, two American and one Swiss. The news had been leaked to the press some time ago. The Pope explains that my presence at this meeting is due to the impact that these analyses have had on public opinion.

Casaroli thinks that the management of this matter has been mismanaged, with a certain naivety. He doubts the result of this investigation and values other data—also scientifically proven—that have highlighted, and continue to highlight, the inexplicable elements of the canvas and its image.

I think he is right. The Pope is hurt by all this, although—as a scientist—he is willing to accept a scientific result.

It is decided that the custodian of the Shroud will make this result public in Turin, since it is not a dogmatic or doctrinal issue. The Pope comments that there is no need to be afraid of the results of science, but that the simple people, who have revered the Shroud as a great relic, following a tradition of centuries, will be disconcerted.

He asks my opinion. I suggest that, on the one hand, it should be made clear that these analyses are not *the last word* on the question; on the other hand, that the Church has no fear of science; and to emphasize that there are unexplained elements in the Shroud that remain unanswered.

It is considered appropriate for him to go to Turin to work with the Cardinal and his scientific advisor, Professor Gonella of the Politecnico di Torino, to present the data to the press.

At the European Parliament

October 8–11, 1988

The Pope was in France from the 8th to the 11th; in addition to the European institutions in Strasbourg, he visited the dioceses of Strasbourg, Nancy and Metz.

On the 8th, the Pope speaks at the European Parliament. Shortly before he entered the hall, the president informed the Pope that it was possible that Ian Paisley, MEP[6] for Northern Ireland, would pull one of his stunts. And so it was: as soon as the Pope gets up to speak, Paisley stands up and begins to read a short text in which he says that the Pope is the antichrist, that the Parliament should not have invited him, etc.

The Pope remains serene until the same parliamentarians get Paisley to leave the room. He then reads a splendid speech. These two ideas especially stick in my mind:

> After the coming of Christ, it is no longer possible to idolize society as a collective grandeur that devours the human person and his irreducible destiny. Society, the State, political power, belong to the changing and always perfectible framework of this world. No project of society will ever be able to establish *the kingdom of God,* that is, eschatological perfection on earth.
>
> Political messianisms almost always lead to the worst tyrannies. The structures that societies give themselves never serve them in a definitive way; nor can they by themselves offer all the goods to which man aspires. In particular, they cannot replace the human conscience, nor its search for truth and the Absolute.

The next day, before celebrating Mass, he visited an institution that cares for deaf and dumb children and adults. Some of them were also blind. He greeted them personally, giving each one of them an affectionate gesture, a few words, a smile, a caress. At the end he improvised these words: "This meeting is the best preparation for the Mass I am going to celebrate next. Some of you cannot hear me and others cannot see me. But to all of you I say: see you at Mass!"

---

6. MEP: member of European Parliament

Carbon 14

OCTOBER 12–13, 1988

We return from France on the evening of the 11th, and on the 12th at noon I leave for Turin. I was met at the airport by Professor Gonella, who accompanied me to the hotel. We meet at five o'clock in the afternoon with the elderly Cardinal Ballestrero, a saintly, humble, and good-humored man. He is conspicuously calm. He has prepared a press release for the following day, which has already been seen in Rome. I explain to him that the interest on the part of the press is very high, because he thought that only about eight or ten journalists would attend. To his astonishment, I tell him that there will be at least a hundred . . . as there will be; among them a large English-speaking group.

The press conference is held the next day at a Salesian headquarters. Great interest. I propose the presentation as an opportunity to make the communiqué known and to raise questions about thosse aspects of the Shroud that are still unexplained. The Cardinal of Turin reads the communiqué and the questions begin. Gonella talks about the limits of science and the value of its results. The cardinal responds quite well. The press conference continues for an hour and a half. At the end I adjourn, satisfied, because the atmosphere has been good and without "scandals" of any kind. Then I am interviewed by the American network *CBS*.

I return to Rome and find a message saying that the Pope wants me to come to dinner tonight. So I do. The whole conversation revolves around Turin. I tell him, in conclusion, that it seems to me that everything went well, within what was to be expected.

Are the Pope's Trips *Useful*?

DECEMBER 12, 1988

Dinner is delayed for a quarter of an hour, until the Pope finishes his business with Casaroli.

As I greet him, he reminds me that the last time I had dinner with him was three months ago, in September, on the occasion of the Shroud of Turin.

Over dinner he tells me that he has seen the first of the TV programs that the *BBC* has produced on the pontificate, and that he liked it. I give him the book that Wynn has just published: he skims a few pages, and then, looking at Dziwisz, says, "For vacation." I gather that, although he reads quite a lot, he doesn't have time to read everything he would like to at any given time, and he organizes himself so that reading doesn't take time away from his work.

He tells us that this morning he received a group of former Lefebvrian priests and seminarians. Then he spoke about the appointment of the Archbishop of Cologne and how some sectors of public opinion have received him. He did not complain about the lack of pressure, but it is clear that he is concerned about the matter.

I tell him that, from time to time, in various parts of Europe, there are those who question the usefulness of the Pope's travels. Naturally, he is well aware of these criticisms. I read him a paragraph from a letter written by Michel Di Falco, spokesman for the French bishops, in which he says that the benefits of the Pope's travels cannot be quantified, apart from the good that his words and his very presence among the people do.

At that moment, one of the nuns who attend to the pontifical apartment was serving us at the table, and upon hearing this, the Pope laughingly remarked to her:

—"Do you see how the Pope is not so bad?"

This is yet another example not only of his good humor, but also of the "Olympic" spirit with which he deals with criticism.

We talk about the *Sala Stampa*. I tell him about some positive and negative aspects, and he concludes by saying that our information strategy needs to be improved little by little.

"La Bottega dell'Orefice."

December 19, 1988

At the Aula Paolo VI, I attended the presentation of "La Bottega dell'Orefice" (The Goldsmith's Workshop), a cinematographic transposition of Karol Wojtyla's "meditation." In my opinion, the text is better, but impossible to bring to the screen. The Pope had seen it a few days ago.

The Aula is full. I reach the front rows and greet some cardinals, among them Poupard and Baggio. I find a free seat and sit down, not realizing that the front row, with the curial hierarchy, is reserved for cardinals. I see out of the corner of my eye that Monduzzi[7] does not look good, but at that moment the lights go out, the projection begins and I stay there.

7. Dino Monduzzi (Italy, 1922–2006) was prefect of the Pontifical Household (1986–1998): his duties included protocol matters. He was appointed cardinal in 1998.

At the US Embassy

December 21, 1988

I was invited to lunch by the US Ambassador, Frank Shakespeare, to watch the program *48 Hours: In the Vatican*, part of a series on various topics, produced by *CBS* with our collaboration. Also at the embassy were Foley,[8] Schotte,[9] Rigali, and Wilton Wynn. I find the program positive and sympathetic.

About Agca

December 28, 1988

It has been commented in some media that Agca has written to the Pope. Today I spoke with Dziwisz and he confirmed that Agca has not sent any letter to the Pope.

False threat

December 30, 1988

The Pope travels to the towns of Fermo and Porto San Giorgio, in the Italian region of the Marche. I came yesterday by car and slept in Fermo, in Villa Nazareth. The Pope arrived by helicopter in the morning. He makes a brief stop in Fermo where he has a meeting in the cathedral, and then goes to Porto San Giorgio, where he celebrates Mass for people of the Neocatechumenal Way. He first greets Kiko Argüello[10] and Carmen Hernández.

Mass is celebrated under a large tent. The Pope skips the text he had prepared for the homily and delivers another splendid homily without any notes.

The local police call me: I have to call my office urgently. When I speak to them, they explain that someone has left a threat on the phone, stating that the Pope is going to suffer an attack. I tell Cibin and Inspector Marinelli. It is not the first time this has happened.

It's all right.

---

8. John Patrick Foley (United States, 1935–2011) was president of the Pontifical Council for Social Communications. He was elevated to the cardinalate in 2007.

9. Jean Pierre Schotte (Belgium, 1928–2005) was secretary general of the Synod of Bishops. He was appointed cardinal in 1994.

10. Francisco José Gómez Argüello Wirtz (Spain, 1939) was—together with Carmen Hernández—the founder of the Neocatechumenal Way, in 1964, in the Madrid neighborhood of Vallecas.

8

Rome and Dissidence

The Pope Thinks of Africa

January 6, 1989

The Pope announces the convocation of a special assembly of the Synod of Bishops for Africa. He gives no dates, nor does he say where it will take place. For years there has been talk of this possible meeting. He himself had been answering questions on this subject at least since 1983. It had remained to give shape to this meeting. He has chosen the formula of a synod. Now it will have to be defined in its details. During these days the first meeting of a commission created for this purpose will take place.[1]

With Pio Laghi

January 10, 1989

Pio Laghi, papal nuncio in Washington, D.C., comes to the office. We talk about the meeting of the bishops of the United States with the Pope that will take place next March. The news has been leaked. In this case it has been Philip Pulella, from *Reuters*, who has obtained the information.

Meetings, Dinners and Projects

January 11 to 23, 1989

Jan. 11. I speak with Giovanni Battista Re, Secretary of the Congregation for Bishops, about the Pope's future meeting with the bishops of the United States. Re is a person I find very interesting, like many others with whom, fortunately, I interact every day, sincere, with a real spiritual restlessness and a great capacity

1. The sessions took place from April 10 to May 8, 1994, and the theme was "The Church in Africa and her evangelizing mission towards the year 2000: 'You will be my witnesses.'" The fruit of the special Assembly was the apostolic exhortation *Ecclesia in Africa*, signed and presented by the Pope in Yaoundé (Cameroon) during his visit to Africa (September 14–20, 1995).

for work. Incidentally, I tell him about the project of connecting with the bishops of the world by computer. He thinks it is fantastic.

Robert (Bob) Lynch, Secretary of the United States Conference of Catholic Bishops, is coming to see me. I show him, in outline, the information plan we have prepared for the March meeting.

Dinner at the Spanish Embassy to bid farewell to Faustino Sainz Muñoz, who was recently ordained bishop and appointed pro nuncio in Havana. Cassidy, Martínez Somalo, Silvestrini,[2] Ambassador Jesús Ezquerra (host) with his wife Laura, Angel Gómez Fuentes (TVE correspondent), the nuncio in Panama, and others attended.

JANUARY 12. The Swedish ambassador is coming to the office with Father Lorth. They want to organize a meeting with Scandinavian journalists before the Pope's trip to those countries. They have good ideas, but I try to disassociate myself from the project: I explain to them that the Holy See, unlike other institutions, does not "invite" journalists as a public relations strategy. Naturally, we will gladly receive all those who ask us to do so.

Today the body of an American pilot shot down during the US air raid in 1986 arrives from Libya. Libya asked the Holy See to mediate for the delivery of the body. I have spoken to the press of "humanitarian reasons" on the part of the Holy See for accepting this request. The US Embassy is a bit uncomfortable because they are humiliated by Libya's gesture. They see it as a publicity stunt by Gaddafi. In reality, they are right.

JANUARY 17. Lunch with the Ambassador of South Africa. He wants to make contacts to whom he can send information about the reality of his country, in view of the Pope's trip next year. He has the difficult task of convincing others that the South Africa of today is something different than what appears in the press.

JANUARY 20. Dinner at the Italian Embassy to the Holy See. The Latin American ambassadors and the Spanish ambassador were present. Nice informal dinner: buffet style. Each one sits where he wants. I chatted, among others, with the Ambassador of Italy, Scamacca, father of six or seven children: a nice and principled Sicilian. Reason for the dinner: to bid farewell to the Cuban ambassador, who is returning to his country.

---

2. Achille Silvestrini (Italy, 1923–2019) at that time was prefect of the Supreme Tribunal of the Apostolic Signatura. Later he was prefect of the Congregation for Oriental Churches. He was appointed cardinal in 1988.

JANUARY 21. I speak with Martínez Somalo on the subject of the constitutions of the Carmelite nuns. The prioress of the monastery of La Encarnación (Avila), a very good friend of mine, called me on the phone and is concerned about this issue.

JANUARY 23RD. The Argentinean engineer Pedro Brunori has been working for a few days now on the project of establishing permanent contact via computer with all the bishops of the world. The idea came to me almost by chance when I started using a computer myself. I have spoken a couple of times with the Pope about this issue and he understands its importance. We have to solve the problem of funding. Cassidy told me it was probably one of the most important issues at hand. We'll see: I pray about this.

Letter From German Theologians

JANUARY 26 AND 31, 1989

JANUARY 26. A critical letter signed by 165 German, Swiss, and Dutch theologians is published in Frankfurt, Germany. It focuses on the appointment of bishops, on the approval—by the Holy See—of professors in Catholic faculties, and on *Humanae Vitae*. Cassidy summoned me to the Secretariat of State to explain the situation. I read the report that was passed on to the Pope and made a brief statement to the press.

A bit of brighter news, it seems that the issue of the Auschwitz Carmel has been resolved, although the solution that has been reached may not be convincing.[3]

Between one thing and another, it has been a great morning: in the afternoon I escape to play tennis.

JANUARY 27. Great press coverage of the letter from the German theologians. My statement yesterday has apparently stung the promoters. Cassidy summons me again to discuss this matter. I tell him that messages of support for the Pope from the European Bishops' Conferences could be promoted: he likes the idea, although I do not know if he will decide to put it into practice. I suggest that Kasper[4] give an interview. He passes me a copy of the letter from Lehman,

3. This Carmel, located next to the former Auschwitz concentration camp, was permanently relocated in 1993.

4. The theologian Walter Kasper (Germany, 1933) was appointed Archbishop of Rottemburg-Stugartt (1989–1999). The Pope called him to Rome, where he was secretary of the Council for Christian Unity (1999–2001) and later president (2001–2010). John Paul II created him a cardinal in 2001.

president of the German Bishops' Conference, in response to the letter. We translate it and distribute it to the press.

Don Stanisław phoned me because he liked what I said to the press yesterday. On another note, he tells me that President Bush had called the Pope on the phone and they had talked for a while.

January 28. Hans Küng, one of the promoters of the German theologians' letter, mentioned me because he did not like the fact that the response of the Holy See to his position was given in a casual tone, and the protest was described as a "local event." They wanted to stir up a great controversy in public opinion. It did not work and they got angry.

January 31, 1989. Conversation in the office with the Nuncio in Germany, Msgr. Uhac about the letter of the German theologians.[5] He tells me that the statements that have been made from here have helped to clarify the issue and the perspective has been broadened. He adds that many of these issues boil down to very specific and local problems of the situation in Germany and some neighboring countries. He himself has been publicly criticized by some, but he has not been impressed: you can see that he is a man of courage. He praises Meisner,[6] the new bishop of Cologne.

Milingo

February 1, 1989

Today I have not said anything to the press, although perhaps I should have said something about Bishop Milingo.[7] He is a unique person. He was transferred to Rome because in Zambia, his own country, he was organizing some very moving liturgical ceremonies, with the expulsion of demons, following unapproved rites. He did this not only in his own diocese, but also acted without permission in other dioceses. The problem has become more complicated because he continues to do the same thing here in Rome.

---

5. Josip Uhac (Croatia, 1924–1998) was apostolic nuncio in several countries and secretary of the Congregation for the Evangelization of Peoples. John Paul II had planned to appoint him a cardinal, but Uhac died a month before the consistory.

6. Cardinal Joachim Meisner (Germany, 1933–2017) was archbishop of Cologne from 1988 to 2014. His appointment had been strongly contested by some sectors of the diocese.

7. Emmanuel Milingo (Zambia, 1930). In 1983 he was asked to resign as Archbishop of Lusaka. He was sent to the Vatican to work in the Pontifical Council dedicated to the pastoral care of migrants.

Thousands of Romans follow him and there are people who come from elsewhere to "see the show." A pro-Milingo demonstration had been called for today in St. Peter's Square, but no one came.

Contacts with Hungary

February 2, 1989

Lunch at the Hungarian Embassy with the Ambassador and Alceste Santini of *L'Unità*, who always acts as a link between the countries of Eastern Europe and the Holy See. For some time now I have been insisting on meeting the ambassador. They are interested in establishing contacts in view of the Pope's visit to Hungary. The ambassador is pleasant, friendly, a man of the Gorbachev era.

Sakharov

February 7, 1989

There appears today in *Time* magazine a letter of correction that we sent for a stupid article (I am sorry to call it that) about the appointment of bishops. It is the first letter of correction I have written in the last five years.

This afternoon the Pope received Andrei Sakharov[8] and his wife Yelena. One hour and twenty minutes of conversation. The interpreter is Irina Alberti.

Dissent: Significant Figures

February 11, 1989

I went on an excursion and, on returning home around five o'clock in the afternoon, I found several invitations to dinner tonight with the Pope. Crescencio Sepe, advisor to the Secretariat of State, is also attending. Main issue: the German theologians and what Bernard Häring[9] has written in *Il Regno*,

---

8. Andrei Dmitrievich Sakharov (Russia, 1921–1989) was a nuclear physicist, winner of three "Hero of Socialist Labor" medals. From the 1960s onwards he began his action in favor of human rights and freedoms, for which he suffered internal exile in the USSR. He received the Nobel Peace Prize in 1975. He died a few months after his meeting with the Pope. Irina Alberti (1924–2000) was a Russian journalist and activist, editor of *La Pensée Russe*, among other initiatives; she returned to Russia in 1991.

9. Bernard Häring (Germany, 1912–1998), a Redemptorist priest, specialized in moral theology, had some disputes with the magisterium of the Church for some of his positions on matters of contraception, etc.

attacking Carlo Caffarra[10] on the occasion of *Humanae Vitae*. The Pope is perfectly informed on the matter.

I have the impression that an attempt is being made to create a climate of "generalized dissidence," which does not correspond to reality. Cardinal Ratzinger has told the Pope that, in recent years, nine hundred requests for *nihil obstat* (approval) to fill professorships in Catholic theology have been submitted to the Holy See; of these, seventeen have been rejected; and of these seventeen, only three are German.

Diffusion of *Perestroika*

February 15, 1989

Vadim Perfiliev, deputy director of the Information Department of the Ministry of Foreign Affairs in Moscow, a Gorbachev man, is coming to see me. He speaks magnificent French.

We talked about the new Soviet situation. There is a need for understanding, a need for dialogue. They wish to establish frequent contact with this "power"—the Vatican—which is a State. You say it this way to avoid recognizing the religious and spiritual reality represented by the Holy See.

His visit is part of the *perestroika* outreach in the West. He invites me to a forum, to be held in London next month, on issues related to journalism.

The Pope with the US Bishops

March 7–10, 1989

Tomorrow begins the meeting of the Pope and the Curia with the bishops of the United States. Thirty-five metropolitan bishops are coming. From what I read, some of them do not seem too happy: as if they do not like public opinion to know that they have been "summoned" by Rome. They are trying to create an unpleasant climate.

The Pope has changed the draft of the speech prepared for him for the inauguration of this meeting. He is proposing something more open, to give way to a dialogue that is sincere from the beginning. He does not want to impose his will.

---

10. Carlo Caffarra (Italy, 1938–2017) was, since January 1981, founder and president of the Pontifical John Paul II Institute for Marriage and the Family. In 1995 he was appointed bishop of Ferrara and in 2003, of Bologna. Benedict XVI elevated him to the cardinalate in 2006.

MARCH 8, WEDNESDAY. The meeting begins and will last until Saturday; meeting desired by some, feared by others, and needed by all.

I am present at all the sessions, morning and afternoon, and I am a witness to the vicissitudes and aspirations of the Church in the American world. I notice the difficulties of living the Gospel in a post-industrial culture, rich, but lacking in some ways a religious sense, and in others, a healthy anthropology. At the same time, it retains great human and spiritual values.

The question arises: what does it mean to be a bishop in America today. The Pope reads an initial speech, short and generic. I have the impression that he wants to hear from the lips of the bishops themselves the problems and situations that he already knows; he wants them to dialogue among themselves under his presidency, and to listen to the cardinals of the Curia.

John May, Archbishop of St. Louis and president of the US bishops' conference, reads his speech: "We come to listen . . . but also to speak." I get the impression that what he says is more intended for public opinion than for those present at this event. I find both Ratzinger's opening statement and that of O'Connor of New York particularly relevant.

MARCH 10, FRIDAY. Today the burning questions were raised. Priestly vocation crisis, marriage instability? What can be done? Listening to them speak, different attitudes appear: those who are resigned, those who are horrified, those who propose to abandon themselves to God, and those who, besides that, are ready to fight and propose solutions.

Some sacraments, such as confession, are discussed. One third of American priests go to confession only once a year.

Listening to some evaluations, one can observe the weight of a great cultural pressure, which leads them to lose their self-confidence, and in some cases the certainty that Christianity offers the key to solve their problems.

I speak with Bishops John May, Edward Pilarczyk (from Cincinnati), John O'Connor—who invites me to New York—and Roger Mahoney, from Los Angeles. The latter asks me if he "can" talk to journalists from his diocese. I replied that, in my personal opinion, he "must." At the end, they concelebrate with the Pope at the tomb of St. Peter. Lunch. Speeches. From what I see and hear, they leave satisfied. Many ask for a copy of Ratzinger's speech.

There has been talk these days of an anti-Roman sentiment. I have the impression that it alludes rather to an obvious cultural clash between, for example, Italian and American ways of doing things. It is a mismatch between the customs of very different countries. Some tend to think, confusing the styles of the various nations with much more essential questions, that the Pope does not understand us.

Is this true? I think not. What happens is that the problem is not reduced to questions of style: some people begin pastoral or sacramental initiatives that move away from the faith and the teachings of Jesus Christ; and here, naturally, they are told that this cannot be done. It is simple fidelity to the Lord's teachings, which are addressed to people of all cultures, races, sensibilities, tastes and traditions.

In these days I have come to realize that it is not a question of culture shock: it is a question of faith. It is not a problem of geographical latitude, but of spiritual latitude.

At the Hungarian Embassy

MARCH 20, 1989

Lunch at the Hungarian Embassy with Cardinal László Paskai[11] and Hungarian Minister Imre Pozsgay, who is in Rome and was received today by the Pope. Also present were Cardinals Etchegaray, Sodano, and Colasuonno, the Flying Nuncio to the countries of the East. Ambassador Pozsgay announced to the Pope that they will study the 1949 trial of Cardinal Mindszenty.[12] He renews his invitation to me to visit Hungary before the Pope's trip, which will take place in the fall of 1991.

---

11. László Paskai (Hungary, 1927–2015), created cardinal in 1988, was archbishop of Esztergom-Budapest from 1987 to 2002.

12. József Mindszenty (Hungary, 1892–1975) was appointed archbishop of Esztergom and cardinal in 1945. He experienced persecution at the hands of the Nazis and then the Communist regime. In December 1948 he was arrested and subjected to torture to make him confess that he had committed crimes against the Communist regime. After a sham trial, he was sentenced to life imprisonment the following year. Physically exhausted, he signed the accusation that he had conspired to overthrow the government, but had the lucidity to add the initials C.F. (*coactus feci*, i.e., "I signed because I was forced to"). During his imprisonment, he fell ill with tuberculosis. He was released by the insurgents of the 1956 popular uprising. After the failure of that revolution, he took refuge in the US embassy in Budapest. In 1971 he was forced into exile. He promised that he would not return until the disappearance of communism. His mortal remains were transferred from Austria to Hungary in 1991.

The Pope on Austrian Television

April 6, 1989

A few weeks ago Kurt Krenn, Auxiliary Bishop of Vienna, came to the office to tell me that Austrian television was preparing a program on the Church in that country and that it would be a great thing if the Pope could intervene with some answers. I asked for the Austrian journalists involved to write to me explaining the content of what they wanted to do. When I got the letter, I passed a note to Stanisław to get a few moments with the Pope. We arranged to meet this morning, at the end of the audiences. I select the questions. The Pope sees me in the Library and jokes, "You always get something." The interview is conducted in German.

Lech Walesa

April 20, 1989

Lech Walesa at the Vatican.[13] This is the second time he has come. Between these two visits, the *Solidarnosc* trade union was banned and Lech Walesa was imprisoned. He is accompanied by his wife and his advisors. The Pope is pleased. He invites him to lunch.

Madagascar, Réunion Island, Zambia and Malawi

April 28 to May 6, 1989

April 28, Friday. We leave Rome early in the morning for Antananarivo. Shortly after take-off I go up to the Pope's apartment. He is praying with his eyes closed. I sit next to Dziwisz and raise the possibility of the Pope greeting the journalists. We have prepared a loudspeaker and microphone system, very handmade, but it may prove useful.

We chatted for a while about other things and when I was about to leave, trying not to disturb the Pope, he called me. I sit down next to him and he asks me about the progress of the *Sala Stampa*. I update him on the progress of the

13. Lech Walesa (Poland, 1943) was an electrical technician by training and one of the founders of Solidarity, the first free trade union in Communist-bloc Europe. He suffered several periods of detention. He received the Nobel Peace Prize in 1983. He was president of Poland from 1990 to 1995.

project to communicate with the bishops by computer, and of Derksen, the Dutch businessman who will finance it. He speaks to me with affection about Holland, which gave so many missionaries to the Church, raised figures such as Blessed Titus Brandsma,[14] saw a blossoming of vocations a few decades ago; and which is now, unfortunately, going through a profound crisis. All sorts of means have been put in place to help them out of it. "What can we do now? Patience," he says calmly, without bitterness, and at the same time, without resignation.

Dziwisz had told me earlier some details of the Pope's life. Among other things, that he usually got up at 5:40 AM and that, as a young priest, he already enjoyed great prestige. A detail about his life of poverty: in Poland he only had one coat, which was not particularly thick. When the cold weather came, he simply put on more clothes underneath.

April 29. Madagascar. We are forced to wait for a long time at the airport of Antananarivo because fog in Antsiranana prevents take off. We are all together—with the Pope—in an airport lounge. The Pope sits in a corner of the room and prays the breviary. When he finishes, he begins to read a work by the ethologist Konrad Lorenz, who died recently.[15] I am not surprised, because I already know that his fields of interest are very varied: theology, philosophy, anthropology, even authors apparently as far away from theology as this Nobel Prize winner in Medicine.

We set off. As we approach our destination, I realize that the pilot has taken a big risk: there are low clouds and mountains. To reach the valley we are heading for, the plane passes very close to the mountains.

The Pope celebrates Holy Mass in Antsiranana. Very humid and hot weather. We return immediately to a small and uncomfortable plane. He has a smile for everyone and some sympathetic gesture.

After getting off the plane, he goes to meet with young people at the stadium and then meets in prayer with representatives of other Christian denominations at the Catholic Cathedral of Antananarivo.

---

14. Anno Sjoerd Brandsma (Holland, 1881–1942), a Carmelite priest and philosopher, had been beatified by John Paul II a few years earlier, on November 3rd, 1985. He was rector of the Catholic University of Nijmegen. He died in the concentration camp of Dachau. Canonized by Francis on May 15, 2022.

15. Konrad Lorenz (Austria, 1903–1989) was a zoologist, ornithologist and ethologist who, starting from his study of animal behavior, moved throughout his life towards the study of psychiatry. He was awarded the Nobel Prize for Medicine in 1973.

April 30, Sunday. Magadascar. Beatifies Victoria Rasoamanarivo,[16] a decisive figure in the evangelization of the country.

Some political opposition parties in Madagascar have written letters to the nunciature requesting a meeting with the Pope. It is considered more convenient that they be received by Casaroli and Cassidy. The meeting took place in the afternoon in the premises of the Episcopal Conference. They converse for almost two hours. I give a brief account of this meeting, in which the Cardinal Secretary of State underlined some points of the social doctrine of the Church, especially the rejection of all violence in social life.

Madagascar lurched to the extreme political left and is now trying to get closer to the West. Gentle, good people, of oriental origin. Very particular cult of the dead. Ecumenism: a large group of Anglican faithful attend, together with their bishop, the Pope's Mass. The Anglican bishop comments: "This is magnificent." It should not be forgotten that in Africa Catholics and Protestants have reached a practical ecumenism, in order to face together the difficulties that Christianity encounters in this land.

May 1st. Reunion Island.[17] Upon entering the plane, the Pope jokingly told me that he felt that the press "is behaving well" with him so far. I had not shared anything with him, so I don't know what could have been the origin of that comment. I think maybe Stanisław called Rome and Sister Eufrosina, one of the nuns who attends to him,[18] was the one who gave her point of view on the state of public opinion. In any case, the Pope would not change the tone of his speeches, even if the opinion was hostile.

---

16. Victoria Rasoamanarivo (Madagascar, 1848–1894), was related to royalty, was baptized at the age of fifteen, and was forced into a marriage of convenience, in which she suffered greatly because of the alcoholism of her husband. Through her tireless devotion, however, he accepted Catholic baptism on his deathbed. She held onto to her faith in times of persecution, supported Catholics in their faith when missionaries were expelled, and carried out numerous works of mercy.

17. Reunion (French: La Réunion; Reunionese Creole: La Rényon) is an island of the Mascarene archipelago, with the status of French overseas department, located in the Indian Ocean, east of Madagascar, and constitutes an outermost region of the European Union. Like the other overseas departments, it is also a region of France and is part of the Republic.

18. The Polish nuns of the community of the Servants of the Sacred Heart of Jesus who took care of the Pope's house were: Sister Matilda (mainly in charge of the wardrobe), Sister Fernanda (management and shopping), Sister Eufrosina (private correspondence and telephone), Sister Germana (kitchen) and Sister Tobiana, who acted as governess (and collaborated with the *Sala Stampa,* sometimes translating texts).

We arrived at five o'clock in the afternoon at the "Guillot" airport of this small island in the middle of the Indian Ocean. Stifling heat. The Pope is received by the French Prime Minister Michel Rocard,[19] accompanied by three ministers, including the Minister of the Interior. The next day, the four of them attend the Mass, which is magnificent, both for the organization and for the participation.

May 2–3. From Reunion Island to Lusaka, Zambia. Saint Denis, the capital, is a modern city: we are in France. Few autochthonous population. The Pope beatifies Brother Escubilión.[20] After Mass, we go to the airport and there, in a small lounge, the Pope speaks with Rocard and his entourage. He leaves in a Concorde for Lusaka: a three-hour flight at Mach-2.

Already in Zambia, I was struck by the deeply ecumenical atmosphere. The Anglican bishop welcomes the Pope in the Anglican cathedral as "leader of Catholics, champion of human rights, successor of Peter." And he thanks "the Spirit of God that the lack of understanding between Catholics and Anglicans is disappearing in Zambia." "The Church," the Pope replied, "is fully committed to the path towards unity, even though we realize, painfully, that there are things that separate us in faith and morals."

There is no mimicry: the differences are clear, as is the mutual affection. Anglicans ask the Pope to bless the first stone of the hall to be built next to the new cathedral. It may well be the first time something similar has happened in the history of Catholic-Anglican relations.

I have already experienced it on other occasions: in these trips there is, on the one hand, what the Pope says and does, and on the other hand, what his presence provokes in so many people. How to value that? Those of us who travel with him witness firsthand the great devotion to the Pope that exists in so many countries, perhaps in a special way in those that have not suffered "Western" cultural influences.

May 4. Malawi. We arrived at three o'clock in the afternoon at "Chileka" airport in Blantyre, Malawi. Hot. Very hot. President Banda, a wobbly and friendly old man, interrupts his speech to embrace the Pope. The atmosphere is very cordial and full of respect, to the point that, in the presidential palace, the lady who served the Pope served him tea on her knees.

---

19. Michel Rocard (France, 1930–2016) was a Socialist politician who served as prime minister (1988–1991) during the presidency of François Mitterrand.

20. Juan Bernardo Escubilión Rousseau (France, 1797–1867) was a Brother of the Christian Schools (De La Salle) known as "the catechist of the slaves."

During the meeting with the young people of Malawi, Kamuzu Stadium was filled with enthusiasm. The Pope looks excited, happy and, at the same time, amused. "In your language," he tells them, "you have a word, *chitukuko*, which means 'help yourself.' The Lord has blessed you by giving you abilities and means to reach levels of life and culture that were not within the reach of your parents and grandparents. Take advantage of these talents to develop your character and all that is noble in life. Malawi now needs people of strong character, aware of their value, but who have the humility to ask Christ for the graces they need."

MAY 9, 1989. ROME. "SYNTHESIS LUNCH." After teasing me about my African tan, the Pope goes—as usual—straight to the point: the ecumenical dimension of his visit to these countries. I tell him that this is one more reason to keep making his trips: although he recalls the same teachings of Christ, by proclaiming them in various places around the world, those teachings find a much greater echo. Since it is a comment that is somehow related to his person, he simply nods, "It is true."

I mention the future Synod of Africa, "in a year or two . . ." The Pope corrects me: "No, for later." I think he has a singular experience of time: he knows that this synod is urgent and, therefore, he is not in a hurry, or rather, he is not impatient for it to begin. I say that on the occasion of the synod we could perhaps think of an important intervention of an international nature that would contribute to resolving some of the enormous problems of Africa. He nods, but realistically comments to me that even he cannot find the means to resolve the situation in Lebanon peacefully.

He is happy with the new formula we have inaugurated for his meetings with journalists on the plane: microphone and ordered questions, thus avoiding repetitions. Until now, the Pope walked down the aisle of the plane and was asked questions, often the same ones. He is also grateful that most of the questions are now asked in a single language—Italian—because this makes him work less and be more precise in his answers.

9

The Warmth of the Nordic Countries

Letters on Lebanon

May 19, 1989

The Pope has written a personal letter to sixteen heads of state and to the Secretary General of the United Nations about the destruction that Lebanon is suffering. Among those heads of state are President Chaim Herzog of Israel and Gorbachev. The letters are going out during these days. This is one more initiative among his many proposals and steps to help solve a situation that is of deep concern to him.

Visit of George Bush

May 27, 1989

Great security deployment throughout Rome and especially around the Vatican. At six o'clock this evening, Saturday, President George Bush visited the Pope. The private part of the meeting lasted fifty-five minutes. At the end of the meeting, his wife Barbara, Secretary of State James Baker, White House Chief of Staff John Sununu and about twenty-five other members of his entourage entered the room.

After the farewell I approached the Pope to ask him for some details of the interview, for the press. When the Pope begins to speak, Casaroli, Cassidy, Sodano and Touran approach him. The Pope explains in detail the issues they have discussed: *perestroika* and the changes taking place in the Soviet Union; the question of Lebanon—a subject raised by Bush—and the difficulty of solving that problem; that Iraq is passing weapons to those fighting against the Syrian occupation forces. The Pope insists that the situation cannot be fixed without the intervention of the superpowers, and tells him that he wrote about this to Gorbachev. Bush is interested and suggests that this can be a "rallying point" with the USSR.

Bush talks about Central America: that Ortega presents one face when he comes to Europe and another in Nicaragua; that everything depends on whether he will call free elections, but that he doubts they will be free. He says that the Church can play a fundamental role in creating a certain climate in the region (and the Pope adds that he is right). He talks about Israel and Baker's speech to the Jews in the United States, where he said that they cannot annex the occupied territories. It is said that the Prime Minister, Isaac Shamir, is a hardliner, but that the Foreign Minister, Moshe Arens, is more so. The United States has decided to help the Soviet Union economically in order to favor internal developments.

I deduce that it was a meeting of substance. You can see how these people value their interview with the Pope: and not only for reasons of public image.

Visit to the Nordic Countries

June 1 to 10, 1989

An immersion in Lutheran Europe. The total number of Catholics in the five countries (Sweden, Norway, Finland, Denmark, and Iceland) is 196,500: it is possible that they could all fit comfortably in St. Peter's Square. In Iceland, there are 1,999: they will reach 2,000 with the Pope. In the whole of Finland, 4,200. And in the neighboring countries, absolute majorities of Lutherans, with their national Churches, linked to the state structures.

The Pope is excited about this trip. He knows the risks: we do not know how the Lutheran bishops and public opinion in those countries will react.

Leaving Rome on the flight to Oslo, I tell him that we have fourteen journalists from the five countries with us and that they would be happy if I could talk to them for a moment. As always, the Pope is available. I suggest to him that, as there is no room on the plane—we are flying in a DC-9—it would be best to have a small group of journalists on each leg of the trip. Today it would be the turn of two Norwegians and a journalist from Iceland. The Icelandic journalist asks the Pope if he knows anything about Iceland; the Pope replies that he knows little, but that he has read, in its Polish translation, the *Edda*,[1] a famous book of local mythology.

June 1. Norway. Mass in the square next to Akershus Castle in Oslo: "For the first time in history—says the Pope—the successor of St. Peter celebrates

---

1. The *Edda* are fragments written in the 13th century of oral stories related to Norse mythology.

the Eucharist in a Nordic country. I am deeply moved. And not only me. I am convinced that you too, my brothers and sisters in the great family of faith, are deeply grateful to God who has granted you to offer this liturgy of thanksgiving." Cordiality: three Lutheran bishops with their wives, several pastors, and some sisters of the Lutheran Church were present.

Visit to the Royal Palace: the King accompanies the Pope to the balcony to greet those gathered in front of the façade.

Ecumenical meeting in the room of the King Christian IV of the castle of Akershus: numerous details of delicacy with the Pope. For example, he is given a small throne that is larger than that of the Lutheran bishop who welcomes him. The Pope, after recalling what unites us, speaks of the doctrine of communion that separates us from the Lutherans.

Meeting with Norwegian Catholics. All—priests, religious, lay people—show their joy in recognizing themselves as part of a universal Church. The Pope is working for a future in which there will be no particularism or national churches.

June 2. Trondheim. Ecumenical meeting in the Lutheran cathedral of Nidaros. One of the highlights of the trip. Double translation of the Pope's speech, printed in Norwegian and English. The people followed his words attentively. He began by underlining the history, culture, and sacraments common to all Christians, in the face of a world that is moving away from God. I read this headline in *La Croix*: "A humble Pope conquers Norway."

June 2. Tromsø. "It is a pleasure for me," says the Pope, "to be in Tromsø. It is the first time I have visited a land north of the Arctic Circle. I know that you have 'the night of two months' a year. And now you are happy for the return of the light. You enjoy bright nights without sunsets. I understand how you must love the light. Jesus Christ said: 'I am the light of the world.' He is the light that shines forever . . ."

June 3. Reykjavik. Iceland. The driver of one of the cars, an Icelandic, makes an observation: "They say that the world is going very badly, but I think it must not be so bad if here are the bishop and the Pope praying together."

Locals have commented that there were more people in the streets than when Reagan and Gorbachev came. Very small Catholic population. The almost lunar landscape of this country is impressive.

An ecumenical meeting is held at the national shrine of Thingvellir. When leaving for the place of the celebration, the Pope decides to go in the same minibus that transports the Lutheran representatives, instead of getting into the car that had been prepared for him. Cold and windy during the open-air celebration.

JUNE 4. FINLAND. Flight to Helsinki. Greeting of the Pope by Danish and Swedish journalists. Arrival in Helsinki. As expected, few people in the streets. Upon entering Bishop Verschuren's house, near St. Henry's Cathedral, he is greeted with colorful regional dances. Warm welcome.

JUNE 5. TURKU. Ecumenical ceremony. Great dignity. The Pope asks before the representatives of the various confessions:

> —"Who am I?" and he answers in a determined voice:
>
> —"Like all of you, I am a Christian, having received in Baptism the grace that unites me to Jesus Christ Our Lord. Through baptism I am your brother in Christ and have been called to the priesthood without any merit on my part and ordained to the ministry of the word, the celebration of the Holy Eucharist and the forgiveness of sins."
>
> "God's will for me was to entrust to me the mission of the special ministry of the Bishop of Rome, successor of St. Peter, in which, according to Catholic teaching, the Lord instituted the principle and the perpetual and visible foundation of the unity of faith and communion."

Refreshment at the bishop's house, together with his wife.

We fly back to Helsinki and I accompany Casaroli for a press conference. Interesting conversation during the trip. He talks about the importance of the press. He says: "I would talk more, but sometimes I have doubts whether what I say would please the Pope. We talk sometimes over lunch and he gets passionate. He has a diverse existential experience."

The press conference is going well: Casaroli and the Lutheran bishop of Turku are present. One of the questions they ask the bishop is how to understand the freedom of a Church that is a State Church. The bishop speaks of economic freedom, with the power to collect taxes, as the basis of that freedom. Then we had lunch: Casaroli, the bishop and his wife, and two officials from the Foreign Office. A pleasant meal and a singular experience. We remember Casaroli's visit to Helsinki in 1975, on the occasion of the Conference for European Cooperation and Security.

From there we go to the Ice Palace for Mass. Full of people. Lutheran bishops with their wives participating in the Mass. I have to assist the wife of one of these bishops who suffers a fainting spell; after first attention, I entrust her to the care of a local doctor on duty.

JUNE 6. DENMARK. *The Confrontation That Never Existed.* For some of the press, there has been a confrontation with the Lutherans. The only thing I have noticed is—perhaps—less enthusiasm on the part of some bishops, and the anecdote of the bishop of Roskilde, who preferred the Pope to speak outside the ecumenical ceremony. He gave a pessimistic and fearful speech, as if to say, beware of this Pope who is too popular. But the common people received him with great sympathy. The neighbors of the houses near the nunciature commented on TV that, in order to make the Pope's stay in that place pleasant, they had cut the lawns surrounding their houses and were trying not to make noise at night so that he could rest. And I have not seen any public gesture, banner, or anything similar against the visit.

During the last decades, the local media—especially TV—had given very little information about Catholics. They only spoke, from time to time, about the IOR[2] or liberation theology. Not a single mention, for example, of the Pope's travels. These ten years of pontificate have not existed for Danish TV; and, consequently, for many Danes. Now, on the occasion of this trip, special programs have been broadcast, and debates and surveys about the Catholic Church have been organized. For the first time the newspapers in this country have given abundant information about Catholicism.

JUNE 8. STOCKHOLM—SWEDEN. Very cordial atmosphere during the whole stay. During the visit to the King and Queen, the Pope greets their three children with kisses. Then he greets the rest of the family: the king's uncle and the queen's mother. Gifts: prayer books for the children—in Swedish—and a photo of himself. The royal family presents him with another photo and letters from Pope Pius IX to Queen Josephine of Sweden and Norway (1854–1876) in facsimile. They go out to the courtyard of the palace, cross it on foot and greet the people from the balustrade.

Lunch at the bishop's house. Meeting with the Prime Minister and then with Mrs. Lisbeth Palme, widow of the assassinated prime minister.[3]

---

2. The Institute for Works of Religion (IOR) is a financial institution of the Holy See established by Pope Pius XII in 1942, although it has its origins in a body created by Leo XIII in 1887. Its mission is to serve the various institutions of the Catholic Church (Holy See, religious orders, clergy, etc.) by guarding and administering the assets entrusted to them and providing them with specific payment services worldwide. According to the 2021 annual report, the IOR has assets of €649.3 million, with a net profit of €18.1 million. During its recent history, the IOR has been involved in some scandals that resonated strongly in the news. Recent pontiffs undertook some reforms to make its structures and regulations more transparent.

3. Olof Palme (Sweden, 1927–1986), leader of the Social Democratic Party, was prime minister of Sweden from 1969 to 1976, and from 1982 until the time of his death by an unknown assassin.

"I remember—says the Pope—that her husband was the first to invite me to come to Sweden, and I said to him: but the bishops have not invited me yet! To which her husband replied: don't worry, I will tell the bishops to invite you right away."

Mass at the Globe. Splendid place. A quarter of the participants are not Catholic. A Lutheran pastor devoutly prays the Creed: *Credo in unam Santam, Catholicam et Apostolicam Ecclesiam. . . .*

Three Lutheran bishops—the Bishop of Uppsala, the Bishop of Stockholm, and a third—approach the presbytery during Communion. They place their crossed hands on their chests, indicating their Lutheran status. The Pope blesses them. They bow their heads—each one separately—and walk away. Four centuries of history weigh on this gesture, which is moving.

This climate of cordiality has presided over the entire trip. I think that the Lutherans of these countries did not expect such a Pope. The Lutheran Bishop of Helsinki told him: "You, as Bishop of Rome, are an inspiration for us."

Oke Malm, a Swedish journalist who has been a correspondent in Rome for years, tells me, amused, about the cordial attitude of the press in Sweden: "These days, when you read the papers, you get the impression that my country is going Catholic. I have the feeling that many Lutherans are perhaps ceasing to consider the Catholic Church as a minority composed mostly of immigrants. I think they are realizing—along with the universality of the Church—their own roots, since this country was Catholic for centuries, until the Reformation."

June 9. Uppsala. Today is Friday. In the morning I attend Mass at the convent where we are staying. The Pope prays in the chapel while Marini, Boccardo, Willebrands and Borgomeo celebrate. He goes through the Stations of the Cross on the walls of this small oratory.

The events continue: an ecumenical meeting in the Lutheran cathedral of Uppsala; a meeting with the university community, Mass next to the old Lutheran church. The fatigue of these days accumulates, with the constant change of countries, climates, cultures, and languages, which causes amusing confusions: a lady handing out leaflets in various languages asks the Bishop of Helsinki: "Are you Italian?" He, confused, replies: "No; I am Catholic!"

We have dinner in the evening at the convent with the Bridgettine nuns in Stockholm. Mother Tekla[4] sings a Neapolitan song: *La Mamma*. It is a unique sight: in the midst of everyone, the Pope, just like everyone else.

4. Tekla Famiglietti (Italy, 1936–2020), abbess general of the Bridgettines (Order of the Most Holy Savior of St. Bridget).

Long conversation with Dziwisz after dinner. He tells me about the Pope's prayer life. It is very often "prayer of adoration." And he confirms to me what we all see, that also during the trips, despite the intensity of the program, he prays, does spiritual reading, prays the rosary, and the Stations of the Cross.

The Lutheran bishop of Uppsala tells the press: "I believe that the Pope is a man sent by the Holy Spirit."

JUNE 10. VADSTENA. Mass in Vadstena, the city of St. Bridget, Patroness of Sweden. Afterwards, as he prepared to leave Sweden, the Pope blessed the first stone of a new Catholic church. It comes from the medieval cathedral of Lipkoping, formerly Catholic and now Protestant, and was donated by the Lutheran Bishop Lonnebo and the Lutheran Diocese of Lipkoping.

JUNE 12. ROME. Dinner with the Pope. I tell him some anecdotes of the trip. Someone comments on the "confrontation" with the Protestants, which has been published in some newspaper. Since I know who wrote it, and that he wrote it without any real evidence, I say that with certain people there are two possibilities: either one passes over them, or one has a heart attack. Everyone laughs at this rather vehement way out, and the Pope says to me amused: "*Non lo faccia*!".[5] After dinner, as I was leaving the oratory, he repeated to me again: "*Non lo faccia!*."

At another point, an episode is told about Pius XI, who commissioned the painting of two frescoes on the walls of the chapel of Castelgandolfo: one is the "Miracle of Vistula," which occurred when he was nuncio in Poland, and the other represents the defeat of the Swedish troops in front of Jasna Gora.[6] During dinner there is a funny episode with the nun who "fights" with a steak . . . Little things that give an idea of the cordial and informal atmosphere, full of deep respect, that surrounds the Pope.

For dessert we had some mangoes given by the bishops of Togo, who are on an *ad limina* visit.

---

5. "Don't do it," in the sense of "don't let him have a heart attack."

6. The Battle of Warsaw between Poles and Russians (August 13–25, 1920) is sometimes referred to as "The Miracle on the Vistula." Although it initially appeared that the Russian troops were winning, they were in fact walking into a trap. On August 16, the troops led by Jozef Pilsudski counterattacked, forcing the Russian soldiers to retreat.

Conversation with Casaroli

June 16–19, 1989

June 16. Long conversation with Casaroli this morning in his office. He called me to talk about how to break the news of the restructuring and appointments at the *Institute for Works of Religion* (IOR). Then we moved on to other topics. He was particularly expansive. He read me the names of the new members of the IOR, who they were, where they came from: O'Connor, American; Lehman, German; Sánchez de Asiain, Spanish, and so on.

I ask him about his vacation. "It's coming up," he tells me, referring to his 75th birthday and his possible retirement. As we were just talking about Willebrands, who is still going strong in his eighties, we joked about it. I found him particularly human, approachable, and open.

June 19. New structure of the IOR. I have met with journalists to explain the new structure. I have prepared it taking into account their possible questions, including some about Marcinkus.[7] As the Statute is still at the reserved document stage, I have not referred to it, although I have explained the new structure as stated in that Statute.

No Resignation in the Face of Lebanon

June 26, 1989

I am going to have dinner with the Pope. I ask Dziwisz if I should prepare a topic. "Lebanon," he tells me.

The Pope focuses on the question from the outset: what more can be done in public opinion to make the leaders and the people aware of the need to put an end to the agony that the country is going through. He explains in detail the situation from a historical point of view and the implications for today. He dwells on the role of Syria and Israel. And he mentions the letter he has written to the heads of state. From some he has received a reply (from Bush, for example); and in other cases he is waiting for it (Gorbachev).

And he asks us, not from a political point of view, but from a human, ethical perspective:

—"What else can we do?"

7. Archbishop Paul Casimir Marcinkus (United States, 1922–2006) was president of the Institute for Works of Religion from 1971 to 1989. His name was mentioned during those years in several episodes of Italian financial scandals.

I say that, for the public in general, the Lebanon issue is no longer news. Unfortunately, people have become accustomed to the images that arrive daily from that country; they accept a situation in which everyone is fighting against everyone else; and they take for granted the disappearance of Lebanon as an independent state.

The only thing I can think of to do, I say, is to publish his letter to the heads of state and highlight those dimensions and the ethical burdens that are lacking in public discourse, which has reduced everything to a merely political question. To give it more continuity, an article could be written with the ideas he has just mentioned, perhaps signed by someone representative of the Holy See, such as Sodano.

He does not give up in the face of the facts. He has written to the heads of state—of the United States, the Soviet Union, France, Germany, Spain, Italy, the Arab League, etc.—. He has spoken several times on that question in his general audiences and in the Angelus he prays from the window of the Apartment. He has asked for prayers. He has received an *ad limina* visit from the Catholic bishops of that area. Theoretically, he has done everything in his power. But he will not give up in face of the catastrophe.

At the end of dinner, when he says goodbye, he tells us, with a relieved expression, that discussing these worries with us has helped him. He feels better, like someone who is relieved of a heavy burden when he shares it with others.

A "Creative" Title

June 30, 1989

Yesterday, the feast of St. Peter, Sepe called me at home to have lunch with the Holy Father today. Subject: reaction of the press to the presentation of a document of the Congregation for Catholic Education on the teaching of the social doctrine of the Church in seminaries. Some of the Italian press has offered a simplistic interpretation, along the lines of: "The Holy See supports social democracy."

We are at lunch with Mejía, Saraiva Martins—Secretary for Catholic Education—Sepe and Agnes, director of *L'Osservatore Romano*. Greeting him, I tell the Holy Father that every time he invites me to lunch I consider it a gift. He interrupts me with a smile to say: "I have calculated the number of times I have invited you to lunch. There are many. It would be time for you to invite me once. . . ."

With regard to the matter at hand, I explain that it began with the eagerness of a local news agency to highlight a topic of "little interest" to the general public: the teaching of social doctrine in seminaries. They ended up disseminating information with a gimmicky title—"Yes to social democracy"—which was later picked up by some Italian newspapers. From *Sala Stampa we* commented that it had been an obvious distortion, that there was no real basis, and everything died down.

At another point, I tell the Pope that I will be going to Spain in a few days to present, with Cardinal Ratzinger, the Spanish edition of the book published in the tenth year of his pontificate.[8] The conversation then returns to the trip to the Scandinavian countries. I affirm that, for me, it was a historic trip. "Indeed it was," he corroborates. I tell him that that trip could be the subject of a book. Perhaps it is a project that he would enjoy. I tell him about a film, *Babette's Feast,*[9] which reflects the Nordic religious climate. I can send him the cassette, if he is interested. He says yes.

The Pope was, as I have already noted on other occasions, very well informed about everything and full of his usual good humor. Long visits to the chapel before and after lunch. At the end, Stanisław tells me, in an aside, to get ready to go with the Pope to the mountains on the 12th.

On the 50th Anniversary of World War II

July 10, 1989

The trip to the Nordic countries comes up again in today's dinner conversation. The Pope's question is: How can we revive or prolong the positive atmosphere of those days? It occurs to me that one possibility could be to invite the Scandinavian bishops here to Rome, perhaps for lunch. The idea seems to have a future. He tells me to tell Willebrands about it.

The Pope is preparing a document on the occasion of the 50th anniversary of the end of World War II and says that among those assisting him in the drafting are Msgr. Roland Minnerath and Father Robert Graham.[10]

---

8. *John Paul II. Pilgrim for the Gospel* (Madrid, 1989). It contains testimonies of King Juan Carlos I, Cory Aquino, Susaku Endo, Teresa of Calcutta, among others, and photographs by Giancarlo Giuliani.

9. Danish film directed in 1987 by Gabriel Axel, based on a story by Isak Dinesen (Karen Blixen). Winner of the Oscar for best foreign film.

10. Roland Minnerath (France, 1946), specialist in Church history; he was appointed bishop of Strasbourg in 1989 and later of Dijon (2004). Robert A. Graham (United States, 1912–1997), Jesuit, specialist in the history of the Church during World War II.

In this connection, I tell him about a request from *Time* magazine: they are also preparing a special issue for the anniversary and they would like to publish a personal memento of the Pope. Although he does not dislike the idea, he wants to know more about the project. (I think it could be a good article: the Pope has told on some occasions that the day Germany invaded Poland he had gone to the Wawel Cathedral in Krakow to go to confession and attend Mass. It was the first Friday of the month. There he was told the news of invasion. He was nineteen years old.)

The document on St. Joseph also comes up in the conversation, and he says that it is almost finished.[11]

---

11. It is the apostolic exhortation *Redemptoris custos*, on the figure and mission of St. Joseph in the life of Christ and the Church, which was published on August 15, 1989.

10

Back in the Mountains

With the Pope in the Aosta Valley

July 12 to 21, 1989

July 12. "How are you getting to the airport?," Dziwisz asks me, early in the morning, on the phone. "By car," I answer. He tells me to be at the Vatican heliport at a quarter to five, to accompany them by helicopter. And so it happens: we go, together with the Pope, Dziwisz, Tadeusz, Gugel and Dr. Sandro Sabato, another very good and nice professional. We arrived at Ciampino; we left the helicopter, and we boarded an "executive" plane.

At one point during the flight, the Pope peers into our compartment and, seeing us, comments amusedly, "How many 'capi' (chiefs)!"

In Turin, a new helicopter takes us to Les Combes, in the Aosta Valley. The house where the Pope will reside is rented. It is a small two-story building, built in stone, isolated and separated by a couple of hundred meters from another prefabricated house belonging to the Salesians.

Our company is as follows: Alberto Carreggio, a priest of the Diocese of Aosta who organized this vacation on behalf of the bishop; the security men—Biocca, Coali and others—and the police team, who have their own small operating room. Marinelli and Volpe, the police chiefs, have lodged in a hotel in Introd, a quarter of an hour away.

July 13. First day of the excursion. The Pope leaves his house at a quarter past ten and starts walking uphill. Half an hour later, he takes off his white cassock and continues walking in gray corduroy pants and a white shirt with a collar. On the shirt, discreetly and to the left, are the initials: G.P. II.

Arriving next to a cross—the *Croix du* Bois—he blesses himself. Splendid panorama, with the Gran Paradiso mountain. During one of the pauses, I make a reference to the document in preparation on World War II. Difficult document, I add. "Yes," he says, "the German people of today are not to blame. A system was created that allowed everything that happened. When I was in Germany in 1980, I talked to Schmidt and said, 'Why did you do that to Poland? Six million dead, most of them Jews . . .' And Schmidt answered me that you had to go back in history, to the Polish partition in the 18th century, carried out by Russia and Prussia. 'I will try to do my best,' said Schmidt, 'to overcome all this.'"[1]

We were chatting standing up, before having lunch in the bush, when he called Don Tadeusz and said: "Come, because this is of interest to you." Later, joking, he said to me: "Now you have to give us a press conference on the matter."

After lunch, as we walk, I have a "philosophical" conversation with Tadeusz. He tells me that the previous year, while climbing the mountains near Lorenzago, the Pope suddenly asked him, "And you don't think that immanentism has already exhausted its historical validity?"

This is the Pope's concept of vacation: walking, constantly thinking, without taking his thoughts away from the issues that occupy him. Sometimes he pauses and concentrates: it is the birth of an idea. His mind is active, he does not only contemplate the landscape from an aesthetic perspective: he looks for the foundation of his ideas.

Tadeusz tells me that it is difficult for him to sleep, and that when he sees the worries that the Pope carries on his shoulders, he marvels at how easily he sleeps. He thinks that this is the fruit of his enormous faith in Christ, who has come to redeem the historical, concrete man. For Tadeusz, the concept of freedom as it is sometimes presented: as freedom uprooted from reason and truth, is a grave error.

As we approach Les Combes, we find a family gathering hay. Big surprise! I take a photo of them. We arrive in Les Combes, a village with only a few houses. I see several families. Shortly before, the Pope had put on his white cassock. The families greet him and invite him to tea. He excuses himself saying that he has already had it. They ask him if he wants to see the village church and he agrees. It is a small church without a tabernacle. The Pope kneels down and prays, by himself, for a long time.

July 14. The Pope is relaxed. Before leaving, in the morning, he asks, "Where are we going today?" Someone explains that a long hike is planned through two valleys, Arvier and Valgrisenche, and that we will go up to 2,100 m at Boregne.—"How?" responds the pope—"We haven't reached 3,000 yet . . ."

---

1. Helmut Schmidt (Germany, 1918–2015), Social Democratic politician who, among other positions, was chancellor of West Germany from 1974 to 1982.

On the way, we meet some peasants who greet the Pope. We continue towards Verconey and La Frassy. Long itinerary. Splendid weather. We stop for lunch at two o'clock, a late hour after a long walk. We met a family in an isolated house. Around five in the afternoon we arrive at the place where the cars are waiting for us. The Pope decides to take a break. He puts on his cassock, sits down on the folding chair we are carrying and prays the breviary. I take some photos of him which I give to the press the next day.

At the end I tell him that in this place it is very easy to raise our hearts in thanksgiving to God. He responds by reciting a psalm. I take a photo with him, which I keep.

In the evening, after dinner, I go to Stanisław to tell him that the next day I will meet with the journalists to tell them something about these days, and that I will bring them some photos. The Pope comes out at that moment—we are outside the house—and wants me to continue the conversation, but I leave them alone and go.

July 15. I do not accompany the Pope because I go to see the journalists. I go to the village of Introd to work with Luciano Mellace, *Reuters* photographer. I want to develop some pictures I took of the Pope while he was walking. We go to see the *Associated Press* correspondent, who has a portable lab. We develop two rolls of film and I select three photos that we distribute to the press. Then, I go to the Introd town hall, where a sort of press room has been set up temporarily, where the journalists meet. There are journalists from *ANSA, Avvenire, Corriere della Sera, Il Giorno* and the local press. I give them a *briefing* on the first two days of their vacation. Then we all go to lunch together in Aosta, at *Cavallo Bianco,* at the invitation of Augusto Rollandin, President of the Region.

The Pope returns at a quarter to eight. They are quite tired because today's excursion included a descent of more than three hours and their knees are hurting. Tadeusz also has an injured knee. They humor me and tell me that I didn't go because I already knew the difficulty of the route. The Pope, in the same tone, asks for their forgiveness, telling them that if they walked slowly it was their fault.

July 16. The whole day was dedicated to the Pope's pastoral work. First, transfer by helicopter to the shrine of Our Lady of Oropa, near Biella. After Mass, a simple lunch. Then to Pollone—also by helicopter—to visit the tomb of Pier Giorgio Frassati.[2]

---

2. Pier Giorgio Frassati (Italy, 1901–1925). Young member of Catholic Action, great mountaineer of the Aosta Valley. He was beatified by the Pope on May 20 of the same year.

Later he went to Quart, to inaugurate a Carmelite convent. He speaks to them about a sanctuary also dedicated to Our Lady of Mercy—the same invocation as here—which is in Vilnius, Lithuania; and he makes an affectionate reference to the Lithuanian people, "so faithful, so heroic, and who have suffered so much." From there, by car, he went to greet the people in the parish of Introd, the town to which our house belongs.

JULY 17TH. Towards noon we are arrive to the Court de Bard (2,261 m), a wonderful plateau where we stop to contemplate a wide circle of mountains, from Mont Blanc (4,810 m) to the Gran Paradiso (4,000 m).

The Pope pauses on the road. I approach him and tell him something about Poland: today it was announced in Rome that Poland would reestablish diplomatic relations with the Holy See; and soon the new president of the republic will be elected. I also add that in Russia there is a huge strike of miners.

Standing up, leaning on the mountain staff, the Pope begins to speak about the countries of the East. He makes a synthesis of the Christian Slavic peoples and then refers to the situation under the Soviet empire and the current injustice. He speaks of his position, as Pope, and his role in relation to the world that was created after Yalta. "Politicians think that perhaps Yalta was not just and that this Pope, because he does not accept this situation, is a destabilizer." I tell him that they could say that in 1980 and 1981, when the change in Poland began and his attack happened. "Ah, yes, the bombing . . . and everything else." He does not say more, but I seem to understand that he inscribes the attack within the logic of that "destabilizing Pope."

We talk for twenty-five minutes, looking out at a splendid panorama. I have the sensation of seeing the whole of Eastern Europe, with its history, its struggles, and its effort to survive in the face of communism. This Pope knows this reality. He is not making an academic, distant, laboratory speech: it is part of his own life and, above all, of his responsibility.

I wonder then: if God has brought a Slav to the seat of Peter, will he not want his influence to serve to undo Yalta and bring justice to those peoples?

At one point in the conversation, when we were talking about the changes that are beginning to appear in Russia, these words slip out: "Perhaps Our Lady of Fatima . . ." In his reasoning there is the force of history, the moral imperative of justice, and the enormous perspectives opened by faith. Also by faith in Fatima.

Although it does not outline a new *ostpolitik*, I have a feeling that the Holy See will carry out its new *ostpolitik* under the leadership of this Slavic Pope. I do not see it as a tactical, short-sighted operation. It is an exercise in historical truth. It does not start from the passive acceptance of Yalta and its subsequent accommodation, but from an original impulse based in history and the principle of respect for the rights of man.

After lunch, we walk back for a while. He sits under a tree on a folding chair and again talks spontaneously about relations with Poland and *ostpolitik.* I sit down on the ground next to him. I tell him that from what he told me earlier, I thought I saw the elements that will have to be taken into account in the new *ostpolitik* of the Holy See.

The basis of this *ostpolitik,* he tells me, will always be the same, although the way of applying it will be different. The USSR has so far acted from a position of military force, of confrontation and cold war. "I remember that Gromyko—may he rest in peace—came to see me at the beginning of my pontificate, in 1979, and then spent years without letting himself be seen. He woke up again when the Americans started with their Star Wars program, SDI.[3] He told me that I could use my influence to stop it. I told him that I had no power to stop it. Then he replied: 'But don't you realize how much power you have?' Gromyko knew his job, as foreign minister of that superpower."

I say that Gromyko did not understand *perestroika.* In his memoirs, published in Italy by Rizzoli, he explains things from his point of view and does not mention his request to the Pope to stop the Americans in their experiments on SDI.

—"Indeed," the Pope tells me, "he did not understand *perestroika.*" But he was the one who proposed the appointment of Gorbachev."

Several of our entourage have been approaching us, telling us some anecdotes. The atmosphere becomes more relaxed. Dziwisz tells an amusing story: Reagan was once asked if he had any regrets and he replied that yes, he regretted falling asleep during one of his audiences with the Pope. We all laughed.

July 18th. We climbed a 2,600 m mountain. At lunchtime the Pope asks me about the comments that have appeared in the media on the reestablishment of diplomatic relations with Poland. I read him a text from *Corriere della Sera.*

Dziwisz then speaks to me on this subject: "The Pope, for years, did not want to re-establish relations with Poland, because he did not want to recognize an officially atheist state with no respect for human rights."

---

3. In 1984, the United States initiated the "Strategic Defense Initiative" (SDI) program—popularly known as "Star Wars"—which sought to create a protective shield against a possible attack by the Soviet Union.

19 JULY. The Pope flew to the Ruitor glacier, at 3,350 m., in a small helicopter of the Alpine Rescue, a French *Alouette* with a single pilot. It seems to me that this is the first time he has flown alone with the pilot. The place is magnificent.

When I get there on the second helicopter expedition, I see the Pope walking on the snow in silence. He looks at the landscape. We prayed the Angelus, as we had done all the previous days. He greeted a group of French people who, astonished, met the Pope in the middle of the glacier. We chatted while contemplating this marvel. Sandro Sabato, the doctor, brings up the subject of how many university students lose their faith when they reach this stage of life. The Pope follows the conversation with interest and asks some questions.

We take some pictures. The day is splendid. I leave my dark glasses with Dziwisz and give the Pope some lip balm. The helicopter returns—it has gone to Aosta to refuel—and we stop at Gran Paradiso. Before lunch, while the Pope rests for a moment, I tell him that I am reading a biography of Buddha. This prompts the Pope to make a series of reflections on Buddhism.

He comments that Christianity starts from what is written at the beginning of Genesis ("And God saw that everything was good"). Buddhism, on the other hand, focuses on the negative, it sees evil in the world. It is a human way of thinking about the world. It is a personal asceticism. As in St. John of the Cross; but St. John starts from faith and Buddha—we do not know where he starts from. Certainly not from revealed truth. St. John of the Cross lives this asceticism to purify himself, to meet God in that state that he calls spiritual marriage of the soul with God. "Of course, God, who is good and loves goodness wherever it exists, can lead this asceticism of Buddhism towards . . . ," the Pope concludes without finishing the sentence.

JULY 20. Long walk with the idea of returning around 5:30 PM, because afterwards a meeting with young people of the diocese is scheduled at the Pope's residence. The itinerary is miscalculated and we arrive late.

In addition, the route includes a long descent that is very uncomfortable for the Pope, because of the slope itself and because he is wearing slippery sneakers that do not grip the terrain well. At a certain point he slips and falls to the ground. He is not hurt, but we fear that he has suffered a dislocated ankle. We make him sit up for a moment. The doctor examines him and we see that there is nothing wrong with him. He changes his shoes; he wears the boots that Coali is wearing, and Coali put on the Pope's sneakers.

We arrive at the cars. The Pope is very grateful for a glass of fresh water from a fountain. As we take off his boots to give them back to Coali, Dziwisz jokes that now those boots will have to go in the Vatican Museums.

Once at home, he held the meeting with the young people and delivered some very nice, off the cuff remarks.

JULY 21. Return day. Vacation is over. Last departure, in the morning: three long hours of walking to return for lunch. The Pope is silent. He sits on the folding chair and spends a long time under the shadows of the trees, contemplating the mountains.

On the way back to Turin by helicopter, we stopped at the "Lingotto:" an old *FIAT* building where they have installed an exhibition of Russian and Soviet paintings. Gianni Agnelli has invited the Pope, and the Pope wanted to go as a deference to the Soviet Union in these times of change.

Thinking back on these days, I noticed that the Pope did not shy away from people, although I think he preferred to maintain a bit of privacy while walking. When there were people on the road he would signal for them to stop the car and greet them. On one occasion he even got out to talk to those who wanted to see him. He gave himself to everyone.

11

A Hard Summer

The Carmel of Auschwitz and the Tragedy of Lebanon

August 13–15, 1989

August 13. I spend a few days away from Rome and, on my return, I find an angry reaction unleashed by various Jewish associations. They are reacting to a statement by Cardinal Macharski, Archbishop of Krakow, on the Carmel of Auschwitz. I give a first reading to what has been published in the international press and call Stanisław: I propose that Macharski must be brought into agreement—at least formally—with Decourtray, president of the French bishops' conference, who had made some critical remarks about Macharski. Stanisław says he will tell the Holy Father. Sepe informs me that the Pope is expecting us tomorrow for dinner.

August 14. As on other occasions at Castelgandolfo, the Pope appeared informally dressed: simple white cassock, a little unbuttoned at the neck, no white sash, no pectoral or skullcap. We started dinner half an hour later—around 8 o'clock—because I was in the garden with Stanisław. I took advantage of the time by talking with Msgr. Thu, who was enthusiastic about Cardinal Etchegaray's trip to Vietnam, the first by a papal emissary in recent times.

The Pope is in a good mood, as always. Brief reference to some Italian topics and then the conversation focuses on the Auschwitz controversy. Naturally, I am interested to know the Pope's thoughts on the ultimate destiny of the convent: whether it will remain there or whether it will be moved in the end. The Pope does not respond directly to the issue: he prefers to analyze the picture, to understand the current situation and its implications.

After reviewing the situation, he reasons like this:

> Here we touch on a problem of a religious nature. For Christians, praying in a place close to where so many people have died is a must. And this cause is shared by everyone in Poland and in the world. There are precedents, moreover, in the case of the *Shoah*: in Dachau there is another

> Carmelite monastery. With the agreement signed in Geneva in 1987, the Carmelites in Auschwitz were told: "this is wrong."[1] Naturally, we must take into account that there are those who think that only silence should reign there. We can accept that those who prefer silence should keep it. But from the point of view of conscience, of religion, one cannot prevent others from praying. Above all, if we start from the fact that these people are already there, and that they have gone there in good faith. Perhaps other reasons should be taken into account: whether inside or outside the enclosure. But that is the logic of my thought.

The promoters of the protest have offered only one alternative: the nuns must leave, which is considered ignoble and offensive by many people. In this situation, Cardinal Macharski published his statement. Possibly, other motivations also play a role: there is a desire to force the Pope to give in, there is also the question of the recognition of the State of Israel by the Holy See.

The Pope's reasoning is clear. Stanisław adds that Macharski has even made the effort—also financially—to buy the new land; that many Polish Jews are outraged by the aggressive actions of groups coming from outside; that all this has provoked a reaction of solidarity with the nuns from the majority of the population; that the problem is, above all, of a diocesan character.

On the Geneva agreement, the Pope says that Macharski has allowed himself to be included in it (implying that, possibly, he was not fully aware of what it entailed). But he formulates his conclusive point of view by saying that the agreement has been signed and, therefore, will be respected as far as possible, in spite of contrary judgments. It is a position of openness, but at the same time it makes clear the essential defects of the agreement.

He tries to understand the attitude of completely rejecting the idea of a contemplative convent near the camp. He says that it is a reaction to what cannot be understood, to the mystery of extermination. In the face of this, there is another attitude, that of Christ himself who, facing his own death, expresses his helplessness: "My Father, why have you forsaken me?"; but then comes the prayer: "Into your hands I commend my spirit."

Once the Pope's thoughts are known, I mention the unpleasant fact of the division between Cardinals Decourtray and Macharski, which is tantamount to

1. On February 22, 1987, an agreement was signed between Hebrew and Catholic representatives. The Catholic side consisted of four cardinals, among them Franciszek Macharski, Archbishop of Krakow, on whose territory Auschwitz is located. Among the points of agreement was the transfer of the Carmel within two years.

serving on a silver platter a motive for new criticisms. The objective would be for both of them to come to Rome, in some time, to talk and agree, and then to announce it themselves, leaving the Holy See on the sidelines.

The Pope points out that perhaps the dean of the College of Cardinals, or the Cardinal Secretary of State, could convene them. Naturally, he would not, because the matter does not per se fall within the competence of the Holy See. If there were a serious division of opinion between two priests, the case would be submitted to the diocesan bishop. In the case of two cardinals, it is a matter for the College of Cardinals. Carried away by an overly "operative" eagerness, I insist a little more and the Pope says: "Well, we don't have to decide everything tonight . . ."

As we finish dinner, the decrees of episcopal appointment of two Czechoslovakian bishops are brought to the Pope. He signs the parchments with satisfaction, saying aloud their names and dioceses. The signature was urgent because Nuncio Colasuonno[2] is going to Czechoslovakia tomorrow for the episcopal consecration.

Another matter on the table was the text of tomorrow's Angelus, which he wished to dedicate to Lebanon. He read what had been prepared for him and said that it was "too soft." He reflects for a moment and adds: "People are dying there and I cannot say this;" expressing, with the gesture, that in the face of the tragedy of Lebanon the words prepared are insufficient. His face darkens. It has to be redone.

Dziwisz tells him that it is too late and he does not know how they are going to be able to do it from Castelgandolfo, where they do not even have a telefax. The Pope insists and asks them to bring him the text of the letter he sent in May on this matter to the heads of state. The letter is in Rome, at the Secretariat of State. The Pope begins to speak, with a serious gesture, in Polish with Dziwisz: I did not understand anything, but it seemed to me that he was insisting on the inadequacy of the text that had been prepared and the magnitude of the tragedy in Lebanon.

That same afternoon he had received Alain Decaux,[3] sent by President Mitterrand, who wished to inform him of France's diplomatic initiative in Lebanon. The Pope says: "This afternoon, when the French minister came to see me, I told him (and he pronounces the following paragraph in French, as if he

2. Francesco Colasuonno (Italy, 1925–2003) was appointed by John Paul II as "flying nuncio" in the countries of Eastern Europe, as soon as the process of liberalizing these countries began. He was the first nuncio in Moscow. The Pope made him a cardinal in 1998.

3. Alain Decaux (France, 1925–2016) was a historian and member of the Académie de France. From 1988 to 1991, in the government of Michel Rocard, he was Minister of Foreign Affairs in charge of French-speaking countries.

were in front of the diplomatic envoy): 'Minister, I appreciate very much the initiative of President Miterrand. But there are people dying there. And it is a scandal that there is no international body intervening to stop this genocide. It is a scandal!' The minister told him that this was also France's position, but the Pope reminded him that "it was not enough."

The tone during this part of the conversation was dramatic. The dinner seemed to have gone awry. The Pope's horror at the Lebanese tragedy was evident. And at the same time his refusal to accept what many consider historically ineluctable—the destruction of Lebanon—was visible.

Silence. Then he looks at me. He changes his tone of voice and regains his usual serenity and cordiality. "You see," he says, "on the one hand there is the Auschwitz issue, on the other Lebanon." I am not sure what he means, but I understand that he is referring to the enormity of the problems that a Pope has to deal with day after day. In any case, it is clear to me that he does not accept the problems passively, but chooses a course of action: actions possible for a Pope who knows, at the same time, of his material weakness and of his spiritual strength.

On leaving the dining room, he insists that a copy of the letter be sent to the heads of state. Sepe asks who will write the text. The Pope says he will write it himself. As we leave, Dziwisz asks that someone come early tomorrow morning to correct the Italian style. The Pope moves in this absolute lack of means and people: there is no telefax in Castelgandolfo, there is no assistant to correct his Italian.

As we say goodbye, Thu tells us that the Pope is determined, if he does not succeed with all these initiatives in favor of Lebanon, to write to bishops all over the world.

That same evening the Pope's letter to the heads of state was sent to Castelgandolfo.

August 15. This morning, taking some phrases from that letter and adding others, he finished the brief speech—an address—that he read at the Angelus. It is an extremely moving text, which I cannot resist reproducing in full:

> On this feast of the Assumption of Mary, I would like to go spiritually on pilgrimage to the various Marian, Catholic, and Orthodox shrines in Lebanon, a country that has been enduring for too many years now divisions and trials, and which is being subjected during these days to inhuman bombardments. I kneel spiritually before Balamand, Bikfaya, Bzommar, Kannubin, Ksara, Magdouché, Zahle and especially before Harissa, overlooking the city of Jounieh, and its towering image of Our Lady who offers her maternal protection from on high. This venerated image is a symbol

of tenderness, a sign of hope for all those who are under daily, cruel, and savage attacks.

Events are taking place before the eyes of the whole world that call upon the responsibility of the entire international society. Lebanon is being destroyed and we are facing, in fact, a threat that affects the entire order of international life. It is a threat of a moral nature, all the more painful because it is a weak state suffering from the violence or indifference of the strongest countries.

In international life, too, the principle applies that it is not permissible to harm the weakest, it is not permissible to kill the weak. Whoever does this is guilty before God, the Supreme Judge, and before the courts of human history. This moral guilt affects all those who do not defend the weak, and could or should have done so.

The beleaguered inhabitants of Beirut write to me: "from our subway shelters, under the whistling of rockets and the explosion of shells that are demolishing the buildings that are still standing, we cry out to you so that you may hear our *De profundis* . . ." I address myself in the name of God to the Syrian authorities to put an end to the bombardments that are destroying the capital of Lebanon and the whole country. I do so that they may not assume the attitude of Cain, who was guilty of the death of his brother.

Today is the feast of the Assumption: You, Mary, Mother of the Redeemer and Mother of Nations and Peoples, Mother of Lebanon, on this day we repeat the 'De Profundis' of our brothers and sisters of Beirut. On this day we repeat the 'De Profundis' of our brothers and sisters of Beirut, to you, Our Lady of Harissa, we turn weeping and praying for the salvation of Lebanon!

On more than one occasion I have wished to go to Lebanon. And every day in my prayer, I go there as a pilgrim. I have been advised to postpone for the time being my physical presence in the region to exercise my pastoral ministry among the brethren, because of the existing situation, which in these days has worsened even more. And that makes me feel in my soul even more strongly the inner imperative to go to Lebanon. I pray that all the difficulties that prevent me from carrying out my pastoral ministry may be overcome."

In the Press Room, the journalists were listening to these words on the radio with great attention. When he was about to finish, Sepe called me from the Secretariat of State: Dziwisz had just read the text, they were typing it up and would send it to me right away. Paradoxes of life: we are speaking to the world about an important subject and we only have a half-made structure.

Dziwisz calls me a moment later to see how everything went. I give him my impression and that of the journalists. But I tell him that next year, the *Sala Stampa* will send a fax to Castelgandolfo.

WYD in Santiago de Compostela: a Respite

August 22, 1989

We returned last night from a trip to Spain for World Youth Day—August 19–21—in Santiago de Compostela. This very morning I was notified to go to lunch at Castelgandolfo. The party was Sepe, Msgr. Tauran—under-secretary of the Council for Public Affairs of the Church—and Mario Agnes. The Pope is very happy. I point out to him that, according to what I was told, there had been a good preparation and a great catechesis of the confession. Like other trips, it seems that this one has had an impact on everyone, including the bishops, who have been able to physically see the great work ahead of them; and the fruit of that work are the thousands of young people—more than 500,000, according to official data—who have participated.

The Pope speaks of Covadonga and of some words he improvised after the Mass: "I said it when I understood what Covadonga meant for the history of Spain and for the cultural formation of the Spanish soul."

He then passed the floor to Tauran to discuss Lebanon. The Pope lives this topic with special intensity. I notice that the Vatican and Lebanese flags are embroidered on the tablecloth. There is talk of the various options underway, the French initiative and the declarations to be made by the representatives of the European Community.

The Pope laments: "They do not want to go beyond the humanitarian" (as if to say that more decisive action is needed to stop the genocide being carried out against Christians). He speaks again of his meeting with French Minister Decaux and announces that next Thursday he will speak with the special envoy of the Soviet Ministry of Foreign Affairs. It is also mentioned that the Nuncio, Msgr. Angeloni, was with General Aoun, who has written a letter to the Pope. The Maronite Patriarch declared to *La Croix* that if the Pope were to visit Lebanon, it would be to see and be with everyone, and not only with Christians.

The Pope's thoughts return to what I consider the heart of the matter: the concerted action of Arab countries to annihilate Lebanese Christians. And he mentions the year 1683, when the Turks were stopped at the gates of Vienna.

He says that 80 percent of the people understand only the language of physical force, and that the West lacks the firmness to stop this massacre of Christians. He stresses how horrible the physical destruction of the Maronites is, but that their moral destruction is even worse. "And meanwhile, the Christian world sleeps!"

Naturally, the Pope is not suggesting a crusade: he is advocating a strong, decisive, convinced positioning to stop this carnage and to break the arrogance in the face of Western passivity. He remains determined to go to Lebanon, even if the problems are enormous. Tomorrow, diplomatic contacts will begin talking with Syria and—let me insist until I succeed—with Iran. We shall see.

Gorbachev's Response

August 25, 1989

Yesterday at Castelgandolfo, the Pope received Yuri Karlov, special envoy of the USSR Ministry of Foreign Affairs. In his meeting with journalists, he told them that "he discussed with the Pope issues of mutual interest such as religious freedom and peace in the world, with particular reference to the Middle East."

Karlov has brought a message from Gorbachev, in reply to the Pope's letter delivered to him by Casaroli in Moscow fourteen months ago. Gorbachev's letter, translated into Italian, is almost seven pages long. It is very cordial, open-minded, and shows great sympathy for the Pope. He speaks of the trip to Italy that he will make next fall. He shows himself to be an optimist. It is a good text.

The Soviet news agency *TASS* gave, just yesterday, a dispatch in which it says that Gorbachev "proposes and asks for collaboration to face the great problems of our time;" announces that he is ready to "develop contacts with the Vatican" and "analyze the concrete ways to promote a wide international cooperation to find solutions to these problems." Some of them, says *TASS*, are "drastic issues of the present time: elimination of nuclear war, consolidation of peace and justice on earth, and protection of basic values of civilization."

A Small Family

August 31, 1989

I'm going to see Cassidy about the convent in Auschwitz. They are studying a solution to the problem. Yesterday I get a phone call from Tullia Zevi, president of the Italian Jewish communities. I tell her that the best thing would be a moratorium of about four weeks without public comments. She tells me that this is not possible. They are determined to continue their public outcry.

Thu has had a car accident. That makes Dziwisz's job even harder. He goes to see him in the hospital in the evenings and then the nuns come: it's like a small family. The Pope has not been able to come yet.

"Nostra Aetate:" No Turning Backwards

September 11, 1989

Dinner at Castelgandolfo. There is again talk of World Youth Day in Santiago de Compostela. Perhaps the next meeting with young people could be held—I suggest—in the United States or in one of the Eastern countries, such as Lithuania.[4]

The Pope refers again to Lebanon, an issue that affects him deeply. He becomes tense.

Auschwitz. He commented that some are beginning to lose their cool for lack of an answer to the problem. The Pope adds that, in any case, "one cannot go backwards from *Nostra Aetate*." That is to say: one cannot ignore the teachings of that conciliar document and go back to the previous era, where there were serious misunderstandings towards the Jewish people. This helps me to understand the core of his thought and action in this and many other matters: fidelity to the teachings of Vatican II.

Balance

September 22, 1989

Lunch at Castelgandolfo. During my absence—I have been in Spain for a conference—the communiqué circulated on the solution for the Carmelite monastery.

It has been a hard summer for the Pope: lack of peace, Auschwitz, Lebanon. The days of July in Les Combes already seem terribly distant.

---

4. In fact, the next one was held in Czestochowa (Poland), from August 10 to 15, 1991, something that seemed unthinkable at the time [Author's Note].

12

SERVI INUTILES SUMUS "WE ARE SLAVES TOGETHER"

South Korea, Indonesia, East Timor, Mauritius, Sumatra, South Korea

OCTOBER 6–16, 1989

OCTOBER 6TH. We make a stopover in Venice to refuel. The trip will be a long one. During the first fifty minutes of the flight I have the opportunity to speak with the Pope, before his meeting with the journalists.

Following other previous conversations, he comments to me about *ostpolitik:*

—"The [specific people involved] are not the important thing. What is important is the history [of these peoples of Eastern Europe] and Providence. Besides, it is not known whether they were the ideas of Paul VI or of Casaroli. Paul VI once told me, when I was a cardinal: 'We try to reach an agreement, but they do not give an inch.' Certainly, Casaroli has been there, but I know better the situation of those peoples."

I ask him if, when he was in Krakow, they viewed the Vatican's *ostpolitik* with fear, or at least distrust.

—"Yes. Most of all, Wyszyński. Me, less so. Besides, we had already seen the bad result of some bishops appointed in Czechoslovakia during the 1960s, after the council. Although they said they had left *Pacem in Terris,* in reality they did not leave it.[1] Those were years of a very confident, arrogant

1. *Pacem in Terris* was a Czechoslovakian association of priests named after John XXIII's encyclical. It was created in 1971 with the objectives of seeking "peace in the world and friendship among nations." But, in reality, it was sponsored by the Communist regime and its real purpose was to control and spy on the clergy in order to influence the life of the Church. Archbishop František Tomášek of Prague forbade priests from joining it. In fact, it began to weaken in the 1980s and was dissolved in December 1989.

communism. Then the situation changed. Who would have said then, for example, that Tomášek, a humiliated and imprisoned bishop, would become what he is today?"

The meeting with journalists took place after the stopover in Venice.

The flight plan, from Rome to Seoul, prepared by *Alitalia,* initially took us over northern China. However, Beijing refused permission, and the flight had to fly over the Pole.

Naturally, one of the questions was along these lines: Holy Father, what would you say to the Chinese government, which has forbidden you to fly over Chinese territory?

It occurred to me at that moment to whisper to him discreetly: "Your Holiness, it is *Alitalia* that has been banned from flying over China, not you."

The Pope, with a wry smile, takes the microphone and responds: "I do not know well the state of *Alitalia*'s relations with the Chinese government. But I think those relations should improve." The reporters laughed at his answer. When the press conference is over and we return to our seats, the Pope thanks me for the suggestion that helped him *fly over* a thorny issue.

October 7–9. South Korea. The reason for this trip is the 44th International Eucharistic Congress. For this reason, he celebrates Mass in Latin, the universal language of the Church, and not in Korean. The Congress will close on October 8 at Youido Plaza in Seoul.

After the Angelus, he remembered the Chinese Catholics, who were living in such a difficult situation:

> In this filial conversation with Mary our Mother, I also mention our brothers and sisters in Christ who live in mainland China. Their geographical proximity, as well as the bonds of faith and culture, place them very close to many of those gathered here. In the depths of my heart there is always present an ardent desire to meet with these brothers and sisters, to express my cordial affection and solicitude for them, as well as to manifest to them the high esteem in which they are held in the other local Churches.
>
> I am deeply moved when I think of the heroic signs of fidelity to Christ and his Church by many of them in recent years. May Christ, through the intercession of Mary, Help of Christians, be their consolation in all their sufferings and in all the challenges of daily life.

The next day we left for Indonesia from the military airport in Seoul.

OCTOBER 9. ON THE PLANE. As we fly to Indonesia, I am told that the Pope is calling me. He is with Cassidy. He wants to talk about the most opportune gestures upon arrival in Dili, capital of East Timor, which is seeking to secede from Indonesia, the country with the largest number of Muslims in the world.[2] For my part, I suggest that if he decides to kiss the ground—as he usually does when he arrives in a country—it might be advisable to warn President Suharto beforehand, so that this gesture is not misinterpreted. Another option is for him to kiss the floor of the Dili Cathedral after the blessing. This second possibility seems better to him. Then it is decided that Bishop Belo, who will receive the Pope at the Dili airport, will carry a crucifix in his hands and he can kiss it.

The Pope gets off the plane a little tense as he greets the Minister of Defense, who is a Catholic: I then realize that at each stage of the trip there will be a Catholic minister, out of the five in the government.

OCTOBER 9. INDONESIA. The reception at the "Istana Negara," the presidential palace, is similar to that offered to any other head of state: the President would have received much criticism if he had treated the Pope differently. In any case, the protocol has been reduced to a minimum: there will be only three meetings, with a slightly longer duration. This means, however, a great tribute to the Pope.

We are accompanied by a minister as a government representative and co-organizer of the trip, something similar to what happened to us in Cameroon.

My impression is that the rulers have achieved a lot in this country, which has a huge and dispersed geography and a population of around 100 million. The archipelago was economically backward until a few years ago. Today, they are self-sufficient in various sectors, such as food, and even export rice. I see, among other negative aspects, forced internal emigration and anti-birth policies.

The Catholic Church is respected. A part of the clergy is still influenced by the atmosphere that was created after the Council, in questions such as the so-called "anti-Roman sentiment" or priestly celibacy. In this sense, the country is similar to Holland. There are many vocations and—something singular in an Islamic country—many adult conversions.

There seems to be no threat—although there was—of communism coming to power. A possible danger is Islamic fundamentalism. We are told that at

2. Dili was founded by the Portuguese in 1520. In 1769 it became the new capital of Portuguese Timor. During World War II it was occupied by the Japanese. On November 28, 1975 it made a unilateral declaration of independence from Portugal, but nine days later it was invaded by Indonesia. On May 20, 2002 it became the capital of the independent state of East Timor.

present there is no repression. Java dominates. One of their great achievements has been the introduction of a common language, which, of course, comes from Java.

The first event in Jakarta is the Mass in a stadium filled to overflowing: perhaps 120,000 people. A tremendous humid heat. In the evening, visit to the president at the palace: a complex and long ceremony which ends, after the speeches, with a beautiful show of typical dances and traditional music. But we are all exhausted and sleepy. Even so, the Pope then meets with young people, priests, religious, seminarians and representatives of the world of culture.

October 10. Mass at the sports field of the Military Academy. On one of the trips I talk to Casaroli about *ostpolitik* and I ask him to receive the *Time* magazine people, who want to talk to him.

October 11. Maumere. We take a jet to Maumere, on the coast. The Pope celebrates Mass at an unbelievable hour for the heat of the day: at 3:15 in the afternoon. Perhaps this is the only possible time for the attendees to have time to leave their homes in the morning and return in the evening. After Mass, we drive a few kilometers to the seminary where we will sleep. It is exciting: along the road, already dark, we see families waving from the doorways of their houses and huts, along with very simple holy images and small lighted lights. There is a great spirit of faith.

We arrived at the seminary and had dinner standing up. We then move to the other seminary for the meeting with the seminarians. The Pope is so tired from the hustle and bustle of the last few days that he almost falls asleep while being addressed. Dziwisz notices and puts the text of the speech in his hands. He perks up a bit when he stands up and answers some questions from the seminarians.

October 12. Dili. Bishop Belo, who was to receive him at the airport in Dili, was supposed to carry a crucifix in his hands and give it to the Pope to kiss. But when he got off the plane I saw that he was not carrying it, and we learned that the authorities had forbidden this gesture, because it had not been agreed upon. It was quickly decided that the Pope would kiss the crucifix before celebrating Mass, placing it on the floor before the altar.

When that moment arrives, the Pope also kisses the floor of the cathedral of Dili: it is almost a furtive kiss that few notice.

I notice a less pious atmosphere, perhaps as a result of the lack of catechesis and the hard circumstances these people have gone through, who have suffered so much during the last decades.

The Pope's homily is very measured: he says, on the one hand, that "a historical change does not mean a danger for the faith, since the Church is universal." And on the other hand, that "rights must be secured in order to lead a more humane life." It is a matter of peacefully resolving current difficulties and achieving social harmony in accordance with one's own traditions.

At the end of the Mass there is a small incident: about twenty young people walk towards the altar with banners that read: "FRETILIN salutes you." Our security stopped them and some chairs were knocked over. We hardly notice because we are leaving the place; and the journalists, who have returned before us, do not see anything. In the evening they call me at the hotel to ask me what happened. But at that moment I am having dinner with the Pope and I cannot attend to them.

I told journalists about it the day after, and some of them exaggerated in their reports. One newspaper headlined: "The guerrillas arrive at Wojtyla's altar." I have to deny it. The rest of them thank me, because their editorial offices have scolded them for not having given news of those "dramatic" altercations, which in reality—fortunately—were a minor and unimportant anecdote. Moreover, I explain to them that the Pope's kiss to the crucifix is a pastoral gesture without political significance.

It is paradoxical that this movement, which now greets the Pope with banners, in the past aimed at uprooting everything non-native: Western customs, religions from outside, etc. The FRETILIN—Revolutionary Front of Independent East Timor—was born as an independence movement that later became a guerrilla movement.

It seems to me illusory to think that the UN will ever solve the problem of Dili, capital of East Timor, where a climate of independence from Indonesia, to which it has belonged by force of arms since 1975, is in the air. The Indonesian government has appointed an Indonesian-Portuguese minister and has opened the country to tourism.

Although the Indonesian government is doing what has not been done in several hundred years, internal tensions are very high. For example, some priests do not want to inaugurate a church just because it has been built by the government and a large part of the clergy is leaning towards a federated independence with Portugal.

The bishop asked the Pope, in view of the situation, not to speak in Indonesian or Tetun.[3] He consecrated the cathedral in the presence of all the priests.

---

3. Tetun is currently, along with Portuguese, the official language of East Timor, which—as has been recalled—achieved independence in 2002. It is an Austronesian language, with many words of Portuguese and Malay origin.

When media professionals ask me about these questions, I explain to them that the Pope's mission is genuinely pastoral: he did not come to solve local political problems. The Pope decided to come to Dili from Indonesia because if he had come at the beginning or at the end of the trip, the Indonesian President would also have come to Dili to receive him or see him off, so the authority of Indonesia would have been further underlined.

The pastoral trip continues. We arrive late in Jakarta. I am in the shower in my room when the phone rings. "You must go immediately to the nunciature," the receptionist tells me. There is a car at the door of the hotel waiting for you." Did something happen? I hurriedly get dressed, pick up my briefcase with the speeches and leave quickly for the nunciature. When I arrive, I see that everything is normal. The Pope has started dinner: Dziwisz, the nuncio, Tucci, and I are with him. He only wants to hear our opinions and views on his stay in Dili.

On Friday the 13th, before leaving, he made a comment to the bishops who came to visit him in Jakarta, which highlights the historic moment that this part of the world is going through:

> "[The Church in Indonesia] is a growing Church, a visible Church, which is reaching its adult stage. In the past it was a Church of missionaries. Among us there are many missionary bishops, especially Dutch, who have brought Christianity to Indonesia. But now it is an Indonesian Church, and most of you bishops are Indonesians, who have taken upon your shoulders the responsibility to carry the Church forward into the future."

October 13, Sumatra. Sumatra Island, city of Medan. In a population of ten million, the archdiocese has 355,000 Catholics: 3.5 percent. Here the Muslim population is higher than the Indonesian average. Today is Friday, a holy day for them, and the streets are full of people eager to see the Pope pass by. It is swelteringly hot, after three days of torrential rains.

In the Mass, which is celebrated in an old racecourse surrounded by palm trees, there are about 100,000 people and a hundred TV monitors, very well distributed among the people. The choir is made up of 3,000 Catholic voices and 3,000 Protestant voices. Upon arrival, the archbishop, Alfred Datubara, a Capuchin, imposes a shawl on the Pope, following a local custom.

The governor of Medan, a Muslim, comes to Mass; he leaves in the middle to go to the mosque to pray; and then returns again.

I speak to the journalists, reticent about Indonesia's political regime. "There is one clear fact, I tell them: the Pope has made the trip the way he wanted to, without any limitation. And he has spoken with complete freedom in the largest Muslim country in the world."

At the end of the Mass, as there are many people in the streets who have come out of the mosques, the Pope decides not to make the return trip in the closed car. And since there was no *popemobile* because the authorities were afraid of a possible attack by some fundamentalist group, it was decided that he would go in a small bus, seated next to the driver: it is a solution that does not provide any security, but in this way people can see him.

October 14–16. Mauritius. Half of the population is Hindu, followed by Catholics and Muslims. Fairly democratic, with some problems that affect post-industrialized countries, such as drugs and family instability. The president has suffered two attacks, more for economic than political reasons. Its economic development model is similar to that of South Korea or Taiwan.

During his stay, the Pope evoked the figure of Father Jacques Laval, a Frenchman from Normandy, who, after obtaining his doctorate in medicine at the Sorbonne, was ordained a priest and came from France in 1841 as a missionary of the Heart of Mary. He worked on this island for more than twenty years, especially with the freed slaves. The Pope beatified him in April 1979.

Languages

October 18, 1989

Back in Rome, during the traditional working lunch that follows our trips, the Pope again made a positive comment about the change in the way the press conference is organized on the plane, which facilitates order. And he brought up an issue I had not expected: that of language. In Indonesia he delivered most of his speeches in English—with the occasional opening sentence in Indonesian—and the local bishop translated into Indonesian or the local dialect, such as Tetun, in Dili.

Although this was the most prudent thing to do on the trip, he does not like what he considers the excessive use of English. "In the audiences, when there are Scandinavian pilgrims, for example, I speak to them in English, and that cannot be. I sometimes use English with pain, because people who come to see me are forced to speak in a language that is not their own. Whenever I address a group of people in their own language, I praise their language and their cultural identity, because I, at least, am proud of mine."

He continues: "I really appreciated in Mauritius that even though the official language is English, the people have kept their French cultural identity.

That's why I think it's necessary to say a few phrases in the language of the people there. In Japan, they helped me to pronounce Japanese by phonetic signs, and I was able to address them in their language. That's why I will have to make, for history, a version in Indonesian of all the speeches I made in Indonesia."

With the German Bishops

November 13, 14 and 15, 1989

On the 13th and 14th a meeting with the German bishops was held at the Vatican. All the residential bishops—not the auxiliary bishops—came to speak about the problems of the Church in their country. Two full days in the *Sala Bologna* during which the Pope listened to all the bishops, one after the other: from nine in the morning until lunchtime, and from five in the afternoon until almost eight o'clock. It always ended late.

The agenda was very broad and, above all, open. Everyone, "without tactics or strategy," as the president of the bishops' conference, Lehman, would say at the end, spoke with enormous freedom on the most varied issues.

I have been in the classroom during all the sessions. On the 13th and 14th I briefed the journalists in two sessions. Perhaps a new praxis is being born: the summoning of an entire episcopate to listen to him, so that they can talk among themselves in the presence of the Pope. This formula helps them to see their problems in perspective, and many problems lose some of their edges. They find solutions and perhaps come away with new ideas.

When he sees me, before starting the sessions, he makes an amused gesture. I notice again that, no matter how intense his situation, he does not lose his good humor or his supernatural perspective. He does not lose his good humor, I conclude, because he is firmly grounded in that perspective.

Vision of the *Ostpolitik*

November 17, 1989

In addition to the two secretaries, another guest came to dinner today: an elderly Polish priest who had been Dziwisz's teacher. The Pope introduced him to me, telling me that he was "an extraordinary confessor." I have the impression that he is living in the Pontifical Apartment. I tell the Pope that it is a pity for me to come at this time of the afternoon when he must be very tired. He answers me that it is better this way, because the conversation stimulates him.

He raises three topics: the congress on AIDS, which ended yesterday at the Vatican; the meeting with the German bishops, and the forthcoming meeting with Gorbachev. I told him that the congress had gone very well, that we had a press conference, that the speakers had planned it in such a way that it did not turn into the umpteenth discussion on prophylactic means. I told him about Pellegrino's speech[4] on the four ethical problems that arose in dealing with these patients: whether one could endanger one's own life to care for AIDS patients; whether one had to care for them, even if they were terminally ill; the question of confidentiality and what to tell their families; whether one could use medicines for their relief or cure without sufficient prior clinical experimentation.

We are talking about the attitude of some Americans—and not only them—who consider this type of disease a scandal, since it restricts the sexual freedom for which they have fought so hard.

I also tell him how the press treated the meeting of the German bishops. He makes some comments on the meetings. I tell him that, in my opinion, the bishops have left the meeting comforted and have left Rome ten years younger.

I brought up the subject of Gorbachev's visit and *ostpolitik*. I was especially interested because I had written a note for the press, as background information in preparation for the visit. I transcribe it in its entirety with the observation that I added the first paragraph later, after a comment made to me by the Pope himself:

> An important precedent for the Holy See's *ostpolitik* was Paul VI's decision to participate in the Conference on European Security and Cooperation in Helsinki. That decision was much discussed and misunderstood: it was said that the Holy See's participation in that conference somehow endorsed and legalized the status quo that existed in Eastern Europe. Despite these criticisms, Paul VI decided to send a delegation from the Holy See to Helsinki and the result was very positive, because that presence was decisive in emphasizing the issue of human rights—including religious freedom—and this was reflected in the conclusions of the Conference.

What we now call *ostpolitik* underwent a decisive change on October 16, 1978 when Cardinal Wojtyla was elected Pope. The presence of the first Pope of Slavic origin in the Church caused an incredible historical acceleration of Vatican *ostpolitik*; and in fact the very concept of *ostpolitik* changed radically.

---

4. Edmund D. Pellegrino (United States, 1929–2013), physician, one of the first specialists in bioethics.

The situation of the peoples and cultures of the East suddenly acquired an unusual importance in the Church and in the world. In this regard, the role of John Paul II has been invaluable. A year after his election, he said in Krakow, on June 3rd, 1979, that he had gone to cry out "before Europe and the world, for the often forgotten nations and peoples of Eastern Europe." One had the impression that Europe's historical consciousness extended to the Urals and beyond. The Slavic peoples, with their historical and cultural richness, with their Christian roots, ceased to be in a certain gloom and entered fully into Western consciousness.

The dissatisfaction with an artificial division of Europe, as established at Yalta, could have been expressed in political terms. But John Paul II did not approach this question from a political perspective, but from a cultural, historical, and moral perspective. The Pope considers that confining peoples to certain systems of thought is not primarily a political question, but an ethical and therefore a human question.

He said during his first visit to Poland: "Christ cannot be kept out of the history of man anywhere in the world (because) . . . to exclude Christ from the history of man is an act against man (Warsaw, June 2nd 1979)."

This is the essential foundation of *ostpolitik,* which goes beyond strictly political categories. The Pope is against any ethical schizophrenia that dissociates politics from morality, both in the past and today.

Tactical opportunism is alien to the thinking of John Paul II: "I go to the roots of history and culture and from there, I look forward," he once said. Thus, *ostpolitik* was posed in terms of the personal identity of the peoples of the East, and not as a tactic to achieve a simple compromise. The goals were much more ambitious; and therefore, perhaps, more risky. However, this approach is proving to be more effective, and above all, more authentic.

This new approach to the problem explains the Pope's bold decisions. When he received the invitation from the Russian Orthodox Church for the Holy See to participate in the Millennium celebrations (June 1988), the Pope decided to send a delegation at the highest level, with the Secretary of State, instead of sending only Willebrands as an expert on ecumenism.

The second act of courage was to send a personal letter to President Gorbachev. There was no guarantee—when we left Rome—that the letter could be hand-delivered. These were two personal decisions of the Pope, which opened up developments to which we are witnesses.

Undoubtedly, one element that has helped a lot in these years is the obvious fact that the Pope's respect for Russia is honest, sincere, and culturally based. Its Slavic cultural heritage is vast, especially in terms of history, literature, poetry, and language. When the Pope speaks of the "two lungs of the Church"—the Latin and Eastern traditions—one has the impression that one is listening to a biographical reflection. No Pope so far has known so well the reality of these Eastern peoples.

The Pope attaches (in *ostpolitik*) extraordinary importance to two factors without which the development of these years would be unthinkable: the very history of the peoples of Europe, without which one cannot understand the reality of today, and the personalities who have maintained in these peoples their cultural and religious identity. I am speaking of personalities of the stature of Cardinal Tomášek in Czechoslovakia or Cardinal Wyszyński in Poland. There is a third factor, which is the first, in fact: the action of Providence.

Gorbachev calls for the moral contribution of Christians, including Catholics, to bring about these cultural and social changes in the Soviet Union. Prior to this, the Pope had said that "membership in the Catholic Church should not be considered incompatible with the pursuit of the good of one's own homeland." In other words, the Pope teaches that being a good Christian and being a good citizen are not different or dialectically opposed realities. It is only fair to recall that there has been no violence in Ukraine or in Lithuania, where the presence of Catholics is more numerous, because Catholic ethics rejects violence as a means to change society. From this point of view, the case of Poland is very eloquent."

The Pope reads it and the only thing he says to me is that my statement at the beginning—to say that everything began with his election—is insufficient. He points out to me that Paul VI made a very courageous decision in allowing the Holy See to participate in the 1975 Helsinki Conference. It was a debatable and disputed decision, because it seemed that the Holy See supported the position of the Soviet Union during those years and, indirectly, the Yalta resolutions. Then it became clear that it paid off to have been there because the question of human rights was immediately raised. I added that first paragraph and the text remained as I have transcribed it. That was the background note that was distributed to journalists.

When we talk to him about his influence on what is currently happening in the countries of the East, the Pope says: "*Servi inutiles sumus*. I have said it several times, and these days I say it to myself more often."[5] What he never adds—as several commentators have observed—is the second part of that Gospel quotation: "We did only what we ought to do."

---

5. Lk 17:10. "Sic et vos cum feceritis omnia quae praecepta sunt vobis dicite servi inutiles sumus quod debuimus facere fecimus." "So you also, when you have done all that you have been commanded to do, say, 'We are useless servants; for we did only what we ought to have done.'"

13

Gorbachev at the Vatican

Preparations

November 21, 1989

Meeting at 12:30 in the library of the Pope's Apartment with Casaroli, Sodano,[1] Tauran, Sepe, and Msgr. Franco. Topic: the imminent meeting with Gorbachev. The Pope comes smiling, as always, and speaking in Portuguese: he has just finished an audience with Portuguese people and takes only a couple of minutes of pause between one thing and another. We sit around the table and the Pope summarizes the data we have so far.

He begins by saying that they have written to each other—he and Gorbachev—in "generic and specific" terms. In August, Minister Yuri Karlov brought him a letter from Gorbachev. "It was a very comprehensive letter," he says, "which did not go into specific problems, but in which he set out the various issues he wished to discuss during his visit." He gives the floor to Casaroli, to explain the conversation he had with Gorbachev in June last year in Moscow.

Casaroli: "Gorbachev did not go into specific issues. He spoke, above all, of the Soviet Union's attitude toward religion. 'We are applying *perestroika* to the political field, to the social field, and also to the religious field. Naturally, this will take time.' He mentioned two issues: territorial boundaries and the diplomatic delegation of Lithuania accredited to the Holy See, which are the two issues traditionally brought up by the USSR against the Holy See. He then spoke of the new relations with the states in terms of collaboration. He was not very specific about the problems. He said he would read the Pope's letter and reflect carefully on its contents."

The Pope gave the floor to Sodano, who on October 20 had been in Moscow to bring a new letter to Gorbachev, this time on the question of Lebanon. It was the third letter he had sent to Gorbachev and the second specifically on Lebanon.

1. Angelo Sodano (Italy, 1927–2022) was at that time Secretary for Relations with States. In 1991 he succeeded Casaroli as Secretary of State, a post he held until 2006. He was appointed cardinal in 1991.

He met with Gorbachev on the same day, the 20th. The question was whether the Soviet Union could convince Syria on this issue. He seemed very interested in the Lebanese problem and appreciated the Pope's concern: "We have a common understanding of the problem," he said.

"I will show the letter to Assad," Gorbachev remarked, "and you have to put pressure on Israel afterwards." Sodano asked him about his trip to Italy and the possibility of visiting the Pope. His answer was immediate: "Of course. What is more, I don't know why they put this visit after the one to Italy."

They then discussed relations with the Holy See. In his letter to the Pope—Sodano told him—he already indicated that possibility. "What do you think?" asked Gorbachev. Sodano spoke to him of three possible solutions: a personal envoy, a permanent delegation or an ambassador. "What exactly does the personal envoy consist of?" He asked. "It is an interesting formula, but there are others. I will talk to the Pope."

"We have too many problems," Gorbachev added. And he referred to the need to "energize the dialogue with the Russian Orthodox Church." "It makes me happy to see a delegation from the Holy See here." Then there was talk of the possibility of the Pope being able to appoint bishops in Russia, a question Sodano discussed with Foreign Minister Shevardnaze. He also met with the Minister of the Cult Kristoranov, who seemed to him to be more closed and less flexible.

The Pope then asked that the letter written to him by Gorbachev, dated August 6, 1989, be read. Sepe read it. It spoke of "contacts and reflections," that "we have already had several relations with you and with the Holy See. This is the hour of the new configuration of the world. This leads us to a new vision of religion: and we have changed our way of seeing things with regard to the Vatican."

I add other ideas in a telegraphic way: "His [the Pope's] activity has influenced us. I have read his speeches. The Vatican contributes to peace. In the field of the formation of conscience: this too is part of politics. Interconnectedness of the world. You may say that this truth is not new (. . .) I agree, but truths become new when they are put into practice. The center of our foreign policy is the interest of the community. And in domestic policy, the interest of the individual. This is our creed, our faith: the reason and morality of man. We are learning to live together: atheists, Buddhists, believers, Muslims. And also the possibility of reaching a new level in relations between the USSR and the Holy See. Sending personal representatives and exchanges of written messages, useful for Europe and for the whole world."

The Pope gives the floor to others. Specifically, he asks me how the meeting should be reported. I would try to arouse interest before the audience, offering background information, and complete this information with a communiqué after the audience.

It is lunchtime. Sitting at the table, we continue to talk. The Pope asks that a memorandum be prepared for him on the subject of the borders within the Soviet Union, in order to be well informed. I do not sense any uncertainty. The whole conversation has been conducted in a relaxed tone. "I think we are now ready for the interview," says the Pope, in conclusion.

Safety Issues

November 23, 1989

Second meeting at the Prefecture of the Pontifical Household with Monduzzi, on the one hand, and the chief of Soviet protocol and the chief of security, on the other. One of the things the chief of the Soviet protocol says is that, at the beginning of the colloquy, the Pope and Gorbachev should be completely alone; then they will call translators. Some security details are determined: for example, three of Gorbachev's security will be in three places inside the Vatican that morning; there will always be one of his security where there are journalists; Gorbachev will be accompanied by two of his personal security, who in the protocol will function as personal assistants. The official entourage is not yet clear. We clarify that inside the Vatican the agents cannot enter with weapons: they enter.

With the Russian Information Service

November 24, 1989

Vadim Perfiliev, Gerasimov's deputy in the Information Service of the Soviet Foreign Ministry, is coming to my office. He is accompanied by the head of Soviet television. We talked about several things: Perfiliey wants to interview Casaroli. No problem on our part. I ask him what time Gorbachev's press conference will take place in Milan on the same day of the interview with the Pope. The TV director, who knew nothing, says to Perfiliev: "I have to come to the Vatican to find out that there is a Gorbachev press conference . . ." I find this funny.

Perfiliev wants to know about my briefing. He suggests that Gerasimov also participate in a joint briefing. I refuse. I tell him that I will speak informatively about the situation of Catholics in the Soviet Union. He does not like it: he says there are many other topics.

Tauran sent me the documentation prepared by the Second Section of the Secretariat of State: for the informative use that I want to make of it, it seems meager, among other things because it does not make any reference to Catholics in the Baltic Republics. I ask him to complete it.

Eastern Rite Catholics

November 27, 1989

As I enter the Papal apartment, while waiting in the lounge, I see on a table two gifts for the Pope: a Chinese language course on cassette (*Linguaphon*), and a small and modest metal altarpiece of a nativity scene; next to it there is a small inscription on parchment-like paper, written in Spanish: it is from the Carmelites of Avila, who ask the Pope for the Constitutions of St. Teresa.

Dinner with the Pope and Sodano. I tell him that, as far as public opinion is concerned, perhaps it is Gorbachev who will gain the most from the audience, because I still do not know in what terms it will be discussed. What worries the Pope, above all, is the information—or the impression—that will reach the Lithuanians and Ukrainians. He asks me if I already know the speech he has prepared, and asks Sodano to pass it on to me. I inform him that I will have a press conference the following day. He points out that, having seen the mood of the press, we can judge again if it is convenient to add something to his speech.

He refers to his interview, that same morning, with Metropolitan Juvenaly. He expressed to the Pope his wish that a message of pacification be sent to the Eastern Rite Catholics before Gorbachev's visit, because he says that there is still a ruckus in Lviv, and he fears that it will increase with the audience. The Pope told him, "But if we don't know where they are; if there are no contacts with them . . ." Casaroli and Sodano also spoke with Juvenaly and asked him why they had delayed the meeting with the Holy See delegation during the last trip to Moscow. "Because there was a fire in Lviv," Juvenaly replied. "Well, if there is a fire, the more firefighters available, the better," they replied.

With Minister Karlov

November 28–29, 1989

I am meeting with journalists to give them information prior to Gorbachev's visit. I announced it only yesterday because I feared an excessive presence in our conference room. I tell them about the various events, the members of the entourage and the reality of the Catholic Church in the Soviet Union. "What is expected?" they ask me. "An improvement of relations between the Soviet State and the faithful, and a possible establishment of permanent contacts," I answer them.

I speak of the positive steps that have been taken in *ostpolitik* during this pontificate, along the lines of my promemoria.[2] Federico Mandillo, from *ANSA*, asks me if I am trying to detract from Casaroli's merits. Mandillo—who is an exceptional connoisseur of Rome's cultural and artistic heritage—is prone to judge world events from an "Italian" perspective. I answer no, but I also remind him that we must not forget the work that has been carried out, along with the Cardinal, by so many other people from different countries, not to mention the impetus being given by this Polish pope.

Minister Karlov came to see me to discuss the audience with Gorbachev. After the conversation I wrote this note which I am sending to the Pope and copying to Sodano:

> "Mr. Yuri Karlov came to see me this morning, in the *Sala Stampa*, at his request. He is the same person who, last August, delivered Mr. Gorbachev's letter to the Pope at Castelgandolfo. He was accompanied only by Mr. Korotkov, First Secretary of the Soviet Embassy in Rome.
>
> *Purpose of the visit*: to make contact—apparently very sincere—to discuss some specific aspects of Friday's hearing. Minister Karlov is a cordial man, very close to President Gorbachev, in tune with the new climate in the USSR.
>
> *On the visit itself:* He has said that Gorbachev is personally taking care of all questions related to the visit to the Pope. "The president himself is preparing the issues he wishes to discuss with the Pope as well as his own speech. I can tell you, confidentially, that what interests Mr. Gorbachev most during his stay in Italy is this visit to the Pope. He has delegated to his collaborators, and to myself, the preparation of political and commercial contacts with Italy. Everything that concerns the visit with the Pope, he is working on personally. He has a deep admiration for the Holy Father."
>
> *On Gorbachev' speech*: "I apologize," he tells me, "but I do not really know when I will be able to give you Mr. Gorbachev's text for the *Sala Stampa*. He has not written it yet, and I am afraid that, as he is preparing it personally, we will only be able to have it when he has delivered it before the Pope." I asked him to remind President[3] Gorbachev that the television broadcast was

2. A formal written note of a diplomatic nature.

3. Gorbachev had been elected chairman of the Supreme Soviet of the Soviet Union on May 25, 1989.

going to be live and it would be convenient for the editors to have an embargoed text beforehand in order to be able to prepare the broadcast.

He was interested in the length of the text. I only replied that in this type of visit—Bush's, for example—the Pope prepares a speech that can be up to four pages long.

As for the language, he told me that Gorbachev could read in Russian, while his translator would translate into Italian. He asked me what the Pope intended to do. I told him that, although the Pope has not yet decided, he could read a few paragraphs at the beginning and at the end in Russian, and the main text in Italian. He told me that this formula would allow Gorbachev's translator to make a simultaneous translation from Italian into Russian.

As for the persons who will make up the entourage, he reports that Gorbachev has not yet decided whether or not to include Metropolitan Juvenaly as a member of the official entourage (Note: today, Nov. 29, the official list of the entourage, which has been expanded to twenty-four persons, and does not include Metropolitan Juvenaly, has arrived at the Press Room).

On the topics to be discussed during the meeting: "Of course, the Holy See has some questions to raise with us. We also have some; for example, that of borders." But I think Mr. Gorbachev will talk to the Pope about the coincidence of Christian values with our *perestroika*. Now we are talking about a democratic socialism in which the fundamental interest is man, something that is also found in the Pope's documents."

On this point, he told me clearly that Gorbachev expects "help from the Holy See for this broader vision of human values; help that is not economic, naturally, but moral."

He also referred to the "moral support" that Gorbachev expects from Christians in the building of Soviet society. He discussed this with Patriarch Pimen.

On the problem of Eastern Rite Catholics, he says that it must be kept in mind that it is a problem to be dealt with primarily in the Orthodox Church. "You know that the civil authorities did not intervene in Lviv during the occupation of the Church." I have commented to him that the state will also have some role in resolving this issue. He insists: "It will be the new law on freedom of conscience, which will be discussed next March, that will solve the legal part of the problem. But our fear is that, after the Pope's visit next March, some impatient Ukrainian will complicate things by mixing them with nationalist issues." I have made him see that the problem of the Eastern Rite Catholic Church should not be assimilated to a Ukrainian nationalist issue. He said that this is a very interesting idea.

About the information: I have told him that we have had a press conference today and that after the Pope's meeting with Gorbachev we will give, following our custom, a communiqué without a press conference afterwards. Since Gorbachev will hold a press conference in Milan together with Andreotti that same day, I will fax him the text of our communiqué—which will be brief—so that Gorbachev will know it before meeting with the press. He has been very grateful for this offer.

The Pope with Gorbachev

December 1 to 4, 1989

December 1. The atmosphere of the hearing was cordial and open. They seemed happy and relaxed, especially after their private interview. Gorbachev was conspicuously expansive, especially when he was with Raisa his wife and the Pope, or introducing the many members of his entourage. The Pope's gift was a mosaic reproducing the image under the high altar of St. Peter's Basilica. The image of Christ carries in his left hand an inscription in Latin: *Ego sum via, veritas et vita. Qui credit in me vivet.*

Gorbachev read his speech in Russian. At the end, improvising, he said that he was leaving with the conviction that he had been heard; he spoke of a possible visit of the Pope to the Soviet Union, and gave thanks for the exchange of ideas during the meeting.

In the evening, the Pope invites us to dinner and gives us his impressions. Mario Agnes is also present. His translator was Father Dziwisz Szlowieniec, S.J., who traveled with us to Moscow during the Millennium celebrations.

"Gorbachev considers and declares that religion is positive for human life and for the life of society," says the Pope. He accepts that they have been wrong. He is a humanist (in the sense that his concern is centered on man)."

Have you had the impression that you were talking to a man with Marxist mental schemes? "It is difficult to identify Marxist elements in his personality. He is a man of principle. He is not a theoretician, but a man who believes in principles to which he must be faithful. He knows how to identify the principles and grasp the essentials. Then, the rest will be a consequence that he accepts."

"He is a statesman, not a pragmatic opportunist. I am convinced that you can't fake what he says. It's difficult to imagine how a man who has grown up in Marxism has become such a person. He told me: we are two Slavs; and we Slavs have been despised for the fact that we are Slavs; but I think that we Slavs are also capable of doing great things."

"I repeated to him what I have been saying for years: 'the Church has two lungs, the Eastern tradition and the Latin tradition. And it needs to breathe with both. 'Very good,' he said. And then I jokingly remarked to him: 'You have given a lot of publicity to the Pope on TV.' And he answered me: 'I also see him often on Soviet TV.'

I ask him if they talked about the Russian Orthodox Church: "We have not talked much about the Orthodox. For the Eastern Rite Catholics, he foresees a peaceful solution, thanks to the law that will be discussed in the Supreme Soviet, which will be based on freedom of conscience."

"All this does not follow from any ideological principle. I think we are facing a kind of conversion. Humanly speaking, one does not understand how his thinking could have reached the present point. Our Lady spoke at Fatima of the conversion of Russia. I prayed a lot for this meeting and I told him so."

"Is it easy to live history in the first person," I ask? "When God wants it, it's easy. It makes life easier for me. When you know God wants it. Sometimes things are easier, sometimes more difficult. He arranges everything."

He speaks in a relaxed manner about his conversation with Gorbachev. I find him happy and at ease. I asked him if he had seen anything on TV. He said no, and I gave him a video that *RAI* had sent me with the whole special program they had made.

DECEMBER 4. Three days later, on Monday, I spoke to Dziwisz and it occurred to me to ask him if the Pope had already seen the video. He replied that he had not. I thought perhaps he had mortified his natural curiosity because of his many activities. These days he is receiving the bishops of Colombia in the mornings, who are on an *ad limina* visit; he has even met with some of them in the afternoons.

An Interview Next to the Nativity Scene

DECEMBER 23–24, 1989

On the 20th, Dziwisz called me to have dinner with the Pope. I had told him a few days earlier about the director of *Il Messaggero*—Mario Pendinelli[4]—who is doing a good job of reporting; I also told him about the possibility of the Pope recording something for TV around Christmas.

4. Mario Pendinelli was director of *Il Messaggero* from 1987 to 1993.

Mario was in a private audience with the Pope, accompanied by his wife, Piera, and his son. He called me that same evening to tell me that he had prepared for this meeting and that he was deeply impressed.

When I arrive at the Pontifical Apartment, the Pope continues to work, this time with Sodano. "So much has happened this year!" he remarks as we walk down the hallway toward the dining room.

During dinner, he asked about the current situation of *Il Sabato* and *30 Giorni*, two publications inspired by Communion and Liberation. A few moments later, we talk about the general climate among the bishops. I tell him that, from what some of them have told me, I see them as more self-confident. "And that is necessary for their mission," the Pope adds. I also comment on what some have told me: that a few years ago, there seemed to be a "principle of uncertainty" by which everything could change; for example, when a seminarian entered the seminary, he was not sure that the norm of celibacy would still be in force when he finished his studies. . . .

Dziwisz suggested the idea of recording a Christmas video for TV, which would be a brief interview on TG1, the first *RAI* news program. I tell the Pope that at first I was not very convinced, but then I thought it would be very positive for people to see the Pope at Christmas, in his own home, next to his Christmas crib. We see him in public ceremonies, during his travels, but never in a private dimension, in his living room.

"I know the Pope doesn't like to talk about himself," I add. Jokingly, he replies: "It's true." But he agrees to do this little interview. As always, he does not ask about the details (how and where to do it, etc.): he leaves it in our hands.

Dziwisz wanted it take place in the *Sala dei Foconi*, but since there was no way to set up a nativity scene there, to give a Christmas atmosphere, we went back to the original idea of shooting in the Papal Apartments: it seems better to me, because it reflects the homey atmosphere we want to show. Frajese had passed on to me in advance the questions he wanted to ask.[5]

The Pope was working in his room. He came out just as we had finished setting up lights, cameras, and the microphone. Despite his long experience, Frajese was very excited: I have to give him a glass of water, because his mouth is dry. The interview goes well, and we stay a little while collecting the material; as we leave, I see that the Pope is already in his chapel, on his knees, praying. Shortly afterwards—around 11:30 AM—he would begin his day of audiences.

---

5. Paolo Frajese (Italy, 1939–2000) was a well-known *RAI* journalist, news anchor, and foreign correspondent.

14

"What Can We Offer the Pope?"

The Noriega Affair

From December 25, 1989 to January 4, 1990

Yesterday, Christmas Eve, I received a late phone call from *CNN* asking me what the Holy See thought about General Noriega,[1] who had taken refuge in the nunciature in Panama. All I knew was that the Americans had invaded Panama and that they were looking for Noriega; little else? I tell them that tonight is Christmas Eve and that tomorrow we will talk.

I go to the office despite the day it is, and find out what has happened, after making numerous phone calls, since no one is in place (it's Christmas!). In the end, I manage to get through to Sodano. He tells me that they have prepared a brief communiqué and faxes it to me. I get some complementary information—not much, because I don't know how things happened, how many people are inside the nunciature, etc.—and I have a face-to-face with the journalists. I do what I can. I am annoyed by the impossibility of doing my job at the appropriate level. Also, there is no one in the office, apart from Sister Giovanna, to translate the communiqué into English.

December 26th. I start the day a bit worried. I call Dziwisz and explain to him that the case is serious, that the Pope is going to be involved in it sooner or later. Half an hour later Sodano calls me and gives me the information I need: the attitude of the United States, who made the decision to let Noriega into the nunciature, and other information. He tells me to go to lunch with the Pope at 1:30 PM to discuss the matter further.

1. Manuel Antonio Noriega (Panama, 1934–2017) led a military dictatorship in Panama (1983–1989) until he was overthrown by the US invasion. He had previously collaborated with the US Central Intelligence Agency. Drug trafficking was among the charges for which he was convicted.

At twelve o'clock I have a briefing with the press and television, and I answer their questions with more knowledge than yesterday. I end up exhausted, but happy. I run to arrive punctually for lunch with the Pope, whom I find serene, smiling . . . and also tired by the activity of this year, and of these days in particular. He plans to stay at Castel Gandolfo from Wednesday afternoon to Saturday.

He starts talking about Romania, about the horror of the events of these days—Ceaucescu was executed yesterday.[2] Other topics come up. I tell him about the interview we did with him for *RAI* and he seems to have liked the way it turned out.

He says that a professor friend of his, who wished him a happy Christmas yesterday, asked him if he was worried about the Noriega affair, and he answered that he was not. At lunch we told him some particulars that he did not know. The position that crystallizes is that we agree to grant him asylum in the nunciature.

I approach the problem from the point of view of American public opinion, which is particularly sensitive to the drug issue, and of the situation of the hierarchy, which can be questioned. The Pope indicates that a note should be prepared to explain to the American bishops the reasons for this asylum. But he does not accept the passive surrender of this person to the United States.

In the evening, the three *RAI* news programs extensively cover this morning's press conference. The images of the *Sala Stampa* are followed by those of President Bush. I try to make it clear that there is no pressure or bad manners on the part of the United States, and that the issue is more complex than the super-simplification to which the American public opinion is victim: if we are the good guys—they think—and they (Noriega and his friends) are the bad guys; how is it possible that the Vatican protects the bad guys?

DECEMBER 28TH. As I have not given any more information, because I do not have it, journalists are buzzing: calls from half the world, especially from that half of the world in which the United States reigns supreme.

In the morning Casaroli calls me. Calm down, don't exaggerate. I take it to mean that there is no need to talk any more. But my impression is that the matter will get bigger and bigger, because there is no easy or quick way out.

---

2. Nicolae Ceaușescu (Romania, 1918–1989) was general secretary of the Romanian Communist Party (1965–1989), president of Romania (1967–1989). His dictatorship, which began with signs of openness, was characterized by progressive repression. He was shot along with his wife, Elena, after a trial broadcast on TV. Romania was the only Soviet bloc country to violently overthrow the Communist regime.

A while later Ken Doyle, spokesman for the US bishops, calls me. He appreciates what we said yesterday, making known the reasons for Noriega's "asylum," and asks me to continue in this line. I see that he is aware of what is coming their way. I summarize in a brief report what Ken has told me and send it to Sodano, with a copy to the Pope's apartment.

Sodano calls me at the end of the morning: he is happy with the outcome of yesterday's press conference. He tells me that O'Connor from New York has called him to document himself on this matter, and that he will send me a copy of the letter he has received from Marcos G. McGrath, Archbishop of Panama City. I am considering releasing it to the press tomorrow.

December 29. I received a copy of the report on the Noriega affair that Sodano sent to O'Connor. It is good. I organize a new briefing and the journalists are happy because they now have something to write about. And, above all, they have the opportunity to talk about the "clash" between the Holy See and the United States. Many of them think that the only thing that counts is to return Noriega. We see more elements, such as diplomatic praxis and asylum rights. The Americans have put loudspeakers blaring rock music next to the nunciature. There are different interpretations: some say it is to distract their guys—and nobody believes that—; others say it is to intercept communications. My impression is that it must be the result of some psychological consultant's advice to break the nerves of those inside the nunciature.

The truth is that in the press conference with the journalists I am a bit aggressive, mentioning the international conventions on the security and independence of diplomatic headquarters. I add that Nuncio Laboa[3] is trying to convince Noriega to surrender. I insist that the resolution may be a matter of days—although I have no evidence that this will be the case. Coincidence or not, the fact is that the tone of the American government is softening.

The next day the press highlighted the "Vatican-USA clash" in the headlines. They take many quotes from the press conference. Casaroli is worried. He had already called me the day before, half an hour after my press conference, because he had seen in TG2 a reference to the efforts of the nunciature to convince Noriega to surrender. As a diplomat, he is horrified by the image

3. José Sebastián Laboa (Spain, 1923–2002) was papal nuncio to Panama, Paraguay, Malta, and Libya. His mediation and conciliation work during the military dictatorship in Panama has been highlighted.

of a "clash" of the Holy See with anyone, let alone the United States. The idea of clear opposition, of contrast, of lively discussion does not suit his character. Discreet negotiation is his thing.

In the middle of the morning, I receive a paper with a few lines written on it, this time from the Secretariat of State, in which some things already mentioned before by *Sala Stampa* are said, with the intention of ending the stalemate. I give it in the daily bulletin of the office and wait to see what happens.

December 30. I spoke to Sodano to tell him that the first phase had gone well, but that it could be dangerous to begin a second phase without information. He confirms that Cardinal Casaroli had asked him to keep silent.

What I think about the situation is this: there is no way to move this and other issues forward without adequate and continuous information. On the one hand, there is the policy and decision line; on the other, the information line. And these two lines are not connected.

Two more days pass with no information. I stall by confirming Msgr. Barlocco's trip to Panama. This makes some Italian journalists happy, because they say that this nuncio is a kind of right arm of Casaroli, and he is going to solve the case. On Wednesday I spoke with Tauran. He tells me that Berloco is very animated, and that he thinks that this could end immediately, although he does not see it that way personally. As there is not much else to do, I decide to go to the mountains for a couple of days.

End of the crisis

January 4, 1990

The little village of San Felice d'Ocre is magnificently silent. The dogs have finished eating. I have my hiking boots on to go out, when I get the message: Sodano has called me. I try three times to connect with him, to no avail. He is with Casaroli. I call Tauran. "Ah, but you don't know anything?" All right, I say to myself, they have released Noriega. That's right.

I call the office: a press conference has to be called at 1:30. I take the car and arrive in Rome at 12:45. At 1:10 I'm in the office. I read the agency dispatches: they don't even agree on how Noriega was dressed. From the Secretariat of State, they pass me the communiqué from the Nuncio and fifteen lines of information for me. I expand with other data and off I go!

The press room is full, with many more cameras than usual. I try, above all, to be confident and affirm what I know with conviction. I leave aside the actions of the nuncio in Panama, I underline the primacy of law. Statements in English, Italian, French, and Spanish. In the end, I am even able to sit down for lunch at a reasonable hour: 3:10.

Dan Rather, from the USA, asks me for an interview for the American *CBS*. May it be God's will. I read the US press: for them, the Nuncio has ceased to be a villain and has become a hero. *Sic transit gloria mundi* . . .

Letters to *Sala Stampa*

JANUARY 10, 1990

A voluminous book could be written with the letters I receive in the *Sala Stampa*. They reflect the psychology of the various peoples who send them. They come especially from Italy, the United States, Latin America, and Spain. I notice some general characteristics—which are not always true, of course—depending on the geographical origin: many of those from the United States are related to issues that public opinion has brought to the forefront. I find that North Americans have an easy pen for writing, giving their opinion on a given issue: they believe in democracy.

From Spain, I receive letters from people who have read my name somewhere and ask me about a personal problem, often a dramatic one: the situation of a prisoner, of an unemployed person, etc. And some Italians—not all, of course—write to ask me for . . . a recommendation!

Influenza

JANUARY 15, 1990

Leaving aside the days of the attack and its aftermath, today is the first time in the eleven years of his pontificate that the Pope has suspended his audiences due to illness.

It is only a flu, but it is strong and with fever. Last Sunday he already had a fever, but he did not want to cancel his visit to a Roman parish. He told them that he did not kiss the children, because he did not want to subject them to his influenza. On Monday he suspended the scheduled audience, but on Wednesday he held the general audience, which is attended by people from all over the world. Although he was still ill, he did not want to disappoint them.

Back in Africa

January 25 to February 2, 1990

We left this morning for Africa. Five countries this time: Cape Verde, Guinea Bissau, Burkina Faso, Mali, and Chad. It's a trip to the Sahel; to the heart of African poverty.

Shortly after taking off from Rome—we flew in an Airbus—I approached him to greet him and to advise him where to direct the journalists' questions. I tell him that the subject of the Eastern countries is still making the headlines and that a Soviet journalist, Pavel Negoitsa, is coming with us for the first time. And that nationalism in the Soviet Union might come to the fore. Listening to me, he makes a distinction: "Nationalism is one thing and patriotism is another." And he explains how in patriotism, elements of one's own cultural and historical identity are safeguarded. "Gorbachev is encountering problems and realities that are the fruit of Russian expansionism of the past."

Cape Verde: an archipelago with several islands and some small islets. Here everything is on a small scale, except for the immense affection the Pope receives from the people.

Guinea Bissau. In the stadium where the Pope celebrates Mass, there is not room for a single soul. It is overflowing, and I am surprised, because the proportion of Catholics in the diocese of Bissau is 6.9 percent. That means that many animists and Muslims have come. Why do they come? I think this may be one reason: in addition to speaking to them about God, the Pope speaks to them about justice and human dignity in a place where poverty, misery, and disease are very present, more perhaps than in any of the Pope's five previous trips to this continent.

We slept in the minor seminary in Bissau. My room is next to the Pope's, with only one room in between. Before he arrives, I take a look from the corridor: his bed is just like mine, very narrow, short, with boards instead of a bed base. They have put an air conditioner in it and it has a tiny bathroom.

At night it is not easy for us to sleep, because next to the seminary there is a hotel, where there is a barbecue with loud music.

The next day, the Pope visits a leprosarium. He touched and greeted each of the sick. On the way back to Bissau, he asks the car to stop and gets out to greet some people who live on the side of the road. They invite him into their huts and the Pope enters for a few moments.

When I see this reality, it comes to my mind that—just like in the countries of Eastern Europe—freedom is in danger here as well. I think this might be a good idea to discuss with journalists, and I tell the Pope about it during the flight. He tells me he agrees. And he adds that when he was in the United States for the first time, he saw that people were not really free there either. He is referring, of course, to a deeper freedom, not determined by economic circumstances or political regimes.

BURKINA FASO. We go from Ouagadougou to Bobo Dioulaso, where the Pope celebrates Mass under a blazing sun, amidst waves of dust.

When he finishes, he boards the plane, a small *Fokker*, where he is given a tiny paper napkin to dry his hands. Then he is offered some candy. He eats one, because he knows that glucose gives him strength, and immediately picks up a book and starts reading.

Last night, when he was having dinner with the bishops of Burkina Faso, he told them that their *wake-up call* on the Sahel situation meant something very profound to him: it was a matter of conscience. "Ten years ago I made an appeal about the situation in the Sahel. Now Providence has allowed me to renew it. Without having made it I could not die in peace." (The words were not exactly these, but the idea was).

CHAD. We go by plane—another small propeller *Fokker*—from Jamena to Mondou, where Mass is celebrated. Then we continue to Sahr. Only a liturgy of the Word was planned, but he is asked to celebrate Mass there as well, because it is the only diocese in Chad that has an African bishop, and he decides to do so. For those of us who are not used to it, the heat is close to humanly bearable.

We returned to Jamena late. And the Pope still has two more events to attend: a meeting in the cathedral and dinner with the bishops of Chad. It has truly been an exhausting day.

Speech by the president of Chad, a Muslim who praises the spiritual significance of the Pope and his actions in the service of mankind.

FEBRUARY 2. We returned from Africa last night. This morning, at a quarter past nine o'clock, Sepe called me and summoned me to lunch with the Pope.

He appears calm and smiling, as usual. When he sees me, he jokes: "First of all, *the stampa. . . .*" Mario Agnes is also there. They talk about the trip. I tell him that we will send the Sahel speech, with a letter from Casaroli, to the ambassadors accredited to the Holy See, and that Etchegaray will come to the

Sala Stampa to speak about the meaning of this speech to the representatives of the media.[4]

The Pope is moved by the joy of these African peoples in the midst of their poverty. He comments on some details of the trip, showing the extent to which he understands and continually deepens his understanding of the realities that he contemplates. I bring up the subject of the basilica of Yamassoukro,[5] which worries me in the public eye. The Pope approaches the issue from an African and not a European perspective, avoiding the latter's tendency to consider that Africans "do not have the right" to certain things we enjoy in Europe:

> This topic must enter into the logic of the African Synod. This synod should be held in various places, and also here. On the one hand, no one is saying anything against the huge mosque built by Hassan II in Casablanca. Naturally, a center for social promotion should be built next to the basilica. On the other hand, the Church in Africa has a certain need to "be present." In Africa, there is much talk of venerating God in his greatness. Therefore, this African initiative for Africa must be respected.

He returns to the theme of freedom compromised by poverty. And again he refers to the United States. "There I realized that social life is subject to business. And everyone is a bit of a slave to it. Those who don't go in that direction end up being excluded." He recalls, on the other hand, the principle of St. Thomas: man needs to possess some material goods to be free, to be able to freely cultivate his humanity.

He comments with admiration on the generosity of the Africans in Mali and adds, laughing, "I told the bishops there that when I go to America or Europe, they say to me, 'how much does the Pope's trip cost?'; and when I go to Africa, they ask me, "what can we offer the Pope?'"

---

4. The Sahel area, south of the Sahara desert, is one of the poorest in the world. In 1984, at the Pope's initiative, the "John Paul II Foundation for the Sahel" was created, which promotes, among other initiatives, projects against desertification and in favor of agricultural development. Most of its beneficiaries are Muslims.

5. The basilica of Yamassoukro, in Côte d'Ivoire, is the largest church in the world with an area of 320,000 square feet. It was built in 1990, and cost $175–600 million dollars. It can hold 18,000 people.

15

"I Don't Know What a Miracle Is . . ."

Czechoslovakia

March 7, 1990

Two days ago, I was in the Pontifical Apartment discussing with Dziwisz some of the things I had pending from the last meetings with the Pope. I also spoke to him about the relevance of the trip to Czechoslovakia next month, since it is the first country in Central-Eastern Europe that the Holy Father will visit, after Poland. And I shared with him some personal reflections on the significance of this trip in the context of the changes we are experiencing in Europe. These are ideas that I have come up with from the perspective of my work at the *Sala Stampa,* in order to give context and background to the information.

In the end, he asked me to send him a note with these points, "in case they might be useful to the Secretary of State." As he asked me for this "appunto" with short notice, I am sending it to him today. Below is the content of those notes, which deal with the reasons for the interest aroused by the forthcoming trip to Czechoslovakia, taken in the thread of what is happening:

1. The events of 1989 in Central and Eastern Europe occurred so quickly that there was no way to develop a historical interpretation of them. The facts are known and obvious; what is missing is the interpretation of these facts. The Pope's visit to Czechoslovakia could be an opportunity to better understand what happened.
2. These events are deeply related to the initial changes in 1980 in Poland, which were dramatically interrupted in December 1981; they resumed in the following years and culminated in free elections and in the last change of regime. Poland's successful evolution was a signal—at the level of the people and leaders—that led to changes in all other countries.

3. It is enigmatic for public opinion that this extensive process of change in Central and Eastern Europe has taken place—with the exception of Romania—in a climate of non-violence.
4. The recent attitude of the Soviet leaders, though undoubtedly important, does not explain the whole phenomenon.
5. The most recurrent question in public opinion continues to be: what has been the role of the Church, of Christian ethics and of the pontificate in this incredible process of change? We can see that this role has been decisive; but we cannot formulate it explicitly, perhaps because of the lack of an interpretation that goes beyond the facts themselves, and because the tension towards the future diverts attention from the elements that have favored the change.

   Public opinion is aware that the Holy Father's upcoming trip to Czechoslovakia has a specific characteristic: a) we are aware that the new leadership in Prague attributes a high symbolic value to this trip; b) we also anticipate that the Holy Father, speaking in Czechoslovakia, will have before his mind the recent reality of other neighboring countries; c) we know that all the other countries of Central and Eastern Europe will listen very attentively to what the Holy Father will say in Prague.

For these reasons, journalists expect the Holy Father to provide, in some of his speeches, ideas that will help us make a deeper historical evaluation of the events of 1989, so decisive for a large part of Europe. Attention will focus especially on the speech he will deliver at Prague Castle on the evening of April 21.

Some of the topics that journalists themselves raise, perhaps in questionable terms, are:

- Since the Enlightenment, attempts have been made to present the Church as afraid of freedom. In contrast, now, historically, the Church is seen as a promoter of freedom and Christians as proponents of freedom.
- Christians, in the defense of freedom of conscience and religious freedom, were first the guardians of freedom and then catalysts for the gaining of other freedoms. What is the relationship between "social" freedoms and religious freedom?
- Some journalists recall the Pope's words on November 9, 1982 in Santiago de Compostela: "Europe, find yourself. Be yourself. Discover your origins . . ." These words can now be read from a broader geographical and historical perspective.

- What does the fact that this "revolution" has taken place essentially without violence have to do with the fact that in these countries there was and still is a Christian ethical "humus"(a culture fertilized by Christian values)?
- The press wonders who was the real protagonist of 1989. It is, at bottom, a question about the action of Providence in History.
- History has done justice to those personalities "misunderstood" at the time—Wyszyński, Mindszenty, Beran, Slipyj, Tomasek—but in doing so, what particular dimension of those personalities now seems most definitive, other than their faith and loyalty to the See of Peter?
- Vaclav Havel in Czechoslovakia, and other artists in other Eastern European countries, have played a particular role in the defense of freedom and national identity. Can we think of art as a particular space of freedom? What is the role of artists in this process?
- Can the future unity of the peoples of Europe be conceived apart from their common Christian roots?
- Towards the future: Is the freedom historically present in the West the true model for these peoples? What are the limits of this "Western freedom" as it is presented today?

Perhaps the public expects the Pope to address some of these issues in Czechoslovakia and thus help the world understand the meaning of the events that have taken place in Europe in recent years.

"The Voice of the Greats"

March 20, 1990

A few days ago, Alberto La Volpe, director of TG2, one of the *RAI* news programs, called me. He wants to make a program, in satellite connection, confronting Gennady Gerasimov, Gorbachev's spokesman; Marlin Fitzwater, spokesman in the White House; and me. I tell him that if he is trying to present communism, capitalism and then the Vatican as the "third way," I am not interested at all. He insists that this is not about that, but about a program to exchange professional points of view, to talk about our work as spokesmen. I like that and accept his approach.

We shot it today around lunchtime, a time that suits the three of us, given the time zones in Moscow, Washington, and Rome. It's a fun experience. We are being broadcast the next day and it seems to have turned out well. It is entitled: "La voce dei grandi" (The Voice of the Greats).

Creating Public Opinion

March 22, 1990

Before I said anything to Dziwisz, he already knew about the program: "You have to *create* public opinion," he tells me. From my point of view, that's the right position: you have to go out and play on the media's playing field.

Viewpoints

March 31, 1990

Sepe tells me that tonight we are going to have dinner with the Pope. As always, I ask if there is anything to prepare, if there are any topics the Pope has said what he wants to talk about. He tells me he hasn't said anything. I prepare some notes on topics I want to report on, and I take with me the book by the English essayist Paul Johnson, *Modern Times,* in Polish translation, which the publisher Leonardo Mondadori sent me a few days ago.

Leonardo has come from Milan to see me a couple of times in the last year and a half. He wants to publish a book on the Holy Father. Naturally, also for commercial reasons and publishing prestige. The last time he told me that he saw this book as a long colloquy with the Holy Father, something like Guitton's with Paul VI.[1] He asked me for suggestions about the author. I recommended Paul Johnson. He called him in London to find out his availability. But Johnson told him that he had two books in the writing stage and that he would not be free until Christmas. Mondadori asked me a few days later if we could meet with Johnson. I discussed all this with Stanisław so he could inform the Pope. We'll see how it turns out.

Before dinner, the Pope brought up the subject of the TV program with Fitzwater and Gerasimov. I had informed Re and he wanted to know more details. During the first part of the dinner I told him about the program, which he had not seen. He seemed amused by it all.

1. Originally published in 1967, this book of Guitton's conversations with Paul VI—*Dialogues with Paul VI*—was an unprecedented publishing event. Jean Guitton (France, 1901–1999), member of the French Academy, was one of the most significant Catholic thinkers of the 20th century. He was the only layman to participate in the Second Vatican Council.

I then mentioned Lithuania's recent declaration of independence, and the Pope immediately focused on this matter. Evidently, it was what he wanted to talk about.[2] The question arose as to whether or not to make any public comment the following day, after the Angelus. Sepe was rather in favor of not commenting on anything. I was rather in favor of saying something. I said that I thought it was appropriate to do so, but tactfully, without confronting the Soviet Union and without abandoning the Lithuanians. It occurred to me to express it in two words: that the Pope prayed that the problem would be solved "with justice and dialogue." Sepe agreed and wrote down those two words. The Pope developed it further and better, so much so that he indicated that a short text be prepared that same evening, which he would pronounce the following day after the Angelus.

When I suggested the phrase "I pray that the situation in Lithuania . . . ," the Pope immediately said: "Yes, pray. We Christians always pray when we need something: an illness, a physical, or spiritual need. I receive thousands of requests to pray for specific intentions: a relative who is sick. . . . And I take all these intentions to prayer, to Mass.

Another topic was the upcoming trip to Czechoslovakia. The Pope told me that he had read my note and asked Sepe if it had been passed on to Father Tomáš Halík, a Czech priest and intellectual who is helping in the drafting of the speeches. Sepe said yes. The Pope asked me if I had spoken to Halík. Coincidentally, a couple of days earlier I had made an appointment with him on the recommendation of Ludmila Grygiel, and I told the Pope that we would meet on Monday morning.

The Pope commented that the draft prepared for the Prague Castle seemed to him "too local;" and that he should transmit to Halík some main points, few and concrete, to give that speech a broader horizon, along the lines of my note: that it should make reference not only to Czechoslovakia but to the rest of the countries of the East, and to the events of that past year.

The Pope, as always, was in magnificent good humor. His visits to the Blessed Sacrament before and after supper became longer. As we said good-bye, I told him to try to get some rest. "Yes," he replies, "and in the meantime . . ." He does not finish the sentence. He smiles and walks towards his room. He carries in his hand the book I gave him before dinner.

---

2. On March 11, following the electoral victory of the Lithuanian Reform Movement (Sajudis) in the first free elections since World War II, the Lithuanian parliament declared its independence from the USSR. The declaration was not recognized by Moscow, which implemented various economic and energy supply sanctions, followed by some military actions. Soviet recognition would come on September 6, 1991.

With my Brother Rafael

April 7, 1990

This morning, accompanying my brother Rafael, I attended the Pope's Mass. A group of Czechoslovakian priests and some lay people were in the chapel. At the end the Pope greeted us and chatted for a while with the two of us. He also spoke to me about a subject close to his heart: the gesture of King Baudouin of Belgium in not signing the abortion law in his country.[3] "Something should be done to support this courageous gesture of the king."

That same morning I called the TV station and spoke to the deputy director: in the evening, the news program on the Telediario showed what *L'Osservatore Romano* had written. I also spoke to Domenico del Rio, who wrote about it two days later. It was not that I convinced them, it was just that the subject was news in itself.

Travel to Czechoslovakia

April 21, 1990

Trip to Czechoslovakia. Initially, the visit was not scheduled, but Václav Havel[4] wanted it so badly that the Pope agreed. The Czechoslovak bishops had invited him several years ago, but it was unthinkable that it would take place under the previous regime.

During the trip to Prague, I took the opportunity to talk to Casaroli about the problems of the East. In his opinion, there are two decisive persons who have influenced the current changes: the Pope and Gorbachev; to which he adds a third figure: Reagan, because of his position of strength at the beginning of the Gorbachev era.

---

3. On March 30, 1990, King Baudouin informed Prime Minister Martens that his conscience did not allow him to sign the abortion extension law passed by parliament, a prerequisite for its enactment. Since the king did not change his mind, a constitutional solution was sought: on April 4, Baldwin delegated to the cabinet the exercise of his powers, invoking Article 82 of the Belgian Constitution, on "the temporary incapacity to reign of the representative of the Crown." The government assumed the Regency and in exercise of it sanctioned the law. A day later, the Parliament declared the temporary incapacity of the king to reign ceased, and he resumed his functions.

4. Václav Havel (Czech Republic, 1936–2011), playwright and politician, was imprisoned several times by the Communist regime. Leader of the human rights movement "Charter 77," he was imprisoned from 1979 to 1984. After the "Velvet Revolution" of 1989, he was elected president of Czechoslovakia. In 1993, after the separation with Slovakia, he was again elected president of the new Czech Republic.

I ask him which figure in the Eastern hierarchy he considers most decisive. Wyszyński—he answers me—is in first place; then Beran. Then Tomášek and Slipj.

On Lithuania: the panorama has been darkened by the sanctions decreed by Gorbachev (or whoever in his name). He thinks that in this situation it is convenient to apply the principle of the lesser evil: it is preferable to hold on, in order to avoid the greater evil: a setback in the changes taking place in the East. Although I would never say this lesser evil to the Pope, who defends with all his heart the sovereignty of the peoples.

I ask him about Zagladin,[5] who recently visited the Pope. "He did not say anything of note: they spoke in very general terms." I continue: would the Holy See accept to be mediator in the Lithuanian case? "—That's what they want too, but more than the Holy See, the local Church should mediate." And he tells me about Sladkevičius, Archbishop of Kaunas, "who is more open, more flexible." "The worst thing," he continues "is not the energy embargo, but the food embargo; because if this continues, the children, the elderly, the people in general will suffer. We must bear in mind that Gorbachev is standing on a volcano. And if that volcano explodes, it is of no benefit to them, to the West or to anyone else."

I visit the Pope during the flight, and I tell him that *RAI Uno* wants to record some words of his for a program dedicated to Czechoslovakia that will be broadcast this very evening. I mention some possible topics: the role of the Church in all these processes; the great figures of the hierarchy in the countries of the East, etc. He listens to me attentively and says that these are only partial details. He is only going to express his gratitude to God for his plans for these peoples. He does not wish to make an analysis, which would require more time, attention, and discernment.

Václav Havel is a writer and a playwright, and this is evident from the moment we arrive at the Prague airport. He begins a most brilliant speech welcoming the Pope:

> I do not know what a miracle is. . . . In spite of that, I dare say that at this moment I am seeing a miracle: the man who six months ago was arrested as an enemy of the State is here today as President of that State, welcoming the first Pontiff to set foot in this country in the entire history of the Catholic Church.

---

5. Vadim Zagladin (Russia, 1927–2006) was Gorbachev's personal advisor and one of the ideologists of *perestroika*.

> I am not sure I know what a miracle is. In spite of this, I dare say that this afternoon I have seen a miracle: today, in the same place where five months ago the canonization of Agnes of Bohemia filled us with joy . . . the principal representative of the Catholic Church will officiate at Mass, and will probably thank our saint for her intercession before the One in whose hand is the inscrutable course of all things.
>
> I am not sure I know what a miracle is. In spite of this, I dare say that at this moment I am participating in a miracle: to a country devastated by the idea of confrontation and division in the world, comes the messenger of peace, dialogue, tolerance, esteem and calm understanding, the messenger of fraternal unity in diversity.

After lunch with the bishops in the archbishopric of Prague, the Pope makes a toast. Speaking in Italian, he thanked Casaroli for the years of dialogue that have borne fruit. He also mentions Nuncios Poggi and Colasuonno, and Father Bukowski.

Upon returning to Rome, we find that Italian President Cossiga is waiting for the Pope at the airport. He wanted to come personally to express the importance he attaches to this trip.

April 23rd. Lunch with the Pope and review of the trip. For him it was especially emotional. "I remember that, on the first trip to Poland, in Gniezno, there was a banner that read: 'Holy Father, do not forget your children of Bohemia.' It seemed an impossible thing, even a year ago . . ." He then speaks gratefully of Havel, with his reference to the miracle. He says he is a believer, with an enlightened background. He adds that reading his *Letters to Olga* shows who his teachers are, from which I gather that he has indeed read the book.

He also refers to the Slovak Church: "It is the first time that it is independent from Hungary. Contemplating these people, one can see that they are not yet free from fear, that they are not completely secure in their 'rediscovered freedom.'"

Breakfast with Cossiga

April 24, 1990

Yesterday I got a call from Ludovico Ortona, head of the press office of the President of the Republic, Francesco Cossiga. He wanted me to go to breakfast at nine o'clock in the morning with the president. Cossiga is friendly, almost familiar. He tells me about the Pope's trip. We go to the dining room. I tell him that this is the second time I am here: the previous time, with Pertini at a dinner.

He tells me that he continues with his hobby: reading theology. He goes personally to the "Libreria Leoniana," near the Vatican, and there he buys his books. He talks about his trips to Spain in the immediate post-Franco period and remembers Ruíz-Giménez,[6] former ambassador to the Holy See.

He is an educated person and is more aware than others of the present times.

6. Joaquín Ruiz-Giménez (Spain, 1919–2009) was director of the Institute of Hispanic Culture (1946–1948), Spanish ambassador to the Holy See (1948–1951), and minister of education (1951–1956). From 1956 onwards he maintained a critical stance towards the Franco regime and promoted political initiatives of Christian Democrat inspiration.

16

The Pope's "Big Dream"

Mexico

May 6 to 14, 1990

Mexico always surprises. We have returned from the Pope's second trip and it has been spectacular, among other reasons, because of the millions of people who got to see him directly. The press has given an estimate of twenty-million, and it may be right.

Of course, it is also the trip in which I have seen the greatest number of people in the streets, participating in the Masses and meetings. It was remarkable to see the people who covered the route from the airport in Mexico City to the apostolic delegation every day. And those who spent the night around the delegation, beginning to greet the Pope very early in the morning. They asked for a blessing; they wanted to see him, they sang. . . .

I seemed to perceive three characteristics of the Mexican people's spirituality: an enormous Marian devotion, a great respect for the priesthood, and a spectacular union with the Holy Father.

As soon as he took off from Rome, as usual, I went to greet him and to orient him on the topics that might come up in the conversation with the journalists. This time I guessed three right: the trip to Cuba, the situation in Lithuania and diplomatic relations with Mexico. Afterwards, I took advantage of part of the thirteen-hour trip to discuss various matters with Casaroli, Re and Stanisław.

With Casaroli I talk about a program that German television is preparing. They want to film a scene of him with the Holy Father. Casaroli says that he does not want to instrumentalize the figure of the Pope for a program about himself, but that he does not mind if it comes naturally.

At one point in the conversation, he reminds me of a phrase that a cardinal—I do not remember his name—once said to him: "*Lasciamo da parte la logica e raggioniamo.*" It seems to me a happy expression of a flexible mentality, perhaps very Italian, that knows how to look for a way out even where there seems to be none: "let's put logic aside and reason."

In this context, he jokingly showed me a copy of *Il Principe,* which he had picked up on the plane as an offprint of the weekly *Epoca*. He brings up the subject of his tenure as Secretary of State and confirms that he wrote his letter of resignation to the Pope on the occasion of his seventy-fifth birthday.

I talk to Re about some things in the office. He tells me that the launching of *VIS*[1] has been resolved as far as the number of people who will work there is concerned. He informs me that the deputy director of the *Sala Stampa,* Giovanni d'Ercole, will be moving to an assignment at the Secretariat of State. A new deputy director, Piero Pennacchini, will be appointed.

I talk to Stanisław. He tells me that, according to the information he has, there will be no Consistory before the summer and possibly not even within the year. I ask him about Casaroli's resignation due to age; he tells me that the Pope replied with another letter in which he accepted his "disponibilità" and in which he asked him to continue for a while longer. He also tells me that they watched the entire program on the spokespersons, "La voce dei grandi," with the Pope, in three days . . . over breakfast. This is how I learn how the Pope uses his time: he even takes advantage of breakfast for these things.

Some memories, almost telegraphic, of the trip:

DURANGO PRISON. As I enter the courtyard, in the open air, I see that they have prepared a podium for the Pope in front of the inmates, who will remain enclosed by barbed wire.

I talk to a prison official and tell him that it is convenient for him to have the key to the small door that leads to the prison where the prisoners will be held. "That poses security problems," he tells me. "I understand," I reply, "but it is very likely that the Pope, as soon as he sees them, will want to greet them personally. . . ." So, they are prepared.

Indeed, a few minutes later he enters the courtyard, indicates his wish to enter, the door is opened and he greets each and every one of the prisoners present there.

The director of this prison told the local press that some of the 1,200 detainees were supposed to have been released days ago, but—upon learning of the Pope's visit—they asked to remain there until this day in order to be able to greet him. The journalists—above all the Americans Clyde Habermann

1. "Vatican Information Service." The VIS is the official news service of the Holy See, providing news and information about the activities of the Pope, the Roman Curia, and events within the Vatican City State.

and Bill Montalbano—are very moved: some give cigarettes to the prisoners, through the wire; and others, like Clyde, who is Jewish, distribute some photos of the Pope.

May 10. Monterrey. Sweltering heat. We had lunch on the plane. We were very tired. We arrived at the archbishopric with about three quarters of an hour to spare before we had to leave for the afternoon events; some of the Pope's entourage did not hesitate and tried to take a nap, even if it was only for those few minutes.

Dziwisz tells Buzzonetti and me that he accompanied the Pope to his room and, as soon as he entered, instead of resting on the bed, he got down on his knees and began to pray. "That's how I left him," he tells us.

When we returned to Mexico City, after ten o'clock at night, we were exhausted. However, before going to rest, the Pope came out three times to greet us from the window of the apostolic delegation. And I don't think he slept much because the people continued to sing to him until very late, and continued to do so from the early hours of the morning.

Every day the same scene was repeated and the Pope gave himself, greeting the people in the evening, when he arrived, and in the morning, before leaving.

There was little rest at night and tiredness accumulated. Those who resided in the delegation could not turn on any light during the night because at that very moment a cheer would sound and they would begin to sing "Mañanitas." They decided that, if they went to the lavatory at night, they would go with a flashlight or a candle. . . . The Pope could have asked the police to move the people away so he could rest. But he did not do so.

The images and memories of this unforgettable trip come flooding back to my mind: the endless applause when the Pope spoke in Tabasco about the need to "return to the Church." The speech in Durango to the industrialists about the errors of both socialism and capitalism in favoring a more humane and just life. The meeting with young people in San Juan de los Lagos. And of course, the visit to Guadalupe.

We returned to Rome at 2:30 in the afternoon of the 14th. I returned totally exhausted, even though I managed to get a few hours of sleep during the trip.

May 15–16. Dinner with the Pope. As soon as I see him, I ask him how he is feeling. He says he is still a little . . . , and he gestures with his hands around his head. I ask him to rest, because it has been a very hard trip, and he replies, smiling: "Yes, but we have to keep going." At dinner, together with Mario Agnes and Sepe, we review the trip. For my part, I refer to the meeting with the intellectuals and I read him some very positive comments from the writer Octavio Paz and others. We then talk about some episodes in Mexico's history. The conversation then delves into the roots of the black legend about Spain.

On the way out I ask Stanisław if the Pope slept well. He tells me no, that he woke up at one o'clock and could not fall asleep. . . . The next morning I call him to find out if he slept that night. Fortunately, he confirms that he did.

Pope's Birthday

May 18, 1990

The Pope's seventieth birthday. Nothing is planned. Dziwisz tells me that this morning Cossiga phoned; that a message arrived from Gorbachev; a message with a gift from the Israeli ambassador; another message from King Baudouin. . . . It is a cascade of congratulations from all over the world. I know that messages have also arrived from Poland from President Jaruzelski and Prime Minister Mazowieski.

Teresa of Calcutta

May 21, 1990

Father Callaghan comes to the office and introduces me to Mother Teresa of Calcutta and one of her sisters. We talk in my office for a long time. At one point I offer her a glass of water: "No," says Mother Teresa, "we don't drink anything between meals, we offer it for the poor."

I show her a book about the Pope's visit to Calcutta. She appears in a photograph. "Is it for me?" I gladly give it to her. Father Callaghan asks her how she is doing: "Fine, in spite of the two pacemakers I have." She tells me that they have already opened six houses in the Soviet Union; another six in Poland; and that she hopes to open one in Bucharest soon. The conversation becomes more and more relaxed, and I tell her that I remember her at the last synod, sitting for hours on end, "wasting time," praying the rosary. "But that's not wasting time," she tells me, as I expected.

"In Calcutta," she says, "they have already given about 40,000 people a ticket to St. Peter's," that is, they have helped them to die well. Then she tells me about some people with AIDS whom they have picked up off the street. She looks happy.

I introduce her to some journalists in the *Sala Stampa*. She gives me a small picture of the Madonna for the car and some medals, which she hands out to the other people. Tiziano, who works in the office, asks for a medal for himself, one for his wife and one for "the child to come." As she says goodbye, she advises me to "always stay young, for fidelity to Jesus."

Malta

May 25 to 27, 1990

May 25. Malta: huge enthusiasm coupled with affectionate disorder. People get into everything. It seems to me a vitalistic and extroverted people, with a slight British touch.

We go to the island of Gozo by boat. On the way back, the ship stops near the islet of St. Paul. There is a phenomenal buzz: dozens of boats, windsurfers, and sailors surround us. The sirens are wailing. Color, intense light, and a radiant sun: a spectacle for the senses, especially at that time of the afternoon. The Pope is seated in the cockpit of the boat, reading the breviary, deeply concentrated.

I admire that he does not raise his eyes when it seems impossible not to, because of the beauty and liveliness of what surrounds us. He remains oblivious to everything until Dziwisz warns him. Then he gets up, goes out on deck, and watches a monumental sculpture of a Christ of the abysses being submerged in the sea.

I am amazed—it is enviable—by his enormous capacity for concentration: when he prays, when he studies. He knows how to guide and control the sensory stimuli that surround him to disconcerting extremes.

He has been asked if he can receive some Dominican nuns when we return to the island. This visit was not foreseen in the program. He accepts immediately.

Although it was a short trip with no time zone problems, the journey was so intense that we returned tired.

And at a quarter to ten in the evening, when those of us who are part of the retinue are getting ready to have dinner, the Pope gets into the car and goes to greet the nuns. Although he never stops smiling, his face shows signs of exhaustion, the result of the continuous journeys and the hustle and bustle of the day.

Risk of Intolerance

MAY 28, 1990

Back in Rome, we had lunch with the Pope to talk about Malta, its history and the character of its people. Then the subject of Lebanon comes up again: he has sent a video message to the bishops and peace has been decreed between the Christian factions fighting, those of Aoun and Geagea. The Pope speaks of this country: he knows the situation and the balance of power well.

He then refers to the lack of religious freedom in some Arab countries. He compares it in some ways to the intolerance suffered by countries under Communist rule. He thinks that in the future this intolerance will constitute a great danger for Christians all over the world.

He then brings up his "great dream": a trip, he says, to the "lands of God: Mesopotamia, Damascus, the Holy Land and Sinai; a trip that my predecessor Paul VI had already begun." He recalls that Sadat had invited him to visit Egypt. Dziwisz intervenes saying: "Yes, that trip to Sinai must be made immediately." This is a reference to the effects of the height of the mountain and to his age. The Pope says: "If the Lord gives me life, I hope to be able to realize this dream of my life."

Today he received a letter from President Vytautas Landsbergis of Lithuania, inviting him to travel to his country, and asking the Vatican to recognize his independence. Gorbachev is mentioned. The Pope says that the present difficulties—economic, ethnic, etc.—come from the system that preceded him. Moving from communism to a plurality of options is a surreal change: it is a remark made to him in Mexico by President Salinas, and he agrees.

The USSR Ambassador with the Pope

JUNE 7, 1990

The Pope received today the first ambassador of the Soviet Union to the Holy See, Yuri Karlov. It is the first audience since this diplomatic channel was established last March 14. Karlov handed him a letter of introduction, signed by Gorbachev and Shevardnadze, Minister of Foreign Affairs: there was no "presentation of credentials" ceremony, but almost. In fact, the formula does not imply diplomatic relations in the strict sense, but the two representatives—Nuncio Colasuonno and Karlov—are diplomats: they are not mere personal representatives.

Karlov has been with the Pope for more than half an hour. I called Dziwisz to find out more. He told me that he had given the Pope written information about the recent "summit" that had taken place in America between Gorbachev and Bush.

For the First Time with Ukrainian Bishops

June 25–26, 1990

Meeting at the Vatican with the ten bishops of Ukraine and the eighteen who are in the Diaspora. I spend some time with them these two days in the Old Hall of the Synod. When the Pope arrives, he is greeted by Miroslaw Lubachivsky, Major Archbishop of the Ukrainian Church, and by Sodano, who made this meeting possible. He then approaches to greet the ten coming from Ukraine: the first time in more than fifty years.

The Pope speaks in Polish, a language they all understand. They then go into an adjoining room and sit around a table. The Pope is accompanied by Lubachivsky and Sodano. The Pope is interested in their stories. He asks under what circumstances they were ordained and about the deaths in Siberia of some of their predecessors. This family reunion began with a song in Ukrainian, spontaneously sung by one of them.

They go into the classroom. The Pope greets the others, one by one. The first meeting begins with a Ukrainian song addressed to the Holy Spirit. They are hard and clear in the formulation of their problems, but there is dialogue. I do not know what idea of the Vatican they are getting; they seem poorly informed, after so many decades of forced separation. The Pope, at the end, says that in the afternoon the people of the Curia will speak, implying that the vision of the problems must be completed with these statements. The ten Ukrainians have lunch with the Pope.

In these years I have seen that in the Holy See there is great respect for the Easterners. At the same time, at times, it is necessary to help, as in this case, to ponder their requests: they insistently ask for the appointment of a patriarch in Kiev; among other things, the appointment of a patriarch—Duprey explains to me—is something that can be done when a country is independent, and Ukraine is not yet independent . . . for now.

There is also the problem of the residential appointments of the hierarchy itself: many of them have been ordained without the Holy See having entrusted them with a specific diocese. That is the reason why they are asking for a synod to be convened.

Lubachivsky tries to delay the celebration of the synod until September, after they have been able to reflect on what has been said during these Roman meetings. But they say that on this occasion they have managed to get visas and that, in September, possibly, they will not be able to get them again; that is why it would be good to stay here for a few days, hold the synod and return with some matters resolved.

They insist on this two, three times. The Pope tells them that if a synodal meeting is held, it must be to deal with questions concerning the Ukrainian Church in Ukraine, excluding everything that concerns the Diaspora. He adds that he understands well that, on their return, the faithful will ask them, "What do you bring us from Rome?" and that they must be answered with something concrete. "You can stay here for a few days," he concludes, "but we have to think about it a little more. We will decide in the afternoon."

In the afternoon it was decided that this synodal meeting would be held the following morning and that the results would be passed on to the Pope, who would do what he considered appropriate.

The next day, I call a press conference with Sterniuk,[2] Hermaniuk,[3] Marusyn,[4] and Nuncio Colasuonno. Sterniuk and Hermaniuk come half an hour earlier to my office and we speak through an interpreter. The meeting with the journalists is rich in information and feelings. Sterniuk recounts the sufferings of his church. Marusyn gives a moving personal testimony. He recalled that he left Ukraine in 1949, and only now has he been able to pray at the grave of his parents. There is applause when he finishes speaking, almost with tears in his eyes.

---

2. Volodymyr Sterniuk (Ukraine, 1907–1997) served as head of the Ukrainian Catholic Church from 1972 to 1991, when Major Archbishop Lubachivsky was able to return from exile in Rome. Always under surveillance and harassed by the Soviet police, he spent five years in prison and labor camps.

3. Maxim Hermaniuk (Ukraine-Canada, 1911–1996), a Redemptorist religious who ministered throughout Canada, where he was ordained bishop in 1951. He presided over the synod of the Ukrainian Greek Catholic Church from 1969 to 1974.

4. Miroslav Marusyn (Ukraine, 1924–2009), appointed bishop by Paul VI in 1974, he became the first member of the Ukrainian Greek Catholic Church to work stably in the Roman Curia. He was secretary of the Congregation for the Eastern Churches and vice-president of the commission for the drafting of the Code of Eastern Canon Law.

17

On Mont Blanc

Meeting in the Aosta Valley

July 11–20, 1990

July 11, Wednesday. The same people as in previous years: besides the Pope, we were Dziwisz, Tadeusz Styczeń, Gugel, Cibin, and the physician Proietti. And the same place as last year in the Aosta Valley.

Stanisław asked me a few days ago if I wanted to come this year. He thinks that, since the initial intention is to give little—or no—information, then the precaution of bringing the director of the *Sala Stampa* is not necessary. I replied: a) for me, coming to those days with the Pope is a gift from God; b) apart from that personal motivation, I think that wherever the Pope goes, for whatever reason, someone who can deal with the press must always go: you can never say *a priori* that it will not be necessary to intervene. "Then you are coming," he said to me. I think, in any case, that he was more convinced by the first reason than the second.

The trip was by helicopter from the Vatican to Ciampino airport. Then by small plane to Turin. From there, again by helicopter to Les Combes, passing over the Gran Paradiso: a splendid view that serves as an appetizer for these days.

I had to deny a month ago the rumors about the Pope's "tiredness." But the image of the Pope being tired has remained engraved in public opinion, especially among journalists who are not permanently accredited in the *Sala Stampa* and do not follow the Pope's grueling day-to-day schedule, precisely the ones who usually cover these vacations.

On arriving in the Aosta Valley, the usual questions: "Will you walk a lot during these days, Holy Father?" "We'll see," he replies; "the years are passing; my strength is beginning to fail. . . . But there could be some surprises. Those last four words set off a cascade of suppositions. And as a fruit of this unbridled imagination, a Milan newspaper, *La Notte*[1] dedicates big front-page

1. The newspaper *La Notte* had been founded in 1952 and ceased publication a few years after this episode, in 1995.

headlines to its own cabal: the Pope is unwell, he has retired to *Val d'Aosta*, and he could resign. Three in one.

July 12, Thursday. While this news was picked up by the press in various places, and so many Catholics and non-Catholics were worried, the Pope headed towards two peaks of about 2,000 m: Plan Bry and Moccosoney. After lunch—and the little nap that accompanies it—the Pope, alone, begins to climb a little more, conversing with Don Tadeusz, on the same theme as last year: immanentism, the philosophical currents that deny transcendence and consider as a criterion of truth one's own inner feeling.

On this occasion I pluck up courage and intervene in the philosophical dialogue. I ask if it is possible that non-immanentist thought moves away from Christian thought or, at least, away from religious thought. Don Tadeusz talks to me about Kołakowski[2] and shares his vision on this point with me. Since I am not an expert on the subject, my conclusion is that there is no definitive answer.

We had hoped to return home around a quarter to five, but that was too optimistic an estimate: we arrived at a quarter to eight. Since this year we have a technological advance—Gugel is carrying a radiotelephone given to the Pope—we were able to warn the nuns of the delay, so that they could prepare dinner more calmly.

When I arrived, they told me that half the world had phoned me about the *La Notte* newspaper.

July 13, Friday. After returning from the excursion, they tell me again that people are still looking for me. At 11 PM I speak to the *ANSA* correspondent on the phone and make a statement on the subject. I also tell him that, as we agreed when we arrived, the next day I would meet them at the Introd Town Hall, where we have "the general base."

July 14, Saturday. Today the newspapers are more thoughtful and are beginning to backtrack.

We leave at 9:45 AM: a good walk. After praying the Angelus in Challancin, they tell the Pope that today is the saint's day of Enrico Marinelli, the chief inspector of Italian security. The Pope says we have to toast: "—But

2. Leszek Kołakowski (Poland, 1927–2009), philosopher and essayist known—among other things—for his critical analysis of Marxism, which cost him expulsion from the Polish Communist Party and exile in 1968.

we only have water . . . ," someone comments; "—Well, even if it is with water . . . ," adds the Pope. And so we do.

As we go upstairs, Dziwisz tells me about some documents that are about to come out, such as the encyclical on morality.[3] He tells me that it is finished and that the first draft was done entirely by the Pope. Then four other drafts were made and, in the end, it was decided that the best thing to do was to go back to John Paul II's original outline.

There is another document in the making, on the centenary of *Rerum Novarum*. It is very important at this time because of the social and political changes taking place in Eastern Europe. One of the ideas that stands out is that it was not capitalism that defeated Marxism.[4]

There is also the apostolic exhortation on the missions.[5] This was not written by the Pope himself, but—in revising it—he introduced numerous annotations and had to completely redo it.

In addition, there are the three letters signed by the Secretary of State—encouraged by the Pope—on labor issues in the Holy See: one was addressed to the heads of the dicasteries, and another to all the lay employees. Once again, it can be seen that the Pope does not let the issues pass: he acts and does not hesitate to get into the hornet's nest.

I tell Dziwisz what the newspapers have written these days about the Pope's health. He tells me that he has not seen any symptoms of diminished capacity in the Pope. "Perhaps if one day he finds himself unable to carry out his mission, the Holy Spirit will say." I gather from his words that the Pope has not spoken to anyone about the possibility of resigning one day for reasons of health or old age. "I would have to find me a superior (to give him my resignation)," was the joke he said a couple of years ago on his visit to *Stampa Estera,* when asked about this.

Dziwisz adds that a sign of his ability to work is that before leaving Rome he left everything arranged: he met with the cardinals with whom he had pending matters and outlined the work for these months.

Then he makes a reference that touches me personally. He says that, on more than one occasion, the Pope has spoken at the Secretariat of State about the new possibilities that have opened up with the *Sala Stampa*. And that he

3. In reality, it would still take some time to come out, since it was published in 1993 under the name *Veritatis splendor.*

4. It was published a few months later, in May 1991, under the title *Centesimus annus.*

5. It would appear as an encyclical a few months later (*Redemptoris missio,* December 1990).

wanted to talk to me these days, which is why he had asked Stanisław if I would also come with them to the mount. Naturally, with this preamble, I don't need to be asked twice.

In the middle of the walk I see the Pope standing in front of a very beautiful landscape. I look at him. He stares at me. I approach him and we start talking while standing and contemplating the landscape. We stay like that for half an hour. I tell him—it is the news of the day in the press—that Gorbachev has triumphed at the 28th Congress of the Communist Party of the Soviet Union, getting his candidate appointed deputy secretary. "That means he was right and it was recognized." He appreciates Gorbachev.

He refers to the recent meeting of the Ukrainian bishops and I give him my impressions of how the press conference went. He tells me about some peculiarities of that Church. The liturgical language of that rite—among Ukrainians—is not Ukrainian, but the Paleo-Slavic language. "That is why I asked Duprey: 'if one day you could concelebrate with the Patriarch of Constantinople, in what language would you do it?' Duprey answered me: 'a solution will be found. . . .'"

I tell him about some of the issues at the office. I see that he appreciates the work done there. I tell him that our problem sometimes is gathering information and I tell him about my odyssey during the Noriega affair. "But we were all in the dark at that time," he tells me with all the reason in the world.

He speaks to me about Germany, about the situation of the Church in that country. As always, I tell him what I think: that part of the problem comes from middle-management, that very high number of civil servants working in the curias and collateral organizations. And I also seem to see, I might add, a certain osmosis into the ways of Protestantism.

The Pope tells an anecdote: "Don Tadeusz told me that on a recent trip to Switzerland he entered a church and, during the prayer of the faithful, a nun went up to the altar and said: 'We ask you, Lord, to take away from this Pope the temptation to do everything himself in the Church.'" The Pope commented with some sorrow, but without drama.

I think that so many sad things happen to the Pope that he might not see in all their dimension the good that his teachings and his fidelity to Christ generate. When I point some of this out to him, he asks me: "Do you believe?" and adds no more.

The conversation continues. I compare the situation in Germany with that of other countries, such as Sweden, where the Lutherans have even more weight, but where there is a friendly diversity, one might say a much less "anti-Roman" atmosphere. The Pope, as usual when it comes to questions of this kind, listens and says nothing.

This same day I take some pictures, looking for some that could be useful for the press. The Pope is wearing the white cassock in both of them. In the first one he is standing; in the second one he is seated and in the background you can see the Mont Blanc massif.

I go to see the journalists and give them the photographs. In the evening, at home, we celebrate the saint of Cibin—St. Camillus—and we have dinner at the Salesians' residence. Marinelli, who celebrated his saint yesterday, St. Henry, is also coming. Towards dessert, the Pope appears. We served him a piece of cake, which he consumed in its entirety. He says a few words and reminds us that in Poland St. Henry and St. Camillus are celebrated together. This is a very fine allusion to the collaboration between Cibin (Vatican security) and Marinelli (Italian security), in which from time to time there are those little unimportant misunderstandings that characterize human life.

Then he jokes about "this traveling Pope who goes around the world and climbs mountains." In this context of friendly humor, he refers with an amused tone to what some media write about him and, turning to me, he adds amusingly: "But that is not his fault. . . ."

July 15, Sunday. Day dedicated to the pastoral activity of the Pope. In the morning we leave for Besac. The Pope's helicopter circles around the Matterhorn and over Monte Rosa; the helicopter we are in will make the same route when we return in the afternoon. After lunch we go to Introd: the Pope holds a general meeting in the village church and then another one for young people only, on the sports field.

July 16, Monday. We are on our way to the *Alpe di Met,* 1,800 meters, and at one of the stops I go up to chat with the Pope for a while. I tell him that since he usually only receives bad news, I wanted to give him some good news which I have seen in the last few days: the 25 percent increase in priestly vocations in the United States this year, and the five thousand people who have been received into the Catholic Church in Sweden after his trip. These are two references that I have picked up from the press. To each piece of news he responds with a "thank God."

With regard to giving only bad news, he tells me with a smile that this is typical of a curia, and that it also happened in Krakow. When he arrived as auxiliary bishop, the vicar general of that time—who was a nice and optimistic man—told him that only problems came there. In fact, in a short time, that man—who is still alive—became a much duller, almost sad man.

Stanisław Dziwisz cites, as an example, the apostolate carried out by so many lay people in the Church. He recalls that around 1968, when it seemed that young people were moving away from God en masse, he became aware of the vitality of the lay apostolate and understood that it was a gift of God, of the Holy Spirit, for the Church.

The news about priestly vocations in the United States allows him to focus on the topic of the priesthood.

> "Father Magee," says the Holy Father, "who was Paul VI's secretary, told me how the Pope lived the drama of the priests who asked to be dispensed from celibacy. Paul VI would bring those long lists to the chapel and almost wept. I remember the first time he brought the list of priests asking for dispensation to Šeper[6] and me—because at that time this matter was handled by the Congregation for the Doctrine of the Faith. When I saw the list, I told him: 'I cannot sign this. I simply cannot sign it.' He said to me: 'Well, I thank you.'"
>
> "I told him that we had to calmly draw up new criteria and wait for some time. Two years went by and this anecdote spread in the Church. After that, fewer requests came in. It is simply not possible to apply to priests a criterion for dispensation different from the one that applies, in the case of marriage, to the stability of the marriage bond."

He continues to speak of the causes that have favored some priests to have an erroneous idea of the priesthood. "They were ordained, and then they asked for secularization . . . it was a fluid idea of the priesthood, based on a very particular anthropology. That's why some people hate this Pope, who has destroyed that idea of ecclesiology and anthropology. Well, not quite destroying . . ." (he corrects himself, as if to say that the word *destroy* sounds too strong).

We continue talking serenely, standing, while we contemplate the landscape. At this moment we are told by radio that we still have an hour's walk to get to the lunch place. We continue walking. At another moment, the Pope passes by a meadow and greets a young woman—Oviana Pont—with her five-month-old baby. I take some pictures of them.

---

6. Franjo Šeper (Croatia, 1905–1981), was prefect of the Congregation for the Doctrine of the Faith from 1968 to 1981.

When we arrived at the appointed place, I dared to show him a clipping from *Avvenire* that contained some considerations of mine about his character: his capacity for concentration, the uniqueness of the centrality of his ministry to his entire way of being. I ask him: "Holy Father, do you think I am right? Because I don't know." He answered me laughing: "I don't know either."

Today's itinerary was tough: Tura, Alpe di Met (1,800 m), below Punta Chalique, La Neove (2,200 m), a small and very beautiful lake—Lago del Falere—next to which the Pope sat to finish reading the breviary.

When he concludes, Don Alberto Carreggio tells him that they have prepared a helicopter ascent for the following day . . . to Mont Blanc! to Mont Blanc! The Pope's surprised face reflected his excitement. He had already been invited to go up on September 7 and 8, 1986, when he was in Aosta on a pastoral visit. But the plan did not work out because of bad weather. So he stopped at Mont Chetif.

He asks Dziwisz, who is still surprised by the proposal, what he thinks. In the end it is decided that it can be done.

Hours later, when we arrived home, on the way back from the excursion, he greeted those of us who accompanied him and said to me, smiling and referring to the long walk: "We have done what could be done. And Dr. Navarro has also done it, trying to emphasize the positive things about the Pope, leaving aside the rest."

I then reflect on these words: we do what we can, period, even if what we do does not solve all the world's problems. It is a lesson in healthy realism.

Dziwisz sees me writing these notes after lunch, notices their contents and warns everyone, in a joking tone:

—In a few years you will see all of this written down and published in a book by Dr. Navarro!

I take the opportunity to ask him if the Pope keeps a diary. He tells me that he does not. He only takes personal notes when he makes spiritual exercises. He tells me about the Pope's holiness and inner life: "I make efforts every day to be better, but in him, that is something that flows naturally. He is a man of great holiness, a contemplative. One day I will tell you about these things, because if I tell them now they will say that I am spreading propaganda."

July 17, Tuesday. Mont Blanc. In the morning two small *Lama* helicopters arrive from Aosta. The Pope is in one of them. Accompanying him are the pilot; the president of the *Soccorso Alpino e Speleologico*; Franco Garda, of the

Corpo Nazionale; Dziwisz and Gugel. In the other one are Cibin, Don Tadeusz, the pilot, a guide, and myself. The Pope's helicopter departs first and our helicopter follows behind. When I move to take some pictures I immediately feel the lack of oxygen and when we fly over Mont Blanc we feel an intense cold: outside it is 6 below zero.

The Pope's helicopter tries to land on Colle Maggiore (4,700 m) but cannot land. He tries once, twice, three times, four times, until the fifth time he succeeds. The space is too small. The summit is only 114 meters higher (Mont Blanc is 4,814 m).

It's a risky adventure, but it's worth it. The Pope must have thrown himself and the others to the ground under the propeller rotor, which has not stopped spinning. He immediately recites a *Te Deum*. Then he blesses Europe and prays for a united and peaceful Europe.

We take a tour of the vicinity with the helicopter and descend to the Monzino refuge, at 2,590 meters. We stay there for about half an hour, while the helicopter descends to pick up the others and take them to the point where we have met. The spectacle is incredible. Nobody in the refuge knows that the Pope is at the summit.

We then fly, following the Pope's helicopter, to the waterfalls of the Ruitor glacier, which the two helicopters climb, very close to the water, in a splendid ascent.

Then we drive to Lake Bellecombe, which is half frozen, to land on the Belveldere, next to the ski resort of La Thuille. The Pope, exultant, talks to Franco Garda: "The small lakes and, above all, the waterfalls, are incredible. And all this in two hours. It would take me about two months to do it on foot . . ."

He is asked what impression he brings back from what he has seen. "There are a multitude of impressions left. Above all, I liked Mont Blanc. I was quite calm (during the landing). I don't deserve it."

While he is talking, a lady appears with her daughter, who have recognized the Pope. The lady says that her daughter always comes here to ski and that she has also taken mountaineering courses. Her name is Elsa Dossetti and she is from Lodi. The Pope greets them. They leave with great emotion. The conversation with the pilot and Garda continues. The pilot says that a week ago it was not possible to land on Mont Blanc because of the weather conditions. He asked the Pope: "Shall we do it again, Holy Father?" The Pope laughs: "We had to wait until the Pope was seventy years old to come. I thank you, I thank you with all my heart."

The Pope is interested in the most frequent causes of mountain accidents and the new free climbing techniques. He comments that "the mountain inspires adoration, it is a natural expression of God's greatness." Garda says: "One feels closer to God." And the Pope: "Certainly, it would be a pity if the spirit of the sacred, which refers us to Something, were to disappear. . . . I am very, very grateful."

A French family arrives. They speak in French with the Pope, recalling his first trip to France, ten years ago. And then the bishop of Vercelli appears with a Carmelite priest who is preaching some exercises somewhere nearby. This, which seemed lonely, is busier than a street in Rome!

We set off. The helicopters disappear and we start the real excursion of the day: Belvedere, La Thuille ski resort, descent to La Thuille. While we are having lunch I decide to go and see the journalists. I phone and let them know that I will be with them between 4:30 and 5:00 PM I descend alone and a jeep of the forest guard awaits me.

We go rather fast, but the road is long and I arrive at 5:15. They are waiting for me and I tell them about the excursion to Mont Blanc and the rest. Two of the journalists—*Il Giorno* and *Il Tempo*—apologize to me for the "joke" they had played on me: they had included in their reports two days ago the loud "cue" that escaped me in my last meeting with them.

July 18, Wednesday. Ascent of Pointe de la Pierre 2,660 m, Colle del Drink 2,800 m, Pila ski resort. At the top of the mountain there is a 360 degree view: there are all the mountains and hikes of the trip, from Mont Blanc to Monte Rosa. At the beginning of the climb, the Pope greets a young Moroccan who works in the fields; the young man reminds the Pope of his trip to Casablanca, teaches him the confession that summarizes the Muslim faith ("La ilaha illa Allah") and greets him in Arabic.

We reached the summit at a quarter to two. As it is a relatively steep mountain, the Pope stops from time to time to catch his breath. "But I don't sweat," he says. "Yesterday on Mont Blanc I did feel short of breath when I was praying the *Te Deum*."

It is windy, and when he stops again, I put my raincoat jacket over his shoulders. When he reaches the summit, he prays a Hail Mary and then says three invocations: *Regina Italiae, Regina Poloniae, Regina Mundi,* which we all answer. And we take a group photo.

On the way up, Father Tadeusz tells me that yesterday, on Mont Blanc, the Pope was exultant. It was the day of St. Eudivigis. He was thinking of that immanentism which led to war for war's sake. He recalled the documents of Pius XI on Fascism and Nazism: *Non abbiamo bisogno* and *Mit brenender Sorge*. On his return, he spoke about these questions during dinner.

July 19, Thursday. Splendid excursion: Arp Vieille, Costone Mont Pelà, San Grato Lake, Grand'Alpe, Bonne towards Valgrisange. We cross a snowy area. We make large tracks to prevent the Pope from slipping. When he passes, he refuses the help we give him. At 11:45 we get the news on the radio that the Italian President Francesco Cossiga, who is with Mitterrand today on the anniversary of the construction of the Mont Blanc tunnel, has sent a message of greetings to the Pope. The reply is written a few kilometers away:

> The Holy Father thanks and wishes a happy day to President Cossiga and his French colleague Mitterrand, congratulating them on the 25th anniversary of the construction of the Mont Blanc tunnel, which has united two peoples, in a portent of peace, friendship, and joy. The Holy Father celebrates this historic meeting between Italy and France from the Italian mountains that shelter him, very close to the French border.

The excursion was very beautiful. Arriving at Lake San Grato, Stanisław says: "Dr. Navarro had asked me to take a picture with the Pope. This is the moment." He takes my camera and shoots a couple of pictures.

July 20, Friday. We return to Rome. In the morning the Pope celebrates Holy Mass at the house where he resided, inviting only the people who have been involved in the care of these days, without the presence of the police or authorities.

I facilitate the entry of several journalists: Pisano from *ANSA*, Mazza from *Avvenire*, the one from *Famiglia Cristiana*, and the one from *RAI*, Aosta. The one from *RAI* asks the Pope about his prayer on Europe and the Pope gives a long answer.

After breakfast, he takes a short walk, and takes the opportunity to sit in the same place as last year and read for a while.

In this atmosphere of farewell, I suggest to Dziwisz that the Pope could send as a gift a small image of Our Lady for the very small wayside shrine that he visited yesterday by Lake San Grato. He agrees that it would be a nice gesture for these people.

We reviewed the trips planned for next year: May, Poland; June, Jamaica; August, Poland and Hungary, and the possibility of going to Fatima on the tenth anniversary of the terrorist attack; and then Madeira and the Azores. I tell the Pope that we are recording a list of all the events of the Pontificate on the computer.

I speak with the Pope for a moment about the documents he intends to publish in the coming months. I tell him that it would be convenient if the documents of the other organisms of the Curia were published at another time, and not at the same time; and I tell him that sometimes it gives the impression that "some documents of dicasteries seem to be made only to justify that work is being done."

"No," says the Pope, "there are documents made with great care, with time."

It was a good correction to my imprudence in formulating a hasty judgment: I have never heard from the Pope's lips a critical judgment on the Curia or on the people of the Curia.

18

"The Certainties of Jesus Christ"

With Philosophers at Castelgandolfo

August 13–14, 1990

We had in Castelgandolfo the "dreaded"—at least for me—philosophical meeting organized by Don Tadeusz, to which he had invited me during the days in the Aosta Valley. As I suspected, the language is very technical. I can see that the Pope likes this atmosphere of academia, where everyone speaks freely about what he thinks. It is a meeting of wise men with an exceptional teacher and scholar.

After Mass in the courtyard at the entrance of the Pontifical Villa, breakfast with the Pope was served. A free time, and at ten o'clock the sessions began, under three monkey-puzzle trees that shade a corner of the back garden.

Wicker armchairs, the same for everyone; the Pope's is a little different. Three portable microphones; a table for the speaker, who normally speaks standing up. A short prayer at the beginning of the first session. A twenty-minute break at about eleven o'clock. It continues until one o'clock, at which time the Pope probably does a little exercise . . . perhaps in the swimming pool.

Lunch with the Holy Father, free time until five o'clock, followed by a session on the terrace overlooking the lake until half past seven, then dinner with the Pope at a quarter past eight, and the end of the day. Thus we spend two days.

The Pope wore a white cassock, without a pectoral and without a soutane, and Polish felt slippers decorated with floral motifs (and, by the way, so worn that they were crying out for a replacement). Optimal mood. Relaxed. Very smiley. Joking around and showing affection. He participates in the sessions as one of the participants, sometimes asking questions. But, most of the time, he listens to what the speaker says.

Among the participants is Sr. Emilia Ehrlich, an Ursuline, who works in the Secretariat of State and was born in Lviv, Ukraine, when it was united with

Poland. She became a nun after the war. She helped the Pope in Krakow with the notes of the book *Person and Action*. She thanks me very much for my "loyalty to the Pope" . . . I try to tell her that I thank her for hers, but I miss my opportunity because we are interrupted by someone else.

Josef Zverina, a seventy-seven-year-old Czech priest and one of the signatories of *Charter 77* for Human Rights.[1] He spent a good part of his life imprisoned, first by the Nazis—from 1942 to 1943—and then by the Communist regime for twenty-two years, for "high treason and espionage." Released in 1965, he had a brief period of normalcy at the Faculty of Theology in Litoměřice in 1968. He was persecuted again during the Czech "normalization" of the 1970s, and from 1975 onward he was banned from all priestly activity by the Communist authorities. Since last spring he was honorary dean of the Litoměřice Faculty of Theology.[2]

The Pope introduces us and we go to the dining room. During the meal the Pope shows interest in the state of theology in the Czechoslovak educational institutions. Zverina says that it is bad, but not for the reasons observed in the West, but because the academic level is now low. Someone asks the Pope if Gorbachev is an agnostic. The Holy Father says that Gorbachev spoke to him about the need for the spiritual dimension of life. Someone present commented that there is a need for a Slavic theology. The Pope replies that perhaps theologians there have not produced much, but at least they have had the gift of discernment: they have known how to keep the good and reject the bad.

At lunch and during the speeches of the sessions we spoke in German and Italian. We would go in and out of the garden of the house through a door near the kitchen, where there were boxes with fruit, sacks, packages, etc. The Pope would also pass by. I felt I was in the country house of a large family, not in a papal palace.

At breakfast the following day, the difficulties in the life of the Church are discussed. The Pope distinguishes between external and internal difficulties. Among the external ones is currently the invasion of sects of various kinds, especially in Latin America. Someone says that they go against the social

---

1. The "Charter" was signed in 1977 by 241 people. It called on the Czechoslovak Communist government to adhere to the principles of human rights contained in the Helsinki Accords (1975), also signed by Czechoslovakia. Although the main signatory, Václav Havel, was imprisoned and the signing of this manifesto was classified as a crime, *Charter 77* brought together an opposition to the regime that would crystallize in the "Velvet Revolution" of 1989, which culminated in the election of Havel as president of the republic.

2. Zverina died suddenly on August 18, a few days after this meeting in Castelgandolfo [Author's note].

doctrine of the Church. There is talk of theologians, and someone comments that Hans Küng has some very beautiful pages. The Pope says that one thing is the fascination for formal beauty and another the fascination for truth, which is, "so to speak, fascination for the real Truth." Then the internal difficulties of the Church are mentioned: disobediences, dissension . . . ; "but this is normal" (in the sense that they will never be lacking).

At lunch on the last day the Pope takes the floor for a moment:

> "Since this morning I have had something in my head that I want to say. Today is the feast day of St. Maximilian Kolbe, that humble and modest Franciscan. His brothers themselves said that he was 'mad,' yes, a 'madman' full of love for God. And in Auschwitz, with his attitude, he was like an antibody to barbarism. And this idea came to my mind: faced with the evil that we see in the world today, faced with the power of the prince of this world who has entered even within the Church, we need those antibodies that by their actions resist and offer a solution. I wanted to say this since this morning, and I say it now (he concludes smiling) during lunch, so that it can be better digested."

In the afternoon, before the session begins, I say goodbye to the Pope and return to Rome, partly because I have some business to take care of and partly . . . because a two-day philosophical discussion is too much for me. Before I leave, the Pope tells me that I have to deal with some negative reaction in France about the consecration of the Basilica of Our Lady of Peace, during the trip to the Ivory Coast. He does not miss a single one.

VIS Problems

AUGUST 20–27, 1990

The obstacle course continues on the *Vatican Information Service*, the idea that I have had for years and which is now in the realization phase. The *VIS* fills a great need for communication between Rome and the bishops, and has obtained very generous management funding that I myself requested from Derksen.

The problem lies in the complexities of the Curia. It is not clear who has the last word in matters and these pass from one office to another without anyone taking the responsibility to decide.

AUGUST 27. Stanisław calls me in the morning to go to dinner with the Pope at Castelgandolfo. I am the only guest. I find him very fit: rested, tanned, relaxed.

A consequence of the days spent at Castelgandolfo, during which he can walk and swim, as well as work a lot. We watch the beginning of the news on TV.

At the beginning of dinner he asks me about *VIS*. I explain the situation. The Pope says, "Then we'll have to say a little word . . ." And so it goes. He confirms that Derksen visited him some time ago in Castelgandolfo and that he was willing to cover the expenses.

Tanzania, Burundi, Rwanda, and Côte d'Ivoire

September 1 to 10, 1990

On the way from Rome to Malta, where we have a stopover, a powerful electrical storm breaks out. The pilots tell Dziwisz that it is the worst storm they have ever experienced.

As usual, I talk with the Pope at the beginning of the trip. I comment on some of the topical issues that are likely to come up in the journalists' questions: relations with Islam; the situation in the Gulf (Iraq, etc.); meeting with Walesa, and the future of Poland.

September 2. Tanzania. We are in this beautiful country from September 1st to 5th. The Pope ordains a group of priests in Dar-es-Salaam, meets with representatives of other confessions, administers the sacrament of confirmation to a hundred young people. A well-established Church, with religious and priestly vocations, especially in Moshi, where the Pope makes a brief synthesis—during his homily—of the history of evangelization in this country. The Church arrived a century ago and all that we see has become a reality, he said, with "patience, perseverance, and humility."

In one of the intervals I talk to Casaroli about *ostpolitik*. He tells me about the 1960s, when he used to make trips to the East. He was sent by Paul VI, whom some cardinals considered "an anti-Polish Pope." Paul VI replied: "We do not work for human glory."

September 5. Burundi. We leave Tanzania for Burundi. The priest who accompanies us—secretary of the bishops' conference—tells me that they are very happy with the visit. The people knew there was a Pope and wondered what he would be like; and now they have seen him up close. In Europe his figure appears frequently on TV, but here few people had seen a photograph of him. Along with curiosity there is the human need to see, and that explains why many people who are not even Catholics have come.

September 7–8. Rwanda. On September 8, he speaks about AIDS to young Rwandans at the Amahoro National Stadium:

> "Rwanda, as is unfortunately the case in so many African countries, must face the scourge of AIDS. I encourage you to lend all your sympathy, help, and solidarity to your brothers and sisters affected by AIDS, and to the people afflicted by HIV. I invite you to pray with me persistently for those affected by this terrible disease. I wholeheartedly encourage and express my respect for the people who care for these sick people and support them morally. I hope that research in biology and medicine will soon discover an effective remedy for this disease."

September 8–9. Ivory Coast. The information officer reads a pungent, sarcastic speech. I realize that the Pope takes tremendous risks on these trips. He is like a trapeze artist without a safety net. At the end the Pope improvises a few words in response and adds: "Certain things can only be understood if you read them on your knees."

Basilica of Yamoussoukro. It is beautiful. It was a personal decision of President Houphouët-Boigny. The basilica belongs to the diocese of Bouakè, erected in 1955.

September 11. We returned to Rome around midnight and I went to bed after one o'clock. This morning, at nine o'clock, when I was still asleep, they called me to tell me that they were expecting me for lunch at Castelgandolfo with the Pope. Sepe and Agnes are coming. Naturally, they talk about the trip.

In the course of the conversation, I commented that we had two risky issues in terms of public opinion: one foreseen (Yamoussoukro basilica) and the other unforeseen (the official's speech). Regarding the first one, we had been able to prepare something; the second one, to tell the truth, didn't draw much attention.

The Pope has to leave the table at the beginning of the second course, as a consequence of the almost inevitable intestinal infections that are brought back from Africa. I feel sorry for him. He comes back a moment later. He doesn't eat anything else and talks mainly about the missionaries. And he expresses a concern: the young African churches, he says, "were born thanks to the apostolic zeal of the European missionaries, and I fear that sometimes these native churches, which are no longer mission churches, lack the zeal and eagerness to bring their animist brothers to the faith."

With Gianni Pasquarelli

September 25, 1990

I am going to Castelgandolfo to have lunch with the Pope with Gianni Pasquarelli, appointed a few months ago director general of *RAI*.

During the fifty-minute trip we talked about the situation in Italy, *RAI*, and the Pope. He is very excited about this lunch. We arrive in plenty of time to first take a walk around the lake.

At lunch he thanks the Pope, as a Catholic journalist, for the changes that have taken place in Eastern Europe, which he attributes largely to his intervention. The Pope tells him, smiling, that he cannot accept that everything is due to his intervention. Then he also thanked him for this pontificate of certainties. The Pope replies: "They are the certainties of Jesus Christ."

19

A Rough Meeting

Gulf War and Kiev

January 21, 1991

Dinner with the Pope. Today's menu of topics is varied: Gulf War; Cardinal Lubachivsky's return to Ukraine; upcoming encyclicals; *Sala Stampa* activity.

Gulf War: he is saddened by the evolution of the conflict. Saddam Hussein[1] has replied to his letter, but to no avail. His reply came on Saturday from Moscow. There they had received the message from his embassy in Iraq, via radio. The text speaks of the dignity of the Arab people.

I comment on the reactions to his intervention and the foreseeable future evolution of this war. Millions of people around the world are waiting for the Pope to continue to speak out for peace and justice.

Cardinal Lubachivsky: Lubachivsky, successor of Slipyj, leaves his Roman exile and returns to Kiev. I suggest that perhaps it is opportune that the Holy See be represented, so that this return is not interpreted in an exclusively local context. The Pope says that Colasuonno, among others, should be present; and he speaks to us about the situation, demonstrating a surprising knowledge of Ukraine, its history and the life of the Church there.

This year's agenda: two encyclicals and four trips: Portugal, Poland, Hungary and Brazil. The social encyclical will be released in April, and the one dedicated to moral issues, perhaps before or after the summer. This second encyclical—he says—will not be like the previous ones, which were documents of spiritual theology, but will have a doctrinal character.[2]

1. Saddam Hussein (Iraq, 1937–2006). Several months earlier, on August 2nd, 1990, he had invaded Kuwait claiming ancient rights over its territory. That was the origin of the first Gulf War, which officially ended on February 28, 1991.

2. The social encyclical, *Centesimus Annus,* was dated May 1st, 1991. The encyclical of a moral nature, *Veritatis Splendor,* would be published more than two years later (August 6, 1993).

We will have to prepare his presentation well, I commented. We may have to go to a European country like Germany to stir the waters and get some collaboration.

Sala Stampa: several countries have subscribed to the *VIS* service. He is pleased to know. In my opinion, we have to move from a merely reactive scheme—waiting for negative news to arrive and responding with denials—to a proactive scheme, in which the media is provided with abundant information of interest about the Church. He nods and adds: "It's like in pastoral activity. Before, it was enough for the priest to wait for the faithful and attend to them; now we have to go and look for them."

As we leave the chapel, after praying for a few minutes, as usual, I suggest he rest. "We've been skiing for a whole day!"—he tells me laughing, referring to the day they spent outside the Vatican last December.

Breakfast with Cossiga

February 4, 1991

Last Saturday, Ludovico Ortona, information advisor to the President of the Italian Republic, telephoned to invite me to breakfast today at 8:45 AM with Francesco Cossiga at the Quirinale. He asked me to send him a copy of what the Pope has been saying about the Gulf War.

The three of us had breakfast in a small room. Cossiga, friendly as always, put the question to me at the very beginning: the Pope's position on the Gulf War has put the Italian Christian Democrats in an uncomfortable situation, because the Communist Party has adopted the same position as the Pope, while they . . .

Cossiga, has elegantly described to me the curious situation of a Communist Party in favor of the Pope's position and some Christian Democrats against it, especially those in the foreground: Andreotti, as head of the government; Forlani, as president of the Christian Democrats; himself, as president of the Republic, and Rognoni, as Minister of Defense. "And couldn't the Pope at least say that Iraq should abandon Kuwait?" That would be enough for him.

The conversation lasted an hour and a half and he addressed the issues with surprising clarity: he told me that Andreotti had called him asking him to put in place the means for the Pope to make this statement. I understand his position. But I also understand—and I fully share—the Pope's position on the war.

With Maria Antonietta Macciocchi

FEBRUARY 8, 1991

Stanisław called me in the morning to see if I could accompany the writer Maria Antonietta Macciocchi, who was invited to dinner with the Pope.[3] I call Macciocchi, whom I did not know personally, and we come to an agreement. She is very excited. During the dinner we talk mainly about Albania and about the apostolic letter *Mulieris Dignitatem*, about the possibility of a book interview with the Pope.

The Eternal Manipulation

FEBRUARY 14, 1991

Yesterday there was a new bombing in Iraq. Many civilian casualties. Tremendous images on TV of charred people. The United States claims that the bombed building was a communications center of the Iraqi army. This morning Paolo Frajese called me, who presented yesterday evening's news coverage very well. I congratulate him and he tells me that Cossiga was irritated by the way the news was given, even though—Paolo tells me—they did not broadcast all the images they had, especially the most terrible ones.

I understand that these reactions may sometimes be motivated by the desire to achieve a higher good. But it saddens me that public opinion is played with in this way. It is the same as always: the presentation of information according to certain political interests.

With the Bishops of the Gulf Area

FEBRUARY 19–MARCH 6, 1991

FEBRUARY 19. This morning we made public the Pope's call for the bishops of the Gulf area, and of other countries involved, to meet in Rome to study the consequences of this war and to put in place the means to confront them.

This is very characteristic of John Paul II: the problem—the war—is still open; and yet he is already preparing how to resolve its consequences. Also

3. Maria Antonietta Macciocchi (Italy, 1922–2007) was an intellectual and journalist who was a member of the Italian Communist Party until her expulsion in the 1970s. She later joined Marco Pannella's radical party. In 1991 she met John Paul II and was fascinated by his personality. Later she dedicated a book to him, *Le donne secondo Wojtyla* (1992) [Women according to Wojtyla].

novel is the speed with which the curial machinery moves from the level of considerations to that of resolutions.

March 4. I spent most of the day in the *Sala Bologna*—in the third *loggia*[4]—following the statements of the patriarchs and bishops of the countries most directly involved in the Gulf War.

The Pope remains silent all the time. He listens attentively to the statements, prays. sometimes he looks worried. At a certain moment—perhaps because he sees me with a serious or tired face—he looks at me with an amused gesture, winking.

March 5. Dziwisz calls me in the morning: “Can you come to dinner?” “Is there a specific topic?” I ask him. He doesn’t know. I spend the rest of the day with the bishops. In the afternoon they work out the final text, drafting it in the form of a communiqué. They finish after half past seven.

At the beginning of the dinner, without dramatizing and with a humorous tone, I commented to the Pope that it would drive him crazy to know that one of the speakers had only given me a ten-line summary of his speech, which was one of the most important ones. The Pope laughs and explains to me that there has not been much time to prepare for this meeting. He then asks me how these talks might conclude. I sense that this is the “theme” of the dinner. He wants to hear new ideas and suggestions on the issue.

I tell him that, in my opinion, there is only one person in the whole world capable of attracting the attention of both the Church and the rest of the world: himself. For this reason, I suggest that he close the meeting personally and in the most solemn way possible. He could do so tomorrow, for example, during the general audience, dedicating his speech to this issue.

He agrees. Dziwisz supports the suggestion and comments that Monduzzi should be told right away, because the audience will be prepared as usual; and Tauran[5] should also be asked to prepare the speech. “Tauran,” he comments, “has told me that he works at night. So he told me.” The Pope intervenes with a humorous comment, waving his hands in denial: “Well, not me. At night, never. At night, I never work.”

---

4. A *loggia* is an open-air space or balcony that is often covered and supported by columns or arches.

5. Jean-Louis-Pierre Tauran (France, 1943–2018) was appointed Secretary for Relations with States (then Council for Public Affairs of the Church) in 1990, a position he held until 2003. That year he was made a cardinal and the Pope made him Librarian and Archivist of the Holy Roman Church and, subsequently, president of the Pontifical Council for Interreligious Dialogue (from 2007 until his death).

I add that the Pope could make a reference in the speech to a possible trip of his to Jerusalem; not announcing a new trip, but expressing his desire to make a pilgrimage to the Holy City, and there meet his Arab and Jewish brothers. He comments that, in fact, during that journey he hopes to follow the route described in the Bible. He could start in Ur, in Mesopotamia; then go to the Holy Land; pray in Jerusalem; climb Sinai; and finish in Damascus. He had already told us about this dream of his during a meal at Castelgandolfo.

6 March. Today, during the closing of the meeting of the bishops of the Gulf area and other countries involved, in the Audience Hall, the Pope expressed his desire to make a pilgrimage to the Holy Land.

We then held a press conference with Michel Sabbah, Latin Patriarch of Jerusalem;[6] Tauran; the Archbishop of Glasgow, Winning; the President of the U.S. Bishops' Conference, Pilarczyk; and another bishop from Lebanon. When Sabbah is asked about the conditions required for the Pope to make this trip, he makes it clear that the fundamental thing is peace, and that only then can he invite him to Jerusalem. Tauran intervenes to say that there has been an evolution on the part of the Holy See: it is no longer demanding a *corpus separatum* for Jerusalem—that is to say, that it be under an international regime, as the UN had requested in 1947—but only an international guarantee that would make it possible to define the peculiarity of that city because of its religious significance.

With Mieli, Director of *La Stampa*

March 11, 1991

I have lunch with Paolo Mieli,[7] who understands me when I tell him that his newspaper (*La Stampa*, of Turin) usually gives rather poor information on issues concerning the Vatican. He asks me to keep in touch with him, and to alert him to some of these issues, which he may not be aware of.

---

6. Michel Sabbah (Nazareth, 1933) was Latin Patriarch of Jerusalem from 1987 to 2008. The Latin Patriarch is, at present, the only title of the Eastern Catholic Churches that is assigned to a bishop of the Latin Church. He has jurisdiction over all the faithful of the Latin Catholic rites in Israel, the Palestinian territories, Cyprus and Jordan. He does not have jurisdiction over the Catholic faithful of the Eastern Catholic Churches living in those areas.

7. Paolo Mieli (Italy, 1946), journalist and essayist. In addition to other positions and numerous TV appearances, he was editor of *La Stampa* (1990–1992) and *Corriere della Sera* (1992–1997, 2004–2009).

Defense of Life and the Threat of Cults

April 4 to 8, 1991

From Rome, one can see the problems with a greater perspective, far from one's place of origin, where one experiences more strongly the influence of local public opinion and the burden of the problems. I was thinking about this during the extraordinary consistory, focused on the defense of life and the threat of sects, which was attended by all the cardinals. At least, all those who have been able to come: there are 112, including those over eighty years of age, who would not enter an eventual conclave.

Ratzinger's introductory report is magnificent. I think that the Pope's meeting with the cardinals stimulates them in a special way, beyond the discussions, presentations, and conclusions that can be drawn. Besides manifesting the unity of opinion, they are a kind of infusion of spirit and strength to preach the faith.

Although the Pope does not say anything during the sessions, his presence encourages all. He listens attentively to the presentations and, at certain times, discreetly prays the rosary.

Ratzinger suggests in his speech that the Bishops formally ask the Pope to write an encyclical on the defense of life. I assume this is something he has discussed with the Pope before the Consistory. The possibility is discussed and everyone is in favor of it. The French group is the only one that prefers a document of a different type, without the status of an encyclical. The question then arose as to whether, before proposing such a document, the episcopal conferences should be consulted. Full unanimity is sought in view of the seriousness of the number of abortions in the world today: between thirty and fifty-million a year.

April 6–8, Saturday. The Cardinals have decided to distribute a communiqué on what they have discussed during these days. It was prepared today by Livio Melina[8] and myself, with the help of Elio Sgreccia.[9] The wording has a firm tone. It is also extensive. The Pope makes a single addition to the text. He suggests that this idea be included: the Church does not ignore the demographic problem. We finish at 9:30 in the evening. On April 7, Sunday, we make the communiqué public, and the next day, during the press conference, it is

8. Theologian Livio Melina (Italy, 1952) was dean of the Pontifical John Paul II Institute for Studies on Marriage and the Family (2006–2016).

9. Elio Sgreccia (Italy, 1928–2019), a well-known expert in bioethics, was appointed bishop in 1992, and secretary of the Pontifical Council for the Family (1992–1996). Benedict XVI created him a cardinal in 2010. President of the Pontifical Academy for Life (2005–2008).

clear that the conclusions of this assembly touch on a human problem, not a "Catholic problem."

Asking, Asking . . .

APRIL 10, 1991

"Let's see what the *fons informationis* tells us."[10] As usual, the Pope receives me with an affectionate joke. Before going on to dinner, we visit the chapel. Today's visit is particularly long. I have the impression that, as the years go by, the Pope devotes more and more time to the Lord.

"Holy Father, tomorrow is Don Stanisław's saint's day," I comment to him as we make our way to the dining room. He tells me about this Polish saint, his martyrdom and his miracles in Krakow. St. Stanisław reminds him of Thomas Becket. The conversation then moved on to other topics.

> *Consistory in favor of life:* "The important thing," he emphasizes, "was the unanimity and the fact that the cardinals asked for a document on this issue. Some journalists have written that I seemed to hesitate before that request." He says this with an amused tone because he often has to tackle unpopular questions alone. He is glad that, in this case, his intervention was requested by "the rank and file."
>
> *Trip to Portugal.* It will focus on Fatima. I tell him that in this trip there seems to be a personal ingredient that did not exist in the previous ones. He says yes, and that alongside the personal aspect of the trip there are also "the great changes that have taken place in Eastern Europe." He considers that Our Lady's intercession has been decisive in this process; as decisive as it was during his attack. I tell him that it would be wonderful if, to underline this aspect, some bishops from the East could be in Fatima. He likes the idea.

I continue with the questions: the date of the next social encyclical, the consistory? After a while, the Pope is aware that he has been giving me information about dates and issues that he had not planned to talk about, and he comments, amused: "The director of the *Sala Stampa* keeps on asking me about one date and another, asking, asking . . ."

I think that he allows himself to be subjected to this interrogation because these conversations give him insight into some external points of view (world

10. "The source of the information."

public opinion), which complement the points of view he receives from within (from the Curia). Perhaps he wanted to confirm a personal intuition, to confirm a piece of information, or to know the position of certain media, environments, or persons.

Swiss Tensions

April 29 to May 1, 1991

April 29th. Tension, nervousness, uneasiness. The Pope's meeting with the Swiss bishops begins. The Pope has instructed me to attend all the sessions, which take place in the *Sala Bologna*. Most of the Swiss bishops have been under strong pressure in recent years from some priests and groups (deaneries, vicariates, etc.) who are asking for the resignation of Wolfgang Haas, bishop of Chur, because he maintains a pastoral line different from theirs and they reproach him for a conservative attitude.

In Rome they have tried to make them see that the "Haas case" is only the tip of an iceberg: the grave state of the Church in Switzerland from the moral and doctrinal point of view. That is the reason why the Pope summoned them to Rome; not to talk about Haas.

In the morning session, some bishops expressed their disappointment in front of the Pope, because they think that the *Haas Case* is being ignored in the program. Corecco himself, Bishop of Lugano—who has supported Haas in various matters—pointed out in his brief intervention that it is necessary to talk about Haas. The interested party, Haas, seated with them in the room, remained silent until it was his turn.

After the Haas intervention, a bishop commented that everything he said was an insult to his predecessor and to the rest of the Swiss bishops. And he calls for his resignation because, in his opinion, he has created "a pastoral problem" within the Church in Switzerland. He says that, as the parable of the good shepherd shows, the shepherd is recognized by his sheep, and since in his case the sheep do not recognize him, he cannot be considered a pastor. . .

When he finishes speaking, there is a sepulchral silence. Ratzinger makes a gesture with his hands, as if to indicate that he has gone too far. The Pope comments to Ratzinger, to take the tension away, in a very low voice, with a smile on his lips, an Italian expression that comes to say that this good bishop *is a little bit in the clouds.*

The rest of the bishops—the majority—think that something must be done, because the situation of the Church in Switzerland is close to schism. Haas' rejection is even in his own diocese: four hundred parishes deny him access and the administration of confirmation. It seems that the bishops are afraid to return to Switzerland without having solved the problem with the only solution they can envisage: the resignation of Haas.

The day ends in a very tense atmosphere.

APRIL 30. But the worst thing happened today, at the end of the morning. We have not been able to give the press the conciliatory communiqué that we had prepared in the *Sala Stampa*, because there is no way out of this conflict.

During lunch with the Pope, Cardinal Ratzinger comments that some prelates seem "to have found a scapegoat for the ills of the Swiss Church and want to sacrifice him." He refers to Haas, but does not mention his name.

The possibility of a joint communiqué is raised. Bishop Bullet says he cannot sign it. He cannot return from Rome with only a generic appeal to prayer, without anything concrete.

There is a moment when the Pope seems to want to intervene; but he does not. At times he follows the debate with the rosary in his hand. At the beginning of the afternoon session, after the prayer to the Holy Spirit, he invokes Our Lady twice, once St. Nicholas of Flüe (one of the three patron saints of Switzerland), and once all the saints.

Little by little, while the text was being drafted—which received various modifications—an agreement was reached. The bishop who had spoken most harshly against Haas asked forgiveness if he had said something that might have hurt someone. Cardinal Gantin[11] said that, since the solution to be adopted involved Haas, he should speak.

Haas speaks again. He recounts some of the events of his life, from his appointment as coadjutor (1988) to his appointment as bishop by the Pope (1990). He confesses that, at times, he has been tempted to ask the Pope for his resignation, but he has not done so because it would mean letting the Holy Father down.

In the end, to everyone's relief, the final formulation of the joint declaration was reached.

11. Bernardin Gantin (Benin, 1922–2008), at that time prefect of the Congregation for Bishops (1984–1998); later he was also dean of the College of Cardinals (1993–2002).

The Pope takes the floor and explains how he has lived these two days. Although he acknowledges that it has been the most difficult meeting he remembers in this room, his words are full of serenity. I am impressed by his reference to the supernatural order. At no time does he allude to the harsh language of these days. He tells them that the Lord will help them and that this is only a step towards the future. At the end, some bishops embrace Haas.[12]

12. Two years later, in 1993, the Pope appointed two auxiliary bishops for the diocese of Chur, hoping to pacify the situation. But the attacks from his critics continued. Even the Swiss government, intervening in the internal affairs of the Church, made a diplomatic request to the Vatican to change the bishop. In view of the situation, the Holy See decided in 1997 to create a new diocese in Vaduz, the capital of Liechtenstein, and appointed Haas, who was born there on August 7, 1948, as archbishop.

20

Conversation about Fatima

"Sempre avanti!"

May 6, 1991

While we wait to go to the dining room, I talk to Dziwisz about the Pope's upcoming trip to Poland, during which he will also visit his hometown. The Holy Father arrives and we go to the chapel, where he prays for a long time.

In the dining room, the conversation moved from one topic to another. With regard to the recent meeting with the Swiss bishops, it occurred to me to comment that one does not know where the ordinary Providence of God ends and the extraordinary begins. I thought it was going to be very difficult to arrive at a joint declaration, accepted by all, because the issues had become radicalized and moved to the personal level. But it was resolved thanks to the presence of the Holy Father because, although he did not intervene during the meeting, he was the point of reference. I try not to personalize his influence too much because I know he does not like it.

He seems happy with the result, although—he adds—the situation of the Church in Switzerland is still very complicated, partly because of the strong influence of a Protestant mentality and a way of functioning that is typical to the political structures of the country, with many committees, delegates, etc. The Pope asks me if the meeting has aroused the interest of the press. I tell him that only in Switzerland and, in part, in Germany and Austria. The mainstream media are not usually interested in such local issues.

Let's move on to the encyclical *Centesimus annus*, published a few days ago. I will give you a summary of the reports of the press. Some Americans were surprised that issues as diverse as ecology, foreign debt, capital, and interest appear organically arranged within the text, forming a unity of meaning. Many considered them to be independent of each other, like those "truths that go mad" of which Chesterton spoke.

"That is because of the anthropological approach," the Pope explains to me. I understand what he means by this: an analysis of these varied realities from the point of view of human nature helps to understand them in a unitary, harmonious, and global way.

I am surprised—and I tell you this—that there are so many favorable receptions when the Pope addresses questions of "social" moral theology and, on the contrary, so many critical responses when he speaks of "individual" moral theology. It makes me see that in "social" moral theology, the individual responsibility is as if blurred, contrary to what happens in moral questions, such as those of a sexual nature, for example. These types of questions concern each person, in his or her individuality. "In modern thought, which calls itself *humanist*," he continues, "there is this escape from man and his personal responsibility. This explains why so many are reluctant to accept the consequences of their own actions, as individuals."

I will tell you a personal anecdote: when I was studying these subjects, the experts did not know where exactly to place the so-called "Social Doctrine of the Church;" whereas nowadays it is more clearly seen that the Social Doctrine of the Church is a part of Moral Theology.

He tells me that he became aware of this when he was teaching at the seminary in Krakow, and that he learned it from Piwowarczyk, a professor of his who was editor-in-chief of *Tygodnyk Powszechny*. He studied these questions in that professor's typed notes, which he still reviews from time to time. "Social doctrine" used to be regarded as something that went on its own. He had the good fortune to have to study, in order to teach them in class, two areas of which he was unfamiliar: the phenomenology of Max Scheller and the social doctrine of the Church. That in-depth study, he tells me, enriched him greatly.

He then talks about the upcoming trip to Portugal. At the end, I show him the project of the book on his person and pontificate that is being prepared by *Novosti*, a publishing house of the Soviet Union. He likes the idea and, above all, that it is entitled precisely "Love and Responsibility," like his well-known book dedicated to human love.

Apropos a comment by Dziwisz, I mention to him an article by the sociologist Francesco Alberoni in the weekly *Panorama* entitled *Dopo Wojtyla, nulla* ("After Wojtyla, nothing"). I would have liked to show it to him. The thesis is that the current prestige of the Pope covers up and hides the situation of lack of faith in the Church; and that, as soon as this pontificate ends, the Church will begin to fade out, almost in a phase of extinction. It is a sad vision, which shows a great lack of hope. The Pope says nothing. Dziwisz closes the subject by affirming that Providence elevates the right people at the right time.

After leaving the dining room, the Pope goes, as always, to the chapel. I accompany him. He remains praying, on his knees, for a long time. Before finishing, he says to me: "*Sempre avanti*" (*Always go forward!*). It is as if he is encouraging me to continue my work, in spite of the fatigue or the little encouragement that these tasks can sometimes produce. And Dziwisz seems to confirm this when he tells me, as we leave: "Many years working with the successor of Peter and then, heaven." And I leave thinking that the Pope never ceases to surprise me.

On the Secret of Fatima

MAY 10–14, 1991

We returned last night from the trip to Portugal, the Pope's second to that country, and the second also to thank Our Lady for her intercession during the attack of May 13, 1981. The stops: Lisbon, Azores, Madeira and Fatima.

MAY 10, LISBON. On the first day, during the Mass in Lisbon, some Timorese boys raised banners saying that Timor was suffering and that human rights were being violated there.

MAY 11, AZORES ISLANDS. The radical press headlined on the front page: "The Pope forgets Timor again."

During the flight to the Azores, I told the Pope about this news and suggested a possible interview with Aura Miguel, a journalist from *Radio Rinascenza* who was on the plane. It seemed appropriate to him to do so. When Aura asked him about Timor, he gave her an exhaustive answer: during his homily in Lisbon he mentioned Indonesia because Portugal's apostolic activity was not only limited to East Timor. He added that the political solution to Timor's problems was a matter for the UN and that, for his part, he had asked that the people of Timor be able to preserve their cultural, linguistic, and religious identity.

As usual, the Pope's presence drew out the faith of the people in all its strength and spontaneity, in full view of everyone. He celebrated Mass on the Island of Terceira, in the Azores, and in the afternoon he went to the Island of Ponta Delgada.

MAY 12, MADEIRA. The press picked up the Pope's words on Timor and the matter was not discussed again. He celebrated Mass in Funchal, Madeira.

FATIMA. Naturally, the center of the trip was Fatima, where we arrived for the Marian vigil. The esplanade of Fatima was crowded, with thousands of candles that illuminated the night: the press spoke of a million people. The Pope went to the *Capelinha*, and there he remained on his knees, praying intensely, while the five mysteries of the rosary and the litanies were prayed. After the transfer of the image of the Virgin to the altar, he entered the Shrine and prayed before the tombs of Francisco and Jacinta.

In his greeting to the pilgrims, he recalled the visit that the image of Our Lady of Fatima made to St. Peter's Basilica on March 25, 1984, for the consecration of the world that was celebrated in the square.

May 13, Fatima. Anniversary of the apparitions. The Pope celebrated Mass on the esplanade and blessed the sick with the Blessed Sacrament. Before the Mass, at 8:30 AM, Sr. Lúcia arrived, accompanied by another Carmelite.[1] Immediately the Pope came and greeted her. They took a picture at the door of the chapel and talked alone for twelve minutes. Then the other Carmelite and the Bishop of Leiria came in and they continued talking for another ten minutes. When I entered the room, Sister Lucia was handing the Pope a rosary and a book of photographs of reproductions of Our Lady of Fatima. The Pope said to her twice, as he said goodbye, "Let us pray together." We returned to Rome in the evening.

President Mário Soares has attended all the Masses celebrated by the Pope. For some, he was only seeking to appear next to a popular figure. I prefer not to make rash judgments: the fact is that he was there. Others said it was the first time Soares had visited Fatima. I do not know. The fact, again, is that he was in Fatima.

I discovered among the authorities Gennady Gerasimov, who was Gorbachev's spokesman for years and with whom I had participated in a TV program on spokesmen. He is now Moscow's ambassador in Lisbon. I went over to greet him.

May 14. Rome. As happens to me when we return late at night, I was still sleeping when I was told to go to lunch with the Pope. Along with the two secretaries, there are Sepe, Agnes, and myself. The conversation revolves around the trip, and touches on some episodes in the history of Portugal. Suddenly, Dziwisz suggests:

---

1. Lucia de Jesus Rosa dos Santos (Portugal, 1907–2005) was ten years old when, together with her cousins Jacinta and Francisco, she declared that the Virgin Mary had appeared to them several times, between May 13 and October 13, 1917, in the Cova da Iria. The sanctuary was erected there, after the Church certified the validity of the apparitions.

—"Holy Father, perhaps it would be time to tell us what you talked about with Lucia and what is the third secret of Fatima."[2]

There is an expectant silence. The Pope begins to speak:

"Lúcia told me about the pressures she receives from many people. They ask her to tell them what Our Lady told her in Fatima. They are people who go there out of simple curiosity, and she, in conscience, cannot go beyond the norms given to her by her superiors."

"It's a curiosity similar to Ali Agca's, when I went to see him and he asked me, 'What's this Fatima thing, why didn't you die when I shot you?'"

"As for the third secret," he says, smiling, "we do not know what it is. . . . At the beginning of my pontificate, Villot brought me all the documentation, and I read it for the first time."

Dziwisz notes: "And he read it again at the Gemelli." The Pope nods: he almost didn't remember.

"The central problem," he continued, "was to elucidate what the 'consecration of Russia' consisted of. I remember that at some public hearings there were groups—of Americans, above all—who shouted at me: '*Consecrate Russia to the Blessed Heart of Our Lady! Consecrate* Russia to the Blessed Heart of Our Lady! Consecrate her!'"

"My predecessors, since Pius XII, had made a consecration, but it was not clear if that was what Our Lady had asked for."

"Sister Lúcia was asked the same question and wrote to me. But we didn't know what exactly 'Russia' meant: the Tsar's empire? Ethnic Russia? Soviet Russia?"

"A few years later, in March 1984, the consecration was made and we asked all the bishops of the world to join in it. I was very happy to learn that the Patriarch of Moscow had joined in that consecration."

He remains silent. After a few seconds I ask her if Sister Lucia thinks that Our Lady's promise—the conversion of Russia—has already been fulfilled.

---

2. From the apparitions of Fatima, the visionaries—Lucia, Jacinta, and Francisco—collected three messages of the Virgin, which were considered to be of a premonitory nature. The first two, revealed by Lucia in 1941, referred to the Russian Revolution and World War II, respectively. The third was kept by the Pope in a sealed envelope until John Paul II decided to make it public in 2000. It is related to the persecution of Christians. As—like the previous ones—its understanding is neither immediate nor univocal, the Pope wanted it to be published together with a commentary by the then Cardinal Ratzinger.

"Sister Lúcia," he answers, "knows that now there is freedom in Russia to live one's religion. But we don't know how to understand the word 'conversion.'"

At the end of lunch, the Pope goes to the chapel and remains kneeling for a very long time. Sepe, Agnes, and I accompany him in silence, as do his two secretaries.

After a while, Dziwisz whispers in my ear: "Thu says that probably the Pope is not aware that you are still here." We continue to pray. When the Pope gets up and sees us, he apologizes, telling us that he had forgotten about us. His heart and mind—I am convinced—are still in Fatima.

Various *RAI* Projects

May 27, 1991

I go to lunch at *RAI* with Gianni Pasquarelli, CEO, accompanied by Sergio Zavoli and Gustavo Selva. A very cordial lunch. We spend the whole time talking about the Pope. Zavoli and Selva are preparing two different programs: Selva, on the fall of communism; Zavoli, a series on the impact of John Paul II on our times, with the judgments of personalities of the time. Both asked me to have the Pope participate in these programs. We talked about what this participation would be and I told them to send me a report on the format of the programs, so that I could study it.

Poland

June 1–9, 1991

We have returned from Poland. An intense trip. A different atmosphere from the three previous ones: it is the first time that the Pope visits his country freed from State Marxism. Latent problems that had been silenced by the previous political and social situation are surfacing. The Poles are faced with the challenge of rebuilding their legislation from the ground up, including the constitution.

Certain sectors of the press seem interested in spreading the image of a de-Christianized and materialistic Poland, despite the high rate of religious and priestly vocations and the evident religiosity of so many Poles.

The Pope has spoken in his homilies about the Ten Commandments. Some of them struck me as particularly accurate. He often improvised: in his homilies, at the end of Mass and in the addresses he gave after lunches in the seminaries where we have been residing.

June 2. Koszalin. During the Mass, a banner is raised among the people, reading, in Russian and Polish, "Moscow is waiting for you." At the end of the Mass, the Pope tells them that the Bishop of Moscow, Tadeusz Kondrusiewicz, was also there. This was a way of implying that he would go when the bishop's invitation reached him, which would mean that the obstacles currently holding up such a visit would have been overcome.

I discover in the Pope's texts a kind of intimate symphony, an inner coherence when it comes to explaining what should be the social and political foundations for the construction of a society that truly respects man. There are some basic concepts, such as the freedom-truth binomial; the neutrality of the State in the face of ideological questions; the defense of life; ecumenism and the Christian roots of Europe.

June 4. Radom. During the Mass celebrated at Warsaw's Radom airport, he delivers a great homily, clear and didactic, on the fifth commandment. After recalling the great wars and massacres of the 20th century: "To this cemetery of victims of human cruelty in our century, another cemetery is added: *the cemetery of the unborn,* the cemetery of the defenseless, whose face is unknown even to their own mother . . ."

June 6. In Wroclawek he recalled the itinerary of his formation, when he returned from Brussels and was preparing his thesis on St. John of the Cross, already finished, to be published in Poland.

July 9. We return to Rome. The Pope arrives at the cortile of San Damaso, next to the Papal Apartments, at about ten o'clock in the evening. "We are expecting you tomorrow at lunchtime," Dziwisz says to me as we say goodbye.

Rome, June 10. Mario Agnes, Tadeusz, and I are with the Pope and his secretaries. Thu tells me that the Pope celebrated Mass a short while ago and that they found themselves with almost thirty kilos of documents to dispatch. They have been sorting through the material all morning before passing it on to him.

During lunch, the Pope says it has been a more restful trip than his first to Poland: he has slept well every day, except the last night in Warsaw; and he has managed his strength better.

He mentions his conversations with Walesa and, speaking of the crisis in Europe, alludes again to the Christian roots of the continent: "Certain Europeans reason like this: 'We can accept God, but Jesus Christ, no. We are autonomous and we will build the world in our own image and likeness.'"

And he recalls the meetings he has had with Russians, Belarusians, Lithuanians, and Ukrainians during this trip.

At the end of the lunch, he commented that Poland does not have to beg to join Europe, because *Poland is Europe,* and has maintained the Christian roots of the European continent, when these roots have been disappearing from other countries.

He frequently refers to "mi tierra," "my land," "my homeland." He is neither utopian nor unrooted; he recognizes his origin and loves it.

21

Vacanze di lavoro "Vacation From Work"

Back in Aosta Valley

July 10–19, 1991

This summer I also accompanied the Pope for several days of rest in the mountains.

July 10, Wednesday. We leave by helicopter from the Vatican at five o'clock in the afternoon. We arrive at Ciampino and a Gulfstream aircraft of the *Aeronautica Militare* takes us to Turin. Then, in another helicopter, to Combes, in the Aosta Valley. The usual "team": Dziwisz, Gugel, Cibin, Styczeń, Sabato, and myself. Upon arrival, a group of journalists tries to interview the Pope, who replies: "Ask Navarro."

When we got home, I was interested to know what he wanted me to say to the press, and he told me that these days of rest were not going to be *dolce far niente*:[1] "I have brought the text of the encyclical on morals to work on it.[2] Then, I have to prepare for the trip to Hungary, with that very difficult language that I have to practice. And the meeting with the young people in Czestochowa awaits us."

I transmit these ideas to the journalists. The next day, the headlines announce: "*Vacanze di lavoro;*" "*Non sará un dolce far niente.*"

On this occasion we left for the mountain a little later than in other years, at about a quarter past ten in the morning, because the Pope works from very early in the morning until that time, probably on the drafting of the future encyclical. He also works for a while after dinner.

July 11, Thursday. First outing. Pleasant excursion of a few hours. We return around 6:30 in the evening. Dziwisz is taking very seriously the advice of the

1. Catchphrase: "a nice to do nothing."

2. As already mentioned, it refers to the future *Veritatis Splendor*.

doctor Buzzonetti, who has told him that the Pope must be given rest, avoiding extraordinary efforts. We climb to lower altitudes and make frequent breaks in the hikes so that the Pope can sit down and rest for a while.

Today we climbed up to the Valgrisenche: Leitin, Mocossonei, Boreigne—at about 2,000 meters, Provenze and Pileo. On the way out I went ahead with another car to wait for the group from the summit. When I arrived, Marinelli told me that the Pope had asked for me on the way out, so I decided to walk down to meet him. When he saw me he told me that he wanted to talk to me soon after. As he was wearing the white cassock, I took the opportunity to take some pictures of him, as he always prefers to appear in photos dressed like that.

I approach at lunchtime, around two o'clock. Tadeusz and Dziwisz were with us. He asked me about the consequences of the recent statements made by Claudio Martelli, the Socialist deputy prime minister of the Italian government, who accused him a few days ago in the press of interfering in social matters "that do not fall within his competence."

He reminds me that, during the trip to Poland, I commented to him that some aspects of his message (such as the neutrality of the State or the defense of life) had a significant influence on the rest of Europe. He wonders if Martelli's attack could be a response? Is Martelli the loudspeaker of some intellectuals who oppose his message?

I express my point of view with a certain vehemence: it seems to me that Martelli's words have no connection whatsoever with his message in Poland. Moreover, I do not foresee any attack against the Pope for his defense of life: Western governments have come to the conclusion that it is not possible to govern without ethical references; and at this moment there is none stronger and clearer than the one that marks this pontificate. I would also add that Martelli, with his attack on the Pope, has stepped out of the official line of his party. Almost everyone has criticized him and he has become an "isolated voice."

The subject of the press in Poland comes up: as the most influential newspaper in the country is currently of a radical nature, he thinks it is possible that it will be attacked in the future for ideological reasons. I tell him that the Polish press is at the moment, in fact, in Western hands and that the owners of these media are more likely to be driven by economic rather than ideological interests.

We are talking about the United States, a country, today, less ideological than the Europeans. Some Americans currently feel somewhat alienated from the Pope because of his opposition to the Gulf War. For this reason, I suggest to him that perhaps during his next trip to Poland, at the inauguration of *Project HOPE*, a children's hospital built by the Americans, he could make a gesture of sympathy towards them. He says he will do so sincerely and jokes that he finds my optimistic outlook comforting. And, as if to show he has no worries, he tells me at the end of lunch that he is going to "try to sleep."

I think he succeeds, although only for about twenty minutes. He has brought two books with him to pray and read on the mountain: the breviary and a biography in Polish of Angela Salawa (1881–1922), a lay woman who worked all her life as a domestic servant, whom he will beatify in Krakow's Market Square next August.

July 12, Friday. I did not go on an excursion with the Pope. I spent the day talking to the journalists in Introd, where I told them some anecdotes of these days along with biographical details that can help them understand his figure in greater depth: most of the correspondents who follow us do not usually deal with the Pope and the Holy See.

July 13, Saturday. The information about the Pope in the press is quite good.

July 14, 1991, Sunday. The Pope carried out various pastoral activities in the diocese of Susa: Mass with the beatification of Eduardo Rosaz (1830–1903), who was bishop of the city and a close friend of Don Bosco; a meeting with young people and nuns—to whom he left his pectoral cross—and a visit to the unique *Sacra di San Michele,* an ancient abbey dedicated to the archangel on the summit of Mount Pirchiriano. It was a Benedictine convent, now run by the Rosminians.

The helicopter tries to land on the summit; it does not succeed and we end up on a soccer field in a nearby town. Surprise and joy of the people. Radio calls for cars to come and pick us up, until we finally leave for the convent. From there, late in the afternoon, we set off back to Les Combes. The helicopter dances so much in the wind that we seriously think about landing in Aosta. Finally we arrive home. I see this interruption of the rest as an inconvenience. But it is clear that the Pope is not only interested in his rest.

July 15, 16, and 17. New excursions. Long conversations with Tadeusz, an acute philosopher, a very intelligent and lucid man; at times, I perceive touches of pessimism due to the environmental difficulties he encounters in the field of German theology, which he knows so well.

Tuesday dawns with bad weather, but no matter. We set off for the *Vallone di Comboé,* and ascend a steep slope following the course of a stream with beautiful waterfalls. It is raining heavily. When we reach the top, we come out onto a meadow surrounded by trees and between them there is a wooden cross formed by two simple unpolished tree trunks. The Pope approaches as soon as he sees it. He takes off his cap and prays with his head down. He is alone. Behind him, Don Alberto Carreggio stops. I approach, pray there and take some pictures without the Pope noticing. He continues praying. He seems to move away, but he comes back. He rests a hand on the cross. Time passes. We leave him alone.

July 18, Wednesday. We walk from Val de Rhennes to Alpeggio Feleuma, situated at about 2,000 meters. When we get to the top there is a family who knows that the Pope is having lunch very close to them, but they do not approach until we invite them to greet him, if they wish. They all come: Emidio Martin, with his wife, Yvonne; his son Aurelio; his seventy-two-year-old mother in law, Anselmina Sanchez; and a Moroccan employee, Mustafa Thiriri, whom they call Stefano. The Pope greets them and gives a rosary to each one. Mustafa-Stefano asks for another one for his wife, who lives in Marrakesh.

In the evening the Pope comes to dine with everyone and recalls the parish in Krakow—St. Stanislaus of Kostka—run by the Salesians, where he used to go in 1938, "when I began studying at the university."[3] There he went to confession and attended Mass. "At that time I was a worker and, since I had the afternoon shift, I could go to Mass in the morning. I remember—I am still seeing it—that one day, when I went to church, I was told that the Nazis had taken all the Salesians from the parish to a concentration camp. Some did not return. In that parish I made the definitive decisions in my life: the priestly vocation, the priestly ordination."

At the end, we sang a happy song, typical of mountain excursions.

July 19, Thursday. Last day of rest. The Pope moves to Cervinia to celebrate Holy Mass. Incredible panorama at the foot of the Matterhorn. During the homily he refers to these days of rest, "which have passed in a state of serenity and of prayer for the whole Church," "freed from daily tasks."

---

3. In June 1938 he entered the Faculty of Philosophy and Letters at the Jagiellonian University in Krakow. He wanted to study Polish philology, and went to live in that city with his father, the only person left in his family. But he was only able to attend classes for one year, because at the end of the summer of the following year World War II broke out. Poland was invaded, the university was closed, and he had no choice but to go to work in a stone quarry for the chemical company Solvay.

Back in the helicopter, he heads to Les Combes to visit the small chapel of St. Laurent. At the door of the church, the whole village is waiting for him: about fifteen people. He enters, prays before the altar, and as he leaves, he says to them some words that he has often repeated during these days: "Deo gratias." I read in the church a beautiful ejaculation to the Virgin: "*Vous, qui avez souffert pour nous, ayez pitié de nous.*"[4]

We return that same afternoon to Rome. A small breakdown in the helicopter delayed our departure. Already on the plane, I sit next to Dziwisz, who says to me in a low voice: "I thank you for everything you have done for the Pope during these days." When I want to interrupt him, he continues: "especially for the heart you have put into it." "Ah, if it is for the heart, then yes." This time, I think about it, but I don't say it.

4. "You who have suffered for us, have mercy on us."

22

Knowing the Obstacles

In his Hometown

August 13 to 20, 1991

August 13, Tuesday. Trip to Poland and Hungary. We leave at eight o'clock in the morning. President Walesa waits in Krakow for the Pope, who then goes to the cemetery—located about ten kilometers away—to pray at the tomb of his parents and his brother.

The entourage does not arrive at the cemetery. The Pope enters alone, accompanied by Macharski and Dziwisz; I also enter and I see that there is a small group of people waiting for him there: a few nuns, a small choir, and several journalists. One asks the Pope about the influence his father—who died on March 18, 1941—had on his life.

"He had a great influence," he says, "because after my mother's death, he played the role of father and mother. He was a profound man, very religious, who taught me the mystery of the infinite majesty of God."

—"Do you have any memories of him?"

"Sometimes at night, when I wake up and it takes me a while to fall asleep, I remember that sometimes he would get up in the night and start praying."

Krakow. Beatification of Angela Salawa: "I have prayed so many times before her relics that these words of hers have remained deeply engraved in my mind and in my heart: 'Lord, I live because you want me to live; I will die when you want me to; save me because you can do it.'"

The Pope celebrated the Eucharist for the first time in that square. Until now, the authorities had prevented him from doing so; some say, jokingly, that they prevented him because of a popular Polish proverb "he who reigns in that square, reigns in Poland."

In the evening, in the bishop's residence, which was his home for years, he received some friends: about thirty people. Then, he meets with two hundred more, mostly relatives of the girls and boys to whom he gave spiritual direction when he was parochial vicar of San Floriano, with whom he organized excursions to the mountains and other activities.

AUGUST 14, WEDNESDAY. WADOWICE. Mass for the dedication of the parish church of St. Peter the Apostle. He lunches with the fifteen priests of his class and greets his schoolmates who are still alive: kisses, hugs, and uncontainable joy. Some kneel down to greet him: his friend Karol is the Pope!

CZESTOCHOWA. Thousands of young people participating in the 6th World Youth Day have been waiting for him in the vicinity of Czestochowa since early afternoon. The press is spreading the word that there are a million of them. In reality, there is no way of knowing the exact number. Young people from Western and Eastern Europe are coming together for the first time for a World Youth Day of this kind. During the opening greeting, the Pope highlights this reality and proposes a goal: "May Europe seek unity for its future and for the good of the whole human family; and return to its Christian roots. These roots are to be found both in the West and in the East."

The young Spaniards are noted for their vitality: shouts, cheers, and songs. The Pope jokes with them. Dziwisz tells me at the end: "They have been good because they have animated the meeting." In the evening I go to pray before the Black Madonna.

THURSDAY, AUGUST 15. *The* act of consecration of all the young people of the world to the Virgin Mary is taking place in Czestochowa. I attended the Mass celebrated by some of the entourage in the chapel of Our Lady and then I met with journalists. In the afternoon the Pope received the members of the theological congress held at the Catholic University of Lublin.

AUGUST 16, FRIDAY. HUNGARY. The Pope celebrated Mass this morning in the chapel of Jasna Gora before leaving for Hungary.

During the plane trip, going through the texts, I realize that in the Pope's speech in the cathedral of Esztergom, there is no reference to Cardinal Mindszenty. I tell Dziwisz about it and he talks to the Pope. At the end, Re is asked to add a paragraph to the speech in which the cardinal is mentioned.

Shortly after we arrive at the "Ferihegy" airport. The Pope kisses Hungarian soil and greets the President. "I come to confirm in the faith the brothers and sisters who belong to the Church, and to offer all Hungarians a Christian vision of the world," he says in his opening address.

The reception may seem cold, but only in appearance. It is the fruit of recent history. The people are responding to forty years of Marxism and official atheism. This means that Catholics in this nation of great Catholic tradition are now few in number, even though a multitude of people came to greet the Pope in front of the Palace of Parliament.

August 19, Monday. Coup d'État in Moscow. The news reaches me that there has been a coup d'état in Moscow and a restriction of movement has been imposed on Gorbachev. I tell the Pope about it and pass it on to the journalists.

Once again, I am faced with an occupational hazard: I have to report something about which I have no more information than the brief communiqué from Moscow, which speaks of Gorbachev's unspecified illness. The journalists, of course, want to know more, but I have no other sources. All I can do is wish the Russian leader an immediate and complete recovery.

We return to the capital in the afternoon. The Pope is meeting with young people in the so-called People's Stadium. In the meantime I go to the hotel to see if they have more information in Rome. I speak with Tauran.

In the evening, during dinner, a text on the Russian question is prepared with Re to be proposed to the Pope.

August 20, Tuesday. In the morning, at the nunciature, the Pope is shown the draft of the possible text: he agrees and approves it. The Pope reads this text at the end of the Mass he celebrates in Heroes' Square in Budapest:

> In the face of the news coming from the Soviet Union (he says, in a grave and serene tone), our prayer becomes more intense to ask God to deliver that great country from new tragedies. I trust in prayer that the efforts that have been made in recent years to give voice and dignity to the whole of society will not be jeopardized. I pleasantly recall the meetings I have had with President Gorbachev on the two occasions he has come to visit me. I have appreciated in him, in a singular way, the sincere will that guides him and the high inspiration that animates him in the promotion of the rights of man and his dignity, seeking the good of his country and of the international community. May the process he has initiated continue.
>
> And you, dear Hungarian brothers, be aware of the great fortune that the freedom you have irreversibly conquered represents for your future. May you know how to appreciate and live in this freedom!

People applaud when he refers to Gorbachev and freedom in Hungary.

These are words that, to my surprise, have an extraordinary diffusion in the Italian and international press, because they imply that the Pope considers this something fleeting that it will pass in a few days.[1]

We return to Rome in the afternoon.

AUGUST 21, WEDNESDAY. Lunch with the Pope at Castelgandolfo, with the trip as a background theme. He has comes from Rome this very morning, after the general audience, and he looks relaxed: he wears slippers of Polish craftsmanship and a white cassock, without a cape or pectoral. When he sees me, he says to me with humor: "I look very inelegant like this."

I ask him about his "relatives:" the group of people with the surname Wojtyla that he greeted in Wadowice. "In reality," he tells me, "there are no living relatives left, except for a second cousin, quite elderly, who was unable to attend."

During the conversation, someone alludes to the Pope's chapel at Castelgandolfo. The subject had already come up at another dinner some time ago. I say I have not seen it. It is near the dining room and when we finish lunch the Pope shows it to us, acting as *cicerone,* explaining the details of the two paintings. On the left wall, a painting depicts the Miracle of Vistula. On the right, another canvas evokes the defense of Chestochowa against the Swedish troops. Pius XI, who had been nuncio in Warsaw, commissioned the paintings.

On our way out, led by Dziwisz, we passed through some of the rooms of Castelgandolfo, including the dining room used by the popes until Paul VI, who was the first pontiff to start using the current smaller dining room.

With Communicators

OCTOBER 4, 1991

I am participating in a luncheon colloquium in Madrid, invited by the "Club de la Comunicación." They are a group of executives from various companies, working in the external communication or marketing sectors. We start at 2:30 PM and adjourn at 6:30 PM. It is a long time, but I see that people are interested in the topics. I start with some professional references about the *Sala Stampa,* but immediately the attention is focused on the Pope: the reasons for his trips, some central questions of his magisterium, etc. There is a lot of interest and little information.

---

1. As it was [Author's Note].

Spain: Dialogue or Not

October 7, 1991

The two secretaries and I joined the Pope for dinner. We return to an issue we discussed last July. At the moment, the Pope notes, many European governments are Socialist, and some socialists have made negative comments in recent months about the Pope's preaching.

As this comment invites me to express my point of view, I say that at present European socialism is not homogeneous, and it is a rather de-ideologized socialism, especially on issues such as private property, economy, etc. Certainly, many are bothered by the Church's continued defense of life and many of its teachings, but they do not attack it head-on because they know it would not be popular.

Before dinner, I went to the Quirinale to see President Cossiga. The press had published an unfortunate comment of his about the Pope, and I called Ludovico Ortona this morning to clarify this. He immediately told me that the president wanted to see me, and we arranged to meet for tea at five o'clock. In reality, Cossiga did not mean what was published. His press office would later write a note: "What is attributed to him, as recorded by the newspapers, does not reflect the thinking of the head of state who nurtures an affection, etc.". I see that the Pope was not at all concerned about this matter.

Brazil

October 12 to 21, 1991

October 12. Second visit of the Pope to Brazil. During the press conference on the outbound trip, a journalist remarked—referring to the opinion of a bishop—that liberation theology no longer makes sense, after the fall of Marxism in Europe. The Pope's answer seemed to me to be very clarifying: "liberation theology rooted in Marxism does not make sense, which is what the Pope criticized, but another non-Marxist liberation theology still makes sense."

What was to be a long and tiring trip, in sweltering heat, had an unusual prelude: at the press conference, one of the journalists sang Schubert's "Ave Maria" to the Pope in Polish, before the astonished gaze of the rest.

October 13. Natal. Meeting with the bishops at the Congress Center. Many things have happened since their first trip. A Salesian priest, who works in the Mission of Mato Grosso, tells me that some bishops have downplayed the spiritual, and this has left a vacuum in these people, who have a deep religious sense and expect to be told about Jesus Christ. Political-social reflections, by themselves, do not fulfill their aspirations. And a considerable number have gone to the sects, which are experiencing a much greater growth than some people think.

OCTOBER 16. CUIABÁ. Today marks the thirteenth anniversary of his election as Pope. There is no celebration; in fact, the date coincides with the hardest day of the trip: unbearable heat, high humidity, continuous displacements. After his meeting with the representatives of the indigenous communities, he meets with thousands of young people in the sports palace. It is an enclosed area and the ambient temperature is similar to the degree of enthusiasm with which he is received.

OCTOBER 17. CAMPO GRANDE. "No person is a single verse. We compose together the same divine poem, which God writes with the help of our freedom," he says to the lepers at the Hospital São Julião. We return late at night and the first thing the Pope does when he arrives is to celebrate a second Mass, accompanied by the local bishop.

OCTOBER 18–21. The intense rhythm continues in various cities. Mass for the beatification of Mother Pauline. Ecumenical meeting in Florianópolis. Meeting with religious sisters. Mass in the archdiocese of Vitoria. Visit to the favela do Lixâo de São Pedro. Address to the children of Brazil in Salvador de Bahia. Meeting with the world of culture. . . .

OCTOBER 22ND. During the return trip, the Pope holds this peculiar press conference on the heights. Tiredness is also evident on the faces of the journalists. We arrive in Rome late at night; before saying goodbye, Dziwisz summons me for tomorrow.

OCTOBER 23RD. When I arrived at the Papal apartment, I discovered that Dziwisz had called me several times during the course of the day to tell me that there would be no dinner because the Pope was not feeling well: intestinal problems. I have dinner with him, Thu, and Dr. Buzzoneti, who has come to attend to the Pope. It seems to be a passing thing.

OCTOBER 24. The Pope has already recovered. I return for dinner, which revolves around the trip to Brazil. I have developed my own hypothesis, assimilating what I have read, seen, and experienced during these days. I am trying to understand what has happened in the Catholic Church of this great country.

For some time—I think—there has prevailed, in the teachings of the ecclesiastics, what we could call "scandal of sensitivity," fruit of the impact produced by the terrible poverty in which so many Brazilians live, a consequence of the enormous social inequalities. This has led, in some cases, to a loss of strength, genuineness and preeminence in the proclamation of the faith.

Then, in view of the disagreements with Rome, a particular ecclesiology has been developed, which is presented as "the project of the Brazilian church." This has given rise to a conflict that still persists. But it seems that a new line of action is gaining strength which, together with the necessary attention to the serious social problems, seeks to satisfy the people's thirst for God: it is the new evangelization, the theme of the future general assembly of CELAM, which brings together all the bishops of Latin America.

Bush with the Pope

November 8, 1991

Visit of President George H. W. Bush. This time I know the topics that could come up in the audience with the Pope, since in the previous days the US ambassador and others from the White House "advance team" have visited the office.

I prepare an outline of a possible press release and show it to Sodano. It looks good to him. At the end of the audience, I read it to the Pope. He changes a word and tells me that one of the topics mentioned has not been discussed. The general tone of the press the following day seems to me to be correct.

On Vatican Radio

November 13, 1991

I am going to give a conference at Vatican Radio at the invitation of Father Lombardi.[2] It was a refresher seminar for radio journalists, in an atmosphere of great cordiality. Tucci comes to greet me, since we practically only see each other on the Pope's trips, even though we work only a few hundred meters away from each other. Paradoxes of Roman life.

2. Federico Lombardi (Italy, 1942), was provincial of the Jesuits in Italy, director of programs and director general of Vatican Radio, and director general of the Vatican Television Center. He succeeded Navarro-Valls as director of the Vatican *Sala Stampa* (2006–2016). President of the Joseph Ratzinger Foundation.

At the Spanish Embassy

November 23, 1991

Lunch at the Spanish Embassy with Queen Sofia, who has come to participate in the VI International Conference on Drugs and Alcoholism organized by Cardinal Angelini.[3]

The Cardinal invited me last night to another dinner at the *Columbus Hotel* with Queen Sofia. This morning I participated in the round table on prevention, from the point of view of public opinion. Several people I already knew participated, such as the president of the International Olympic Committee, Juan Antonio Samaranch, and the expert in family education, Rafael Pich.

Heads and Tails

November 25, 1991

As usual, when I go to dinner with the Holy Father and his secretaries, he makes a joke before I begin. Today he said to me:

—"Thu gets very happy every time he comes to dine with us. What do they say in *Sala Stampa*?"
—"Holiness, it is said that the Pope works a lot."

He smiles and suggests that we talk about the media and its influence on society. I tell him that I was happy to read the book *Karol Wojtyla,* by Luca di Schiena: it is a good book, based on press reports, which indicates that many media offer quality information.

There is no united front. We return to a conversation we had this summer in *Val d'Aosta* regarding the criticisms from some socialists of the Pope's preaching.

I restate my opinion on the non-existence of a "united front" and add that the pontificate's message is getting through to public opinion. Many people—and also some governments—realize that it is necessary to have ethical principles, and the ones that are being proclaimed most forcefully are those proclaimed by the Church.

Spain. Referring to the recent *ad limina* visit of the Spanish bishops, he comments that in their reports they speak of a constant aggression, from the media,

3. Cardinal Fiorenzo Angelini (Italy, 1916–2014) was at that time president of the Pontifical Council for the Pastoral Care of Health Care Workers (1985–96).

against life and the stability of the family. I try to complete this picture, adding that there are also other elements, such as the high percentage of Spanish gynecologists who have declared themselves conscientious objectors to abortion.

Continuing with the thread of the conversation, he comments that in Poland there are also some who try to corner the Church in the sacristies.

Listening to him, I discover that his questions are not the result of a fear of difficulties: he wants to analyze the possible obstacles in order to respond to them adequately.

Synod of Europe. The Pope says that Kondruciewicz, apostolic administrator of Moscow, is discovering many more Catholics than he expected: in Moscow alone there are about fifty-thousand. That is the reason why his see must be in Moscow, and not in St. Petersburg.

How will the synod proceed? "When I announced it, I felt compelled to convene it. I don't know if now though, with the difficulties in Yugoslavia, I will be able to do it."

I would add that it seems likely to me that the bishops of the East will speak their sufferings of the past and those of the West the difficulties encountered by the Church today. Those difficulties are obvious, but today's world also presents a number of encouraging features, which perhaps the Pope could mention. In so-called "modernity" there are, along with certain confusions, many positive values.

As I say goodbye, I ask him if he is sleeping well. "Normally, yes; although it depends . . ." and he points outside. I don't know if he's referring to the seasonal weather changes or to deeper issues.

As I make my way out of the apartment, I ask Thu what the Pope usually does at this time of day. He tells me that he spends time first of all browsing through some Polish newspaper; then he reads some essay (he has just finished, for example, a book by the Archbishop of Paris, Lustiger) and later he reviews the texts of the next day's speeches. He goes to bed around eleven o'clock.

23

"It's the Church, not the Pope"

Three days in Vienna

February 1, 1992

I am in Vienna from January 29–31, at the invitation of Erich Leitenberger of the *Kathpress* agency, to give a lecture to journalists on the occasion of the feast of the patron saint, St. Francis de Sales. I also took the opportunity to reciprocate an invitation extended to me years ago by the Austrian government. Leitenberger and a government interpreter accompanied me for three days.

I had lunch in Vienna with Cardinal König, Archbishop Lázsló of the Eisenstadt diocese and some government officials. I was able to talk with the Minister of Education and President Waldheim. It was an intense trip: Mass celebrated by Cardinal Groër, a visit to Graz, etc. A program to which was added at the last minute a meeting with the editors at the *Kathpress* and, at my request, a visit to Viktor Frankl,[1] who received me with great cordiality.

It has been a very interesting stay as a whole. Naturally, they do not see me, but the Vatican. So I hope that it will help to overcome some of the reservations about the Holy See that are perceived in certain Austrian circles.

A Possible TV Interview

February 3, 1992

"Let's see what the *Direttore* has to say to us about how the world is going and thus receive some *enlightenment*," the Holy Father says aloud as I enter the dining room of the Pontifical Apartment.

1. Viktor Emil Frankl (Austria, 1905–1997) was a neurologist and psychiatrist of Jewish origin, founder of logotherapy. He survived several Nazi concentration camps, where his parents and wife died. As a result of that experience he wrote one of his best known books, *Man's Search for Meaning*.

I tell you about my recent trip to Austria: contacts, human atmosphere. But I also wanted to raise with him the possibility—which I have been thinking about for some time—of doing an interview on TV. The Pope does not see the need, but Dziwisz and I agree—and we tell him so—that it looks better on TV when he speaks "without papers." Dziwisz asks how long it would take to make such a program. I say it can be done little by little: in Rome or in Castelgandolfo.

As I entered, I passed Sodano, who was just finishing his divine office with the Pope. He jokes: "Let's see who has the biggest dossier."

Senegal, Gambia, and Guinea

February 16 to 29, 1992

Meeting with the Pope on the plane to Senegal, before his meeting with journalists, I am struck once again by the accuracy with which he expresses his ideas and recalls names and dates. His thought, agile and rigorous at the same time, without emotional or other distortions, is that of a profoundly serene man.

Seeing the journalists on the plane—all Westerners—he jokes with them, saying:

—"Not one African! All white! Are we still in the colonial era?"

No two papal trips are the same. This one has some important singularities. One of them is the admiration that some Muslim leaders have shown for the Catholic religion. The president of Senegal is married to a Christian. A delightful atmosphere reigned at the Marian shrine of Popodigine. The Pope spontaneously added these words during his homily: "We invited Our Lady to come, and she has come and is here with us."

February 21. In Dakar, capital of Senegal, meeting with young people in the Demba Dio stadium, carried out with excellent organization. The Pope was very happy and thanked them three times at the end. The celebration of the Mass, with elements of the African liturgy: a marvel.

There are two sights of this trip that have had a special impact on me. The first is on February 22, when we visited the "Maison des Esclaves" ("slave house") on the island of Gorée. The Pope was moved by the thought of the thousands and thousands of slaves who passed through here on their tragic journey to America. He leaned against the doorway overlooking the Atlantic and spent some time in prayer, contemplating the sea.

Giuliani took a formidable photo of those moments.[2]

The second image is when I caught him at the Nunciature in Dakar, very early in the morning, before the start of the day, still, leaning on the balustrade of the staircase and with his eyes closed, praying. We could see him praying intensely, "filling himself with God," before beginning a long day of activity.

On February 23 we arrived in Gambia. In a meeting with the young people at St. Augustine's High School in Banjul, he told them not to let their youthful ideals be stolen and that "true happiness is in *being*, not in *having*."

On February 24, in Guinea, he spoke similar words to young people about progress, both spiritual and material, which were widely applauded. That same day he ordained three new priests and met with, among other groups, Muslim religious leaders at the People's Palace.

I note a phrase from the President's speech at the end of the trip: "You are the best witness of our needs."

Tensions with the Patriarch of Moscow

March 2–3, 1992

Meeting between a delegation of the Moscow Patriarch and a delegation of the Holy See in Geneva. Topic: discussion of the pending problems following the changes in the former Soviet Union and the establishment of the Catholic hierarchy in those lands.

Metropolitan Kirill[3] heads the Patriarch delegation; Cassidy, the Vatican delegation, composed of Pierre Duprey, Salvatore Escribano, Msgr. Franco, from the Second Section of the Secretariat of State, and Father Arranz S.J., who acts as translator with his excellent Russian. Also participating are Archimandrite Josef Poustoutoff (whom we met during our trip to Moscow for the Millennium), Fr. Nestor, and the Orthodox priest who represents the Moscow Patriarch at the World Council of Churches in Geneva.

When I heard about this meeting, I commented to the Pope that it would be a good opportunity to change the public atmosphere of confrontation between Moscow and Rome. The Pope encouraged me and he told me to talk to Duprey. I did. It was discussed with Kirill, whether a press conference would

2. Italian photographer Giancarlo Giuliani has covered all of John Paul II's trips for the magazine *Famiglia Cristiana*.

3. Vladimir Mikhailovich Gundyayev (Russia, 1946), Kirill of Smolensk, was at that time chairman of the Moscow Patriarch's Department for External Church Relations. In 2009 he was elected Patriarch of Moscow, succeeding Alexis II.

be held. Ambiguous answer. After some discussions with Cassidy, I was asked to join the delegation to deal with press matters.

I go without a program and with little information on the state of relations between Orthodox and Catholics in the new context of Eastern Europe. As soon as the talks begin, I realize the dimension of the problem. Since September 1990 there have been no meetings between the Patriarch and the Holy See.

The meeting on the 2nd will take place at the Orthodox representation headquarters and, the following day, at our representation to the United Nations.

Kirill does not hold anything back. He is clear; not aggressive, but unequivocal. On several occasions he makes the point that, if there is no progress on the issue of Catholic parishes in Ukraine[4] and on what he calls Catholic "proselytizing" in Russia, there is no point in speaking in fine words of ecumenism and, therefore, of continuing to meet. His position is difficult. He visited several agencies of the Holy See last year and was received by the Pope. A few days later, the reestablishment of the Latin Catholic hierarchy in Russia was reported to the press, without anyone in the Curia giving Kirill prior notice. This made him look bad in the Patriarch. In my opinion, he is right. He wants to take concrete and positive results away from this meeting. When we return home in the evening we are more aware of the tense atmosphere.

Kirill has spoken of the need for a "sign" from Rome. But what sign? It occurs to me that the Pope could give a church to the Ukrainian Orthodox, the means to build it, leaving them wide latitude as to where to build it. The idea struck a chord with the members of our delegation. That same evening consultations were held with Rome.

Talks are resumed in our representation at 9:30 AM. Kirill states his problems and demands. Nestor is more harsh and aggressive. Cassidy talks about the Pope's gesture. It leaves them a bit bewildered. They are grateful. They do not know how the Ukrainian Orthodox will respond: they could say—Kirill adds—that the Catholics have taken all the churches from us and that the Pope is now giving them one. . . . It is resolved that he will take the offer to Moscow and they will decide at the meeting at the end of the month with the Ukrainians.

The atmosphere changed, but the sharper tone returned when, in the afternoon, it was time to draft a press release. Kirill wants a terse text setting out the differences and determining a mechanism for consultation between the Catholic bishops and the Orthodox before erecting parishes and "other Catholic

4. In the new context of freedom, Ukrainian Catholics of the Eastern Rite began to demand—sometimes by occupying churches—the return of parishes that had been seized during the Communist era and handed over to the Orthodox Church.

works." Clearly, he wants in his possession a document that, upon his return home, will make others see that he has been tough and that he has obtained some assurances from Rome.

During the subsequent discussion, which becomes very long, I unsuccessfully attempt a quasi-amendment to the whole text: I get nothing because, in addition to Kirill's resistance, I have raised the issue in terms that are not very possibilistic, instead of raising things in a fragmented way. Only one point is changed. It ends at 12:40 PM.

In the afternoon, Italian TV takes some shots of the meeting table and, in the garden, Cassidy and Kirill make some statements. In my brief interview I say that the origin of the conflict lies in the seventy years of totalitarianism. We prepare the informative material and it is sent by fax to the *Sala Stampa* and to the Secretariat of State. We return to Rome.

The Pope on an Article by Gorbachev

March 4, 1992

Yesterday *La Stampa* of Turin published an article signed by Gorbachev on the influence of John Paul II on the changes in Eastern Europe. Paolo Mieli, editor of the newspaper, and Ezio Mauro, deputy editor, showed that text to the Pope last February 15. It was written in Cyrillic and bore Gorbachev's signature.

I accompanied them during the private audience the Pope granted them in the Library. He was handed a small white dossier on whose cover, handwritten in blue ink, Gorbachev had written "O Pape Rimskom" (*About the Pope of Rome*): a title more typical of an office memorandum than of a press article. Inside the dossier were two pages in Cyrillic characters, initialed, also in blue ink, with his signature, broadly and generously oriented to the right. He was also given some sheets of paper with a translation of the text in Italian.

The Pope made some remarks and when the audience was over, Mieli and Mauro asked me if they could come to the *Sala Stampa* to reconstruct what the Pope had said. We worked together and came out with a text of the Pope's words. I reread it calmly, made some small suggestions and they proposed to me that they publish it the day after Gorbachev's article appeared.

That day is today. They got it out very well, and both Mieli and Mauro were grateful, although I have the feeling that they overestimated my intervention. Actually, I only participated in the reconstruction of the Pope's comments, and in the approval to publish it, agreeing on some details over the phone. For their newspaper it is a good article. I am told that Gorbachev's article has been published by 115 newspapers all over the world. I suppose something similar has happened with the Pope's comments.

This is the text of what the Pope said in that conversation, which we have reconstructed fairly faithfully:

> *Memory of Gorbachev.* "I keep a very strong and precise memory of my meeting with Mikhail Gorbachev, when he visited here. I think he is a dignified, principled, spiritually very rich man, a charismatic man who has had a determining influence on the events in Eastern Europe. He does not declare himself a believer, but he spoke to me about the great importance he attaches to prayer, to the inner dimension of man. I believe that our meeting was arranged by Providence."
>
> *The Slav Pope:* "As he himself writes in his article, during our meeting Gorbachev spoke to me with sympathy and warmth about the 'Slav Pope.' He told me that he was happy to have found here, in the Vatican, a Slavic Pope like himself and, therefore, a Pope able to better understand the problems of his world. I replied smiling, reminding him that I am a West Slav. He told me that it doesn't matter.

"It is not by chance that the Pope wanted to name Saints Cyril and Methodius co-patrons of Europe. They represent the point of intersection between Slavic identity and Latin identity."

> *The Pope and the East.* "I have read Gorbachev's judgment of the Pope's role in the events that changed Eastern Europe during the last few years. I am convinced that he really thinks as he writes, and he says so frankly. When the Synod of European bishops, in its final document, wanted to underline this specific role of the Pope, I asked them not to do so. It is the Church that has counted in this process, not the Pope. Everything that can be attributed to the Pope is the fruit of his fidelity: fidelity to Christ and to man."
>
> *Spiritual change in the East.* "It is possible that some may not be satisfied with Gorbachev's judgment. It is necessary to evaluate recent events in depth, identifying the real causes of the phenomena that have occurred. For example, there are those who—like Popper—are convinced that economic difficulties are the ultimate cause of the crisis in the Communist systems of Eastern Europe. And, certainly, this argument has its weight. But we must not forget something very important: it has not only been a crisis of communism: there has also been a *perestroika*. And *perestroika*, among other things, means 'conversion.'"

"This means that in the crisis and in the failure, in the convulsions that have occurred and are still occurring, there is a spiritual element, an inner change. On the other hand, it must be so and could only have been so. Man is made up of two elements, and an exclusively spiritual interpretation of the events in the East would be wrong, just as an exclusively material interpretation would be wrong, incapable of looking beyond the purely economic dimensions of this crisis, because man is spirit incarnate."

The political role. "Gorbachev speaks of the political role the Pope has played within the world scene. I don't think one can speak of a 'political role' in the strict sense, because the task of a Pope is to preach the Gospel. But in the Gospel one finds man, respect for man, and consequently, human rights, freedom of conscience and of everything that belongs to man. If this has a political value, then yes, that term—'political role'—also concerns the Pope. But always speaking about man, defending man."

An unthinkable transformation. "In 1978, when I was elected Pope, I could not have imagined that I would witness such a radical transformation as the one that has changed the face of Eastern Europe. I could not imagine it because it was unimaginable. And not only then: even in that great, unforgettable year 1989, the year of *the Velvet Revolution,* as Czechoslovak President Havel called it. It was a sign, a light, a harbinger of what came later. I especially remember the canonization of St. Agnes of Bohemia, which took place here in the Vatican in November 1989, attended by so many pilgrims from those countries."

The coup in the USSR. "When the coup d'état took place in the Soviet Union, I was in Hungary. We immediately made a statement in which the Holy See, upon the official announcement of Gorbachev's illness, expressed its wish that he might recover as soon as possible. And the next day, during the celebration of Mass in Heroes' Square, in the center of Budapest, I added a few words during my homily, to speak about what was happening in Moscow and worrying the whole world . . ."

The trip to the USSR. "A lot has been said about this trip. Mikhail Gorbachev invited me and I think he has a sincere desire for this trip to become a reality; and not only him, but also his successor; although we cannot properly speak of his successor, because Boris Yeltsin is president of Russia and not of the USSR, like Gorbachev. But it is necessary to continue working before making this trip. It is necessary to continue working."

Macciocchi's Book

March 6, 1992

I have just returned from the meeting with the Russian Orthodox in Geneva. The Pope invites me to dinner for a briefing. He has not yet spoken to Cassidy. He asks me about the impact of Gorbachev's article that has appeared in *La Stampa* and Maria Antonietta Macciocchi's book, commenting on *Mulieris Dignitatem*. The Pope thanks her for writing that book and tells Dziwisz to invite her to dinner.[5]

Blessed Josemaría

May 22, 1992

Dinner with the Pope. A few days have passed since the beatification of a priest with whom I had the good fortune (or rather, the gift of God) to live with for five years: Josemaría Escrivá. I am filled with gratitude to our Lord every time I think of him. Along with him, the Church has beatified a Sudanese nun, Josefina Bakhita.

When the Pope enters, he tells me about the beatification. "A great spectacle," he says, referring to the ceremony in the Square. He was especially impressed by the composure of the people. During dinner, the subject continues to be discussed. They ask me questions and I talk about the Christian formation provided by Opus Dei, something the Pope knows and appreciates.

At another point in the conversation, we spoke about the usefulness of the press review that collects news clippings and articles of special interest. I tell him that Paul VI had already had a *Rassegna Stampa*, which never omitted the criticisms or the sectarian news, but that sometimes the positive things were forgotten. I add that, from my point of view, this omission corresponds to a mentality according to which it is enough to read everything negative to be informed. This seems to me to be wrong, because it is also necessary to be informed of the positive. To do otherwise is to contribute to creating a siege complex in the face of criticism. The Pope listens with interest to this discussion on press reviews.

---

5. Some time later, I accompanied Maria Antonietta during that dinner: she came in a long black dress. She deeply admires the Pope, who was especially interested in everything she told him about China. [Author's Note]

In Angola, Sao Tome, and Principe

June 4 to 10, 1992

Upon arriving in Luanda, the capital of Angola, I find that the government has entrusted the Pope's security to a group of Spanish policemen, who will accompany us during these days.

Huambo. The Pope arrives at the presbytery before celebrating Mass. On the altar, a large crucifix with African features. He kneels, rests his hand on the crucifix and prays for eight minutes with his eyes closed. Today is Friday and perhaps he is making the Stations of the Cross.

June 5. Lubango. The Pope's presence in these places that have suffered so much after almost thirty years of war (fifteen to achieve independence and another fifteen years of civil war) helps to reinforce the perseverance of religious vocations. I am impressed by the enthusiasm of the local religious who care for the most needy people of this country.

The number of children attending the celebration of the Word in Lubango's Revolution Square is striking. The Pope addresses them affectionately, with the language of an experienced catechist.

June 6. As we fly to Sao Tome I review the speeches he is going to deliver and notice that there is no reference to slavery, though this island was a place of transit in the slave trade. I tell Dziwisz about it and Re writes a paragraph, which is made available to the Pope. During the farewell at the airport, the president changed his original speech to comment on that reference to slavery that the Pope introduced at the end of the Mass.

Family and friendly atmosphere. Peaceful and sensitive atmosphere. I read on a banner: "*Joao Paolo II, world leader of peace, of unity, of justice, of freedom, of progress.*"

June 7. Luanda. We return to the capital, where the Pope meets with the members of the Episcopal Conference of Angola, Sao Tome, and Principe. Marxism has been very present in these countries, as in his native land. It is the feast of Pentecost and at a certain moment he begins to speak in Italian, with a tone of confidence. He recalls his first Pentecost celebration in Poland, when the world was still divided into two blocks: "It was 1979. Then what happened, happened. From 1979 to 1989 and now, in 1992, we are here. It is the same process, even if the places are different. They are linked to each other because the same system tried to implant ideological atheism in one place as in the other. On the other side is the Church, which does not follow a program: it follows the Word of God, the promises of Christ."

June 8. Cabinda. The Pope celebrates Mass at the airport, almost on the border with Zaire.[6] A few days ago several people died near here, due to border clashes. Impression of absolute poverty.

The local people find it incredible to have the Pope in their own land, so far away from everything. I am amazed to see the small group of Franciscan missionaries working here. I see where they live, with practically nothing. The Pope has lunch with them, at the mission, in a small and modest room. The bishop is a Franciscan. Before the afternoon ceremony, the Pope visits a family living in a shack. It is somewhat impromptu. He sits with them and they chat for a few minutes. A catechist accompanies us.

At the hotel in Luanda, I talk to Cardinal Tomko[7] about Czechoslovakia during the years of communism, which the Pope has recalled so often during these days. He tells me that the Holy See appointed four bishops in 1972: two were directly from *Pacem in Terris,* and the other two were close to that movement that sympathized with Marxism. It did not work. He left his country—Slovakia—in 1945 and was only able to see his mother many years later, in 1968, since until then he was not given a visa to travel there. Some time later he also had difficulties attending her funeral.

June 11. On the plane, as we return from Africa, I see that the Pope is writing the text of Wednesday's general audience. When he finishes, he hands it to Nowacki for translation. I am struck by the original text: five pages written in Polish with very few corrections. He usually writes an aspiration in the upper right-hand corner of each page. On this occasion it is not an isolated aspiration. The phrases of the five folios compose a Marian prayer:

> "*Totus tuus ego sum / Et omnia mea tua sum / Accepi te in mea omnia / Praebe mihi cor tuum / Maria.*"
>
> (I am all yours, / And all that is mine is yours, / I welcome you in all that is mine, / Give me your heart, / Mary.)

Everything he writes "forms part," in some way, of his prayer to Our Lady.

On the last page he wrote this note, addressed to the translator: "*Prego umilmente corregere e completare*" ("I humbly beg to be corrected and completed.")

---

6. Zaire is now known as Democratic Republic of Congo. The name Republic of Zaire was used from 1971 to 1997—during the period of Mobutu Sese Seko.

7. In 1972, Jozef Tomko (Slovakia, 1924–2022) was a Slovak bishop. He was created a cardinal more than a decade later, in 1985, by John Paul II and appointed prefect of the Congregation for the Evangelization of Peoples (1985–2001).

24

"I'm Going to Be Admitted to the Hospital"

At the Universal Exposition of Seville

June 28–29, 1992

June 28. I am traveling to Spain with Sodano, who is presiding over the ceremonies of the Holy See Pavilion at the Universal Exposition of Seville (EXPO). On the plane I read him some possible questions that, I think, Spanish journalists might ask him. We are received at the airport by the Nuncio, Mario Tagliaferri.[1]

Lunch at the nunciature: we talked about the religious situation in Spain. Tagliaferri thinks that in this country there are no well-trained Catholic lay people in public life and that he thinks the Italian model (Catholics united in politics under the same party) is much better.

Personally, I have my doubts. What seems clear to me is that the parties in power in Italy, in the last ten years, have respected pluralism more than in Spain, where there has been a kind of purge of Catholics in public life.

Seville. The EXPO. Interview for *Canal Sur*, the regional television. Visit to the pavilion of the Holy See: the Discóbolo de Mirón, showcases with documents linked to the evangelization of America and the discovery, such as the testament of Christopher Columbus. Paintings by Murillo, Zurbarán, Goya, Caravaggio, El Greco. At the end, meeting with journalists.

Madrid. Interview at Moncloa[2] with Felipe González.[3] Ambassador Ezquerra, Sodano, Tagliaferri and Mons. Broglio. Sodano asks the President why a series

1. Mario Tagliaferri (Italy, 1927–1999) held diplomatic positions for the Holy See in numerous countries. He was apostolic nuncio to Spain from 1985 to 1995, and was later appointed nuncio to Paris, where he died.

2. Moncloa is the official residence of the Spanish prime minister.

3. Felipe González Márquez (Spain, 1942), was secretary general of the Spanish Socialist Party from 1974 to 1997 and president of the Spanish government from 1982 to 1996.

of pending matters have not yet been resolved: assistance of chaplains in the prisons, meeting of the mixed Church-State commission, etc. Lunch followed in the adjacent palace with Vice-President Narcís Serra and the Ministers of Foreign Affairs, Education and other personalities, together with several bishops, such as Suquía and García Gasco, President and Secretary of the Bishops' Conference.

In the afternoon, Serra comes to the nunciature. Then we will meet with the permanent staff of the bishops' conference.

Back in Rome, Sodano asks me to accompany him in the car from the airport. When we arrive, Re is waiting for us. We have to prepare the communication of the Rota's sentence on the marriage of Caroline of Monaco.[4] Lunch at the *Sala Stampa*. I invite the journalists for the afternoon, because I have spoken with Di Falco, spokesman for the French bishops, who confirms that several newspapers already know the sentence of nullity on her marriage with Junot.

The Surprise

July 10–20, 1992

I linger for a while chatting with Dziwisz before the Pope comes. I tell him about the rest period in the mountains—always too short—which will begin in five days. He does not confirm anything, which surprises me, because it will be very soon. I ask him if I should accompany them on this occasion and he evades the answer: it depends on what the Pope says during dinner. What will happen? A moment later the Holy Father enters: "Let's see with the Director in what situation we find ourselves . . . ," he comments amused. "We find ourselves, Holy Father . . . about to leave for the mountains," I reply. "*Vediamo, vediamo*," ("We'll see, we'll see") he says, as we head towards the chapel, before moving on to the dining room.

On his way out, he walks, clicking the heels of his shoes. It's a joke with Dziwisz. "He just doesn't want me to make noise when I walk," he tells me, laughing. Dziwisz explains to me that the Pope sometimes wears these shoes, one size larger than his size, because they are very comfortable; but they rattle a little when he walks. . . .

"What is the word out there?" the Pope asks me. I talk to him about the anticipation for his upcoming trip to Santo Domingo and other topics. I get the

4. The couple divorced, childless, on October 9, 1980. In 1992, the Catholic Church granted the princess an annulment from Philippe Junot, a Parisian banker.

feeling, from the way he sits, that he is not feeling quite right: as if he is in some kind of discomfort. His dinner, usually very light, is reduced to only mashed potatoes. He does not take any cheese.

I speak of the need for a few days of rest in the mountains, evoking the Neapolitan saying: "*Quando il corpo sta bene, l'anima balla*" ("When the body is well, the soul dances"). I add that St. Thomas Aquinas said something similar.

"Of course," commented the Pope with good humor, "because St. Thomas was also Neapolitan, from Campania."

After a brief pause, he adds: "So you think we should go to the mountains?"—"Yes, Holiness," I tell him, with the impression that there is some obstacle I am unaware of. We finish dinner, get up from the table, head back to the chapel, and before we enter, he stops:

"I have to tell you something. I'm going to be admitted to the hospital this Sunday."

I freeze, although I try not to let it show. He tells me in a serious tone, but without drama. And he adds something else about the possibility of an intervention.

We move on to the oratory. What will it be? An ENT procedure, to solve the problem of his hypoacusis, the hearing loss? But, by the way he says it, it must not be that. We prayed for a few minutes.

On leaving, I tell him that this is one more occasion to pray for the Holy Father. He thanked me and asked me to continue praying and to pray for him. Dziwisz comments that a few days ago Brother Schutz from Taizé called him and told him that the Pope was going to suffer.[5]

> —"The Pope suffers a lot," I added, not knowing quite what to say, and not daring to ask what was going on, "but more than physical pain, he suffers for the Church."
>
> "That's true," he comments to me.

This is the first time I have heard him admit that he suffers.

Before saying goodbye, Dziwisz brings me two texts that have been prepared for Sunday (today is Friday): the announcement of his admission to the hospital, which the Pope himself will read at the end of the Angelus prayer, and

5. Roger Schulz (1915–2005), Swiss Protestant monk. He was the founder of the ecumenical Taizé Community, composed of Protestant, Orthodox, and Catholic brothers. He died as a result of stabbing injuries caused by a deranged person.

the information that I have to communicate to journalists. I read them, tell the Pope that I have enough with these texts, and say goodbye.

But Dziwisz is worried and eager to talk. He accompanies me and we sit in the next room, where the liturgical vestments are laid out for the Swiss bishops who are on an *ad limina* visit. He tells me about the tests the Pope has undergone in the last few days, the preparation for the analyses, his ailments. . . . And to think that, in the meantime, he has maintained his normal schedule. The only change was on Monday when, to save him work, he was given only one audience.

He informs me that the tumor found on him seems malignant. From the way he tells me, I understand that it is serious. And I begin to pray, asking God for a miracle.

July 12, Sunday. I have been with Re, who seems optimistic: he tells me that in ten days everything will be solved and that I don't have to change my rest plan, because he is not going to change his. I am less optimistic, after talking to Dziwisz on Friday.

At twelve o'clock, there is only one Japanese journalist, Hiroshi, in the *Sala Stampa*. I suggest he turn on the TV and listen to the Pope. After the announcement, there is a big commotion: journalists start coming and we have a press conference. They ask me questions and then more questions about an issue for which I have only an elementary, but significant answer: it is an intestinal dysfunction that may lead to a probable surgical intervention. I stress that it has nothing to do with his last trip to Angola.

I have lunch in the *Sala Stampa*, where I continue to work all afternoon. At about six o'clock Re calls me to tell me that the Pope will go down to the San Damaso Courtyard at a quarter past seven and that, from there, he will go to the Gemelli, in case I want to be there for the farewell.

Giovanna, who even at this hour is still working in the *Sala Stampa*. While I wait for the Pope, I talk with Buzzonetti. I ask him what he foresees. He thinks there is an 85 percent chance that it is a malignant tumor. I see that he is carrying an envelope with the X-rays.

As the media will want to know the results immediately, we agreed to prepare in advance two communiqués depending on what happens: one stating that it is benign and the other—if their forecasts are confirmed—informing that it is a malignant tumor. But, he asks, who is qualified to make the second announcement? Buzzonetti tells me that not even the Secretary of State can decide on his own. The Pope himself must authorize it, and he is nervous because he does not know if they are going to let him raise this issue before the intervention. I leave him my telephone numbers; we agreed that we will call each other every day and we will be in contact.

Arriving at the courtyard of San Damaso, the Pope jokes with the nuns who are waiting for him before he gets into the car. The atmosphere is very cordial. They do not know what is wrong with him and think it is something small.

"If you want information," the Pope tells them, laughing and pointing his index finger at me, "ask him."

JULY 13, MONDAY. Great commotion in the press; they appreciate that the Pope has personally announced his admission to the hospital.

I speak to Dziwisz on the phone: he has had a CT scan and "everything is clean." This means that they have found no signs of metastasis: this is the first good news in all these days. I keep praying and asking for a miracle.

JULY 14, TUESDAY. There is tension in the press and a great deal of interest. I tell them that he is still undergoing tests and that, as soon as they are finished, we will communicate the diagnosis. I speak on the phone with Buzzonetti and with Dr. Candia of the Gemelli Polyclinic, to reach an agreement. We agreed to have a simultaneous reading of the communiqués, both at Gemelli and at *Sala Stampa*.

JULY 15, WEDNESDAY. SURGERY. Re calls me to tell me that Sodano is waiting for me to accompany him to the hospital. He is worried because the statement prepared by the doctors is too technical and he thinks that people will not understand it well. He wants me to go to the hospital and work with the doctors to prepare a more understandable text.

I go with the Cardinal in his car. We go through a side entrance to the hospital, to avoid the group of journalists that has gathered at the door, and head straight to the tenth floor.

Next to the Pope's room there is a small chapel. We pray before the Blessed Sacrament. The Pope's skullcap—he is still in the operating room—has been placed on the altar.

During the long wait—an hour—we talked about the difficulty Buzzonetti encounters in getting the Pope's entourage to follow his instructions when it comes to preventive measures. The Pope travels frequently, has very little free time, and checkups are postponed again and again. Buzzonetti has been proposing for some time that a series of tests be carried out, even if he does not have any symptoms, but he has not succeeded.

At about eleven o'clock in the morning, I see the doctors arrive. They take the Pope directly to his room. They have written a technical, descriptive, and realistic communiqué, but—as they refer only vaguely to the *tumorous nature of the lesion*—the good news will not be sufficiently clear to the general public: the adenoma is benign.

On the other hand, Buzzonetti and Cruccitti, the surgeon, as experienced physicians, would like the text to be less emphatic, until all possible extremes have been confirmed. In the end, an agreement is reached and a brief paragraph is added to emphasize the benign nature of the tumor, indicating that the surgical intervention will be "curative and resolutive." Sodano signs it as "seen."

Buzzonetti, somewhat calmer, shows me, taking a deep breath, the draft of the other communiqué (the one that would have been published if the doctors had told us, after the operation, that the tumor was malignant).

Sodano enters the Pope's room. Dziwisz comments that the doctors have said that, because of the characteristics of the tumor, it seems miraculous that it was benign. He is happy. Tobiana and all of us are there.

Buzzonetti, however, is still nervous: partly because of the accumulated tension and also because of his responsibility as a physician. He thinks that even after having done these two biopsies—preoperative and intraoperative—there may be elements of dysplasia (abnormal cell growth) that could prove to be malignant. In any case, the information that goes to the press is accurate, complete, and clear. Cruccitti tells me that the size of the adenoma was seven centimeters.[6]

I was scheduled to meet the journalists at twelve o'clock, but I postponed the press conference until a quarter past one because the Pope spent more time than expected in the recovery room and we went over the wording of the communiqué several times.

I have agreed with Dr. Candia not to accept questions, because rather than clarifying the situation, they could be an element of confusion in these delicate moments. And we have drafted four points that clarify some excessively technical terms.

Press conference: great interest and remarkable order, despite the fact that, to complicate things, we are undergoing construction in the *Sala Stampa*. I have to read the text in English for some of the news people. We finish very late. I go home exhausted. And I still have six or seven more interviews for television and several for radio. But I am happy and thankful to God.

6. 27.6 inches.

JULY 16, THURSDAY. New communiqué on the first hours following the operation. Dziwisz tells me that yesterday, before the operation, the Pope had gotten up at four o'clock in the morning to celebrate Mass and to perform his practices of piety, because he foresaw that after the operation he would not have been able to do them. After the operation, he asked Dziwisz to read him part of the breviary and pray the rosary aloud, and he joined in these prayers on his part.

JULY 17, FRIDAY. I do not go to the hospital. Dziwisz informs me by telephone of the state of the Pope's health. I call Sodano and ask him to please tell the doctors to stop talking to the press: I fear that some of them are giving too many interviews.

As usually happens in these cases, a controversy begins to brew, because some American and Italian doctors do not hesitate to affirm that such a thick lesion should necessarily have been diagnosed earlier. Naturally, all this makes poor Buzzonetti uneasy, as he cannot speak of the great difficulties he has to overcome to have the Pope undergo preventive tests (for example, a preventive colonoscopy every year). There is always a trip, a consistory, scheduled meetings that complicate things. I tell him to be calm: I will take care of this.

Buzzonetti would like to give the press a text showing the asymptomatic nature of this lesion, highlighting the analyses—stool and otherwise—that he has been doing during this time.

Sodano, who is currently on his way to the hospital by car, asked me on the phone to read Buzzonetti's report and give him my opinion. I tell him that I do not think it is appropriate to give it in these circumstances. He then spoke to Buzzonetti and asked him to leave it to my discretion.

Two days later, when the matter calmed down, I gave an interview to Alceste Santini, of *L'Unità* on these questions and I emphasize Buzzonetti's professionalism.

L'Indipendente has published a negative article about Stanisław—"*Tutti i poteri di Don Dziwisz*" ("All the powers of Don Dziwisz")—presenting him as "the all-powerful man" of the Curia, as if he commands more than the cardinals themselves.[7] I give it to him telling him not to worry, that it is not important. In the afternoon, he calls me at home: "You know that nothing in that article is true. But if you ever see anything in the way I act that might give rise to it, you should tell me fraternally." It is an act of humility that impresses me.

---

7. *L'ndipendente* was a Milanese general newspaper, published daily from November 1991 to November 1994. It was successively published for several periods, but ceased publication definitively in 2007.

JULY 18, SATURDAY. Stanisław invites me into the Pope's room. He is in bed with a nasal probe. When he sees me he says: "Come closer, come closer." I kiss his hand and tell him that this illness has been a gift for the whole Church: we have all prayed a lot. In this type of situation—and this one is no exception—I get "soft" and tears come to my eyes. . . . The Pope says: "It is necessary to fulfill in our flesh what is lacking in the passion of Christ." And he adds: "Even if everything is fulfilled by Christ, we can always add something."

Seeing him like this, well groomed, serene, with a nasal probe held in place with adhesive tape, makes me feel an enormous tenderness for him.

On the bedside table, his rosary. On top of a small chest of drawers, next to his bed, an image of *Maria Bambina* (*Mary Bambina*). And an armchair, where he rests for a few hours.

Both yesterday and today he concelebrated Mass with Father Stanisław. This means that he has not missed any day of celebrating the Eucharist, although at the Mass they celebrated shortly after his operation, in the afternoon—according to what Dziwisz told me—he could only say the words of consecration.

Yesterday I reported all this to the press, because I think it can do a lot of people some good.

I speak with Dziwisz about the Pope's Sunday Angelus: possible themes and how to record it with the Vatican Radio technician.

Sodano calls me in the afternoon: the doctors already have the result of the definitive histological analysis and they would like to give it to me on Sunday. He asks for my opinion. I tell him that on Sunday the Pope will say the Angelus, and that should be the only information of the day. Confusion can be created and there is no hurry to give that analysis. He agrees and tells me that he will tell the doctors. He asks me to be reachable on Sunday morning.

JULY 19. SUNDAY. BORSELLINO. National uproar: Judge Borsellino has been assassinated in Sicily.[8] I suggested to Sodano by telephone that, given the magnitude of the event, a message could be sent to the Bishop of Palermo and another to the President of the Republic, Oscar Luigi Scalfaro. He is fine with that. I am working with Dziwisz on some ideas for the telegram on behalf of the Pope.

8. Paolo Emanuele Borsellino (Italy, 1940–1992) was an Italian magistrate who, together with Judge Giovanni Falcone (murdered a few months earlier, in May) led the judicial proceedings against the *Cosa Nostra* mafia gang. He began his work under the orders of chief prosecutor Rocco Chinnici, who had himself been assassinated in 1983.

July 20, Monday. I go to the hospital at 9:30 AM and I am present at the meeting with the doctors to outline the communication on the histological analysis. We agreed with Dr. Candia to explain some complementary concepts, especially what concerns "dysplasia." I talk to Buzzonetti and give him my interview in *L'Unità,* which he did not know about. I talk to Sodano, who had invited me to accompany him in the car to the Gemelli.

Press conference. I have to get into medical issues and use precise terminology. I see that, at least, I am getting some return on my professional past.

Doctors think that the Pope should remain in the hospital for several more days: he is weak and often falls asleep. He has not eaten since he was admitted on Sunday and is being fed by drip.

Until July 26, Sunday, *when he leaves the hospital.* I go to the Gemelli every other day. Always in the morning to talk to Dziwisz, who appreciates it. One day Buzzonetti accompanies us.

25

Replenishing Forces

In Lorenzago del Cadore

August 17, 1992

A few days ago Dziwisz called to tell me that on the 17th we were leaving for Lorenzago del Cadore, accompanying the Pope in this stage of his recovery. We left Ciampino airport at 9:30 in the morning in a DC-9 of the *Aeronautica Militare* to Treviso. From here, by helicopter, to Lorenzago. We are the usual group: Cibin, Gugel, the doctor (this time Giampiero Gasparro) and Tadeusz Styczeń.

We arrive at Lorenzago around 11:30 AM Buzzonetti accompanies us there. That same day, after dinner, the Pope takes a walk in the small garden of the house, and very early the next morning, around 6:30 AM, before Mass, I see him walking again.

August 18. First outing. I talk to Dziwisz about the possibility of the Angelus on Sunday, and I manage to convince him to have it at home instead of at the Castello di Mirabello. I also propose that it not be transmitted live on television, since it would be a contradiction to the relaxed atmosphere that we want to give to these days. He tells me that the Pope is slowly recovering. During the past few days, in Castelgandolfo, he has suffered a dental abscess, which was cured with antibiotics, and a urinary infection. He does not eat too much. According to Buzzoneti he does this among other reasons, so as not to gain weight.

In the afternoon we make our first outing on the road near the house: an hour in all, with several stops. I ask the Pope if he has seen Gorbachev's recent comments about his influence on events in the East. Gorbachev claims to have been inspired by the Pope's encyclicals. "Do you see?, " he says to me with a smile, "sometimes it pays to write an encyclical!"

Hearing him say this comforts me: he is regaining his usual good humor. At the next stop he asks me, generically, what's going on in the world. He wants to be informed. We talk—Tadeusz is present—about the Bosnian problem and the perplexities raised by international intervention. He talks about the moral conditions that justify interventions: it must aim to "disarm the aggressor." It is clear that he has thought about the moral justification of such an intervention.

He adds that it was very good that Cardinal Etchegaray was in Sarajevo precisely on August 15, the feast of Our Lady. It was the Pope himself who sent him, as an expression of solidarity in the face of all that they are going through.

I take some pictures of him praying the breviary under the trees.

AUGUST 19. We take a walk along the route that they have called the "John Paul II Trail." I tell him that tomorrow I will go to see the journalists and I tell him, through Dziwisz, that I need some photos. He agrees to let me photograph him. He keeps asking me about Bosnia and tells me that something similar could happen in Kosovo. During the stops he prays the breviary; while walking, he carries the rosary in his right hand and the *alpenstock*—a long stick—in his left. In the evening he stays at home.

Long conversation with Tadeusz: he talks about Ratzinger's lecture in Salzburg. He values Ratzinger very much and is worried about his health. I tell him that, indeed, he needs a person in his dicastery to help him, so that he can be more free to devote himself to thinking and writing. On another matter, he confided to me a domestic detail: since the Pope spends more time in bed these days, Sister Euphrosyne reads to him while he rests.

AUGUST 20. I'm going to see the journalists. There is a good group. When the list of those who will come to the Angelus on Sunday is finalized, there are forty-eight. I give them a run-down of our trip and explain in detail the itinerary that the Pope will follow on the first full-day trip.

AUGUST 21. READINGS IN POLISH. The Pope has left the house in a good mood: "*Buongiorno turisti; turisti e escursionisti!*" ("Good morning, tourists; tourists and hikers!"). We go to Valbona, in the municipality of Cortina d'Ampezzo. We arrive after an hour's drive and start the hike at the Tre Croci pass. Long descent, smooth. Stop for lunch at the edge of a forest. Splendid view of the mountains: the Marmarole, the Cristallo, and others.

As soon as he finishes a light and brief lunch, the Pope begins to read, as if he considers food almost as a nuisance to be rid of as soon as possible, in order to dedicate himself to the real activity, reading. He lies down for a while in the tent that we have brought with us this year. His breviary, bound in white, the one he takes with him on his trips, is written in Polish. Today he has brought several publications with him: the magazine *Znak,* the magazine of the University of Lublin, *Ethos,* and a book on contemporary religious theater. All in

Polish: this universal man preserves and nurtures an extraordinary interest in the themes of his country and in universal issues written in his language.

He seems to be improving day by day: he wants to talk, he jokes and communicates with others. At one stop he spontaneously recalls when he first "escaped" from the Vatican, unescorted, in 1982 or 1983, in a car driven by Józef Kowalczyk,[1] to go to the mountains.

Today he had fish for dinner, that one of our people brought yesterday, and he is preparing tomorrow's Angelus. A group of Catholic Action from Treviso and a group of refugees from Bosnia are coming.

August 22. In a shepherd's hut. We leave home at about 10:15 AM, by car on the 336-A trail. Itinerary: Forcella Mezzarazzo, Forcella Ghirlo, *fienile* (haystack) Ghirlo at 1,440 m. The road is a bit long, and we fear it will be hard. We hesitate to continue, but the pope keeps going. We arrive around one o'clock. Sunny. At Forcella Mezzarazzo we meet a young family: a father and two children, girl and boy. We chat with them as the Pope approaches. They suspect nothing. The lady is the first to recognize the Pope. Her name is Loris Tremonti.

We continue walking and a few minutes later it starts to rain. We take out our umbrellas. We arrive at the *fienile*, the haystack, under a downpour and thunder. The shelter is closed. Some of the security guards begin to make maneuvers to force the lock. The Pope dissuades them. We take shelter under the eaves of the roof.

The Pope laughs and comments: "*La Croix* says that this Pope goes out into the bush against the advice of his doctors." "An act of rebellion?," I ask. "Yes, a rebellious Pope. And then Dr. Navarro-Valls appears saying that the Pope is very docile to the doctors." It's an amusing reference to a comment I made to the press while the Pope was in the hospital. He laughs heartily. We continue, while the Pope speaks in Polish with Dziwisz, who then tells me: "The Pope told me that he would laugh more, but that the scar is still pulling a little and hurts."

We follow a path between tall bushes: it is a complete immersion in nature, between water, thunder and vegetation. At about half past one, we discover a wooden hut, a shepherd's hut, with the door open. We decide to have lunch there. At first, the Pope takes a seat at the door of the hut and we take shelter

1. Józef Kowalczyk (Poland, 1938) was in charge of the Polish section of the Secretariat of State from its creation in 1978 until 1989. He was then appointed nuncio in Warsaw after the restoration of diplomatic relations with Poland (1989–2010). He was archbishop of Gniezno and primate of Poland (2010–2014).

under some trees. Then, when the downpour of rain comes, he enters the hut and we take shelter under an uralite porch. Faced with this peculiar situation, it occurred to me to comment to Gasparro: "This is an unprecedented page in the history of the Church." I don't realize that, inside the hut, everything we say outside can be heard.

After lunch, the Pope rests for a while inside the shelter. It stops raining and we light a fire to dry ourselves. A little later the Pope approaches the fire, sits down on the chair we have brought him and reads from his breviary. These are delightful moments.

On the way back we meet the family of Gigi Vecellio, the *miscredente* (agnostic), as he defined himself, whom the Pope visited the first year he came to these parts. His wife, Dea, tells me that her husband has had a kind of reliquary made in Milan to keep the glass in which the Pope drank orange juice. . . . The Pope greets them. Another family and a young man approach me. The man is the son of the restaurant manager at the Mauri Pass, where I had lunch a few days ago at the invitation of Mario Tremonti, mayor of Lorenzago.

Dea Vecellio offers the Pope some "fritelle"[2] that she brought in a metal container. The scene gave me the opportunity to take a picture of them that I shared with the press a few days later. We returned at about half past six.

Today it seemed to me that the Pope was having some difficulty hearing our comments. I also noticed a tremor in his left hand, which he corrects by resting it on a table or chair.

August 23rd. Angelus. The scheduled groups of people attend the Angelus in the house. The Pope is especially funny and witty with them. He makes a mistake when he begins the Angelus for the second time and graciously rectifies it. I greet Buzzoneti, who has come with his son Luca.

August 24. We drive to Ciampo de Ra Fontane, 1,900 m high. At the top, a splendid lake with views of the mountains: Croda de r'Ancona, Zuoghe, the three peaks of Lavaredo, Monte Piana, il Cristallo. . . . On the way we met a forester, Herbert Comploy, who did not expect to see the Pope in these places. He stops in astonishment: "*Ma è possibile? Guarda che roba!*" ("But is it possible? Look at these things!").

He accompanies us throughout the day. I talk to him during lunch. "I have never had such an experience in my whole life. I didn't know what to do. He tells

2. The "fritelle" are fried sweets that can be shaped as fritters. Sometimes they are also salted.

me that every day he climbs the mountain with his ten year old son, but that today his son slept at home. He adds that when he tells him that he has seen the Pope, his son will tell him that he knew about it before and that's why he didn't take him with him today. It can be seen that he is a religious and good man; a Ladino of language and culture.[3] He speaks of the surprise that his wife will have: "When I tell her, she will not believe it. It will be hard to convince her that it is true."

In the afternoon, we continue walking. We stop to pray at a World War I cemetery. During the walk, I have a long conversation with Tadeusz: philosophy, thought. "I am a priest, I am sixty years old, and only since five years ago have I begun to understand what 'the truth shall set you free' means." I ask him about his personal history. He was born in 1931 in Wolowice, Krakow, into a deeply Christian family, and studied with the Society of the Divine Savior, which had been established in Poland in 1900, and which he joined years later. After his ordination to the priesthood, his provincial told him that he should continue studying. He thought he was referring to a career in music, which he was passionate about; but no, he was referring to philosophy.

He studied theology at the Jagiellonian University (Krakow) and attended Karol Wojtyla's classes. He then followed him to the Faculty of Philosophy of the Catholic University of Lublin and was his assistant in the Department of Ethics. Wojtyla supervised his thesis. After he completed his doctorate and teaching qualifications, he officially succeeded him in the chair with the title of Professor of Philosophy. Wojtyla came and visited him frequently.

August 25. Fit. I go to see the journalists. I tell them anecdotes from the trip. Before leaving, I take some pictures of the Pope with some nuns who have come to greet him. The Pope, joking, says to them, pointing at me, as if to draw attention away from himself, "Do you know who this gentleman is?" As I said, I see him in good shape.

August 26th. Sanferminero air. Ascent to Misurina, up to the refuge at the top. It is a good walk. Intense sun and an extraordinary mountain landscape. When we stop, the Pope begins to remember: "Today is the day of Our Lady of Jasna Gora. In 1978, on this very day, John Paul I was elected Pope. A year later I wanted to visit his homeland, Canale d'Agordo, and then the Marmolada. Cossiga, who was Prime Minister at the time, was also there. We encountered a snowstorm. . . ."

3. Ladin is a Rhaeto-Romance language spoken in the Dolomites (ancient Retia).

I ask him how he learned of the death of John Paul I. "I was on a pastoral visit in a parish outside Krakow. A parish without a church. And the driver of the car came to tell me that the death of the Pope had been announced on the radio. It was Friday. I returned to Krakow; on Monday I officiated at the funeral Mass and on Tuesday I left for Warsaw and Rome."

At half past one, we stop for lunch. In the meantime, we are approached by some cows grazing nearby. I lead them away, with a newspaper in my hand, in the purest Sanferminero style.[4] Dziwisz comments: "He had to be a Spaniard and a bullfighter to boot." The Pope is amused by the comment and laughs with pleasure.

I talk to Tadeusz about the Pope. Is he more of a philosopher than a poet, or the other way around? The Pope wants to obtain an adequate explanation of reality using philosophy; and he turns to poetry to express what philosophy cannot say, like St. John of the Cross, whom he admires so much. He tells me that he himself did not know—despite working with him—that Wojtyla was a playwright, because he signed under a pseudonym. He found out some time later.

August 27th. At the Antonio and Antinesca hut. The most pleasant part of the day is the arrival, already on the way back, at the Forzella di Zovo refuge. The Pope greeted the managers, the couple Antonio De Bettin, and Antinesca Casanova, with whom he had a pleasant conversation. The Pope was interested in the family and the history of the shelter. "I built this shelter with my hands," said Antonio. "Bravo, I know well that mountain people are very hardworking," he commented. I took the opportunity to take some photos.

August 28. The noise of the water. Val Padeon, Torrente Felizon. He asks me about some current issues: elections in Lebanon, news from the United States, the question of abortion in Germany. . . . Afterwards, I talk for a while with Tadeusz about the various legislations on right to life issues. We stop for lunch next to a hunting lodge. To our left rises Monte Cristallo, to the right Pomagagnon.

After lunch, there is a heavy downpour with lightning. The Pope spends about an hour in the tent. Arriving home in the evening, he comments: "It has been fourteen or fifteen years since I have heard the sound of water on the roof of a tent."

4. In Pamplona, around the feast of San Fermin on July 6th, famous bullfights are held in large arenas.

August 29th. I go with the journalists and also develop some photos for the press. Last night I had dinner with Victor Simpson—from the *Associated Press*—and his wife, Daniela, who had come to greet me.

August 30. Overcoming "tests." Angelus in Domegge. Friendly and familiar atmosphere. The Pope speaks of "his superiors at the Gemelli (Polyclinic)" and of the two tests he had to pass: the first, the Angelus at home, and the second, the Angelus in the square of Domegge di Cadore. In the afternoon, he remains at home. I go for a walk upstairs and meet Stanisław. We sit and chat. At one point in the conversation he comments to me, "I realize more and more that what is fundamental is the personal relationship with God."

August 31. Matters of public opinion. We climb Malga Campobon and finish at Malga Manzon. We go by car and then walk to the 2,041 m summit. Lunch. The Pope has consommé with tortellini, minced meat with chard, fruit, a glass of wine, and two cups of hot chocolate that Tadeuzs and I give him.

Before lunch, the Pope spoke to me about an article published in the weekly *Der Spiegel* on the decline of Catholics in Germany. He asked me if I knew any German journalists. I told him about the correspondent of the *Frankfurter Allgemeine Zeitung*, Heinz-Joachim Fischer. Over lunch we continue to talk about public opinion issues. The upcoming World Youth Day in Denver is also mentioned. He hopes that many young Latin Americans will also participate.

September 1st. *About the snow.* Last night it snowed and this morning it is cold. I go down to the village with Gasparro. In the afternoon the weather improves and we make an outing: we go again to Monte Zovo.

September 2nd. Last departure and farewell. Mass in the morning in the chapel of the Castello. The bishop of Treviso and his predecessor come. Later, a short outing. The Pope lists some concrete themes on which I must work: Russia, the Third World and the Far East. He goes into detail, pointing out goals. I see him completely recovered.

26

Taking the Initiative

Santo Domingo. V Centenary

October 9 to 14, 1992

In recent months, a controversy erupted over the meaning of this five-hundredth anniversary of the evangelization of Latin America. It is a historical question about which much remains to be investigated. Most of those who have dealt with these questions have been English and Dutch Protestants. Some of the existing bibliography is unreliable because of its lack of historical rigor, objectivity, and equanimity. Often, for ideological or political reasons, the facts mentioned reflect prejudice and biased approaches.

The Pope convened a symposium some time ago to study evangelization in America. The proceedings have just been published. They are interesting and open up new perspectives, but a certain sector of public opinion prefers to be carried away by visions of little historical foundation, which are part of what I consider to be a superficial and noisy contestation.

October 9th. Already on the plane, on our way to Santo Domingo, I go to see the Pope and we talk about these matters. The subject of the "request for forgiveness" is in the air. This request, apparently justified by certain excesses that occurred during the time of evangelization, could be manipulated ideologically, as if it were a question of asking forgiveness for evangelization itself. In the meeting with journalists, the Pope commented that Bartolomé de las Casas had already made a confession of sins centuries ago, a recognition that is closely related to another fact: the development of the doctrine of human rights carried out by the theologians of Salamanca. "It is something that must not be forgotten," the Pope emphasizes.

It is a significant trip, because it will also inaugurate the fourth general conference of the Latin American episcopate. Sodano will be the first president; and twelve members of the Curia will attend. I have been asked to participate. I even have a pontifical appointment. I am an "expert."

After the meeting with the journalists and lunch, Dziwisz tells me that the Pope wishes to speak with me again. In this second conversation, he tells me about the *ad limina* visit of the German bishops, an issue he had already mentioned during his stay in Lorenzago. He wants this visit's impact on public opinion to be studied. As he knows that I will be staying in Santo Domingo for a few more days for the Conference, he asks that we have a meeting on this matter when I return to Rome.

He is aware of everything: a number of news and articles have been published in the German press that are highly critical of Rome and contradict important doctrinal issues. Lehman believes that the real situation is not as serious as the media portrays it. The Pope comments that they are too closed in on themselves.

He then speaks of his address to the Pontifical Academy of Sciences on the occasion of the closing of the studies on Galileo Galilei, and of the presentation of the new "Catechism of the Catholic Church" in two months' time, on December 6, 7, and 8.

I see it once again: he lives intensely in the present and, at the same time, he keeps an eye on the upcoming events, to prepare them well. He takes time from wherever he can: he takes advantage of the flight hours to better outline the issues, to make them concrete, and to tie up loose ends. For example, noticing a great tension on the question of forgiveness, he makes some changes to his speech, addressing this idea in the context of the words of the Lord's Prayer: "Forgive us our trespasses as we forgive those who trespass against us. . . ." Before the dinner with the Latin American bishops, he tells me that I should see Lozano,[1] from the Secretariat of State, to discuss this matter.

October 14–29, 1992. At the end of the trip, I stayed in Santo Domingo for the General Conference of the American Episcopate. Those were intense days. Some Brazilian bishops had prepared an excessively "horizontalist" text: they proposed that the central theme should be the promotion of man, without further spiritual considerations.

No less than thirty-three working commissions were set up to prepare the texts. Predictably, when everything was presented in the classroom, the length was so great that it was almost impossible to summarize them in a text of reasonable length.

1. Francisco-Javier Lozano (Spain, 1943) was then in charge of the Spanish language section of the Secretariat of State. He would later become nuncio to various countries.

The drafting commission—led by Dom Luciano Almeida, assisted by several experts appointed by the Holy See—was in charge of making this synthesis. The vote was positive. Sodano, who presided, acted with authority. There were votes even on the morning of the closing, on the 28th.

The idea, insistent on the part of some, of making a penitential act for the alleged errors of the Church in her evangelizing work, was rejected. My impression is that the intention of this proposal was to hold the whole ecclesial institution responsible, rather than specific evangelizers; in this way, the guilt and responsibility for these errors, committed by individuals, with names and surnames, was to be diluted into the institutional sphere.

During these days, Sodano asked me to be present at his conversations—at the nunciature or at the hotel where the rest of the Curia cardinals were staying—and with the people with whom he spoke about difficulties and problems. He also asked me to be present when he talked with Medina, one of the two secretaries, or with other presidents: López Rodríguez, Cardinal of Santo Domingo, and Dom Serafim Fernandes de Aráujo, of Belo Horizonte.

On two occasions, always on Sundays, I have organized an outing to go for a walk on the beach and clear our heads a bit. Two Brazilians, Cardinal Arns and the Secretary for Divine Worship, have had a small traffic accident, fortunately without injury.

I have also helped them in the news coverage of the conference. Thanks to that, I have met many people.[2]

A Gift From the Pope

OCTOBER 31, 1992

Dziwisz calls me to go to dinner with the Pope, who arrives with the white neck strap (pallium) in his hand. He asks me, jokingly, "Do I have to wear this?" Then he combs his hair: "Don Stanisław, who is always looking out for me, insists on this, especially," he remarks good-naturedly, pointing to his hair.

He wants me to tell him about the Santo Domingo Conference. He is going to meet shortly with the cardinals who attended to study the document. I tell him—half jokingly, half seriously, thinking of the thirty-three commissions and the positions of each one—: "Holy Father, after being there I have concluded

2. One day, Sodano asked me to join him for dinner with Father Maciel at the hotel. We talked about the events of those days. Of course, when I spoke with Father Maciel I was far from imagining what later became known [Author's Note].

that if the Primacy of Peter did not exist by divine decision . . . it would have to be invented." He quickly replied, in the same tone: "No; if it did not exist by divine will, it could not be invented."

He speaks again about the *ad limina* visit of the German bishops. He informs me that we will not be able to hold the planned meeting and begins to list all the Tuesday meetings he has been scheduled for until December. I spoke to him about the possibility of his appearance on German television at Christmas. He does not answer me and leaves that decision up in the air, as if to say: "We'll see."

When we finish, Dziwisz gives me a book: an Italian translation of the *Diary of Sister Faustina Kowalska.* I ask the Pope if he could dedicate it to me. He goes to his secretaries' room and writes: "*To the most dear J. Navarro-Valls, Joannes Paulus PP, 31.10.92.*"

And he speaks to me about priestly celibacy, which has been criticized in the press in recent weeks. He wants the Church's position on this issue to be well presented. He seems particularly interested about this: "A new task for you," he tells me.

Meeting on Priestly Celibacy

November 3, 1992

The Pope has indicated that we meet at the Secretariat of State, Re, Schotte, Sepe, and I to discuss a response to the criticism on priestly celibacy.

Sepe fills us in on the situation: some priests belonging to presbyteral councils in various European cities have manifested, in different ways, their opposition to the maintenance of the present discipline of celibacy. They speak of "optional celibacy," of ordinations of *viri probati*, etc. It seems that they have collected signatures and have reached 80,000 already. At least a couple of European bishops have joined.

Everyone presents their points of view and proposes initiatives. For my part, I suggest the possibility of organizing public conferences in various cities of Europe on the question. Some personalities—bishops, prestigious theologians—could give them at the suggestion of the Holy See. Several names come up: Ratzinger, Lustiger, Kasper, Suquía, and others. Re notes the idea, which he is going to run by the nuncios in those countries.

This meeting, along with many other actions, is proof that the Pope never adopts a passive attitude. He does not resign himself and he moves his collaborators.

"Not for the Pope, but for the Church."

November 12, 1992

Dziwisz jokingly says, when the Pope enters: *"Il dottore Navarro viene alla sua udienza di tabella."* The Pope replies: "*Forse sarebbe meglio chiamarla Udienza da* tavola."[3] We go to the chapel and then to the dining room.

There is no specific topic, but I have mentally prepared a list of possible issues. We begin with the decision of the Anglican Church to open the door to the ordination of women. I comment on the reactions of the press: in Europe they are not all favorable to this measure. I also refer to the reaction of the Holy See to this decision and, in this regard, I tell him that we at *Sala Stampa* are looking for ways to better communicate what is being done in the Holy See and what the Pope is saying or suggesting. In this sense, it seems to us that it is better to give abundant information on the various topics, to take the initiative, not to limit ourselves to reaction. He nods. It must be done this way, he says: "Not for the Pope, but for the Church."

Another topic is priestly celibacy: I tell him about the proposals that came out of the meeting the other day, such as promoting a series of conferences on this issue in various European capitals, led by public figures in those countries: for example, Cardinal Daneels, in Brussels; Lustiger, in Paris; Ratzinger, in Vienna; Suquía, in Madrid, and so on. He likes the idea.

I tell him in more detail as well about a program that the German public television (*ZDF*) would like to make at Christmas. They want to record your words at the end of the *ad limina* audience of the German bishops and film you next to the nativity scene. It sounds good to him.

At FAO

December 5, 1992

This morning the Pope was at FAO.[4] He included in his speech the concept of "humanitarian intervention," which justifies an intervention within a country for ethical reasons. National sovereignty can be violated if there are serious

---

3. It is a play on the words "tabella" and "tavola" in Italian: "Dr. Navarro is coming to your *tabella* audience (office audience scheduled in the agenda)," says Dziwisz. To which the Pope replies: "It would be better to call it a *tavola* audience (table audience)," since they are about to have dinner.

4. *Food and Agriculture Organization* (FAO) is a United Nations organization whose purpose is to combat world hunger and support the transition to sustainable agriculture. It is headquartered in Rome.

humanitarian reasons that make it advisable. It is the idea I was talking with him about this summer, while hiking in the mountains, in connection with the Bosnian case: "It is lawful to disarm the aggressor, even by exercising a certain amount of violence." It is now a matter of developing the appropriate legal doctrine around the idea.

The Pope is suffering during these days because of the tragedy in Somalia: it seems that there is no choice but to intervene from the outside if we hope to prevent people from continuing to die in a country that lives in a permanent state of political and social chaos.

Future of *VIS*

December 18, 1992

"Very well. I don't deserve it," he replies when I ask him how he is. Indeed, I find the Pope very well. He has regained the kilos he had lost and may now weigh perhaps even a little more. Of course, I am happy to see that he eats his dinner with appetite now, contrary to what was usual for him.

He is interested in knowing "what's going on" and having the window to the world open. I tell him about the German television program—*ZDF*—and give him the questions suggested by Werner Kaltefleiter. He reads them and nothing changes.

Bosnia: I have the feeling—and I tell him this—that at the moment your voice is the only one being heard in the media and, above all, the only one being listened to.

Vatican Information Service: I inform the pope that it is launching. I tell him that translations will be made into other languages: German, French, "Polish too?" he probes amusedly, with a certain sardonicism. He asks me if it could become a sort of news agency of the Holy See: I reply that perhaps it could become one eventually.

Again in Front of the Nativity Scene

December 23, 1992

At 9:00 AM Werner Kaltefleiter and the *Vatican Television Center* staff are already preparing for the recording of the interview, which takes place at 9:30 AM. The Pope sits next to the crib at the end of the hallway near the entrance to the dining room. As usual, he accepts with docility the indications suggested by the professionals: how he should stand or where he should look.

27

Assisi, Again

Preparing for the Assisi Meeting

January 4, 1993

We are meeting with the Holy Father to prepare for the prayer and fasting meeting in Assisi on the 9th and 10th. Etchegaray, Arinze,[1] Duprey, Marini, Re and I will be accompanying him. Christians, Jews, and Muslims will meet for the second time, again at the invitation of the Pope, to fast and pray together for the gift of peace for Europe, and in particular for Bosnia-Herzegovina.

The Pope has the approved texts on the table. I see his signature in red pencil on the dossier with the acronym *JP*.

—"I wonder where we're going to put the fast," he says as he begins.

They tell him that the whole Sabbath afternoon will be a fast.

—"And on Sunday, nothing?" he asks.

That is his first concern: the sacrifice offered to God.

He immediately goes to the absence of the Orthodox. You can see that it hurts him. And a lot. "It's a paradoxical situation, but the paradox should not be emphasized," he says. "It's better to let it go. Those who have decided to come are welcome. We don't judge, even if we don't understand."

I suggest to him that I could comment something in the press to show that their absence cannot be explained. He immediately tells me no, not to do so. "Certainly, this is a slap in the face of the Pope," he observes, "but we are brothers in Jesus Christ. Therefore, if one brother behaves badly, the other cannot also behave badly." He thus points out the primacy of charity and, therefore, forbids that the Orthodox be shown in a negative light.

He wants prayers to be said in all the languages of Europe, East and West. This means that Marini, who organizes all liturgical aspects, will have to modify

1. Francis Arinze (Nigeria, 1932). At that time he was president of the Pontifical Council for Interreligious Dialogue. Later he was prefect of the Congregation for Divine Worship (2002–2008). He was appointed cardinal in 1985.

the program to include petitions for peace in all European languages, both in the vigil ceremony and during the Mass.

As we were leaving, the Pope told me in an aside that perhaps it would be a good idea to share these ideas with a journalist, so that the spirit of the day will be better understood.

Assisi

January 9 and 10, 1993

January 9. Assisi. Arrives by helicopter at five o'clock in the afternoon. He immediately goes to meet a group of handicapped children; he welcomes the representatives of other Christian confessions, Jewish and Muslim communities, and goes with them to the Hall of Friar Elias, where they eat bread and salt together, following an ancient rite that symbolizes peace. A single loaf of bread is broken for all, and salt, which gives flavor and life. In his speech he refers to the motivation for this meeting:

> Each of us knows that one's own religious conception is in favor of life and against death; it is in favor of respect for every human being in all his rights and against the oppression of man by man; it is in favor of the peaceful coexistence of ethnicities, peoples and religions, and against violence and war.
>
> The spectacle of the horrors of the wars being waged on the continent, especially in the Balkans, cannot but impel us to have recourse to the characteristic means of those who believe: prayer. This is our strength and our weapon. In the face of the instruments of destruction and death, in the face of violence and cruelty, we can only have recourse to God with our words and our hearts.
>
> We are neither strong nor powerful, but we know that God does not leave unanswered the plea of those who turn to him in sincere faith, especially when the present and future destiny of millions of people is at stake. This is the meaning of our vigil.

Each religious community then withdraws to pray separately. The prayer vigil, presided over by the Pope, takes place in the basilica, with the presence of members of various Christian confessions and some Muslims. Pierre Duprey reads the messages of the Patriarch of Constantinople, Bartholomew I, and the Serbian Patriarch Pavle.

The Pope does not have dinner or a snack. Before the first ceremony of the afternoon he is offered something liquid and drinks some tea. In the evening, several people who have suffered the hardships of war recount their terrible experiences.

The lower basilica is filled with young people, who spend the night in prayer.

January 10. In the morning, before we begin to receive the delegations, I find him praying in his chapel. My room is nearby and I walk past the door. He meets with the Muslims and recalls the testimonies they heard last night from the lips of people who have fled the Balkans.

"The most tragic aspect of this war, as of any war, is the fact that those who suffer most are usually ordinary citizens—parents, the elderly, women and children—people who simply want to take care of their families, work, live and fulfill their religious duties in peace. It is to these people, whose voices are rarely heard in international fora, that we must turn our attention first and foremost."

"We stand in solidarity with the victims of oppression, hatred, and atrocities (. . .) Both Christianity and Islam instill in us the effort to persevere in the search for justice and peace for them and for all the victims of conflict. We have a duty to help everyone, because all human beings are created by God and we are all members of the same human family."

Muslims attend Mass: it seems to me that this is the first time I have seen it. The visit of Oscar Luigi Scalfaro, President of the Republic, Giovanni Spadolini, President of the Senate, and Giorgio Napolitano, President of the Chamber of Deputies, is very significant: the three main Italian institutions, also belonging to different political sectors.

A collective lunch in the large refectory of the friary in Assisi. During the toast, the Pope speaks of the Franciscans and cordially encourages them to continue to live their spirit of poverty. In the afternoon he visits the tomb of St. Francis and meets with 170 nuns, mostly Poor Clares. At a quarter past six he returns to the Vatican.

With Venevisión Producers

January 15, 1993

We spent two days meeting with producers of the Venezuelan television channel *Venevision*. We came up with some ideas: a soap opera with human values, connecting with *Telepace* to bring news of the Pope's activities to America.

John Paul II had a marked sense of humor. He responded with a quick laugh or smile at the comments of those around him, in this case, from Joaquin Navarro-Valls.

© Vatican Media used with permission

The historic encounter between John Paul II and Mikhail Gorbachev on his arrival at the Vatican. Navarro-Valls is taking notes of the exchange of greetings to pass on to journalists.

© Vatican Media used with permission

An in-flight press conference, which became better organized over the years, without losing its spontaneity.

Violeta Chamarro, the president of Nicaragua, greets the Holy Father at the airport. She asked me how we could allow the pope to work so much at his age. "You ought to take better care of him, and make him rest."

It was a privilege to meet Mother Teresa of Calcutta. I always remember her words, in response to my question about how she carried on her work among the most destitute: "To try to make sure that these people who have lived so badly treated, like animals, could die as they are, as children of God."

His days in the mountains enabled a relaxed and comfortable time with friends, although he could not avoid the company of security people.

Accompanying the Pope during these rest periods was a privileged time to carry on longer conversations. These discussions helped Navarro-Valls to better know and to pass on the Pope's thinking in his work with the media.

For John Paul II, the days in the mountains were a great gift, even when his state of health limited his enjoyment. In his contact with nature, with its grandeur and beauty, he saw the creative hand of God.

His trips at various times followed less traveled routes, which from time to time led to unexpected encounters with local people or with hikers, and at times ended with a conversation over coffee or tea.

In spite of an acquaintance with Cardinal Ratzinger for more than 20 years, Navarro-Valls always admired, among other traits, the humility of the "intellectual pope," Benedict, who received with simplicity the suggestions that were made by his collaborators.

Interview on *ZDF*

January 16, 1993

I take to the Pope a very light anorak that they gave me in Madrid for him. I give it to Dziwisz. Dinner topics: Assisi, Catechism of the Catholic Church, interview on German television *ZDF*, my interview on Polish television about the Pope's health and meeting with the producers of *Venevisión*. The Pope tells me that Lehman, president of the German Bishops' Conference, has written to him telling him that he liked the *ZDF* interview.

At the end, I ask him about the two documents that are expected: the encyclical on moral theology and the one dedicated to life. Regarding the first one, he tells me that it will be published after the Catechism comes out, where many moral questions are clarified; in this way the encyclical will expand some aspects of the Catechism. About the second document, he tells me that it will come out next year, which the UN will dedicate to population and the family.[2]

Tobiana, one of the nuns who takes care of the Holy Father. She is a bit angry because some photos, taken by them and developed in the photographic service of *L'Osservatore Romano*, were later stolen and sold to a weekly magazine. They were images of the Pope's daily life.

An Interview in the *Telegiornale*

January 22–23, 1993

January 22nd. In the middle of the afternoon I get a call from the *Canale 5* news program: they are going to give a "bombshell" report on the Pope's health. The English journalist and writer Peter Hebblethwaite states that the Pope is seriously ill; that his life expectancy ranges from one to four years; that the hospital of San Raffaello in Milan, where he has been visited, has confirmed all this, etc. They insist that I go, and I decide to go on *TG5* live. "Sometimes," I say, "news is published that responds more to the desires of those who write it than to true information, based on reality. Naturally, Enrico Mentana, the *TG5* journalist, asks me who has this wish, and if there is someone who hopes for an early disappearance of the Pope. He gives me the opportunity to be clear.

January 23rd. Apparently, from the bits and pieces that have been reaching me, yesterday's interview was convincing. Dziwisz calls me to say: "Everyone says it was very good: thank you, thank you, thank you."

2. They are, respectively, *Veritatis Splendor* (published the following August 6th) and *Evangelium Vitae*, which will be published two years later (March 25, 1995).

I do not deny that I consider these "solo escapades" quite risky, going on the air to speak on behalf of the Holy See. Still, there are journalists—such as the veteran Benny Lai, who began covering the Vatican in 1951—who do not believe that I take such initiatives without consulting the Holy See first. Nor do I try to convince him.

Trip to Benin, Uganda, and Khartoum (Sudan)

FEBRUARY 3–10, 1993

FEBRUARY 3. As we head for Cotonou, the capital of Benin, before the Pope meets the journalists on the plane, I discuss with him the possible questions that he might be asked. I suggest that the meeting take place after breakfast has been served and before lunch.

He starts joking, as usual: "I am here to bother journalists again. It is not my fault; it is Dr. Navarro-Valls' fault, as always. Today we have little time, because this trip is relatively short."

We arrive in Cotonou and in the afternoon the Pope celebrates a Mass with priestly ordinations at the Friendship Stadium, which lasts almost four hours.

FEBRUARY 4. We flew to Parakou in a French military plane, designed for the transport of paratroopers, no comfortable accommodations, not even for the Pope. Canvas seats. I am inwardly angry. The Holy Father does not complain. I ask him if he has been able to sleep well. "*Non tanto bene*" ("Not so well"), he replies.

In Parakou, a meeting is held with the Muslims. Once again, the tolerant Islam of Africa is evident, because they quote texts of the Pope in Assisi and talk about the Muslims of Bosnia.

"In Benin," says the Pope, "Christians and Muslims have been living side by side for a long time. It only remains for me to encourage the efforts of both to advance in mutual knowledge and respect. Your country has known times of glory and times of serious difficulties. The time has come for all the inhabitants of Benin, regardless of tribe or religion, to work together to rebuild the country. The development of Benin, in which Muslims, Christians, and members of the traditional religion must participate, must benefit all strata of the population, free from any form of moral, physical, or psychological violence."

During the celebration of the Mass in the municipal stadium, the procession with the offerings takes place: one of them is nothing less than an Arabian horse. The Pope waves to the native who is leading the animal. As he perceives that the latter has not seen him, he insists on his greeting. It is a detail of his gratitude to each person he meets.

That same day he meets with a representation of voodoo followers.

On the return trip to Cotonou, Sodano gets seasick and I give him medical attention. I take him to the pilot's cabin, where he remains for the rest of the trip.

February 5. Uganda. President's Palace. When he arrives at my side, the Pope stops and introduces me: *"Monsieur President: le Dr. Navarro-Valls, Chef de Presse. C'est tres important"*("Mr. President, Dr. Navarro-Valls, Head of Press. It is very important"). These gestures from the Pope towards me leave me somewhat confused. They show that he values and is very mindful of communication . . . and, at the same time, that he is having fun teasing me with elegance, without the others noticing.

Before leaving the archbishopric and after praying in the chapel, he met with a group of nuns, who received him with great enthusiasm. How distant at this moment the pseudo intellectual criticisms and sophistry of certain European circles seem to me! It is clear that these women are profoundly happy and faithful to their missionary vocation.

February 6. As soon as he enters the plane, he begins to pray the rosary. Then he begins to read, as usual. On this occasion, a book by John Meyendorff, entitled "Byzantine Theology," translated into Polish. Byzantine Theology . . . in Africa! For the Pope, a man of universal mentality, this is nothing new.

We arrived in Gulu: great poverty. The Pope celebrates the Mass of the Good Shepherd in the esplanade of "Kaunda Grounds." There are some groups of refugees from Sudan. Two bishops distribute a letter addressed to the Pope in which they object to his visit to Khartoum, capital of Sudan, because of the repression there. I commented to Sodano that it would be good to share this information with journalists: "Yes, it is necessary that it be known."

We return to Kampala in a small plane and arrive home at four o'clock, so we have a late lunch. In the afternoon, meeting with the young people at the Kampala stadium, which is packed to capacity. Twice the power goes out and we are completely in the dark. But that does not diminish the strong impact of a little girl's story: Veronica, thirteen years old, sick with AIDS after an assault she suffered one night when she was leaving school.

February 7. The Pope prays at the Anglican Shrine of Namugongo, where some Ugandan Christian martyrs, who were burned after being tortured, are venerated. We pray together, Catholics and Anglicans. They say to the Pope: "Yes, the fire brought them together; but it was the fire of the Holy Spirit." He kneels before the images of the martyrs and spends a long time praying.

He then celebrates Mass at the Catholic shrine of the Ugandan martyrs. He begins his homily using the local language: *Baana bange abaagalwa, Mbalamusizza mwenna. Mwebale okujja. Katonda Kitaffe tumugulmize* (Dear sons and daughters, I greet you all. Thank you for being here. Let us praise God our Father). In the afternoon he announced to the bishops the elevation of this shrine to a Minor Basilica.

FEBRUARY 8. How little is needed to live and how many superfluous things there are in our latitudes, I think when I see the material conditions of so many people.

The Pope celebrates Mass on the esplanade of the Archbishopric. During the homily he calls for harmony and peace, so that "we may all cooperate in the common task of rebuilding the social fabric of Uganda. The tragic events of the recent past have left a painful legacy."

A few hours later, he delivered a magnificent speech to the members of the diplomatic corps, in which he showed them the great challenges facing African countries:

> But who should solve Africa's problems? There is no doubt that it is the peoples of Africa themselves who must build their own future. . . . No, Africa cannot accept a new colonialism. Its nations are independent and must remain as such. This does not mean though that the help of other members of the family of nations is not necessary and desirable. On the contrary, such help is needed more than ever. But to be truly effective, such help must not reflect a relationship of subjugation, but one of interdependence.

FEBRUARY 9–10. SUDAN. After a Mass in a stadium and a meeting on the Synod of Bishops for Africa in Rubaga Cathedral, near Kampala, on February 10 we headed for Khartoum, the capital of Sudan.

The president receives the Pope at the airport. The Pope's greeting speech is a lesson in social ethics. On the way to the city, thousands and thousands of people, mostly Catholics, greet the Holy Father. They are migrants from the south who have settled here, trying to survive. Some carry wooden crosses in their hands as a sign of identity.

During the visit to the president at his residence, I notice that when they leave to talk in private, one person is taking notes of the conversation. In view of the situation, I also decide to stay and take notes of everything that is said. The president speaks in Arabic, the interpreter translates into English and the Pope answers in English. Sodano is also present.

We celebrate Mass in the "Green Square," in honor of Blessed Josephine Bakhita.

The Pope has not stopped working at any time during his trip. Between Kampala and Khartoum, he writes the text of the general audience he will have next Wednesday in Rome, corresponding to the first part of the trip. Twenty minutes after taking off from Khartoum, he gives Henrik the complete text with his comments on his stay in Sudan.

FEBRUARY 11. Once in Rome, we had dinner with the Pope, with the experiences of the trip as a background theme.

To the Women of Sarajevo

MARCH 8, 1993

Some feminist groups have stirred up a controversy following the letter the Pope sent to the Archbishop of Sarajevo, asking him to help create a supportive climate for the poor women raped in Bosnia, so that they will not consider the child they have conceived as an enemy. During dinner we commented on this protest and I warned that the Pope is concerned about the plight of these women, not about the criticism that might come his way.

I inform him of the book that is being prepared in Spain on the occasion of his trip and the 15th anniversary of his pontificate. Smiling, he says: "Publish it after my death." It is not that he thinks he is going to die soon: it is a way of saying that he does not much care about the favorable comments that will appear in it. I tell him that it is a book that will undoubtedly do a lot of good.

Do not Interfere in the Political Climate

MARCH 25, 1993

Italian political life, in these first months of 1993, is particularly convoluted: cases of corruption and illegal financing in the parties, crisis of traditional political parties, strong divisions in the Christian Democracy (DC), etc. In this climate, I receive the information that today Mino Martinazzoli—Secretary General of the DC—is coming to have lunch with the Pope. Several people ask me to announce it to the press.

In the current atmosphere, it seems to me that giving news of the visit could be interpreted as a bet by the Pope for a political party, and that in the end it will just create controversy with other political parties in which there are also Catholics. I spoke with Stanisław and Sodano, and I decided not to give this information.

With Mother Teresa

April 1, 1993

The book *Solo per Amore,* published by Pauline Editions, on celibacy, was presented in the *Sala Stampa.* Bishop Lehman, Cardinals Moreira Neves and Sanchez, Sepe and Mother Teresa of Calcutta came to present the book. I receive them in my office and we sit down to chat for a while. I serve them a glass of tonic water: I know that Mother Teresa will not drink, and she tells me so. We prepare a little of the interview.

Some journalists focus their attention on Mother Teresa. One, in particular, asks her:

—"What would you say to one of your nuns who wanted to stop being a nun because of celibacy?"

Respond immediately:

—"I would say, 'Pray, pray, pray. You are the bride of Christ and you have to share His passion with Him. Now you are with Him in Gethsemane.'"

And she adds: —"Of course I can't force it. . . ."

I had lunch with Sodano and took the opportunity to discuss a few things: his interviews with *Catholic News Service* and the *EFE* agency; the request of *La Stampa* to interview an Italian bishop on the subject of Catholics in Italian political life (Sodano proposed the name of Saldarini, archbishop of Turin, the city where the newspaper is published).

Mercy of the Pope

April 4, 1993

I am going to discuss with Dziwisz some pending questions from the last conversations with the Pope. At the end of the conversation, some details of piety that the Holy Father lives with great naturalness come up in the conversation. In the evening, when he visits the chapel before retiring, he lies down on the floor and kisses it. In the mornings, he lies down on the floor—perhaps when making the day's offering—and prays like this for a while. The secretaries and the nuns who attend the apartment do not interrupt him; they know that sometimes he lies down on the floor to pray in the chapel or in his room when no one is watching.

At this hour—half past five—he is alone in his workroom, writing. He never complains about the amount of papers and documents that come to him. He writes a lot. At the moment, a document on ecumenism. In the afternoon he prays the breviary on the terrace.

"He continues to govern the Church," Dziwisz tells me, "with his initiatives, with his indications." He has not observed any sign of diminished energy or loss of strength in him. This is something that I also see every day."

Back from Seville, Huelva and Madrid

June 18, 1993

Yesterday we returned from Spain, where the Pope was from the 12th to the 17th. The enthusiastic response of the people was particularly evident in Madrid, with demonstrations that were also scenic, such as the thousands and thousands of multicolored papers that were thrown from balconies as he passed through the streets, just as in 1982. On this occasion, the trip also had a personal dimension: the Pope briefly received my brothers and sisters with their wives and children at the nunciature.

Today we had lunch with him at Castelgandolfo: Sandri, Agnes, and myself. I ask the Pope if he was surprised by the people's response. He was a little surprised. I tell him that the sectarianism of some media leads to a distorted image of the real Spanish Catholicism, which does not reflect—from my point of view—the work of evangelization and catechesis that so many Catholics have carried out during the last decade.

The conversation continues along these lines and we talk about some periods in the history of Spain: Asturias, Covadonga, the Vandals. The Pope mentions the Visigoths and their king Recaredo. . . . Again, I am surprised by his knowledge of European history and his memory.

28

"Somewhat Impaired, but Not Completely"

Back to Lorenzago di Cadore

July 7–16, 1993

We returned, as in previous summers, to Lorenzago di Cadore. We followed the same itinerary as in previous years: by plane to Treviso and then by helicopter to Lorenzago. Already on the day of arrival, after dinner, the Pope is seen walking a little in the garden of the house.

The next morning we set off for the first hike: Passo della Digola (1,650 m). We meet a couple, who greet the Pope with astonishment but naturalness. The green landscape blends with the steep rocks of the mountains. When we return, Gigi Vecellio and his wife Dea come to the house with a basket of mushrooms for the Pope.

The following notes correspond to those days, but some are undated:

July 9. Mount Rusiana, 1,600–1,700 m. We make a climb of about four kilometers [two and a half miles]. Along the way, we greet a woodcutter, Francesco Vecellio. Arriving at the top after a two and a half hour walk, the Pope says he wants to continue.

Every day the schedule is the same: We leave around ten o'clock and return around half past seven in the evening. Some days I go down to the village to meet the journalists and for this reason I do not join in the outings.

The Pope jokes, as usual, during the walks: one of those days, while I was taking pictures of him, he hummed: "How wonderful, the Pope is in Seville!," recalling in Spanish what the people sang during his trip last month. You can tell he has stuck with the tune.

On another occasion, while we are walking, I speak to him again about the possibility of making a television program in the form of an interview. And the interviewer? he asks; and he himself suggests the French writer André Frossard, who has dedicated several books to the pontificate: "Frossard already knows the Pope."

July 12. Excursion to Mount Rite, where we can see some defensive works from the First World War. The summit is at 2,183 m. At lunch, we take the huge loaf of bread that was given to him yesterday during the offertory procession at the Mass in Santo Stefano di Cadore. He jokes, "This is the bread I earned yesterday!"

On the way up, a few snowflakes fall. Then, after lunch, a wind and hail storm leaves the landscape completely white. We protect ourselves as best we can. It starts to cool down. Already in the afternoon, as we descend, we meet a group of people who have attended the Mass celebrated by a religious who comes here every year. The Pope enters the house and chats for a while with him. He is still dressed in liturgical vestments.

Another day we reach the *malga* Pian Formaggio (1,800 m.). It is called "malga" in this area because of the rustic houses that the shepherds use in the summer for themselves and for the cattle. We talk again about the possible TV program. The last day in the morning we take a walk along the "John Paul II Trail."

Here everything becomes simple and natural: one day, at night, around half past ten, I see the Pope go out to the balcony of his room to close the shutter, but it is stuck and will not come down. To my astonishment, I see him take a chair and climb up to try to fix it.

I would say that the chapel, the mountains and the books have been for him the three focal points of these days, the great poles of attraction. As far as the books are concerned, we carry them in our backpacks and he reads them, as always, even during the stops along the way. After one of these stops, when he stands up, he insists on personally carrying the folding chair he has been sitting on, and walks with it in his hand.

One morning a criticism of Cardinal Ruini appears in the newspapers.[1] The Pope calls him on the phone to express his solidarity with him. He tells me to go to Lithuania to help with the preparation of his next trip in September. He is now working a bit on the languages of those countries; in fact, he has brought some recordings in Lithuanian, Latvian, and Estonian to listen to them.

1. Camillo Ruini (Italy, 1931) was Cardinal Vicar of the Pope for the Diocese of Rome (1991–2008) and President of the Italian Bishops' Conference (1991–2007).

Preparation for World Youth Day Denver

August 2, 1993

We talked about the preparations for the trip to Denver for the World Youth Meeting. We accompanied the Pope for lunch at Castelgandolfo: Sandri,[2] Boccardo (from the Pontifical Council for the Laity, which oversees the Youth Days), and myself. Dziwisz is in Poland.

Regarding the content of his speeches for Denver, the Pope says he wishes to speak clearly from the outset about the defense of life. He will address that issue when he is received by President Clinton, who holds a very different point of view.

But there is also talk of other topics. "The chapel here has no Stations of the Cross," says the Pope, "so I do it outside, in the corridor." It is a corridor near the dining room, which has a series of framed plates with scenes from the Stations of the Cross. Thu, one of the secretaries, will later tell us that sometimes, when he gets up at six in the morning, he sees the Pope in that corridor, on his knees, with his head leaning against the wall, while he does the Stations of the Cross.

With US Ambassador Flynn

August 5, 1993

Raymond Flynn, US Ambassador to the Holy See, is coming to the office. He wants to talk about how to present the Pope's meeting with President Clinton to the public. Although he does not say so clearly, at the end of the conversation he raises the real reason for his visit. "What if a journalist asks the Pope or Clinton if they talked about abortion?" I tell him that the Pope does not normally answer questions asked about the content of his audiences, because he is a priest. As for Clinton, let him answer as he sees fit. The ambassador is aware that the abortion issue will occupy part of that audience and that the public already knows the positions of both leaders.

---

2. Leonardo Sandri (Argentina, 1943). At that time he was an advisor to the Secretariat of State for General Affairs (1992–1997). He would later be appointed substitute to the Secretariat of State for General Affairs (2000–2007) and then prefect of the Congregation for Oriental Churches. He was elevated to the cardinalate in 2007.

Preparing the Trip to Lithuania

August 27, 1993

I am in Lithuania from August 21–26, as the Pope suggested to me when we were in Lorenzago. The goal is to prepare information for the Pope's planned trip: he wants very much to go to Lithuania, but he is well aware of the difficulties.

I am introduced to Sigitas Jereys, a young Lithuanian Franciscan who helps out at the nunciature where I am staying. The country is emerging from a terrible history. I talk mainly with local journalists and government organizers of the trip. We call a press conference at the nunciature with about thirty journalists. I am interviewed on TV by a gentleman recycled from the Communist network, a system that still holds the keys to power and communication in the country.

During my meeting with the prime minister, he tells me about his reservations towards the Poles, recalling the history of poor relations between the two countries. Both the prime minister and the president are former communists.

Today, dinner at Castelgandolfo where I recount my take-aways from the visit. The Pope recalls some facts of Lithuanian history. Then he reviews the events planned for the trip. He decides not to speak about the withdrawal of the Russian troops remaining in the country. With the experience of the days spent there, I suggest a theme for the meeting with the priests: servants of the people who should not serve the people. He tells me that if, in reading the speeches, I see any point that I think it would be opportune to add, I should say so.

An Interview That Did not Take Place

September 19, 1993

In the last few days there have been too many activities and I have not been able to explain things to the Pope as I would have liked to. So, the TV interview we were working on, whose questions we had decided to entrust to the Italian journalist Vittorio Messori, who had already prepared them, came up.

That is one of the topics coming up today at the dinner with the Pope. I am sad that the plan is not going ahead. At one point in the conversation, the Pope makes a comment that intrigues me: "You have to keep in mind what the interviewer wants to ask. One could respond by having these questions as an outline and then rework the answers. I do not rule out the idea. . . ." The thing remains up in the air, but the fact is that the Pope keeps the sheets of paper of the questions.

Cardinal's Noodle

OCTOBER 4–10, 1993

I learn in Lithuania a small anecdote of the Pope in this country. Shortly after his election, he sent, with a priest friend, his cardinal's "noodle" hat to the shrine of Our Lady of *Ausros Vartai* (Gate of Dawn).

"No mention of the Council"

NOVEMBER 4, 1993

Last night I called Stanisław to tell him that I had returned from a trip to Spain. He told me that during my absence the Pope had told him a couple of times that he wanted to talk to me. I go to see him first thing this morning and he tells me about an interview with Jas Gawronski, who had insisted on talking with the Holy Father for a book. They talked over dinner, then Jas sent the text, which Rylko reviewed, and on the 2nd they saw it published in *La Stampa*.[3]

When I meet the Pope, he almost apologizes for the interview, as if to say that he was not entirely happy with its outcome. But what surprises me most, because it is unexpected, is the reason for his dissatisfaction: "There was a Second Vatican Council and the interview did not mention it at all."

On another matter, he tells me that we will have to think about the TV interview that in the end did not take place and whose questions he kept. He does not add more.

An Enigmatic Question

NOVEMBER 6, 1993

This morning, while working at *Sala Stampa,* I get a call from Dziwisz: "What are you doing Tuesday night?" I tell him I am doing whatever he tells me. He suggests I be available in case the Pope wants to see me. Sounds a bit enigmatic to me.

A Day in the Mountains

NOVEMBER 9–10, 1993

This morning Dziwisz calls me again and asks, "Shall we meet tonight?" When I ask him, as usual, if I should prepare something, he tells me tersely, "At a

---

3. Stanisław Rylko (Poland, 1945) worked at that time in the Polish section of the Secretariat of State. He was president of the Pontifical Council for the Laity (2003–2016). He was appointed cardinal in 2007.

quarter past six." I think he wishes to discuss something with me. "What are you going to wear?" he adds. Then I am really puzzled. We are clearly talking about two different things. I deduce that he is pulling my leg. He laughs and asks if I can come and see him for a moment.

Ten minutes later I am in the Apartment. "We are going with the Pope to San Felice d'Ocre." I tell him that I am very happy for the Pope, that he will be able to rest there. In San Felice, which is in the Abruzzi region, there is a country house, Tor d'Aveia, which is used in summer by the young people of Opus Dei who study in Rome.

At six o'clock I am back in the cortile of Sixto V, where there is only one guard. I see Valentino Pinci, the chauffeur, in the car, an armored, metallic, light-colored *Croma*. I carry a small suitcase in my hand with my things for the trip. I call Dziwisz, who tells me to go up to the apartment so that we can wait for the Pope together.

The Pope arrives a few moments later, wearing the black cape. The Pope, Dziwisz, Angelo Gugel, and I descend in the elevator. There is no one in the Cortile except the guard. The Pope enters the backseat of the car, in-between Dziwisz and Angelo. Dziwisz offers him a black beret and I install myself next to the chauffeur. Thus, well covered, it is difficult for anyone to recognize him. We leave the Vatican through the side door, the Perugino door. One car goes in front and another, a police car, behind.

We drive through Rome. It's fantastic: we stop at traffic lights, wait a few minutes because of a traffic jam . . . and nobody notices that the Pope is in the car.

When we reached the beginning of the highway to L'Aquila, the car in front of us stopped. Angelo, having accomplished his mission of hiding the Pope, gets out of our car and gets into the other one. We continue our journey. We stop to pick up the highway ticket and then to pay the toll. On the way, wanting to distract the Pope, Dziwisz brings up the subject of Freemasonry, perhaps because of a newspaper story. The Pope asks me what I think about it.

> – "Holy Father," I tell him, "I am not a great friend of 'great conspiracies' and 'world orchestrations,' although I understand that people are seduced by hidden plots and that sort of thing. I think that most of the actions against the Church are the work of individual people, radicalized, who coincide in their way of thinking."

Dziwisz speaks in a relaxed tone, very different from that of a work meeting (it is only a conversation to liven up the trip) of the famous "lists of Masons," sometimes published by the press, in which there used to be some ecclesiastics.

I tell him that I do not believe the lists. The Pope interjects: "Neither do I. At the beginning of my pontificate I did not believe in them. At the beginning of my pontificate they came to me with those lists in which there were several cardinals of the Curia. . . ."[4]

The conversation drifts to Denver and the encounter with young people. I tell him that, in my opinion, Denver is helping to change the horizon of the Church in North America. We then reviewed the various Youth Days: Buenos Aires, Santiago, Czestochowa. . . . "Because of the setting and the climate," the Pope said, "the best was Czestochowa, but Denver has had very good results. Now, when the North American bishops come to see me, they start talking about Denver."

The Pope feels like chatting and thus the first three quarters of an hour of the trip goes by. Then he turns on the back light of the car and starts reading. I pray for a while. Later, the Pope prays the rosary.

We arrive in San Felice in an hour and forty-five minutes. I get out of the car and open the door for him. He is welcomed by a priest, Francisco Vives, and a medical colleague, José María Araquistáin. He talks briefly with Prefect Marinelli and others from the police who have accompanied us on the trip; then he goes to greet the Lord in the chapel.

We move on to dinner, where he has a few good-humored words with the girl waiting on table. Later he says that, at this time of year, he remembers more and more often—"perhaps because I am getting old"—his priestly ordination.

Then, he speaks of his trip to the Baltic countries and praises the work of the nuncio, Justo Mullor. He also recalls his last trip to Spain: Madrid, Seville, his meeting with the King and Queen of Spain. . . . And he goes on to talk about Denver.

The dinner is simple but well presented. Often, before being served, the Pope tells them: "I don't deserve it."

After dinner, the girls who are in charge of the administration of the house enter the dining room; he greets them one by one, and they sing several songs for him, giving him a text with the lyrics. He makes amusing remarks to them, and says that they are "very good girls," before giving them his blessing.

---

4. The next day, remembering this conversation, Dziwisz told me that some time ago a person had come to see him to tell him that there were two collaborators of the Pope who belonged to Freemasonry: Ruini and me! Dziwisz told that gentleman that the Pope had full confidence in Cardinal Ruini and in me, and that the person who spread these suspicions only wished to sow distrust [Author's Note].

He greets the Lord again in the oratory and goes out into the garden. He wears an anorak under his large black cloak. He takes a pleasant walk to a hermitage, some four hundred meters away, chatting with Stanisław and Francisco Vives. I follow behind with Cibin. The sky outside is dark. The night is stupendous, with a starry sky. He goes in to pray to the Virgin and stays there for a while. Then we return with the light of a lantern. He retires, probably to read for a while. He looks happy and relaxed.

We chatted in the living room, while we peeled some chestnuts that Marinelli had brought and that the administration of the house have roasted wonderfully.

NOVEMBER 10. The Pope celebrates Mass at 7:30 AM, which we all attend. After breakfast, we hike to Campo Felice. We have brought the famous folding chair, so that the Pope can rest better.

While we have lunch on the mountain, we have a long conversation. The pope is linking topics and memories, and we only have to insinuate a question from time to time to keep him talking.

> *Priestly vocation.* "Yes, when I was a child I thought about becoming a priest, when I was an altar boy. But then came a period when I became passionate about literature and Polish philology. I was especially interested in the philosophy of language. Later came the theater and I forgot about the priesthood. I thought I should start a family, although an inner voice told me: '*Non la troverai mai*' ('You'll never find it')."

I considered becoming a priest. I went to talk to Bishop Sapieha, who accepted me into the underground seminary, and I began my studies in secret. He told me that I could not tell anyone that I was studying to become a priest, not even my father, who died in 1941.[5] .

I started studying with a book on Metaphysics. Aristotle's concepts—matter and form, potency and act, essence and existence . . . It changed my vision of the world.

Then began the period of manual labor, which I consider as a gift from divine providence, preparing me for what was to come. I worked for four years: two in the quarry and two in the factory. During the first two years I had little time to study. In the second two, my work consisted of controlling some

---

5. Karol Wojtyla, a member of the Polish army, was born in Lipnik, Poland, on July 18, 1879, and died on February 18, 1941.

pressure clocks; I did it in about two hours and then I studied. And my colleagues would tell me: your job is to study theology. . . .

On November 1st, I was ordained to the priesthood. Yes, alone. I was ordained by Sapieha and the next day I celebrated my first Mass, my first three Masses for the dead, in the crypt of the Wawel Cathedral.

"I knew and suffered the cruelty of two systems. One was more refined in its manners, but also more cruel and savage."

Wanda Półtawska:[6] "The Nazis put her in a concentration camp. When she got out, she couldn't sleep. She wrote a book (says the title)[7] and from then on she regained sleep. Yes, it was a catharsis."

We ask him about his disciples, Szostek and Styczeń. He jokes, "Shostec is a disciple of my disciple Stytzen and is therefore 'my grandson' in that sense."

Council years: "I was the only Polish bishop able to attend all the sessions of Vatican II. This was also providential. The communists gave me a passport because they thought: 'with this one we might be able to achieve something.'"

Ali Agca: "When I went to see him he was perplexed. He wondered why he had not killed me. The journalists wrote that he wanted to convert during those days, that he had asked for forgiveness. . . . All he said to me was that he did not understand why he had not succeeded in killing me; and, as he had heard about Fatima, he asked me: 'Explain Fatima to me.'"

Secrets of Fatima: "After my election, Villot—who was then Secretary of State—brought me the Fatima dossier and the envelope containing the text of the third secret, which had not been made public. I read it and did not understand exactly what it meant. Some time later, when I was in the hospital after the attack, I remembered the third secret, and asked for it to be brought to the hospital and read it again."

"Then came the consecration of Russia to the Heart of Mary. I made it with the formula: *I consecrate to you those countries that you carry in your Heart.* And that same day they called me on the phone to tell me that the Russian

6. Wanda Półtawska (Poland, 1921), physician and writer. As a member of the Polish resistance, she was interned in the Ravensbrück concentration camp where she was the victim of several experiments that caused physical symptoms for the rest of her life. Among other works, she wrote *Diary of a Friendship*, in which she recounts her long friendship with John Paul II, who was her confessor for a time and helped her overcome the traumas she had suffered during her internment.

7. I did not take note of Póltawska's book; but, quite possibly, she cited her autobiographical work *I boję się snów (And I Am Afraid of my Dreams)*, which she published in 1961 [Author's Note].

Orthodox bishops had also made the consecration, joining me in my consecration. If I had used another formula, they would not have accepted it. A few days later, Sister Lucia wrote to me to tell me that now everything had been done as Our Lady had requested."

It started to get a little chilly. I suggested that we should protect ourselves and get some rest. The security people accompanying us had set up a tent nearby, and the Pope took refuge there to rest for a while. He came out early, because of the cold, and we set up the folding chair next to the fire we had lit for him to warm up. There he read the breviary.

Some time later, we walked back to the place where the cars were waiting for us. The afternoon was splendid. We walked down through beech trees of ochre, gold, and red, all the shades of autumn. The Pope sat for a few minutes in front of them and commented: "Finally, the best." It was half past five in the afternoon.

The Pope returns to Rome giving thanks. As I said goodbye, I gave him a kiss, as I would have done with my father.

An Urgent Call

November 11–21, 1993

Today I leave the office early because I am going to have lunch and a meeting with a group of student priests at the Pontifical Universities in Rome. I get home around 4:00 PM. When I arrive, I receive a notice to call Dziwisz urgently. Apparently, he has called me several times: I realize that I forgot to activate the "pager" when I left the office this morning.

I call and Angelo Gugel gets on the phone. "Do you know yet, doctor?" "My God," I think, "something has happened and I haven't heard about it." He puts me through to Buzzonetti: "The Pope fell this morning and dislocated his right shoulder. This afternoon we will go to the hospital to have it relocated." I ask just two questions: general anesthesia? who will operate? Buzzonetti confirms the first one and tells me the name of the doctor: Professor Fineschi, head of the orthopedics and traumatology department at Gemelli.

I summon the staff and open the *Sala Stampa*, which is usually closed by that time. The journalists don't know anything yet. Or rather, they know that he has fallen, but nothing more. It was this morning in the *Aula delle Benedizioni*. The Pope was receiving representatives of the FAO (*Food and Agricultural Organization*). At the end of his speech, he began to descend the steps to greet the attendees to the right. Mr. Wagner of the FAO advanced to the left. The Pope began to change direction and fell . . .

Since it does not seem right to me that the images of the Pope's fall should be circulated, I call Re from the office to ask him that the *Vatican Television Center* not distribute them. Re tells me that, apparently, there are no such images, but that he will check. He calls me later: indeed, there are no pictures except those of an FAO photographer who was asked for the film, which he handed over without any problems.

I am calling some journalists to alert them, because the *ANSA* agency has reported that the Pope has just entered the hospital.

At the end of the operation, Buzzonetti calls me from the hospital: everything went well. Anesthesia time: fifteen minutes for bandaging plus three to four minutes for the actual bone setting. He reads me the medical report. Briefing with journalists and TV cameras. Personalized interview with several networks.

I speak to Sodano on the phone. I ask him if he wants me to accompany him to the Gemelli. He says yes. We leave at 8:08 PM. We arrive at the same area of the hospital he used when he was operated on two years ago. We are told that the Pope is sleeping. We talk in the front room with Dziwisz. A while later, we are informed that he has woken up. We go into the room. He is in bed. We can only see his head and a little of his left hand. I tell him: "Holy Father, the Lord always sends you some cross, small or big; he never forgets you." The Pope replies with good humor, "Do you see how [God] is good?" Since he is not in pain, there is no need to give him painkillers.

At ten o'clock in the morning of the following day, he left the hospital. On that day and the following ones, speculation continues in the press, based on the medical reports, because we have given all the data. A long article in *La Repubblica* reports alleged Vatican rumors—no names given—that speak of a fall due to fainting. It adds that the Pope had previously had minor fainting spells and memory loss. All false. I give a long and clear denial, which the press picks up the following day.

On Sunday, the Pope decides to lean out of the window for the Angelus prayer: he blesses with his left hand. He skips the Wednesday general audience and on Saturday attends the Congress on Childhood, organized by Cardinal Angelini. He wears the red mantle that covers his immobilized arm. At the beginning of his greeting in the Paul VI Hall he says:

> The Pope wishes to greet everyone. As you can see, he is a Pope with a handicap. Handicapped yes; but not completely destroyed. [Laughter and applause]. As you can see, I wear the red cape for solemn occasions: now

> I wear it even on everyday days to cover up my handicap and not to give an occasion to the photographers, who would like everyone to see that the Pope cannot move his right arm. . . . [laughs] I say that this is their job . . . but the very dear Dr. Navarro-Valls will explain everything to you. . . . Yes, I am somewhat impaired, but not completely.

A few days later, we published the criteria for the Pope's appearance at ceremonies and events. The planned schedule will be maintained, except for those events that could compromise the perfect immobilization of his right arm. Therefore, all public liturgical ceremonies will be suspended. He will participate in other events, such as the traditional visit to the monument to the Immaculate Conception in the Plaza de España on December 8.

"I Dictate Things Now."

December 12, 1993

I was away from Rome for a few days and on my return I received a call from Dziwisz. Thu, who receives me at the door of the Apartment, tells me that the Pope, after his fall, began to dictate the texts he was supposed to write, and now he has continued with this habit. "It's a great good thing," he says, "because he gets less tired and more productive." I am taking three books to the Pope: one by the Spanish writer José Luis Olaizola, another by Vittorio Messori, and another by Luigi Accattoli. I give them to him after greeting him, while we go to the chapel.

At the beginning of the dinner they talk about his fall. He comments with a smile on the inordinate interest he has aroused in the press. I tell him it is inevitable. "It has been providential. Now I dictate things and I get a lot more done. No, my arm hasn't hurt at any time. They tell me that at the moment of the resetting I winced, but I don't remember. The anesthesia was very special, because I saw the doctors, but I don't remember any pain. Now I am doing the gymnastics prescribed for me" (Thu told me that some days of the week a physiotherapist comes to help him with the recovery exercises).

And we talk about this year that is coming to an end, so intense. "Yes, it has been a year of great activity: Albania, the Baltic countries, Denver." He also told me that he was answering the questions Messori had prepared for that TV interview that never took place. "I am writing the answers. So far there are about thirty-seven pages. If it gets to about seventy, they could be published. It's not a TV interview any more, but there is a text there. . . ."

Agreement with Israel

December 30, 1993

The fundamental agreement between the Holy See and the State of Israel was signed today in Jerusalem. The Pope was the driving force behind this agreement. Faced with the inertia of bureaucracy, he acted with his typical innovative audacity.

The Pope told me some time ago: "When Reagan came to see me, he asked me why we did not recognize Israel. And I told him: my disposition is optimal; we could exchange ambassadors tomorrow. But they would have to take some steps as well."

What has happened? Well, Israel has recognized the Palestine Liberation Organization (PLO) as an interlocutor to initiate a peace process. Now—since the Madrid Conference and, above all, after the secret negotiations that brought Rabin and Arafat to Washington—the State of Israel and the Palestinians are talking about their future, both of them renouncing violence as a method of settling their differences. With this step, the Holy See no longer has any problems in establishing diplomatic relations with Israel.

These have been very busy days for me as well. I asked the Second Section of the Secretariat of State—Tauran—to prepare a memorandum on this question, to be given to the press, explaining the position of the Holy See. They have already done so and Sodano has approved it. Yesterday afternoon Tauran called me to talk. I was joined in the conversation by Celli and Gatti, who work in foreign relations for the Secretariat. After reading the memorandum, I asked them some questions about Jordan and the possible reactions of the Arab countries.

This morning the Jordanian ambassador came to see me. Yesterday he was called by the Minister of Foreign Affairs of his country, which is negotiating a similar agreement with the Holy See. The minister wanted this to be mentioned at the meeting with the journalists, because he felt it was only fair. I reassured him by confirming that it was planned to mention this issue, and he thanked me for it.

I had a long briefing with the journalists about all this material. And after convincing Tauran, I also gave them the text of the agreement. I think it was worth the effort.

29

The Family on the Horizon

About the Former Yugoslavia

January 4–5, 1994

Yesterday and today, meeting in the *Sala Bologna* with the Pope, on the situation in the former Yugoslavia. Members of the Roman Curia and some experts are participating. On the afternoon of the 3rd, Re called me at home to see how news coverage could be organized. Half an hour later he called me back. He had spoken to the Pope, who agreed to the news outline. "If you are not busy, you could attend the meeting," Re tells me. I admire his elegant way of presenting things.

It begins at 9:30 in the morning. The Pope enters and greets everyone. He reads his speech, written entirely by him, as Cardinal Etchegaray later confirmed to me. The other participants followed. The Pope attended throughout the morning and part of the afternoon, with great attention. At the end of the morning session, he signaled me to accompany him and Sodano to his apartment. He asks my opinion and I comment that the message will have to be well defined, taking into account that the resonance it will have in Belgrade will be different from the one it will have in the West, since they are two different audiences.

In the afternoon Etchegaray read his text, which I considered good, in a somewhat homiletic style. Tauran had taken some of these ideas and had elaborated another text, of a more informative nature. We discussed which of the two would be more suitable for dissemination to the general public. In the end, a genuinely informative text was approved and I was commissioned to write it. I wrote it at night, at home. In the morning I went to the Second Section to have it corrected and translated into French, and returned to the *Sala Stampa*. The text is approved with some additions.

Before concluding, I suggested to Sodano that a short paragraph could be prepared for the Pope, since it would be opportune for him to mention this matter during the general audience. Sodano approved the idea and entrusted it to Tauran.

Today, when we were waiting outside the Aula at the beginning of the meeting, Rylko read to Sodano a translation of three pages that the Pope himself had written in Polish that very evening. It is a very beautiful text: "We will not solve the problem of Bosnia without Jesus Christ." The primacy of prayer. It was decided to give it to Etchegaray, who is working on a message to be sent to all the dioceses.

Available

January 29–30, 1994

I am outside Rome. I talk to my office and they tell me that Dziwisz is looking for me. I call him: he asks me if I can come to see him tomorrow. I return to Rome and he asks me if I can be "available" on Monday at six o'clock in the evening. This time that word alone is enough for me to understand. It is a question of accompanying the Pope on a day of rest outside Rome.

Sixteen Declines and Three Drops

January 31–February 1, 1994

I arrive at six o'clock at the Cortile of Sixtus V. I go up to the apartment and a moment later the Pope comes, wearing his black cape. The car is waiting for us downstairs. The Pope, Dziwisz, and Gugel follow behind; I walk together with the chauffeur. We drive through Rome and on the L'Aquila highway, the car in front of us stops, Gugel gets out of our car and gets into the other one; we continue in the direction of San Felice d'Ocre. We repeat the plan of a few months ago.

On the way, the Pope begins to talk about the ceremony in which Tadeusz Styzcen was awarded an Honorary Doctorate at the University of Navarra. He says that Tadeusz—who passed through Rome on his way back from Pamplona—has returned enthusiastic. And, taking into account that the university is promoted by Opus Dei, he jokingly tells me: "Now he wants to become a member of Opus Dei. . . ."

He then mentions his recent audience with the Russian Prime Minister; I ask him if he has invited him again to visit Russia and he says no, but that he told Cadinal Sodano that this trip cannot be delayed indefinitely. We discuss the situation in Bosnia.

We arrive at Tor d'Aveia around eight o'clock. Francisco Vives and some students from Cavabianca[1] welcomed him. The Pope shows great confidence in those he meets. This "anomaly" of a Pope leaving the Vatican for a walk in the mountains does not worry him at all. During dinner, we spoke of the many

1. International seminary of the Prelature of Opus Dei in Rome.

good things of our time and of the "springtime of the Church," an expression often used by the Pope.

Turning to those waiting at the table, he jokingly added: "*Con queste brave ragazze, belle ragazze, come non è primavera?*"[2] He was interested in the presence of Opus Dei members in various Eastern European countries: Poland, Lithuania, Latvia, Byelorussia, Ukraine, and Russia. Vives gave him some data: in some they are just beginning; in others the first vocations are coming.

We comment on the situation of the family in some of these countries. The Pope asks about the the Work in Slovakia, Slovenia, Hungary, and Romania. Vives explains the situation in each country. "And in the Asian part of Russia?" Then he asks about China. He has been giving an overview of that part of the world.

When the waitress encourages him to eat a little more, he replies with a smile: "Everything is very good. But I can't eat so many good things. I mustn't get fat, unlike Don Francisco, who is very thin: he could put on ten kilos more and nothing would happen." At another point he says: "If the nuns [who usually attend to him] were to find out that I have eaten so much, they would be surprised."

Vives explains to him that some women of Opus Dei are doing a retreat course these days at Tor d'Aveia. The Pope asks about the priest who is preaching and how the retreat is organized. I tell him that it is usually done in silence, with various acts of piety (Holy Mass, Stations of the Cross) and various meditations preached by the priest. He was also interested in the organization of the women of the Work. Vives tells him that they depend on the prelate, as do the men, and that they govern themselves in all aspects.

Later on, we talked about the crisis in Eastern Europe and he added: "This crisis is now manifesting itself, but it existed before; in any case, they have the resources to get out of it."

The girl waiting on table tells him that tomorrow is a Marian feast and that February 14 is an anniversary of the Work: the beginning of the apostolic work with women. The Pope then raises his glass and pronounces his toast for that date: "I wish you to grow and multiply."

Returning to the girl's comment, he asked about those beginnings. Vives explained that in 1928 Josemaría Escrivá had thought of working only with men, but God had arranged things differently. "When I too," the Pope commented, "when I began to do apostolate with young people, I thought the same thing: I will go to the boys. No girls."

2. "With these fine girls, beautiful girls, how can it not be spring?"

Meanwhile, those who work in the administration of the house begin to enter the dining room to greet him. They sing several songs for him. At the end, he tells them: "When God finished creating the world, he said that everything was good; and then, that it was very good. The same thing happened with Opus Dei. The Work was not completed until the women came. Only then was it possible to say: everything is fulfilled, everything is complete, everything is very good. How much the woman is worth!"

At the end, he has a few words of affection with them, praising their songs and the care of the house. Francisco Vives comments that, through their professional work, they help many people live with a Christian spirit. The Pope, pointing to those who take care of the kitchen, emphasizes: "To live . . . and to survive."

In the garden, while strolling, he continues to speak about women in the Church. He recalls his catechesis on women in the book *Uomo e donna lo creò* (*Man and Woman He Created Them*). And he adds: "Women have a great capacity for sacrifice. And also physical strength. That is why they are able to endure pregnancies and the terrible pains of childbirth. When they are corrupted, they are capable of the worst things. But often, when that happens, the culprit is the male."

The next morning, after Mass—which we all attended—and breakfast, we left with the Pope for the mountains. We go to the Gran Sasso. On the way, we leave the car for a caterpillar-tractor, which takes us to a snowy slope. The Pope puts on his skis and starts to descend. In the first attempt he falls because he is still getting used to this sort of activity after the incident with his arm. He then makes several descents between morning and afternoon, with a break for lunch. The day is splendid, with wonderful sunshine and no clouds. We finish around half past five.

He returned to Rome happy. It had been a perfect day of rest. I tell him that he has made a good number of descents: "Yes," he says smiling, "sixteen descents with three falls . . . like our Lord."

Two Hours with Tad Szulc

February 9, 1994

The journalist Tad Szulc is coming to see me this afternoon and I am with him for a couple of hours.[3] He is writing a biography of the Pope. I had been

3. Tad Szulc (Tadeusz Witold Szulc) (Poland-United States, 1926–2001), a Polish-born journalist, was a foreign correspondent for *The New York Times* from 1953 to 1972. He later published books on international politics and a biography of John Paul II: *Pope John Paul II: The Biography* (1996).

following him for a long time when he first told me about the project. I presented it to the Pope during a trip, and now Dziwisz has invited him to lunch in the Papal Apartment. Naturally, it would be naive to think that the whole book will be roses. In fact, when I press Tad a bit on whether I will be able to read the manuscript, it becomes clear that his plans, though well-intentioned, include aspects of the pontificate that he considers controversial and he quotes the theologian Charles Curran to me on the issues of overpopulation and sexual morality.

Our conversation was devoted to Eastern Europe in the past years and to Gorbachev. I clarified some points he was confused about: I had spoken with Jaruzelski and he almost got the impression that Jaruzelski was the person who had persuaded Gorbachev to go to see the Pope. . . . I told him about our trip to Moscow in 1988, about Gorbachev's visit in December 1989, about Ali Agca.

With the German President

March 3, 1994

The President of the Federal Republic of Germany, Richard von Weizsäcker, is coming today for an audience with the Pope. They have a long interview. When it is all over, I approach the Pope to find out the topics of the conversation. "And one thing that is not for publication: he has insisted a lot on the trip to Russia. I told him: 'President, for that you will have to insist (with the Russians).' The authorities want this trip, but right now with the Orthodox it is more problematic." He insists that it is not for publication, but only as background information.

On the Pope's Resignation

March 5, 1994

Has the Pope ever thought of resigning the pontificate because of old age or illness? I do not know. Undoubtedly, someone around him has thought about it, possibly without reaching a convenient conclusion. I know that Cardinal Castillo Lara has secretly commented that he thinks that John Paul II could resign—in due course—because of old age.

The illness of two years ago—the colon tumor—may have made the Pope think. Also, perhaps, the slight tremor in his left hand: some signs of old age. I don't know: he has never brought up the subject, at least not when I was there.

Stanisław once asked me what I thought about the possibility. I replied that it seemed crazy to me: two Popes, one retired and one elected, would be the basis for a good division in the Church. The "progressives" or the "conservatives" would already have an "institutional" excuse to swirl around one of the two.[4]

Naturally, this conversation in no way proves that the subject was the object of the Pope's consideration. But it could also be an indication to the contrary.

Vaclav Havel

MARCH 7, 1994

Audience with Vaclav Havel this morning. The Pope told me that they talked about Bosnia-Herzegovina, Germany, Russia, the separation of the Czech and Slovak Republics. He tells me that he is a religious man. He thinks it is a good thing to have had these audiences with the President of Germany and with Havel. He is looking forward to the visit of Yeltsin and Clinton in June. He seems happy.

International Travel and . . . Poetry

MARCH 12, 1994

Dinner with the Pope. Only Dziwisz is there. The conversation is pleasant and covers a wide range of topics. From the preparation of the United Nations conference on population ("Bishop Tauran has spoken to me about this conference and is preparing his intervention") to the upcoming trip to Croatia. "Tauran has spoken to me about that conference and is preparing to speak") to the upcoming trip to Croatia. Telegraphic notes on some of the topics he spoke to me about.

The Pope's Letter on the Family, published a month ago on the occasion of the International Year of the Family, is being widely circulated in France. The Pope confirms to me that he wrote it in its entirety.

Regarding the meeting with Havel a few days ago, he tells me that perhaps *L'Osservatore* has given too little space to this news. "Havel is a nice and cultured person. He asked me to bless him. I think he did it out of conviction. He made a very good impression on me."

---

4. That is what I thought at the time. Naturally, almost twenty years later, history would show a very different scenario [Author's Note].

Lebanon is always on his mind. Looking ahead to a trip, he says that local authorities "have two concerns: security during travel and the fear that the Pope's visit will become a confirmation of Syria's presence in Lebanon. But this visit is an occasion to tell the truth about Lebanon's independence and sovereignty. The mere fact of visiting the president, the country, the government: that is already a sign of sovereignty. As in Poland, the authorities, Edward Gierek and the rest, wanted these visits because they were a sign of sovereignty [against the USSR]."

He is very happy that the text of this year's Stations of the Cross was written by Bartholomew, Patriarch of Constantinople. "It is unprecedented," says the Pope. This month the dialogue with Moscow continues. There is a meeting in Geneva: "Kirill is coming."

Sarajevo. The Pope says we should go as soon as possible, because the city is now protected by the United Nations. "People are waiting for it. Of course, it would be better to go to Belgrade and Sarajevo. We have done everything possible with the Serbian authorities, but they say nothing. I see that Patriarch Alexis[5] travels a lot, but public opinion does not give him enough attention. The Nuncio was telling me that Alexis has been in Bulgaria, but no one is talking about it. Then Bartholomew went. That has had more impact because it is an area influenced by Constantinople. We will see. The trip should take place in June, before it becomes impossible to plan it."

Other projects. He adds that the meeting of cardinals for the preparation of the year 2000 will take place first. "I have already written the first project," he says. And then, the African Synod. "We have quite a bit of work in progress."

Survey of US clergy. I am talking with the Pope about a survey on the American clergy published by the *Los Angeles Times*. According to this survey, the young priests who have been ordained in recent years turn out to be more "conservative" (as the newspaper calls them, to indicate that they are more faithful to the faith they have received) than the previous ones. "It is the same thing—the Pope comments—that Cardinal O'Connor tells me. Especially after Denver. In October we will have another meeting with young people in New York."

5. Alexis II (Estonia, 1929–2008) was Patriarch of Moscow and all Russia (1990–2008). He was elected successor of Pimen a few months before the dissolution of the Soviet Union, becoming the first post-revolution patriarch elected by the Orthodox Church and not by the Communist political power.

Croatia and other countries. I tell him that, with so much work to do, we'll have to rest well this summer. "In July and August," he says, "because in September we are going to Croatia. If the Yugoslavian problem is solved this year, it would be providential, because there, to a certain extent, is the key to the entire Orthodox East."

We get up and he says that, after all this walking around, he's going to read poetry. "Specifically, the poems I wrote fifty years ago. I'm reading them with interest: how could I have written that? Now they don't seem so bad to me. . . . I compare them with those of Milosz[6] when he was in France and Berkeley and it seems to me that mine are much better!" he concludes with a laugh.

I leave the Papal apartment after more than an hour of conversation on a wide range of issues, which show the Pope's universal interest. He does not follow events, he drives them. He does not allow himself to be carried along by public opinion, he stimulates it; and, to a great extent, he creates it. He does not wait passively for favorable historical circumstances: he uses the means at his disposal to direct history towards Jesus Christ.

Álvaro del Portillo

March 23, 1994

Andrés Vázquez de Prada woke me up at six in the morning to tell me that, during the night, a few hours after returning from a pilgrimage to Jerusalem, Don Álvaro, prelate of Opus Dei, died.[7]

Before going to work, I went to Villa Tevere, the central headquarters of Opus Dei, where the funeral chapel was already set up. I kissed Don Alvaro's forehead and hands, so many memories! I begin to ask his intercession for many things.

Numerous bishops and cardinals came to pray; among others, Cardinal Ratzinger. I leave for the office and the first call I receive, when I arrive, is from Dziwisz, giving me his condolences, very affectionately.

In the evening, at a quarter past six, the Pope arrives at Villa Tevere. "*Sia lodato Gesù Cristo*" (Praised be Jesus Christ!), he says as he enters. He kneels

6. Czeslaw Milosz (Poland, 1911–2004), poet and translator, Nobel Prize 1980.

7. Álvaro del Portillo Diez de Sollano (Spain, 1914–1994), the first successor of St. Josemaría Escrivá at the head of Opus Dei. He was beatified on September 27, 2014. Bishop Javier Echevarría, who was then Vicar General, succeeded him in office (1994–2016).

on a kneeler, in front of the recumbent body of Don Álvaro, and prays for about ten minutes. They suggest that he recite a response, but he prefers to begin with the Salve Regina. Then he recited three glorias and two invocations for his soul. At the end, during the farewell, the Vicar General of Opus Dei, Javier Echevarría, thanked him for his visit: "*Si doveva, si doveva*"[8] answered the Pope. I also thank him when I greet him.

I start receiving messages of condolences from various places. Schotte tells me on the phone: "You already have two saints." Father Tucci tells me that he has offered the Mass of suffrage for his soul. Tauran, Re. . . . I receive letters and messages from Macchiocchi, Aura Michele, Gasbarri, and many others, for which I am very grateful.

With the Jews

April 4, 1994

Tad Szulc brings me the issue of *Parade* in which he has published his article-interview with the Pope on the Jews. It is good. It came about thanks to his friendship with Dziwisz. *The New York Times* immediately echoes it, with an article by A.M. Rosenthal, its former editor.

Since the Pope's visit to the synagogue in Rome and the uninterrupted series of meetings with Jewish communities all over the world a long road has been traveled. I think that at the beginning there was, on the Jewish side, a certain amount of caution, as if they were not entirely sure of the Pope's sincerity.

The controversy over Waldheim's visit to Rome is now behind us. So too the controversy over the Auschwitz convent. Now, with the establishment of diplomatic relations with Israel, the panorama seems to have cleared up.

Letter to Families

April 6, 1994

The International Year of the Family is still very much on our minds. A couple of months ago, the Pope published his splendid *Letter to Families*. Some additional initiatives have been planned along the same lines, such as the meeting with families in October and the visit to the UN headquarters.

8. "It had to be done, it had to be done."

In the midst of this situation, the UN convened the meeting on population in Cairo, with a clear anti-birth orientation. And the Pope has shown that he is not willing to remain silent. His attitude is not one of accepting the inevitable or resigning himself to lamentation. He rebels. He knows that if he shouts he will be heard. And he shouts.

Three days ago Jerome Lejeune died—the well-known French geneticist who discovered the gene defect that causes Down syndrome—and the Pope sent a letter to Cardinal Lustiger, Archbishop of Paris, in which he also referred to the attacks on the family. Everything suggests that this will be an important area of work in the coming months.

30

Parkinson's

A Book of Questions and Answers

April 28, 1994

I am going to Verona. I take with me something quite unexpected: the Pope's answers to the questions that Vittorio Messori had prepared for the TV interview that did not take place. It is a very good text: 177 pages.

I transmit to Messori some criteria about the Pope's interview-book, which he will have to work on. He asks me to send my points to him in writing so that he can keep them in mind. We then spent some time chatting about his life, about his encounter with Christ through his reading of the Gospels, about his first best seller (*Ipotesi su Gesù*), and about his other books.

Another Fall

April 29–May 15, 1994

In the morning, while I am praying before breakfast, Re calls me: the Pope fell last night and "hurt his knee." —"Is it necessary for me to come urgently?"— "No, it is not necessary; but it would be good for you to meet with him this morning, as soon as he arrives at the Vatican."

A few minutes later, Sodano calls me. He is a bit more explicit about what happened, but he does not offer much information either. In view of the situation—I have no idea of the seriousness of what has happened—I decide to go immediately to the Vatican. I take a cab and go to see the Cardinal, whom I find dictating to his secretary a statement with the medical data: fracture of the neck of the femur with a deviation of fragments.

We discussed whether or not it is appropriate to say that the Pope's fall occurred in his bathroom. At the beginning, I was in favor of not putting that circumstance in the communiqué, and limiting myself to commenting it orally to the journalists. But we left it as it was, and only afterwards I realize that I was wrong: it would have been better to leave it out.

I give a first briefing to the journalists around 9:50 AM, ten minutes before the Pope is taken by ambulance to the hospital. I speak with Buzzonetti to coordinate the information.

At ten past eleven I go to the hospital with Re. We go straight to the trauma operating room. In the next room is Dziwisz, alone, reading the breviary, his right arm in a cast from a dislocation he sustained on the mountain. He tells us that the Pope fell last night, just before eleven o'clock, as he was leaving the bathroom. He alerted Dziwisz, who immediately called Buzzonetti. They x-rayed him and very soon had a clear diagnosis. "This is what I was missing for the year of the family," the pope said. He was given some light painkillers, with which he was able to sleep for a few hours. Before leaving for the hospital he concelebrated Mass from bed.

We wait in the operating room. Everything goes well, but slowly. The operation itself lasts two hours: a good part of that time is taken up by the preparations. The hours go by, and they seem interminable to me. I pray the rosary, walking up and down the corridor, next to the connecting door. They bring me some sandwiches that I take right there, while I hear some confused noises coming from the operating room.

The surgeons finish the operation around a quarter to four in the afternoon. They confirm that everything went according to plan. Fineschi explains the operation in detail while showing me the X-rays. They have implanted a prosthesis. I take with me an X-ray of the fracture and another one of what it looks like after the operation. "A new small cross for the Pope," I tell Dziwisz. "Not so small," he replies, with good reason.

They bring a draft of the medical report. I suggest changing a word to make the text more understandable. The doctors sign it and I rush off to the *Sala Stampa* where the journalists are waiting for me for the briefing. We start around five o'clock in the afternoon.

There is a colleague who finds it very suspicious that the Pope was not immediately transferred to the hospital after the fracture. I reply that it was not necessary to proceed with an emergency admission for the simple reason that the diagnosis had already been made and was very clear.

I give a series of interviews to various European television stations and to several radio stations in Latin America. At the last minute, I still have an appointment for a *RAI Uno* program at eleven o'clock in the evening: but I am so exhausted by the stress of the day that I am no longer in a position to talk about anything. Tomorrow will be another day.

April 30. I go to the hospital in the morning. I arrive while the doctors are still there, and Professor Fineschi tells me that the Pope is well. They mobilize him a little. He has his first breakfast after the fall. I have another briefing in the *Sala Stampa* at about twelve o'clock.

At five o'clock in the afternoon the Pope concelebrated with Dziwisz. It was a quieter day than yesterday.

May 1st. Late yesterday afternoon he had a slight fever, I was told this morning when I arrived. But since he does not want to miss his weekly appointment in St. Peter's Square, in the morning he records the brief speech that accompanies today's *Regina Caeli* prayer, which will be broadcast at noon. At the end, he spontaneously adds: "I wish you a good Sunday, a good month of May, a true springtime."

Today, since I did not go to the office, I had some time to think about the events of the last few months. And I come to a strong conclusion: these falls—the one of the arm, and now the fracture of the femur—have to do with the fact that there is a creature that acts together with the Pope to prevent him from doing his work, the devil.

May 5. In the morning, at 9:45 AM, I visit the Pope in his room. I find him well, with a relaxed and calm face. His enormous spiritual strength contrasts with his great physical vulnerability. He smiles.

During the conversation I tell him something I have considered in prayer. The devil must not be too amused by the Year of the Family. . . . "Of course!—The devil doesn't want me to do this Year of the Family. But I will." And he adds laughing: "Sometimes they tell me that I am a pillar; well, now I am a pillar upside down" ("*una colonna capovolta*"). As I see that he is feeling better and feels like talking, I tell him that I was with Messori a few days ago, on the occasion of the book he is writing, and I tell him about my conversation with him.

May 15. This morning, around a quarter past nine in the morning, I enter the area reserved for the Pope. I find him walking with the help of a walker. He is attentively calculating each step he takes, as if savoring the beginnings of his reconquered autonomy. A nun and one of the doctors watch him, attentive, so that he does not lose his balance. He continues to take small steps, as if asking for approval after these exercises. It reminds me of my mother when she was in a similar situation. She too, after an identical operation, as she began to take her first steps asked me, "Am I doing it right?"

He returns to his room. A short time later I stop by to see him. He is lying on one of the narrow hospital beds. Someone has placed an image of Our Lady of Fatima on his bedside table. "Holy Father, it is wonderful to see you walking again," I tell him.

He asks me about Messori's book: I answer that I think it will do great good, especially for intellectuals. And I add that I am praying that we can go to the mountains in July. "Maybe, he says, with less steep trails." You can tell he's excited at the thought. Doctors are inclined to advise against it, because of the risk of further falls, but he would like it immensely.

I ask him what he is thinking about these days. He tells me about the ceremonies on the occasion of the fiftieth anniversary of the battle of Montecasino, because, together with the destruction of Warsaw, those ruins symbolized the birth of the new Europe.

He then comments on more personal matters. "I spent May 13th in the hospital. The day I should have died. But God did not want me to die, because he wanted the Pope to. . . . And I have also been thinking that I was born on May 18, at five o'clock in the evening, around the same time they tried to kill me. The church was very close to my parents' house, and at that hour, after praying the rosary, they used to sing the litanies. Possibly, the first music I heard in this world were the litanies to the Virgin."

I tell him that he seems to be improving rapidly. "Yes," he says with a smile, "I have told Professor Fineschi that he and I have only one option left. He has to cure me and I have to get well, because there is no place in the Church for an emeritus Pope."

And he adds, like a child telling a little joke: "On Sunday, at the window. . . ." That means that he wants to be at the Vatican next Sunday and look out to pray the *Regina Coeli* with the pilgrims coming from all over the world. At the moment, it seems that the doctors are not as convinced as he is.

I pass by the chapel that has been installed in the adjoining room. I greet the Blessed Sacrament and see, on the altar, a small glass container. Dziwisz explains to me that it is a reliquary containing tears from the image of Our Lady of Syracuse, brought by the bishop of that Sicilian city.

As on so many previous occasions, the Pope facilitates my work. The anecdote with Professor Fineschi is indicative of his attitude, and allows me to deny the possibility of a possible resignation, a favorite and somewhat obsessive theme of some journalist colleagues during these days. He does not tell me what I should report to journalists, but the freedom and confidence with which he speaks to me allows me to know his thoughts and make them known.

"Parkinson's Case"

May 17, 1994

The Madrid newspaper *Diario 16*[1] published an article stating that the Pope has been suffering from Parkinson's disease for three years. It also adds that he is taking two antiparkinsonian drugs, and cites their names. As sources, it mentions "a Curia cardinal" and "Vatican Radio." Two days later, *Il Messaggero,* of Rome, reproduced the contents of this article in a report by its correspondent in Madrid. I am forced to intervene.

Some time ago, Buzzonetti told me that the Pope did not have Parkinson's disease. Now he has changed his mind and thinks that he has been suffering from the disease for two years, and that one of its first manifestations is the slight tremor in his left hand. He has not taken any medication, because of possible side effects. The Secretary of State's office knows nothing.

Buzzonetti tells me that a neurologist from the Catholic University of Milan examined the Pope. I do not know what his opinion was. He suggests that I should not be too specific in the denial. I speak, therefore, of "irresponsible reporting," because no sources are cited to support what is written; and I deny that the Pope is taking the drugs cited in the article.

The news explodes with all its virulence. But the denial prevails. I have to give several interviews for various TV stations, radios, and newspapers.

The next day Dziwisz tells me that he has telephoned a doctor friend of his in Warsaw who apparently knows the Pope. This man's version is that the Pope's left hand tremor should be attributed to an accident he suffered when he was young. Frankly, with all due respect, this seems to me to be an unfounded hypothesis. Surgeon Fineschi says on TV that the Pope does not have Parkinson's; anesthesiologist Manni does the same. But neither of them is a specialist in this field.

I see that some in the Vatican are so influenced by what public opinion says that they raise this issue only because it appears in the newspapers, and not because it actually exists.

When the weekend arrives, the doctors decide that the Pope will not leave the hospital. I did not go to the Gemelli on Saturday, but first Dziwisz and then Buzzonetti told me by telephone that he would remain there for the time being. In addition to his recovery, they have decided—with very good judgment, in my opinion—that, in order to avoid his having to return for the periodic checkups, it is best to have him undergo these tests now. He will have to remain seven

1. Newspaper published from 1976 to 2001.

or eight days more, resting and inactive: this means a new cross for him, who feels the weight and the urgency of the Church.

Dziwisz is worried. I try to reassure him, telling him that once public opinion has been reassured, it would be a good idea to have him checked by a good specialist.

Return to the Vatican

May 27, 1994

The Pope returns to the Vatican in the afternoon. In the morning he received a visit from Cardinal Ratzinger, who brought him a copy of the English edition of the "Catechism of the Catholic Church," which has just been published.

With President Clinton

June 2, 1994

Audience with President Clinton, which takes place in the context of the Pope's constant concern about various aspects related to the family, human love, and the defense of life. The document prepared for the UN Conference on Population and Development, to be held in Cairo in September, also deals with these issues.

At the end of the audience, the Pope leaves the library leaning on a cane. I ask him about the matters discussed. "I have made him see the responsibility of America and his own responsibility. He always affirms that it is an important issue, both for them and for us, for the world. At least, that's what he claims when you talk to him. I have told him that in the United States there is a large majority that does not accept abortion. There are groups that want to impose it on the whole country and influence the Cairo conference. We will see. I think we still have a lot of work to do on our side."

While the Pope is in the audience, I speak with Dziwisz and he tells me that he has seen him walking well and without a cane inside the apartment.

Plenary Meeting of Cardinals

June 13 and 14, 1994

A plenary meeting of cardinals was held on June 13 and 14. A total of 114 of the 139 living cardinals participated in this consistory. Twenty-five were unable to attend due to illness, old age, and various other reasons. Re asked me to attend the sessions, which were held in the Synod Hall.

I take notes of the various statements and organize two briefings. As usual, these meetings start with the "bolt-hole" mentality: "as these are private matters, there is no need to say anything to the press." But since the reality is that journalists ask questions, I give them what information I can, before fantasy replaces reality. In the meantime, I try to convince the cardinals of the need to hold a press conference.

I raised it formally on the occasion of the closing of the Consistory. I said it to Sodano, and not to others, who do not quite understand the importance of public opinion. I invited several cardinals and the secretary of the College of Cardinals, Mejía. It went well, because thanks to the previous meetings we had with them, the journalists had plenty of information on the topic under discussion: the preparation for the Jubilee of the Third Millennium.

First Dinner After the Fall

June 17, 1994

I have seen the Pope a few times during his recovery period, but today is the first time I have had dinner with him again. When I arrive, I see that he is walking on the terrace, leaning on a cane. His face has not yet regained its usual liveliness, and he looks tired. It must be hard. Used to moving around freely, he now uses a cane because of the prosthesis. This is precisely what has happened to him, who has to lead the way for so many, who must always be in the foreground.

Dziwisz suggests to him over dinner that, in his situation, it is better not to celebrate the June 29 Mass at St. Peter's. "To be present yes, but not to celebrate." I try to support Dziwisz by arguing that it is not necessary, that no one expects him to celebrate. . . . He replies, "Well, we'll see."

As always, what the Pope wants is to review some topics, in my case also bearing in mind the dimension of public opinion. I propose, to begin with, the consistory. The Pope had proposed to the cardinals, among the issues discussed at the meeting, a review of the errors committed throughout the history of the Church. The cardinals suggested that, in any case, the present era should be examined and the errors of other centuries should be dealt with prudently at a later date. This point, which was the only one that could seem controversial, was treated positively by the media, which presented the Pope as more audacious than the cardinals themselves.

He looks happy for the consistory. He asks who is the oldest cardinal among those who have come and recalls that he was forty-seven years old when he was made cardinal: "And there was a cardinal younger than me: Alfred Bengsch, from Berlin, who was 45."

He comments that Cardinal König, who was seated next to him during lunch, has been kind and positive. "But then, especially when he is interviewed on some topics, he is rather a bit critical," he adds with a wink.

He is interested in what the press has said of his illness and what is being said about his presumed resignation. I tell him that speculation about his health is inevitable, to a certain extent, for a person who has been at the forefront of world news for fifteen years. Dziwisz specifies: "sixteen."

On the subject of resignation, I tell him that I recently discussed it with journalists. I talked about two episodes in which the Pope himself addressed the question. During a visit a few years ago to the *Stampa Estera,* he responded to a question about whether the Pope could resign with these words: "I would have to look for a superior. . . ." I also brought up his recent comment to Fineschi, at the Gemelli, that "there is no place in the Church for a Pope Emeritus." Immediately, he told me: "Yes, I remember that I told him that."

We talked about the book with Messori and about another book he is dictating to Rylko with memories of a biographical nature. In this regard, he comments that—as he was born in 1920, in the middle of the Russian-Polish war—if the Poles had not won the battle they call the "Miracle of the Vistula," all subsequent history would have changed.

I tell him that, as I read the memorandum he sent to the cardinals at the consistory, I realized that it is a document with more projects than memories, a document that looks to the future, something typical of young people. He is amused by this statement and comments with humor: "Oh, really? Have you noticed that?" And he begins to joke affectionately with Thu, his secretary from Vietnam: "And Msgr. Thu, which way are you looking?"

—"I look to the future," Thu replies, "and dream of the day when Vietnam is free of communism."

"Now," I commented to the Pope, "after such an intense year, it would be good to rest a bit." He nods serenely. Dziwisz takes the opportunity to insist that, precisely for that reason, to rest, it is not necessary for the Pope to celebrate Mass at St. Peter's on the 29th. The Pope does not add anything. It is clear that he has not decided yet.

Dziwisz explains that every day the physiotherapist comes to "teach" him how to go up and down the stairs, kneel down, etc. I ask the Pope if he feels pain. "No, I only feel a little discomfort when changing position." In fact, I see that when we enter his chapel, he kneels on his kneeler, on which he can lean, and not on the floor, as on other occasions.

To Clarify your Doubts

July 11–12, 1994

This morning I accompanied Professor Manuel Martínez-Lage to Castelgandolfo, to check whether or not the Holy Father has Parkinson's disease.

A few weeks ago, I spoke to Dziwisz suggesting that, for the sake of clarity, a specialist could come to Rome, such as the Spanish doctor Martínez-Lage, whom I knew from the Clinic of the University of Navarra, where I underwent medical check-ups from time to time. Logically, this would have to be done with the knowledge and approval of Buzzonetti, who knows Dr. Obeso, a doctor who works in Martínez-Lage's department. The proposal stayed there.

The possibility of a Spanish specialist coming to examine the Pope must have aroused jealousy in someone and they told Buzzonetti, who did not know Martínez-Lage personally, a series of falsehoods about him. Buzzonetti, naturally, told this to Dziwisz, who phoned me, saying: "We don't want him."

I thought it best to put all these facts on record in writing, and I sent Dziwisz a fax on the afternoon of July 5th in which I said, in summary, that the accusations against this person were simple slander and that I certainly would not have proposed him if I were not one hundred percent sure of his personal integrity and professional worth. I informed Buzzonetti in similar terms.

Dziwisz answered me saying that the best date for him to come would be the week of July 9–17, with the exception of the 13th. I told Martínez-Lage and we agreed that he would travel to Rome on the 10th to examine the Pope the following day, that is, today.

I pick him up at the hotel and on the way I fill him in on the Pope's symptoms. From what I tell him, he thinks it may be Parkinson's disease.

We are welcomed by Dziwisz: friendly and cordial, as always. Buzzonetti is waiting for us in a small room. The four of us sit down and Buzzonetti begins to explain the Pope's medical history: precedents, high blood pressure and its treatment; the interventions (after the attack, removal of 70 cm [28 in.] of small intestine and after the adenoma, removal of 40 cm [16 in.] of large intestine). A test with L-Dopa at low dose: average positive result, etc.

He then goes to see the Pope. He is in his bedroom, which is a rather small room. The small size of his bed is striking: simple, with a modest headboard in gilded bronze. I find nothing personal, except for one detail: a painting of Our Lady of Chestochowa on a console table and, in front of it, a small frame about 6 by 3 cm [2.5 x 1.18 in.], with a photograph of his parents. An armchair. And books.

The Pope receives us standing leaning on the cane. Martínez-Lage begins to ask him questions, and asks him to explain what is happening to him. The Pope answers: "I believe that God sends me these signs (his illnesses) and I try to understand them." It is his way of living all this. He refers to the attack. Then, to the tremor in his hand. When asked about sleep, he says he slept only three hours tonight.

He begins to explore him. I help him undress: he gives me the pectoral, the ring and then the cassock. He takes off his shoes and lies down on the bed. Martínez-Lage does the whole neurological examination. The Pope lets him do it. It is an exhaustive examination, lasting about half an hour. Dziwisz, who had gone out, returns and discreetly asks me if there is still a lot left. The Pope shows no signs of impatience, something I find striking in such a long examination.

He sits up and takes a few steps, as requested. He sits up for the hand movement examination. He finishes the examination. Martínez-Lage and Buzzonetti leave the room accompanied by Dziwisz.

I stay to help him get dressed. He tells me that after the insertion of the prosthesis he can no longer put on his socks. When I start to put them on, he stops me: "No, Sister Tobiana will give me a hand now. . . ." But I say to him: "Holy Father, let me put on his socks at least once in my life . . ." He smiles and lets me do it. As we are finishing, Dziwisz returns.

We return to the room. Martínez-Lage confirms the diagnosis of Parkinson's disease. Several therapeutic possibilities are discussed: pharmacological treatment and stereotactic surgery. Dziwisz listens attentively. The Holy Father is coming. Martínez-Lage tells the Pope, in Spanish, with great delicacy, that he suffers from Parkinson's disease, in a mild form. I translate his words into Italian. The Pope raises his hands up to show the tremors. He is serene and serious.

Martínez-Lage explains to him the two possibilities: one therapeutic and the other surgical. The Pope listens attentively, without commenting. He thanked the doctors for their presence and left. Thus he receives the painful confirmation of his illness.

We continue to talk to Dziwisz. Although he does not show it, he is quite affected by the diagnosis. He asks about all the details: foreseeable evolution, treatments—especially surgery; if there are doubts about the diagnosis. . . . The care of the Pope depends on him, and he takes the necessary measures to take full charge of the situation. At the end, before asking a new question, he says: "*Datemi una qualche consolazione*" (Give me some consolation), as if asking that among so much bad news, at least some good news be given to him.

Martínez-Lage explains, again, that the form is mild, and that if in two years no tremors appear in the leg or in the other arm, it will be a very good sign. Surgical intervention could be done after five years to avoid the side effects of L-Dopa medication. All this seems to bring some relief to Dziwisz. Although the news has been very hard for him, he never loses his composure.

We don't see the Pope again that morning. He is in the garden. A plan is made for the next day: a diagnostic test consisting of administering 500 mg. of levo-dopa and following the patient's reaction every hour, starting at a quarter past nine in the morning. Dziwisz accompanies us to the exit. Buzzonetti asks me if I can pick him up tomorrow so that we can come together, because he is without a car.

Lunch with Martínez-Lage, and we commented on the exceptional moments we have experienced.

July 12. Very early in the morning, I pick up Martínez-Lage at the hotel and we go in search of Buzzonetti. We arrive early at Castelgandolfo and have a coffee in the only restaurant open by the lake. Dziwisz meets us at the appointed time. He says that the Pope has taken the prescribed dose at breakfast and has had no signs of gastrointestinal intolerance. At a quarter past nine Martínez-Lage and Buzzonetti go to the Pope's room. When they came out, Martínez-Lage said that his reaction had been excellent. The tremor had disappeared. The Pope was lying on the bed, dressed. He has not suffered any nausea or dizziness: only a slight feeling of discomfort that he attributes to his head.

When Martínez-Lage shows him that the tremor has disappeared, the Pope says: "Thank God." There is no trace of the stiffness in his arm either. He asks Manolo about his family; he is interested in his children.

As we leave, Dziwisz offers us a coffee brought by Sister Tobiana. We talk a little about everything, with a greater sense of relief than yesterday. At 10:15 AM the visit to the Pope is repeated: the test continues its course and at that time some of the tremor reappears, as expected, just like it was an hour later. Then the Pope takes a short walk in the garden.

Dziwisz shows Martínez-Lage some of the rooms of Castelgandolfo and part of the garden. We pray the Angelus next to the image of the Virgin. Dziwisz tells us that the Pope comes to greet her every day. We approach the area where the Pope is reading: Martínez-Lage asks him and the Pope says he feels fine, although he still feels a little dizzy. He wants to know if he will be able to swim today: Martínez-Lage tells him that in the afternoon there will be no problem.

I talk to the Pope about Messori's book and ask him to write the first page in Polish. That text would be reproduced on the back cover. He likes the idea.[2] He comments that Tadeusz has suggested to him to introduce a small variant in a question. I tell him that there is time to change whatever is desired.

We went on to lunch. The Pope is in his usual good humor. He still rests his left hand under his chin: it is a gesture he has been adopting over the years so that the tremor is not visible. Hopefully he won't have to do it anymore!

In honor of the guest, he recalls his trips to Spain: Asturias, Madrid, Seville. At the end of the meal—today he has an appetite and earlier he told us that he slept well last night—he bids an affectionate farewell to Martínez-Lage, giving him some rosaries for his wife and children.

First Time on the Phone

JULY 29, 1994

Dziwisz phoned me from Castelgandolfo. He tells me that they had been looking for me and that the pager didn't work. He wants to congratulate me on my birthday. As we talk, he tells me to wait a moment. A few minutes pass and . . . I hear the Pope's voice: "*Buona sera, come sta?*"

I get excited. I tell him I'm fine and ask him how he's feeling. "*Così, così*," ("so, so") he replies. I tell him that I have seen him in the general audience and he gave the impression that he was well. "*Yes, sono le apparenze*." Clearly, he has not fully recovered.

He asks me about Messori's book. I tell him that there is very good news: an Arabic translation has been ordered. He is happy: "*Ah, vedi. Allora debe venire a racontarci*" ("Ah, look. . . . Then he has to come and tell us about it").

He asks when I returned to Rome. I reply and add that many people have told me that they are praying for him. He thanks me with a slow voice. After a few seconds we say goodbye: "*Sia lodato Jesucristo*" ("Praised be Jesus Christ"). It is the first time I have spoken to the Pope on the phone. He sounds tired. But to know how he is I need to see his face and his gestures.

2. Indeed, I received that page two days later [Author's Note].

31

"Man of the Year"

In the Aosta Valley

August 1994

It is raining when we arrive at Les Combes. This contributes to a certain disorder in greeting the people who have gathered to welcome the Holy Father. Dziwisz and Tadeusz accompany him, along with Angelo and Cibin. We also met the same people as in previous years: Alberto Cerise, "nature guide," and Don Alberto.

This year the marches through these parts of the Aosta Valley are much shorter because the Pope walks with difficulty. He is not in pain, but he suffers from a curious functional disability, which varies from day to day, and even at different times during the same day. This causes him a certain psychological blockage, like an insecurity. He confirms it when, in response to a question, he tells me, "I feel as if all this is going to fall out of place. . . . " He makes great efforts to walk, with the desire to overcome this inability.

August 18. During this morning's excursion I have a long conversation with the Pope, in which we move from one topic to another. It's a time when I wish I could stop the clock.

> —"In our days," he tells me, "many peoples have regained their freedom, especially those of the Central European nations that emerged after World War I, such as Poland, Czechoslovakia, Hungary—today's Hungary, not that of the Austro-Hungarian Empire—and the Baltic countries. During the Second World War these peoples regained their identity by throwing off the yoke of the State; but they fell under a more terrible, more brutal, stronger yoke. On the one hand, Hitler; on the other, Stalin. And for the first time in history, the peoples of Ukraine, Belarus, Caucasia, Asia have constituted themselves as nations.

Hearing him talk about Russia, I commented that it would be a great thing if the Pope could meet the Patriarch of Moscow, Alexis, on his trip to Sarajevo.

—"It would be good," he tells me, "if we could meet in that context, but it is not the only place where we can meet, because I think it is difficult for him to meet the Pope of the Catholics if Pavle, the Patriarch of the Serbs, is not present.[1] It seems that the Muslims do not want Pavle to go, because they say that he has not condemned the errors of his compatriots, which is not entirely true, because he has done something. For example, he affirmed the existence of a moral order, as opposed to war conquests.

He asked me if the congress held at Castelgandolfo had any interest for the outside world. It is clear that he liked the question. He makes reference to the summer conferences that, with the help of Tadeusz Styczeń, he organizes to keep up to date on philosophical and other scientific issues.

"The topic was very interesting because of Ricoeur's initial approaches,[2] who spoke of memory as the element that builds the personal and national identity of a people. That influenced everything that was said afterwards, especially in the historical analyses that were made about America, Germany, Poland, Russia. . . ."

—"Holy Father," I asked him, "a somewhat personal question: do these meetings help you to learn new things or to confirm intuitions that you already have?"

"They don't serve me so much to learn, but rather to confirm some intuitions," he tells me, without hesitating in his answer. When I meet with physicists, I don't learn too much from them, because they have very specialized knowledge, but I become familiar with a certain terminology, categories and language."

—"What about the field of philosophical and humanistic thought?"

"In these meetings I am not a mere listener, because I have worked in this field, especially in the area of philosophy. I have dealt, above all, with the question of the person, which leads to many other aspects, mainly of an ethical nature."

We talked about the book-interview *Crossing the Threshold of Hope*, with Vittorio Messori, due to come out in October. "I would not be too optimistic about this book, but those who have read it told me that it could be useful." I

1. Orthodox Patriarch Pavle (Paul II of Serbia) (1914–2007) held that office from 1990 until his death. He had previously been Orthodox bishop of Kosovo for thirty years.

2. Paul Ricoeur (France, 1913–2005), philosopher and anthropologist, especially relevant in the fields of phenomenology and hermeneutics.

tell him that this book could be very interesting for the general public, because it uses more accessible language.

About the next synod, which will be dedicated to religious life, he tells me that "it will be important: perhaps the most important of all. The world of the religious is in a difficult situation. But they are also in crisis in a positive sense, because new forms of consecrated life are emerging."

We continue walking in silence. I ask him if he has brought any other work with him for these days in the mountains.

> "I have to prepare the keynote speech in Sarajevo. It is very important. And then the one at the United Nations, although that's still a long way off."

We talked for quite a while. While we were chatting he was walking well. I tell him so.

> —"When the Pope forgets that he has had hip surgery, he walks very well. When he remembers, he walks less well." He is amused by the comment and laughs heartily.
>
> —"Look . . . I don't always remember how I walk. But I can't forget, because I see how others walk, and I also remember how I walked myself until last year" (laughs).

From the mechanical point of view, it is already solved, I tell him. Now you just have to incorporate it into your own life.

> —"That is more difficult. Last year, after the operation on my abdomen, everything was solved: a little fasting, and I immediately started to regain strength. There were no problems at all. A month after the operation we came to Lorenzago and I was walking as usual. Now I've been going for three months and I can't do it."

He reviews the time since last summer and the horizon ahead: "We have certainly experienced decisive events. And now, Sarajevo. And we have to publish the letter for the preparation of the year 2000, which I have already discussed with the cardinals. The work on the document on the value of human life is quite advanced. But you have to wait a little bit, because we are also working on an ecumenical document. Perhaps it will end up being an encyclical: we will see."[3]

---

3. The encyclical *Ut unum sint,* on ecumenism, was published on May 30, 1995. The other two documents mentioned are the apostolic letter *Tertio millennio adveniente,* in preparation for the Jubilee of the Year 2000 (November 14, 1994), and the encyclical *Evangelium vitae* (March 30, 1995).

At another point, the meeting of the young people in Denver was mentioned. I comment on what I have already said on other occasions, that some things can only be explained because the Pope is there. Without the Pope's presence, the gathering of almost a million people would be unthinkable.

"Yes, of course. It can be said that the Petrine charism is inscribed in some way in the Church and through the Church also outside of it. As Vatican II reminds us in *Lumen gentium*, the Church is all of us. There are three circles: those of us who formally, sacramentally, belong to her; the other Christians; and then, all people of good will."

August 20th. Magnificent weather: sunshine every day and warmth. This morning, during the excursion, we had a long conversation, just like the other day. This time we talked about God's grace.

"Protestants say that the will of man has become so corrupted that it is incapable of doing anything of its own accord. There is only grace. But, in reality, the will has not become so corrupted, it can still do much. It is a form of pessimism, which can be seen in the report of the World Council of Churches on the subject of the Cairo Conference. They say that the position of the Holy See, of the Catholic Church, is too aggressive."

I comment that the Reformation, which wanted to protect man's autonomy and freedom from the Church, has ended up developing a pessimistic anthropology, with a man who is not capable of heroism without the help of grace. Paradoxically, at present, there are Swedish Lutherans who listen to the Pope with attention.

"Yes. One of the best visits was the one I made to the Scandinavian countries; that climate was very good in Sweden, and also in Denmark, especially among the people. The queen was very friendly. Something similar happened even in Norway. I remember that, in Trondheim, the bishops waiting at the door of the cathedral said to me: 'How many centuries we have been waiting!'"

"Recently, a Swedish Lutheran bishop told me: 'Rome is our mother!' This phrase is more rare to hear coming from a German Lutheran. It is the homeland of Luther. Just as Switzerland is the homeland of Zwingli and Calvin. And this also influences the mentality of Catholics in these countries. It can be seen, for example, in the protests following the publication of the text on the ordination of women to the priesthood."[4]

I tell him that without the clarity provided by some of his encyclicals and other documents, we would continue on a slope that would lead us to total subjectivism.

4. Apostolic Letter *Ordinatio sacerdotalis,* addressed to the Bishops of the Catholic Church, on priestly ordination reserved to men, dated May 22, 1994.

"It would lead to complete uncertainty," he says, "to a situation in which priests could say: we don't even know what our future might be. Perhaps the same thing would happen to us as happened to the Anglican Communion in England. That is, as far as this part of the world, Europe, is concerned. Here there are some challenges. In other places it is different."

At this point in the journey, the Pope begins—half seriously, half jokingly—to do some exercises with the operated leg. They were exercises that I had taught him yesterday.

On the Way Back from Cairo

September 16, 1994

Cairo, International Conference on Population and Development (ICPD), from September 3 to 14. I was not in the initial delegation, nor had the possibility of attending crossed my mind. But the pressure of public opinion was increasing because the Pope had mobilized the whole Church: bishops, nunciatures. . . .

Before leaving for Valle d'Aosta, a preparatory meeting on the Conference was held at the Secretariat of State. There, in view of the panorama that was emerging, I announced that they would need someone to manage public opinion, because the Holy See was going to Cairo as the "star" of the Conference. They look at me and ask: "Couldn't you go? I reply that I have scheduled a trip with the Pope to Croatia and then another to Sarajevo, which is a very delicate arrangement."

I organize a briefing to offer the Holy See's point of view to the Conference, and the *New York Times* puts the article on the front page. I am lost: Msgr. Renato Raffaele Martino,[5] head of the delegation, speaks from New York with Sodano, who goes to the Pope. Then Dziwisz tells me to get everything ready to go to Cairo. But first there is the rest break with the Pope on the mountain. There I jokingly tell the Holy Father that if he sends me to Cairo, it is because he does not want me to accompany him to Sarajevo.[6]

---

5. Renato Raffaele Martino (Italy, 1932) was at that time Permanent Observer of the Holy See to the United Nations (1986–2002). Later he was president of the Pontifical Council for Justice and Peace and of the Pontifical Council for the Pastoral Care of Migrants and Itinerant People. He was elevated to the cardinalate in 2003.

6. The trip to Sarajevo was scheduled for September 8, 1994; therefore, the dates coincided with those of the Cairo Conference. In the end, the trip could not take place on those dates. "To the motive of not exposing to serious risks those who await the Pope in the Bosnian capital," the Vatican communiqué said, "was added the concern that the trip to Sarajevo at this time could be misunderstood and increase tensions."

Back in Rome, after the trip to Valle d'Aosta, I organized a second briefing on the Cairo conference, in which I made a reference to the Vice President of the United States, Al Gore, which provoked controversy. I limited myself to saying that his statements that "the United States has not sought, does not seek, and will not seek to establish an international right to abortion" contradict the draft document on population, of which the United States is the main sponsor.

At that time, I published an article in the press to explain the critical attitude of the Holy See towards the draft document of the Conference (on which there was a broad lack of consensus). I highlight the positive aspects of the text, despite the fact that they are generic, impractical statements. I emphasize that the Catholic Church, "with its 21,575 health institutions throughout the world—1,800 in Africa—has achieved, in number and quality, what no country or supranational institution in the world has been able to do for the health of women and children, and for the spread of responsible parenthood in places and countries where the objective social and family circumstances require it."

My criticism focuses on Chapters 7 and 8 of the document, which contain the terms "reproductive health" and "sexual health," two ambiguous concepts, not approved by any international organization, which are at the core of the ideas proposed for approval in Cairo.

Among the methods to promote "reproductive health," "fertility regulation," which includes abortion, is cited. Abortion is thus proposed as an *essential component of "reproductive health."* Thus, whenever the term "reproductive health" appears in the text, it assumes the meaning of "the right to safe, effective, accessible, and acceptable abortion." *Accessible* means that governments should subsidize abortion, with no limitations other than individual choice. In short, discretionary abortion without the limits now imposed by current legislation.

In the same chapter, it is proposed that abortion, accessible "to all individuals of any age"—thus also to adolescents—should guarantee "their right to privacy and confidentiality." This would eliminate the right of parents and family to be informed before performing an abortion on adolescents.

But what is even more repulsive is the treatment of abortion as an *essential dimension* of health policies, both nationally and internationally. And what a large number of national delegations reject is the idea that abortion should be proposed as an *important part of international development policies*. Underlying such an idea seems to be a neocolonial conception of the relationship between rich and poor countries.

I recall that at the previous UN Conference on Population (Mexico, 1984), the international community solemnly signed the clause that "in no case should abortion be promoted as a method of family planning." Now, at the insistence of some Western countries, that same statement has not been approved. President Clinton has said that in the United States federally funded abortion will not be a method of family control. However, that same statement appears in parentheses in the document that goes to Cairo.

It is also striking that only seven pages of a 113-page document on development are devoted to development, while the concepts of "reproductive health" and "sexual health" are repeated more than a hundred times.

On September 1st, I leave for Cairo with Martino. It has been one of the most tiring and exhausting periods of my work at the Holy See so far.

Ratzinger's Greatness

October 19, 1994

Presentation in Milan of the book-interview of the Pope, *Varcare la soglia della speranza* (*Crossing the Threshold of Hope*), the fruit of that TV interview that was never made. Intense day. Press conference with Vittorio Messori and the publisher, Leonardo Mondadori, at three o'clock in the afternoon, with about two hundred journalists and photographers. At six o'clock, the official presentation, with the President of the Italian Parliament, Irene Pivetti and Cardinal Ratzinger, together with some 400 guests.

Around 10:30 PM, we return to Rome in President Pivetti's small plane. I confirm, once again, Ratzinger's spiritual caliber. For him, this has been a real beating; he had almost no time and, nevertheless, when days ago I allowed myself to tell him that he had to do it, because it was the Pope's book, he accepted in spite of the effort. Today he devoted the afternoon to this matter. On the plane, he almost fell asleep.

The Cane

October 22, 1994

I have dinner with the Pope. He is accompanied only by Dziwisz. I guess Thu will be out. He jokes, as always, before dinner. This time on the occasion of the cane "for which we are grateful," he says, "to Dr. Navarro." And then he demonstrates that he can walk without using the cane.

There is a little story about the cane. The Pope carried a brownish-colored wooden cane, which I did not like at all. When we were in the mountains this summer, while the Pope was resting, I measured it; and when I returned to Rome, I bought him a black cane, made of ebony wood, with a simple handle, and I sent it to him at Castelgandolfo. He liked it, and it is the one he uses now.

At the dinner, the presentation and reactions to the book-interview *Varcare la soglia della Speranza* are discussed. "Ratzinger showed me the text he had prepared: it is splendid," says the Pope. We then move on to other topics. For example, I inform him of a biography about him that has appeared in France, of which I had no news. But another matter worries me: a few days ago I read the program of the trip he will make in January to the Philippines, Australia, and other countries, and I thought it was too much. I told him that it would be better to shorten it, that it is ten days and it is very long. He says that there are three beatifications and that the only difficulty will be the time changes.

On leaving the oratory after dinner, he recalls that we are "at the beginning of the 17th year of the pontificate. With the help of God and Our Lady. Before, there was the attack: they say it came from the East. But now the difficulties are coming from the West, as in Cairo. We have to start working now on the International Women's Conference. I am told that there are no economic interests here (in Cairo). There were also economic interests on the occasion of *Humanae Vitae*."

I inform him that in December my second five-year term at *Sala Stampa* will come to an end and that we should start thinking about a replacement. "Don't worry," he replies with a smile.

Before leaving, he gives me an autographed copy in Italian of *Varcare la soglia della speranza*: *"Per Dott. Joaquín Navarro-Valls, con gratitudine."* During dinner the Pope looked tired. Dziwisz tells me: "He has had a very intense day today, and with you he does not have to make an effort to hide it." I feel honored and at the same time worried.

A Scoop

NOVEMBER 6, 1994

I have been to Wilton Wynn's house. He announced that he was going to give me a scoop. And indeed he did: *Time* has decided to name John Paul II "Man of the Year" for his struggle to lay the foundations of a moral order in our time.

Wilton asks me for an interview with the Pope for himself and for the Paris correspondent, who is in charge of putting together the story, and also to be able to attend Mass with the Holy Father. Greg Burke, who works for *Time* in Rome, is also in the meeting. We will see.

Questions about *The Man of the Year*

November 19, 1994

The Pope enters, jokingly: "*Questo Papa zopicante . . .*" ("This Pope who limps . . ."). I comment to him, also as a joke, that bishops and popes have always carried a cane; that originally this cane would have been for support and that later it remained as a ceremonial element. . . . He is amused.

Today at dinner I tell him about *Time's* initiative to designate him "Man of the Year."[7] I explain the significance of the honor and that there has only been one other pope who received this title: John XXIII in 1962. We look at the list of award winners in the entire history of *Time*. He is surprised that Hitler also received that title. I explain to him that *Time*'s criteria for "Man of the Year" takes into account all factors, good or bad. I talk about the worldwide dissemination of this rating, and also that there will be no shortage of controversy and criticism. I tell him that some questions have been sent to me, although I have my doubts about the advisability of answering them. In the end, it is he who asks me for them: "Looking at the questions, you can understand the reasons."

Then he asks about the presentation of the Apostolic Letter on the Year 2000 (*Terzo millennio adveniente*). I tell him that the journalists have focused their attention on the idea of the Church's examination of conscience, of asking for forgiveness. He comments that this cannot be the *leit-motiv* of the preparation, but he also adds that without this sense of sin "one cannot pray, one cannot go to Mass." I don't know when the idea of asking for forgiveness came to him, but it is certainly something he has been maturing for some time.

A few moments before dinner, Dziwisz told me in an aside that some complaints had reached the Pope about the choice of publishers for the publication of the book-interview. I explain to him that if the book has reached such a wide circulation it is because it has entered other circuits, since it went to commercial publishers and not to specifically Catholic publishers. He sees this clearly, but considers that, in order to avoid hurting anyone's feelings, now is not the time for the Pope to receive the group of foreign publishers in audience, something I had suggested.

7. In 1994, the international impact of this *Time* magazine initiative was much greater than it would be today (2023).

The Pope's Health

DECEMBER 2, 1994

This morning I was talking to Dziwisz about the Pope's health. I am concerned, I tell him. It seems to me that the Parkinson's is progressing and I wonder if we are doing all we can to take care of him medically. I suggest that perhaps it is time for an international consultation to clarify the diagnosis definitively, orient the appropriate therapy and, if the disease progresses in spite of everything, to fully accept God's will.

Dziwisz asks me which symptom I see as the most evident. In my opinion, the Pope's "expressionless faces" at certain times are a very clear indication. He tells me that he is not sure it is Parkinson's; that a doctor (he said the name, but I did not know him) says that if it is Parkinson's it is a very mild form. He is concerned about the situation, says it is the cross that those of us who are close to the Pope bear, but that the L-Dopa medication he took this summer produced many side effects: the Pope was unwell. It is not that he doubts Martínez-Lage's ability, but he is not sure if it really is Parkinson's disease.

I add that all this is one more reason to convene, under Buzzonetti, an international consultation to clarify the diagnosis and therapeutic orientation. I see Dziwisz get very upset. I tell him to forgive me, but I can't talk to anyone about this. "So, you put everything onto me . . . ," he tells me and my heart is moved a little because, indeed, he is the one who suffers the most.

We had this conversation while the Pope was in the Library, receiving the President of Lithuania, Algirdas Brazauskas. At the end of the audience I greeted the Pope. He tells me that the conversation was about the history of Lithuania: they talked about the difference between the Russian domination and the period when they were federated with Poland. The Pope says to me again: "*Vede, il Papa sempre zopicando . . .*" ("You see, the Pope is still limping . . .").

His limp is evident. In addition, the little finger of his right hand is bandaged as a result of a small accident: Thu inadvertently closed the car door on the 27th, before the Mass with the new cardinals. Consequence: an injury, loss of the nail and fracture of the phalanx.

No Interview

December 3, 1994

I have spoken several times with Tom Sancton, *Time's Paris* correspondent in charge of the "Man of the Year" project. The last one, during a lunch of several hours at Wilton's house. It's a worthwhile project, but one that has risks: I think *Time* will achieve a positive thing in which there will be no shortage of shadows.

The Pope prefers not to do anything that might give the impression that he supports the initiative. For this reason, although he has been left with the questions, he has decided that he will not respond. I inform the *Time* people of our decision. Naturally, they would have liked to be able to interview the Pope, like any other public figure to whom this discretion is granted. I give five of them, including the managing editor and an editor from headquarters who has come from New York, tickets to Wednesday's general audience.

December 7. I inform Dziwisz that the *Time* people will be at the audience. He calls me and tells me that the Pope will greet them for a moment when the audience is over; he asks me to accompany him. The Pope, in fact, receives them in a small room and is very friendly with them. He thanks them for this election and jokes about the fact that *Time* made Stalin and Hitler "Man of the Year" in the past. Sancton takes the opportunity to try to get some statements. I feel sympathetic and ask the Pope what the common ground is when he speaks in his writings of social ethics and individual ethics. "The person," the Pope says at once. Some photographs are taken. In the evening we have dinner together, and we are joined by Wilton Wynn and Greg Burke.

Front Cover Upside Down

December 19, 1994

I am in Spain for a few days. I have a conference on Cairo in the Conference Room of Caja Murcia. Lots of people. Then, synthetic repetition in the Casino of Cartagena, my hometown.

My aunt Amelia, a real character, passes away during these days. In the morning I was with her chatting and laughing. At night she went into a coma and died two days later. I am sure she is in Heaven. She asked to be admitted to Opus Dei when she was already seventy-nine or eighty years old. And she never lost her joy and apostolic spirit.

Dziwisz called me these days to have dinner with the Pope. When I got back I called him and he told me to come tonight. We are the Pope, the two secretaries, and myself. There seems to be no topic in particular: he wants to give a general overview of a number of issues that he sometimes suggests for conversation and others come up naturally during the conversation. He limps. He carries the cane. But today his face is normal. He arrives later—ten to eight—because he has been meeting with Sodano.

When we sit down to dinner I give a copy of *Time* to the Pope. He glances at it, without pausing. He will probably read it later, without hurrying. On the cover is a magnificent photo-painting of him, in the foreground, with a slightly ironic expression. He leaves it on the table, but with the cover upside down. Then I ask him: "Holy Father, don't you like photography?" He answers with a smile: "No, on the contrary, maybe I like it too much." During the conversation that follows he recalls the people who came to see him while the article was being prepared.

We talked about the trip to Manila: "Some people tell me that this trip should not be made for three reasons: time zone change, heat, and distance." He says it like this, and I think he throws it out there to see what we say. I tell him that, in my opinion, the trip should be done, but he has to prepare well. Prepare by resting in Castelgandolfo. Doing physical exercise, getting a little more sleep. . . ." "Maybe it will be necessary to go back to the swimming pool," he says. I insist that it is important to tire the body. I explain to him that this moderate physical tiredness is a good thing.

We are talking about *Varcare la soglia della Speranza,* already at one million copies in Italy. I tell him that letters are now beginning to arrive from readers who are grateful for its contents. And I read him one that arrived in my office from a reader in Turin who says he has "rejuvenated" his faith by reading the book.

"Let's go to the oratory." He prays for a long time. And when he comes out he says: "If these things help. . . ." He refers to *Time* and thinks about who will read it. I tell him that this serves as a kind of *praeambula fidei,* which can help to clear the path to faith. Before saying goodbye we still make some jokes and I think, as I leave, that at least tonight I have made him laugh a little.

32

My Father and the Pope

Medical News

January 11, 1995

Dziwisz called me at home three days ago to ask me: "Do you remember where you bought the cane?" And he told me the story behind the question. Someone had commented that the cane was a bit long, and they shortened it; but, when the Pope tried it out, they saw that it was too short. So I spent two days looking for another one all over Rome that was identical to the previous one. Thank God, I found it and yesterday afternoon I took it to the apartment.

I asked him about the Pope's health. "During these days," he told me, "he has been examined by a Swiss doctor, to see how he is assimilating the prosthesis. Fortunately, everything is going well: we just have to be patient. Another specialist confirmed that everything was fine from the mechanical point of view. The problem is that he has learned to walk with small steps, and now he has to learn to walk normally." There is no bio-incompatibility problem, because no cement was put in the prosthesis. And the doctor has recommended that he stop physical therapy. With what Dziwisz has told me, I am a little calmer, because I thought that there could be a rejection reaction to the prosthesis.

A neurologist with expertise in Parkinson's disease has come from London. He has confirmed that the diagnosis is correct: he suffers from a mild form of Parkinson's disease. He recommends not to continue with pharmacological therapy for the time being, but later and in small doses. Dziwisz had told me that the doses he was taking last summer were causing him significant side effects of tiredness and fatigue. I ask him if this decay manifested itself in a reduction in the field of interests, insomnia, lack of appetite, less sociability, etc. Nothing of the sort. Although I see the Pope better, I am still concerned about the trembling of the left hand, especially during the celebration of Mass and during the prayers.

The Philippines, Papua New Guinea, Sri Lanka and Australia

January 22, 1995

Last night, after a thirteen-hour flight, we returned from our rather arduous trip to Manila, Port Moresby, Colombo, and Sydney. The Pope was happy, in spite of the effort.

We left Rome on January 11. At the beginning of the flight, at night, I went to see him to ask him if he wanted to greet the journalists. There was no need to press too hard: he came right away. He joked with them ("as you can see, I carry a cane and the cane is used to hit—*bastonate*—those who don't behave well, perhaps even some journalists . . ."). He referred to his motor deficit and spoke of "psychophysical" difficulty, which is a broad understanding of the problem.

The Manila stop, where the 10th World Youth Day was held, was ultra-massive. So many people, mostly young people, attended the Mass on January 15 that we were stranded at the nunciature because there was no way to get to the area where the Pope was to celebrate: the crowds had blocked the esplanade and all the access roads. It was decided to use the helicopter to travel from the nunciature to Malacañang Palace, the president's residence; and then, in a small helicopter, from there to the back of the altar. Several flights had to be made. It was impressive to contemplate the immense waves of people from the air: around four million people.

The Pope recalled, in a way that I found very beautiful, the fact that all Christians are called to be saints.

"Every Christian," he stressed, "participates in Christ's mission in a unique and personal way. Bishops, priests, and deacons participate in the mission of Christ through the ordained ministry."

And from there he made a detailed enumeration:

> Religious men and women participate in it through the spousal love that is manifested in the spirit of the evangelical counsels of chastity, poverty, and obedience. Lay Christians participate in the mission of Christ: fathers and mothers of families, the elderly, the young and children, the simple and the educated, farmers, workers, engineers, technicians, doctors, nurses and health personnel.
>
> The mission of Christ is also shared by teachers, lawyers, and politicians. Writers, people who work in the theater, in the cinema and in the

> media, artists, musicians, sculptors, and painters. All have a part in the messianic mission of Jesus Christ. So do university professors, scientists, specialists in any field, and people in the world of culture. In the mission of Christ a part belongs to you, citizens of the Philippines and peoples of the Far East: Chinese, Japanese, Koreans, Vietnamese, Indians; Christians of Australia, New Zealand, and the Pacific; Christians of the Middle East, Europe, Africa, and America.
>
> Every baptized person has a part in the messianic mission of Jesus Christ, *in the Church and for the Church*. And this participation in the mission of the Church constitutes the Church. The Church is a living participation in the mission of Christ. Do you understand this?

A delegation from mainland China attends the Mass. Among them are some priests from the Patriotic Association who wish to concelebrate.[1] They number about thirty in all. Sodano wrote to the nuncio that, before doing so, they should make their profession of faith. But everything is confusing. Cardinal Sin says that they have already made it, apparently with the Jesuit Zuloaga, with whom they have come. However, since this cannot be confirmed and we do not know if they have concelebrated or not, I avoid commenting on it with the journalists.

The Pope would like to receive these priests. We tried to get in touch with them, but there is such a great movement of people in the city that we were unable to do so.

Papua New Guinea. On January 16, we flew from the Philippines to Papua New Guinea, where we found what we could call a "frontier" missionary Church. There was an atmosphere of joy and enthusiasm among the people. Fortunately, a light rain was quenching the intense heat.

The following day, we traveled to Port Moresby, where the Pope beatified Peter To Rot, the first Blessed of New Guinea. He wanted to do it in the same land, Rakunai, where To Rot was born in 1912 and where he suffered martyrdom during the Japanese occupation. On July 7, 1945, he was poisoned and suffocated by the doctor in the prison where he was confined because he was a catechist.

---

1. The Patriotic Association of Chinese Catholics was the instrument used by the regime to control the Catholic Church, as opposed to the so-called underground Church, faithful to Rome. In recent decades, however, there were many "patriotic Catholics" who recognized the authority of the Pope.

SYDNEY. All very well organized, with demonstrations of affection and crowds attending the two main events: the arrival at the Domain and the Mass the following day, in which he beatified Mary MacKillop (1842–1909), an Australian nun who founded schools, convents, orphanages, shelters for the homeless, the elderly, ex-prisoners, and prostitutes, both in Australia and New Zealand. The misunderstanding of the local bishop caused her to be excommunicated for five months.

Thank God, the Pope is resisting well all these efforts. In addition, they have placed a kind of forklift behind the altar, to prevent him from having to climb up on foot.

SRI LANKA. We arrived at Katunayake International Airport in Colombo around 3:00 PM. It is scorching hot. The Pope travels the thirty-five kilometers [twenty-two miles] from the airport to the presidential palace in a popemobile without air conditioning. I can't figure out if the problem is that the air conditioning doesn't work or that they can't get in touch with the driver to turn it on. The fact is that the Pope goes on for a while under a blazing sun, until at a certain point of the journey they are forced to stop.

The Pope gets out of the vehicle and heads towards a neighboring church. Buzzonetti and I approach him. He walks with difficulty and seems to be suffering from congestion. We enter a tiny sacristy. It seemed to him—he tells us as he sits down—that he was about to have one of his migraine attacks. His last one was in 1979. I look for something for him to drink and refresh himself. I find, upstairs, in a small refrigerator, two bottles of Sprite and a bottle of water. The Pope drinks the Sprite while Buzzoneti tends to him medically. I dip a handkerchief in the cold water and put it on his forehead. Little by little he recovers.

It is decided to continue the tour in an air-conditioned car, but when the Pope sees the people waiting for him in the streets, he climbs back into the popemobile. When he arrives at the palace he is clearly tired. Nevertheless, the ceremony with the speeches and the private audience takes place.

Some journalists—who have noticed the Pope's fatigue when they noticed the delay in the itinerary and saw on TV the unscheduled entry into a church, raised the alarm. Imagination runs wild and it is useless for me to explain to them, as I have done, the real reasons for the stop.

In the evening the Pope dines alone and goes to bed. The next morning I find him recovered.

> *Problems.* The local Buddhist leaders have communicated that they will not attend the interreligious meeting. The problem goes so far that the Buddhist architect who designed the altar where the Pope will celebrate has been forced to flee the country.

I make a statement: "We appreciate the fact that a Buddhist architect has built the altar for the beatification Mass. We are also pleased to note that some Buddhists will be present at that event. We understand that, because of issues related to Sri Lankan circumstances, Buddhist leaders have decided not to attend the meeting with leaders of other religions present here."

I speak at length with Buzzonetti about the Pope's health. He tells me about the English specialist and tells me that now he is not receiving medication, but he will start immediately with a small dose of L-Dopa, hoping for a cumulative effect. "His Parkinson's is not serious," the specialist said, "but in the case of a Pope it constitutes a notable inconvenience, because of the public activity he carries out." He ruled out the possibility of an intervention with stereotaxis.

Intention Sheets

February 16, 1995

The Pope receives me, as usual, with good humor:

> —"Let's hear what Dr. Navarro-Valls has to say!"
>
> —"No, Holy Father," I tell him, because it is true, "it is I who have come to listen!"
>
> —"No, no, I'm the one who listens!"—"I do nothing else all day! I'm basically just a listener (*un ascoltatore*)!"

During dinner, I tell him that editions of *Crossing the Threshold of Hope* are being prepared in Lithuanian, Ukrainian, and Swedish. I tell him that it has already been translated into Chinese, in Taiwan, and that the person in charge, Msgr. Janusz, was ordained a priest by him.

At the end of the dinner, returning to the subject of the book, he commented to me: "Don't you think that in the end it was better not to do the interview on TV? Perhaps we should think about another book of that style. The important thing is the questions, and Messori asked some very good questions."

I inform him that a few weeks ago the journalist and writer Peter Hebblethwaite, who never spared invectives on the Pope, whom he considered a reactionary, passed away. The Holy Father knew him personally. He was a secularized priest and very critical of the papacy. Upon hearing the news, he concentrates and prays aloud a prayer for his soul: "*Requiem eternam dona ei Domine . . .*"

The Pope reviews the year's travels, the two encyclicals coming out soon, and the preparation of the international conference on women to be held in Beijing in September, coinciding with the dates of his trip to Africa. He stresses again the importance of this UN conference. As there is some confusion among the various dicasteries involved in the organization and prioritization of the conference, a joint meeting has been convened to prepare for it. And, to my surprise, he tells me to attend the conference.

> —"I can see that His Holiness does not want me to accompany him on his trip to Africa," I tell him, remembering that something similar happened when he told me to participate in the Cairo conference. He tells me, in the same tone, that this trip is not complicated and that the important thing now is to prepare well for the Beijing meeting.

When he finishes, I ask him if he manages to find time to walk. He tells me that he spends half an hour every day. In addition, he does the prescribed exercises, which take him two to three hours a day.

And we enter the chapel. I notice that, as he prays, he bends down to read a sheet of paper that has been placed on his kneeler. Thu then explains to me that many people from all over the world write letters to the Pope asking him to pray for their intentions. They classify them, translate them, make a synthesis of the contents, and pass them on to the Pope, who reads them when he prays in his chapel and celebrates Mass. I review some of these intentions. The name of the person, the country from which he writes, and the intention for which he prays to the Pope.

Two Demons

March 4, 1995

I find the Holy Father cordial and joking, as always, although with a serious face, due to his illness. He plays with the cane in his right hand.

His new encyclical, entitled *Evangelium Vitae,* will be released on the 25th of this month. He reflects on the defense of life in the current situation. "When I was in Poland, I spoke of two demons: that of the East and that of the West. Or, rather, of a single demon with two faces. The demon of the East, brutal and bloodthirsty, tries to uproot the idea of God in the soul of man. And that of the West, more subtle and less brutal perhaps, has great power of seduction."

In Copenhagen

March 6, 1995

I am going to Copenhagen with the Holy See delegation to the *World Summit for Social Development*. Tauran phoned me a few days ago to ask me if I could attend. The atmosphere is very different from the one we found in Cairo: it is clear that, this time, the American delegation does not want any controversy with the Holy See.

On Peace In the Holy Land

April 7, 1995

Samuel Haddas, Israel's ambassador, invites me to breakfast with Jossi Gal, deputy director general of the Israeli Ministry of Foreign Affairs. An intelligent man, he talks to me about the current situation in the Middle East and the difficulties in this third phase of the peace process with the Palestinians.

"What if Arafat is missing," I ask him. He tells me that the situation would become very difficult, although there are moderate Palestinian leaders who could replace him. "The current danger," he says, "is the extremism of Hamas and Jihad."

He informs me about some multilateral initiatives and projects done together with Jordan and Egypt; and speaks highly of the brother of the King of Jordan.[2]

They place high value on a future trip of the Pope to Israel because they are convinced that it will serve to create a positive climate for the peace process. He even proposes a date: 1996. Next year, he adds, marks the third millennium of Israel, with the proclamation of King David. I suggest that the head of state write a personal and private letter to the Pope. This very morning he has arranged to meet with Tauran.

Haddas reminds me of an initiative, which he has already discussed with his government, to plant a forest near Nazareth, dedicated to John Paul II, in which trees brought by pilgrims to the Holy Land would be planted. Before saying goodbye, he invites me again to visit his country.

---

2. El Hassan Bin Talal (Amman, 1947).

The Origin of a Biography

Spring 1995 (no precise date)

I don't remember if I have recorded in these notes how the idea of commissioning Weigel to write a biography of the Pope[3] came about. We were having dinner one day, some time after Tad Szulc had written his book. The Pope asked me what I thought of the book. Apparently Sister Emilia had told him it was very bad. I told him that no, it was not bad, but that it was insufficient. What was needed was a complete biography, with good documentation.

The Pope replied: "Publish it after my death." Holy Father," I told him, "then many books will be published; it is now that we need this documented biography." And, as with the rest of the questions concerning his person, he did not show too much interest. But since there was no clear "no," I felt authorized to move.

I discussed the matter with Leonardo Mondadori,[4] and began to look for a possible biographer. Different names came up, and thanks to Leonardo, an American publisher sent me several books by contemporary authors. Among them, Robert K. Massie, who had written a wonderful biography of Peter the Great, and his well-known *Nicholas and Alexandra*. But Massie, who has mastered the technique of historical biography, did not, in my opinion, have the necessary background required for this project. The author had to have a good knowledge of the Catholic faith, to be fluent in doctrinal and theological matters, or those related to ecclesiology.

I was in the middle of my search when I wrote to Michael Novak,[5] who replied by return mail from the United States telling me that the right person was George Weigel. I contacted him shortly thereafter.

---

3. George Weigel (United States, 1951), theologian, writer. Author of numerous publications among which his biography of John Paul II is the best known: *Witness to Hope* (1999).

4. Leonardo Mondadori (Italy, 1946–2002), president of the *Mondadori* publishing house (1991–2002), founded by his grandfather Arnoldo. Shortly before his death, he wrote an autobiographical book in collaboration with Vittorio Messori: *Conversione. Una storia personale* (2002).

5. Michael Novak (United States, 1933–2017), philosopher and Catholic diplomat. Author of more than twenty-five books on philosophy and theology of culture, including *The Spirit of Democratic Capitalism* (1982), Templeton Prize winner.

Preparation of the Beijing Conference

April 11, 1995

Tuesday of Holy Week. At half past eleven the Pope received the students of the UNIV university congress in the Paul VI Hall. It was a festive, joyful, and enthusiastic meeting.

At ten to one o'clock, a little late because the audience was extended, we met to prepare for the Beijing Conference. The Pope was visibly satisfied after the meeting with the young people.

During the meeting and the meal that followed, together with the Pope and his secretaries, there were Sodano, Re, Tauran, Sgreccia, Cordes, María Isabel Tellería, from the Secretariat of State, and myself. Each one presented his point of view. Tauran reported on the preparation—the *PrepCom* was closed a few days ago—objectively and with equanimity: there are indeed many negative aspects. Many issues are going to be addressed with the same language that was used in Cairo.

During lunch we continued to formulate initiatives and ideas. Some decisions were made: meeting with the ambassadors, doing something special for Africa, etc.

The Pope, after listening to us with great attention, encouraged us, saying, "*E poi c'è la Madonna*," meaning "we will always count on Our Lady's help." In truth, we will need special help from Our Lady, because the Beijing Conference presents a very bleak and difficult panorama.

An Unforgettable Stations of the Cross

April 14, 1995

Sister Minke de Vries, a nun from the Protestant community of Grandchamp, Switzerland, prepared this year's Stations of the Cross, and a Russian Orthodox participated. Last year the Patriarch of Constantinople, Bartholomew I, was present.

"All this indicates," says the Pope, "that we are approaching the Third Millennium, with the desire to be ever closer, ever more united, because Christ unites us in his Cross, in his Resurrection, in his Mystery, *Mysterium passionis, Mysterium paschale*."

Unforgettable Way of the Cross: the Pope carries the Cross, limping and with many physical difficulties. He only goes through three stations. At some stations the cross is carried by women, a young man and an Orthodox priest of the Moscow Patriarch.

My Father

MAY 8, 1995

I am in Spain. Today, in the early hours of the morning, my father passed away. Watching him suffer during the last few days has been a great sorrow for the whole family and, at the same time, a gift from God. His last lesson: the profound and silent serenity he maintained in the hospital; not a gesture of impatience; his fortitude, his suffering without making others suffer, without even trying to communicate that he was suffering. I never want to forget his eyes looking at me. . . .

He was conscious until the last moment and was able to receive Communion every day. In the evenings I would ask him if he had said his prayers, and he would recite a Hail Mary. He would say the first part: *Hail Mary, Hail Mary* . . . ; but then he was silent, because of the fatigue of breathing. From time to time he would ask me for something, and how sad it was that sometimes I could not understand him. Last night the choking was more frequent. Yesterday I was talking to his doctor and to the hospital doctor: the only thing to do was to give him cortisone introvenously. It seemed to relieve him.

After a bout of restlessness and breathing difficulties—always conscious—he rested for a few hours and died around six o'clock in the morning. At that time he was accompanied by my niece Conchita. God will take him to his bosom. I know he will intercede for me from Heaven.

It was fortunate—or rather, a gift from God—that I was able to be at his side during these last days of his life. In other circumstances, because of my work, I might not have been able to do so, as I was traveling, accompanying the Pope, for example, to another part of the world.

We received a telegram from Rome signed by the Pope, in Spanish. In the middle of the morning, while I was with my mother at the morgue, Dziwisz called my parents' house. They gave me the message and, at noon, when I returned home with my mother for lunch, I called him back. He was very affectionate and at the end he said to me: "Wait a moment, because . . ." And I heard the Pope's voice: "Navarro-Valls? *Come sta? E la sua mamma? Preghiamo insieme* . . ." ("How are you? And your mother? Let us pray together . . ."). We were very moved, both my mother and I, and tears came to our eyes.

My father left us some papers with three handwritten instructions for when he passed away: "Do not grieve too much. Pray for me. Do not forget the poor." I owe him very decisive things in my family upbringing: my religious sense, my love for Our Lady and a large part of my vocation, which he always respected.

May 9. A representative of the Nuncio in Madrid and the Bishop of Orihuela, on behalf of Msgr. Re. The Holy Father's words of condolence were read. There was a large number of people. At the end, many of them thanked me for the favors my parents had done for them during their lives.

Mid-May: I had dinner with the Pope, who was particularly affectionate and kind to me. I thanked him for so many expressions of affection. I also thanked Dziwisz. It was surely he who had arranged for the telegrams to be sent, at the Pope's request, and for a bishop to be present, as well as many other details of affection.

"Month of May" with the Pope

May 24, 1995

Dziwisz, the Pope, and I had dinner with Mario Agnes and Msgr. Sandri. Two days ago we returned from a short trip to Prague and southern Poland. I ask the Pope if he cried during this visit to Poland, as *RAI* had said.

> —"Externally, no; but when the helicopter started to descend and I saw the people of the mountains in their [traditional] costumes. . . ." Undoubtedly, the sight of "his people" thrilled him.

After dinner, as the Pope makes his way to his chapel, Dziwisz reminds him that they have not done the "month of May," and makes a gesture inviting us to join them, specifying beforehand: "But we do it in Polish."

I tell him at once that I will join them and we take a small elevator up to the terrace of the Papal Apartment, which has a Stations of the Cross on one of the walls. "Look at the fifth station," Dziwisz tells me. I see, in fact, that the face of the Cyrenean, by the sculptor Enrico Manfrini,[6] has the unmistakable features of John Paul II.

---

6. Enrico Manfrini (Italy, 1917–2004) was a well-known and prestigious sculptor, author of some doors of churches and cathedrals (such as the one in Siena), as well as sculptures of the last popes, from Pius XII onwards.

There are some flower pots. Dziwisz tells me that they were planted by him and the Pope. "Look at those little fir trees: they are the ones they send us at Christmas. We have transplanted some of them and they have sprouted."

In a corner of the terrace there is a small altar with a simple image—about 60 cm [24 in.]—of Our Lady of Fatima. "We put it here a year after the attack," Dziwisz tells me.

We stand in front of this image and the Pope starts a song. He is accompanied in Polish by Dziwisz and the nuns who attend the apartment. It is a long and beautiful song, with stanzas that end with verses—always the same—in praise of the Virgin.

It lasts quite a long time: between seven and eight minutes. They sing another song and we end with the "*Ave, Ave Maria*" from Fatima in Polish: I accompany them in Spanish. They sing very well and the Pope does the harmony.

I am moved by the Pope's devotion and naturalness, as well as by the spontaneity, familiar and simple, of these moments.

The Pope shows us the rest of the terrace. We go up to the upper terrace, from which there is a magnificent view of Rome. "*Ma di sera*—says the Pope—è *ancora più bella con tutte le luci*" ("But at night it is even more beautiful, with all the lights").

Beijing Conference: Speak to the People

May 27, 1995

Working meeting on the Beijing Conference at the Secretariat of State, from 9:00 AM to 1:00 PM. At the end of the meeting, we will have lunch with the Pope. Tauran, Martino, and I are there. In the face of all the difficulties, the Pope renews his commitment to deal with this issue without discouragement.

He writes a letter to all the women in the world. He proposes some names for the delegation that will go to Beijing. And when Martino tells him that at the preparatory session in New York they systematically responded to some of the proposals of the Holy See by putting them in parentheses, the Pope advises: "Then, when they speak, say also 'in parentheses, in brackets'!" He tells us at one point that if we encounter difficulty, to turn to the people: "*Rivolgetevi alla gente*," that is, tell the public what is happening. It is a splendid line.

33

A Problematic Conference

A Window onto Mont Blanc

July 10–22, 1995

Ten days of rest for the Pope. Actually, only eight, because we arrive there on the first day around dinner time, and the last day is the return. They have been days of long walks and prayer. The Pope has walked a lot and sometimes without limping. When he walks a good distance he almost forgets the discomfort of his leg.

We set out each day around ten o'clock in the morning and, as the days go by, we come back later and later, until we are regularly arriving back around eight o'clock, dinner time.

On July 21 we were on the great glacier of Tza de Tzan, about 3,500 meters above sea level. A marvel. It is on the border with Switzerland. In front of us was the west face of the Matterhorn. As he contemplated it, while walking on the snow, the Pope asked for the breviary: it is clear that he needed to praise God with words of Scripture and the Liturgy of the Church. I have witnessed this on numerous occasions. He shares everything with the Lord: his worries, his sorrows and, in this case, his joys.

The war in Bosnia continues and we speak frequently of the attacks, the dead and the threat of the fall of the Bosnian enclave of Zepa. This situation brings about the consideration of "humanitarian intervention" and just war once again. I tell him that certain media are trying to get him to "bless" the armed intervention decided upon in London. We also talk about the forthcoming Beijing Conference, which is of great concern to him. His *Letter to Women*, written precisely on the occasion of this conference, has just been published.[1]

He gets up every day around five o'clock in the morning. At half past five he goes out onto the balcony of his small room, from which he looks out over Mont Blanc. Cibin tells me that he saw his chapel light on at 3:30 AM.

---

1. The *Letter to Women* is dated June 29, 1995. In a way, it completes the vision that John Paul II had presented in the apostolic letter *Mulieris dignitatem* (1988).

We go to the Chabanne Valley, to the Plain Bry, to the Laod Lenteney, where several horses and cows graze. There we meet Mrs. Perrouchon, the owner of the cattle, who is happy to see the Pope walking on her land.

One day, while discussing upcoming trips, the Pope tells me that there is a possibility of a meeting between him and Patriarch Alexis of Moscow in Hungary. I expressed my joy and added that this would make a visit of the Pope to Moscow more feasible. He answers: "I don't think so. . . . But everything is possible, because it is Our Lady who prepares everything." The tone of this statement is so sincere that I understand to what extent he trusts in Our Lady, knowing that where the future is dark, there is also the hand of Mary making the impossible a reality.

He also mentions the possibility of the trip to Israel and comments again that he would be very excited to follow in the footsteps of Abraham through the various places. It is his great dream.

"What Else can We Do?"

AUGUST 13, 1995

I arrive to Castelgandolfo at 8:00 PM and I am told to go to the pool area. The Pope is swimming. While he finishes his exercises, I chat for a while with Dziwisz, who tells me that a specialist in orthopedics (Dr. Pool, I seem to remember) has come from Germany and has been working with the Pope. He recommended a more intense and specific physiotherapy, and has left a couple of people from his team in Rome to help him carry it out.

Then he tells me about the tremor in his left hand. He has started taking a new medicine (he gives me the name), in doses of three half tablets, and asks me to talk to Martínez-Lage to get some guidance about it.[2]

I join the Pope as he comes out of the swimming pool: smiling and relaxed. As we drive to the "palazzo," the driver stops at a place in the garden from where, at the end of an avenue, a sculpture of the Madonna can be seen. "Will you sing with us," the Pope asks me, as he gets out of the car. From there, about 200 meters from the image, he intones, accompanied by Dziwisz, the "Mary, Queen of Poland," which the Poles traditionally sing at nine o'clock in the evening. I join in humming the melody. We return to the car and head for the dining room.

What more can we do in view of the Beijing Conference, the Pope asks. There are many people working on this issue, but—as always—he asks all his

2. I spoke the next day with Martínez-Lage and told Dziwisz his suggestions[Author's Note].

collaborators for ideas, looking for new suggestions and initiatives. We are talking with the Italian Prime Minister about promoting public statements by some European, American, African and Asian cardinals. Tomorrow Cardinal Sodano will come, he tells me, and he will talk to the Pope about this.

IV World Conference on Women in Beijing

August 25–September 18, 1995

August 25. Rome. I have a press conference on Beijing. Great interest on the part of the press and great difficulty on my part to make myself understood and to transmit my message. I speak to them of values, of equality and dignity, but some of them only understand what could be a "cut"—according to a certain mentality—of sexual liberties. Yesterday I sent Celli the text of my intervention. They make some corrections and remove what may seem controversial. Surely it is for the best.

August 27–31. New York. Since I received the letter from the Cardinal Secretary of State asking me if I could be part of the delegation of the Holy See for the IV World Conference on Women, we have had quite a few preparatory meetings. This is the last one.

Renato Martino, Msgr. Diarmuid Martin,[3] Sheri Rickert,[4] John Klink,[5] Msgr. Frank Dewane,[6] Gail Quinn,[7] Mary Ann Glendon[8]—who will be the head of the delegation—and I have spent these days gathered in one room, discussing various aspects and preparing our statements. It is a difficult task, because the document that the organizers have prepared is full of the ideas of radical feminism, which treats marriage as a form of slavery for women, pits them against men, and for whom children are a kind of shame. Although the proponents of this movement are not in the majority, they are very active. And the US delegation—sad to say—is moving along the same line of thought.

---

3. Diarmuid Martin (Ireland, 1945) was secretary of the Pontifical Council for Justice and Peace (1994–2001). He was archbishop of Dublin from 2004 to 2020.

4. Sheri Rickert was a New York lawyer, legal advisor to the Holy See Mission to the UN.

5. John Klink was president of the International Catholic Commission for Migrants and consultant to the Pontifical Council for the Family.

6. Frank Joseph Dewane (USA, 1950) was undersecretary of the Pontifical Council for Justice and Peace (1995–2001). Since 2007 he has been bishop of Venice, Florida.

7. Gail Quinn, director of the Pro-Life Secretariat of the US bishops' conference.

8. Mary Ann Glendon (United States, 1938) was a professor of law at Harvard University. Years later, she was US ambassador to the Holy See (2007–2009). She has been president of the Pontifical Academy of Social Sciences for nine years.

AUGUST 30, BEIJING. We have arrived in Peking thinking that we were going to have the support of some unconditional allies; but the reality is that no one supports us. We get ourselves set up and settled in. We test the transmissions and detect some problems. First skirmishes in the previous meetings. Only a few of us from the delegation are here. The rest will arrive later.

SEPTEMBER 3, BEIJING. Mass at the Argentinean embassy. Some people from the Latin American embassies attend. All the members of the delegation of the Holy See are present, except for a Vietnamese nun who has not yet been granted a visa. A woman from Hong Kong is part of our delegation. Her name is Teresa; she speaks Mandarin Chinese and she is a great help to us in everything, thanks to her silent and efficient work.

Official opening of the Conference at the Palace of the Great People's Assembly, in Tiananmen Square. Careful show, "Socialist" style, with some high quality acts—magnificent, the troupe of acrobats—in which there is no lack of some incredible Spanish in Chinese adaptation: the act of the *bullfighting children*! They announced the duet of "La Traviata" as "The Fallen Lady."

In the afternoon, at the Beijing International Conference Center, the conference opened with a splendid speech by Benhazir Bhutto[9] on the family and women. It is interesting: the most prominent women of this Conference—Bhutto and the Secretary General, Gertrude Mongella[10]—have received their early training in Catholic educational institutions.

SEPTEMBER 4–18, BEIJING. We meet twice a day with all the members of the delegation in a suite of the Holiday Inn Lido Hotel, where we reside. Mass is celebrated there at seven o'clock in the morning.

Teresa has succeeded, after going through numerous formalities at the Chinese Foreign Ministry, to obtain a visa for the Vietnamese nun, who manages to meet with us almost at the end of the Conference.[11]

There have been many days of intense work. I return, like everyone else, exhausted.

---

9. Benazir Bhutto (Pakistan, 1953–2007) led the Pakistan People's Party or PPP. She was the first woman prime minister of a Muslim country (1988–90 and 1993–96). She was assassinated.

10. Gertrude Ibengwe Mongella (Tanzania, 1945) held several ministerial positions in her country; she was the first woman president of the Pan-African Parliament.

11. In addition to the names already mentioned, the delegation also included Patricia Donahoe, Teresa Chooi, Peter J. Elliot, Pilar Escudero de Jensen, Janne Haaland Matláry, Claudette Habesch, Kathryn Hawa Hoomkwap, Irena Kowalska, Joan Lewis, David John Malloy, Anne Nguyen Thi Thanh, Luis Jensen Acuña, Lucienne Sallé and Kung Si Mi.

New York and Surrounding Area

October 4 to 9, 1995

The main reason for this trip to New York, Newark, New Jersey, Brooklyn, and Baltimore is the Pope's visit to the United Nations on the fiftieth anniversary of its founding. Months ago the Pope prepared the draft of the speech in Polish, which he passed on to the Second Section of the Secretariat of State for them to work on. Bishop Harvey[12] told me that it was a very good text.

On the 5th, at 6:30 AM, the Pope celebrated Mass at the headquarters of the Vatican diplomatic mission to the UN to pray for this appearance. He was accompanied by Father Tucci, the nuns who take care of the residence, and some other people. In the afternoon he celebrated a second Mass, as scheduled in the program.

In his speech to the General Assembly, he recalled the need to assume the "risk of freedom:"

> Modern totalitarianism has been, first of all, an aggression against the dignity of the person, an aggression that has gone so far as to deny the inviolable value of his life. The revolutions of 1989 were made possible by the efforts of courageous men and women who were inspired by a different and ultimately deeper and more vigorous vision: the vision of man as an intelligent and free person, the repository of a mystery that transcends him, endowed with the capacity to reflect and to choose, and therefore capable of wisdom and virtue.
>
> Decisive for the success of those non-violent revolutions was the experience of social solidarity: in the face of regimes sustained by the force of propaganda and terror, that solidarity constituted the moral nucleus of the "power of the non-powerful," it was a foretaste of hope and a warning of the possibility that man has to follow, on his path through history, the path of the noblest aspirations of the human spirit.

The speech was warmly applauded by all. He then went to the office of the Secretary General and greeted several high-ranking UN officials. Secretary General Boutros Ghali accompanied the Pope to the "Meditation Room," an interfaith

12. James Michael Harvey (USA., 1949) was then working in the Secretariat of State. He was appointed advisor to the Secretariat of State (1997–1998) and then prefect of the Pontifical Household (1998–2012). He was elevated to the cardinalate in 2012, when he was appointed archpriest of the Basilica of St. Paul Outside the Walls.

meditation space at UN headquarters. He thought he was going to be there for a few seconds, but the Pope stayed there alone, praying for ten minutes.

In San Marino

OCTOBER 15–16, 1995

OCTOBER 15. I go to San Marino as "spokesman of the Pope" following every step of the ceremonies of this small republic. We go in the car, the bishop of the diocese, an official of the Republic, and myself. Upon arrival, we visit the Minister of Foreign Affairs and discuss relations between the Holy See and San Marino.

Meeting with the Minister of Culture. Visit of the city and lunch. After lunch, we drive back to Montefeltro and San Leo, two Romanesque churches. The population of this small and beautiful country awaits us, with the mayor at the head. I visit the Castello where Cagliostro was imprisoned and died and observe the coins and lira bills thrown on the floor by many of those who visit his cell.[13]

I am interviewed by two local TV stations and meet with the local people, who ask me various questions about the Pope. I take a break at the hotel and spend some time in prayer. Then I have dinner with other authorities and give a lecture in a theater, broadcast live on local TV. It is the most lively part of the evening.

OCTOBER 16TH. Formal audience with the two Captains Regent; that is to say, with the two heads of State of this Republic. I say a few words and sign the Book of Honor, and I return to Rome grateful for the kindness of these people and, at the same time, quite tired.

These ceremonies are an unavoidable part of my job: I am received as the "spokesman for the Pope," and although these encounters allow me to clarify some questions and talk about various aspects of the faith—the priesthood, women in the Church, the family . . . —I do not like them, nor do I feel comfortable with them. Every time I conclude one of these activities, I say to myself: "Navarro, this was the last one." But then new invitations come to me and I accept them again, because I think they are a good opportunity to talk about God, the Church, and the Pope, even though I personally hate having to do "the little number."

---

13. Count Alessandro di Cagliostro (1743–1795) was a well-known alchemist, occultist and founder of a branch of Freemasonry.

It amuses me to compare the image that people have of me when I go to these places with the image that I—who am the one who really knows the full score—have of myself: a poor yokel stuck in a big role. I tend to take it all as a big joke, but what else can I do? I have no choice but to get used to—at least, outwardly—the life of a public man that this job requires.

Echoes of the Yugoslavian War

November 18, 1995

Dusan Miklja, Minister Counselor of the Yugoslav Embassy, comes to see me at the office. He is an intellectual who has published ten books. He leaves me a memorandum on the ethnic cleansing carried out by the Croatians (especially against the Serbs) during the last war.

He complains about the attitude of *L'Osservatore Romano.* He says that its opinion has not been sufficiently balanced in speaking about the Yugoslav issues. It is possible that he is right. We have arranged to meet on further occasions.

Vatican.va

Christmas 1995

During the Christmas season, we opened the *vatican.va* website with a message from the Pope during his *urbi et orbe* address. In just a few days more than a million people accessed the site. We set up a mailbox so that people could send e-mails and we received thousands and thousands of messages, some of them touching, especially the requests for prayers for various needs.

34

Nebulous Communication

Amnesty for Agca

January 19, 1996

The Holy Father is in good spirits, as usual, but the passage of time and the progression of his illness can be seen in his less expressive face and the more frequent recourses to Dziwisz when he tries to remember something.

I tell him that we have received a letter from Ali Agca in the office and I suggest that perhaps we could ask that he be granted amnesty, as he says in his letter: "I, after all, have not killed anyone." The Pope is fully willing to ask for it, but comments: "He did not kill the Pope . . . because Our Lady did not want him to."

During dinner, the visit of French President Jacques Chirac, who is coming tomorrow, is discussed. It is important for the Pope. On another note, I tell him about the good reception of the website.

With Mondadori in Cortina

January 28, 1996

I spent the weekend in Cortina d'Ampezzo with the publisher Leonardo Mondadori. I suggested to him some time ago the possibility of organizing a spiritual retreat with some of his friends from Milan and he liked the idea. A few days ago he called me to tell me that he wanted to do it this weekend, even if he had to attend alone. So Pippo Corigliano, director of the Opus Dei information office in Rome, who is also a friend of his, a priest, Umberto de Martino, and I went there. We met in Milan and Leonardo took us to his house in Cortina. It was all snowed in.

The retreat consisted of two meditations by the priest, two ascetic and spiritual talks given by Pippo and myself, and the recitation of the rosary before lunch.

The atmosphere is one of great trust and Leonardo is very sincere when it comes to talking about the mistakes of his life—two failed marriages among other things. The environment of Milan in which he moves is not very moral, according to his own definition. He was very happy at the end and he told me that we have to organize another one with his friends next October.

Internet

January 29, 1996

The Internet: the never-ending adventure. I had to take the initiative at the Holy See with this, and it occurred to me to take the plunge unconsciously. I spoke to the Holy Father about the possibilities of the Internet. He immediately grasped the idea. I also told him about the difficulties there would be in making it happen, because of the complexities of the Holy See. "But who will have to decide? Isn't it me?" he asked with a touch of irony. He told me to write a letter to the Secretariat of State and send him a copy.

I had already spoken to Re about this a few months earlier. His first reaction, and I understand it, was: let's organize a meeting. But I get a tremendous panic about these meetings: we talk, we talk, we try to reconcile extremes. . . . I suggested that we leave it for later. In any case, the meeting took place and, unfortunately, it was of no use. Nothing was proposed, some were against it, and others were jealous of their own jurisdictions. This was on November 11, 1995.

Things seemed to be bogged down. I spoke again with Re. Finally, a relatively ambiguous letter came out, signed by the Cardinal Secretary of State, which was sent to all the dicasteries: the idea and its realization were approved, but nothing was said about who and how it was going to be carried out, so as not to anger the jealous ones. And so, we set out . . . In the memorandum he had sent to the Secretariat of State, in addition to an approximation of the costs, he stressed that in this project "the Holy See must enjoy true independence and must not have any links with public or governmental bodies at any level."

At Christmas, thanks to the work of Sister Judith Zoebelein,[1] the home page with the Pope's *Urbi et Orbi* message was inaugurated. Although it was a success, there are many within the Vatican who look at all this with indifference. It is not malice, it is a lack of sensitivity to things that fall outside their immediate experience. To use Machado's words,[2] "they despise everything they ignore."

1. Judith Zoebelein (USA, 1948), a Franciscan Sister of the Eucharist, worked on the Vatican website since its inception in 1995.

2. Antonio Machado (Spain, 1875–1939), poet and playwright, representative of the so-called "Generation of '98."

Guatemala, Nicaragua, El Salvador and Venezuela

FEBRUARY 5–12, 1996

Throughout my life, I have met with magnificent communication professionals and what we usually call "journalists of breed." But as has happened in previous trips, there is no shortage of others who raise non-existent problems and imaginary conflicts, which only increase the already abundant number of difficulties posed by each trip.

On this occasion, I have learned that some are trying to pit Fernando Saenz, the new archbishop of San Salvador, who is Opus Dei, against Archbishop Oscar Romero. They consider that Saenz is more or less to blame for the fact that Romero has not been beatified yet. They ignore the fact that Romero chose Saenz as his confessor and spiritual director, because of his great friendship with him, after having been directed for years with Juan Aznar, another Opus Dei priest. Not to mention the great affection Romero had for the founder, Blessed Josemaria. In fact, he was one of the first to ask the Holy See to open his cause for beatification.

They do not know all this, or even the fact that Romero spent the day he was assassinated—March 24, 1980—in the company of Saenz and several priests of Opus Dei. He was with them from the morning until the early afternoon, participating in a priestly meeting. Saenz himself took him by car to the Hospital of Divine Providence, where they said goodbye at three o'clock in the afternoon. At a quarter past six he was killed by a bullet fired from outside the church while he was celebrating Mass.

When we take off from Rome, I go to where the Pope is preparing for his meeting with the journalists. He tells me to come back in half an hour because he is doing his personal prayer. When I come back, we talk about the countries we will visit.

When we come to El Salvador, I tell him that it is possible that some journalists will contrast Romero with the new bishop of El Salvador. The Pope did not know that Fernándo Sáenz had been Romero's spiritual director and that they had maintained that friendship until the end of his life.

As I expected, during the question and answer session, a journalist speaks to him about the Saenz-Romero antithesis. The Pope clarifies things and the supposed antithesis is deflated, which allows him to devote attention to the genuine issues of the trip.

FEBRUARY 5. GUATEMALA. We arrive in Guatemala City around four o'clock in the afternoon, local time, after a very long drive. For our bodies it is night; and late at night. However, the Pope carries out the planned activities. In his speech at the airport he alludes to the struggles of this country during recent decades, among them the earthquake that twenty years ago yesterday caused more than 20,000 deaths.

The ceremonies continue with the greeting to the faithful in the Cathedral Square and the official reception at the presidential palace. The Pope is extremely exhausted after so many hours without rest. According to our "biological clock," which follows Rome time, it is not long before dawn.

February 6. Zacapa. The helicopter carrying the Pope to Esquipulas is forced to return because of bad weather. Someone says that the Pope has become ill. I have to fight another "windmill," this time his imaginary illness.

When we leave Guatemala, a journalist asks me how the audience with Rigoberta Menchú, Nobel Peace Prize winner, went. Instead of saying that I had no news, I routinely answer "fine"(I did not receive any news that there had been any problems with any audience). Then I find out that there was no hearing because Menchu did not show up. Nice blunder on my part! It serves as a lesson for me not to forget that, in this profession, one should never act "by rote," with unthinking response.

February 7th. Managua, Nicaragua. The reception in Managua is very cordial and spectacular, especially considering how things were during his previous trip, under the Sandinista government. As we were leaving the airport, I saw a large banner: "Welcome to Nicaragua, Holy Father." It is signed by . . . Daniel Ortega, the president during our previous trip, which was characterized—to put it mildly—by a total lack of courtesy.

Afterwards, Holy Mass for families at the Malecon Park. The Pope refers to the 1983 trip:

> "This visit," he said during his homily, "is taking place in very different circumstances from the previous one. Those who remember the one thirteen years ago, know that the Pope came to Nicaragua and celebrated Holy Mass, although he was not able to really meet with the people. Much has changed in Nicaragua since then. For this reason, both your nation and the Pope himself were eager to have the opportunity for a new pastoral visit, which would be a true encounter."

The President of the Republic of Nicaragua is Mrs. Violeta Chamorro, who is very cordial and affectionate with the Pope during the reception. But then, when she learns that I am Spanish, she gives me a real tirade, directed at me and at all of us who work with the Holy Father. She does not understand, she tells me, how we allow the Pope to work so much at his age. We should take much better care of him, make him rest. I thank her, because they are words born of affection. If she only knew how much I carry this concern in my soul! (And what to say about Stanisław!).

FEBRUARY 8. EL SALVADOR. Upon his arrival at Ilopango International Airport, the Pope made reference to his previous visit, in which "I witnessed the suffering of a people torn by the pain of a fratricidal war that sowed death, violence, divisions, resentment, widowhood, and orphanhood. For this reason, I invited them to follow the path of sincere and constructive dialogue." He added that during these years he had followed "with interest the progress of the negotiations, which culminated in the historic Chapultepec Agreements, in Mexico, on January 16, 1992, thus concluding a process initiated precisely in the Apostolic Nunciature of San Salvador, and led first by the Episcopal Conference and then by the United Nations."

I talk to the archbishop about the possible beatification of Romero. For now, he tells me, the bishops are still divided.[3] After lunch, I suggest to Dziwisz that, in my opinion, during his visit to the cathedral, the Pope should go down to the crypt where Romero is buried, since the program only includes a meeting with the catechists. Dziwisz tells the Pope, who will indeed pray for a long time at the Archbishop's tomb.

FEBRUARY 9. VENEZUELA. From El Salvador we return to the airport in Guatemala, where the official farewell takes place and we fly to Venezuela. He goes to Retén Judicial de Los Flores de Catia prison to greet the inmates.

FEBRUARY 10TH. The Pope travels to Guarané. There he celebrates Mass for the inauguration of the new Shrine of Our Lady of Coromoto.

The activities follow one after the other. And along with them, the imaginary news by some, who claim that the Pope had to breathe oxygen because he was suffocating at the end of the Mass. Another bubble that needs to be burst.

FEBRUARY 11. Farewell at the "Simon Bolivar" airport. The Pope finishes his trip with a bad cold due to the temperature changes and intense air conditioning.

---

3. Indeed, almost twenty years passed: Oscar Romero was beatified on May 23, 2015 in San Salvador and canonized by Pope Francis on October 14, 2018, in St. Peter's Square in Rome.

February 15. In Rome, dinner with the Pope. We recall anecdotes from the trip. And he asks at the end, "Do you think these trips are useful?"

Fidel Castro's Letter

February 20, 1996

I am talking to Tauran. On Monday the Cuban Minister of Foreign Affairs is coming to see him and it is possible that he will protest the statements I made during the recent trip, when I was asked why the Pope did not go to Cuba and I said that it was because he had not been invited.

Tauran tells me that Fidel Castro wrote the Pope a letter on May 14, 1989 in which he said:

> In the course of the interview I had last December 30 with His Eminence Card. Etchegaray, I expressed to him the willingness of our government to receive you in Cuba on the occasion deemed most propitious. I would like to personally ratify this disposition and express to you on this occasion the testimony of my highest consideration.

The Pope responded to Castro on June 30 of that same year, telling him that he appreciated his invitation. Since then, there has been nothing more. Naturally, I knew nothing of that interesting exchange of letters.

The Pope with Fever

March 13–16, 1996

Re called me at home this morning at 8:30 AM to tell me that the Pope is not feeling well and will not be attending the weekly Wednesday Audience: "He has a slight fever."

When I get to the office I call Dziwisz. The Pope is in bed, with a high fever, 102.59 degress Fahrenheit, and he has had colic. I talk to Renato Buzzonetti. He says it is a febrile syndrome. Buzzonetti doesn't want to say that it is the common flu, because the fever may be the result of something digestive and he is not sure yet. I talk to Re again and prepare my report.

My great help in these cases is being able to speak directly with Dziwisz, who gives me first-hand the nuance of the situation, which allows me to calibrate the information. Buzzonetti would like to say nothing at all. We have good relations, because we can talk doctor to doctor, but he finds it difficult to understand the demands of public opinion around a personality like the Pope.

Besides, journalists' hunger for information is infinite. When I give them the little information I have, they try to get more. . . . Some of them, even inventing. Flu, not flu? I tell them: "You can say whatever you want. I prefer to stick to the objective data and that is what I'm giving."

The summit on terrorism begins today in Sharm el Sheik, attended by Mubarak, Peres, Clinton, and others. The Pope was planning to refer to this issue during the general audience. Since it did not take place, I remind Re in case he considers it appropriate to propose that a message be sent on behalf of the Pope.

I cannot avoid the dance of TV interviews. This morning I speak about the Pope's illness on six channels, one after the other. Late in the afternoon I talk again with Dziwisz. He tells me that the Pope has slept a lot, has been able to rest, and has less fever.

March 14: His fever has gone down. But I learn that yesterday, even with fever, the Pope got up to pray in his chapel. And that this morning he concelebrated Mass with Dziwisz. Buzzonetti heard about it and got angry, naturally. I think that the Pope cannot live without the Eucharist and I understand him. And I also understand Buzzonetti.

I go back to talk to the journalists. They are dissatisfied with the little information I have given them, and rightly so. I have told them that the fever has gone down, but I have not been able to tell them anything about the diagnosis, simply because we do not have it.

Buzzonetti tells me that yesterday morning, when he went to see him, he found him singing softly. Despite the fever, he is still cheerful and optimistic.

March 15. Long conversation with Buzzonetti. No clear diagnosis. Fever decreases in the mornings and increases—although less than on the first day—in the afternoons. There is a slight jaundice, which is not detectable in the eyes but in the skin. In the analysis there is bilirubinemia.[4]

His hypothesis is that as a consequence of the cholecystectomy operation during the second abdominal operation, or as a result of the operation after the attack, adhesions may have formed, obstructing the flow of bile into the duodenum and causing biliary retention. There cannot be calculi and it also excludes a viral hepatitis, because in that case he should not have fever. And he does not

4. Bilirubemia is the abnormal presence of bilirubin in the blood. Bilirubin is the pigment resulting from the degradation of red blood cells in the spleen. It is normal to have a certain amount of bilirubin: when there is an excess, jaundice occurs, which is characterized by yellowing of the skin, membranes or eyes.

rule out that this condition could end up in the operating room. For the time being, he is providing antibiotic coverage.

The Pope asked him, "What have I got?" and he explained his two hypotheses. Dziwisz thinks Buzzonetti always assumes the worst. And Re moves on the same skeptical wavelength.

I tell Buzzonetti that today we have to say something, even if we cannot give a diagnosis, since the press is still speculating. The poor man is in a delicate situation. I suggest that we say, at least, that "his digestive system is affected." He agrees. And we draw up the text of the communiqué that I give to the press.

It's a fish that bites its own tail. If I said that I am only willing to communicate what the medical reports say, so that I can play it safe, the journalists will be angry with Buzzonetti and not with me. And when I give these nebulous statements, they get angry with me and not with Buzzonetti. But if I were to say that the diagnosis has not yet been confirmed, speculation would run wild.

In addition, the Pope has a different perception of his own state of health, which he transmits to his collaborators. As soon as the fever goes down, as he has a great capacity for recovery, he thinks he is already well, and starts to carry out his plans once more.

Re finds him looking well and speaks of a possible trip to Siena on Tuesday. Dziwisz doesn't rule out the possibility of a three-hour beatification Mass at St. Peter's this Sunday. Buzzonetti, logically, proposes that the Pope cancel all his engagements for several days. They do not understand Buzzonetti, because the Pope gives every impression of being recovered, and they think he is acting with exaggerated prudence.

At last Buzzonetti manages to get the date of the Siena trip postponed until March 30, and he gets the Pope to come down to St. Peter's Basilica next Sunday and only for the first part of the ceremony. I know that it is difficult for the Pope to make the decision to leave early, because he thinks of the people who have come to greet him; but in the end, he agrees.

March 16. I am issuing a communiqué to announce the changes in the Pope's schedule. Yesterday afternoon he had an ultrasound and an X-ray. The result was nil and Dziwisz was ecstatic, as was everyone else. This led them to reaffirm their idea: "Buzzonetti is a great doctor, but he always tends to assume the worst, like all doctors." Buzzonetti, with good judgment—which I agree with—explains that the fact that nothing has been seen does not exclude the possibility that there is something we have not seen. . . .

The Last *Trovata*

March 25, 1996

The same author who had already written a couple of years ago about the Pope's health, published an article yesterday in which he stated that the Pope had cancer, "probably of the colon," and possibly Parkinson's disease. Naturally, the news appeared in the Italian press and Dziwisz called me immediately to see what we should do. I reassured him.

I tell journalists that the latest *trovata* (the latest witticism) about the Pope's health comes from a Spanish newspaper, and that I am authorized by the Holy Father's doctor to say that the Pope undergoes regular medical examinations "and shows no symptoms of neoplastic disease."

I would add that it is enough to look at the Pope's scheduled activity to rule out this hypothesis. Today we have given them the programs for the trips to Siena and Tunis. Tomorrow we will provide them with the program for the trip to Slovenia, and I will confirm all the Pope's activities during Holy Week.

Istanbul, UN Conference on Habitat

June 17, 1996

Yesterday I returned from Istanbul, where the United Nations Conference on Habitat II was held from June 3 to 14. Somewhat calmer than Cairo and Beijing. But only "somewhat." The last day I went to sleep at four in the morning.

The delegation from the Holy See was composed of Msgr. Martino, Diarmuid Martin, Frank Dewane, Patricia Donahue, John Klink, Jim Reinert, a Honduran couple—Leonardo Casco and his wife Marta Lorena,—and myself.

The conference theme did not, in itself, require us to clarify our position on too many issues vis-à-vis other delegations. But it soon became clear that some wanted to insist on issues of moral consequences that had already appeared in Cairo and Beijing: reproductive health, sexual health, etc., terms that in their particular vocabulary are synonymous with abortion.

The US delegation again puzzled me because, without warning, they proposed to make six references to these issues instead of the two planned, trying to ideologize the document, whether or not it was relevant. I told the press about it. The news appeared in all the newspapers. In the end, the US delegation backed down.

The Canadians wanted to remove any reference to family by replacing that word with *Afamilies@* or Agender@, so that not only homosexual unions, but any type of "gender relationship" would be considered family. Brazil adopted a similar position. The attitude of the European Union, free, on this occasion, from the ideological pressure exerted in Beijing by some Spanish socialists, was more balanced.

On the other hand, pro-abortion NGOs were surprised to see that our pro-life proposals were approved and found an echo not only in Latin America, but also in Muslim countries.

At the Conference itself, little attention was paid to the media, which allowed me to speak at length with some correspondents of international agencies who demonstrated with great clarity the position of the Holy See on the issues that were of most interest to us. We strongly supported—against the initial opposition of the US delegation—the human right to decent housing. And our proposal was approved.

This morning the Pope received in his library the members of the delegation. Afterwards, Msgr. Martino, Diarmuid Martin, and I had lunch with the Holy Father. Martino commented that Leonardo Casco and his wife Lorena have done a great job. The Pope emphasized again that the presence of the Holy See in these international forums was necessary.

On June 8, I had sent Dziwisz a letter to inform the Pope of the progress of the conference. Together with some of the considerations I mentioned in the previous lines, I expressed my surprise at the total lack of initiative on the part of the countries of Central and Eastern Europe. Why is this happening? I venture an answer: as I see it, these peoples, who aspire to be accepted into the "club" of the European Union, do not want to "interfere" with its proposals so as not to risk being slammed in the face with the door.

35

A Resigning Pope?

On the Return from Cadore

July 23, 1996

We have spent Wednesday, July 10 until today, Tuesday, July 23, in Cadore. They have been days of peace and long conversations while walking in the mountains. We are the usual group, plus Buzzonetti, who is with us for the first time. Dziwisz asked him to come, which is logical, because if the Pope is in need, we are more at ease with him than with one of the younger doctors.

The first day the Pope stayed at home reading. In the afternoon we took a short walk on the nearby trails. The rest of the days we went out into the mountains, as usual. On the first excursion I talked with the Pope about his recent trip to Germany (June 21–23) and the good it had done, contrary to what some have written. I gave him some objective data that had reached me: the impact on the people, the fact that the Germans were able to hear and see him on TV, without filters or commentary.

I told him about it because I knew he had read the criticisms of Küng and Drewermann preceding the trip, and perhaps the discontented murmurs that some groups, very much minorities, promoted in Berlin still resounded in his ears.

July 13. As we were walking up the mountain, we were overtaken on the path by a German tourist in his forties, with his twelve year old son. Seeing the Pope, he recognized him at once and greeted him. He told the Pope that he was from Jena, a city in the former East Germany, and told him that this was his last day of vacation. He would never have imagined that he would meet the Pope right there, walking with his little Mathias!

—"Those of us who have lived in East Germany," he said, "are very grateful to you for everything you have done."

They continued to converse in German and Tadeusz translated for me. He did not seem to be a Catholic, but he was certainly aware of the full debt that the East Germans owed to John Paul II.

July 14. In the afternoon, we went for a short walk around the house. I told the Pope that the previous day's meeting with the German had been a kind of confirmation of what we had discussed two days earlier about his trip to Germany. He listened to me in silence, without saying anything.

> —"Everyone knows," I added, "the great mental and physical effort that these trips involve, but they are worth it, because things happen on them that would not have happened if the Holy Father had not gone."
>
> —"Well, but I have to tell you that I . . . I like to travel!" —he said with a smile.
>
> —"Perhaps the Lord makes use of that too," I replied.
>
> —"So you think," he added amusedly, "that the Pope should continue to make trips?"
>
> —"No doubt about it!"—I exclaimed. And I remembered a comment he made during a meeting with journalists on a trip to the United States in 1987. One of them told him that it had been calculated that he spent 7% of his time outside Rome . . . The Pope replied, pretending to be serious: "Really? What a scandal!"

We now turn to the participation of the Holy See in the major international conferences of the United Nations. He is convinced that the effort made in defense of human dignity has been worthwhile.

> —"When we met in Newark," he then told me, "Clinton told me about the great collaboration that the American delegation was giving to the delegation of the Holy See at the Beijing Conference."
>
> —"Holy Father, unfortunately, that's not. . . ." —and I told him in detail about the discussion I had in Newark with a person from the White House who wanted this supposed collaboration to be mentioned in the joint communiqué of the White House and the Holy See. I flatly refused to have such a falsehood mentioned, because they did not help us nor did they collaborate with us in any way. Quite the contrary. That effort to appear, during the Pope's stay in the United States, as a "collaborator with the Holy See" was blown to bits.

I told the Pope about Janne Haaland, the competent Norwegian university professor who had been part of the Holy See delegation to the Beijing conference, and the story of her conversion to Catholicism. He then brings up his upcoming trip to France, and the criticism of some people, who claim to be agnostic, about "the expense of the trip."

July 15. We arrived by car on the shores of a small lake. The Pope, happy as usual, sat down to pray the breviary. But on this occasion he did it singing, in a low but audible voice, with the classic semitone.

Each day we went to a different place. We were accompanied by extraordinarily good weather. I went down to the village—Lorenzago di Cadore—to develop the photographs I had taken of him and distribute them to the journalists. I chose four in which the Pope looked really good. The next day I showed them to him. He began to look at them carefully, but immediately put them down and moved on to something else.

We head towards the Colesei. During these walks, in a discontinuous but evident way, I discover some changes. Sometimes he has a hieratic face—which I attribute to Parkinson's—with a smaller range of expressiveness. The walks have been shorter, about a kilometer, with a good deal of effort on his part. The smile, which was a habitual gesture for him, appears now only now and then, although I did manage to make him laugh when I put on a red clown's nose while taking a photograph of him.

—"Do you remember all the trips we've taken over the years?" he asked me on one of those walks.

—"No, Holy Father. There have been so many. I am unable to remember them all."

And he told me that he had been given an album with photographs of his youth, with which he has remembered his excursions in the forests of Poland and his kayaking on the lakes.

One day, after lunch, while I was reading under a tree, Dziwisz approached me. He asked me what the world of the press and the circles of the Curia would think about a possible resignation of the Pope. I tell him that this question was discussed on the occasion of the Pope's 75th anniversary, but that at the moment it is not in the foreground.

However, it is clear that the Pope has thought about it. And he may well have asked Dziwisz to raise the issue with various people.

—"And you, how do you see it?"

—"I see that there are reasons for it and reasons against it," I tell him. Reasons against it: a Pope in Rome and a resigned Pope in Poland could lead to new divisions in the Church. But there are reasons in favor, with their advantages: John Paul II, who has changed so many traditions of the pontificate, could change one more and set a modern precedent that would allow future Popes, disabled or very old, to resign with ease.

When Dziwisz leaves, I keep thinking about it. This question about a possible resignation is logical, but at the moment it seems to me to be without much foundation. The Pope has suffered several health setbacks, but, in my opinion, none of them would justify a resignation today, because none of them completely incapacitates him.

Another thing is the psychological pressure that these illnesses put on the Pope, who is always in the spotlight of public attention. Perhaps—knowing his way of being and thinking—he might consider the possibility of resigning as a temptation, as a dereliction of his duties before God.

Dziwisz thinks about the many health setbacks he has suffered: truly, how many illnesses he has had since the attack! But he cannot get used to the idea of a resigned Pope, living in hiding somewhere, and another Pope in the Vatican. He told me that he had asked Martínez Somalo about it and he had told him that he doesn't even consider it to be a possibility. I don't know how many other people he has talked to about this.

The next day, I have another conversation with Tadeusz Styczeń on the same subject. He tells me that he was talking to the Pope about this matter after his hip surgery.

> —"I told him," Styczeń told me, "that God is the one who gives the call and that only God can revoke it with death." But the Pope told me: 'Yes, but God can revoke it not only with death, but also with incapacity.' I did not know what to say to him. On another occasion, when I saw the faces of the people who were waiting for him in Lorenzago every day when he returned, I told him that I could not deprive of his presence all those people who loved him so much. He remained thoughtful and said nothing to me. And I added: 'Holy Father, when Bach was dying, in disastrous family circumstances—he was almost broke and his children were selling his scores to get money to get drunk—he wrote one of his most wonderful works, which has a passage that evokes God's call to Bach himself . . .'"

The Atlanta Olympics have begun during these days. The Pope alludes to them after praying the Angelus in Pieve. In the evening Samaranch calls me from the United States asking me for a telephone or fax number to contact the Pope. I give him our fax number and after a few hours he sends a message, as president of the International Olympic Committee, thanking the Holy Father for his words after the Angelus. When I tell the Pope about it he says to me:

—This means that the Pope is *saying* something. . . .

Sometimes I wonder if he is aware of the extent to which his figure and his words count, weigh, and influence today' s world.

When I returned to Rome, I asked the office to draw up a list of the Pope's travels, detailing the dates, countries and cities he had visited, which I gave to the Pope, and the next day Dziwisz told me that he had been consulting it in detail after dinner. Nostalgia for the years when he enjoyed a striking physical strength?

Panonhalma, Hungary: Too Much and Too Bad

SEPTEMBER 9, 1996.

Last Saturday, September 7, I met with journalists in Gyor during the Pope's trip to Hungary (September 6–7). The day before, I had denied a dispatch from *Agence France Press* about the Pope's health. The journalists, of course, asked me about it, and I ended up talking too much. And, moreover, badly. I mentioned Parkinson's for the first time, and I also referred to the stomach problem.

Naturally, the next day the Italian newspapers echoed my words. I thought of the predictable—and justified—anger with me on the part of the Secretary of State and, above all, Buzzonetti.

Undoubtedly, the ambiguity with which the Pope's state of health has been reported in recent weeks is a problem for me. But, at the same time, I felt that—in the midst of these difficulties—something had to be risked.

I hope this will be useful and helpful in the future. And I am not only referring to my "technical" ability, but also to my search for holiness, because it is something that hurts and humbles me.

"It is Past Time that Overcomes All Weaknesses."

SEPTEMBER 27, 1996

The theme of the dinner at Castelgandolfo was the trip to France (September 19–22). We three accompanied the Pope: Sandri, Mario Agnes, and myself. Three unforgettable moments stand out: the meeting with the families, the meeting with the sick in Tours, and the Mass in Reims.

I tell the Pope that the trip was a miracle. TV has helped a lot, providing almost complete coverage of the ceremonies. I think it has contributed to the fact that some newspapers, with *Le Monde* at the forefront, have changed their attitude to the power of images.

We spoke for a few moments about John Paul I, because the next day a memorial Mass was being celebrated in memory of the deceased pontiff.

When we finished dinner, the Pope let slip a phrase that is not easy to interpret: "The time has passed that overcomes all weaknesses." None of us present fully understood his meaning. I thought those words were related to his current situation: he knows that in a few days he will return to the operating room for an appendectomy operation, which adds to his numerous bodily and spiritual sufferings, turning his existence into a cross.

Appendicitis Operation

October 8, 1996

On September 14, we issued a statement on the clinical diagnosis: the Pope suffers from recurrent appendicitis which necessitated surgery, which took place this morning.

In the clinical bulletin and in the informative data for the press given by Dr. Crucitti, the three issues to which I alluded in Hungary are mentioned: laparotomy intervention and the existence of some adhesions. The third one refers to Parkinson's disease and is contained in the sentence: "As far as the problem of the extrapyramidal syndrome is concerned, there are no new data. No further examinations have been made and the specialists continue to be attentive to the development of this disease, as usual."

I go to the Gemelli early in the morning. I go up to the tenth floor and from there I call Re, who is with Dziwisz on the ninth floor, next to the operating room. He comes in and tells me that the operation started shortly before eight o'clock. Buzzonetti left the operating room for a moment to confirm that it was appendicitis. Later I meet Francesco Crucitti, Manni, and the rest of the medical team. Manni tells me: "Reading the newspapers of the last few days, I see that there are some who wish to report and others who do not wish to do so at all."

Dziwisz tells me that the Pope got up at three in the morning, prayed in the chapel, read the breviary and recited the rosary, because he was not sure if he would be able to do so after the operation. He celebrated Mass at five o'clock this morning.

On this occasion, when he came out of the anesthesia, his face had an expression of serenity and not of suffering. When he was taken to his room after the operation, he was conscious and, at his request, the medical report was read to him. During these days he has not taken the prescribed drug against Parkinson's disease, and he is feeling better.

Regarding Sunday's Angelus, I suggest that perhaps the Vatican Radio technician could come and record the Pope in his room. Then, he could lean out of the window for a few seconds to give the blessing. That brief public appearance will comfort and reassure the thousands of people around the world who pray for him and are anxious about his health.

Vatican Number Three

October 15, 1996

The Pope's words recorded for the Angelus on Sunday the 13th show how he lived these days: with total abandonment to God, placing his life in the hands of Our Lady—he recalled the *Totus tuus*—until the year 2000.

Then, he gave the blessing from the window and made some improvised and amusing remarks, saying that, for him, in this period of his existence, Vatican number one is St. Peter's Square; Vatican number two, Castegandolfo, and Vatican number three, the Gemelli Polyclinic.

The media are still talking about Parkinson's disease. Dziwisz has told me not to say anything about it, because we are still not clear about the diagnosis: "It could be a consequence of the accident he had when he was young," he says.

The Pope was discharged today. At this time, the priority is not public opinion, but to define the diagnosis. Later on, we will study the best way and the most convenient moment to make this diagnosis known. This is what I propose to Dziwisz and Sodano.

An Article at Midnight

October 30, 1996

On Sunday the 27th *Corriere della Sera* published a full page article by Hans Küng with his usual attacks against the Pope. In the evening, I called Messori to propose to him, since he is an expert on John Paul II, that he write an article in response. He did so that same night. He finished writing at three in the morning, and when I had the article in my hands, I called *La Stampa* of Turin to see if they would publish it. La Spina, the deputy editor, told me that since *La Stampa* and *Corriere della Sera* are like "cousins"(both are owned, to a greater or lesser extent, by Fiat or the Agnelli family), it would be better if *Corriere* would publish it.

This mixture of competition and friendship between two of the leading newspapers never ceases to amaze me. The next day I speak with the editor of the *Corriere* and they decide to publish Messori's entire article, which takes up a full page. As it is a good article, it is also published in Austria and other countries.

About Weigel's Book

November 6, 1996

The Pope is back to his usual rhythm of work after the operation he underwent last October. I saw this today when I arrived at 7:30 PM and upon entering the apartment, I greeted Tauran, who had just left the Holy Father's office. We begin dinner immediately: the Pope does not allow himself moments of relaxation between one activity and another.

These are intense days for him. Today he had a general audience in the morning, and throughout these days there will be a succession of celebrations for the fiftieth anniversary of his ordination to the priesthood. Five cardinals and more than a thousand priests and bishops who were ordained in the same year, 1946, are also taking part.

I see him relaxed and friendly, as always, but tired. With less tremor in his hands, but with a stiffness in his expression and some movements that denote the progress of the disease, which I am more and more convinced is extrapyramidal.

He greets me in the living room and smilingly asks me how long it's been since we've seen each other:

—"Since the hospital, after your appendicitis operation, Holy Father."

We discussed several issues. First, Küng's article. And once again, I see that he does not make the slightest word of criticism against anyone.

Dziwisz asks about the book Weigel is preparing. I know that the Pope does not like us to talk about questions that refer to his person. That is why I tell him: "Holy Father, John Paul II no longer belongs to Karol Wojtyla; he belongs to the Church; he is a page of the Church. This book is intended to shed historical light on that page of the Church."

He smiles at this reasoning. And that encourages me to continue:

—"The book will be more valuable to the extent that all its statements are historically well dated and documented. That is why you have to find a system so that all the historical material you need about these years can be passed on to you. For example, in the future, there may be a historian who will say that John Paul II did not deal with China at all during his pontificate. For this reason, we should now give Weigel the letter that the Pope wrote to Deng Xiaoping,[1] to which the latter did not reply. . . ."

Since the Pope seems to agree, we propose with Dziwisz a system to facilitate Weigel's work. At the end, as usual, we go to the chapel, where we pray for a long time on our knees in front of the tabernacle. On this occasion, among other intentions, I ask God for the miracle of the Pope's healing.

When Dziwisz escorts me to the elevator, he tells me that Weigel has sent a series of questions to the Pope. He asks for my opinion. I suggest that they leave the Pope alone for now, because many of those questions concern data that Stanisław Rylko can easily answer.

1. Deng Xiaoping (China, 1904–1997), an important political leader who fell from grace during Mao's Cultural Revolution, but later became the Supreme Leader of the People's Republic of China and a reformer, although he approved of the brutal repression of the protesters in Tiananmen Square (1989).

36

Tremors in Sarajevo

A Unique Dinner

January 23, 1997

I have returned from Milan after an unusual dinner. Host: Leonardo Mondadori. Guests: Henry Kissinger, Gianni Agnelli, Mario Monti—commissioner of the European Union—, the U.S ambassador, and two other people. Unfortunately, I didn't quite understand who they were, and me.

Leonardo sent me the plane ticket and I decided to go. I was seated next to Agnelli, a man with a normal manner, not at all aloof, just like Kissinger, and I took the opportunity to talk about the Pope.

Kissinger told us an anecdote from his time as US Secretary of State, when they were making great efforts to improve their relations with China. He went to Beijing and met with Deng Xiaoping, who was then number two. During the conversation he told him: "There is something that unites us: neither the United States nor China have anything to ask of each other." The next day he met with Mao, who was already aware of their conversation the day before, and told him, "You say that both the United States and China do not need each other at all. If that were true, I would not have invited you." To which Kissinger replied, "Neither would I have accepted your invitation."

Kissinger told me that he would like to speak with the Pope and left me his fax number in New York, commenting that before his next trip to Europe he would contact me, in case that opportunity arose.

Lunch with Sodano

February 6, 1997

I had lunch today with Cardinal Secretary of State Sodano who, from time to time, invites me. We are alone, as usual. I tell him what happened at dinner a few days ago with Agnelli and Kissinger.

Sodano asks me about the book Weigel is writing: I explain the genesis of the idea.

He tells me that he finds the Pope tired whenever he meets with him in the afternoons. The Pope meets with some of his collaborators one or two days a week. On Monday, Sodano himself goes; on Tuesday, Re; on Wednesday, Tauran; on Thursday, Sodano again; on Friday, Ratzinger; and on Saturday, Gantin or someone else. The meetings usually last from 6:45 to 7:30. I told him that the Pope has told me on some occasions that it is difficult for him to write at night and that he prefers to write in the morning, even if it is very early.

The Cardinal gives me news of his brother, who has had an accident in Asti—he was hit by a car—and has suffered an intestinal obstruction. At the end I tell him that it would be very useful for me to attend a meeting they are going to have at the Secretariat of State with several nuncios about the presence of the Holy See in international organizations. He tells me that he will send me the schedule so that I can attend.

In International Organizations

March 3, 1997

Two days of meetings, from 9:00 AM to 7:00 PM, with a break for lunch. Sodano, Tauran and several cardinals are meeting in the *Sala Bologna* with the nuncios to various international organizations of the United Nations. The aim is to study the presence of the Holy See in the UN, to see what is currently being done and what can be done. The various nuncios relate their personal experiences and comment on the difficulties they encounter.

These difficulties are magnified in New York because it is there that the issues of greatest ethical and moral impact are raised, especially birth control and the new anti-natalist and anti-family language. Ratzinger presents a profound analysis of the problems of our time, offering us, so to speak, the context in which we move.

What Else Can Be Done?

March 8, 1997

The Pope receives Mary Robinson, President of Ireland, in audience. Meanwhile, I tell Dziwisz that even though I know that we have used all the means at our disposal, calling on the best specialists in the world to attend to the Pope's health, I still ask myself, if we couldn't we do more, even if it is not easy? And he tells me something perfectly understandable: that the Pope, after so many consultations, operations, diagnoses, treatments, and exercises, "is fed up with doctors and medicines."

> —"What else can be done?" he asks me. And we conclude that—even though the Pope accepts what God sends him—we must continue to consult with good specialists until we are completely sure of the diagnosis. Then, we must change whatever is necessary in terms of work habits, attention, etc.

Finally in Sarajevo

April 16, 1997

On the 12th and 13th we travel to Sarajevo. As we are approaching with the plane, we are informed by radio that they have discovered a large quantity of explosives—more than 100 kilos—under a bridge located on the route from the airport to the city.

We are told that the explosives were connected to a detonator and a radio command. The SFOR forces (Stabilization Forces of the UN) have prepared several helicopters to move us from the airport to the city, instead of going with the popemobile. The Pope is informed so that he can decide. Before giving an answer, he asks: "Are there people on the road waiting to see the Pope go by?" And then he decides to go by land, in the popemobile.

The Pope, perfectly informed of everything, makes no reference to this attack. But I wonder if, from a human perspective, we have adequately assessed the real danger posed by this trip.

A couple of days later I have dinner with the Pope in Rome and we recall some of the events of the trip. The impact of the TV footage has been very strong.

During the Mass at the Sarajevo stadium, a snow and wind storm arose and the temperature dropped dramatically. The altar had no protection whatsoever. In the sacristy, before the Mass, the Pope was well protected with a sweater and a raincoat under his alb and chasuble. But when the storm started, he began to shiver intensely: partly because of the cold and partly because of his illness. Piero Marini, the master of ceremonies, very gently held his left arm to contain the trembling, but I got the feeling that the Pope got a little scared and told him to call Dziwisz. His presence reassured him. In those moments you can see how much he trusts and relies on Dziwisz.

Surprisingly, at the end of the ceremony, he joked with us, "I'm sure more than one of us will catch a cold after this, but I'm not up for it."

Prague

April 27, 1997

From April 25 to 27, he traveled to Prague on the occasion of the anniversary of St. Adalbert. The Pope is in a good mood and more expressive than on other occasions. The evolution of his illness is irregular, or at least not constant, because his symptoms manifest themselves differently at different times. When the plane takes off from Rome and he greets the journalists, he laughs as usual and starts joking with them. I get the impression that the very departure from the Vatican—with the weight of so many problems—has a positive influence on him and his facial expression becomes freer.

During this trip, Vaclav Havel shows great affection for the Pope. It is clear that he sincerely appreciates him. An ecumenical event is held in the Prague Cathedral, which is attended by all the Protestant leaders. Some of them did not want to participate in the previous trip.

A Letter from England

June 26, 1997

Busy evening. I had committed myself to participate in the presentation of a book by a member of parliament, when Dziwisz calls me to tell me to come to dinner at 7:45 PM. This was a "complication" that I gladly accepted. I attended the book presentation and ask that, as I will have to leave earlier, a cab be waiting for me at the door at 7:15 PM.

I arrive a few minutes before the scheduled time at the apartment and Msgr. Mietek[1] tells me that the Pope is still in the chapel. I enter and see that he is seated, with a standing light to help him read. I kneel down and wait in prayer. It is not the usual five or ten minutes, but half an hour. Mietek beckons me to a waiting room, but I return the signal saying I prefer to stay where I am. The Pope is reading the breviary. He makes frequent glances at the tabernacle,

1. Mieczysław Mokrzycki, familiarly called "Mietek"(Poland, 1961), was appointed second secretary to the Pope in 1996, replacing Msgr. Thu. After the death of John Paul II, he continued for a time as second secretary to Benedict XVI, until the latter appointed him, in 2007, coadjutor archbishop of Lviv (Ukraine). A year later he was appointed archbishop of Lviv.

without hurry, without turning around, immersed in his prayer, forgetting about time. To see him praying like this, immersed in God, without consulting the clock, moves me and edifies me.

To the eyes of a person without faith or religious culture, this chapel from the time of Paul VI might seem "tragic." It consists of an altarpiece and a life-size crucified Christ, surrounded by the representation of two crimes, two murders, those of St. Peter and St. Paul. To see the glorious Christ, one must look up to the ceiling and contemplate the stained glass window with the image of the Risen Christ. John Paul II has only added a small icon without a frame, Our Lady of Czestochowa, to the left of the cross.

When he finishes, he gets up leisurely, remains kneeling for a few minutes, takes his cane and leaves. He greets me and we go to the dining room. The two secretaries are also there. Before we sit down, Dziwisz reminds us that this is the thirtieth anniversary of his cardinalate.

After we bless the meal, I ask him if I can read him a letter. It is a short message, which came to me from England. It is signed by an unknown man who recounts his life story. For a time he was a director of a trading house and was happily married, until he had problems with alcohol and drugs and became a beggar sleeping on the streets of London. He happened to read Tad Szulc's biography of the Pope and found within it the hope and strength to change. Now he has put his life back together and wants to thank the Pope. Dziwisz tells me to leave the letter on the table. The Pope does not comment.

Later, he asks me what is being said about the refusal of the Patriarch of Moscow to meet the Pope in Graz. I explain to him that the entire press has commented on it, in general, in its proper context. It is evident that the responsibility lies with Alexis II, since the Pope did all he could. I tell him that now there will be talk that the Ecumenical Patriarch of Constantinople will not send a delegation to Rome this year for the feast of St. Peter. Stanisław adds that it is better not to say anything to the press. I say that it is preferable that I explain the situation to some journalists. I assure the Pope that I will not be uncharitable, but that it is better to say how things stand.

Shortly thereafter, Dziwisz gets up and goes into the next room to do an errand for the Pope. While Dziwisz is absent, I ask the Pope if he will allow me to suggest an idea to him about Don Stanisław. I tell him that perhaps he could be appointed prefect of the Pontifical Household, now that Monduzzi is retiring, and ordained a bishop. Dziwisz would continue to do the work of the Pope's secretary, living in the Apartment, etc. but since the prefect's main role is to prepare the Pope's audiences, there would be no one better than him. It would be the continuation of what he already does now. The Pope says: "That's a good idea." And he adds, "I don't deal much with that kind of appointment, but I share the concern of how to promote D. Stanisław." The idea is not mine, it is a suggestion made to me by a priest who knows of the Pope's concern. Mgr. Mietek, who was at the table, says that such an appointment would be a great thing.

I tell the Pope that a year ago, after dining with him at Castelgandolfo, he shared a phrase that has stayed with me and I would like him to explain it to me. The phrase was: "È arrivato già il tempo che supera tutte le debolezze" ("The time has come that overcomes all weaknesses"). The Pope recalls the occasion: "Yes, it was after the trip to France." And he adds, "It is one of those phrases that are said. . . ." It seems as if he does not want to comment on it, out of modesty. I tell him that I interpret it as meaning that he no longer cares about physical weaknesses, illnesses. He immediately answers me: "Yes, that's what I meant."

He speaks of his physical situation: "A Pope whose arm trembles; who breaks his leg. . . . The voice still works, but. . . ." It is like an external self-definition. He says it without lamenting: he simply states the fact. I tell him: "Holy Father, this is how we see that God does everything, almost without the need of human beings."

The Pope replies without hesitation: "Ah yes; that's how Poland, France, and the rest are understood." It is clear that he attributes to the grace of God the good reception that his message has had in these countries during his recent trips. These are miracles that God works precisely when the physical limits are most evident.

Dziwisz, who had already returned, wants me to elaborate on these ideas. I add that, at the beginning of the pontificate, the figure of a young Slavic Pope, who skied and swam, almost "hindered "—in a certain sense—the reception of the Gospel message. It was an image that attracted by itself. Now that people are more familiar with the figure of the Pope, it is possible that they will listen more to the message of Christ that he transmits. At least, that's what I think.

I also take this opportunity to suggest, as delicately as I can, that in the present circumstances it would be good for him to take a little more care of himself physically, and dedicate some time daily to guided physical exercise.

The Pope answers me: "Every day I exercise twice: in the morning and in the afternoon." —"But, Holy Father, does anyone accompany you to lead you," I ask. —"No, I do them alone; they are exercises that I learned when Emma and [. . .] came here (he refers to the physiotherapists of the German orthopedic surgeon who was at Castelgandolfo a few summers ago).

And he moves on to another matter. When he finishes, he signs the letter from the Englishman that I have left on the table, telling me to return it to its author. I tell him that I will do so. And he tells us that we have to finish because "we have to sing to the Sacred Heart." When I say goodbye, after kissing his hand, I give him a kiss on the cheek.

Questions in Naples

June 5, 1997

I am going to Naples for the Communication Summit organized by the news station *Telecom*. I have been awarded the 1997 Comunicatore dell'Anno prize, the third recipient. The previous winners were Nicholas Negroponte, from the Massachusetts Institute of Technology in Boston, and Jim Clark, founder of *Netscape*. I have had to give several interviews these days to *La Repubblica, La Stampa, Il Mattino,* on radio and various TV channels.

This award was also given to the Italian architect Renzo Piano, who designed, among other buildings, the Beaubourg Museum (Georges Pompidou National Center for Art and Culture) in Paris.

The award ceremony took place yesterday morning at Castel dell'Ovo. After the words of the president of *Telecom,* Guido Rossi, a question and answer session was opened, initially with questions from the panel, composed of Italian intellectuals, writers, and academics.

To my surprise, instead of raising issues related to the world of communication, all the questions have to do with substantive issues of this pontificate, problems of doctrinal depth. This gives me the opportunity to explain some of the teachings of the Church in the almost three hours of the interview.

It is a "secular" environment formed by deputies of the PDS—ex-Communists—, who are very interested in the teachings of the Pope. The general tone is respectful, except for a question from Paolo Flores d'Arcais, known for his secularist militancy. At the end, and during lunch, I am treated with cordiality, and I have the feeling that it is not simple courtesy. For people far from or unfamiliar with the faith, the Christian message always opens great perspectives.

Renzo Piano is very interesting to me. And I think we understand each other well. I hope to see him more often. He tells me that he is building a church on Padre Pio's land and that he has been impressed by his contact with the pilgrims who go there. He told me that he will send me documentation about the project.

37

The Air of Paris

Back in Aosta

July 20, 1997

I returned yesterday from the Aosta Valley, where we were from the 9th to the 19th of this month. Ten days of rest and relaxation: too few for what the Pope deserves . . . and needs. Along with splendid landscapes, we had, in general, good mountain weather: sun, rain, and even hail. But we were able to go out in the mountains every day.

We are the usual small group: Dziwisz, Tadeusz Styczeń, Renato Buzzonetti, Camillo Cibin, Gugel, those in security, and Enrico Marinelli. I see more and more clearly our insignificance around this Holy Father who, even with his physical limitations, is always, even visibly, a giant in the history of the Church.

I have long conversations with the Pope as we walk. The editor of *La Repubblica*, Ezio Mauro, sends me on Saturday the 12th a fax with a message from Joseph O'Dell, a death row inmate in the state of Virginia, United States, who will be executed on Wednesday, July 23. O'Dell's message mentions the Pope twice and asks him to be spiritually at his side at the moment of execution.

As we walk I tell the Pope about this message. He asks me if anything has been done for this man. I tell him that a message has been sent to the governor of Virginia asking for an act of clemency. He asked me about the date of the execution: it coincided with Wednesday's public audience. He asked me if that day was St. Bridget's day . . . And he added: "God alone is Lord and Master of life and death."

These words give me a clue on how to handle the subject with journalists. The Pope continues: "Naturally, society has the right to legitimate self-defense." I remind him of his words in *Evangelium vitae* and the practical idea he gave: given that penitentiary institutions are secure and prevent those who have already done harm to society from being a threat to life again, there will be no situation which justified the death penalty.

We continue talking about the encyclical *Evangelium Vitae*. The Pope says that this encyclical is an evolution of *Humanae Vitae*, in the sense that it starts from the teachings of Paul VI and develops them. In this regard, I ask him if he had anything to do with the final drafting of *Humanae Vitae:* "I saw the text, but nothing else."

He comments to me about the bad reception that *Humanae Vitae* had in the public opinion. I will tell you my point of view regarding communication. When Paul VI convened the commission of experts, public opinion was informed of the different positions that existed within that commission, but the Pope's reasons were not well explained; and only the part of the document in which he said "no" was commented on, as if that "no" were a personal refusal of Paul VI and not a teaching of the Church.

We pause on the road and, contemplating the landscape, the Pope recalls the mountains of Zakopane: "How many times have we been skiing there!" he says, turning to Tadeusz Styczeń. Tadeusz then tells me that, indeed, they took advantage of the times when there were no people: "He told me: today there is no one, let's go skiing!"

The Pope adds that he can no longer do some things. And he whispers, "What I have injured the most is this leg." This phrase is revealing to me. I think this is how he sees and understands his ailments. He attributes his current limitations to the fractured femur and not to his neurological disease.

Later, when I discussed this with Buzzonetti, he confirmed that he had the same impression. The Pope has not yet conceptualized, has not yet accepted the limitations deriving from Parkinson's. He told me that he had given Dziwisz some photocopies of a medical book so that the Pope could learn more about the consequences of his illness, which he had not yet grasped.

After lunch I discuss with Dziwisz the reply to the editor of *La Repubblica* about the letter of O'Dell. I wrote it after the conversation with the Pope. I go down with a jeep of the rangers to an area where the telephone signal reaches. I read Ezio Mauro those sentences, which make the front page headlines of *La Repubblica* the next day.

On July 13, conversation while walking. The Pope tells me about a Polish mountaineer, Wanda Rutkiewicz, who on October 16, 1978, the very day of his election to the pontificate, summited Everest. "Then she came to see me and came to my Mass, and afterwards we chatted. He told me that he only realized the coincidence some time later. She died years later climbing in the Himalayas and they still haven't found her body. She was the third woman to climb Everest and the first to climb K2."

He talked to us about all this as we marched along the Vallone di Youlaz, next to a stream that ran to our left, at an altitude of 2,150 meters. Shortly after, the sky darkens and after lunch it begins to rain heavily. The Pope takes shelter in a large tent that has been prepared for him; we, in the cars or under some raincoats. One of the forest rangers takes out an accordion and we sing mountain songs in chorus next to the tent in which the Pope is sheltering, listening from inside.

The weather worsens and we all have to take refuge in the first part of the tent, where we continue singing for a while. It is so simple and, at the same time, so unusual that it seems natural: a mountaineer Pope, with various ailments and diseases, resting and reading under a beach tent (practical, but somewhat ridiculous in the mountains), while a group of forest rangers and collaborators sing alpine songs.

It's nice here. On the way back, Buzzonetti stumbles and hurts his ankle. We return home late.

July 17. I speak to my office every morning. Ciro Benedettini, the deputy director, tells me that journalists are asking about a letter from the Pope to Yeltsin asking him not to sign the new law on cults in the Russian Federation. This law has been passed in the Duma and in the Upper House, and only Yeltsin's signature is needed for it to become law.

It turns out that from the Secretary of State—in this case the Second Section—they have sent that letter and we had not been informed by the office. I know it is not worth getting angry. But I think that this letter of the Pontiff should be made public and I say so to the Pope. Then, I make all the necessary arrangements until, finally, we manage to send it to the agencies this very afternoon.

And it is timely because, the next day, I learn from the press that the Patriarch of Moscow has written to Yeltsin asking him to sign the law! At least, today's information shows the position of the Patriarch and—at a far distance—also that of the Pope. And thus public opinion—at least the Western one—can know the Pope's rationale.

This is precisely the first question he asked me as soon as we got underway this morning. I tell him that it was providential that yesterday it was decided to distribute the text. "Providential . . . but not so much for the Patriarch." In fact, I think, this will be one more small obstacle on the way to a possible meeting with Alexis II. Apropos of all this, I comment on how surprising I find this way of thinking of some Orthodox, who consider all of Russia as a single "canonical territory." "But we are not interested in territories, but in souls!" says the Pope.

We continue walking. The Pope adds that he is reading a book by Riccardi[1] that deals with the thinking of fundamentalist Islamic groups. I tell him that there was a very interesting historical experience in Spain, in Toledo, when Jews, Muslims, and Christians lived together in a prosperous community that was also rich from the intellectual point of view. The Pope knows this history, and speaks of Averroes and Avicenna. With Tadeusz he recalls a verse of a Polish poet who mentions Toledo.

Then he says that the last city from which the Muslims were expelled in Spain was Granada. We move on to talk about Isabella the Catholic. "Her process of beatification was stopped because of protests from the Jews; perhaps we will have to wait, as with St. Eduviges, six centuries . . . ," says the Pope. The expulsion of the Jews is mentioned: "Yes, that's how they came to Poland." There is a silence that the Pope breaks with an expression, as if thinking aloud, "How God writes straight with crooked history!"

July 17. Tadeusz offered to read me an essay he is preparing on the Ethics of Wojtyla, analyzed by his disciple. In that article there are some sentences that I do not know if they came from the Pope or from other authors. I ask the Pope directly. "Yes," he tells me, "that phrase—person is the self-transcendence of freedom in truth—is from the book *Person and Action*." This leads me to comment that there are those who emphasize that the English translation of Wojtyla's book (*The Acting Person*) was very important. The Pope says that "the thesis of the translator (with whom he still writes) is that Wojtyla crystallized his thought during the translation of the book . . . " He adds no more.

It has been a great few days. The Pope has rested and is more relaxed. Buzzonetti asks me if he seems better, because he has increased his dose of levodopa a little. I tell him that I notice more facial expression.

1. Andrea Riccardi (Italy, 1950) is professor of history at the University of Rome III. Founder of the Community of Sant'Egidio (1968), which promotes dialogue, ecumenism, and international solidarity.

Paris. XII World Youth Day

AUGUST 25, 1997

From August 21 to 24 we were in Paris for the XII World Youth Day. It was extremely hot and the places where the ceremonies with the young people were held were not protected from the sun. The Pope suffers a lot. In the afternoon, on the Champ de Mars, the podium has no protection and the metal chair that had been set up for the Pope has to be replaced because it accumulated the heat of the day and burns when touched. The Pope is protected with a simple umbrella, which is clearly not enough shelter.

One of the days, upon returning to the nunciature before lunch, the Pope entered the chapel that had been prepared for him next to his room, knelt down and prayed for two hours. Buzzonetti told me this. Clearly, it is his intense prayer life that gives him the energy to endure these efforts.

Buzzonetti also told me that this summer, in Castelgandolfo, the Pope had a slight fever and was scheduled for a medical examination. The Pope told him that the next day, Wednesday, he had the general audience at the Vatican and, therefore, he had to get up . . . at four in the morning! Undoubtedly, it was to keep to his personal prayer plan.

During the vigil at the Longchamp racecourse, the Pope suffers, along with the heat, the effects of severe fatigue because he has been greeting numerous groups of people in the nunciature—a building without air conditioning. He arrives at the vigil so exhausted that it is difficult for him to keep his balance during the ceremony. Marini holds him up on several occasions.

The Mass on the 24th is a long ceremony that once again represents a notable effort for the Pope. There is an extraordinary participation of young people. The Prefecture of Paris gives a figure: one million, two hundred thousand. All forecasts, which spoke of half a million at the most, have been surpassed by a wide margin. This is food for thought. I was talking in Paris with Henri Tincq, from *Le Monde*. He was also surprised—like everyone else—by the flood of young people during these days.

On leaving the nunciature, the Pope had the car slowed down—at four o'clock in the afternoon, under a blazing sun—to greet a group of young people who were waiting for him, singing, in the street. As usual, he does not "conserve" himself. He gives himself to everyone and everything.

38

Cuba

Preparing the Ground

October 20–26, 1997

I have been in Cuba from the 20th to the 26th helping to prepare for the Pope's visit next January. Before leaving, I ask Dziwisz to have the Pope sign a copy of *Crossing the Threshold of Hope* to give to Castro, if the opportunity arises. I am going with the work program that the nuncio, Beniamino Stella, has prepared for me. No trips to other cities: I want to stay in Havana to see what the talks with the authorities yield. When I arrive at the airport I meet Caridad Diego, head of the Office of Religious Affairs, and other members of the Ministry of the Interior and security. We greet each other cordially, and I meet the Havana correspondents in the airport terminal.

That same afternoon I have a long conversation with the Nuncio and some of the Cuban bishops—the Cardinal of Havana is in bed with the flu—who update me on the situation. My first impression is that of a totalitarian regime, Communist in its formulation, which does not admit anything that is not organized and controlled by the party. How can this be reconciled with a Church to which the majority of the Cuban people belong?

At the moment the Church cannot celebrate ceremonies outside the churches; there are very few clergy and they do not allow more priests to enter; it is impossible to establish schools with a Catholic orientation; the Catholic press is not officially allowed—although there still is one. In the nunciature itself our conversation is accompanied by the permanent sound of stereophonic music, to neutralize the spy microphones that are surely distributed throughout the house.

During the following morning—October 21—I speak for the first time with Caridad Diego in the Central Committee. I am accompanied by the Nuncio and the representative of the Ministry of the Interior and Isidro Gómez, from the Central Committee, from which I conclude that even Mrs. Diego is "supervised," as well as the rest of the people in the party. I bring an initial agenda prepared jointly with the Nuncio.

We agree that it is in their interest as well as ours that the Pope's trip be a success. And if it is not, because of them, public opinion may become very critical against freedoms in Cuba. Naturally, the concept of success is understood differently by them and by us. In any case, our positions are not opposed.

They have thought of their little tricks: for example, to fill the squares with people loyal to the regime; to broadcast on TV the liturgical ceremonies, but only in closed circuit for the press centers and not for the people. We do not leave any issue unaddressed. As we gain more clarity, I believe that the prejudices melt away on their part. They begin to see that we do not have a "hidden agenda." After almost two hours, there are still things to say and I ask Caridad Diego to meet again. We set the appointment date for the 24th.

Cards Face Up

October 24, 1997

After the first meeting, I ask Caridad Diego that the second meeting be alone, without the other two people from the Ministry of the Interior and the Central Committee. "I had also thought about the usefulness of this arrangement," she replied.

I began the meeting by saying that it was always best to be completely honest and show all our cards from the beginning when we wanted to go ahead with our conversations. We have done this already, at our first meeting, in which we saw that their interests and ours coincided in creating the conditions for the Pope's visit to be a success.

I said that something had happened that was not only very unpleasant, but also potentially very serious from the point of view of public opinion. A few days before, while I was talking to them, a hidden microphone had been discovered in the house of the bishop of Camagüey. The microphone had been implanted by some workers who were checking the roof of the house. To be absolutely sure, I myself had checked the microphone while holding it in my hand.

Naturally, this had deeply humiliated the Cuban bishops. It also implicated the Holy See in some way, because it occurred in the context of the talks in preparation for the Pope's visit. With great delicacy, the bishops had decided not to raise the matter with the authorities until after my departure from Cuba.

Caridad Diego's reaction was one of surprise. I don't know if she was sincere or not: "Above all, it's strange," she said, "that I have to learn this from you. I added that I didn't want to discuss the subject, but that I couldn't help mentioning it to her."

I told her that the Pope's trip had awakened an extraordinary interest in world public opinion. Cuba will be under the watchful eye of thousands of journalists; some of them, for political or simply sensationalist reasons, will look for excuses to make the trip a kind of scandal. "I think you have a great opportunity for Cuba to surprise the world in a positive way during these next few days. Also, I know that several foreign ministries in Europe and elsewhere have decided to redefine their policy towards Cuba after the Pope's visit. Do you agree with me on this basic approach?"

She replied that, indeed, she agreed and that it was the appropriate way to begin discussing the different topics. At this point I added that the Holy Father wanted, already in his first greeting after his arrival in Havana, to be able to thank the President for some gestures that facilitated the preparation of the trip. And I began to enumerate these topics:

> *Entry of religious personnel.* There were about a hundred applications to enter the country and currently there was a great need for priests. So," I said, "it does not seem impossible to me to ask that at least half of those waiting—fifty priests—can obtain a visa before January 21. For the Church everyone is needed, but it is up to you to decide who will have priority in the granting of the visa. She replied that the issue was being studied; that a similar criterion applies to the priests as for other petitions for immigration to the country, etc. I told her that they were not similar problems, that we were not saying who should come in and who should not, but that it was an issue that could not be postponed and that I would talk to the president about it. She was open to it, but it was clear that the decision was not up to her.
>
> *Television broadcasts.* I said that I had realized, in the previous day's conversations with the general director of state television, that their plans were to broadcast the liturgical ceremonies, even with a large use of cameras, but only for the journalists' press rooms. This, certainly, would have saddened the Holy Father, but it could also mean a disaster for Cuba's image. In fact, thousands of journalists would immediately realize that the images of the Pope were not reaching the people, that he was a virtual Pope for the consumption of the press, and not of the Cubans. It could also happen that journalists would boycott the press centers to go and see "the real Pope and not the virtual TV that only a few Cubans can see."

At that stage of our conversation, José Ramón Balaguer, one of the twenty-four members of the Political Bureau, Caridad Diego's hierarchical superior, had entered the room and wanted to greet me for a moment, out of pure courtesy. Listening to my argument, he stayed until the end of that part of the meeting and then said to me, "Thank you, because we had not anticipated what you were saying. We'll have to think about it again."

Modes of television transmission. I explained that the Holy Mass is a ceremony that requires specialized personnel from the point of view of both the image production and the commentator. After a long discussion, they agreed to have another *RAI* producer with experience in religious events and the presence of two commentators in the program: one from Cuban television and the other a priest proposed by the Cuban bishops, who had some experience in transmissions of this type.

Holidays in the places visited by the Pope. I said that it would be discourteous to the Pope not to declare public holidays when the Pope visits different cities. I suggested that this could be approached as a civil courtesy to a Head of State.

Transportation for the faithful. She immediately said to me: "Don't worry, the squares will be full of people." To which I replied: "But Caridad, what people? Of course you can transport many Cubans to the places, but we are interested in the Catholics who want to come." I added that "even if it is not the case with Cuba, because I know your desire to collaborate with the Church," I could not help but remember what happened years ago in Nicaragua, when Daniel Ortega filled the square with his people. That destroyed his public image abroad.

Then she told me that they had many objective difficulties because of the lack of means of transportation. At this point I told her that I well understood their material limits, "a consequence also of the injustices of which you are victims;" but if the reason for the difficulties was economic, perhaps some associations of Catholics—perhaps Germans or others—could provide some buses. I begged her, in this climate of sincerity, to tell me if I should really take interest in this project, in which case everything would be done in a proper way, without anyone knowing, so as not to hurt their image.

Christmas holiday. I told her that I was going to take this matter up directly with the president, but that I also wanted her to be informed. I mentioned that this was probably the only request the Pope had made to the president at their meeting in Rome.

That the president receive the cardinal. In response to this request, the lady reminded me of a pastoral letter that had been written years ago, at a very difficult time for Cuba due to the new international sanctions, and that both the letter and the timing had done the president a great disservice. I said that it had already been a long time, that public opinion was waiting for such signs, and that the preparation of the Pope's visit could be an opportunity to receive the Church Committee. In the end she told me that "this, no doubt, will be done."

Permission to print. Edition of a small booklet so that the faithful can follow the Mass. This was a request of the Cuban bishops. The booklet would be accompanied by a short devotional booklet with some common prayers (Our Father, Hail Mary, Creed, etc.). An agreement was soon reached and half a million copies will be printed by a state publishing house.

The meeting lasted about three hours. Caridad Diego took notes of everything in order to make a complete report to her superiors. The atmosphere was always cordial, never tense; anecdotes, even personal ones, were often told. The initial decision to speak frankly about the issues favored an atmosphere of transparency. And the meeting certainly made it easier for her to become aware of some problems on which they had already made a decision, but which now had to be reviewed, because they also went against their own interests.

Of course, they are thinking of this trip in terms of international public opinion. But it is precisely this consideration that will perhaps encourage a change in their position on certain issues, when they have understood the risks they could run if they do not rectify some decisions already taken.

A Conversation with Castro

October 25, 1997

At the dinner with Castro were the nuncio, the secretary of the nunciature, Piero Marini, and Giovanni Viviani. Carlos Lage, number two of the regime, José Ramón Balaguer (from the Political Bureau), Caridad Diego, and Castro's personal secretary were there.

Fidel Castro was very thin. White hands. It is possible that he is sick, but not of prostate illness (unless he has been operated on) because he was with us for six hours straight without needing to leave. We greeted each other at 8:45 PM and said goodbye at 2:30 in the morning.

We had a standing *aperitif* in the Palace of the Central Committee—where he will receive the Pope—with a few small, well-served oysters and chilled champagne. Over dinner we talked about everything from the universe and the galaxies to international relations. Castro showed great interest in the Pope: his work schedule, his travels. We recalled episodes of the history of the colony and the suicidal action of Admiral Cervera when leaving Santiago de Cuba in front of the American squadron. Not a single reference to present-day Cuba, nor to the Revolution.

I commented that I was bringing him something on behalf of the Holy Father and he told me that we would have time after dinner. They offered wine at dinner, which I did not take. Castro, with good humor, pointed out that it was *Vega Sicilia*: the wine he offers on important occasions. —"In that case, President, I accept the wine," I said, in the same cordial tone.

After that, he began joking and asked how to avoid the possibility of the Pope being poisoned; I told him that we were not too worried about it. In the same tone, he commented that when he offered wine to his guests, he always tasted it first. Continuing the joke, I told him: "Perhaps you should do the opposite: offer it to the guest and if he survives . . . you drink it."

At the end of the long dinner, he suggested that we talk together, just the two of us, with no one else present. The conversation, which took place in a climate of informality, cordiality, and spontaneity, allowed me to see that he was well acquainted with each and every one of the topics I had discussed during the previous days with Caridad Diego and the Minister of Foreign Affairs. He was perfectly aware of our demands.

I began by handing him the copy of *Crossing the Threshold of Hope*, which the Pope had given me with his signature and dated a few days before, as a gift to Castro. He was very grateful. —"Does it have photos? I already have the one on the cover," he commented.

I stressed to him that it is not normal for the Holy Father to send such a detail to other heads of state—at least, as far as I know—but that he had a good memory of their previous meeting at the Vatican. "He is a great man," he said. And he added: "I was impressed by that meeting we had, so intimate."

I told him that during the previous days I had met with some of his collaborators, to talk about the upcoming visit of the Holy Father, and I asked him if he would be willing to talk about these matters. "We want the visit to go well, tell me about these things," he replied.

I told him that the Pope's visit to Cuba had awakened an interest I had not seen before. I was sure that several thousand journalists would come to Havana. It was a great occasion for Cuba to surprise the world, including those who would like to find reasons to criticize the country. For that reason, the trip had to be a great success. Castro told me he felt the same way.

> *Christmas Feast.* "You know," I told him, "that [the celebration of Christmas in Cuba] is a desire that the Holy Father carries deep in his soul; it seems to me that the Pope spoke to you about this. The Pope hopes that. . . . " Castro replied, "Yes, it is an important question, but would it be only for this year?." I did not want to answer directly. I only replied that this issue was being raised now, in connection with the Pope's visit.
>
> "Mr. President," I continued, "the Pope wishes to publicly thank you and your collaborators for your visit, as soon as he arrives in Havana. For that reason, we would like to create the conditions for him to make this gratitude manifest before the international community. That is why, from our point of view, it will be necessary to do something about Christmas." He did not give me a definitive answer, but it was obvious that he was considering this question.
>
> *Entrance of priests and religious.* I told him that it was a question related to the pastoral preparation of the visit. I mentioned the figure of fifty, half of those who had applied for visas.
>
> —"When I returned from Rome," Castro replied, "after meeting with the Pope, some priests came in. I insisted that we urgently needed these people for the pastoral preparation of Cuban Catholics."
>
> "You know," he added, "that the Cuban Revolution is not anti-Catholic and not a drop of blood of the Cuban clergy has been shed. If you think, for example, of the war in Spain. . . . " I replied, "I am fully aware of that. Also in Mexico there was a systematic persecution of the clergy, which has not happened here. That is a merit of the Revolution in Cuba."[1]

He added that, in 1992, thanks to his personal insistence, "and not without some difficulty and opposition," it was approved that Catholics could be members of the party, and the Constitution of the Republic was modified. Now Cuba is not an atheist state.

By way of conclusion, he said: "I have to discuss everything you have said with my collaborators. You know that here things must be approved with everyone's consent. But you can be sure that I will talk about what you have suggested."

1. This was not exactly the case, but it did not seem to me the time to start a debate [Author's Note].

From the way he said it, I got the impression that he is certainly the one who decides, but because of the different positions within the State apparatus, his decisions must not appear as the result of external pressures or as the fruit of internal "weakness." Therefore, so that the internal apparatus does not become ungovernable, he must reach a consensus on the part of all.

He continued: "I have already decided to intervene personally to explain the Pope's visit. I have not done so before because we have been very busy lately with the first Party Congress and then with the funeral ceremonies for Che Guevara. But now I intend to devote more time and attention to the Pope's visit. I can tell you that I have on my desk a list of twelve questions on this subject and some of them are the same ones you have told me about."

I mentioned these other issues to him in the same terms that I had used in presenting them to his collaborators: transportation for liturgical ceremonies, live TV broadcasting, declaring half-day holidays in the cities visited by the Pope. . . .

I also commented to him that, if he considered it appropriate, the Pope would love to receive "the President's brothers," referring to Raúl and Ramón, and their two sisters who, I believe, are practicing Catholics. He answered me by saying that the Revolution always distinguishes between the family dimension and the political one, and that it would not be appropriate for the Pope to receive his brothers in the official residence. I asked him if he would like the Pope to receive them at the nunciature or some other suitable place; and he thanked us for our availability.

The conversation lasted about three quarters of an hour in total. The tone was informal, and pleasant: we were both seated on the same two-seat sofa. There was no moment of tension or sense of discomfort about the subjects we were discussing. I think that, after having read the reports that had been sent in, Castro wanted to have a personal contact to get an idea for himself about our suggestions and requests. He certainly did not seem ready to give definitive answers, but neither did he dismiss any of the requests as "unrealistic."

Open Mass

October 26, 1997

Following the scheduled program, on Sunday, October 26 we attended one of the Masses that the government had allowed in an open space in preparation for the Pope's trip. The reproduction of the Virgen de la Caridad del Cobre, which represents the union of the Cuban people, presided over the ceremony.

Before leaving, a few journalists came to see me at the airport, where I read them a communiqué prepared in agreement with the Nuncio.

Some Clarifications

November 15, 1997

From some of Re's comments to me on the phone, I think there has been some misunderstanding about the nature of my mission to Cuba last month. Some at the Secretary of State's office seem a bit miffed, as if I had invaded their "diplomatic" turf.

The fact is that the issues I spoke about in Cuba—TV transmissions, declaration of feast days in the cities visited by the Pope, etc.—had not been discussed in advance by anyone from the Holy See and, therefore, the Cuban government had decided on its own.

I understand that, in this case, some do not understand that what matters to the Cuban authorities about the Pope's trip is its impact on public opinion, and that they do not understand either that my statement at the Havana airport was precisely intended to exert a little pressure from public opinion.

In order to put it in writing, I sent Re a letter on this subject, in which I said that the communiqué was drafted with the nuncio and carefully corrected several times. The idea was to make public the problems still open, and which the authority had undertaken to resolve. Thus it would be the press itself who would exercise a certain control over the authorities, without directly involving the Holy See.

A few days later Re phoned me to tell me that he wanted to answer me in writing, but that since I had left on a trip, he was now doing it by phone to thank me for the letter and to confirm that it had been a misunderstanding. As we all want the same thing, that was the end of it.

A Letter to Caridad Diego

(Undated) December 1997

I have just sent a letter to Caridad Diego to make a decision regarding the TV broadcasts of the trip. This is one of the paragraphs:

> As I told you, in twenty years of the Holy Father's pontificate and apostolic travels, Cuba would be absolutely the first country in which the people would be prevented from following the celebration of the Holy Mass

live on TV while the images of those acts, already produced, are passed on closed circuit to the press rooms and hotels. I can easily foresee, and it will not be difficult for you to foresee as well, the *disastrous* results for Cuba of such an operation in terms of international public opinion. Any kind of explanation would be, for foreign journalists, "gasoline on fire:" every justifying comment would serve, in my opinion, only to underline the magnitude of the unjustifiable.

Suggestions for Speeches

December 19, 1997

I meet Vicente Juan Segura, head of the Spanish language section of the Secretariat of State, in the office. He talks to me about the preparation of the Pope's speeches. He brings the drafts already prepared and asks me for suggestions on the contents, also taking into account the experience of my recent trip, in order to be able to include them before passing the speeches on to the Pope.

I see that the subject of the embargo has not yet come up. I tell him about what I have seen these days and explain to him that, to the extent that the Pope speaks clearly about the embargo issue, which Castro will like, to that same extent he will be more severe with issues related to human rights. I tell him that the "pastoral character" of the trip implies ethical principles and the embargo is one of those issues that in no case can be avoided. He is fine with the reasoning and includes in the draft the idea I suggest to him: the embargo "is ethically unacceptable."

I also spoke to him about including some phrases that would be effective in terms of their content and that would have a strong impact on public opinion. Specifically, that it would be good to include a phrase such as: "May Cuba open up to the world and may the world open up to Cuba," something that had repeatedly come to my mind during my visit to the island. Naturally, these are ideas and suggestions on which the Pope has the last word.

Another Biography about the Pope

December 21, 1997

He has finished the Synod of America, which has kept him very busy, not only because of his presence in the plenary meetings, but also because he has been inviting the various bishops to lunch.

Last night I had the opportunity to have dinner with the Pope, who immediately focused on the two topics he wanted to talk about: the synod and the trip to Cuba. Regarding the first, I told him that little has been said about it in the press and that, possibly, they will address the issue when he publishes the post-synodal exhortation.

As for Cuba, the problem of the plane offered by President Castro for the return trip from Cuba, which does not seem to convince our organizers, is one of the issues discussed. Re calls me today to ask about this subject. It is a question of seeing what strategy we can follow to gently dissuade the Cuban authorities. Some suggest a security approach. I tell him that it would be best to approach it from a perspective that directly affects the *Sala Stampa*: the number of seats available for journalists.[2]

I brought the Pope a copy of the book *Man of the Century*, dedicated by the author, Jonathan Kwitny. Contrary to what I thought, the Pope did not know it nor had he heard of it. It is about 600 pages long and is in the nature of a "biography of the pontificate." The author tells the Pope in the dedication that he admires him "more than any other man on this earth, with the exception of my father," and wishes him "the second miracle," a probable reference to the upcoming trip to Cuba.

Back to Help

January 6, 1998

What a story this is about the preparations for the trip to Cuba! The Nuncio, Beniamino Stella, has already written twice to Sodano asking that I return there the week before the Pope's visit, to help them with the inevitable last minute surprises. The Secretariat of State has not given a definitive answer. And the Cuban ambassador assures them there is no need for me to come.

In the meantime, the Nuncio writes to me several times insisting that I go, adding that the Cardinal of Havana is also in favor of such a visit.

I receive a letter from Alina Fernández, Fidel Castro's daughter in Miama.[3] She sends me a copy of her book for the Pope. Her wish is that someone intercede with Castro to recognize her as his daughter.

2. This was done, and the Cuban government accepted [Author's Note].

3. Alina Fernández Revuelta (born March 19, 1956, Cuba) is a Cuban anti-communist activist. She is the daughter of Fidel Castro and Natalia Revuelta Clews.

In Cuba, the Previous Days

JANUARY 17–19, 1998

Back in Cuba. I have been given the green light. I arrive in Havana where I meet the Nuncio and others. That same night we have dinner with the Cardinal. The situation has changed, in the sense that Castro's requests have been fulfilled. There are still some doubts about the broadcasting of the visit to the whole country.

JANUARY 18. Long interview with Isabel Allende, Vice Minister of Foreign Affairs. I clarify with her the news published in *El País*: the discovery of the microphone in the house of the bishop of Camagüey. Without telling me explicitly, it is clear that she thought that the Holy See had leaked this information to the press. I assure you, because it is so, that there has been absolutely no interest or management whatsoever on the part of the Holy See in that matter. She believes me.

I talk to her about a possible humanitarian measure with some detainees in Cuban prisons. "It is a very delicate matter," she tells me. There is no answer, as I expected, because those decisions are made at another level. But I know that this request will end up on Castro's desk.

JANUARY 19. I have dinner with Caridad Diego and we go over some pending issues about which she cannot give me an answer. She is intrigued by my presence here and laments that Cardinal Ortega has decided to organize a procession on Sunday morning to carry the image of the Virgen de la Caridad del Cobre from the cathedral to the Plaza de la Revolución.

We solve some problems regarding the arrangement of the cameras in front of the altar in the Plaza de la Revolución, so that they do not detract from the view of the attendees. We also outline some organizational issues regarding the press center in Havana and the transmission of speeches. I give an interview to *Televisión Española* in which the question of political prisoners comes up.

Eusebio Leal, who is carrying out the restoration of Havana's historic center and has direct access to Castro, comes to the nunciature. We talk about many things, both of us aware that Castro will end up being informed of all this.

I go to sleep. At 11:00 o'clock at night, Caridad Diego calls me: "Joaquín, I wanted to give you some news that will make you sleep well: the Mass in Santiago de Cuba will be broadcast live to the whole country." I thank her and, of course, I sleep better that night.

The Pope in Cuba

JANUARY 21–26, 1998

The 21st is the day of the Holy Father's arrival. Before leaving the airport I get a phone call from the plane to tell me that the Pope has spoken to journalists and answered several questions about Cuba. I ask them to send me the text. An Italian journalist asks him:

> —"Holy Father: Fidel Castro continues to speak of revolution. How does Christ's revolution combine with Castro's?"
>
> —"It would be necessary to specify what the word *revolution* means," the Pope replies, "because it has different meanings: one can speak of *Christ's revolution* and *Castro's revolution.* And also *Lenin's revolution.*"
>
> "But it means different things. The revolution of Christ means revolution of love, while in other cases it means revolution of hatred, of revenge, of victims."

The journalists have transmitted their dispatches to the agencies from the plane and while we are waiting for the plane to arrive, Isabel Allende informs me that there is a dispatch from *ANSA* stating that the Cuban Revolution is a revolution of "hatred, revenge, and victims."

I tell him that I am surprised because I have read the text of what the Pope has said and it does not coincide with that. When the Pope arrives, I go to Havana in the car with the Cardinal Secretary of State and we prepare a text for a statement of mine in which I say more or less the following: "The Pope's reference to revolutions other than Christ's revolution does not refer to Cuba, but to different historical and geographical circumstances."

When we arrive in Havana, I call the agencies, the Cubans are reassured, and we start our trip in peace.

The next day we go to Santa Clara. In the afternoon the meeting with Castro takes place. After Mass I speak with Isabel Allende to inform her that this afternoon Cardinal Sodano will present a long list (more than a hundred names) of people in prison, asking for a gesture of grace on the occasion of the Pope's visit.

She is surprised by the subject. I tell her that I am going to prepare a communication for the press and that, if she wishes, we can see it together. She agrees to come to the hotel after lunch. I read her what I have prepared and she suggests changing some words. As it does not change the general meaning, I agree. She leaves happy. When we go to the Palace of the Revolution, Felipe, Castro's secretary, asks me if I can change a word in my statement: instead of "the authorities have accepted (the request)," "the authorities have received." I modify it.

I suggest that Cardinal Ortega be placed next to the Pope when Castro and the Pope come out to the door of the Palace to pose for the photographers and the televisions. This is how it is done. The idea is to make it clear, with this gesture, that the Cardinal is the person with whom the authorities should deal when the Pope returns to Rome.

I asked Dziwisz, a couple of days ago on the phone, to bring a small crucifix for the Pope to give to Castro during their private meeting. When we return from Santa Clara this morning, Dziwisz tells me that he has brought it: it is a small gold crucifix of his, about 4 cm [1.5 in.] in size. The Pope gives it to Castro while they have a personal conversation.

Then, when the Pope introduces me to Castro, he says, laughing, "Do you know him?" To which he replies, "Sure, we were having dinner together." I also see that he has decided to bring his brothers Raúl and Ramón and their sisters to the Palace. They wait in a separate room and the Pope approaches to greet them. One of the sisters tells him that she would like to give him a hug. The Pope accepts the gesture and she embraces the Pope in tears.

After the meeting I have a briefing with the journalists, who are surprised, because they did not know anything about our request of grace for the imprisoned.

The Mass in Camagüey, on the 23rd, is very warm. Isabel Allende thanks me for the way in which we have communicated to the press about the prisoners.[4]

4. The trip was very special, and continued for two more days, but my notes end here [Author's Note].

39

Tragedy in the Night

Lenten Dinner

February 26, 1998

It is the second day of Lent and the Pope had only a little vegetable and fruit salad for dinner. This is the rhythm he keeps during the whole of Lent. At his request, he was not given the glass of wine he normally drinks.

We accompanied the Pope, Mietek and me. Dziwisz is outside. During the dinner conversation, many different topics come up: Boris Yeltsin, Cuba, the Asian synod that is being prepared, the trip to Nigeria. . . . and the reactions to Dziwisz's recent appointment as prefect of the Pontifical Household.

Estermann

May 4–5, 1998

May 4. Around 10:00 PM, Cardinal Sodano calls me on the phone. I find it strange that he does it at this hour. "Doctor Navarro, have they called you yet?" "No . . . , what is it about?" And the shocking news: a Swiss Guard went to the house of Alois Estermann, head of the Swiss Guard, and shot his wife.

He adds that the situation is terrible and that people will say that "these people in charge of the Pope's security are killing each other. . . ." I realize he is telling me something terrible, but I don't quite know exactly what has happened. I ask him about Estermann: "Dead too. Same as the Swiss guard. Without getting a clear picture of the matter, I tell him that I'm coming to the Vatican right away and that I'll call him from there.

I enter through the gate of Santa Ana and see the sorrowful faces of the Swiss guards. I park the car and ask for Estermann's house. They point me in the right direction and I go upstairs. The door is open; there are some guards on the stairs; I see Danzi; Cibin and Buzzonetti. I talk to him and he explains: Alois Estermann and his wife Gladys have been killed, and Cedric Tornay, the young Swiss guard who shot them, has committed suicide. Three dead.

Just this morning in the *Sala Stampa* we had heard the news of Estermann's appointment as the new commander of the Swiss Guard. Shortly afterwards I congratulated him on the telephone and he asked me to pray for him. He was a man of extraordinary human, professional, and spiritual qualities, which I had the opportunity to see, above all, during his many trips with the Pope.

I pray for the souls of the three of them; I think of the Pope's pain when he heard the news and I ask myself what I can do to report on what happened tonight.

I decide that my source of information should be Buzzonetti. He explains to me what he has seen: the three bodies lying there, the gunshot wounds. And nothing more to do from a medical point of view.

Who is responsible for the investigation and the first decisions? Buzzonetti has advised two legal experts. One of them is Professor Arcudi: "They have been our consultants for twenty years and are very competent people."

We continue talking as we walk down the stairs. A few minutes later the forensic doctors arrive. The person in charge of the investigation is the lawyer Marrone, who is called *the Sole Judge* in the Vatican, but who does not have, as is logical, experience in this type of event.

The medical legal consultants ask for gloves and white coats to be brought to them. They go up to the scene and begin their work.

In the meantime, I chat with several of those present: the wife of a Swiss guard, who lives in the apartment below the Estermann's, tells me that she was alarmed to hear some strange noises. She does not remember the shots, only two bangs (possibly the result of the bodies falling to the ground). She went upstairs to see what was going on. She entered the house, whose door was open, and upon seeing the scene, she called the police.

I then speak with Major Hasler, who gives me some details about Cedric Tornay, the time he had been in the corps, his unstable character.

A Swiss guard adds some personal impressions: Tornay should not have been promoted to sub-corporal because, he says, he was an undisciplined person. He adds that he had an Italian girlfriend and had broken up with her.

I talk again with Major Hasler, who shares a relevant fact: the murderer thought he was going to be decorated on May 6, during the Swiss Guard's celebration, but he learned three days ago that he had not been included in the list of awardees.

I begin to glimpse, vaguely, a possible motivation: a man with an unstable personality, perhaps psychopathic, who has been accumulating in his mind grievances, alleged or real, until finally they burst out in a violent explosion.[1]

While forensics continue to work at Estermann's house, I call Sodano on the phone and tell him that I will say something to the press tonight and that I am waiting for forensics to finish their work to have documented data.

Then I call our deputy director, Ciro Benedettini, tell him that something serious has happened and ask him to come to the office and wait for me there. I call Pisano, a journalist with the Italian news agency *ANSA*, and tell him to stand by because I am going to give him some news this very evening. "No, it's not about the Pope. It's something else, but serious. I give him my phone number."

I look at my watch. It's been almost two hours since Sodano called me at home and forensics is about to finish. I enter the room. A terrible scene. Three corpses in two square meters. I don't see Estermann's face; I see Tornay's and Gladys's: he is in prone position and she is leaning against the corner of the room, sitting on the floor, with her right leg in an irregular position. She is wearing a gray tracksuit. Blood. I pray for them.

I start writing some notes for the press. I sit down with Marrone and Buzzonetti, and between the three of us we finalize the text. I read it to Sodano on the phone and quickly go to the office while they begin to remove the bodies: Estermann's is the first. While he is being removed, some blood stains fall on the steps of the staircase and the entrance of the house.

I tell Ciro about the tragedy and we get on the phone to transmit the text we have prepared to the agencies. I add a brief hypothesis about the development of the events to prevent some people from starting to think of it as a crime of passion. However, when I read the news to Pisano the first question he asks me is: "Were they dressed?"

MAY 5. I called a press conference in the morning and made a series of phone calls. One of them to Marrone, who has come to the office to bring me some data; and another, to Buzzonetti, who informs me that they have already finished the first autopsy (Estermann's) and have certified that he has been shot twice. He will let me know the results of the other two autopsies as soon as they are finished.

---

1. Some of the hypotheses about which some journalists speculated, without any basis, several days later: a crime of passion in a context of homosexuality or related to Estermann's wife [Author's Note], did not occur to me at any time.

I speak again with Major Hasler. He informs me that there is a letter from Estermann to Tornay, reprimanding him for a serious fault: not having slept one night in the Swiss Guard barracks.

This seems to reflect on the possible motivation of the event. At around 1:15 PM, thanks to this piece of information, I have a relatively complete picture of motives that help to explain the event.

I find myself in the room with almost three hundred journalists, with about twenty televisions. The press conference lasts a little over an hour, during which I follow these points:

The facts:

- A few minutes after nine o'clock at night, noises were heard. A neighbor of the building entered the house—the door was open—and saw the bodies in the living room next to the hall.
- Under the prone body of Vice Corporal Tornay was his weapon. The only weapon found there was the regulation revolver that had been assigned to Sub-Corporal Tornay: a Sig Sauer 75, Swiss, 9 mm caliber.
- That gun usually has six bullets, five of which had been fired. The autopsy and the expert analysis of the scene will reveal the trajectory of the bullets.

Hypothesis:

- Autopsies are currently being carried out, so we must wait for the results and analysis to provide us with new elements of judgment.
- According to the data available to us at the moment, the most reasonable hypothesis—and in my opinion, it is more than a reasonable hypothesis—is that it was all the result of an act of madness that matured in the mind of a man who harbored the humiliating thought that he was not being sufficiently recognized and valued.

There are several data that justify this hypothesis:

- The weapon under the assailant's body was his own regulation weapon.
- The sub-corporal complained bitterly yesterday to some of his colleagues, because he thought he was not being valued enough. At seven o'clock in the evening he gave one of them a letter to deliver to his family.
- Captain Colonel Estermann had sent Sub-Corporal Tornay a letter, dated February 12 of last year, in which he reprimanded him for the serious infraction he had committed against the Corps Regulations: specifically,

for his unjustified absence during a night in which he did not return to the barracks.

- The sub-corporal had complained in recent days to his colleagues in the Swiss Guard about not being included in the list of names to be decorated tomorrow, May 6, the day of the Corps' feast day, during the swearing-in of new recruits.

Research:

- From the very beginning, the investigation has been in the hands of the Sole Judge (magistrate) of the Vatican City State, lawyer Gianluigi Marrone.
- Once the investigation is completed, the results will be handed over to the Promoter of Justice (a position similar to that of the Attorney General of the Republic), Professor Nicola Piccardi, who will be in charge of investigating the case.

Estermann:

- He was a person of extraordinary human, professional, and spiritual worth.
- His appointment was received with great satisfaction by the entire Swiss Guard.
- The Holy Father particularly appreciated him because he was at his side during the Ali Agca attack and watched over his safety during his many trips abroad.
- His wife, Mrs. Gladys Meza, was born in Venezuela on January 24, 1949 and graduated in Canon Law and Civil Law from the University of the Lateran.

Funerals: will take place tomorrow at the altar of the Cathedral, in St. Peter's, officiated by the Cardinal Secretary of State. Among those attending will be the almost three hundred relatives of the new recruits, who had come for the celebration. (In the end it was decided to separate the funerals: those of Estermann and his wife, in St. Peter's; that of Tornay, in the parish of St. Anne, at the entrance to the Vatican).

Burial: the family will decide the place and manner of burial.

Commander Buchs, who had just retired, returned to the temporary command of the Swiss Guard.

The sub-corporal was born in Monthex, in the canton of Vallais, on June 24, 1974.

Reactions

MAY 10, 1998

Taking stock of these days, I see that the foreign press—especially the English language—has given information in line with the facts. In the Italian press, there have been those who have followed an even-handed line, evaluating the objective data, and those who have reacted by approaching the news from the perspective of "dietrology": what is "behind" . . . ?

A section of the local press, in fact, thought they had "a big issue" on their hands: a murder-suicide in the "Pope's house." And they have begun to promote two assumptions about which they have written incessantly, despite not having *any* evidence in both cases: that there was a background of homosexuality or a "triangle" between the people who died.

The fact that this approach fell apart during the first press conference provoked some disappointed reactions: it was all too simple and too soon clarified! Similar reactions have been reported in other newspapers. Later on, Tornay's letter to his mother was published, confirming the information we gave.

Some people do not forgive me for saying at the first press conference that, for me, with the available data, the case was closed. They may be right: although it was totally obvious that I was not referring to the judicial investigation, I think it would have been better not to have used the expression "closed," in order to avoid such sensitivities.

40

Letters that Touch the Heart

Quiet Walks

July 8–21, 1998

Days of rest with the Holy Father in Lorenzago del Cadore. Sites already visited; some others still to be discovered. In the background, the contrast between the random excursions, with long distances and somewhat risky climbs, of other years; and the current ones, with small walking tours, always in places without unevenness, and with great effort on the part of the Pope.

A conversation with Dziwisz reflects the situation. We were standing one day in front of a destroyed World War I fort. The Pope, sitting some distance away, was reading. Dziwisz asked me: "What do you think about the question of the Pope?" It was a way of probing what I thought of the possibility of the Pope resigning for reasons of illness. I answered him, as on other occasions, that the problem could be raised on a theoretical level, and then there would be room for an hours-long discussion. It could also be raised at a practical level, and then the matter would be different. At that level, I told him, I saw no problem, since the Pope could go ahead, even if he had to take some precautions.

And I mentioned some examples: to delegate small things; not to undergo the great fatigue of some trips, to follow a physiotherapy plan that included about forty-five minutes of directed physical therapy every day, or at least three days a week. He told me that, for much of the year, this plan had been followed and there had been a consultation with doctors to examine the disease, with specialists from various countries.

I told him that for years I have been asking for the miracle of a cure for Parkinson's, and that I do it every day after Communion. "The Pope prays a lot for this . . . ," he adds. What he means to tell me—and this is how I interpret it—is that the Pope prays a lot about his illness and, above all, in case he has to resign from his ministry because of it. And so I see, once again, that the subject of resigning is still on his mind. It must be a very hard test.

On Saturday 11 we are on the Alpe de Nemes, at 1,995 meters above sea level. I have a long conversation with Tadeusz. I ask him how he thinks the Pope is doing. His answer: worse than last year. He tells me that his sister, who died at the age of sixty, suffered from Parkinson's disease. That the problem is the connection between the soul (psyche) and the body; this is how he explains the disease. The soul can be brilliant—and that is what he sees in the Pope—but its connection with the body fails.

A little further on, and changing the subject of the conversation a little, he speaks of a lack of harmony between the Pope and the Curia: the excessively "diplomatic" spirit of the Curia. He says that their intention is good, but that sometimes it seems that they are not on the same wavelength.

As we speak—it was after lunch—the Pope is resting in his tent. I hear him moving around inside and call Dziwisz. He comes in, stands with the Pope for a moment and then calls us. The Pope is sitting on the folding chair we carried up the mountain, relaxed, and with his feet up on another chair. As he has just woken up, he has a very relaxed, happy expression. And I tell him: "Holy Father, you have an expression of great happiness." And he replies: "What a delight!" I sit down on the floor next to him. There is again talk of the possibility of making that trip to Ur,[1] which for him is a dream, a subject we already talked about yesterday as we walked. I tell him that it would be a great sign for the whole world and I ask him if he already had that "dream" before he was elected Pope. "No, before the pontificate I was thinking about the millennium of Poland and the protagonist was Cardinal Wyszyński. Then I began to think with new categories, with the categories of the Jubilee of 2000."

Dziwisz takes the lead and jokes with one and all. He asks me how many years I have been in office. I tell him fifteen. Then, turning to the Pope, he says: "Holy Father, we will have to start thinking about a change . . ." The Pope laughs.

At another time, Tadeusz pointed out to me that the Pope carries the missal in the car, and reads the readings of the Mass of the day and also those of the following day. It is a way of preparing for the next Mass. Indeed, I have seen that scene several times.

On another occasion, while walking with the Pope, we talk about Spanish literature. He pauses for a long time thinking about Calderón de la Barca and then tells me: "I have read it; it is splendid. It has been translated into Polish

1. Sumerian city state founded 3800 BC and located in present-day Iraq.

by a wonderful poet." He asks me for names of contemporary Spanish intellectuals. I name a few in different areas: poetry, literature, philosophy. He is currently reading a book by Julián Marías[2] about Christianity. He then moves on to history: Granada, the colonization of America. He asks me about the royal family: he has seen on TV, he tells me, news about the birth of Infanta Elena's first child. His mind works like a charm.

On one of the days we went to Borno, the village of Msgr. Re. We travel there and back by helicopter. It is a very special day for Re: it is his homeland and the day is his own. We have lunch at the parish priest's house. In the afternoon we visit a rustic "baita," as mountain dwellings are called here, belonging to Re's father. The Pope greets the whole family over tea. From there we return by helicopter to Lorenzago. The newspapers will later speak of Re's "investiture," and there are even those who venture to say that he is one of the cardinals "in pectore" whose name the Pope reserved for himself at the last consistory.[3]

Against the Current

September 18, 1998

For three days, from the 18th to the 20th, we accompanied the Pope on his apostolic visit to Brescia and Chiavari. Once again the Pope goes against the current: in this case not against the current of the dominant ideas, but against the current of the years and of his illness. He does not lose his good humor, but his physical limits are always obvious.

London Journalist

September 24, 1998

Charles Moore, editor of *The Daily Telegraph* of London, whom I met this summer in England, is in Rome this week. He says he wants to prepare a good article about the Pope on the occasion of the 20th anniversary of his election. Moore wrote an article in the *Sunday Telegraph* a couple of years ago entitled "Why I shall become a Catholic," in which he explained his entry into the Catholic Church, which got a lot of coverage. We spoke for several hours over the last few

---

2. Julián Marías (Spain, 1914–2005) was a philosopher and essayist, main disciple of the philosopher José Ortega y Gasset. The book mentioned is precisely entitled "On Christianity" (1997).

3. In reality, the two cardinals "in pectore" that the Pope had announced at the Consistory of February 21, 1998 were Marian Jaworski and Jānis Pujats, whose names will be made public by the Pope at the Consistory of February 21, 2001, the occasion on which Msgr. Re will also receive the cardinalate.

days on various occasions. I set up appointments for him with Ratzinger, Szoka, and Etchegaray. I presented him to the Pope at the end of Wednesday's audience.

Stepinac: Breaking a Myth

OCTOBER 9, 1998

Lunch with the Pope. It is the usual meeting that follows a trip, on this occasion Croatia, where we were last weekend (October 2–4). On one of the topics, the criticisms of the beatification of Cardinal Stepinac,[4] I put forward my point of view: there was a negative myth created and exploited by the Yugoslav Communist authorities for forty-five years. This myth implied that Stepinac was a collaborator with Ante Pavelic's "ustashia" regime, that Serbs and Jews had been murdered in that period, and that Stepinac had done nothing. . . . To destroy that myth it was necessary for the Pope to do what he has done, of course after a serious investigation. Inevitably, there has been some critical reaction, but the myth has been destroyed.

I give the Pope the new book by Accattoli, Vaticanist of *Corriere della Sera*: *Karol Wojtyla: l'uomo di fine millennio*. The Pope's question: But will this do any good for the Church? I tell him it will certainly do good: the Pope is inseparable from the Church.

During lunch, as we are approaching the anniversary, I ask him about some details of his election. He recalls that it was a Monday; I discreetly inquire about the time; he answers that it was around five in the afternoon.

At the end, Mietek helps him to get up. The Pope says with a smile: "He always helps me . . ." and adds in French: "*Après moi le déluge!*" ("After me, the deluge!"). Class and humor in all circumstances.

More getaways

OCTOBER 12, 1998

Tomorrow the Pope will not be in the Vatican. And I'm glad, because even on Sunday he can't rest one bit. Yesterday, for example, he had the long ceremony for the canonization of Edith Stein: a great joy, no doubt, but also a great effort.

---

4. Alojzije Viktor Stepinac (Croatia, 1898–1960) was archbishop of Zagreb from 1937 until his death. After World War II, the Communist regime of the then Yugoslavia sentenced him to sixteen years in prison. Pius XII elevated him to the cardinalate in 1952 in response the severance of Yugoslavia's diplomatic relations with the Vatican.

It seems to me that now these Tuesday getaways into the open air, to the mountains, are becoming more frequent.

Pope Live

October 13, 1998

In the evening, program on *RAI Uno* by Bruno Vespa on the occasion of the 20th anniversary of the election of the Pope. Numerous guests and many connections from all over the world: Gorbachev, Jaruzelski, Walesa, Ali Agca, etc. And the surprise of a phone call from the Pope himself, which takes place in the middle of the program and is broadcast live. The idea came from Dziwisz: "I am the secretary of the Holy Father . . ." and then the voice of the Pope: "Mr. Vespa, I thank you for what you have said." I learn later that he also called to thank him for the tribute concert conducted by Riccardo Muti, who had been one of the connections.

A Missed Opportunity

October 26, 1998

Today Tauran is in Jerusalem. He delivers an important speech on the position of the Holy See regarding the Holy Places and, above all, Jerusalem. The text is clear and strong. But we knew nothing about it and it reaches us in the office around 1:45 PM. It is given to the press, but without time to point it out to journalists as "something important."

The following day, in fact, a few references appeared, but nothing significant. Conclusion: a missed opportunity for not thinking about the dynamic of public opinion, also for international political issues.

The Reputation of the Swiss Guard

October 29, 1998

Pius Segmüller, the new commander of the Swiss Guard, is coming to see me in the office for the second time in a short time. His problem is real: with the tragedy of Estermann's murder, the corps' reputation has been damaged. Especially in Switzerland, where a novel about the murder has already been published. He says that the good name should be restored, also to encourage the recruitment of new soldiers, which is now problematic.

In our first meeting, I told him that the fundamental problem is to make the result of the investigation public. With the long silence since this tragedy occurred, reservations, doubts, and suspicions have increased. Some people have the idea that something is being kept quiet. And those who can clarify matters here are not in a hurry to publish the results of the judge's investigation.

Kabila

November 23, 1998

I see the Pope receiving Laurent-Désiré Kabila,[5] president of the Democratic Republic of Congo. He is a very controversial figure, with a not inconsiderable record of war and violence. He has come to see the Pope because he wants the support of the Holy See in order to get the foreign troops out of the Congo, some of whom he himself brought into the country as allies in his battle against Mobutu.

The Pope is currently attending the Synod of Australia and the Pacific. I received him during an interval in one of the small rooms attached to the Synod Hall. On his way out, he tells me: "*Sembraba un agnellino*" ("it looked like a little lamb"). I tell him that the bishops of Rwanda have protested this visit. "Yes, I knew it." His comment afterwards is for the synod: "The synod is going very well."

New Ideas

December 2, 1998

The fact that the Pope is looking for new ideas seems to me to be a good sign that his ailments are not affecting him at his core. At today's dinner he talks about a bit of everything, but I think that what the Pope wants is—in effect—to hear suggestions, proposals for new things that can be done.

At one point in the conversation, I tell the Pope that he, who has been caught up in the whirlwind of the mass media from the beginning, could perhaps address this topic in a profound document. . . . The Pope listens. He rarely gives an immediate answer, positive or negative, to these things. He thinks about them. He thinks them over. Then he tells me that there are two documents ready and he is waiting to find the right date: one on the elderly and the other on artists. As if to say: it is not the time now to add another document

5. Laurent-Désiré Kabila (Congo, 1939–2001) had overthrown Mobutu Sese Seko in 1997. He was assassinated and succeeded by his son, Joseph Kabila.

to the list. He also speaks of the recent Bull proclaiming the Holy Year 2000. A concrete and practical document.[6]

Some Questions from Weigel

December 16, 1998

I am accompanying George Weigel to dinner with the Pope. He is finishing the biography and brings some biographical questions to confirm.

"Had you thought of becoming a Carmelite when, before entering the underground seminary, you made some spiritual exercises with them?" "No; perhaps it was in my mind, but it was resolved when Bishop Sapieha told me to go to the seminary and then I would see it. I already knew St. John of the Cross because Jan Tyranoski[7] had introduced him to me."

"In March 1981, some books say that you received the Soviet ambassador and in that conversation you spoke about the issues of the moment: Russia, Poland, etc." The Pope did not remember the interview. Dziwisz went to check in his notebooks, where he wrote down all the Pope's activities, and found that the audience did indeed not take place. George raises other questions and the Pope answers everything.

Influencing International Awareness

December 17, 1998

Tonight the United States is again bombing Baghdad and other targets in Iraq. The alliance this time is the United States and Britain. I feel that something needs to be said. I have prepared a draft and I am talking to Tauran.

The Pope receives the letters of credence from four ambassadors and in the common speech he addresses to them, the Secretary of State has decided to put something on this subject. I see the prepared text and Iraq is not even mentioned. There is a vague reference to the endangered peace in the Middle East.

Possibly such treatment is appropriate, but I cannot help thinking that there is a moral problem here on which the Holy See could shed a little more

6. *Incarnationis mysterium*, Bull of Convocation of the Great Jubilee of the Year 2000, dated November 29, 1998.

7. Jan Tyranoski (Poland, 1901–1947) was a tailor in Krakow, a friend and mentor of the young Karol Wojtyla, whom he introduced to Carmelite spirituality and the theology of Louis Marie Grignion de Montfort.

light. This very moderate line seems to me not to be the Pope's line. But it is already too late: he is about to receive the ambassadors. I consider it a lost opportunity to influence the international conscience through public opinion.

Letters

DECEMBER 25, 1998

One family: the man is forty-four years old; his wife is forty-one years old; eight children. She has been suffering from cancer since 1994. They write me a letter, and another one to Dziwisz, because they would like to come to a Mass of the Pope.

An eighty year old man from Alicante sends me a packet of "cereals with cocoa." He says it works very well for him, and "if it works well for one-year-old children, why shouldn't it work for an old man?" He suggests giving it to the Pope. He has heard on TV that the Pope was not doing well. "What a joy if this could rejuvenate the Pope a little!"

These are two samples of the type of letters that arrive in my office. Some of them leave me devastated. I try to answer them all. I imagine what the Pope must feel when he reads thousands of letters like these. They are those papers he keeps in the kneeler of his chapel and meditates on in front of the tabernacle.

A Telegram to Castro

DECEMBER 28, 1998

When I was having dinner with the Holy Father a few days ago, I told him that Castro had approved as definitive the restoration of the Christmas holiday in Cuba. He was very happy about the news. The idea arose to take advantage of the occasion to send Castro a personal message from the Pope.

Today we gave the press a copy of the telegram that the Pope sent to Castro dated December 23, thanking him for that decision: "I wish to express my deep appreciation for the decision to return to Christmas Day its festive character for all Cubans, in accordance with their tradition, and at the same time I am pleased to send you my sincere congratulations on the occasion of the imminent Christmas holidays."

41

Grace for a Condemned Man

Mexico and St. Louis (Missouri)

January 22–28, 1999

Mexico is the same as always: colossal enthusiasm and a remarkable display of affection for the Pope, which grows unceasingly during his repeated visits to this country. "It is a people that does not let anyone sleep," the Pope said at the press conference on the outbound trip, no doubt recalling the serenades and mañanitas in his honor. It is the eighty-fifth trip outside Italy.

In St. Louis (Missouri, USA) I propose that the Pope intercede for a death row inmate, Darrell J. Mease, a Vietnam veteran who is to be executed on January 27, the penultimate day of the Pope's stay here, for having murdered three people.

I came up with the idea when I arrived, and although it is something completely out of the planned program, I dare to raise it when I see the profound impact that the Pope is producing in this city. I talk it over with Sodano; he agrees and we call Mel Carnahan, Governor of the State of Missouri, directly on the phone.[1]

Then the governor's secretary calls me and wants to know more details: names, dates, what is the status of the Secretary of State. I clarify and she tells me that the governor will be coming to Archbishop Regali's residence at lunchtime.

At the same time—1:30 PM—the Pope is having lunch with the cardinals and bishops.

As soon as he arrived, the question was put to the governor, who thought that he was going to be asked for this grace because of an argument based on the validity of the sentence or the legal usefulness of the death penalty. I deduce

1. Melvin Eugene "Mel" Carnahan (United States, 1934–2000), Democratic Party politician, was governor of Missouri for six years (1993–99). He was a Protestant Christian. He died a year later in a plane crash while campaigning for senator.

this because he is accompanied by a lawyer who brings with him many documents, probably from the trial. To his surprise, we tell him that he is being asked for a grace, to free this man from the death penalty on the occasion of the exceptional event of the Pope's coming to this city.

Certainly, the Pope has spoken clearly and emphatically on numerous occasions about the need to abolish the death penalty, but this was neither the time nor the place to argue it; besides, we know that Carnahan has declared himself in favor of abortion and the death penalty. After overcoming his initial surprise, he says he will consider the issue from that perspective and give us an answer.

Shortly after arriving at the hotel they telephone from the governor's office, to communicate that he is willing to grant the favor, but they are studying in what way it can be carried out and, then, the way to explain it to public opinion. "Is there a possibility that the Pope could ask the governor directly?" Knowing the Pope's way of thinking, I answer them in the affirmative: that gesture could take place in the cathedral itself since the governor will be in the front row, with the rest of the authorities. The Pope could greet him for a moment and ask him to do so. That is fine with them.

The governor's press secretary then called me to discuss how the news could be released. I suggest that they do it the next day, presenting it as a response to the Holy Father's request, without going into the juridical dimension of the case. And I ask him to fax me what he communicates to the media.

In the front row of St. Louis Cathedral are, among others, President Clinton and Governor Carnahan. The Pope approaches, and tells him, with great simplicity and in a terse manner, the last name of the person condemned to death:

—"Have mercy on Mr. Mease."

The governor replied with the same brevity:

—"I will do it."

At the airport, before saying goodbye, I greet the governor with thanks, assuming that he has made his decision to suspend the execution. In fact, he has not yet announced anything about it.

We return to Rome on the 28th at 1:00 PM. I am home in the afternoon when I receive a phone call. "Apparently the governor has commuted the sentence." Before answering anything I call my office and ask Sister Giovanna if any mail has arrived from the Governor. It has. She sends it to me. The text reads as follows:

> Yesterday afternoon Pope John Paul II asked me to commute the death sentence of Darrell Mease. The Pope said these words to me: "Have mercy on Mr. Mease." In reaching this decision, I took into account the extraordinary circumstances of the Pope's request and the historical significance of his visit to St. Louis City and the State of Missouri. After careful consideration of this direct and personal request, and out of a deep and abiding respect for the Pontiff and all that he represents, I decided last night to grant his request. I have commuted Darrell Mease's death sentence to life imprisonment without the possibility of parole.

Beautiful words, after a generous decision at the end of a splendid journey.

Back in Cuba

March 3, 1999

I am returning to Cuba from February 22 to March 2nd to participate in the II Assembly of the Latin American Catholic Union of Journalists (UCLAP). Nuncio Stella is waiting for me at the airport, but no one from the government's office for religious affairs: it is a way of pointing out that the activities of the UCLAP, and of the thirty or so modest Catholic magazines on the island, are outside the law, although everyone knows about them. The nuncio has arranged several meetings with some of the people I interviewed a few months ago.

Besides the activities of the UCLAP-Cuba assembly, I spend my time accompanying bishops in the parishes of their dioceses, meeting with doctors and other people, giving some conferences. The interviews with the Cuban authorities are very cordial. In the Central Committee of the party I meet with Caridad Diego and Isidro Gómez. Caridad apologizes for not having attended my lecture the day before. Of course, it would be too much for them to attend an event about the Catholic publications—which formally do not exist. We dealt with the topics I had agreed upon with the Nuncio and which have as their substratum the improvement of the life and freedom of Catholics. We also met with Isabel Allende, Vice Minister of Foreign Affairs, in an atmosphere of great cordiality.

When some non-Cuban diplomats ask me for suggestions on how the US Administration should behave with regard to Cuba, I come to the conclusion, and this trip confirms it, that what they can do is decree a lifting of the embargo against Cuba with regard to food, medicines, and sanitary materials. This measure only has advantages. It removes Castro's excuse of the embargo as a tool to control his people; it creates a favorable feeling towards the United States in Cuba; it benefits the Cuban people, and it gives the international community a positive sign.

The highlight of the visit was lunch with the president. Castro received me in his office. We sat down, I thanked him for his attention and gave him the book *Gift and Mystery*, in Spanish, which the Pope had signed as a gift for him. I gave him two videos of the Vatican Museums, also in Spanish, about which he is interested. He asks about the types of art they contain and other information about the Vatican. He shows interest in everything, but I think he distinguishes the substantial from the accessory. He knows perfectly well what I had done these days and even that I gave up going to Varadero beach (I did not accept the invitation because I knew it would be full of tourists). We talked about the Pope's trip. We had lunch in a dining room annexed to his office. We were the nuncio, Caridad Diego, and a doctor, José Ramón Balaguer, from the Party's ideological committee and former ambassador in Moscow.

During lunch he talks endlessly about the training plan for Latin American doctors. He speaks in depth about public health statistics in Cuba and other countries and spends an enormous amount of time on the subject. When I realize that he isn't turning the conversation to matters that interest us, I say that I would like to talk to him about a few issues, and I mention Church-State relations in Cuba.

I told him that there is something of special interest for the Pope, and that is the Jubilee of the year 2000. He is interested; he asks where the word jubilee comes from, its meaning, etc. I explain to him that at that time the Church will make a great effort of evangelization and that in Cuba they will need a great amount of written material. And I go to the concrete: I tell him that the Pope would like to send a printing press to Cuba to edit all that catechetical material. Caridad whispers to me: "And to edit *Vitral*" (*Vitral* is the Church magazine that has given them the most headaches . . .).

To reinforce the request I tell him that the Holy See is now "out of ammunition" when it has to explain to other countries that they must change their attitude towards Cuba, and that we need new arguments to convince them that there are substantial changes in the country. Castro says: "Well, that printed material is being brought from abroad, perhaps it could be printed here." I insist that it should be done before the Jubilee begins and he adds, "Good, but don't make me decide now. . . ."

We continue talking about the Jubilee and I tell him about the possibility of transmitting live the opening of the Jubilee. I explain what it is about and say: "This is something very important." I also mention the possibility of the bishops being able to speak regularly on the radio for a quarter of an hour on Sundays, because it is a pity that whoever wants to hear something religious has to tune in to *Radio Martí* (which broadcasts from Miami).

As the new penalties for crimes of prostitution, pimping, sale of minors, etc., have been discussed before, I tell him that the problem in these fields is one of lack of values and not so much of criminal law. He accepts this point of view. And I go back again to the printing press and the diffusion of values. "Yes, a great diffusion of values is necessary," he says.

Castro has a look that is at once that of an old man, a man of energy, a utopian dreamer and a dictator. His memory is fresh. His capacity for arithmetic is intact: when asked about the size of the Vatican, I mistakenly tell him two soccer fields, but then I specify that it is 44 hectares. He immediately does some mental calculations and says that it is about sixty soccer fields. . . .

He is sensitive to good humor and informality, but it is necessary to be patient at first—sometimes for a long time—until he abandons the pose of the enlightened autocrat. After that, you can joke with him without problems. He eats little and an almost exclusively vegetable diet. At our dinner he ate two grapefruits, a tomato and lettuce salad, and two light portions of cheese. I think he had a coffee. He does not smoke. Naturally, he sometimes abandons himself to his utopian dreams. On this occasion, the repeated narration of his medical-social plan that he is trying to export to all of Latin America. He gives me a box of *Habanos Trinidad*, which I didn't know about. They are excellent.

Difficulties at Work

March 14, 1999

As time goes by, the difficulties of my work do not diminish, but rather seem to increase. On the one hand, there is the gathering of information to feed the interest of public opinion. This simple task is becoming more and more difficult. On the other hand, there is the sensitivity in the Secretary of State, and other agencies, to "playing the game" of public opinion to turn it toward our favor, while respecting the "laws" of journalism. And, thirdly, there is the direct access to the Pope. Naturally, all three aspects of these difficulties can be explained by the Pope's diminished vitality due to age and illness.

Obtaining information is becoming more and more complicated. Those in charge of the Secretariat of State tend to close themselves off, to multiply "prudence" and to become more cautious. They always play on the defensive and are never proactive. Their motto is: "Don't say anything, but if they ask . . ." Thus, the initiative always comes from others, from those who launch rumors, but never from us. They do not consider proposing our agenda to the media, but merely correct the media when they err too grievously.

When the Pope had greater vitality, he himself imposed these things in some way on his collaborators. Now I do not feel like arguing again with a Pope whose energies have been so much reduced, and the occasions to comment on things, to receive his indications, or at least to know his thoughts on the issues better, have also been reduced.

I regularly go to his audiences when the people he is interviewing have a particular significance for public opinion. For example, three days ago, at the end of his audience with the President of the Islamic Republic of Iran, Mohammad Khatami, I asked him about the content of their conversation. He told me the topics discussed, the nature of the conversation and even his view of the man ("I find him a providential person for this moment"). All this helped me to elaborate the communiqué I gave immediately afterwards. If I had confined myself to the official note that was passed on to me, I would not have conveyed the true character of that visit.

All of the above are facts that I can confirm and I consider them as a natural evolution, at least in part, of the characteristics of my work. But I do not hide the fact that they weigh on me.

Kosovo

April 1, 1999

It is Holy Thursday. And we are in the middle of the NATO war with the Yugoslav Republic over Kosovo. Everything possible is being done by the Holy See: meetings with the ambassadors of NATO countries and the UN Security Council and the OSCE (Organization for Security and Cooperation in Europe), etc. Today Tauran is going to Belgrade to meet with Orthodox Patriarch Pavle and Yugoslav President Milosevic. Naturally we spread the news of these efforts.

I listen to the *BBC*: everything is a war report, military actions, the "drama" of three American soldiers taken prisoner by the Serbs. . . . But of Tauran's trip, who is carrying a personal message from the Pope to Milosevic, they do not say a word in their 12:00 newscast: it is not news. This means that their logic is very narrow: just bombing until Milosevic gives in on Kosovo. There is no consideration of negotiation, of diplomatic action. There is a simplified logic of military action and this, in turn, reduced to aerial actions without the intervention of infantry troops.

Rugova

May 10, 1999

Visit of Ibrahim Rugova, leader of Kosovo. He is accompanied by Msgr. Vincenzo Paglia.[2] He sees the Pope and, after the audience, he comes to the office and I introduce him to the journalists. He makes a statement after I deliver an introduction. He seems to me to be a man of great worth: moderate, aware of his responsibility, religious, cordial but not emotional.

Marathon in Poland

June 5–17, 1999

We returned last night from a long trip to Poland: a tremendous program of activities, trips, meetings, and ceremonies that the Pope, in reality, can only undertake with a superhuman effort.

In addition to the official program there are a number of unannounced activities that we planned before departure: visits to churches and meetings with people. During the twelve days he visited twenty cities. The helicopter rides are long—sometimes almost two hours—and we arrive in the destination city after nine o'clock at night. On the way back, we are all very tired. So is the Pope.

On June 8 we traveled to Wigry, a former monastery that the Polish government has converted into a tourist hostel. It is in the Polish lake district. The Pope is scheduled to rest here during the afternoon and for the following day. Upon arrival, we sailed on the lake for an hour and a half.

A boat trip on the lakes is organized for the following day. The Pope goes in silence. He prays and recalls his youthful sojourns in these places. Before embarking in Augustów, he visits the home of some farmers: Stanisław Milewski, his wife, and their five children. The reason for this stopover is that the Pope might give a sign of encouragement to the Polish rural sector, which is going through many difficulties in this time of transitions.

2. Vincenzo Paglia (Italy, 1945) was at that time pastor of the Basilica of Santa Maria in Trastevere. In the context of the activities of the Community of Sant'Egidio, of which he was one of the initiators, he worked for the pacification of Kosovo, achieving the liberation of Rugova. He was appointed bishop of Terni (2000–2012), president of the Pontifical Council for the Family (2012–2016), and president of the Pontifical Academy for Life (2016).

We board the boat, but I have the impression that there are too many of us and it takes away from the intimacy. As the sky is overcast and there is sometimes a light drizzle, the Pope sits on the low, inner deck of the boat. People greet him from the shore as we make our way along the lake. We arrive at a small shrine of Our Lady at Studzienczna. The Pope pays a visit. He greets quite a few people, as word has spread. Lunch, rest, and return to the boat.

I call the journalists to give them some information, and—with the help of a translator—I have a press conference on the phone for more than half an hour. We take some pictures with the Pope. He is now on the open upper deck of the ship.

We pass Lake Orle by the Augustów canal, and the excursion is over. I doubt that the Pope had much rest. But at least he was able to pray for a few moments in peace and reminisce about the years of his youth. We return home by car.

The next day we visit three cities: Sieldze, Drohiczyn, and we return to Warsaw in the evening. He presides over two ceremonies that have an ecumenical flavor due to the presence of Orthodox, Eastern Rite Catholics, and Catholics from Belarus and Ukraine.

In Warsaw, a day later, he delivers a significant speech in the Polish Parliament (*Sejm*). It is the first time he addresses a national parliament in the presence of the three branches of government—executive, legislative and judicial—together with the diplomatic corps.

When he is greeted by some religious leaders, the Chief Rabbi asks him to remove the Cross that was placed next to Auschwitz, as a souvenir of his first trip in 1979. The Rabbi's words are heard on TV and become the news of the day.

In the afternoon I see that the Polish Hebrew communities issue a very harsh statement against the Rabbi. They say that he will cease to be Chief Rabbi within a week; that his words only represent his personal position; that the language and the occasion were inappropriate; that the subject is still an open question, but that it was neither the time nor the way for it to be dealt with.

The next morning, when we go to the nunciature to pick up the Pope, I learn that while he was alone in the bathroom, at about 5:40 AM, he fell, hit his head in the shower and got a wound in the right temporal region, which required three stitches. I immediately went up to his room. The doctors who were on duty in the ambulance, inside the nunciature, have just finished stitching him.

Buzzonetti and Patrizio Polisca, the other young doctor accompanying us, ask the surgeon to come in to determine whether or not to perform a brain CT scan after the trauma. Buzzonetti has doubts and Polisca is rather in favor of doing it. At this point the surgeon arrives. His opinion is, to everyone's great relief, that a CT scan is not necessary. The Pope begins the day with a bright white patch on his forehead.

For me, this signals that the Pope is beginning to lose autonomy: his two falls have taken place when he was alone, in the bathroom.

We leave without delay for Sandomierz. I ask the Polish doctor accompanying us if he can ask the doctor who did the suturing in Warsaw to keep the gauze used for the treatment. When I returned to Warsaw in the evening, I was given a plastic bag with everything that had been used for the treatment: syringe for the anesthesia, gauze, etc. I bring those three gauze pads with the Pope's blood on them with me, thinking of the future.

I am preparing my journalist briefing: "This morning, before leaving his residence at the nunciature in Warsaw, the Pope suffered a fall which caused a lacerated-contusion wound in the right temporal region. The clinical guidelines, and in particular the cardiovascular ones, are normal, etc."

News about the Pope's trip to Armenia, scheduled for a month from now, is emerging. Catholicos Karekin I, leader of the Armenian Orthodox Church, is seriously ill with cancer. We are told that an envoy of his—the Archbishop of the Armenians in New York—wishes to speak with the Pope. It is assumed that he will ask to cancel the trip, although with the polite formula of postponing it. From the information I have, Karekin I wants to see the Pope, but the Synod and others do not. Here, too, are misgivings to be healed.

The meeting with the envoy takes place on the very day of the Pope's arrival in Warsaw. As expected, the proposal was to postpone the trip. They decided on the alternative of a quick trip to visit the Catholicos in the airport and also hold a brief meeting with the Catholic minority at the same airport.

I prepare a brief communiqué to inform the press. The reference to Catholics is removed from my words, so as not to create friction, and the day after the Pope's fall I give the news: "At the end of the Pope's trip to Poland, the Holy Father will go to Armenia for a private visit with Catholicos." It is an announcement that causes a certain sensation. The expression "private visit" came to my mind after some thought because the other expressions—ecumenical trip or pastoral trip—did not fit in this case.[3]

The journey continues. And the fatigue accumulates.

---

3. In the end, this private trip could not take place either. A few days later, on June 29, John Paul II sent a personal message from Rome to Catholicos Karekin I, who died that same day. The trip to Armenia would take place in September 2001.

On the 14th we go to Lowicz, where it is warm. In the afternoon we go to Sosnowiec. There, on the contrary, it is cold. The Pope begins to feel ill. In the helicopter that takes us to Krakow, Buzzonetti gives him a Novalgina pill because he has a fever. When we arrive in Krakow late in the afternoon, his temperature has risen to 100 degrees Fahrenheit.

A large number of people are waiting in the inner courtyard of the archbishopric. To avoid the pope having to stop to greet them, Dziwisz instructs the popemobile to go directly to the door of the residence. But there is no elevator in the building, so he has to walk up the two floors to his room.

The next day, I go early to the archbishopric from the hotel where I am staying. I talk with Dziwisz and Buzzonetti. The Pope has a fever of 100.4 degrees. We write a brief statement to the press: "Since yesterday afternoon, the Pope has had a moderate rise in temperature of probable viral origin. He has been advised to suspend all engagements for the day." He was scheduled to celebrate Holy Mass in Krakow on the millennium of the diocese. Before the Mass I have the press briefing. Sodano celebrates the Mass and Cardinal Macharski reads the homily.

That afternoon I stay in Krakow. I go to the archbishopric, talk to Buzzonetti, go shopping in the city and make some statements for Polish television, which will lead the 7:30 PM news. The Pope is better, but he still has a slight fever. And since a concert has been prepared for him in front of his residence, he gets up and appears for a moment at the window to wave. . . .

The next day the fever is gone. The Pope celebrates Mass in Stary Sacz, where he canonizes Blessed Sister Cunegonda.[4] Cardinal Macharski reads the homily. In the afternoon, we go to Wadowice. In the Liturgy of the Word he makes continuous references to his childhood and youth in this city where he was born. And when he returns in the evening, instead of going directly to the residence, as planned, he visits three other churches.

On the 17th, the last day in Poland, the Pope celebrates Mass "privately" in the cathedral of Wavel: there are about 950 people. The program doesn't include anything else, but the Pope goes to Czestochowa and, before that, he goes to Gliwice, the city where he could not go the day he was in bed. He tells the people who are waiting for him: "I had to come, and I didn't come. Today I didn't have to come, and I came: I, a Pope like that, I wouldn't put up with it!"

---

4. St. Kinga Cunegonda (Poland, 1224–1292) was queen of Poland, venerated as patroness of Poland and Lithuania. After the death of her husband, Boleslaus V, she entered a convent of Poor Clare nuns.

Visit to Our Lady of Czestochowa, to whom he entrusts his pontificate. After lunch and a short rest, return by helicopter to Krakow. Long farewell ceremony. Return to Rome exhausted.

A few days later, we reviewed the entire trip with the Pope during a lunch at his apartment.

A Cryptic Language

July 1, 1999

The debate on overpopulation is taking place in New York as part of the International Conference on Population and Development ICPD+5, which began on June 30 and ends tomorrow, July 2nd. The aim is to implement the action program of the Cairo Conference.

Among other issues, they discuss the use of condoms, the rights of parents to decide on abortion by minors, the use of abortion as a means of population control. In all this debate, one could say many things about the position of the Church in a convincing way. One could try one more time to repropose what was already proposed during the Cairo Conference.

Yesterday we received a call from the corresponding office and they confirmed that they would send us something about the Holy See in the conference. The truth is that I was expecting an elaborate document, a position statement that would take into account the international disinformation on these issues, and even the persecution and attacks that our representation at the United Nations is receiving in New York—and in the international press.

At the end of the morning I simply receive a few lines stating that "the Holy See will ensure that this important meeting will give a new impetus to an authentic development based on respect for the dignity of the person and the family." Naturally, in the face of the massive clamor and commotion of these days, these few lines are cryptic and completely ignored. I do not intend to offload the responsibility onto others: the mistake was mine for not having known how to anticipate and direct this a little better.

42

Toward the Great Jubilee

Reading Vacations

July 7–20, 1999

It is only a few days of rest, but the Pope does not want to be away from Rome any longer. This time Buzzonetti is staying in Rome because he has to have a pacemaker reimplanted, and another doctor, Giampiero Gasparro, is coming in his place. The only change in the schedule is that we leave a little later in the morning, at 10:30. The Pope devotes this time to reading. We return around 7:30 PM.

The Pope's walks in these lands of the Aosta Valley are shorter and shorter: a short walk at noon and another in the afternoon. Most of his time is spent reading. He has begun to read a book published in Poland with the biographies of the 108 he beatified in Warsaw on his recent trip. One day, while we were walking, he spoke to me about them with admiration.

He then read a philosophy book by a contemporary German author; some copies of the magazine *ETHOS*, edited by Tadeusz Styczeń, and other volumes.

Dziwisz told me that when books arrive, the Pope puts them in a pile with the intention of reading them when he has time. From that pile, the nuns and Dziwisz himself take some of them, but the Pope finds them and puts them back in the pile. . . . On one occasion I told him that he read a lot and walked only a little. He replied that he was given a lot of books and he wanted to look at them (in fact, he reads them carefully).

"What do they say about the trip to Ur?" he asked me one day. I told him about the press's interest in that trip, announced for next February. We talked about how Abraham is not as present as he should be in the Christian tradition. "Yes," said the Pope, "we should broaden the perspective of our faith to include Abraham." He added that he had recently had a meeting with

Cassidy, Etchegaray, and Fitzgerald[1]—Arinze was away—, to discuss various aspects of the trip.

As we walked through Brusson, we talked again about the Middle East. I told him that it would be a good idea to explain the purpose of the trip, especially in the United States, so that the news would not be limited to a meeting with Saddam Hussein. One possibility, in this regard, could be to devote the public hearings of the month preceding the trip to explaining his thinking. He thanked me and recalled his trip to Israel in 1965; we ended up talking about Muslim-Christian relations.

Shortly after, the name of the philosopher Roman Ingarden, who was a collaborator of Edith Stein, comes up in the conversation. The Pope would like Edith Stein, whom he canonized last October, to be declared Patroness of Europe. "Perhaps at the next European synod we could talk about that," he adds. But the problem is that there are so many candidates. I tell him that I also have "my candidate:" Teresa of Ávila. He replied that the candidate of the Italians is Catherine of Siena.[2]

On the 15th Shimon Perez called from Israel. Samuel Haddas, who was the first Israeli ambassador to the Holy See, probably gave him my name. He tells me about a calendar that his foundation has made and that will be distributed among Israelis and Palestinians, aimed at the children of both groups. He would like that publication to carry a few words from the Pope; a blessing. I tell him that it could be a good idea, but that the material would have to be sent to the nuncio in Israel. I then referred this call to the Holy Father. He is positively surprised that a Hebrew would ask the Pope for a blessing.

We speak again of the journey to the Middle East, of Mount Horeb—today Sinai—and of God's manifestation to Moses: "I am who I am." The Pope adds that this expression has given rise to numerous commentaries, including philosophical ones. He recalls that the readings of the Mass of the day speak precisely of this scene.

---

1. Michael Louis Fitzgerald (United Kingdom, 1937), of the Missionaries of Africa, an expert in relations with Islam, was secretary of the Pontifical Council for Interreligious Dialogue (1987–2002) and later president of the same body (2002–2006). Subsequently, he was nuncio to Egypt (2006–2012). He was appointed cardinal in 2019.

2. Three months later, he published the apostolic letter *Spes aedificando* (October 1, 1999), naming St. Bridget of Sweden, St. Catherine of Siena, and St. Teresa Benedicta of the Cross (Edith Stein) co-patronesses of Europe.

On one of the walks, Dziwisz tells me that the Pope is doing better than last year. I think so too.

Own goal

July 30, 1999

A few months ago, in February, an anonymous book was published in Italy full of murmurings and cruel and sarcastic comments, along with other true things, about the Roman Curia. The book hardly had any effect on public opinion.

Suddenly, from the Vatican itself, a case is brought against its author. It was discovered that it was a monsignor working in one of the dicasteries. The Tribunal of the Rota was asked to stop printing the book and prevent the possibility of making any new editions. And, as was foreseeable, stories appeared in the Italian and international press about the book, about the persecution of its author, and about the scandals in the Vatican. Phenomenal publicity when nobody was talking about the book anymore. Now, after the court's decision, copies have sold out and all the country's newspapers have echoed the scandalous story: "A harsh settling of scores between monsignors," they said.

Today, a news item in *ANSA* reports that the book is already at the top of the list of best sellers in Italy in the "essay" section, with 100,000 copies in circulation; according to another agency, it is the best-selling book of the last seven days. I think it is a magnificent example of a goal in one's own net.

Thinking about Christian Unity

September 6, 1999

The unity of Christians occupies the Pope's thoughts. And, as a step in that direction, the relationship with the Orthodox. The trip to Romania (May 7–9) was an important step in this direction. But how many difficulties on this road! Now, in view of the Great Jubilee, the Pope published a letter about the trips he would like to make. It is that "dream" of which he already spoke to me a long time ago.[3]

Before the summer, he had a meeting with Cassidy, Etchegaray, Sodano, and Re to see what could be done to make that project a reality. Cassidy wrote an exploratory letter to the Orthodox patriarchs—Athens, Moscow,

3. *Letter on pilgrimages to places linked to the history of salvation*, June 29, 1999.

Constantinople—not so much to announce a trip as to see where he could meet with them in a "pan-Christian encounter." Also, to see if such visits could be made to the biblical places: Athens, where Paul preached, Damascus, etc.

India and Georgia

November 5–9, 1999

Before embarking on this new trip accompanying the Pope, I have given a couple of interviews to the Indian media: one to the weekly *Outlook* and the other to the Indian state television.

There are two main events: in India, the presentation in Delhi of the apostolic exhortation *Ecclesia in Asia;* and in Georgia, in addition to the invitation of President Shevardnadze, the visit to Patriarch-Catholicos Elias II.[4]

The trip to India takes place in the midst of a climate of unrest. During the last few years there have been numerous attacks against priests and religious in different regions of the country, especially in Orissa. An Australian Protestant missionary and his children have been murdered. And before the trip there have been several anti-Catholic demonstrations. They had called for a march—which the government prevented—from Goa to Delhi to protest against the Holy Father. They wanted the Pope to ask forgiveness for the alleged "atrocities" committed by Portuguese missionaries in Goa and the request that conversions to Catholicism in India cease.

During the flight I approach his section of the plane—we are traveling on a *Boeing* 747—to talk to the Pope. But I find him praying, eyes closed, hands clasped, sitting in his seat. I don't want to interrupt him and I tell Dziwisz that on this occasion it is not necessary for the Pope to meet the journalists now.

Then, before lunch is served, I go back upstairs and sit next to him. He interrupts his reading of a book on Polish literature. We talk about the trip and then I ask him if he has already read his biography written by George Weigel. He tells me that he has started and that he is currently reading the chapters about Poland. "There are many events," he tells me, "that he had forgotten about."

I talk to Buzzonetti during the flight. He tells me that on October 24 a group of neurologists confirmed the diagnosis of Parkinson's disease and suggest continuing therapy. It is a normal evolution. His right hand also trembles from time to time. And he confirms that the right treatment is being carried

4. Elias II (1933) was elected Patriarch of the Georgian Apostolic Church in 1977.

out. So I think that it is not that things are being done wrong, but just that we would like them to be done differently.

We arrived in Delhi, a city of 7,206,000 inhabitants, with an archdiocese of 81,000 Catholics.

The next day, the official reception ceremony takes place at the presidential palace. I greet Sonia Gandhi, who is among the personalities attending the ceremony.

The Pope has three official meetings that day: the first with the President of the Republic at the presidential palace; the second with the Prime Minister, Shri Atal Bihari Vajpayee, at a nearby residence, Hyderabad House; and the third with the Vice President, Shri Krishan Kant. I am present during the interviews. All three speak about the non-denominational nature of the country's constitution.

The President of the Republic—Kocheril Raman Narayanan—tells him that he is from Kerala and that he studied in a Catholic school. He reminds him of the Pope's previous trip in 1986, and tells him that, although there is "religious freedom" in India, there are still some "intolerant fringes." He spoke of neighboring countries, such as China, where "there is political suspicion towards religion."

The Pope alludes to the legacy we must leave to humanity in the third millennium: peace and interreligious dialogue. At no time is there any direct mention of the lack of religious tolerance suffered by Catholics in India, although the three leaders indirectly allude to the issue.

Sodano is the one who brings up these topics during the three conversations. With the Prime Minister they talk about the feast of Divali (the Hindu feast of light): "Possibly, the presence of the Pope among us will bring a new light."

I think the most brilliant and spontaneous of the three is the vice president. He comments to the Pope that since the foundation of the nation is the family, his preaching on the family is beneficial for the new millennium that is beginning. If you break the family you break the society. "India should be a haven for all religions, because we believe that religion and culture are synonymous. However, culture is not synonymous with nation." He adds that they still have a long task ahead of them: the spiritualization of politics.

After these interviews the Pope goes to the Raj Ghat, the park where Mahatma Gandhi's memorial is located. He goes barefoot in front of the monument. At the end, he is asked to sign the book of illustrious visitors. I take the opportunity to tell him that I have taken note of a Gandhian phrase that he could add along with his signature, and I put the text in front of him. It seems appropriate: "No culture can survive if it attempts to be exclusive."

Georgia. At the airport of Tbilisi, Georgia, it is cold and there are strong gusts of wind. The Pope begins to shiver as TV cameras film him. When he greets Catholicos Elias II during the ceremony he holds at the end of the day in the Patriarchal Svetitskhoveli Cathedral in Mtskheta, his shivering becomes noticeably worse. Dziwisz tells me that the Pope has had a fever since he left Delhi, possibly of an intestinal nature.

The next morning I spoke to the media to explain that the Pope had suffered a lot from the cold. They were alarmed, but what I told them about the cold reduced some of their concern.

Shevardnadze behaves in an affectionate and cordial manner during the meeting with the world of culture. At the end of the Pope's Mass, which takes place in a sports hall, he approaches the microphone and thanks him once again for his presence in Georgia. The Patriarch, who seemed to me at the beginning a bit stuffy and distant, is now more cordial as well.

During the trip back to Rome, Father Tucci gave us a phenomenal scare when he suddenly lost consciousness and fell to the ground. He undergoes an electrocardiogram. Fortunately, the cause is not circulatory. It seems to have been an acute digestive problem.

"We Have to See Each Other"

December 21, 1999

Curia meeting with the Pope for Christmas greetings. At the end I approach the Pope, who jokes with me touching my face, as if he were blind and did not see me: "*Dobbiamo vederci*" ("We have to see each other,") he tells me amusedly.

I reply, touched by his affection, that I am willing to see him whenever he wants. He smiles, amused. Despite the stiffness of his face, his eyes remain as lively as ever, something that comforts me.

Transmission in Cuba

December 23, 1999

I read in the press that in Cuba it will be possible to see the opening of the Holy Door with which the Great Jubilee will begin. Castro has agreed to what we requested in that conversation last February. One of the requests was to allow the live transmission of this ceremony. He did not give an immediate yes then; but he did not say no either. Now he has given permission.

Opening of the Jubilee

DECEMBER 24, 1999

Opening of the Holy Door and the Jubilee. God has allowed the Pope to see this day. St. Peter's Basilica is full. Angela Buttiglione, commenting on the *RAI* live broadcast, says that there are about 7,000 people inside the church and about 15,000 in St. Peter's Square. I am told later that her estimates fall short: in fact, there are 8,200 people in the Basilica—all seated—and 56,000 in the square.

There is the feeling of a new beginning: people are praying, asking, waiting. In the *Sala Stampa*, about fifty journalists follow the scenes with great attention and even applaud when the Pope opens the Holy Door.

These have been days of hard work for everyone in the office, amidst a succession of difficulties and unforeseen events: the connections with the system we have prepared have failed; there is no way to send the texts through the Internet, etc. Fortunately, I have some exceptional colleagues who stay working until one o'clock in the morning.

The Pope is not going to Castelgandolfo during these days, contrary to his usual custom. Dziwisz explains to me that he has made the decision to stay in Rome because of the large number of pilgrims who have come for the Jubilee.

43

The Holy Land

The Pope's Prayer

January 4, 2000

When I arrive, the Pope is in his oratory. As usual in these cases, instead of waiting for him in a small room, I go to the chapel and accompany him in prayer. He doesn't even know I'm there. Sitting in his place, with a standing light that had been placed to make it easier for him to read, I saw that he was holding the breviary in his hands. He is in no hurry. Time seems not to exist. Even his movements are slow. He conveys the impression that he is doing the most important thing. A quarter of an hour passes. He carefully closes the zipper of the book cover. He rises, kneels, lets his head rest in his hands. Finally, he stands up, I greet him and walk with him to the dining room.

The theme of the dinner is the beginning of the Jubilee. I comment a bit on the traffic disruptions in Rome, but add that, in reality, they are due more to Christmas and New Year's Eve than to the inauguration of the Jubilee on Christmas Eve. "The Pope who complicates the lives of Romans," he adds humorously.

Then we talk about the upcoming opening of the holy door at St. Paul Outside the Walls and I mention the leaders of the Christian confessions who, from the news that has reached me, have announced that they will participate in the ceremony.

At the end, when the dishes have been cleared, Dziwisz brings the Pope the dossiers and papers from the Secretariat of State to sign. He takes the documents to him there and then to save him the effort of moving to another room. Dziwisz escorts me out; we chat before saying goodbye and, among other things, he mentions that the Pope spends several hours each day in prayer.

Jerusalem: Preparing the Trip

January 25, 2000

I am in Israel collaborating in the preparation of some aspects of the Pope's upcoming trip to the Holy Land, scheduled for the end of March. I reside in the

Apostolic delegation in Jerusalem. The Nuncio is Msgr. Pietro Sambi, and the secretary is Msgr. Eugene Nugent. The day after our arrival, Saturday, we go to Bethlehem. We meet with the local—Palestinian—authorities and review what needs to be prepared.

My plan is to organize things so that during the trip everything will be transmitted live to the press center in Jerusalem, since there is no room for journalists in many of the places he will visit. After the business meeting, we follow the route the Pope will take as he heads to the Grotto of the Nativity. It is a very small place. I say it could be covered with two fixed TV cameras (no operator). There are some very vertical steps that the Pope would probably not be able to go down: I suggest that it would be convenient to put a handrail or something for him to lean on.

We return to Jerusalem. In the afternoon we have a meeting with the media committee appointed by the local church. They are capable and smart people, but logically, inexperienced with this sort of thing. I give them some ideas to start working, and take one of them, Wadie Abunassar, with me to all the meetings these days to give him some authority in front of the Israelis.

Saturday: meeting with the Israeli side. Moshe Fogel is the head of the government press office. We discuss some points, but I realize that he cannot decide because he is subordinate to the security people. We go to the Old City. Arriving at the Holy Sepulcher we find that we will have to come back another time, as the Armenians are in the middle of a full ceremony.

The next morning I leave with Wadie for Bethlehem and buy some souvenirs for the people in my office. I get a call from Rome. The *Sunday Times,* London, has published an article about the Pope's health. According to an unnamed doctor in London, who is supposedly treating the Pope, within two years we will have the Holy Father in a wheelchair. . . . They suggest not to answer anything, but I think that if we do not say anything, this thesis will be perceived as true. I decide to intervene. I talk to Buzzonetti and Re. And so, from a place between Bethlehem and Jerusalem, I make a statement about the Pope's health. I mention other predictions in this same sense, launched previously, which have proved to be unsuccessful. I stress that an article cannot be taken into consideration without recognizable sources and accurate information.

The afternoon is spent in a meeting at the apostolic delegation with the various television entities involved in the trip (Palestinian, Israeli, *RAI, European Broadcasting Union,* and government press office). After a long negotiation, we reached an agreement: all the events will be rebroadcast to the press center and made available to the local channels. Each TV station will be in charge of covering a part of it.

Arafat

February 15, 2000

In the morning, the Holy Father receives Yasser Arafat, who has managed to extend his trip to the Holy Land through a visit to Jericho. After the audience, the Pope tells me that the Palestinians "naturally think of their own interests." In other words, he is aware of Arafat's personal calculation in this invitation, but he does not mind agreeing to it.

In the evening I go to dinner with the Pope and we talk a little about the Arafat meeting and about the visit he will make to the Holocaust memorial in Jerusalem. I also tell him about a subject that worries me: the World Gay Pride March that has been planned in Rome in July, in the middle of the Jubilee. I tell him that, given the inevitability of this march, the best thing to do would be to convince the Italian authorities to have it take place on the dates when the Pope is out of Rome. The Pope said he was fine with that. And I ask his permission to propose it to the mayor of Rome, Francesco Rutelli.

The trips to the Holy Land and Sinai start again. As he bids us farewell, he says: "Next week, to Sinai." Earlier, speaking about the trip, Dziwisz comments that in Sinai the central theme is the Ten Commandments. And the Pope adds: "And also the name of God . . . Yahweh. It is the occasion in which God defines himself."

With the Mayor of Rome

February 18, 2000

This morning I went to the town hall in Rome to talk to Rutelli. The appointment had been arranged two days ago by telephone, because he was in Strasbourg. Already a week before, I had called Senator Ombreta Fumagalli Carulli—undersecretary of the Ministry of the Interior—to explain the plan to request the change of dates of the "gay" march in Rome to the days when there were no Jubilee events. She understood the reasons well; I gave her the updated calendar and the next day she passed me a copy of the note she had sent to Rutelli in this regard.

Thus, when I arrived at the appointment at the town hall, Rutelli gave me a photocopy of the letter he had already prepared to send to the Italian organizers of the march. Rutelli himself is in an unpleasant situation. He has let me know that it is not fair to say that the Holy See knew nothing about this march, because they had spoken to them two years ago. And he tells me the name of the Monsignor who acted as interlocutor.

Change of Dates

February 23, 2000

Rutelli calls me. He tells me that he sent the letter to the Italian leaders of this event. Their reaction has been negative and even virulent. They have split into two groups. They have established contacts with the American organizations. But Rutelli tells me that he will now act. He seems convinced that it is preferable to change these dates.

The Pope in Egypt and Sinai

February 24–26, 2000

One of the Pope's dreams is fulfilled: the trip to Egypt and Sinai, a visit to the place where God made his name known and gave Moses the tablets of the Law.

Mubarak[1] receives the Pope at Cairo airport. He makes a very good speech. We go to the Apostolic Nunciature; the entourage goes to the Sheraton Hotel. That same afternoon there are two significant visits: Shenouda III,[2] leader of the Coptic Orthodox, and the Grand Sheik of Al-Azhar University, Mohamed Sayed Tantawi.[3]

The two meetings are very cordial, which—considering the expectations of some—is surprising, especially in the case of Shenouda. There are no written speeches, but they are improvised. Shenouda speaks of Egypt as a "Holy Land," referring to the Holy Family who, he says, were here for "three and a half years."

For his part, Mohamed Sayed Tantawi is an educated man, probably an intellectual. His words are extremely cordial. Like Mubarak at the airport, he praises the Pope's attitude to the problems of the Middle East and to the Palestinian people. There is an exchange of gifts and I see, with some horror, that the Pope gives Tantawi a huge picture of the Holy Family . . . against the whole Muslim tradition of avoiding human images and representations. The Pope's valet, Angelo Gugel, looks very pleased when he passes him the gift.

---

1. Hosni Mubarak (Egypt, 1928–2020) was president of the Arab Republic of Egypt for thirty years (1981–2011). He resigned in 2011, following the protests of the so-called "Arab Spring." He was convicted and acquitted in a series of trials for which he spent six years in jail.

2. Shenouda III (Nazir Gayed Rufail) (Egypt, 1923–2012) was leader of the Coptic Orthodox Church from 1971 to 2012.

3. Mohamed Sayed Tantawi (Egypt, 1928–2010) was Grand Mufti of Egypt (1986–1996). Mubarak then appointed him "dean" of Al-Azhar University, considered the most prestigious Sunni Islamic school.

The Pope celebrates Mass the next day in an indoor sports stadium, which is packed with the faithful. Before the Mass, news reaches me of violent clashes between Catholics and Muslims in Nigeria, with more than 200 dead. I informed Re, proposing that the Pope make some reference to this. I press, because it seems important to me, and a paragraph is prepared for the Pope to read after the Mass.

In the afternoon, the ecumenical meeting in the Catholic Cathedral of Cairo, Our Lady of Egypt, took place in the same cordial atmosphere. There are representatives of the non-Catholic Christian confessions. Shenouda and the Pope spoke. He is even more cordial than yesterday and in his impromptu speech he says to the Pope: "I love you." The Pope repeats the same formula a little later.

The next day, we took off for Sinai in a Hercules C-130 military aircraft. There is no view of the landscape because it has no windows. Halfway through the flight, I look out of the cockpit and see the sandy desert of Sinai, sometimes interrupted by rocky massifs, and to the right the Red Sea. We land at a small airport and from there, after a twelve mile drive, we arrive at the Monastery of St. Catherine.

The abbot, Archbishop Damianos, is cordial. I am told that he has overcome his previous reluctance and, above all, those of his superiors of the Orthodox Patriarch of Jerusalem, on whom he depends. They take the Pope inside the small church of St. Catherine. They show him around a bit, but the Pope is eager to kneel down to pray. When he can, he does so at length. Then they show him some of the treasures they have there: the 5th century Codex Syriacus, a chalice, ancient codices, icons, parchments. . . .

The time comes to go down to the small place where one can see the roots of the bush where God revealed himself to Moses. We all take off our shoes and as soon as the Pope gets there, he kneels on the ground and I hear him murmur, in Italian, "*Io Sono colui che Sono*" ("I am who I am"),[4] the words with which God defined himself to Moses. He prays for a long time in silence. Then he visits the bush, still blooming, and the well of Jethro. Then he goes outside, where he will read his special speech. Damianos withdraws and leaves the Pope there. He cannot pray with him! He will return at the end. Later, while they are having lunch, they have a pleasant conversation, in sharp contrast to the fact that they cannot pray together, something which surprises me so much when it comes to Christians.

---

4. Cf. Exodus, 3:13–14.

To Accompany the Pope

March 2, 2000

This morning Dziwisz called me to ask me to come and have dinner with the Pope. He told me that he was dining out with some classmates at the Polish House on Via Cassia. If I came, I could keep the Pope company. Otherwise he would have to dine alone with Msgr. Mietek. With his great delicacy, he gave the impression that I was doing him a favor. I thanked him very much and told him not to hesitate for a second to ask me for this kind of "favor."

When I arrive, the Pope is dispatching Sodano, as he usually does on Thursdays. I wait in the chapel until 7:40 PM. I greet him and then we go into the dining room. He has a difficult and slow gait. He has lost expressiveness in his face. He has lost his smile.

We discussed some moments of the trip: the meetings with Shenouda, Mubarak, the Sheikh of El Ahzar and, above all, the visit to Sinai. He confirms that his thoughts were indeed on the words with which God made his name known.

He talks about the upcoming trip to the Holy Land and comments that it will be more difficult because of the many nuances that they must keep in mind. I tell him about how we have prepared the television coverage for the entire visit.

Speaking of the Holy Land, I tell him that someone told me that they had found some pages of his in Krakow, addressed to his priests, written when he returned from his trip to Jerusalem in 1963. Yes, he remembers that text. He asked where the pages were found. I told him that they were in the archives of the Curia in Krakow.

At the end of dinner, at the same table, he prepares to sign and dispatch the papers that have been brought to him from the Secretary of State's office. I notice that the first thing he reads this time is the press summary.

Forgiveness Day

March 12, 2000

First Sunday of Lent. Day of Forgiveness. An unprecedented liturgy in St. Peter's: asking God's forgiveness for what Christians of all times have done wrong—have sinned—by engaging in scandalous behavior, sometimes even in the name of the Church, and against other people. This morning's ceremony in the Vatican Basilica was moving.

The Pope presented the idea of Forgiveness Day at the consistory of cardinals a few years ago. I attended and saw the reaction—negative and surprised—among the cardinals. The Pope insisted on the proposal. Today, at last, the day he had been waiting for.

I think that the request for forgiveness came directly from the Pope's prayer. The tenacity with which he pursued it, despite the "opposition" of so many ecclesiastics, is typical of John Paul II. He welcomed the miseries of others, made them his own, "institutionalized" them within the Church, and publicly asked for forgiveness. Certainly, ecclesiology will be enriched by this gesture.

Public opinion—or at least published opinion—is divided. Each one interprets it in his own way. For me it is evident that the Pope's request for forgiveness is addressed to God. Forgiveness from God, for the excesses committed in history by some Christians against Jews, Muslims, agnostics, etc.

In the Holy Land

March 20–26, 2000

Trip to the Holy Land: Jordan, territories of the Palestinian National Authority—Bethlehem—and Israel. The attention was exceptional. TV stations from half the world were there. The Americans have multiplied their transmissions and programs. The media deployment was at full capacity.

The Pope has prepared well for this trip. Before leaving, he wanted his speeches to be read in various dicasteries: the second section of the Secretariat of State, Oriental Churches, Union of Christians. . . . They were very balanced texts.

Jordanian King Abdullah II began his private audience with the Pope by asking him for suggestions for the peace process. It has been a latent theme throughout the trip. I stayed for that audience so as not to leave the Pope alone.

The day in Bethlehem was for the Palestinians. And they were not disappointed. The Pope used the expression "torment" for the Palestinian odyssey; a torment that has lasted far too long. I tried to give statistical information on the number of Palestinians living as refugees in camps: it was only fair to do so. The Pope's emotion in the Bethlehem grotto was palpable. Two cameras—one of them fixed—showed those moments. The Pope then goes down to the manger. He asks for a chair, sits there and calmly prays his breviary.

President Ezer Weizman's speech at Tel Aviv airport set the tone for the Israeli attitude: no mention of Jesus; Jerusalem, united and eternal capital of Israel; "here is peace. . . ."

The voices in Israel are many and contrasted. It is a fact that the Jews of the Holy Land know very little about the Catholic Church and the Pope. They even ignore—at least 22 percent—the fact that the Holy See maintains diplomatic relations with Israel. The Orthodox groups are almost insulting.

The day of the 23rd begins with the celebration of Mass in the Cenacle. Apparently, since the Turks expelled the Franciscans from this place, no Mass has been celebrated here; at least, there is no official record of it. Concelebrating with the Pope are the cardinals and the twelve Catholic bishops of the area. At the end of the Mass, the Pope wishes to be alone in his thanksgiving. He kneels on the floor with his elbows resting on the altar as the entire room is cleared. Then he sits down and stays there for another twenty-five minutes. Discreetly, I remain with him.

That same morning we meet with the two Chief Rabbis of Israel at the headquarters of the Chief Rabbinate. They show great courtesy and understanding. In the private meeting, Lau, the Ashkenazi rabbi, says: "Holiness, we know that sometimes we ask you for things that you cannot give. . . ." This cordiality does not, however, prevent him from declaring, two days later, that the Pope's request for forgiveness at Yad Vashem—the Holocaust memorial—was insufficient.

Visit to the Grand Muftí of Jerusalem, and then to the Western Wall, relic of the Temple of Jerusalem. The text of the written prayer that the Pope left there, between the cracks of the millenary stones, reads as follows:

> God of our fathers,
> you have chosen Abraham and his descendants
> that your name might be made known to the nations:
> We are deeply hurt by the behavior of so many,
> in the course of history, have made these your children suffer,
> And, at the same time that we ask for your forgiveness.
> We want to commit ourselves in a true fraternity
> with the people of the covenant.
>
> Jerusalem, March 26, 2000
> (and the signature of the Pope)[5]

The Pope asks to go to Jericho. There are logistical problems: the area—Israeli authorities say—is full of bombs, it is not safe. The Pope insists and succeeds. They take him alone in a helicopter.

---

5. "God of our fathers, you chose Abraham and his descendants to bring your Name to the Nations: we are deeply saddened by the behaviour of those who in the course of history have caused these children of yours to suffer, and asking your forgiveness we wish to commit ourselves to genuine brotherhood with the people of the Covenant."

44

A Light in the Window

Pope's Birthday

May 17–19, 2000

Yesterday I spent the Pope's 80th birthday in Lublin, in eastern Poland. The John Paul II Institute of the Catholic University invited me to give a lecture on the Holy Father on that very date. The story began this summer during my days of rest in the Aosta Valley. As always, we were there with Tadeusz Styczeń, his disciple. He gave me a long "interview"—a conversation—about my personal history and my work at the *Sala Stampa*. Then he invited me to come to Lublin on the date of the 80th anniversary. I vaguely said yes, and that was that.

I started to prepare the text of the lecture. Then it was translated into Polish.

At Fiumicino airport, on my way to Poland, I phoned Luigi Accattoli who, ill at home, was "chasing" me to do an interview for the *Corriere*, on the occasion of the Pope's birthday. We talk for a long time and I give him the answers, asking him to read me the final text when I arrive in Poland, to get an overall idea. In Warsaw, another long phone call to complete some things.

Tadeusz is waiting for me at the airport, and we go to lunch with one of his assistants. Another interview, this time for the Polish Catholic news agency. Drive to Lublin and dinner at the hotel.

The following day, May 18, press conference at 10:00 AM followed by a TV interview. Lunch at the hotel. At 4:30 PM, the ceremony in the Aula Magna of the University: words of the Rector, words of Styczeń, my lecture with questions, reading of poems of the Pope with organ accompaniment. Then Holy Mass celebrated by Archbishop Jósef Zycinski and dinner. In the middle of dinner, they accompany me to the TV studios because they want to lead off the national news with an interview. Then it's off to sleep.

The next morning, I go to Mass at Tadeusz's house. Then we go to the Institute and from there I have interviews with a couple of newspapers.

When I talk to *Gazeta Wyborcza*, Adam Michnik, its promoter and editor-in-chief, invites me to visit him: "a symbolic visit." And I rush off to Warsaw, making a stop at the newspaper before heading to the airport. The schedule is so tight that Adam is waiting for me at the door with some of his editors.

Vladimir Putin

JUNE 6, 2000

The Pope received Vladimir Putin, the new president of the Russian Federation, yesterday afternoon. On his first trip as president, Putin came to see the Pope and to visit Italy. I speak with Sodano in the morning. We draft a communiqué. It is not likely that Putin will go to see Sodano: in fact, he is interested in meeting with the Pope. Sodano has arranged that, while Putin talks to the Pope, Tauran will talk to Ivanov, the Foreign Minister.

But in the afternoon, shortly before the audience began, Sodano called me: it was decided that the Pope would speak with Putin and a few minutes later, Sodano, Tauran, and Ivanov would come in to continue the conversation together.

The interview between Putin and the Pope lasts almost thirty minutes. The Pope is interested in the conversation and devotes more time to it than expected. When the final bell rings, Sodano and Tauran enter with Ivanov. They spend a few minutes chatting, the gifts are handed over and Putin's entourage enters: twenty-two people, including the mayor of Moscow.

As the Pope bids him farewell at the door, Putin still insists on the interest he attaches to the collaboration that exists between the Holy See and Russia "in international institutions, above all, for the maintenance of international peace."

When Putin leaves, Sodano, Tauran, and I approach him. I address the Pope directly, asking him for some information about what was discussed, to inform the journalists. "He has insisted on the union between East and West, and the importance he attaches to the Holy See in this," says the Pope. And he adds his impression of the person: "A new man for a new situation." That is the focus of the conversation and his impression of Putin. That's enough for me. I ask him if there has been talk about his possible visit to Moscow. "No, that has not been discussed."

Two Lists of Cardinals

January 29, 2001

Yesterday, at the Angelus, the Pope announced that on February 21 he would appoint seven new cardinals, whose names he read out. A week ago he had already communicated a list of thirty-seven. Why these new seven today? I ask for clarification, but the explanations I receive are not very convincing. And why does Karl Lehman, from Germany, now appear as Cardinal?[1]

In this situation, I cannot talk to journalists because I do not know what to tell them. Today, as I feared, the newspapers speak of internal pressure and of a change of opinion on the part of the Pope. At moments like these, I think then of those who want public opinion to be "benevolent" towards the Holy See, but are unwilling to give out information; unwilling to feed the flow of information.

I try my best to reconstruct what happened. The Pope had wanted to make Lehman a cardinal. But he encountered some opposition within the Curia, which argued against it. So what he did was include another German candidate on the list, so that between the two a certain balance of sensitivities would be established. That explains the confusion: an initial announcement without Lehman and a second list that included Lehman and the other cardinal.

Obviously, it was not easy to report on this situation in a way that was well understood. And, of course, the solution was not to explain away this mess either.

Lefebvrianos

March 22, 2001

Today the commission, chaired by the Pope, is meeting on the case of the Fraternity of St. Pius X (Lefebvrians).

It has been a long process, mostly led by Cardinal Castrillón Hoyos. In principle, they were willing to reach an agreement with the Holy See. Castrillon received an email today from the Superior of the Fraternity, Falley, telling him that what they want is to celebrate the Mass with the rite of St. Pius V. And there doesn't seem to be any major problems with that.

---

1. Lehman's appointment was unexpected for many observers due to Lehmann's relatively liberal views on abortion counseling and giving the Eucharist to divorced and civilly remarried parishioners.

However, not everyone follows the same line. There is one bishop, Williamson, who refuses any understanding and continues to insult us. He is the only one of the four Lefebvrian bishops who opposes the agreement.

Today we are issuing a brief communiqué confirming that these contacts exist. I only know that the Pope, accompanied by Castrillon, received the Superior of the Fraternity and that, for now, nothing has been signed.

Among Colleagues

April 4, 2001

Jorge Arandes, president of the Spanish Professional Association of Press, Radio and Television Reporters, is coming. It turns out that I have been awarded a prize, a silver microphone, which was brought to me today. I was accompanied by three other members of the association's board of directors. I thank them sincerely for the recognition and we talk for a while about professional matters.

Ukraine

June 23–27, 2001

In this trip I realize once again that what is really decisive is the presence of the Pope, and his interaction with the people. More than his speeches, his physical and moral presence make a difference. In Ukraine it is estimated that 4 percent of people are hostile to religion, 44 percent are non-believers, and the rest, divided among various confessions. It is known that there are also dissensions between Latin and Greek rite Catholics.

On June 26, the Pope presides over the first beatification ceremony in the history of Ukraine.

With Bush

July 23, 2001

Today, President George W. Bush is coming to Castelgandolfo. I speak with Laura, his wife, and one his daughters, Barbara. Dziwisz tells me that the Pope has a fever and an ear infection. What began to bother him in Aosta has worsened. He wears a discreet hearing aid to hear better.

The "Milingo Case"

August 2001

This month of August has been marked by the "affair" of Emmanuele Milingo, former Archbishop of Lusaka, Zambia, transferred years ago to the Vatican Curia because of pastoral anomalies in his country, of which he was the clear protagonist. In the Curia they do not know how to deal with him. Now in Rome and its surrounding areas, Milingo has gained quite a large following.

The fact is that Milingo disappeared for a while and reappeared in New York, announcing that he will marry a Korean lady—Maria Sung—following a ceremony of the Moon sect.[2] In the Vatican the news comes out in the most unusual way. One day Re receives a call from Don Gino Belleri, the priest who founded the "Libreria Leoniana." He tells him that he wishes to communicate "something very important." He tells me that the nuns who take care of Milingo's home had just come to his bookstore. They told him, in tears, that Milingo had called from New York to tell them to pack their belongings and return to Zambia, because he was going to get married in New York.

Re calls me and tells me all this. There are no further details. The only thing to do now is contact Milingo directly. Msgr. Martino, nuncio to the United Nations, tries to reach him. The archbishop of New York tries; they try from the nunciature in Washington. No one can talk to him. They all collide with Moon's followers in the person of a certain "Reverend" Shenker, spokesman of the sect.

Re, prefect of bishops, passes the matter to the Congregation for the Doctrine of the Faith, whose secretary, Bertone,[3] initiates a canonical process. But there is no way to communicate with Milingo. I am interviewed by *RAI*: I say that this situation does not call into question priestly celibacy but rather religious syncretism.

The announced ceremony takes place in May and is a major media topic. Milingo speaks repeatedly that he wants to have a child, that he does not want to leave the Church, etc. The Congregation for the Doctrine of the Faith gives

---

2. South Korean Christian sect founded by Sun Myung Moon in 1954, also known as Unification Church, or the Holy Spirit Association for the Unification of World Christianity.

3. Tarcisio Bertone (Italy, 1934) was secretary of the Congregation for the Doctrine of the Faith (1997–2003) with Cardinal Ratzinger as prefect; in 2003 he was appointed archbishop of Genoa and elevated to the cardinalate. In 2006, Benedict XVI appointed him Secretary of State, a position he held until 2013.

an ultimatum: if he does not retract and return to the discipline of the Church by August 20, he will be expelled from the priesthood and excommunicated.

When I return from my vacation on August 20, I find myself in the middle of a major media uproar, so I have to take charge. I think the first thing to do is prevent the Holy See from looking like they are the ones managing this story. It was said that Milingo had returned to Italy; that someone had taken him to Castelgandolfo—which was true—and that the Pope had told him "to return to Jesus Christ." He had been taken to a house of the Focolare near Castelgandolfo. People began to say that the Holy See had "kidnapped" Milingo.

I have three goals. First: that the Holy See does not appear in the foreground. It is better that everything be oriented as what it is, a purely human affair between Milingo and Mrs. Sung, which ended with the return to normality, without giving credence to the "Moon marriage" of New York. Second: to put some pressure on the people of the Moon sect, who have come to Rome and are giving interviews, always in the name of Mrs. Maria Sung. Third: to try to put an end to the affair as soon as possible.

Milingo was outside Rome with Don Pepe, a Focolare priest. We needed to let people know that Milingo had returned to the Church by his own decision, renounced his "marriage" by his own decision, that he would talk to Mrs. Sung, and that—naturally—he was not kidnapped by anyone. In fact, this was the only official statement of mine on the case.

I convinced Bertone that it was time for Milingo to speak on TV to say that he was the one who had managed the case and decided what to do, that he was not coerced by the Vatican, that he did not want to return to Maria. I contacted Fabio Zavattaro of *RAI*, Luigi Accattoli of *Corriere della Sera* and Orazio la Rocca of *La Repubblica*.

I go with Bertone to Cardinal Chelli's house to meet with Milingo. He is with Don Beppe. We have a relaxed conversation. Chelli asks us to stay for lunch. We accept. In Milingo I see a person with a very particular "forma mentis" (way of thinking), very singular. I bring him four questions with his answers for the interview this afternoon. He reads them and accepts. He asks me to take some points from the answers. I tell him that Moon's people are threatening to ask for damages for Maria's separation. I ask him if he signed anything in New York that could be construed as a civil marriage. He denies it. And he gets angry at this threat from the Moon sect's representative, Shanker.

Later in the afternoon Zavattaro, Accattoli, and La Rocca come. The interview is recorded in San Calixto. It is seen that Milingo has taken some ideas from the note I gave him, but he gives his own answers. After the interview, we try to adjust the content. In the evening he appears on the *RAI Uno* news and the next day his statements are published in *Corriere della Sera* and *La Repubblica*.

The Moon group changes their language. They become defensive. They begin by accepting that the end of the story is the only one: Milingo has returned to the Church.

On August 29, I get a phone call from Shanker. They are nervous. They want to finish everything as soon as possible. He tells me that Maria is now slipping out of their hands, that she is not obeying them. Naturally, I record the entire conversation. I pressure them, saying that if they don't agree to see Milingo and Maria today, it will take several more days and that won't be good for them.

After some back-and-forth, it was agreed that the meeting would be held at the "Hotel Arcangelo." I had thought of not attending the meeting, but Bertone suggests that I attend. I accompany Milingo to the planned room and we wait. After a while Maria arrives: silent, serious, restrained. They meet and we leave them alone, but they remain in sight, since there are three rooms in the place with no door separating them.

An hour and fifteen minutes later, I get fed up and decide to leave. Naturally, there is already a cloud of journalists at the door. I don't say a word. I go to my office to send the agencies the letter that Milingo has given to Maria during their meeting.

In the evening—around 9 o'clock—I get home and call Dziwisz to inform him; and Bertone, who knows nothing of how the meeting went. It is the end of a story that has filled the newspapers this August. The information published the following day is balanced.

On August 30, Shanker calls me. They want to bring me Milingo's things: his pectoral cross, cassock, briefcase. I tell them to come to my office sometime in the mid-morning the following day. When they come, at two o'clock in the afternoon, they tell me that Maria has sent Milingo's things to the laundry and that they won't be there until six o'clock in the evening. I don't tell them to go to hell, but I think about it.

They return at six o'clock in the evening. Shanker gives me his word that the photos they took at the meeting with Sung and Milingo will never be published. They bring everything that belongs to Milingo. I see in his attaché the forms for consecration, Moon's book with various pamphlets, a text of the lecture Milingo gave in Korea—full of praise for Father Moon and Mother

Moon—and a dated diary of Milingo from the days between his "marriage" and his arrival in Rome. There is nothing in it directly related to Maria Sung and much more related to an effort to understand—and accept—Moon's theories. That helps me to understand Milingo's unfortunate decision.[4] It all started from the head, from a syncretic indoctrination of Moon's ideas. The "marriage" was then included in a confusing theorem on the generation and perpetuation of the *Moonie* "Church."

The next day, Shanker and companions return to New York and Maria, I believe, returns a day later.

September 11

September 11–13, 2001

In a telegram to US President George W. Bush, the Pope expresses his "deep impression at the unspeakable horror of today's inhuman terrorist attacks against innocent people in various parts of the United States."

The following day, the Pope dedicates his general audience to the terrorist attacks in the United States, describing them as "a dark day in the history of humanity." And on Thursday the 13th, he receives the new US Ambassador to the Holy See, James Nicholson, and he assures him that he prays for America.

Kazakhstan and Armenia

September 22–27, 2001

Since the terrorist attack on the United States on September 11, the media have taken a closer look at everything related to Islam. Kazakhstan offers the image of a tolerant and unbelieving Muslim world. The country of a hundred ethnicities.

For many, the Pope is an extreme pacifist. Or at least, they want to present him that way, so that when the Americans carry out some warlike action they can say that the Pope is with the pacifist and anti-American sector.

In the first speech at the Astana airport, the Pope speaks of peace, but in the context of a country, such as Kazakhstan, which has made an anti-nuclear choice after the Soviet Union experimented with nuclear weapons on its soil.

---

4. In the years following this episode, Milingo was to be the protagonist in other actions (illegal ordination of bishops) that would lead to his excommunication (2006).

In spite of everything, many journalists read this text as an option for peace, in the sense of denying the United States any right to an armed reaction to the aggression it had suffered. Sodano, who has remained in Rome, detects this interpretation and tells Sandri so, and the latter communicates it to me.

At lunchtime I invite Phil Pullela—from *Reuters*—and I make some statements to him, in which I say that those who try to present the Pope as an extreme pacifist and those who describe him as an extreme warmonger are mistaken. In Christian ethics, the value of peace is subordinate to the common good.

But I am wrong to make these statements only to one journalist and I miscalibrate the reaction of the rest of the press. When *Reuters* releases the story, the other journalists get angry—rightly so—and come to see me at the hotel.

On the return trip, the Pope calls me and asks me what I thought of the trip. I gave him my impression. But I also tell him about the risks of these misleading presentations by some newspapers. He tells me that the Americans also have the right to defend themselves.

When we return to Rome, I have to leave immediately for Spain to take part in the Psychiatry Congress in Madrid. The Pope speaks at the Angelus that Sunday and twice uses the word "justice" in the context of the "terrible tragedy" of September 11.

War in Afghanistan

October 7, 2001

Military operations begin in Afghanistan. Confusion continues over the Pope's attitude to this complex reality, which some simplify without realizing the nuances, and others try to simplify for their own interests.

But extreme pacifism is not the same as the search for peace. And the legitimacy of self-defense cannot be forgotten. To emphasize one extreme or the other, without nuance, can lead to situating the Pope's teachings in favor or against a certain "side."

Slander Stings

November 11, 2001

A Polish weekly has published an article full of slander and falsehoods against me, Sodano, and others. They accuse me of boycotting meetings between journalists and the Pope, and of accepting gifts in exchange for putting people from the media in contact with the cardinals of the Curia. It is shocking to read such things.

I contact a Polish lawyer—Bednarkiewicz—and an Italian one—Vittorio Caporale—to look into possible legal action. But they both give me the same advice. It is better not to go to court, when it is only a question, as in this case, of the publishers seeking a scandal at all costs. This is the advice I would have given to someone else in my situation; but, in my case, I prefer to go to other professionals.

Preparing for the Assisi Journey

December 10, 2001

We are going to Assisi in three cars for an inspection visit in preparation for the Day of Prayer for Peace in the World on January 24. We are, among others, Harvey, Marini, and Father Lombardi. We have looked into the different possibilities and it seems that everything will work out. We will have to be back before the 24th though.

Justice, Peace and Forgiveness

December 11, 2001

Today we release the message for the day of Fasting for Peace, in which the Pope speaks of justice and forgiveness. "Without justice there is no peace; without forgiveness there is no justice."

Although, in my opinion, it is not a brilliant presentation, at least it clarifies our position on the condemnation of terrorism, on self-defense, along with the sense of forgiveness, without which there can be no real justice.

I think that this text puts an end to a period of ambiguity and a certain confusion, because there were different voices within the Church that addressed the question on another level, in practical and immediate terms, while the Pope spoke—above all—of asking for peace and working for peace. I hope that from now on we will be able to speak about this issue in a more unified way.

The Lighted Window

December 13, 2001

When I arrive at 7:30 PM, the Pope is praying in his chapel. I enter unnoticed and accompany him. He is kneeling at his kneeler, quietly singing a melody while reading a book. It is not his breviary. I don't know what he is singing, but it is not a Gregorian psalmody. He continues praying, singing, for a while, oblivious to everything else, on his knees, next to the Lord.

When he gets up, I leave the chapel and accompany him to the dining room. Dziwisz and Mietek are there. Dinner is very light: white rice cooked in the oven; lettuce salad and fruit. Seeing that he eats so little, I ask him what he will do tomorrow, during the Fasting Day for Peace.

> —I asked Sister Tobiana, who said: "The Holy Father, he fasts every Friday of the year!"

And so I learn that he is in the habit of fasting every Friday. I ask him about the intentions of his Mass: "Yes, for the end of terrorism, for peace." I tell him that his proposal to fast for peace has attracted a lot of attention from sectors far removed from Christianity, such as the Italian Communist left. We talk for a while about current issues and I see once again, with joy, that he is still aware of everything.

We comment on some articles that have appeared in the press recently that speak of a Pope isolated amidst the Curia. The Pope listens. I say that these articles are not credible or they intend to emphasize something else. And I mention one of them, signed by Accattoli. I say that my interpretation is that the author wanted to emphasize that bold and new initiatives always come from the Pope, and that, at times, in the Curia they are not understood or are not followed willingly.

He asks if there is any news about the Day of Prayer for Peace on January 24. I tell him that we have already been to Assisi. Then, I don't remember why, he begins to joke about how old he is, with his usual good humor, loose and relaxed.

At the end I tell him that he should go out sometime between Christmas and New Year's, to get some fresh air. As we say goodbye, Dziwisz tells me that they have decided not to go to Castelgandolfo this Christmas because the house gets quite cold. Besides, the Pope wants to stay in Rome because he knows that pilgrims find it comforting to see the light from his window on.

45

Abuses

An Orthodox Choir

January 1, 2002

At the Mass celebrated today in St. Peter's, a choir of women's voices from Moscow sang "with the blessing of Patriarch Alexis II." They were thirty-six young women who sing at the liturgies of the Moscow Patriarch. "I appreciate Russian liturgical singing very much, and I always feel very close to your culture, especially your religious culture," the Pope told them as he greeted them. It is a minimal sign of thaw between the Patriarch of Moscow and Rome. But on this long road every small step is important.

Day of Prayer for Peace

January 24, 2002

Assisi. A new initiative of the Pope in the wake of Assisi I (1986) and Assisi II (1996). To prepare it, we had a series of meetings at the Secretariat of State with Harvey, Marini, Sandri, and the three pontifical councils involved. Some questions had to be answered: who to invite, apart from the representatives of confessions and Churches; what form to give to the ceremony; the elaboration of the texts. During this period we have traveled twice to Assisi; the second time, in the same train with the Pope. The idea of the train came from Father Sapienza, from the Prefecture of the Pontifical Household, and I think it has been a success.

Seeing so many leaders of religions coming from all over the world, one cannot avoid the question: why are they coming? At the invitation of the Pope, no doubt, who at present is the only one who can afford to invite them with a reasonable chance of receiving affirmative responses. And this is something that is publicly recognized in Assisi; for example, by Rabbi Israel Singer of the World Jewish Congress. There is also the desire to contribute something concrete to the great theme of world peace; and also the desire not to be "left out" of an important event. But why did you take this initiative? Do you expect results?

I think the first answer is that there are things that must be done because they can be done. There is an imperative in this that goes above any fear of not achieving results (peace). At Assisi we launch an idea. It is a precedent for future history. You never know how an idea will develop.

"There is no religious intention that can justify the practice of man's violence against man." In the light of historical experience, this affirmation of John Paul II is still new. . . . It is an idea that has the possibility of a future. It can spread, penetrate consciences and ways of thinking, to the point of acquiring the force of an ethical principle of universal value.

During the ceremony, I go to the *RAI* production room. There I greet Galli della Loggia, historian and well-known columnist for *Corriere della Sera*. He asks many questions. History—he says—teaches that religions have caused wars. I tell him that there have been instrumentalizations that, in the light of the Pope's words, were a tragic mistake.

Dioceses in Russia

February 11, 2002

Today we communicated the Pope's decision to elevate the four existing apostolic administrations in the Russian Federation to the category of dioceses. I have spoken these days with Cardinal Kasper to gather documentation on this whole subject. With this information I prepared today's statement.

It is said, among other things, that Catholics in Russia are recognized as having the same organization and pastoral care as Russian Orthodox living in the West (there are Russian Orthodox dioceses in Vienna, Berlin, Brussels, etc.). And that it is not really a question of introducing new ecclesiastical structures, but of restoring those already existing at the beginning of the Russian Revolution, bringing them up to date with the present situation.

At the same time, it is recognized that, as things stand, it is difficult to define precisely the number of Catholics in the territory of the Russian Federation. It can be stated, not far from the truth, that the figure is around 1,300,000.

The reaction in Moscow was predictable, but at least public opinion got our point of view across. And that helped.

Scandals

MARCH 10, 2002

On Saturday, February 16, Stanisław called me at home. Two topics: one is a scandal in Poland because of certain accusations against the bishop of Poznam; the second is that the Pope is suffering from a pain in his right knee and will not go tomorrow to visit the Roman parish he was scheduled to visit. The second is easy: I prepare a text for the press and announce that the Pope will have his usual Angelus appointment.

The first issue is more delicate. One cannot give the impression—as some would like—that the Holy See wants to "cover up" this matter. On the other hand, one must be respectful of everyone's rights, including the alleged perpetrator and the alleged victims of sexual harassment. I give a brief statement that has a great echo in Poland, and less so here, since in Italy the issue is not news.

The following week, Dziwisz calls me again: the Pope is still in pain. I tell him that we will let the press know without any problem. He is a little worried about the possible negative effects of making this information public. I reassure him that this information does no harm, quite the contrary. Both the previous week and this week I spoke with Buzzonetti beforehand, to confirm the precise medical terms.

Finally, on Tuesday March 5th, Sandri tells me that the Pope will not come down for the general audience the following day, Wednesday, because of the same knee discomfort. I prepare the communiqué and give it to the press. And nothing happens.

Meanwhile, American public opinion is in turmoil because of the scandal of some priests accused of pedophilia in various dioceses. Melinda Henneberger of the *New York Times* calls me on the phone about this issue and, among many other things, I tell her that I believe that a candidate for the priesthood who is homosexual should not be ordained. The statement sparks a controversy in the United States. There are those who write that there are wonderful priests who are homosexuals; others say that if homosexuals were not ordained, it would be a huge problem for the Church there, since many American clergy are homosexuals, including some bishops. The *Boston Globe*, which is the newspaper that has uncovered the scandal in Boston, has published a long article with such statements.

The fact is that there is no document in the Holy See that explicitly says that a homosexual should not be ordained. I discussed this with Giuseppe

Pittau, secretary of the Congregation for Universities and Seminaries, and he confirms that such a document does not exist, although—apparently—one is being prepared that addresses that question.[1]

The Pope's Medical Care

March 12, 2002

The Pope continues to have pain in his knee, although this week he has kept his Wednesday general audience.

Renato Buzzonetti underwent surgery after Christmas for a sarcoma in the hamstring flexors of his right leg. I spoke to him on the phone. I told him I would come by his house to pick him up and we would go for a long walk in a park somewhere. Afterwards, we could have lunch together. That's the plan we made.

In my long conversation with Renato, while we were walking in Villa Doria Pamphili, we naturally talked about the Pope. It is a subject that worries him because of his responsibility as his doctor and because of the objective difficulties he encounters in caring for him as he would like to. It is complicated to take him to the hospital for proper check-ups. At least now, fortunately, he is doing exercises with a physiotherapist.

In anticipation that the Pope may have a problem with laryngeal obstruction while eating, an aspirator has been installed in the room next to the dining room. Because of the ear infection problem, which he had last year in the Aosta Valley, Renato has recommended that he avoid high altitude excursions.

To complete the picture, my dentist, Ezio Benagiano, who is also the Pope's dentist, tells me that he needs to see the Holy Father, but he always receives the reply that he does not have time. It seems that there is never time for proper care. There are other priorities.

At another point in the day, I also spoke with Piero Marini. He is at home because he has undergone knee surgery for a meniscus problem. So the Pope, his doctor, and his master of ceremonies, are all walking with a cane, although neither Buzzonetti nor Marini's condition has been reported.

---

1. On November 4th, 2005, the Congregation for Catholic Education published a document dedicated to this topic: "Instruction on the Criteria for Vocational Discernment in Relation to Persons with Homosexual Tendencies before Admission to the Seminary and Holy Orders."

Contacts with Orthodox

March 13, 2002

This morning a delegation of six people from the Greek Orthodox Church is coming to my office. Two days ago I was with them at a dinner at the Greek Embassy. The atmosphere was excellent: open, friendly, and cordial language. I don't know what they have in their heads, but their hospitality was great. I think that before the Pope's trip to Greece in May last year, this kind of relationship would have been inconceivable.

It never ceases to amaze me that the Greek Orthodox still refuse to pray even an Our Father with Catholics.

The Drama of Sexual Abuse

March 22, 2002

For more than a month, the scandal of sexual abuse of minors committed by priests in the United States has been at the forefront of the news. It is still too early to get a complete picture. My opinion is that this is a very painful tragedy that must serve to purify what is rotten. And I believe that part of the purification—for me, at least—also consists in putting up with the arrogance of certain sectors of the press. Along with many truths, the subject has been treated with a "crusade" approach that has omitted elements of our defense.

It is difficult to pass judgment on some aspects of this drama. The bishops are accused of having covered up conduct that, in addition to seriously violating the moral law, is a legal crime. Should they have communicated to the prosecutor any accusation made by victims—or presumed victims? This is the attitude they have adopted. But now they are required to do more. They must immediately communicate to the police or the judicial authority any accusation, even anonymous ones, and before they themselves investigate the likelihood of guilt.

The situation has many implications. But some of the press tries to look for causes where there are none. Some supposedly "solid" news organizations argue that the root of the problem is the Church's rule on priesthood being only for celibate men. Others analyze the climate of a Church that, by distinguishing crime—criminal or civil—from sin, allows abuses like this to take place. Many comments take a slant that I consider superficial.

On the other hand, it seems impossible to make any voice heard on the part of the Church. Every day I am under an enormous pressure of questions and calls from American journalists accredited in Rome. And there is no way to respond if, as I believe I must, I am to speak about facts and not about general issues of moral theology. There is no voice that dares to enter this hornet's nest of public opinion.

I have on my agenda the presentation of the Pope's letter to priests. In it there is a paragraph in which he refers to this topic. But as things stand, Cardinal Castrillón, prefect of the Congregation for the Clergy, who will present the letter—will be devoured by aggressive questions. I talk it over with him and I see that he is aware of the problem, and that he would almost prefer not to come to present the letter . . . , which would be even worse.

A temporary measure comes to mind: to the first question on the topic, respond with a written statement that addresses some aspects of the problem, and do not accept other questions on the same subject. He is relieved with this formula. What I am also trying to do is frame Castrillón's text as the response, for now, of the Holy See to the issue. And I am also trying to avoid leaving Castrillon alone—that is to say, as the only one responsible.

The press conference proceeds as planned: a fire extinguisher; a defensive soccer match; the lesser evil. Questions are asked on every possible and imaginable topic. At least, the press the next day gives prominence to the words of the Pope's letter, even though there are jabs at Castrillón. Curiously, the American press does not give the substance of Castrillon's argument. The *New York Times* focuses its interest on the formal aspect of the press conference itself, rather than on its content.

American Cardinals are Coming

April 23–24, 2002

A few weeks ago I learned—through the press—that a meeting of cardinals from the United States has been convened at the Holy See with people from the Curia to discuss the situation that has arisen in the country as a result of the cases of pedophilia in the clergy.

Little by little, this extraordinary meeting, in which the presidency of the United States Conference of Catholic Bishops and the heads of various offices of the Holy See will also participate, is taking shape. At first, it seems that it will be organized by the Congregation for the Clergy; then, partly because of the reactions and the interest it has aroused, we realize that it needs to be more prepared. The scheme changes: the Cardinal Secretary of State will preside.

For my part, I try to see what informative line can be adopted. I come to the conclusion that there is none, because the informative dimension is not present in the mentality of the meeting's organizer.

I try, at least, to draw up a brief paragraph that gives an idea of the agenda and the purpose of the meeting during these days. But the day before I intend to give the news, I am told that nothing should be given. Therefore, we start with an unprecedented expectation of public opinion and not even an idea that circumscribes and explains its purpose.

But, in good conscience, I could not leave things like this. In anticipation of the situation, and taking into account that all the American television networks have been accredited in Rome these days and many special envoys have come, I coordinated with the spokesman for the bishops of the United States, Msgr. Francis Maniscalco. He will be the one to speak out, since the Holy See does not seem to be willing to say anything.

A daily schedule of briefings with groups of bishops and the press is established. I tell him to do what he wants at the North American College, but not in the Sala Stampa. If there is nothing I can say on my part, at least let this whole merry-go-round of public opinion be fed in some way by what they say.

While the meeting was in progress, I finally received a call to tell me that Sodano wanted me to attend the meeting, which was being held in the Sala Bologna, in order to prepare the final communiqué. I follow the discussion that takes the form of statements read by the representatives of the Curia.

Two drafts of the communiqué were prepared: one written by the Americans (McCarrick) and the other by the Curia (Castrillon and Bertone). They are two different viewpoints, difficult to reconcile. For example, Castrillón wants something about the inadvisability of ordaining homosexuals; McCarrick opposes it on the grounds of not further inflaming public opinion.

The meeting ends around 8:00 PM and a lukewarm, but not entirely bad, communiqué finally comes out. Maniscalco asks me to hold a press conference. I agree, but the text still needs to be typed out and translated into English. Also (patience!) the Holy See's server is down. The result is that the conference takes place at 11:00 PM when we are still at the press conference with Gregory, McCarrick, and Stafford.

Toronto. Guatemala City. Mexico

August 3, 2002

We returned yesterday from our trip with the Pope to Toronto—for the XVII World Youth Day—Guatemala, and Mexico: almost 22,000 kilometers [13,671 miles]. The Pope has puzzled us once again. His health was bad since the previous trip to Azerbaijan, and everyone expected that he would not move, that he would not be understood when speaking. However, the Pope decides to descend the stairs of the plane on his own in Toronto, even though the freight elevator was ready for his descent. He delivers the arrival speech in a clear voice and the people are taken aback.

He spends a couple of days at Strawberry Island, and that's good for him, too. I see him on the 26th when I go there with fourteen boys to have lunch with him. On the way back, I explain on live TV how things went.

The rest of the program goes as planned: the Pope, making an effort, speaks in a clear and strong voice. At the vigil, we estimate that around 400,000 young people attended; this is the figure that appears in the press. At the Mass, we think it was around 800,000. The Canadian press is very much in awe.

I tell reporters that the Pope would like to go to the meeting of families in Manila in January 2003. I did not know that Sodano had written to the Philippines saying he would not go. But during this trip the Pope tells Dziwisz that he would like to go.

Guatemala: great. The streets full of people. Kilometers of flower tapestries line the route where the popemobile will pass. They tell me that there have been 20,000 volunteers who have distributed all along the route to make these works of art. At the Mass, the local police told me, enthusiastically, that 800,000 people attended. I prefer to be more prudent and say, for my part, that there were more than 500,000.

Mexico is . . . Mexico. Several million people in the streets. Tiredness and effort are noticeable in the Pope, who continues to do all he can, but his voice is less clear than in Toronto. The canonization ceremony of Blessed Juan Diego, in the Basilica of Guadalupe, is splendid. The traffic is so chaotic that the procession gets stuck in traffic.

On the 5th, back in Rome, we go to lunch with the Pope at Castelgandolfo. What interests him, as he says, is to "find out" how the trip went. Because he has lived it intensely from the inside.

46

Just War?

Krakow: So Many Memories

August 22, 2002

From the 16th to the 19th in Poland for the eighth time. On this occasion, it is a trip of memories, of thinking about and appreciating the experiences that built the character and life of John Paul II. And at the same time, a visit to propose new priorities. Concretely, on this trip he proposes a "new pastoral of mercy for the Church."

I had time to talk to him on the afternoon of the 17th, when he was receiving the civil authorities and a long series of private groups at the archbishop's residence. Many memories? —"Yes, so many; I used to come to this very room to talk to Cardinal Sapieha when I was a worker at Solvay." But it seems to me, Holy Father, that you are not what is called a sentimental man. —"Insofar as . . . ," he replies, with an incomplete sentence.

Yes, feelings exist and play their part, no doubt about it. But he controls them. He lets them come to the surface now, perhaps to amuse himself by the vast changes his life has undergone. Yesterday he recalled, at the end of the consecration ceremony of the sanctuary of the Divine Mercy, that by these places "I used to pass by when I was a boy, with my wooden shoes, when I went to work in the quarry. Who would have said that that boy would be here today dedicating this temple!" Again, he references the memory of that time when he worked as a manual laborer while maturing in his vocation.

Improvisations also the next day, after the Mass in the great Blonia esplanade: "I wish I could tell you 'until I see you again'. . . . But my life is in God's hands." And when the people chanted, "Stay here!," he responded with irony: "Some would like me not to return to Rome . . . !" Perhaps a reference to some journalistic speculation published before the trip. But, when—a day later—he asks them to pray for him, he does so with a phrase that—in these years—has become a conscious and heartfelt refrain: "Pray that I may lead to the end of my ministry."

On one of the trips I spoke with Sodano about the possible trip to Manila. He had already written a letter to the nuncio to announce that the Pope would not go. But since the Pope himself—on the trip to Toronto—made some comment that he would like to go, Sodano tells me that the nuncio has been told to keep the letter to himself for the time being. "Imagine at the ridicule we will get if I say he's not going and then he goes . . ." In September, the President of the Philippines will travel to Rome. No doubt she will insist to the Pope that he make the trip.[1]

As I am preparing for a press conference with Franciszek Macharski, I ask the Pope if there has been any response from Putin. He tells me that a letter has been received in which he reaffirms good relations with the Holy See, but says nothing about the case of Bishop Mazur.[2] Therefore, the answer we agreed on, in case the subject comes up in the meeting with journalists, was: "A letter has been received which begins by recalling the good relations with the Holy See. . . . It is a letter that is considered as interlocutory and open to future developments."

On the afternoon of the 18th, the Pope visits some places related to his youth in Krakow privately. He enters the Wawel Cathedral and spends half an hour in prayer before the main altar. His physical condition does not allow him to go downstairs to the Crypt, where he celebrated his first Mass fifty-six years ago.

Canonization of St. Josemaría

October 6, 2002

Canonization of Josemaría Escrivá, founder of Opus Dei. I see no other prayer than *Gratias tibi Deus, gratias tibi* ("Thanks be to you, Lord, thanks be to you"). In it, the words go to God and also to the new saint for his fidelity, for what he has done with his life, of which all of us who are present today in St. Peter's, those who are not here and those who will come, are in some way the fruit. For me, it is particularly moving. He is a saint I have known and dealt with.

The ceremony was a marvel for many reasons, among them the number of people present, and for what these people let us glimpse into their own lives.

---

1. In the end, the Pope would not travel to Manila. But he wanted somehow to participate in the IV World Meeting of Families by means of a TV connection from Rome (January 25, 2003).

2. On February 11, 2002, John Paul II appointed Bishop Jerzy Mazur as Bishop of Irkutsk in Siberia, but on April 19th the Russian authorities expelled him from the territory of the Russian Federation without explanation. On April 23, 2003, he was appointed Bishop of Elk (Poland).

From half past eight in the morning I am on the *RAI* direct broadcast with Vittorio Messori and Giuseppe de Carli. When the Mass is about to begin, I leave them and follow it from the sanctuary. The Pope gives a wonderful homily, not too long. Then he improvises a speech at the end of the Mass.

At the end of the ceremony, Dziwisz calls the Prelate of Opus Dei, Echevarría, to greet the Pope, and when the Pope is about to get into the vehicle (a "Compagnola") with which he will travel to the end of via della Conciliazione to greet the crowd, Dziwisz offers one of those gestures that characterize his personality: he invites the Prelate to also get into the vehicle behind the Pope. And this is how the Pope travels the entire itinerary: with Dziwisz and with Echevarría.

In the afternoon, I call Dziwisz to talk about the day. I told him that for me it was a day of thanksgiving. Dziwisz tells me that the day was also great "for its theological significance." He was referring to the spectacle of faith in the square, which seemed like a living explanation of the universal call to holiness, which is at the heart of St. Josemaría's message.

The Scandal Continues

October 18, 2002

On the 14th, the president of the US bishops' conference, Wilton Gregory, and his vice-president and secretary are coming to Rome. They are traveling to receive a response to their proposals of last June on how to deal with the serious problem of pedophile priests and its painful consequences.

It is up to the Congregation for Bishops to prepare the response. The orientation has fluctuated. Re, prefect of that Congregation, was rather inclined to give an answer along the lines of: "Since you approved these norms *ad experimentum*, go ahead with them and we will see each other in a year's time." And a draft had been prepared along these lines. But the thesis of the Congregation for the Doctrine of the Faith, not to give any approval nor to consider the *experimentum* valid, prevailed. Thus, Re's final response is to point out that there are reasons of ambiguity of language and non-harmony with the universal law of the Church, which prevent approval. Proposal: to form a mixed commission—four members from the Holy See and four from the United States—to modify the original text.

Gregory accepted and proposed to immediately begin the work of the new mixed commission, but the Americans had to propose their names, while the Holy See had already indicated theirs (Castrillón, Bertone, Herranz, and Monterisi).

The subject comes out in the press with different nuances. There is talk of partial rejection of some aspects of the rules. This is the idea that Gregory has let pass. The reaction in America is disparate, depending on the sector being questioned. It seems to me that there is a sense of relief among American priests. Some say it expressly: at last there is someone who defends us, in the sense that it is taken into account that the accused is not automatically guilty. Among the bishops, the predominant comments are that nothing has changed, that it is only a question of fine-tuning the original text, and that in the meantime the norms remain in force as they were approved.

At the Italian Parliament

November 14, 2002

Today the Pope went to the *Camera dei Deputati*, where he delivered a much applauded speech. This is another historic first: never before had a Pope visited the Italian parliament. The visit was not at all easy. But it was a success.

I spoke with Pier Ferdinando Casini, president of the Chamber, a few weeks ago. We had lunch together to prepare for the visit. Then we had another long conversation. He accompanied me to the Aula and we saw how it would be arranged. About the gift to the Pope, he told me that he was thinking of an edition of the Italian Constitution. As he asked me for suggestions, I recommended that he follow rather the biographical-personal line. In the end, the gift consisted of a scale copy of the bell of the Wavel Cathedral in Krakow, which rings on great occasions of Church and State.

We spoke on the phone several times afterwards. Casini had sent his speech to Dziwisz. He then asked him to read it to Msgr. Fisichella, who is also chaplain of the Chamber. Casini told me, "I joked with him, because he has made corrections to me and I told him that he was worse than the Holy Office." Casini is afraid that the Pope's speech—which he had not previously read—would go into some very specific topics.

The day before the visit, around 9:00 PM, I called Casini on the phone. With the experience of the last few months, I told him that it would be good if some deputies applauded the Pope at various points in his speech. Not to create a positive reaction, which I had no doubt of, but because the applause would allow the Pope to pause briefly, breathe, and better deliver his speech. He told me not to worry, that I was sure they would applaud more than I imagined. In fact, it went so well that the deputies interrupted him more than twenty times.

It was interesting to note how the deputies of one tendency applauded more when the Pope mentioned a theme "proper" to their areas. On the left, the themes of peace and the fight against unemployment. On the right, the family and the free schools. There were very few deputies who did not attend: La Malfa, from the Masonic area; Cossutta, from the Veteran-Communist area, and few others. The Pope was happy and in good spirits. After the speech, while he was sitting in the Hall of Ministers waiting for his colloquy with the President of the Republic, Ciampi, he made a nice sign to me, almost a military salute: a joke as if to say that he was putting himself at my orders.

The next day I spoke to Casini again. He was happy and relieved. He told me that when he read the speech in the morning—which we had sent him before the official event—he was a little uneasy because of the direct references to specific issues of Italian politics. But then, he was surprised at how well received it was.

Giovanni Agnelli Dies

January 30, 2003

A few days ago Giovanni Agnelli, president of *FIAT*, a large corporation in Italy, passed away. It was known that he was ill—prostate cancer—, but at no time had a note or communiqué been given, either about his illness or about the developing prognosis.

I cannot help but think of the contrast his story holds with the information system we have followed here every time the Pope has been ill. In spite of the difficulties, we have always given all the opportune information. I note this as a simple observation, without value judgments or comparisons.

Iraq War Rumors

February 4, 2003

It seems that the beginning of a war with Iraq is approaching. The position of the Holy See has appeared in a fragmentary and incomplete way. Public opinion knows that the Holy See is against it, that the Pope is against it, but it seems to me that there has been no clear moral formulation on this issue.

There is general talk of just or unjust war, but what people seem to be waiting for is whether "this" war is just or not. So far, perhaps the clearest enunciation was presented by the Pope in his address to the diplomatic corps last

January 13. There he repeated the idea that only in very specific circumstances can a war be considered just:

> And what about the threat of war that could befall the people of Iraq, the land of the prophets, people already exhausted by more than twelve years of embargo? War is never a means like any other that can be resorted to in order to settle disputes between nations. As the Charter of the United Nations and international law recall, it can only be adopted in extreme cases and under very strict conditions, without neglecting the consequences for the civilian population, during and after the operations, even if the aim is to ensure the common good.

When the audience with the Holy Father ended, both the US and Iraqi ambassadors were enthusiastic about this formulation, indicating that it is open to various interpretations.

The problem is: with what we know now, is this war allowed or not from the point of view of the two cited sources, or from the point of view of morality?

More about Iraq

March 4, 2003

The climate of international uncertainty surrounding the Iraq crisis continues. Different episcopal conferences and non-Catholic Christian confessions have echoed the statements of the Holy Father and the Holy See: Martino, Tauran, Sodano.

Later, the position of France and Germany crystallized against war, favoring the role of UN inspectors to achieve the disarmament of weapons of mass destruction, without recourse to military action. Europe appeared divided, and NATO members were also divided when Turkey asked them for preventive assistance.

All this has contributed to isolate—relatively speaking—US President George W. Bush. The United States has tried, especially at the beginning, to seek an ethical "cover" for this war. Condoleeza Rice, Bush's national security advisor, developed the concept of "preventive war." But she soon had to abandon it: criticism on the level of principles and from the practical point of view is too easy. The objectives of this war have been changing: first, to disarm Saddam; then, regime change in Iraq; finally, to establish democracy in the Middle East.

The Pope's position and prestige have made the Holy See—or rather, the Pope himself—an international point of reference. The German Minister of Foreign Affairs, Fisher, visited the Holy See on his return from New York, where he participated in the Security Council meeting. Then it was the turn of Kofi Annan, Secretary General of the United Nations. Then came Tarik Aziz, Saddam Hussein's envoy. Then came Tony Blair. Finally, José María Aznar, who unconditionally supports the American position.

On all these occasions I spoke to the Pope immediately after each audience. Good impression of Annan: he told the Pope that he was a pessimist—like Fisher before him—and that there was nothing to do but pray. Aziz communicated to the Pope the well-known ideas: we are a moderate Islamic country, not a fundamentalist one, etc. And he made their fear of a new war clear.

The Moral Problem of War

MARCH 29, 2003

The war in Iraq continues and its repugnant face is beginning to show: civilian deaths, prisoners, anguish, terror, violations of international law. Public opinion remains divided. The battle is being fought both in Iraqi cities and on TV. Everyone is trying to gain consensus with half-truths and lies.

But it seems to me that in all of this the underlying moral issue is being ignored: is it a just war or not; is the situation we see every day on TV, with its procession of deaths and suffering, moral?

The Holy See's line has been developed by Tauran. His argument is intelligent: this war violates international law. That is why my statements after Bush's speech, precisely at the moment when it was decided to start the war, were along these lines: "Whoever decides that the peaceful ways made available by international law have been exhausted assumes a great responsibility before God, his conscience and history."

The Pope, for his part, recalls the general principle of Christian morality on the "just war:" war is the last resort and must be in accordance with very specific criteria (proportionality, etc.). From the moment the war began, the Pope's words are aimed at asking for peace, praying for peace and feeling close to those who suffer.

At the same time as the war in Iraq, the crisis in North Korea, which is developing nuclear technology and refusing to allow inspectors from the UN's specialized agency to enter. The Americans—with Colin Powel—say in this case, that the way to deal with it is through multilateral consultations. This seems to be a different path than the one they are following with Iraq.

Colin Powell Hearing

June 2, 2003

The Holy Father receives Colin Powell, Secretary of State of the United States. It is the first contact at this level since the war in Iraq. While the Pope was speaking with Powell, I discussed a different topic with Dziwisz: the proposed European Constitution which, in the preamble, speaks of European roots in terms of the Greek and Roman heritage and then goes straight to the Age of Enlightenment, skipping the whole Christian tradition, which it does not even mention.

Dziwisz asked me what could be done to inform the Pope. I mentioned several proposals: mobilization of the European Episcopal Conferences, the Catholic universities, and some rectors of other universities; with the Greek Orthodox—who had expressed their sensitivity to this issue—a joint declaration could be sought. I have also told him that I could go to Madrid and talk to Aznar personally. In short, many things could be done, since there is still time.

When the audience with Powell was over, I spoke with the Pope. He tells me that it was a long conversation, and that they discussed, among other things, the new prospects for peace in the Holy Land and in the Middle East. The Pope is happy with the conversation. A final curiosity: he tells me that when they were leaving he asked him if he was related to Baden Powell, founder—among other things—of the scout movement. Colin replied that he did not know for sure, that he had to do more research.

I tell the Pope briefly about the preamble of the Constitution. I mention some European politicians, such as Chirac, and the Pope makes a gesture which I interpret as an expression of disappointment.

The European Constitution

June 8, 2003

Dziwisz tells me that "what we talked about the other day (about the new European Constitution) I told the Pope. And I know that the Pope has already said something."

In fact, the Pope spoke to Sandri and told him that some ideas had to be put into action, to provoke initiatives from episcopal conferences, intellectuals, etc. Sandri then told Cardinal Sodano. This explains the ease with which Sodano gave me the green light to go to Spain to talk to Prime Minister Aznar.

I arrive in Madrid at midnight. The Nuncio is waiting for me. At 11 o'clock the next morning I was received by Aznar at La Moncloa. I did not know Aznar, but it seemed to me that he was one of the presidents of the governments of European countries who could act in this field, if the reasons were explained to him.

I pointed out to Aznar the absurdity of omitting in the preamble of the European Constitution any reference to Christianity. The conversation lasted half an hour. Aznar left a few days later to participate in the closing of the semester of Greek presidency in Thessaloniki, where the draft constitution was to be delivered.

Some time later, the press reported that Aznar had asked for the inclusion of a sentence referring to Christianity in the context of Europe's roots in the preamble. He had also raised the same issue in the meeting he had with the leaders of the European People's Party.

A Congratulation

July 26, 2003

Today is my saint's day and I am spending a few days away from Rome. The pager went off and I saw that it was Dziwisz. I immediately called him on the phone. They are in Castelgandolfo. I thanked him for his congratulations, which I received in writing a few days ago. He congratulated me again and told me: "The Holy Father sends you his best wishes. Already yesterday he prayed for you and also this morning. And he sends you his greetings with *riconoscenza*—with gratitude. We remember you. I told him that I was very grateful for what he was telling me and that in these days of rest I was praying for the Pope, his work and health.

I asked him if the Pope was still writing the book of memories of his years as bishop. He told me that he had already finished it and was correcting some details. But he added that he had written a new book, with recollections and assessments of the century that has passed. And he commented that the Pope himself had asked Tauran to read it to see if it should be published or "go directly to the archive," because it contains many judgments about situations and people. This is fantastic news, and also shows his vitality. I hope, of course, that the book does not go to the archive![3]

---

3. The first of the aforementioned books was published on May 18, 2004, under the title *Get Up, Let's Go!* The second book, *Memory and Identity,* was published on February 23, 2005, a few weeks before the death of John Paul II.

47

"No puede más" ("I Can Give No More")

The Pope's Limitations

August 15, 2003

Yesterday Thursday—August 14—I go to Castegandolfo in the morning. I have a long conversation with Dziwisz. We talk about the two books that the Pope has recently written: the one of personal memories about his years as bishop, and the other, reflections on Europe. The first is already finished; Ratzinger has seen it. The second has been read by Tauran, who has made a few minor changes. Then it went through Sandri for stylistic adjustments, and now Sodano is reading it.

I tell him about my planned editions for these two books. I also propose to make a new edition for the book of poems—*Triptico Romano*—, which could be distributed by the weekly *Panorama* around October 16, the anniversary of the election. He tells me it is a good idea; we will have to talk to the *Vatican Typography* for the management of the copyrights.

Dziwisz then elaborates. He says that the Pope is not well these days, that he has problems with low blood pressure—also in connection with the heat—and that when he celebrates Mass in the morning he ends up completely sweaty. Then his underlying concern comes to light: "How long can it go on like this?"

And not knowing how or when this can end, the subject of resignation is raised again. "How do you see it?" I reply, "Stanisław, years ago you first asked me the same question. Then I told you that resignation, in my opinion, was not an option. Now the question arises again because the physical limitations are obvious. But at the same time it does not arise because God wants to tell those of us who are close to the Pope—but not the Pope himself, who lives on a different level from us—that we have to live abandoned, to live for the day because he does not want us to see his greater plan. We have to live without thinking about tomorrow, which God wants to hide."

"Something like what the Pope wrote in his encyclical on Our Lady: the itinerary of faith.[1] She did not see everything from the beginning, she did not know what was going to happen tomorrow, and she lived from day to day, abandoned to God. And about resignation: perhaps God wants to make us see that the Church is something different from other organizations that always have someone young and dynamic at the head. A few years ago, in the face of certain pronouncements, there was criticism of the Pope. Now, nobody criticizes the Pope. There is, naturally, criticism of the Church's doctrine by non-believers, but they do not dare to criticize the Pope personally. . . ."

Dziwisz was thoughtful. And after a bit he said to me, "What you say, have you been thinking about it for a long time or did it just occur to you now?" I told him that I had thought about it a lot and that I say it to myself frequently.

Dziwisz's question leads me to consider once again that it is not only a matter for him: the Pope himself must be asking himself this question in the face of this progressive incapacity, which is becoming more and more evident. And this suggests that his suffering is perhaps not primarily physical, but rather moral. He is not spared doubts. Probably, neither is there any lack of petitions to God that the end of his life not be prolonged for too long. What happens if this situation lasts and the progressive disability continues? He can no longer walk. He cannot stand without support. His diction is sometimes almost unintelligible. There are breathing and swallowing problems. And there is a Church to govern; a daily public activity to exercise; a continuous global visibility. Resignation?

Despite the serious issues we have discussed, we say goodbye with a smile. I ask him if he will go to Poland. I think it would be great, and perhaps even necessary, if he could get away for a few days. He laughs and tells me that he is fine here. Actually, he understands that it is necessary to be with the Pope in this situation. Mietek went to Poland for a few days, but I don't think he will go.

He tells me that the Pope is thinking about the possibility of a new consistory of appointment of cardinals for October, taking advantage of the fact that they will all come on the occasion of their anniversary.

---

1. The encyclical is *Redemptoris mater* (On the Blessed Virgin Mary in the Life of the Church), dated March 25, 1987.

Slovakia: The Cross Live

September 14, 2003

Trip to Slovakia, from September 11 to 14, presided over—at least in terms of public opinion, and also among the entourage—by the state of the Pope's health.

It all started at the Bratislava airport upon arrival. Laboriously, the Pope is lowered from the plane with an elevator. The national anthems are played and the president reads his speech. The Pope begins to read his speech. The effort is beyond his strength. The pronunciation becomes unintelligible; the breathing rhythm becomes irregular and impedes his voice. He stops. He tries to continue, but does not succeed. Then, the Slovakian monsignor who accompanies us is called. He approaches the Pope and the president. The president's microphone does not work. He uses the Pope's, but has to adapt it to match his height. A few minutes pass in the process. All too obvious and dramatic for the press that follows us, only a few meters away, the whole maneuver. Simultaneously, there is a bit of disorder with the operation to take down an armchair from the plane for the Pope, necessary for the next stage in the nunciature. Result: an uncontrolled feeling of alarm. The next day, it was be the only topic in the international media.

We arrived at the nunciature. If it has been laborious to get the Pope into the popemobile, it is an odyssey to get him out. Mietek and Dziwisz try to lift and transport him. Uselessly: they have neither the strength nor the practice to do it. Others approach: everything gets more complicated. Cibin acts and with his strength he lifts him up to start the transfer to the chair on the mobile platform next to the popemobile. It seems that one of the Pope's legs had somehow got stuck in the support of the car seat. The result is a respiratory crisis of the Pope; a laryngeal spasm that is terrifying: his breathing becomes gasping and extraordinarily noisy: it can be heard in the garden at the entrance of the nunciature. Everyone stands still. Buzzonetti, who is next to me, remains stuck where he is. Among other things because there is nothing to do. It was an agonizing few minutes for the Pope and for all of us. Finally, the platform is moved and the Pope is transported to the nunciature.

I made a statement to the press about the fact that the Pope's speech was read by a Monsignor: "It is natural that, taking into account the effort that the Holy Father makes on these trips, we try to alleviate that effort as much as possible." This somewhat de-escalates the situation. In fact, the press picked up these words the following day in an attempt to bring some clarity.

The limitations of the Pope's condition are dramatically evident. Not only can he not walk: he cannot even stand. He cannot move his legs. His diction is extremely laborious as soon as he articulates a few words: especially if he has to read from a text. Undoubtedly, emotional pressure also plays a part.

At 12:30 PM, the Pope receives the President of the Republic, the President of the Parliament, and the Prime Minister in successive audiences at the Nunciature. All with their families. His general situation has normalized, but it is a new fatigue for him.

In the afternoon, at 5:00 PM, the Pope travels sixty kilometers [thirty-eight miles] to Trnava. The maneuver to make him get out of the popemobile is again tiring. And when he enters the cathedral on the mobile platform, he again has a respiratory crisis. He was taken directly to the sacristy instead of going to the presbytery, and about ten minutes passed until he returned to normal. The journalists, who followed everything live on TV, were alarmed once again. In addition, they saw paramedics from the local services heading towards the sacristy with a defibrillator. Arriving at the nunciature, on my way back from Trnava, around 8:00 PM, I see that the Pope does not get out of the car. Ten minutes go by and he is still inside: Mietek—his other secretary—is reading the breviary and the Pope is listening . . . until they finish.

But the Pope, in everything and in spite of everything, continues to carry out his ministry. Thus, once he has finished his speech—read by Cardinal Tomko—when he sees a group of handicapped people in their wheelchairs, he has them bring him there to greet them. It is a touching scene to see him, a handicapped person, comforting and caressing other handicapped people.

The rest of the trip, which is complex because every day he goes to a different city, is treated in the press under the theme of the Pope's health. And this is not surprising. In addition to the motor problems of Parkinson's, there are also the limits of age and a benign prostatic hypertrophy that causes relative urinary incontinence. He suffers, but he is not oblivious to the progress of the trip. Shortly before he had seen me, he made a gesture and I approached him to tell him about the atmosphere among the journalists.

It is an enormous cross for the Pope. His humor is often good and he jokes—or tries to joke—; the smile appears on his face made a mask by Parkinson's disease. But there are times when the disease takes over. In Castelgandolfo this summer there were some days when he could not get out of bed. When he went on excursions, sometimes he couldn't even get out of the car. All summer long he was unable to use the swimming pool.

"Malgré Tout . . ."

September 16, 2003

Two days have passed since we returned from our trip to Slovakia and the Pope invites us to lunch at Castelgandolfo. Almost as soon as lunch begins, he has to be taken out in a wheelchair because of his urinary problem. He returns a few moments later and follows with interest what we tell him about the trip.

I tell him that he has done a lot of good for the people in Slovakia; also by letting them see him with so many physical difficulties. He remains thoughtful for a while and then says: "*Non omnis moriar,*" a phrase from the poet Horace ("I will not die completely"), which I interpret as a way of saying that not everything has been lost in his journey, that something remains there. And he adds in French: "*Malgré tout . . . ,*" that is, in spite of the limitations.

Dziwisz asks him in his jesting manner: "What does the Holy Father think of his collaborators," referring to us. And the Pope answers: "*Abbastanza sopportabili,*" quite bearable. He continues to tease us . . . in spite of everything.

Dramatic Shades

October 14, 2003

We are almost on the eve of the 25th anniversary of the election of the Pope. And these dates have dramatic overtones. The Pope can hardly speak. He cannot move except in a wheelchair. His every appearance is a suffering for him and for those who listen to him. In the Wednesday audiences he can read only a paragraph and sometimes with effort. At the Sunday Angelus, he can hardly be understood.

I spoke on the phone yesterday with Dziwisz to tell him about the presentation of the volume with the philosophical works of Karol Wojtyla. He is excited to tell the Pope about it later. I told him not to worry, that everything would go well, and that the days ahead would be very intense. He told me that "we will see." I assure him that many of us are praying. And he says again: "We will see." It is the first time in these years that Dziwisz expresses to me his doubts about the Pope's life span.

25 Years of Pontificate

OCTOBER 16–20, 2003

OCTOBER 16. The day of the 25th anniversary of the Pope's election arrived. The Mass of the day was celebrated in St. Peter's Square. I was able to read very little of his homily which, by the way, is magnificent. It is a text entirely his own, which allows us to penetrate—at least a little—into his heart. He read only the beginning and Sodano completed the reading of the rest.

The voice of the Holy Father during the Mass was confusing: Ratzinger spoke simultaneously with the Pope during the Eucharistic prayer, so that his voice "embraced" the voice that did not come from the Pope. Although it was still early in the morning, at the signing ceremony of the post-synodal exhortation on the ministry of bishops (*Pastores Gregis*), the Pope read only a small part of the text.

The televised image of the Pope—enlarged and broadcast all over the world—produces sadness and admiration at the same time. And this was the tone of the following days. He attended the concert—Beethoven's Ninth Symphony—given in his honor in the Paul VI Hall on the 17th. He was once again unable to read the text.

On Saturday, the 18th, after his meeting in the Paul VI Hall with the cardinals and presidents of the episcopal conferences, I attended the lunch offered by the Pope. Sandri read the words prepared by the Holy Father. Already during the first course, the Pope had to leave the room. I was sitting with Buzzonetti and Dziwisz—until Dziwisz left—and Buzzonetti said to me, "Dziwisz asks me, 'And why can't the Pope speak now?' I tell him, 'But don't you realize that he can't anymore?'" It's hard to accept this situation when you've seen him for years in top form.

I have greeted several cardinals in recent days. They do not know what to say beyond expressing their admiration for the Pope's tenacity. I see the same thing in the numerous newspaper and TV interviews I have had to give on the occasion of the anniversary. The underlying theme is always the Pope's health. Sometimes I think the comments are superficial, but I always see affection and good intentions.

On the 19th, beatification of Mother Teresa of Calcutta. It was a privilege to have known her. I will always remember her words, in response to a question of mine about how she summed up her work with the most abandoned: "To see to it that these people, who have lived mistreated like beasts, can die as what they are, children of God; that is: washed, combed, fed." It was in 1986, during the Pope's trip to India.

In the evening there are fireworks in the Gianicolo. The Pope looks out of the window of St. Peter's Square: he reads only a few words, but that is enough to excite the people. On the 20th there is an audience in the Paul VI Hall for pilgrims. He reads only a paragraph, with some effort.

Mel Gibson's *The Passion* Controversy

December 15, 2003

The producer of *The Passion of the Christ,* Steve McEveety, brought the Pope a copy of the film. He was accompanied by his wife, and colleague Alberto Michelini, who acted as an intermediary, with his son Jan, who participated in the filming. The Pope saw the film with Dziwisz on two evenings—December 5 and 6. The Pope liked it. He must have commented that the film showed what had happened. And that was possibly what Dziwisz conveyed to the four, when he returned the tape to them a day later.

Alberto called me on the 8th in the morning and asked me if I wanted to see the film. I said yes and, in the afternoon, Steve, with his wife and Jan, came over, and we watched it in my living room. I also invited Juan José García-Noblejas, a film professor.

At the end of the film Steve told me that he was very hurt that Dziwisz told them that the Pope could not say anything publicly about the film. "It broke my heart," Steve said. I commented to them that maybe we would say something after all, and that's how it turned out.

A few days later, I received a message from Steve informing me that Dziwisz had told them that the Pope had commented: "*It is as it was,*" that is, that the film showed how things actually happened. And he asked if he could use that quote. I gave him the green light without thinking too much: if the Pope had said it and if Dziwisz had told him. . . .

It was a mistake on my part, because that quote from the Pope began to appear in the US press. The most quoted article was by Peggy Noonan in the *Wall Street Journal.*

In the meantime, I told journalists who asked me about it that I did not usually comment on the private activities of the Holy Father. In fact, I asked Dziwisz and he told me that he preferred that I not say anything.

Voices from "anonymous sources" in the Vatican began to appear, some saying that the Pope had said that and others saying that he had not. A *CNS* journalist, Cindy Wooden, wrote a letter to Dziwisz asking him to confirm or deny the Pope's statement. And Dziwisz told her that the Pope had not said that. And so a storm broke out in the American press. Because that denial was understood as the Pope distancing himself from the content of the film.

Several days later, in agreement with Dziwisz, I made a statement indicating that "after having consulted with the Holy Father's secretary, I can confirm that the Pope has seen the film." I add a positive judgment on the film and end by saying that the Holy Father is not in the habit of making public comments on a work of art, a judgment that remains open to various aesthetic evaluations. . . . It's like a bobbin lace, because what I say implies that the Pope has said something, but not for public consumption.

Then I discover that Steve, with good intentions, has given a copy of my e-mail correspondence with him to some journalists, in which I advised him to use the Pope's primitive quote. The confusion was already at its maximum! To a journalist from Dallas, who asks me insistently, I end up telling him that what is attributed to him is inauthentic. Second mistake. For her part, Peggy Noonan returns to the arena and writes a new article feeling deceived and bringing me into the ring.

A few days later, the controversy of the American Hebrews against the film broke out, and this whole episode was relegated to a discreet background and disappeared. Truly, my role in all this has not been brilliant.

Suffering From the Cold

January 8, 2004

I had a conversation with Dziwisz and suggested to him that it would have been good for the Pope to have left Rome sometime around Christmas because, even if he can't walk, at least seeing the snowy landscape from the car would have given him a rest. But he told me that what happens now is that the Pope suffers from the cold.

I also suggested that they watch their meals a bit because the Pope has been gaining weight. Dziwisz blamed it more on the medications. He tells me that he is doing physiotherapy and that, with a little help, he manages to take a few steps in his room.

"Alzatevi, Andiamo!"

March 24, 2004

Today at the Excelsior Hotel we are presenting the Pope's new book, *Alzatevi, andiamo!* Or rather, what we are doing is to announce its upcoming release for the Pope's birthday, next May 18. There are about sixty journalists, and several

TV stations. The basic elements of the book are talked about and the reverberation in the press is wide.

The story has been long and curious. Dziwisz asked me to take care of the publishing operation, following the experience of *Crossing the Threshold of Hope*. I called Leonardo Mondadori and Rizzoli (Ferrucio de Bortoli): we agreed that one would get *Alzatevi, andiamo!* and the other, the Pope's book on Europe [*Memoria e identità*].

A problem arises with the *Libreria Editrice Vaticana*, which wants to be included in this scheme. In the end, it was agreed that they would be mentioned as the copyright holders.

Twelve Days in the Mountains

July 17, 2004

We spent the 5th to the 17th of July in the Aosta Valley with the Pope. Along with Styczeń, Buzzonetti, Cibin, and myself, this year Patrizio Polisca, who helps Buzzonetti as a doctor, is also coming. These are days of calm and peace. As the Pope does not walk and cannot stand up, an ingenious and simple system of a wheelchair with wheels has been prepared with which he can be put in the car. Then, when we get to the finish line, we transfer him to a chair to make him more comfortable. We went hiking every day, including one day when it rained a lot, but the Pope still wanted to go: he was protected in a tent and we were protected under some tarpaulins.

I talk to him one day while we are preparing him to take some photographs. I tell him that only God knows the pastoral effectiveness of these years of his pontificate. I add that he—an old and celibate man—is teaching many people to understand human love as well. "And how is this?" he asks me. "Because his effort is an example of how to love," I reply with conviction.

He changes the subject and tells me that he hasn't slept at all that night. "And I need it so much . . . ," he adds. I feel very sorry for him and tell him that I will pray all day today so that he can sleep at night. A while later Dziwisz approaches and says: "The interview with Dr. Navarro-Valls is over." And the Pope graciously replies: "But this time it was me who did the interview." On my way back to Les Combes I told the others in the car to pray for a particular intention of the Pope, without specifying what it was.

One day we go to Vallone de Youla, a place where we were on July 11, 2001. There is a small house, which the owner leaves at our disposal, from which we can contemplate a wonderful waterfall in front of which the Pope was enraptured for a long time. It was there that the poem which opens his book of poetry *Tríptico Romano*, published last year, was born. The owner has placed a stone inscription on the façade with the date of the Pope's visit in 2001.

On excursions, the Pope always remains seated in the tent. He no longer reads. The readings are done aloud by Sister Tobiana. This year is the first time that she always accompanies us on the walks.

Normally, we leave by car between 10:45 and 11:00 AM. We return between 5:30 and 6:00 PM. The Pope greets the people who are waiting for us near the house. These groups are increasing every day. They have discovered that, in order to stop the car, it is enough to show the Pope small children. He never fails. On the last day, at the time of the farewell greetings at the house, a group of young mothers from the area "infiltrated" the area, bringing children born in the last year. Also, during the march to the airport we are interrupted by frequent stops on either side of the route. "Be good to us!" they shout as our car passes. Hearing this, I find it hard to avoid a lump in my throat.

I give a quotation from the Pope to the press: "I know that you will be sorry to leave so much beauty; I am sorry too. Because here you touch the hand of God."

Virgin of Kazan

JULY 22, 2004

During the days of my stay in the Aosta Valley, I prepared a statement on the restitution of the icon of Our Lady of Kazan to the Russian Orthodox Patriarch.[2] In fact, a Vatican delegation will go to Moscow on August 28 to deliver the icon. I prepare some sentences that I then show to the Pope and distribute from my office in Rome.

I suggest to Dziwisz that, because of the risky implications of the trip, it might be advisable for me to travel with the delegation to Moscow. Dziwisz also considers it prudent and tells me that he will discuss it with the Pope. Days after my return to Rome, I receive a letter from Sandri saying that the Pope has indicated that I should be part of the delegation.

---

2. The icon of the Virgin of the Mother of God of Kazan is the Marian image most venerated by the Russian Orthodox. The icon given by the Holy See to the Patriarch of Moscow had been kept by John Paul II in his apartment for ten years. It was donated to him by the Marian association "Blue Army," which had bought it in 1970, after many vicissitudes. There are several theories about the identity of the original 16th century icon. Some argue that it was destroyed.

With the President of the Senate

AUGUST 4, 2004

A few days ago, the President of the Italian Senate, Marcello Pera, called me. He wanted to talk. We arranged to have lunch today at the Palazzo Giustiniani, the Senate's representative annex. He sent me an armored car with an escort. We are alone, under a stupendous portrait from the school of Velázquez. I see that there are others by Guido Reni. We talk about philosophy. He is a professor of the philosophy of science in Pisa. His focus is philosophical and cultural relativism. He recently met with Ratzinger about this issue and would like to publish something along the lines of their conversation.[3] He would like me to give him a hand.

The conversation is personal and cordial. He says he has no faith, but there are issues that concern him and that are "Christian." We talk about America—he is pro-American—, about the Pope—whom he admires—, about Italian politics—he has been anti-Communist since his university years in Pisa. He is not a politician in the conventional Italian sense and assures me that he has no interest in what is called a "political career."

Dziwisz's Concerns

AUGUST 12, 2004

I was in Castelgandolfo this morning to talk to Dziwisz. Long conversation: forty-five minutes. He looks good. He still has the tan he got in Aosta, perhaps reinforced by some later escapades. I brought up two main topics: the trip to Moscow with the icon of Our Lady of Kazan; and the Pope's new book. But many other things also came up.

About Moscow, I make him see what the climate is in Russia and also in regard to the Patriarch. The technical expertise done on the image, which indicated that it was an icon from the end of the 17th or beginning of the 18th century, was poorly done. There were no technicians of note there either on the Russian side or on the Vatican side. Moreover, from the reports and other conversations I have had, the Russian side was positively interested in affirming that the icon was not primitive. They wanted to reinforce the idea that it was not the authentic icon of the Virgin of Kazan, but a later, albeit valuable, copy.

3. Published in book form, co-authored by Ratzinger: *Without Roots: Europe, Relativism, Christianity, Islam* (2004).

Thus, the end result is the statement contained in the joint statement of 2003, which dates the icon to around the 18th century. Now we have the problem of avoiding statements on our part that could provoke negative reactions from the Patriarch before the ceremony of the handover.

About the Pope's book on Europe, I tell him that it is necessary for the manuscript to be ready at the beginning of September so that Rizzoli can take it to the Frankfurt Book Fair, which will allow contracts with many publishers in the world. He sees this as very possible and tells me about the Pope's way of writing: he reads beforehand and takes notes, but when he writes, he does not need to consult any book, but writes in one go and almost without correcting afterwards.

I tell him that I see that the Pope has improved after his stay in the Aosta Valley. He tells me that yes, it is evident. But he lets his doubts and fears about the current situation show through. "And of the resignation . . . ?" I tell him that it is no longer even a topic that is alive in public opinion, and we repeat the same considerations that we have made other times and that he knows better than me. We agree that the important thing is that his collaborators follow the thought that the Pope has expressed throughout these years. Dziwisz affirms that even now, when the Pope sees that something is not going well, he clearly shows it so that the course is rectified. And speaking of collaborators, he mentions that Tauran is also ill, and also with Parkinson's; it is a pity, moreover, because he thinks that in the future he would have been a magnificent candidate for Secretary of State.

He tells me about the upcoming trip to Lourdes. He tells me that Chirac will be there and that the French ambassador has already come several times worried that the Pope, in his arrival speech, in front of Chirac, might mention some polemic topic, such as the Christian roots of Europe, to which Chirac has represented the most significant opposition. He tells me that the Pope, at the time, sent Tauran to Paris with a personal letter to Chirac, and that the latter did not even receive him. Now the Pope has decided not to raise the issue.

I tell him that I am going to Spain for three days and he comments that it is not enough. I explain that I'm going alone for my mother's anniversary, who is turning ninety. "And what present can we give her?" He accompanies me to the courtyard where I parked the car. He has been very cordial and affectionate.

Our Lady of Kazan in Moscow

AUGUST 31, 2004

From the 27th to the 30th I am going to Moscow as a member of the delegation sent by the Holy Father to donate the icon of the Mother of God of Kazan to the Patriarch of Moscow. We travel in a Falcon plane of the Presidency of the Italian Council of Ministers. Three and a quarter hour flight.

At Sheremetyevo airport, we are received by Archpriest Chaplin, who always acts as spokesman for the Patriarch; a bishop of the Patriarch. Of course, Kondrusiewicz, Archbishop of the Archdiocese of the Mother of God in Moscow and President of the Conference of Catholic Bishops of the Russian Federation, is also present.

We went to an airport lounge and, seated, exchanged greetings and resolutions. Welcome from the Russian side: the donation of the icon is an act of "love and justice." This will be the formula, repeated ad nauseam by all the ecclesiastics of the Patriarch, every time the Pope's gesture is mentioned.

Appreciation and hope is expressed that "it will help to heal the wounds between our Churches." The two topical points of these "wounds" are mentioned: what they call proselytism and the destruction of churches in Ukraine, but there is also hope that the best will be done to heal them. Overall, the tone is slightly improved from other occasions.

We drive to the "Danilovskaya Hotel" of the Orthodox Patriarch, located next to the Danilov Convent, which will be our residence in Moscow. We have lunch right away. The good atmosphere of courtesy continues. Chaplin—who is vice-president of the Moscow Patriarch's Department for External Relations and therefore works with Kirill—had proposed a technical meeting to me with his people on "Church and mass media." He told me that it would be a matter of passing on experiences. With the accumulated delay and my haste to telephone Rome, our plans came to nothing. I proposed to him that we spend two days in Rome or Moscow to work more calmly on these topics. He likes the idea.

I work out over the phone the last details of an interview about the trip that I left unfinished in Rome. I add some positive elements about the weather and expectations upon arrival.

The evening ends with a reception at the Moscow Nunciature. Greetings to old Russian friends: Krasikov, who was with us in 1988, when he worked for the *TASS* Agency; the former Russian ambassador in Rome, etc. I also see Sergio Canciani, from *RAI,* to whom I will give a statement tomorrow after the ceremony.

The hope that the icon of the Virgin spend its last night at the nunciature so that Catholics who wanted to see it could do so, since some had asked to be able to pray before the Virgin, was not successful. The "raison d'état" prevailed and the icon stayed with us at the hotel.

The next morning, we go to the Kremlin. We arrive directly at the Dormition Cathedral, and the Orthodox liturgy begins: three and a quarter hours, always standing. Patriarch Alexis II receives the icon from the hands of Kasper and pronounces a few words of thanks, in which there is only a generic mention of the difficulties between the two Churches. As we leave the cathedral we record the statement for *RAI*. Other journalists ask me to comment, and I do so in English for everyone.

The Patriarch leaves the Cathedral and goes to the adjacent building, where lunch will be held. On the way, he answers questions from journalists. One journalist—I am told that of the Polish television—formulates an interesting question, but one that at that moment is certainly not diplomatic. He asks about the Pop's trip to Moscow. The Patriarch answers that it is not being considered at the moment.

Lunch with the Patriarch and official dinner in the evening. As I remembered from my trip in '88, at all dinners and meals they serve vodka from the beginning and you are expected to drink it with every toast. As there are rounds of up to six toasts, the situation becomes critical. I decide to show clearly that I will only drink a few drops with each toast.

Bishop Mark bids us farewell at the airport. He delivers the message for the Pope and insists on something that has already come up on previous occasions: "It is in our interest that public opinion in Europe and in the world sees the good climate that exists between the Orthodox Church and the Catholic Church."

My conclusion is that they want the image of mutual conflict to fade; they do not want to be seen as intolerant towards the Catholic minority in Russia. But, at the same time, they do not seem willing to concede anything on the ground of Orthodox hegemony in Russia or, in the case of Eastern Rite Catholics, in Ukraine. In other words, I think life will continue to be hard for Catholics in these places.

There is undoubtedly a national element to this whole problem: the Catholic presence in Russia includes few ethnic Russians. Currently, for example, among the 226 Catholic priests in Russia, about 180 are Polish or of Polish origin.

48

Back at the Gemelli

Twenty Years at *Sala Stampa*

December 7, 2004

A few days ago, on December 4th to be exact, it was twenty years since I was called to carry out this work in the Vatican. Bishop Dziwisz heard about the anniversary and said that an audience with the Holy Father would be organized to celebrate it. Today, at 11:00 AM, the audience took place, in which all my collaborators participated in the *Sala Stampa*. It was the only audience scheduled for that day.

The Pope received us in the library, the place of his official audiences. I approached him to greet him and he wanted me to sit on his right side to introduce him to everyone in the office. Each one of them, after greeting the Holy Father, took one of the armchairs that were prepared to his right and left. And when we were all seated, a Monsignor began to read the text of a letter the Pope had addressed to me. Naturally, I was rather uncomfortable because it is one thing to receive a letter with such a text, and another to hear the solemn reading of the text in front of other people. When it was all over, I approached him again to kiss his hand and thank him for his affection. Everyone greeted the Pope again and he gave them a medal as a souvenir of his last trip to Lourdes.

From that text, I remember, above all, the words in which God's help is invoked so that I may reach—through this professional activity— the goal of all Christian existence: holiness.

Dinner with Colleagues

December 20, 2004

Some accredited journalists in my office—at least thirty of them—offered me a dinner tonight on the occasion of the famous twenty years at the *Sala Stampa*. Cindy Wooden was one of the organizers. Also Phil Pullela, who was kind enough to ask for messages from American colleagues who had worked here and are now back in the United States.

It was a very pleasant time. I was pleasantly surprised that Sandro Magister, from *L'Espresso,* who every time he writes about me, gives me a lot of hard jibes, was also there—and right in front of me at the table. . . .

The Impact of Limitations

December 24, 2004

I call Dziwisz today to wish him Christmas greetings. We talk for a while. I tell him that people are waiting for the Pope's Christmas Eve Mass, which as always will be broadcast on TV. He whispers that perhaps they are curious to see how the Pope is doing? I tell him that most people support the Pope and that his example does them a lot of good.

I tell him some anecdotes showing the great impact the Pope is having in this period of severe physical limitations. I refer to recent comments—among them, that of the Mayor of Rome, Walter Veltroni—of children who are collecting money through personal sacrifice to go to Youth Day in Cologne next August. . . .

He tells me at the end: "You don't know how good it is for me to hear these things. . . ."

The poor man has been leading an amazing life for many years, not only in his personal assistance to the Pope, in all his needs, but also in the preparation of audiences, etc. This life of constant effort—having continually before his eyes the Pope's impoverished condition—sometimes prevents him from seeing beyond, from looking at the world and the extraordinary fruits of the pontificate, precisely now when it seems weaker.

The Pope at Gemelli

February 1–4, 2005

Eleven o'clock at night. I sleep happily. Urgent call from the Vatican Operations Room. From Sandri. They pass it to me. Excited voice: the Pope has been transferred to the hospital. Respiratory problems. I try to gather the essential data: at what time, with whom, how, etc. In the meantime I hear another phone ringing nearby. It's Buzzonetti. I hear him start to dictate a brief statement that Sandri simultaneously transmits to me.

I hang up and hesitate for a moment. What's the priority right now? Going to the hospital? No. The priority is to tell the press what happened. And I start writing the note to send it with the automatic alarm system, which we set up a year ago in my office. I am going to transmit it over the Internet, but I realize that the Vatican connection is not working. It is impossible to make thirty phone calls to as many agencies. . . . I call the *ANSA* agency. And then I start sending messages. I finish at half past one. The text I send is: "The flu syndrome that the Holy Father has suffered for three days, this afternoon was complicated by an acute tracheitis and a spasm of the larynx. For this reason, it was decided to admit him urgently to the Gemelli Polyclinic, which took place at 10:50 PM today, February 1st."

The next morning I go straight to the hospital. I talk to Dziwisz and Buzzonetti. Laryngotracheitis with laryngospasm. The Pope could have died of asphyxia. He was intubated and was able to breathe for some hours. Parenteral feeding. Urinary catheter.

After the first evening communiqué, I inform the press that the Holy Father is in the room assigned to him, on the tenth floor of the Gemelli Polyclinic, not in the resuscitation services.

Rodolfo Proietti, head of the resuscitation service at the Gemelli, talks with Buzzonetti and prepares the press release. I print it out in my office and send it to the Clinical Director to be read to the journalists at the Gemelli, while I simultaneously communicate it to those accredited in the *Sala Stampa*: "During the past night, respiratory support therapies continued to stabilize the clinical picture. Cardio-respiratory and metabolic parameters are currently within normal limits. Therefore, the diagnosis of acute laryngotracheitis with episodes of laryngospasm is confirmed, as I had already communicated last night. In the course of the night the Holy Father rested for a few hours."

The following two days I provided this official information:

February 2. "The Holy Father's general and respiratory conditions are developing positively. The acute laryngotracheitis is in a phase of regression and there has been no recurrence of the episodes of laryngospasm that prompted the emergency hospitalization. The Holy Father had a peaceful night's rest."

February 3. "The Holy Father's state of health has improved. John Paul II is being fed regularly. Instrumental and laboratory tests confirm the stabilization of the clinical picture. In light of the favorable evolution of the respiratory pathology, a new statement will be issued on Monday, February 7 at noon."

And then I added: "From his room at the Gemelli Polyclinic, tomorrow afternoon the Pope will follow on TV the ceremony of the Feast of Our Lady of

Confidence, Patroness of the Roman Major Seminary, which will be celebrated in the Paul VI Hall of the Vatican. The text of the address prepared by the Holy Father will be read by the *Sostituto* of the Secretariat of State, Archbishop Leonardo Sandri. As for the Angelus prayer on Sunday, February 6, it is known that it is an appointment very dear to John Paul II and one he does not want to miss. Tomorrow I will be able to be more precise about the plan for the recitation of the Marian prayer.

February 4. It is not much as information, but in reality it is much more than the medical data provided when great personalities—François Mitterrand, Giovanni Agnelli, and so many others—were ill and even when they died. And with some of these we were not even told the causes of death.

Naturally, for the media that is still not enough. In today's briefing, an American journalist from *CNN* asked me why "so much mystery," why not give more? I answered: "I believe, objectively, that we have given much more than in many cases has been given with public figures from your country. What I can't do is keep feeding your work twenty-four hours a day."

Every morning I go to the hospital, go up to the Pope's rooms, talk to Dziwisz and Buzzonetti (once the doctors have finished their visit), and prepare the information. I do all this outside the official "structures:" if there is a slip-up, it will be mine.

As it would take hours to get to the Gemelli in Roman traffic, every morning at 8:30 AM I am met by an Italian police car preceded by two motorcyclists who, in a few minutes, take me from the office to the hospital and then bring me back. I am very grateful for their offer to do this. From home to the office I go in my car, with Enrico Spigone as my driver.

The morning conversation with Dziwisz is a pleasant, personal, and enjoyable chat. We talk about everything. On the first day in the hospital he was dressed in liturgical vestments. He is getting ready to celebrate Holy Mass with the Pope. Something he will do every morning.

Problems with the Angelus

February 6, 2005

Yesterday I spoke with Dziwisz about the best way to pray the Angelus. It could be done with the Pope sitting in his armchair, from the window next to Dziwisz's, which overlooks the main entrance of the Gemelli; but it is preferable not to open the window, since the day is cold. The TV, from below, could capture some images.

As this Sunday morning was a little quieter, I took the opportunity to go for a walk on the beach for a while, as I was really quite tired. On the radio I hear the Angelus: Sandri reads, they open the window, and the Pope's voice sounds terribly bad because there has been a defect in the connection.

I return home, and I start to get calls from the various newspapers: an agency—*APCOM*—has given the news that the voice of the Pope, in reality, was recorded. I don't know where they got that story from, but the "news" has a tremendous negative potential: it implies that the Vatican is deceiving. There is a risk of "zero credibility" for what will be said in the future.

I call Father Lombardi, director of programs at Vatican Radio. He tells me that, from the information he has at the time, it seems that the recording had been made beforehand. With that information, I decide to do nothing. Shortly afterwards I call Dziwisz and tell him how things are going. He doesn't give me an answer, but he understands the risk.

I then receive a call from Roberto Calvigioni, who is the technician in the room with the Pope. Roberto had just spoken to Dziwisz and called to give me first-hand information: nothing was recorded; the error was exclusively technical. The transmission was further complicated because, at the moment of giving the blessing, Mietek—one of the secretaries—passed the Pope a sheet of paper with the text of the blessing: that sheet—seen from the perspective of the TV cameras—covered the Pope's entire face, perhaps giving the impression that he had wanted to hide it.

It was almost seven o'clock in the evening when I made an official denial from home to all the agencies, saying that the voice heard was that of the Pope at the same moment he pronounced the words of the blessing, and that there was no sense in talking about a previous recording of his voice. It was what many were expecting.

The Word "Resignation"

February 7–9, 2005

On the morning of the 7th, Sodano's secretary asked me for my opinion on the advisability of the Sodano attending the inauguration of an extension to the Holy See's bookstore in St. Peter's Square. It is preferable that he not go, I tell him, because the atmosphere among the journalists is excited and he would encounter complicated questions.

In the end, they decide he should go. And when he arrives he is asked a flurry of questions, among them what he thinks about the possible resignation of the Pope. "Let's leave the issue of resignation to the Pope's conscience," Sodano replies. He then explains that the Pope knows better than anyone what he must do, and that he continues to govern the Church. But the Secretary of State has now pronounced the word "resignation" in relation to the Pope, and once the door has been opened, there is no way to gather the oxen. . . .

The press goes wild. At the same time, I am in a room of the Senate presenting the book on the Pope written by Alceste Santini, Vaticanist of *L'Unità*. And as soon as I finish, I am cornered by several TV journalists who ask me what I think about what Sodano said about the Pope's resignation. Naturally, I do not respond to the question. When I get home, I check the agencies to see what hornet's nest has been unleashed. The phone starts ringing. I do not answer and go to sleep.

The next day, the press puts this topic on the front page of the newspaper. And I see that the reaction has been similar worldwide. When I arrive at the hospital, Dziwisz has already read some Italian newspapers. He is very upset.

We moved to a private room. The Pope is still intubated, but improving. I ask Dziwisz about any comments the Pope may have made in the last few days. He tells me that a while ago he asked if they could raise the top of the bed a little. While doing so, the Pope commented that St. Peter was put on the cross upside down, while he asked for his head to be raised. . . .

Every day I talk to Dziwisz about different things. He mentions to me some of the Pope's appointments that are still pending. For example, the replacement of Cardinal Lustiger, in Paris, for reasons of age: he passed the age of seventy-five at least two years ago. It reminds me of that time when his appointment was proposed, many years ago, everyone was against it except Cardinal Felici. The Pope, however, appointed him anyway.

We talked about an article by Accattoli in *Corriere della Sera* on "the men who govern the Curia today." Dziwisz, who always sees any article on these topics as threatening, say: "Yes, they govern, but with the Pope and under the Pope's direction."

In the afternoon, Cardinal Re called me at home. A journalist from the *Adnkronos* agency asked him about the famous resignation. He answered: "It seems to me out of place and inappropriate to talk about it, especially on the occasion of a simple flu." But, Re told me, he did not want to appear controversial in comparison to Sodano. The risk is that the press will interpret his words in that sense.

The following day, *La Repubblica* attacks the issue from that angle, with an article by Politi. The day before, Petrosillo in *Il Messaggero* has described Sodano's comment as naive. And, to complicate matters, the elderly Cardinal Mejía appears with a supposedly technical commentary on the issue, while another cardinal, ignorant of the whole controversy, asks me what he should say to some interviewers who ask him something about a commentary by Sodano about which he knows nothing.

Our informative approach continues to be that of giving objective clinical data, adding some personal details from these days and, from time to time, a bit of humor in the midst of this tension, as when I say that the Pope follows the evolution of his illness through the newspapers.

The Pope Returns to the Vatican

February 10, 2005

In the morning there is an expectation that the Pope could be released from the hospital. I spoke first with Dziwisz and then with Buzzonetti. They had already prepared a statement saying that the tests carried out showed no other pathologies (he had also undergone a stress electrocardiogram and a CAT scan). Buzzonetti, cautious, speaks of an imminent departure, without saying when.

Vatican and Italian security are studying the possible route back to St. Peter's. I confirm, once again, with Dziwisz that the Pope is leaving the hospital this afternoon. We talk in the small room that serves as a chapel, adjacent to the one occupied by the Pope. He is praying the breviary. I ask him, "Am I saying that the Pope is leaving today?" "Be prudent," he replies. Given the situation, I decide to take that for granted. I go to the office and have a press conference.

In the afternoon I speak with Dziwisz a couple of times on the phone. There is no change of plan, but there is still discussion about which means of transport to take. I suggest the minivan we used last summer in the Aosta Valley. It sounds good to him, but then he calls me again to tell me that there are too many journalists. And he decides on the popemobile. It doesn't go badly, although we have to work to place the car in the area where the Pope will exit. The end result is that the Pope sleeps that night in his apartment. *Laus Deo!*

Back to Gemelli

February 24, 2005

I am in the office. At 9:15 AM the phone rings directly from my desk. It is Dziwisz. After greetings, he tells me: I'll put you through to Buzzonetti. Buzzonetti informs me that the Pope is not well; that today a consistory of cardinals is scheduled, for some causes of canonization and beatification, and that the Pope will not attend. Let it be said that his personal physician has advised him to remain in his apartment. Perhaps the Pope could follow the ceremony with a TV connection. . . . He advises me to be prudent and to "leave the doors open."

It is clear: the breathing difficulties—laringo-spasm—have returned, and it remains to see how it evolves. Dziwisz tells me that there is a letter from the Pope to Sodano delegating the presidency of the consistory. I take notes for the communiqué I will give in an hour and inform my collaborators in the office.

About forty-five minutes go by. Renato Buzzonetti calls me again: it is better not to make the announcement. They are thinking of admitting the Pope to the hospital. As he speaks on the phone, he uses the expression "to make a *gitarella*"—a little trip—but I immediately understand what it is all about. A new communiqué is written: due to the flu syndrome, the respiratory difficulties are returning, which makes it advisable to admit him to the hospital for further observation and possible treatment.

The truth is that the thought of taking the Pope back to the hospital is devastating. Already the night before, those breathing difficulties had appeared: an agonizing sensation of suffocation . . . The cross always!

A little later, Buzzonetti calls me again: they have decided to leave the Vatican at 11:15 AM, but he suggests that, in order to avoid being admitted to the hospital in the midst of a cloud of journalists, he will call me as soon as they enter the Gemelli and I will then report the news. I think this is very sensible.

As I understand the pressure Buzzonetti must be under and that he might forget to tell me, I call Domenico Giani, head of Vatican security, who tells me that they are arriving at the hospital. A few minutes later, Buzzonetti calls me after all to confirm the arrival. Then I read to the journalists the text I had already written and printed. There was already some nervousness among them because they were watching the Consistory with the Pope absent via closed-circuit TV. None of them imagined that the cause was the hospitalization.

I probably should have gone to the Gemelli in the afternoon to follow the Pope's progress from there and see if there was any news. I did not go. Towards mid-afternoon, rumors began to emerge from the hospital about a possible tracheotomy for the Pope. Later it was Domenico Giani who called me. With cryptic language he tells me that "they are already downstairs," and that it will be "an hour and a half." I ask him to put me in touch with Buzzonetti. He goes to look for him. He calls me later to tell me that "he is inside." We agreed that he would pass any information on to me as soon as they were done.

It is the confirmation that the Pope is being operated on. The calls are numerous: they want to know if what some are saying is true. It is time to decide what to do. And I decide two things: not to answer any calls for the moment (letting it be understood that I am in the hospital) and to test the telematic connections to be sure that, when I have to say something, I will be in a position to send the information. And I wait for news.

At 9:00 PM Giani calls me and informs me that "they have already finished." A little later it is Buzzonetti who calls from the elevator: "In a moment, when I go up to the tenth floor, I will give you the information." It is 9:45 PM when I manage to send everything. And from that moment on, the phone stops ringing.

At the Gemelli and Back

February 25–March 13, 2005

Thanks to the police escort, I am at the hospital at 8:45 AM on the 25th. Like last time, I come early every morning to collect the information. This also makes it easier for Dziwisz to have a chat and get some fresh air. While I am there, I regularly give medical information to the press, which is always received with great expectation. The conference room in the office is full every day and there are many TV cameras.

The Pope, Dziwisz tells me, also suffers from a fungal infection of the larynx, and we have to wait until it disappears before making forecasts. When he recovered from the anesthesia he wrote on a piece of paper: "What have they done to me? But I am always *Totus tuus* . . ." He has already uttered a few words. Yesterday he fully articulated Mietek's name.

In the briefing I have in the *Sala Stampa* I say that, since his return from the hospital on February 10th, the Pope had not had a fever, had followed a normal diet, and had resumed his activity. During those days, moreover, a doctor specialized in resuscitation, Dr. Camaioni, was on duty in the apartment in case of need. I also reported that the tracheotomy was performed to ensure "adequate ventilation and to help resolve the laryngeal pathology." I concluded by confirming that "he is now breathing better, has a noticeable sense of relief and does not need assisted breathing."

A few days passed and it was decided that the Angelus of Sunday the 27th would be led by Sandri from the sacristy in St. Peter's Square. At the end of the Angelus, the Pope waves for a moment from the hospital, with the windows closed. He also makes a gesture pointing to his neck wound, as if to say: I cannot speak. The people are grateful for this gesture. At his side, Sodano appears for a moment.

About this unforeseen appearance of the Pope, Domenico Giani tells me—the next morning—that Dziwisz had asked someone to bring the Pope's wheelchair from the Vatican. And so they were able to move him to the room from where he greeted everyone.

On Monday night the Pope had a "crisis of anger," so to speak, which consisted in the fact that he did not want to see the doctors. Something similar also happened years ago, after the femur operation. On that occasion he did not want to see the doctors either, as a "silent protest."

Some newspapers are speaking of an alleged letter of resignation by the Pope. And they also speak of a study commissioned by the Pope to the canonists of the Holy See on the appropriateness of a Roman pontiff's resignation.

I ask Dziwisz about those two issues. "No study has been commissioned on that subject. The Pope asked Ratzinger, Re when he was Substitute, and Martínez Somalo, as Camerlengo, for their opinion. This was in the years 92–93." Dziwisz also informs me that John Paul II went so far as to write a letter—I understand he means an "apostolic letter"—on this subject, which was never published and is not even preserved in the archives. It was a document that dealt jointly with the resignation of the bishops at the age of seventy-five and also that of the Pope. Dziwisz clarifies—and probably this was part of that document—that it deals with two very different situations, the resignation of the bishops and that of the Pope, since the emeritus bishop remains a bishop, but what would be the situation of an emeritus Pope?

He confirms to me that there is absolutely no personal letter of resignation from the Pope. There is no letter because there is no superior to whom it could be addressed. On a different matter, he also confirms to me, from conversations he had with Msgr. Macchi, his secretary, that Paul VI never thought of resigning.

On Saturday, March 5th, I do not go to the hospital, but I speak with Dziwisz. He confirms that the solution for the Angelus on Sunday, March 6, will be the same as last week: Sandri will lead it from St. Peter's and the Pope will wave from the window. We also make a plan for the ceremony with European university students to be held at St. Peter's this afternoon and we say goodbye.

On Sunday the Pope appears at the window after the Angelus. I see that he has Sodano and Lajolo on his left and right.[1] On Monday I commented to Dziwisz that the image was not bad: the Pope with his collaborators. And Dziwisz answers: "Precisely, that is why we have done it."

1. Giovanni Lajolo (Italy, 1935) was at that time Secretary for Relations with States of the Secretariat of State (2003–2006). He was appointed cardinal in 2007.

Days go by. I continue to go to the hospital in the mornings, chat with Stanisław and then with Buzzonetti. I give the medical bulletins and hold the press conferences, providing the necessary information and skipping some questions that do not adhere to informational needs.

Understandably, there are moments when Dziwisz needs to talk to someone who inspires him with more confidence so that he can, in some way, explain his difficulties. In those moments, we speak of the mysterious dimension of this second relapse of the Pope; a mystery that can only find its answer in the Cross of Jesus. From the Pope's pain, God will be drawing much good for the whole Church. Evidently, these are things he knows better than I do, but I think it is good for him to be told them by someone from outside. In fact, he tells me: "Hearing you speak like this helps me a lot."

We began to make plans for the Pope's possible departure from the hospital. I suggest that the best time would be Sunday afternoon, March 13th: then there would be no problems with the Angelus, since the formula of the previous Sunday could be repeated, with the Pope waving from the hospital window, while Sandri reads the text in St. Peter's. The next day he tells me that the doctors have given the go-ahead for this plan.

On Friday, March 11th, Buzzonetti writes the medical report stating that the Pope is improving and that a new statement will not be issued until Monday, March 14th. I propose that it would be better not to say anything about a new statement on Monday, since—in principle—he will be released from the hospital on Sunday. We change the sentence saying that "a new medical bulletin is not expected before Monday."

I tell Buzzonetti that it is better for him to bring me the brief text on the Pope's departure from the hospital on Saturday, March 12th. A few words are written and we agree to distribute it at 3:00 PM on Sunday, March 13th. But on that day, at 1:00 PM, I see that there is a threat of the news being leaked from the hospital itself. So I ask Father Ciro Benedettini, deputy director of the office, to release the communiqué at 1:00 PM. And in fact we are saved by minutes.

Dziwisz calls me in the afternoon. They have decided that the pope will leave the hospital in the Mercedes pulmino used by Cardinal Deskur, in which it is easy to put a fixed chair. This is how it is done: the Pope is seated next to the driver, and they have placed a TV camera inside the car which gives good coverage.

The Pope sleeps in the Vatican.

Although the decision for him to leave the hospital had been made the previous Friday, there are those who interpret his departure as a spontaneous decision by the Pope, and against the advice of the doctors.

49

Emotion and Serenity

The Last Holy Week

March 20–27, 2005

March 20, Palm Sunday. Cardinal Ruini will celebrate Mass; the Angelus will be recited by Sandri, as on previous Sundays, and the Pope can then wave for a moment from his window. And so it is done.

But the image offered by the Pope is very sad. Bent, he puts his hand to his eyes; he unintentionally hits the lectern. . . . The camera turns away from him soon after. Dziwisz calls me in the afternoon. I tell him—so as not to depress him—that it did not go badly, but the Pope should be given a new cassock, with a slightly higher and wider collar, so that he can breathe through the tracheotomy.

On Monday evening, the 21st, a general alarm went off among journalists. Repeated calls came from the United States. The commotion seems to have come from *Sky News*. The news spread that the Pope had died. I do not even accept the situation of having to deny a supposed death of the Pope. I tell any journalist who manages to get in touch with me that every time there has been an update on the Holy Father's state of health, we have reported it ourselves. "So," they ask me, "does this mean that you are denying the news? No, I am not denying anything; I am simply affirming that every time there has been an update on the Holy Father's health, we have communicated it; and this will continue to be the case in the future."

I understand the journalists' anxiety, but I do not allow their anxiety to become "my" anxiety. I turn off all the phones and go to sleep. Domenico Giani called me from the Vatican; he tells me what I already know: that all this furor is unleashed. There is nothing to say.

The next morning, Tuesday, March 22nd, I call Dziwisz and meet him at the Apartment. On my way there, I meet Buzzonetti at the Cortile Sixto V. He doesn't talk much. He takes it for granted that I know, and I act as if I know . . . I give him my night emergency phone number.

Dziwisz welcomes me and we talk. He asks for coffee, as if we were in the hospital, where we used to have coffee together every morning. He tells me about the Pope's feeding difficulties. They have discovered that the diet of semi-liquid food was insufficient. They have begun to supplement it with nasal tube feeding. But they have been advised to do a PED: a small abdominal opening to access the stomach directly through a tube. To perform it, he tells me, they have to do a gastroscopy in order to determine exactly where to open. He asks my opinion. I try to play it down, because if the doctors have advised this, it means that there is no other less traumatic way to feed him.

I realize—once again—the vast weight of the cross that the Pope has to carry. It is not so much the physical pain, but that progressive impoverishment of a man who stands before the gaze of humanity. . . . And so I say it once again to Dziwisz: there is no way to understand all this except by looking at the Cross of Jesus Christ.

He tells me that yesterday morning the Pope watched on TV the meeting of the UNIV university students in the Paul VI Hall. He then asked me: "What can we do during these days?" I tell him that, if the Pope is up to it, tomorrow, Wednesday, he could lean out of the window for a minute to greet the pilgrims in the square. On Holy Thursday, nothing. On Good Friday, if possible a couple of minutes at the end of the Stations of the Cross in the Colosseum, on TV from his chapel. And on Easter Sunday, a few minutes at the end of the Mass, at the time of the Angelus, from his window.

He asks me who should read the Pope's Easter message. If Sodano will celebrate the Mass, Sandri can read the message and the Angelus. I tell him again that it is necessary to make a new cassock for the Pope with a wider collar so that he can breathe without inconvenience and at the same time that he can be buttoned up. If you want, I could call Gamarelli, the tailor, and tell him to have it ready in twenty-four hours.

Wednesday, March 23rd: great confusion, rumors from one side and from the other. The most comical case is that of *Il Messaggero*: half a dramatic page on the Pope's health and the other half on the possible replacement of Sodano by Re, supposedly something the Pope would do at Easter. . . .

I call Dziwisz and then he passes me on to Buzzonetti, who does not want to give any information, as is his tendency. I tell him that, in the face of the great information vacuum, everything ends up as rumor and confusion. He agrees to give something like this: "The Pope's convalescence continues with a slow and progressive improvement. He is feeding normally and continues with the respiratory exercises of phonation." I agree to spread that around, but with the "progressive" part removed. But later, at 11 o'clock in the morning, as the Pope looks out of his window for a minute to bless the pilgrims, I decide not to give anything. It would be interpreted as wanting to correct the image people have seen. Dziwisz calls me a little later to ask how it went. I tell him fine, although the Pope's face was a mixture of suffering, expressionlessness and shock. I ask Dziwisz if the Pope was moved there. He confirms that he was.

GOOD FRIDAY, MARCH 25. I call Dziwisz to ask if I can come to see him. "Where are you?" At home, I answer him. He thinks I am far away. In reality, I am at the Pontifical Apartment in fifteen minutes. A few minutes later, Buzzonetti arrives.

The Pope's condition is as follows: he is very low in red blood cells (2.8 million) and organic defenses. He is in a state of anemia. Buzzonetti thinks that this nutritional deficit was already present in the hospital, but its consequences have only revealed themselves now. That is why he has been given a permanent nasal tube to nourish him. They have also decided that, as soon as he regains his strength, he will be taken back to the hospital for a procedure that will allow him to be fed directly through the stomach. Once this is done they will be able to remove the nasal tube. But it will be two or three weeks before he recovers.

In the meantime, when the Pope appears at the window—on Wednesdays and Sundays—they remove the probe. To reintroduce it they have to apply a light general anesthesia, to avoid discomfort and because—since the Pope does not have the capacity to swallow now—otherwise the probe doesn't go down. That is what they have done in the Pope's last three appearances at the window. Dziwisz asks me what to do this afternoon with the Stations of the Cross.

I reason that, under these conditions, the removal and reinsertion of the probe is not a possibility. We agree that it would be foolish to have to anesthetize the Pope every time the nasal probe has to be reinserted, just to be seen on TV. For the Stations of the Cross, Dziwisz wonders about the possibility of the Pope being seen for a moment with the probe. I rule it out, arguing that this image of the Pope with the nasal probe would then remain symbolic of these days and, in my opinion, would not respect the minimum of privacy for a sick person like the Pope.

I propose a third option: that the TV camera films the Pope with his back turned, seated in his chapel; that it zooms in on the crucifix and then opens on the figure of the Pope seated, with his back turned and also a little to the left of the Pope—the nasal probe is on the right—but without showing the probe. After talking about it for a while, we decide that this is the best solution.

Later on, we will need to decide what to do during the two weeks, more or less, that the Pope will have to continue nasal feeding. I discourage the removal and insertion of the tube on Wednesdays and Sundays. At most, it could be removed on Easter Sunday for the *Urbi et Orbi* blessing. But only on that occasion.

I also suggest to Dziwisz that, on one of the occasions when they do blood tests on the Pope, he should ask the doctor to take a small vial from him and keep it as a relic for when the canonization comes. Dziwisz had not thought of that possibility. He said to me: "But how can I keep it?" I tell him to ask the doctor to put some anticoagulant inside to preserve it. He thanks me for the suggestion.

As we were leaving, I saw the Pope being carried from his room to the chapel in his wheelchair: not the armchair they use for ceremonies, but a classic wheelchair for the sick. He was wrapped in a white quilt. It seems as if his figure had been dwarfed. I see him and I am moved. Tears come to my eyes. I tell Dziwisz, to justify myself, that "lately I get more emotional than when my father died." We go back to the room and now it is Dziwisz who has to console me. He tells me that the Pope suffers a lot, that it is the mystery of the Cross.

In the afternoon I call Dziwisz again to ask him if he would prefer me to come and help him with the preparation of the transmission. This is not necessary.

In the evening I follow the Stations of the Cross on TV. The image of the Pope is dignified and moving. It takes place as we had agreed this morning: zoom on the crucifix, opening on the Pope with his back and across. Under the altar, they have installed a TV screen on which the Pope can follow the transmission from the Colosseum. It is a good image. But, instead of giving it only once at the beginning of the Way of the Cross, they repeat it from time to time during the hour and a half that the Way of the Cross lasts. At the end, they place a wooden crucifix in the Pope's hands. This repeated exposition is a risk, people may wonder why he is always with his back turned. How is it that the Pope's face cannot be seen? But the intensity of the moment prevails and few—at least, in the journalistic chronicles—ask themselves these questions.

Dziwisz calls me on Saturday to ask me for suggestions about Easter Sunday. I tell him that it is enough for the Pope to lean out of the window and give his blessing. It is enough of a sacrifice for him to have to take the probe out and put it in. Later, at mid-morning, he calls again: would it not be possible, if the Pope does not speak, to put the Pope's voice recorded on some other previous occasion . . . ? I tell him that I don't like that. That from then on they will always ask if the Pope has been dubbed, etc. "All right, you have convinced me."

On Easter Sunday the Pope appears at the window of his apartment. There is great excitement among the people. A microphone is brought to him. The Pope is constricted and cannot speak. The microphone is taken away and he gives his blessing in silence. The people, many people in the square, cry.

When I talk to Stanisław in the afternoon, he tells me: "I know you are calling me to encourage me ("*tirarmi un pò su*"). The problem is that the Pope was talking well all morning. And then, at the window, he was blocked." I told him that the people had been moved, that many were crying, that there were more people in the square than ever before.

We agreed to meet again on Tuesday morning to talk about the future and how to present this new stage of the Holy Father's life.

The Situation Worsens

MARCH 31

EASTER THURSDAY. In the afternoon there were rumors of a worsening of the Pope's condition: someone must have seen doctors entering the Vatican. I call the apartment and speak to Dziwisz. He confirms the truth of these rumors. He immediately passes me to Renato Buzzonetti, who informs me of the general conditions: a septic crisis starting from a urinary tract infection accompanied by cardiocirculatory collapse. Blood pressure is very low; fever very high. The collapse has been somewhat overcome, but there is no stability yet. The Pope is conscious. Buzzonetti dictates a brief medical report that I give that same evening and I tell him that I will leave my phone on.

We are Leaving

APRIL 1, 2005

At 6:00 AM Buzżonetti calls me. Conditions are still serious. He dictates a new communiqué, this time more explicit. We released it half an hour later. It speaks of "septic shock with cardiovascular collapse;" and it adds that "the Holy Father's wish to remain at home was respected" and that the clinical picture evolved negatively during the night. It was specified that he was "conscious, lucid, and calm," that yesterday he received the Eucharist—Viaticum—and this morning he concelebrated Holy Mass.

Before 9:00 AM I go directly to the Pope's apartment without passing through the office. I am first with Dziwisz and then with Buzzonetti. I see that in the corridor there are some trays with leftover food. Undoubtedly, the doctors and nurses have been on their feet all night. I enter the Pope's chapel and stay there for half an hour. One of the nuns who attends the apartment comes in and out carrying flowers. On the altar, there is the small image of the Risen Christ that is always placed there during the Easter period. When I finish praying, I enter the Pope's room.

He is in his bed, which has been repositioned and is parallel to the side windows that do not face the plaza. Behind the headboard, the medical instruments for respiratory support. He is intubated with a nasal tube for nutrition; the tracheal cannula is connected to a respiratory support device; one of the doctors helps by compressing the rubber balloon. At the moment there are in the room Dziwisz, the three nuns of the Apartment, Wanda Półtawska, Buzzoneti, two other doctors—one of them is Polisca, and two nurses.

The Pope is conscious and tries to say something to Sister Tobiana, who cannot understand him. Sister Tobiana is kneeling beside the bed and is holding the Pope's right hand. They give him a large piece of cardboard with a marker, but I don't think they can decipher what the Pope is writing. He is suffering. Breathing difficulty is evident.

I am there for a while praying. Before leaving, I go over to kiss the Pope's right hand: a hand with bruises from the punctures, and very cold. He wears a woolen scapular and a golden cross. That cross, Dziwisz will tell me later, came from Cardinal Sapieha, to whom St. Pius X gave it; it has relics of saints. As I leave, I see Sodano talking in the corridor with Dziwisz. They must publish some appointments already approved by the Pope and on which the date of the day he signed them will be noted.

Then I go out with Buzzonetti and we talk about the situation. It is very serious. We agreed to meet twice every day: in the morning and in the afternoon.

At 12:30 I have the briefing with the journalists. There is a great silence. I say that I imagine they will have a lot of questions but I will answer only a couple of them. The first question I don't remember. The second one is asked to me by Andreas English, a German journalist: "And from a personal point of view, how are you living this moment?" That's when the tension escapes me and my emotions get out of control. I answer: "Personal feelings have no place here. . . . Certainly, it is a new image of the pontificate: the Pope in his bed; suffering, very serene, with an inevitable difficulty breathing."

These words came out broken and with a lump in my throat, which appeared live on TV halfway around the world. It seems that many people were moved more by my public emotion than by the words I said. I was talking about the very serious condition of the Holy Father. Perhaps it helped people to better understand that something very big was happening. It introduced an element of truth, of true humanity, which I had certainly not deliberately intended to communicate.[1]

In the afternoon I return to the apartment. I enter the Pope's room and see that he is asleep. I speak again with Dziwisz and Buzzonetti. Buzzonetti thinks there is nothing to be done from the medical point of view. Dziwisz is serene. I ask Dziwisz for some words the Pope has said these days. He tells me: "I bless the Church. I bless my diocese of Rome. I bless everyone, without excluding anyone." I take note of these words and keep them in case I can say them at another time. In the afternoon, the three nuns who were taking care of the Pope at the Gemelli came. I thought they were going to relieve the Polish nuns, but in fact they only came to see the Holy Father.

At 6:30 PM I give another communiqué in which it is stated that "the general and cardio-respiratory conditions of the Holy Father have worsened again. An increasing arterial hypotension is detected, while breathing is shallow. A clinical picture of cardiocirculatory and renal insufficiency has been determined. The Holy Father, with visible participation, joins the continuous prayer of those assisting him." I leave my cell phone on all night.

A Day of Sadness and Joy

April 2, 2005

Today, at 9:37 PM, the Pope passed away. I feel unable to analyze the situation: neither the fact itself, nor in relation to the Church, nor in relation to myself.

I went into his room at night. He was still in bed, with a bandage around his head.

I have not been able to say any prayers of suffrage for his soul. I am fully assured that he is already enjoying the presence of God.

---

1. A few weeks later, I was still receiving messages, letters, cards, etc., from people who personally expressed their condolences for the Pope's death or joined me in my grief. Former presidents; ministers; people I did not know; journalists—even those who were (or presumed to be) great cynics; newspaper editors. . . . I received messages from everywhere with that same tone of shock, of participation in a pain they perceived that I undoubtedly felt [Author's Note].

"Santo subito"

April 2–9, 2005

On Saturday 2nd, I returned to the apartment in the morning, but I did not enter the Pope's room. During the day we gave two communiqués in which the extreme seriousness of the situation was evident.

Shortly after the Pope's death, I spoke with Buzzonetti, with the doctors present in the apartment and with Martínez Somalo, the Camerlengo. The communiqué of the death is written. I omit a phrase that Buzzonetti wanted to put: "The Holy Father lost consciousness at 7:00 PM." Dziwisz does not accept the Pope's unconsciousness: he says that, if he was spoken to, he understood. Besides, I have had a doubt because I see that later the viaticum was administered to him—a drop of the precious blood, Dziwisz will tell me later—and I doubt whether we can say it was given to an unconscious person.

Dziwisz has spoken to the Camerlengo about his desire not to expose the Pope's body. He would not want to be remembered in that way. For him it would be better to expose the coffin. Already the day before, when he told me, I tried to dissuade him. It is Martínez Somalo who finally convinces him.

I leave the Apartment that night before they start dressing the Holy Father because I have to go back to the office to keep up with the great demand for information.

The information I have been giving these days I first record on video with the *Vatican Television Center in* English, Spanish, and Italian. Then I repeat the briefing in front of the journalists. In this way, the TV stations can choose one of these three languages. In any case, I see that the big networks such as *BBC, CNN, FOX* and others choose to broadcast live, with simultaneous translation, my meetings with the press.

On the first day, *FOX* gives the news of the Pope's death, followed by *CNN*. The former rectifies this mistake; the latter blames the Italian press. In any case, the information these days is very good. There has been a great emotional participation all over the world.

The effort has been tremendous for everyone at *Sala Stampa*. I think a great job has been done. Many journalists recognize it and even say so. The number of accredited journalists in Rome has grown exponentially in recent days. The total number exceeds 6,000, including radio and TV technicians. During all this time, we had promised the journalists that they would be the first to receive the news. Now I think, with healthy professional pride, that we have fulfilled it: the Pope died at 9:37 PM and at 9:45 PM the news reached the news agencies all over the world; at 9:50 PM it was communicated to the people gathered in St. Peter's Square.

Personally, these have been strange days. I am very sad, first of all, for the Holy Father's suffering and then for his death. At the same time, I recognize that he is no longer suffering. Finally, I have complete certainty that he is enjoying God. I pray to him now.

On the 3rd, the Pope's body is exposed in the Clementine Hall, the place of so many audiences. I get there before the Curia people start coming. On the right is Stanisław, the nuns, Buzzonetti . . . , on the left some cardinal. Dziwisz calls me. I approach him and we cannot say anything to each other: he cries and I cry. Sobbing, I tell him that yesterday I could not pray anything as a suffrage. He tells me that the first thing they prayed last night in that room, after the Pope's death, was a hymn of thanksgiving, the *Te Deum*.

I return in the afternoon. In the evening, they prepare the body: "temporary conservative hygienic treatment," Buzzonetti tells me. It is carried out by specialists in forensic medicine from one of Rome's universities (Tor Vergata), together with a private doctor. He has not been embalmed.

One of the *cerimonieri* who work with Piero Marini told me that he had helped in the dressing of the Pope's body. He was worried, because he thought it would be very difficult to undress and dress him with the rigidity of almost two days of death. On the contrary, he tells me, the body was flexible as if he had died at that moment. Dziwisz confirmed the same thing to me the next day: "The doctor told me that, in the 25 years he has been doing this work, he has never found a body in this condition."

Transfer of the body to the Basilica. Dignified and solemn ceremony. The procession begins in the Clementine Hall. All the cardinals, archbishops of the Curia, archpriests of St. Peter's Basilica. The Pope's body is visible, clad in red vestments. I go behind him, with Dziwisz, Buzzonetti. . . . It's a long way: down the stairs, through the first loggia, then the stairway leading to the Bronze Door. When the body comes out of that door and overlooks the square, there is a burst of applause and tears. And so it goes up the sacristy and arrives at the door of the basilica. Before entering, the *sediarios* [assistants] turn it around so that the people can see it. The applause is renewed.

The procession continues through the nave of the Basilica towards the baldachin. The body is placed on a catafalque in front of the altar of Confession. It will remain there for three days so that the people can pay homage to him. It will be an unforgettable few days. The queues form immediately and thousands and thousands of people will pass by day and night. The Basilica is closed at night only during the hours necessary for cleaning. There is an extraordinary order. People wait up to twelve hours to be able to spend just one minute in front of the body of John Paul II. The Italian Civil Protection coordinates volunteers to collaborate in the organization, distributing water and, at night, some blankets to those in need.

At the same time, preparations for the funeral begin. And the problems of accommodating all the delegations that have announced their presence begin. The number of people assigned to each delegation is reduced: three for the Kings and Heads of State; two for the Heads of Government. The problem is also logistical: how to guarantee access to the Tabernacle for so many personalities, who come with their entourage and escorts, at the same time and place? We are working in close collaboration with the Italian authorities.

When President Bush arrives in Rome, he says he wants to go directly to the Basilica to pay homage to the Holy Father. He comes in the afternoon, accompanied by his wife. Two days later, King Juan Carlos makes the same announcement. When he landed at Ciampino, the head of his security called me to tell me that the king wanted to come with the queen and the head of government—Zapatero—to the Basilica. I tell him the itinerary he has to follow, and ask him to call me again when they are about to enter the Vatican. I call Dziwisz on the phone to let him know. He comes down immediately and we meet them at the side door of St. Peter's. They stay in the basilica for a while.

It can be said, without fear of exaggeration, that the day of the funeral was a very special day in the history of the Vatican, which has seen so much. Not only because of the number of people, but also because of the number of official, civil, and religious delegations. With the exception of the royal houses, which are in the front row, the delegations follow a strict alphabetical order of countries. This solves the problem of protocol. But there is still the "anomaly" of Israel and Iran, whose delegations are seated next to each other. Not only does nothing happen, but they shake hands during the rite of peace!

Towards the end of the Mass, amidst the applause of the people, banners began to appear with the words "*Santo subito*" ("Declare sainthood now!") They are from the Focolare, but there is a complete solidarity of all the people with this wish.

After Mass, the body is transferred—in its coffin—to the Vatican Grottoes. I accompany him. A few of us are there: Sodano, Dziwisz, Marini, Buzzonetti, the nuns of the Pope's apartment; Comastri, archpriest of the Basilica;

Ratzinger, as dean of the College of Cardinals. . . . The Rosary, the litany of the saints in Italian, and the *Regina coeli* are recited. The Pope is laid to rest in the earth, in the tomb occupied by John XXIII until his beatification, when he was transferred to a chapel of the basilica. The next day, the access is opened to all the people who want to go to pray before the tomb: an endless praying line.[2]

After the funeral, the period of "Sede Vacante" follows in which the main activity is focused on the cardinal electors. They meet in the Synod Hall, presided over by Ratzinger, as Cardinal Dean. I see him every morning. And I exchange impressions with him, if I have any doubts about the affairs of these days.

The day after the funeral I told him about the impact of the banners, this kind of "popular canonization," reminiscent of other periods in the history of the Church. Don't worry," he told me, "this topic will be left for the new Pope."[3]

There is a problem of not having biographies for all the cardinals, which would be useful for the cardinal electors. I tell Ratzinger that in my office we have some updated biographies for journalistic use. He asked me if it was possible to make a booklet out of them. We order it from an outside printer, making sure it is ready in twenty-four hours. And so Ratzinger distributes that booklet to the cardinals.

Conclave: Benedict XVI

April 18–19, 2005

I arrive in time before the ceremony starts. It is 4:00 PM I greet Buzzonetti and Polisca. I don't ask them anything, but I think that they will be the two doctors who will attend to the cardinals during the confinement. The procession departs from the Hall of Blessings. When the cardinals enter the Sistine Chapel, the choir is still chanting the Litany of the Saints. The senior cardinal, Ratzinger, takes the last place. As I expected, the setting is impressive, with Michelangelo's Last Judgment dominating the atmosphere. It is a very orderly ceremony: each cardinal takes his assigned place in the four rows that run the length of the nave, two on the right and two on the left. They proceed to take the oath, one by one, after Ratzinger has read the text. I pray in this waiting

2. And so, continuously, until May 2nd, 2011, the day after his beatification, when it was moved to the Chapel of St. Sebastian, in the right nave of the basilica [Author's Note].

3. That comment of his later made me think how far from his mind was the possibility of his own election [Author's Note].

time, pray for the new Pope and for the electors. I look at the faces of some of the cardinals. How to predict the future? At the end, Piero Marini—with a voice that is neither imposing nor affected, but serene—pronounces the *extra omnes* with which he invites the few visitors to leave the chapel. Piero closes the door from the inside. The conclave begins.

I go to my office. There are few people in the square. Will there be smoke? The day before yesterday Ratzinger told me that it would be the conclave itself who would decide whether there would be a vote on the evening of the first day. I wait to see what happens.

Around 5:00 PM Domenico Giani calls me. He uses cryptic language to tell me that they are voting. What is his source? Probably the commander of the Swiss Guard who, outside the door, must sense movement inside the Sistine.

Indeed, around 7:00 PM, smoke begins to rise. At first it is gray, but then it darkens to an unmistakable black. Although no one was expecting any surprises, the square has been filling up with people. You never know.

Tuesday 19. Black smoke in the morning. About 5:30 PM smoke begins to rise again. Gray. Persistent gray that does not become black. New smoke. Gray, not black. Third smoke: with good will, it can be called white. . . . A whole doctoral thesis could be written on the color of the smoke, but I think that this momentary uncertainty is part of the unique character of the conclave. The bells are now ringing and confirm that the Pope has been elected. All that remains is to wait.

People rush through Rome in the direction of St. Peter's. In a short time, the square is full of people. And then it is crowded.

While we are all waiting, looking towards the loggia. I receive a curious phone call. A young lady asks me—on behalf of the King of Spain, no less, she tells me—to please tell her who has been elected Pope. We exchange a few sentences and I realize that she may be a naïve trainee journalist who really thinks that I know the name, and she uses her best skills to get it out of me and thus obtain a world exclusive. I bid her a kind farewell.

Shortly after, the *Protodiacon*—Cardinal Medina—appears and pronounces the name: *Josefus Cardinal Ratzinger*.

I pray for him at that very moment, and I think that, from now on, public attention will focus on the differences in style, on the new direction, on the new themes. Everything is new and, at the same time, everything is the same. Perhaps few—it is not news!—will comment on the fascinating mystery of continuity with Peter, after twenty centuries in which everything has happened and in which, not infrequently, the end of the Church was seen as imminent.

Ratzinger, already Benedict XVI, appears self-possessed; he is sparing in his gesture, smiling, the sleeves of a black sweater peeking out from under the white alb! I suppose it would be cold in the Sistine, but I also interpret it as a sign that he was not prepared for what happened. He says a few words. He gives the blessing, which I receive on my knees in the *Sala Stampa*. Shortly afterwards I speak to Sandri and give the first news of the new Pope's itinerary. I have to appear on several TV news programs.

Just that day I had accepted an invitation to lunch with Luigi Accattoli. The restaurants near the Vatican were full of journalists from all over the world and, if they had seen us, they would have thought I was leaking information for *Corriere della Sera*. For that reason, we went to *Taberna Giulia*, on the other side of the Tiber. Naturally, we talked about the *papabili*. Here the spokesman knew the same amount as the journalist. Who? European? Latin American? Ratzinger hypothesis? I tell him my opinion: "I love Ratzinger, I read everything he writes, I admire him. I can tell you that the only Pope with whom I would be willing to continue in the *Sala Stampa* would be Ratzinger. But I don't know if he will be elected and I don't know if he would accept. Of course, I think there is no candidate of his spiritual and intellectual stature."

50

I Have Been Privileged

With the New Pope

April 20–21, 2005

The day after the election, Wednesday April 20th, the Pope's first departure took place: he went to his old apartment in *Piazza di Città Leonina,* a few meters from the Vatican, to collect his things, especially his books. He has decided for the time being not to live in the *Torre di Giovanni XIII,* in the Vatican gardens: he will remain in the Santa Marta residence, in a suite called the "Patriarch's" suite, until some work is finished in the Pope's apartment.

Now that the pressure of these weeks is over, I feel uneasy. To think that now I have to start all over again, as I started more than twenty years ago with John Paul II, is a bit difficult for me. Above all, because I lack my direct source with the Pope and the invaluable help of my regular contact with his secretary, who gave me the "tone" of the topics. I would like to escape. On the other hand, I would like to help, if I can.

I decide to take the initiative. On Friday afternoon I telephone Don Georg, Ratzinger's secretary.[1] I tell him that when possible I would like to speak to the Pope. He tells me that he was expecting my call. "Now the Pope has 'a stone in his stomach,' which is the scripture for Sunday's homily. I will call you to let you know when he will be available." Around 10:00 PM he calls me and tells me to come the next day at 9:30 AM.

I go to Santa Marta a little before that time. I get on the elevator with a smiling man, whom I greet, but I don't know who he is. In fact, I find out later that he is the tailor, who is coming to make the Pope's cassock. He enters before me. While

1. Georg Gänswein (Germany, 1953) moved to Rome in 1993, where he worked in the Congregation for Divine Worship and the Discipline of the Sacraments, and in the Congregation for the Doctrine of the Faith, directed by Cardinal Ratzinger, whose personal secretary he was since 2003. In 2012, Benedict XVI appointed him prefect of the Pontifical Household and conferred episcopal ordination on him (2013). After the resignation, he continued as the closest collaborator of the Pope Emeritus.

I wait, Cordero Lanza di Montezemolo, the former nuncio to Italy, arrives. As an expert in heraldry, he is making the coat of arms for the new Pope. He has made a drawing in which there is no longer the tiara but a miter with three crowns.

I go in to see the Pope. As it is the first time, I kiss his ring and tell him that I am a bit excited. I tell him that I have received a lot of news from all over the world, also from non-Catholics, assuring him that they are praying for the Pope. "If it weren't for that, I wouldn't be able to carry the weight," he replies gratefully.

Once seated, I explained to him: "Holy Father, several times I spoke with John Paul II about leaving this job, because it has already been too many years. The Pope jokingly told me, remind me in five years. Now, I will do strictly what the Pope tells me." Benedict replies: "No, at least for the first year, you continue in this work." I tell him: "Holy Father, this is a job that can only be done if there is direct access to the Holy Father. If anything could be done in these past years, it was because of this: both in normality and in the days of John Paul II's illness and death. The mentality in the Curia is not easy: 'Don't say anything if the journalists don't ask, and if they ask then say what you must. . . .' But it is a very reactive behavior, not at all proactive. Public opinion is like a big container: the first one to fill it, that one can propose his topics and the others follow him. If the others propose the issues, then there is no other way but to follow behind with denials. Let me give you an example."

The Pope nods: "Yes, that's right." He assured me that I would have access to him personally when I needed him; to call him on the phone. That I would have his support. All this reassures me a little.

I told him about the meeting I would have the next day with the journalists who had come these days. I also thought it would be appropriate for him to receive a few people for more direct contact. He asked me how we could select these people without upsetting the others. It seemed to me a very prudent observation. I told him, and he was fine with it, that they would be media directors only, and that there were only a few of these. Before leaving, I asked for his blessing.

Some Confusions

June 4, 2005

First weeks of the new pontificate. The Pope is going at his own pace: almost no changes. Audiences with all or almost all the prefects of the dicasteries of the Holy See.

I am still answering messages that arrived after the death of John Paul II. And refusing to accept invitations to conferences and awards. I know it is all a consequence of TV exposure during the illness and death of John Paul II, and an expression of affection for him, but I find this celebrity unbearable.

In the meantime, I see a movement of involution shrinkage in the informative action of the Holy See. There is a lack of information. But I am aware that at the end of the year I will leave this assignment and I do not think it convenient to condition the work of my successor.

A couple of potentially dangerous issues have arisen for the Pope. Both have echoed in the United States: the dismissal of the editor of *America magazine*—Thomas J. Reese—and the confusion surrounding the possible trial of Father Maciel, founder of the Legion of Christ. My only effort has been to try to keep both from implicating the Pope.

As far as Father Maciel is concerned, the matter was activated because Sandro Magister published an article in *L'Espresso*. Alvaro Corcuera, current Superior of the Legionaries, calls Sodano and they issue a statement saying that there is no trial and there are no plans for one.

But we learn that the communication came from the Secretariat of State and not from the Congregation for the Doctrine of the Faith, which is the competent body in this matter. Confusion. One of the lawyers representing the accusers appears in my office. I do not want to add to the confusion and I avoid receiving him with an excuse, but I clarify things off the record to John Allen, a reporter for the *National Catholic Register*, so that the Pope does not appear unjustly implicated.

In Cartagena

June 30, 2005

I spend a few days with my mother in Cabo de Palos, in Cartagena. One of those days, Georg Gänswein, the Pope's secretary, telephones me. He tells me that he just wanted to confirm that I will go with the Pope to his vacation in Valle d'Aosta; that I should not worry about some contrary voices; that someone had said that perhaps it was not necessary for me to go, but that I will go. He tells me that we will talk.

In the Aosta Valley with Benedict

July 28, 2005

First vacation in the Aosta Valley with Benedict XVI. Everything the same and everything so different. The same plane trip from Ciampino. The same pilot. Almost the same people. And yet . . . it is a new Pope. It is a new stage.

When we arrive home, I notice that a piano has been installed in the small room that serves as his study. But he has not brought the sheet music with him. The next day Georg explains to me that the Pope made two packages: one for Castelgandolfo and one for the Aosta Valley. The scores were in the first one. The next morning someone went in search of sheet music and got the Mozart *Sonatas.* Every day the Pope will be heard playing the piano for a few minutes after breakfast, before lunch and in the evening after dinner.

Georg wants to talk to me and we chat during two long walks. I explain to him my vision concerning the job: the problem of the lack of information and the near impossibility of organizing an information strategy without it. Georg is very explicit. Without naming names, he explains to me what some people have said to the Pope: that I was a close friend of Dziwisz and that allowed me to bypass the structure; that there was a lack of cooperation on my part. That, in short, a change was desirable. Georg understands that, in reality, what some people are looking for is to regain "lost power," so to speak. Personally, I understand the situation and even those reactions. Frankly, I don't give them much importance.

The plan for the days in *Val d'Aosta* is always the same: the Pope works in the mornings and afternoons. At 6 PM, we leave by car for the mountain behind the villa and he walks for thirty-five to forty-five minutes, in a flat or gently sloping area. He talks or prays the rosary with Georg. At some point he exchanges some impressions with him. "I hadn't imagined that you could have a vacation like this," he says. He is surprised by the peace, the intimacy, the *privacy* with which he can walk and write. I tell him that the journalists say he is writing an encyclical: "No, I will write the encyclical in Castelgandolfo; now I am writing a book that I started three years ago, also during a vacation period."[2]

On Thursday the 21st we leave for Courmayeur. We only inform the employees of the cable car that will take us to Mont Blanc. Naturally, there are people who recognize him and the Pope greets them. We climb the first stretch up to the Pavillon du Mont Fréty. We visit the alpine botanical garden, the highest in Europe. We climb again to the Torino Hut, at 3,350 m., an altitude at which the Pope already feels the lack of oxygen. I bring him a chair, he sits down and we wait a few minutes before continuing. The third section takes us up to Punta Helbronner, at almost 3,500 m. We sit in a small covered bar. Around him are Buzzonetti, Cerise, Cibin, Georg and me. The Pope accepts a cappuccino, and eats some

2. The book would be *Jesus of Nazareth,* published in three installments: the first came out in 2007.

cheese. We talk about the great spectacle of the landscape. On the way down he greets many more people. I take a picture of him praying before a crucifix. We return for lunch. The afternoon is spent writing.

On one of these days, the 25th, a journalist called me around 7:00 PM to ask for my reaction to the Israeli protest. I then learned that the Nuncio in Israel had been summoned to the Ministry of Foreign Affairs. They wanted to convey to him the government's protest because the Pope—at the previous Angelus—had spoken of terrorism and mentioned various places with victims without mentioning Israel. This must have happened that very morning. I go to see the Pope, who is on his way back with Georg, after a walk in the garden. I tell him the facts and tell him that I think it best to respond right away. The Pope asks Georg to speak to the Secretariat of State so that he can say something to the press. Shortly afterwards, Lajolo calls me: they have prepared a text, which he reads to me. I ask him to send it to my office for distribution, and I will inform Father Ciro, the deputy director.

The next day, the newspapers picked up these declarations. I was celebrating my saint's day and in the afternoon, during the walk, the Pope called to me, congratulated me and told me that he had prayed for me at Mass. And he adds: "Thank you, you have defended the Pope." I tell him that I am the one who is grateful that he prayed for me, and that the rest is part of my job. I accompany him for the rest of the walk.

Process of Beatification of John Paul II

October 24, 2005

On Friday the 21st I go to the inauguration of the exhibition "John Paul II and Rome," promoted by the Mayor of Rome, Walter Veltroni, at the Victoriano. I meet Stanisław there. "I called you on the phone," he tells me. We agreed that I would go to see him at the House of the Poles, in via Cassia. I also spoke with Monsignor Oder, the postulator of the cause for the beatification of John Paul II. He told me that he wanted to speak with me again in case I had any suggestions about the list of witnesses for the process.

I go to via Cassia the next day and spend an hour chatting in the garden with Dziwisz. I tell him that in December I will probably tender my resignation. He tries to dissuade me in the opposite direction. I tell him that I am tired and that, besides, I cannot do the job as I would like to. But we talk, above all, about the process of beatification of John Paul II. I specifically hint to him that the postulator might need more people to help him with the work.

A Conversation with the Pope

December 1, 2005

I am going to see the Pope. In the new style, I have been summoned with a formal letter from the Prefecture of the Pontifical Household. My audience is at 6:15 PM. Earlier, the Pope had another one with Cardinal Etchegaray. They take place in his apartment, in the large hall at the entrance. The Pope is alone. There are no papers on his table. He is relaxed, sitting with his legs crossed.

I am ready to tell him that the time has come for a change in the *Sala Stampa*. But I cannot put it that way, because he begins by asking for my opinion on the information from the Holy See. I tell him that, without any judgment on individuals, the current climate—from my point of view—is not positive, fundamentally because of a lack of prior information. I give him some concrete examples.

He also asks me about L'Osservatore Romano, Vatican Radio, and the Pontifical Council for Social Communications. "Do you know that Cardinal Szocka believes that the balance sheet of Vatican Radio should be reduced?" he asks me. I informed him that a meeting had been held on that subject a few months ago, because the cardinals were concerned. We also talked about the problem of sending documents to the bishops before sending them to the press and the risks of leaks that this entails. I explained to him that this is largely solved by sending them via the Internet one or two days before publication. He is happy to know that this possibility exists and refers that he had the same problem when he was in the Congregation for the Doctrine of the Faith.

He asks me for suggestions on possible changes. I tell him that—from the point of view of my office—a good experience has been the factual changes made by John Paul II, without waiting for major structural changes: for example, encouraging the presence of the *Sala Stampa* in some meetings of cardinals, special synods, delegations, etc., in order to have a communication criterion in those activities.

At one point in the conversation I spoke to him about a consideration I had read in one of his books, about the possibility of "lightening" the structures of the Curia. He replied that this would be part of the plan of an organic reform, as if to indicate that this, if anything, would come later, or with another Pope.

A Letter to the Pope

February 1, 2006

Several months have passed since the election of the Pope. I have considered that a prudent period of time has elapsed for me to formally present my replacement to the Pope. After meditating on it, I am giving Georg Gänswein my letter of resignation, in which I say to the Holy Father:

> Most Blessed Father:
>
> Twenty-two years ago, to my great surprise, I was asked to be the Director of the *Sala Stampa*, an assignment far removed from my first professional dedication—medicine—and very different from my work in the field of journalism as a foreign correspondent, a job to which I dedicated myself professionally for some years. The fact that I had not sought this assignment and that when it was proposed to me I was very afraid to accept it gave me a certain confidence, thinking that this was possibly the Lord's will.
>
> After all the time I have spent with John Paul II and Your Holiness, I thank the Lord for all that I have received: much more than I could have imagined and than I am able to realize now. I know that one day the Lord will ask me to give an account of these years and, above all, my personal response to so many graces.
>
> At the present time, Holy Father, I think the time has come for a change in the direction of the *Sala Stampa* of the Holy See. For offices similar to the *Sala Stampa*, to have the same person as director for more than twenty-one years is an extraordinarily long and almost unprecedented length of time.
>
> Additionally, some unexpected personal and family circumstances lead me to ask Your Holiness to accept my resignation from this assignment. Should my substitution require some time, I could say, with Your Holiness' permission, that "the Pope has accepted my proposal to leave this charge and has asked me to remain in it until a new director is appointed." This would allow me to devote greater attention to the new circumstances of which I have spoken to you.
>
> I wish you to know that the first of my prayers to the Lord will always be, until the end of my days, for the person and intentions of the Holy Father, as it has been for all these years.
>
> Asking for his paternal Blessing,
>
> Dr. Joaquín Navarro-Valls

The Pope Accepts

February 3, 2006

Georg called me to tell me that the Pope has granted my request, but that he wants me to remain in my job until the summer.

On the same page of the letter I sent him, Benedict XVI himself wrote, in his own handwriting, these words: *Proprio così: ho accolto la disponibilità—donec aliter provideatur.* The translation of these indications, typical of the usual "administrative" language in the offices of the Holy See, could be this: "Exactly so. I accept the availability. Let another person therefore be found to replace you."

My Mother's Death

March 6–7, 2006

Today my mother passed away. A month ago she had a stroke and was in a coma. Since then, I have been by her side practically all that time, morning and evening. Most likely she didn't notice anything and didn't suffer. The ones who have suffered have been my brothers and me. Seeing her like this, unconscious, day after day, with difficulty breathing, has been very hard. We all took turns so that she would not be alone at any time. At night, Maria and Esperanza, the two women who accompanied and cared for her during these last years, took turns.

The Wednesday before she had her heart attack, she called me on the phone, as she did every Wednesday. With her usual good humor, she advised me to take care of myself, "because you're getting on in years," she told me amusingly. And she added: "I'm getting on in years too." That was my last conversation with her. At the funeral Mass, the telegram sent by the Secretary of State on behalf of the Pope was read.

A Letter From the Pope

March 2006

On my return to Rome, I was met with an enormous number of messages of condolence: from the mayor of Rome, from government ministers, from cardinals. But my great surprise was to find an autographed letter from the Pope, written in his characteristic small handwriting:

> At the end of the Spiritual Exercises, I hasten to express to you my most sincere condolences for the death of your dear Mother, assuring you of my prayer

for the soul of the dear deceased in this hour of sorrow. The death of a mother always involves—even after a long life—a wound; and a part of ourselves goes definitely with her. In communion with the Body of Christ we always know that "whether we live or die, we belong to the Lord" (Rom. 14:8).

I would like to take this opportunity to thank you for the wonderful interview you gave to *Deutsche Tagespost.*

With these wishes, I remain yours in the Lord:

Benedict XVI

Proposals for Replacement

May 15, 2006

Yesterday I was with the Pope in a private audience in his apartment. The main topic was my resignation. He proposed that we talk about my replacement. He tells me that Father Lombardi has been suggested to him by the Secretary of State. It is obvious that Federico Lombardi can do it wonderfully, but he seems to me a person who already carries a lot of weight, with Vatican Radio and the Vatican Television Center. I would also add that he would have to leave his other assignments. The Pope nods immediately.

Then he asks me if a woman couldn't do it. I tell him that it would be great and that there is a woman working at *Sala Stampa*—Lina Petri—who has the necessary training, together with the experience she has acquired over the years. He likes the idea and tells me to send her a note, which I did this morning.

We agreed that I could stop by again when he returns from his trip to Valencia in July, for the family day.

On the Maciel Case

May 19, 2006

The Marcial Maciel case, founder of the Legionaries of Christ, broke out. For years there were repeated accusations of alleged sexual abuse of seminarians and priests of his congregation. Nothing had been proven; no formal investigation had been initiated by the Roman Curia. On the other hand, the more than positive work of the Legionaries in many countries seemed to speak against those accusations.

In the Curia, Maciel was appreciated by many people, with Sodano at the head. I had dinner with Sodano and Maciel on one occasion, during the meeting of Latin American bishops in Santo Domingo. Stanisław also approved of him and had contacts with some Legionaries. Naturally, without imagining that in the life of this man there was something unconfessable. John Paul II, seeing the apostolic dynamism of the Legionaries, also appreciated the congregation and its founder.

It should be recalled that a few years ago, accusations of pedophilia were raised in the public arena against two cardinals: Bernardin in Chicago and Pell in Sydney. Both of them made themselves available for any examination and in a short time the falsehood of those accusations was proven. All this created a climate that favored the tendency to dismiss new accusations like those that Father Maciel received in public opinion.

Maciel himself had publicly denied these accusations. As a sample, I attach a copy of a letter he sent to an American newspaper in 1997:

> As to the allegations made against me in the *Hartford Courant* on Sunday, February 23, I wish to state that in all cases they are all baseless libels and falsehoods, as during the years these men were in the Legion I never in any way committed such acts with them, nor did I make such advances to them, nor was the suggestion of such acts ever mentioned.
>
> During the time these men were in the Legion of Christ and even after they left, I spared no sacrifice to help them as much as I could, as I have always done with every person the Lord has placed under my care. I do not know what has led them to make these totally false accusations twenty, thirty, and forty years after leaving the congregation. I am all the more surprised that I still have letters from some of them well into their 70's expressing their gratitude and our mutual friendship.
>
> Despite the moral suffering this has caused me, I bear them no ill will. Rather, I offer my sorrow and prayers for each of them, in the hope that they will regain peace of soul and remove from their hearts whatever resentment moved them to make these false accusations.

After reading this letter, which was widely circulated, it was really difficult to believe the accusations against him.

In 1998 the Congregation for the Doctrine of the Faith received accusations against Father Maciel for crimes reserved to the exclusive competence of that body. A specific competence that had been granted by John Paul II to that dicastery headed by Cardinal Ratzinger.

In 2002, Father Maciel published a statement similar to the 1997 one, in which he denied the accusations and expressed his sorrow for the "offenses" that some former members of his congregation had caused him.

On April 22, 2002, he assured, among other things: "Before God and with total clarity of conscience I can categorically affirm that the accusations that have been made against me are false. I have never had the kind of repulsive behavior of which these men accuse me, and nothing could be further from my way of treating others, as is evident to any of the thousands of Legionaries who know me."

Nevertheless, the Congregation for the Doctrine of the Faith initiated an investigation on the basis of the accusations and according to the competencies that John Paul II had issued with the *Motu Proprio Sacramentorum sanctitatis tutela,* promulgated on April 30, 2001.

That's how things stood when, two days ago, on May 17, John Allen, a reporter for the *National Catholic Reporter,* came to me and told me that he had information that the process against Maciel had been completed and that he had been found guilty of the charges against him. He wants a comment from me. I ask him for a couple of days before he publishes anything and before I say anything. He agrees and sends me—at my request—a text with what he knows or thinks he knows.

He tells me that the Congregation for the Doctrine of the Faith, with the authorization of the Holy Father, has imposed a number of restrictions on Father Maciel's ministry, including a ban on celebrating public Masses and a prohibition on giving speeches or interviews. The Legionaries have also been instructed not to celebrate a public Mass at the time of his death.

He adds that, according to his information, Father Maciel has not been expelled from the clerical state. The restrictions, however, amount to a conclusion that he is guilty of the sexual abuse charges brought against him. The Congregation completed its investigation at the end of 2005. In early 2006, the documentation was shown to cardinal members of the congregation resident in Rome. They were asked to give their opinion—based on the documentation—on the credibility of the charges. The decision they reached was to impose these restrictions. This result has been communicated to the nuncio in Mexico, Maciel's place of residence, and to the superior of the Legionaries of Christ, Father Alvaro Corcuera.

He also says that the more than twenty accusers provided testimony that included not only oral and written recollections, but also, in at least one case, videotapes. The documentation has been described as "overwhelming" and leaves no doubt as to the veracity of the charges against him.

John Allen asked me to specify some data: the concrete list of restrictions, the reasons expressed by the Congregation, and also how to explain—in the light of these conclusions—some of the praise that Maciel had received from John Paul II and high Vatican officials.

"As I told you in person," John concludes, "I know that other journalists, mainly in Mexico, are working on this story. It is destined to become public, and probably in a very short period of time. I would like to present the truth as fully, accurately and responsibly as possible, which is why I am coming to you."

The subject seems to me to be very serious and John's attitude is loyal and professional. Information must be given on this. Trying to keep silent, on this and other cases, would be deleterious.

I immediately went to see Levada, Prefect of the Congregation for the Doctrine of the Faith.[3] I tell him that this topic has already reached the press, but that it has to be given, even if it had not reached the press. He tells me that they have decided not to give anything. I replied that the subject seemed so serious to me, because of the consequences of the accusations of cover-up that would be attributed to the Holy See, that I would immediately go to see the Pope. At this, he asked me if I could wait for an hour. I told him that I could wait an hour, but not a day.

A few hours later he tells me that the Pope is expecting us at his apartment in the afternoon.

Levada, Sodano, and I are standing next to the Pope. The Pope gives me the floor to introduce the subject. I simply say that in this situation the Holy See has to give the information and give it immediately. Otherwise, the press as a whole, but especially the American press, will accuse John Paul II and also him—Benedict XVI—who was Prefect of the Congregation when the process began, of being a cover-up. Despite the doubts of some of those present, the Pope told them to prepare a statement for public opinion. And so that meeting ended.

The next morning Levada gives me the statement that we broadcast from the *Sala Stampa*.

---

3. Cardinal William Levada (United States, 1936–2019) replaced Cardinal Joseph Ratzinger as prefect of the Congregation for the Doctrine of the Faith when the latter was elected pope. He served in that position from 2005 to 2012. He had previously served as archbishop of Portland (1986–1995) and San Francisco (1995–2005).

The Pope in Auschwitz

May 25–28, 2006

Trip to Poland. It is a tribute that Benedict XVI wants to pay to John Paul II. The emotion and the response of the people is striking: almost as if it were a new trip of John Paul II. I am surprised by the Pope, who reads some of his homilies in Polish: a remarkable effort that he makes with undoubted success.

We are in Krakow on the last day; Auschwitz is scheduled for the afternoon. The visit of a Pope to this place is always a bit problematic because of the attitude of some Jews; in the case of a German Pope, the difficulty increases.

After lunch I read the Pope's speech, which was magnificent. I see, however, that he did not include the word *Shoah*—holocaust—, which is particularly significant for the Jews. If the Pope does not pronounce that word, I would not be surprised if some representatives of the Jewish world end up saying that the Pope is trying to Christianize the history of Auschwitz. And a bitter polemic would be organized, which would end up being the only international memory of this trip.

So I decide to go immediately to the Pope's residence in the Archbishop's Palace in Krakow, which is very close to my hotel. I go up to his room and am met by Georg Gänsweing. I tell him that I need to speak to the Pope immediately. He calls him—perhaps he is praying or resting a bit—and comes to meet me asking me a bit alarmed, "What is it, Dr. Navarro?" I explain, "Your speech is magnificent, both historically and theologically. But a word is missing, *Shoah*. . . ." There is no need for me to continue. With the text in his hand, he asks me: "Where do you think we should put it?" I reply, "Wherever you want." He asks me if it would go well in a certain sentence of the speech. I tell him that it goes very well. He writes it by hand in the place indicated. And then he says it could also go somewhere else. And so he writes it again.

He thanks me. I thank him back, stressing that "it's my job," and leave the room touched by the example of humility shown by this "intellectual Pope," who accepts a suggestion with such simplicity.

An Extraordinary Experience

July 11, 2006

Today, as agreed with the Pope, the appointment of Father Federico Lombardi as director of the *Sala Stampa was* published.

I told the press: "I am very grateful to the Holy Father for having accepted my willingness, so often expressed, to leave, after many years, the post of Director of the Press Office of the Holy See. I am aware that during this time I have received much more than I have been able to give and even more than I am now able to imagine."[4]

The experience of the past years has been extraordinary. For many reasons.

In the last few months, I have been able to see first-hand the greatness and simplicity of Benedict XVI.

With John Paul II—in the more than twenty years that preceded him—a collaboration of trust, informality, and speed had been established that went beyond the chronic slowness of the Curia. With the Pope everything was easier, even on those occasions when, because of the nature of the issues, things were in themselves difficult. Direct and continuous access to his person allowed me to have my finger on the pulse of things and, therefore, to be able to adapt what was communicated in the *Sala Stampa* to the true reality of what was happening. I recognize that this is not the norm. I have been privileged. But above all I am privileged because I have been able to see a holy man up close.

4. "Sono molto grato al Santo Padre che ha voluto accogliere la mia disponibilità, più volte manifestata, a lasciare l'incarico di Direttore della Sala Stampa della Santa Sede, dopo un così lungo numero di anni. I am conscious of having received in these years much more than what I have been able to give and perfectly more than what I am now able to fully understand."

EPILOGUE

"In His Own Way"

JOAQUÍN AND I GOT ALONG QUITE WELL. Not only because of our natural fraternal affection, but also because of circumstances in our lives that made that feeling even closer.

For example: I owe my life to Joaquín. I have already mentioned elsewhere our common love for spearfishing. On one occasion when we were together looking for a big fish, I spotted a rather large octopus. I speared it. I tried to keep it from going into its lair ("tana") and grabbed the handle of the speargun I was holding. It released a large cloud of ink (defense mechanism) and, with little visibility, I continued to fight. It hid and I reached out my hand. The octopus (one of the most intelligent animals) launched a pair of thick tentacles, which surrounded my hand and pinned it to the bottom. I couldn't get free. I looked up for help and Joaquín jumped on the octopus and cleanly cut the tentacles that imprisoned me, which allowed me to shoot to the surface, arriving very short of air.

Some time later, I returned the favor, albeit on a smaller scale. One night when I was returning from a poker game, in which I had won a quite respectable sum of money (pesetas, at that time), I found Joaquín debating with my father about the amount needed for a very important trip. The discussion ended in a draw. He was very tight with money. Without his realizing it, I stuffed all my winnings into his suitcase and into his clothes. He never knew the author of the "donation."

I share this because he often shared with me confidences (those he could tell) about his work. Hence, the book to which I attach this note contains many anecdotes, some of which are familiar to me. In the book "The Spokesman," which I published in 2020, and in which I collect twenty testimonies of personalities from all over the world about Joaquín's life, I too record some of them.

The editor, in his Introduction to this book, gives an account of the vicissitudes of the book. I would like to add a confidence: Joaquín wanted his Memoirs to be published after his death and after some years had passed. However, my family—still during Joaquín's lifetime—encouraged him not to delay it so long. That is why very shortly before his death he gave a good push to these Memoirs of his time at the Vatican, while maintaining his terms.

Although I had read these annotations in rough form and made some suggestions to Joaquin, I must congratulate the editor, Diego Contreras Luzón, Professor of Information Analysis and Practice at the Faculty of Communication of the University of the Holy Cross in Rome, for having coordinated the excellent work of arranging and revising them.

These Memoirs are made "in his own way," precisely the title of a well-known song (*My Way*), which Joaquín sometimes sang with his guitar and which he especially liked.

Allow me to tell a particularly intimate anecdote about him. When leaving the funeral in Rome, my brothers and I carried the coffin to the hearse, which would take him to the cemetery. Suddenly, the song played on my cell phone without my activating it. It touched me because it seemed to me that, in some way, it was conveying to us that his soul had arrived in a safe harbor.

Rafael Navarro-Valls
Professor and Honorary Life Professor
of the Complutense University, Madrid

INDEX

L

M